Lecture Notes in Artificial Intelligence   1835

Subseries of Lecture Notes in Computer Science
Edited by J. G. Carbonell and J. Siekmann

Lecture Notes in Computer Science
Edited by G. Goos, J. Hartmanis and J. van Leeuwen

W0042380

Springer
Berlin
Heidelberg
New York
Barcelona
Hong Kong
London
Milan
Paris
Singapore
Tokyo

Dimitris N. Christodoulakis (Ed.)

Natural Language Processing – NLP 2000

Second International Conference
Patras, Greece, June 2-4, 2000
Proceedings

Springer

Series Editors

Jaime G. Carbonell, Carnegie Mellon University, Pittsburgh, PA, USA
Jörg Siekmann, University of Saarland, Saabrücken, Germany

Volume Editor

Dimitris N. Christodoulakis
University of Patras
Computer Engineering Department and Computer Technology Institute
26500 Patras, Greece
E-mail: dxri@cti.gr

Cataloging-in-Publication Data applied for

Die Deutsche Bibliothek - CIP-Einheitsaufnahme

Natural language processing : second international conference, Patras,
Greece, June 2 - 4, 2000 ; proceedings / NLP 2000. Dimitris N.
Christodoulakis (ed.). - Berlin ; Heidelberg ; New York ; Barcelona ;
Hong Kong ; London ; Milan ; Paris ; Singapore ; Tokyo : Springer, 2000
  (Lecture notes in computer science ; Vol. 1835 : Lecture notes in
  artificial intelligence)
  ISBN 3-540-67605-8

CR Subject Classification (1998): I.2.7, F.4.3, I.2, H.5.2

ISBN 3-540-67605-8 Springer-Verlag Berlin Heidelberg New York

Springer-Verlag is a company in the BertelsmannSpringer publishing group.
© Springer-Verlag Berlin Heidelberg 2000
Printed in Germany

Typesetting: Camera-ready by author
Printed on acid-free paper   SPIN: 10721991   06/3142   5 4 3 2 1 0

Preface

This volume contains the papers prepared for the 2nd International Conference on Natural Language Processing, held 2-4 June in Patras, Greece.

The conference program features invited talks and submitted papers, covering a wide range of NLP areas: text segmentation, morphological analysis, lexical knowledge acquisition and representation, grammar formalism and syntactic parsing, discourse analysis, language generation, man-machine interaction, machine translation, word sense disambiguation, and information extraction.

The program committee received 71 abstracts, of which unfortunately no more than 50% could be accepted. Every paper was reviewed by at least two reviewers. The fairness of the reviewing process is demonstrated by the broad spread of institutions and countries represented in the accepted papers.

So many have contributed to the success of the conference. The primary credit, of course, goes to the authors and to the invited speakers. By their papers and their inspired talks they established the quality of the conference. Secondly, thanks should go to the referees and to the program committee members who did a thorough and conscientious job. It was not easy to select the papers to be presented. Last, but not least, my special thanks to the organizing committee for making this conference happen.

Patras, June 2000   Dimitris N. Christodoulakis

Organization

Program Committee Chair

Christodoulakis Dimitris (University of Patras), Greece

Organizing Committee

Diamantopoulou Chara, (CTI), Greece
Gakis Panagiotis, (CTI), Greece
Galiotou Eleni, (Technological Educational Institute of Athens), Greece
Grigoriadou Maria (University of Athens), Greece
Gourdoupi Lena, (CTI), Greece
Kontos John (Athens University of Economics and Business), Greece
Kontodimou Penelope, (CTI), Greece
Malagardi Ioanna, (General Secr. for Research and Technology), Greece
Orphanos Giorgos, (CTI), Greece
Ralli Angela (University of Patras), Greece
Tsakou Ioanna (CTI), Greece
Vouros George (University of the Aegean), Greece

Conference Secretariat

Penelope Kontodimou

Program Committee and Referees

Ananiadou Sophia (Salford University), UK
Anastassiadi-Simeonidi Anna (University of Thessaloniki), Greece
Babiniotis George (University of Athens), Greece
Berwick Bob (MIT), USA
Blache Philippe (Université de Provence), France
Chanod Jean-Pierre (Xerox Research Centre Europe), France
Di Sciullo Anna-Maria (Université du Québec à Montréal), Canada
Filokyprou George (University of Athens), Greece
Gafos Diamantis (University of New York), USA
Galiotou Eleni, (University of Athens), Greece
Grigoriadou Maria (University of Athens), Greece
Iordanidou Anna (University of Patras), Greece

Kokkinakis George (University of Patras), Greece
Kontos John (Athens University of Economics and Business), Greece
Koster Kees (University of Nijmegen), The Netherlands
Ligozat Gerard (Université Paris-Sud), France
Malagardi Ioanna (General Secretariat for Research and Technology), Greece
Moens Marc (University of Edinburgh), Scotland
Morin Jean-Yves (University of Montreal), Canada
Petrits Angelique (Commission of the European Union), Belgium
Ralli Angela (University of Patras), Greece
Sag Ivan (Stanford University), USA
Stamison-Atmatzidi Matina (University of Patras), Greece
Theologitis Dimitris (Commission of the European Union), Luxemburg
Tsalidis Christos (Computer Technology Institute), Greece
Vagelatos Aristides (Computer Technology Institute), Greece
Vouros George (University of the Aegean), Greece
Wehrli Eric (University of Geneva), Switzerland
Wilks Yorik (University of Sheffield), UK
Zweigenbaum Pierre (DIAM - SIM/DSI), France

Sponsoring Institutions

ALTEC Group
Computer Technology Institute
ComputerBank Networking S.A.
Hellenic Republic, General Secretariat for Research and Technology
Hellenic Republic, Ministry of Education and Religious Affairs
Infoquest S.A.
INTRASOFT S.A.
ION Publ. Company
Microsoft Hellas
National and Kapodistrian University of Athens
OTEnet S.A.
Patakis Publications
University of the Aegean
University of Patras

Table of Contents

Tokenization, Morphological Analysis

Lexical Knowledge Representation

Parsing

Parsing, Discourse Analysis

Anaphora Resolution

Anaphora Resolution, Machine Translation

Machine Translation, Language Generation

Man-Machine Interaction, Word Sense Recognition/ Disambiguation

Information Extraction

Parsing Asymmetries

Anna Maria Di Sciullo[*]

Université du Québec à Montréal

Abstract. We extend the Integrated Asymmetry hypothesis in considering the relations between principle-based linguistic models and corresponding parsing models with respect to their account of inverse and covert asymmetries. We present an integrated model of language knowledge and language use relying on the logical definition of asymmetry. Our integrated model keeps the relation between the grammar and the parser maximally simple while it keeps constant the specificity of each system. The integration of asymmetry-based parser in IP systems improves their performance.

1 Asymmetries

We assume that Universal Grammar is designed to derive and represent linguistic expressions in terms of asymmetrical relations and that "Universal Parser" is designed to recover natural language asymmetries. We consider further aspects of the hypothesis we proposed in [20], which bears on the interaction of the grammar with the Intentional-Conceptual and Acoustic-Perceptual performance systems. We define the logical relation of asymmetry in (2).

(1) Integrated Asymmetry Hypothesis
Universal Grammar is designed to optimally analyze linguistic expressions in terms of asymmetrical relations.
Universal Parser is designed to optimally recover natural language asymmetries.

(2) Asymmetrical Relation
r is asymmetrical$=_{df}$ $(\forall x)$ $(\forall y)$ $(rxy \supset \sim ryx)$.

We focus here on the relation between Linguistic Models and Natural Language Processing with respect to the treatment of inverse and covert asymmetries. Inverse asymmetries hold in expressions where the Universal Base Hypothesis ([30]), that is the basic specifier-head-complement order of constituents, does not obtain at Spell-out, thus at the Acoustic-Perceptual interface. Covert asymmetries hold in expressions where one term of the asymmetry, either the head, the complement or the specifier, lacks phonetic features, and thus is not visible

[*] This work is supported in part by the Social Sciences and Humanities Research Council of Canada grant to the Major Collaborative Research Project on Asymmetries in Natural Languages and their Treatment by the Performance Systems (Grant no. 412-97-0016).

D.N. Christodoulakis (Ed.): NLP 2000, LNCS 1835, pp. 1–15, 2000.

or interpreted at PF, even though their conceptual features must be visible and thus interpreted at the Conceptual-Intentional interface.

Both linguistic and parsing theories have dealt with inverse and covert asymmetries in phrasal structures, including passive, raising, control, wh- and QP expressions.[1] We focus here on the treatment of inverse and covert asymmetries below the word level, and more specifically we consider inverse and covert asymmetries in derivational morphology. [2]

We assume that specifier-head-complement configurations are part of the derivation of word-structure, as we argued for in [13], where we showed that the combinatorial properties of affixes and roots were best stated in terms of configurational properties. Categorial selection (sub-categorization) lead to over generation and renders derivational morphology irregular, as it fails to express the relation between the structure of affixes and the structure of roots. Thus, an affix such as -able projects an empty specifier position which must be linked by the complement of the verbal projection it composes with. Ergative and unergative verbs may not combine with −able. Likewise, the specifier of the nominal affix −er must be linked by the specifier of the verbal projection it composes with. Ergative verbs may not combine with −er, and so on. Thus, affixes do not combine with categories, they combine with configurations.

It is a challenge for both linguistic and parsing theories to account for the fact that in many languages of the world, including English, the complement selected by an affixal head does not follow the head and that moreover the latter is in some cases covert, as in denominal and deadjectival verbs such as in to embattle and to enlarge.

The organization of this paper is the following. We first present our integrated model. We then identify the main features of a prototype for morphological analysis incorporating the asymmetry-based grammar. Finally, we consider the incorporation of asymmetry-based modules in information processing systems.

---

[1] See [5]-[8] and related works. for discussion of the complement/non-complement asymmetry in syntax with respect to extraction from islands, some examples of which are given below.
  (i) a. ?Which car did John wonder how to fix?
      b. *How did John wonder which car to fix?
      c. Who do you wonder whether Mary likes?
      d. *Who do you wonder whether likes Lucy?
      e. Where do you wonder if Mary went?
      f. *Who do you wonder if went to school
[2] The facts in (i) illustrate the specifier(subject)/non-specifier asymmetry in compound formation. In languages such as English, as well as in many other languages, a complement as well as an adjunct can be the non-head of a compound, whereas this is not the case for the subject and the prepositional complement.
  (i) a. Money-giver to research *Government-giver of money
      b. Research-money-giver *Research-giver of Money

2   The Grammar and the Parser

The following identifies the specificity of our proposal with respect to the theory of grammar as well as with respect to parsing theory in principled based models of parsing. In such models, Singular grammars instantiate specific parameters of Universal Grammar (UG) ([5]-[8] and related works) and parsing is the processing of UG principles and parameters ([3], [25], [27], [29] and related works).

2.1   The Government and Binding Theory

Let us start by considering GB Theory ([5]) and related works), and corresponding Principle-Based parsing models, in particular the "generate and filter" model ([3], and related works).

The GB model consists of a set of derived levels of representation to which specific principles apply. Each level differs with respect to the set of principles it is subject to, even though certain principles apply to more than one level. The corresponding parsing model consists of a set of rules generating structural descriptions and a set of filtering devices implementing the application of the principles to the internal and external interface levels.

An example of principle based parsing in morphology is the PAPPI ([27]) implementation of configurational selection ([13])). The morphological analyzer recovers argument structure properties of complex words on the basis of the interaction of X-bar Theory and Linking. The parser accepts only the cases where the argument-structure properties of the affixal head are satisfied by the configurational properties of its complement domain. No parse is found when the configurational properties of the complement domain of the affixal head do not satisfy its argument-structure selection.

Configurational selection ensures a larger empirical coverage than models where selection is based on categorial selection, as the latter are limited to the immediate sister domain of a head. However, we observe that complexity increases exponentially with specifier-head order, and placing the specifier to the right substantially increases parsing efficiency ([22]).

2.2   The Minimalist Program

The Minimalist Program ([7]) and related works) is based on a set of features, a set of operations (structure-building: MERGE and displacement: Attract/Move/Delete) and a set of Conditions (basically economy conditions on derivations, e.g. Minimal Link, as well as on interface representations, e.g. Full Interpretation). The corresponding parsing model, that could be thought of as the "check and generate" model, recovers asymmetrical relations on the basis of the interaction of feature structure of lexical items and the Conditions of the grammar. We discuss the properties of such a model for parsing inverse and covert morphological asymmetries, thus providing support to Asymmetry-Based parsing, as defined below.

With respect to the current theories of grammar, our proposal is compatible with the anti-symmetry framework [30][3] as well as with the Minimalist Program [8][4]

The contribution of our proposal to these lines of research lies in the centrality of (2) in the grammar. Firstly, phenomena previously accounted for in terms of symmetrical c-command, or in terms of bare sisterhood, are reanalyzed in terms of asymmetry. Secondly, our proposal extends to areas that have not yet been analyzed in terms of asymmetry, including lexical representations and morphological configurations, as discussed below.

With respect to the theory of parsing, the originality of our proposal lies in the close connection between the grammar and the parser. The parser recovers the feature structures of linguistic expressions on the basis of the analysis of local asymmetrical relations. The feature structures include both formal (lexical/functional) and semantic (argument, aspect and concept) features, allowing for full formal/semantic recovery at each step of the parse.

The originality of our integrated model lies in the hypothesis that while the grammar derives complex feature structures, no feature can be interpreted optimally by the performance systems if it is not presented in canonical asymmetrical format. Thus, asymmetry is also central to the interface condition ensuring the visibility/ interpretation of feature structures by the performance systems.

3   A Model of Grammar

Our proposal restricts the Minimalist architecture of the grammar to the following.

```
                  Morpho            Computational
          Lexicon Syntax                 Space
(3)               Phono                  /   \
                                       LF     PF        (IUA)
                          Conceptual-Intentional   Acoustic-Perceptual
```

The restrictions cover each module of the grammar, i.e. the lexicon, the components (morphology, syntax and phonology), the computational space, the interfaces (Logical Form (LF) and Phonetic Form (PF)) as well as the condition on structural descriptions generated by the grammar, the IUA, which we discuss below.

---

[3] According to the Linear Correspondence Axiom ([30]), the linear order of terminals is a function of the asymmetrical c-command relation of the non-terminals. X c-commands Y iff X and Y are categories and X excludes Y and every category that dominates X dominates Y ([30:16]). See also [8], [26], [35], [36] for different definitions of c-command.

[4] According to [8], the symmetrical operation SET-MERGE, further restricted by the selectional properties of heads, derives head-complement structures and the asymmetrical operation PAIR-MERGE derives adjunction structures. . In both cases, asymmetrical relations are part of the operations and the conditions determining the linear order of terminals, as well as the restrictions on the composition of non-terminals.

The first restrictive property of our model is that lexical features are presented in the same format. Both formal and semantic features associated with lexical items are encoded in terms of the same set of asymmetrical relations.[5]

The second restrictive property of our model is that, even though autonomous with respect to the sort of features they include, the operations of each component generate asymmetrical relations. The derivation of the different sorts of linguistic expressions - words and phrases - takes place in the same space and is driven by the conceptual necessity to obtain Canonical Target Configurations (CTC) at the interfaces with the performance systems, as discussed in [14].[6] These configurations, generally referred to as specifier-head, head-complement and adjunct-head relations, are asymmetrical relations. They satisfy the definition in (2), as in each case, there is an unidirectional relation that goes from one member of the relation to the other and not conversely. Assuming that the grammar manipulates feature structures, formal head-dependent asymmetrical relations can be defined as follows:[7]

(4) The features of a complement are properly included in the features of the head it is a complement of.

(5) The features of a specifier are partially excluded from the features of the category it is the specifier of.

(6) The features of an adjunct are excluded from the features of the category it is adjoined to.

Interpreted in terms of inclusion and exclusion relations between feature structures, the formal head-dependent asymmetries are distinct but nevertheless related relations. This makes complements distinct from adjuncts ([7], [30]) while it allows specifiers to be identified with adjuncts ([30]).[8]

Formal (categorial) head-dependent asymmetries in (4)-(6) are not isomorphic to semantic asymmetries in (7)-(9), as the same semantic relation may be supported by different formal head-dependent relations.

(7) An argument satisfies an argument position of the predicate it is an argument of.

(8) An operator binds a variable is its local domain.

(9) A modifier identifies an unspecified feature of the category it is the modifier of.

---

[5] This differs from standard assumptions, where different notations are used to encode different lexical properties, such as sub-categorization frames, argument structures and lexical conceptual structures.

[6] This property of our model makes it distinct from current models of grammar. For example, it differs from a model incorporating Distributed Morphology [28], where parts of morphological derivations are carried out by the rules of other components. Our model also differs from a theory where morphological rules may insert/eliminate/reintroduce affix morphemes in the derivations, as in [1].

[7] Objects are categorically selected by heads, (4), while subjects and adjuncts are not (5), (6); subjects are external to the VP but internal to v, (5); adjuncts are external to [v [VP]], (6).

[8] Our model is compatible with [10], where syntactic modification, either adverbial or adjectival, is restricted to specifier-head relations in the functional projection of lexical categories. In our model, adjunct-head relations are not part of the derivation of syntactic expressions, they are limited to the generation of morphological expressions.

The relations in (7)-(9) also qualify as asymmetrical relations. Each instantiates a unidirectional relation that goes from one member of the relation to the other and not conversely.

In our model, conceptual features are visible/interpretable at the conceptual interface only if they are part of CTCs, whether they are part of syntactic or morphological expressions.

Thus, in derivational morphology, the predicate-argument asymmetry is instantiated in the relation between category-changing affixes and roots; the modifier-modified asymmetry is licensed in the relation between scalar affixes and roots; the operator-variable asymmetry is licensed in the relation between superlative affixes and roots. While the semantic asymmetries are canonically supported by the adjunct-head relation under the word-level, they are supported by the complement-head and the specifier-head relations in phrasal syntax. The following examples illustrate this point.

(10) a. Nobody is *able* to drink this.
      b. This is not drink*able*.
(11) a. Zev protects Stan *too much*.
      b. Zev *over*protects Stan.
(12) a. Homer is *more* happy than Bart.
      b. Homer is happi*er* than Bart.

In (10a), the predicate-argument relation is instantiated by the head-complement relation holding between the verb *able* and the VP *to read this*, and by the adjunct-head relation in (10b), which relates the adjectival affix *-able* and the verb *read*. In (11a), the modifier-modified relation is instantiated by the specifier-head relation relating the adverbial phrase *too much* to the VP *protects Stan* and by the head-adjunct relation in (11b), which relates the prefix *over* to the verb *protect*. In (12a), the operator-variable relation is instantiated by the degree operator *more* in specifier-head relation with the variable it binds in its domain, and in (12b) by the superlative suffix *-er* in adjunct-head relation with the adjective *happy*. Thus, asymmetrical relations range over syntactic and morphological expressions in specific ways.

Another restrictive feature of our model is that it includes a unique condition on the interpretation of the expressions generated by the grammar.

(13) **Interpretation Under Asymmetry** (IUA)
      a. An interpretation is optimally obtained under a unique local asymmetrical relation.
      b. A local asymmetrical relation optimally supports a unique interpretation.

Our model is distinct from current models of grammar and related parsing systems. It differs for example from GB theory ([5], [6]) as the integrated asymmetry model includes a unique condition on derivation and representation, contrary to the multiple GB sub-principles (X-bar, Case-theory, Government Theory, Binding Theory, Theta-Theory). The IUA subsumes the heterogeneous GB sub-principles which, in our view, are particular instantiations of the basic asymmetry of the grammar and need not to be stipulated as such.

4 A Model of Parsing

We assume an integrated theory of language, where the performance system (UP) is designed to use the asymmetrical properties of the linguistic expressions generated by the grammar (UG) in an optimal way. In this perspective, let us take the general principles underlying asymmetry-based parsing to be the following :

(14) Asymmetry-Based Parsing
   a. The parser makes optimal use of the asymmetrical relations in the grammar.
   b. The operations of the parser are controlled by the IUA.
   c. The parser provides an incremental analysis of linguistic expressions.

We are thus proposing a direct implementation of the asymmetry of the grammar in the computational model: the asymmetrical properties of the competence grammar are directly used by the processor. That is, the system integrates universal asymmetrical relations as well as grammar-specific parametric values. The lexical database includes the idiosyncratic properties of underived items, couched in terms of asymmetrical relations. The actions of the parser are oriented by the identification of local asymmetrical relations at each step of the parse, including categorization, attachments and dependencies between categories. In our model, computational operations are oriented by natural language asymmetries and not by language- independent heuristics. The IUA is used as an overall control device that ensures the legitimacy of the choices undertaken by the parser.

(15) Control
   a. Search until an asymmetrical relation is identified.
   b. Search for formal and semantic asymmetry at each step of the parse.
   c. In case of multiple choice, choose the more local asymmetrical relation rather than a non-local one.

Our parsing model differs from the "generate and filter" model that implemented GB Theory, as the decisions of the parser at each step of the parse are oriented by recovery of asymmetrical relations. We expect the problems of over-generation and speed associated with the early principled-based parsers to be significantly reduced in a parsing model that incorporates an asymmetry-based grammar.

The IUA's role as an overall control mechanism is motivated by our understanding of the processing of structural complexity.

Structural complexity arises in situations where more than one asymmetrical relation is available at a given stage of the parse. The complexity in the processing of multiple dependencies and garden paths can be treated in a unified way, as we will see immediately.

Multiple attachments are cases where a given asymmetrical semantic relation can be supported by more than one formal relation of the same sort. Garden paths are cases where different sorts of asymmetrical relations are available.

Alongside phrasal cases of multiple attachments, illustrated in (16a,b), structural complexity may also arise below the word level, as exemplified in (16c,d).

(16)   a. John saw Bill on the hill.
   b. John photographed Bill with a knife.
   c. John rewired the house.
   d. John reopened the theater.

The structural complexity arising from prefixed verbal constructions, such as (16c), is a consequence of the licensing of more than one local asymmetrical relation, inducing a repetitive/restitutive interpretation or only a repetitive interpretation for the event denoted by the verbal predicate.

Garden paths are more difficult to process than multiple attachments, as contrary to the latter, they present a situation where different sorts of asymmetrical relations are possible at a given point. With syntactic garden paths such as (17a), *the horse* is mis-analyzed as the subject of the VP, a specifier-head relation, instead of being analyzed as the head of a restrictive relative clause. The presence of the complementizer *that* in (17b) dismisses the garden path effect. With morphological garden path, such as (17c), the iterative prefix is mis-analyzed as part of a head-complement relation within the verbal projection, instead of being analyzed as an external modifier of the verbal projection. The presence of the intervening internal prefix *en-* in (17d), entering into a head-complement relation within the verbal projection, forces an adjunct-head analysis for the iterative prefix, and dismisses the garden path effect.

(17)   a. #The horse went past the barn fell.
    b. The horse [that went past the barn fell]
    c. #They reforced their positions.
    d. They [re[en-forced]] their positions

Garden paths are worse for the processor than multiple attachments because, contrary to the latter, the former present a situation where more than one sort of asymmetrical relation is virtually possible at a given point of the parse in the grammar of the language under consideration.

The IUA predicts that the optimal interpretation will be that induced by the more local asymmetrical relation. This makes the correct prediction for multiple PP attachments, where the PP is optimally analyzed as a modifier of the VP and not as a modifier of the whole sentence, as well as for the restitutive/repetitive interpretation of the prefixed verbal structures. In the case of garden paths, the IUA also makes the right prediction. The local asymmetrical relation is preferred and leads to mis-analysis.

Thus, in our integrated model, the grammar and the performance systems manipulate linguistic expressions via unique local asymmetrical relations. Morphological as well as syntactic expressions containing either polysemic morphemes or virtually multiple formal asymmetrical relations at any given point are not interpreted optimally.

4.1   Parsing Morphological Asymmetries

We consider one consequence of our proposal for parsing morphological structure with inverse and covert asymmetries.

As parsing is oriented by asymmetrical relations in our view, it can also optimally parse inverse asymmetries triggered by visible morpho-syntactic features. We will show that covert asymmetries, that is grammatical relations not supported by phonetic features, can also be recovered optimally given configurational primitives and feature structure specifications.

4.2   Morpho-conceptual Parsing

We present the main features of a prototype implementing the asymmetry-based grammar for the analysis of morphological structure. We refer to this prototype a CONCE-MORPHO-PARSE.[9]

---

[9] CONCE-MORPHO-PARSE is a refinement of MORPHO-PARSE [16], which was designed to analyze the categorial and argument-structure properties of complex words.

The morphological parsing is performed by a Unification Grammar and a LR(1) control structure. The prototype builds morphological trees for words (W) identifying the Head (H), External Prefix (EP), Internal Prefix (IP), Suffix (S), Root (R) morphemes. It recovers the asymmetrical adjunct-head (AH), head-complement (HC) and specifier-head (SH) relations the morphemes are a part of, as well as covert asymmetries not supported by PF visible morphemes, but supporting conceptual feature structures.

A unification-based chart parser provides the parse trees with categorial and conceptual feature structures. Unification is useful in implementing an asymmetry-based grammar, as asymmetry holds primarily for pairs of feature structures. Thus, feature unification under head-complement asymmetry is possible only when the features of the complement are properly included in the features of the head; feature unification under adjunct-head relation is possible only if the features of the adjunct are not included in the features of the head; feature identification under specifier-head asymmetry is possible only if the features of the head are partially excluded from the feature structure of its head. The LR(1) grammar controls Unification and implements the IUA Condition, as the operations of the grammar apply only if the relevant symmetrical relation between two feature structures is met. The prototype builds trees on the basis of the recognition of head-complement (HC), adjunct-head (AH) and specifier-head (SH) relations, as only these asymmetrical relations are accepted by the parser.

A description of the morpho-conceptual parsing of the right edge of words is detailed in [16].We present here the analysis of the left edge of words with CONCE-MORPHO-PARSE, incorporating the morpho-conceptual analysis of prefixes detailed in [18] in the asymmetry-based grammar.

The parser analyses a string of morphemes from left to right and assigns, for every word (W), a parse tree which correctly differentiates external prefixes, basically modifiers and operators, from internal prefixes, basically predicates. This makes the correct predictions with respect to the argument structure properties of prefixed words, in particular, that external prefixes do not change argument structure while internal prefixes do, as well as accounting for their aspectual and quantificational properties. This is not the case for current morphological analyzers, where all prefixes are treated on par, as we will illustrate below.

In our model, formal asymmetrical relations are paired with semantic relations (predicate-argument, modifier-modified and operator-variable relations). While category-changing suffixes are part of predicate-argument asymmetry, derivational prefixes also participate in the modifier-modified asymmetry as well as in the operator-variable asymmetry. CONCE-MORPHO-PARSE recovers these asymmetries given the Unification grammar, the LR(1) control structure and the morpho-conceptual lexicon.

CONCE-MORPHO-PARSE recovers predicate-argument, modifier-modified and operator-variable asymmetries. The first relation is licensed under argument saturation, the second relation is licensed when there is an identification relation, the third relation is licensed when an operator binds a variable. The parse trees derived by CONCE-MORPHO-PARSE present a fine-grained analysis of complex words, as illustrated here with the parse tree in (18) for the prefixed de-adjectival verb *re-enlarge*.

While MORPHO-PARSE implemented the morphological theory of [24], CONCE-MORPHO-PARSE implements the theory of asymmetry ([17], [18]). It analyzes word-internal formal and semantic asymmetries. The prototype is implemented by Christian Thérien in the Asymmetry project at the Université du Québec à Montréal.

```
              W
              !
             AH
        PE - -!- -    AH
        Re+      HC- - !- - S
(18)    [Rel]_F    !        [V]
       [AGAIN]     !      [BECOME]
           PI- - ! - -R
           [Rel]    [state]
           [IN]     large
           en+
```

Categorially, CONCE-MORPHO-PARSE associates an adverbial feature (Rel$_F$) to the prefix *re-*, which is the adjunct in the asymmetrical adjunct-head relation formed by the prefix and the rest of the structure. However, this asymmetrical relation cannot be recovered at this point of the parse, as there is no such relation between the iterative prefix and the directional prefix *en-*, which is the second element analyzed by the parser. As there is no asymmetry between the first and the second prefix, they do not form a constituent. There is however an asymmetry between the directional prefix *en-* and the root adjective *large*. It is a head-complement relation, given the lexical specification of the prefix *en-* and the adjectival root *large*. The Unification Grammar correctly parses the head-complement relation. This relation, encoding a more local asymmetrical relation, is parsed before the adjunct-head relation. This ensures the connection of the already parsed head-complement structure to the covert verbal head of the structure. Finally, the Unification grammar attaches the external prefix to the last parsed relation.

It is crucial to note here that the category of the covert head of the structure [V] as well as its conceptual feature [BECOME] are derived by the parser, as the prefix *re-* locally identifies the verbal event (e) category it is adjoined to, as specified in its lexical entry. In the case at hand, the event denoted by the predicate is inchoative [BECOME], given that the verbal projection includes an adjective. Inchoative verbs are change of state predicates and states can be categorically realized as adjectives.

The configurational as well as conceptual distinctions between complementation-predication on the one hand and adjunction-modification on the other, are not expressed by current morphological parsers. Furthermore, there is no way for a parser that does not license phonetically null categories to assign the correct categorial structure to deadjectival (and denominal) verbs in English without losing the generalization expressed by the Relativized Head Rule (Di Sciullo and Williams, 1987) according to which the categorial head of the word is the rightmost member of that word marked for categorial features. CONCE-MORPHO-PARSE recovers covert structures on the basis of formal and semantic asymmetries, given independently needed conditions such as the Relativized Head and the Adjunct Identification Condition ([15]).

Summing up, our prototype assigns the correct categorial and semantic structure to complex words on the basis of the recovery of formal and semantic asymmetries. Moreover, it is able to restore covert formal and semantic feature structures on the basis of decisions taken locally.

5 Application

We discuss an application of our hypothesis: the incorporation of asymmetry-based parsing in Information Processing. We present a view of information processing (IP) that relies on asymmetry-based natural language processing. Our line of reasoning applies to IP systems in general, including information extraction and information retrieval systems, even though each differs with respect to its internal architecture, type of inquiry, type of results and the evaluation measure adopted. We will not discuss of these differences here.

As existing information processing systems are beginning to integrate articulated lexical knowledge ([11], [34], [4], and related works) we expect that a refinement of their architecture with asymmetry-based parsing will increase their performance.

Amongst the IP approaches incorporating linguistic modules, we find the following architecture for Information Extraction which includes grammatical as well as lexical modules.

(19) **IE architecture**

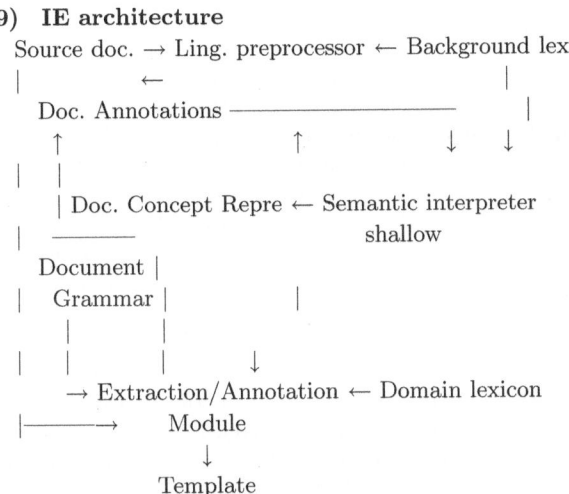

The following diagram presents the modules of a linguistic processor incorporating morpho-conceptual and syntactic-conceptual analysis.

(20) **Linguistic processor**

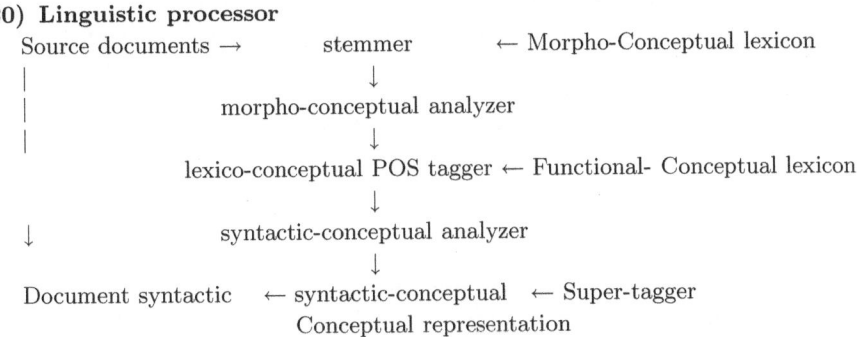

The integration of CONCE-MORPHO-PARSE and other asymmetry-based modules in IP systems optimizes their performance.

While stemming algorithms such as [33] do not rely on word-internal information, in our model parts of words provide categorial and conceptual features that contribute to the form and content of the information they convey. Processing of these features is necessary for IP in more than one way. Morpho-conceptual features are part of the feature structures of single words and they constitute the basis upon which decisions about the properties of their local syntactic context can be anticipated. These predictions are not based on statistical calculus, but rather on morpho-conceptual knowledge.

In our model, IP reduces to one case of grammar use by a performance systems. That is, we take the performance systems to be able to use the formal properties of the grammar to extract or retrieve information from texts. Thus, an IP system is an automated performance system that interprets the linguistic expressions it is exposed to on the basis of the asymmetrical properties of these expressions in order to retrieve or extract specific information. We take these properties to be mainly grammatical in nature and not exclusively statistical.

However, most functioning IP systems are exclusively based on stochastic methods, such as the Boolean search criterion.[10] The use of such methods is based on the view that the representation of the meaning of natural language expressions is independent of the very properties of these expressions. On the other hand, morpho-conceptual systems are natural language dependent. Even though, as is the case for any system, they constitute a simplification of the object they define: they are similar to their object in such a way as to allow new knowledge to be obtained about it.

While it is acknowledged that IP systems based on strictly probabilistic methods achieve high levels of performance ([12], [31], and retated works), it is generally admitted that these systems have now met their limits. Several works indicate that the use of natural language processing methods in IP systems contribute to improving the performance of these systems ([32], [34], and related works).

Different factors contribute to the non-optimality of IP systems operating on strictly probabilistic methods. One factor is that stemming algorithms, such as the Porter algorithm, do not remove affixes on the basis of morphological structure. Such algorithms cannot be parametrized to apply to languages with non-concatenative morphology, such as Arabic. In contrast, IP systems based on natural language asymmetries may do so.

Another factor that limits the performance of IP systems is that documents are indexed on the basis of unanalyzed lexical items (key words). Such processing is not optimal because the meaning/information conveyed by texts is not expressed by unanalyzed lexical items. In our model, the information conveyed by lexical items is a function of the asymmetrical relations holding between their parts, as illustrated above in (18). It is likely that IP algorithms that recover word internal conceptual feature structures will present a closer approximation to semantic information than algorithms based exclusively on stochastic methods.

Our proposal affects the following modules of the linguistic processor: the stemmer, which identifies the canonical form of words, the morphological analyzer, which

---

[10] In Information Retrieval systems for example, indexing of the query consists in its translation into Boolean proper forms, while indexing of the documents consists in the identification of document profiles by means of the selection of descriptors (significant words) for document profiles using a descriptor dictionary.

identifies word-internal structure, the part-of-speech taggers, which identifies the category of lexical items and the post-taggers, which identifies the constituent structure of phrases. We expect that IP systems will gain in optimality if they include asymmetrical relations. Such systems will achieve the following: a fine-grained conceptual analysis of word-structure, a fine-grained categorial analysis of word-structure, disambiguation before part-of-speech tagging and greater precision in super-tagging.

Assuming that IP systems are series of text filters, as depicted above in (20), the first filter submits a text to morphological and lexical analysis, assigning tags, including morpho-conceptual feature structures to words. The dictionary plays an important part in tagging. In particular, the lexical entries for derivational affixes and functional categories carry important information about the syntactic and the semantic structure of the linguistic expressions. The initial tagging is performed on the basis of a limited dictionary consisting of function words. The function words are specified in the functional-conceptual lexicon in our features in asymmetrical format. For example *to* is either a preposition (Rel) or a complementizer (Rel$_F$), a predicate (PRED (r)) or an operator of an event OP (e), with the conceptual properties TO (Loc) or INF (e).

A comparison of the words contained in the text against the lexicon is performed, a sentence at a time, by a sequential merging process. As a result of the look-up process, any word found in the text will have received one or more tags. The majority of content words not listed in the lexicon are tagged using morphological information about the suffixes, in the morpho-conceptual lexicon. Disambiguation is performed by analyzing formal and semantic asymmetries in local domains.

The performance of IP systems incorporating (20) is superior to systems that do not include natural language processing modules, as well as systems that do so but are not asymmetry based.

The accuracy of the processing increases with respect to both the precision of the information extracted from texts as well as with respect to the relevance of the documents retrieved. The system is able to access the same referential entity supported by inverse and covert asymmetries. This is not the case for other systems, such as Cassiopée (Alta Vista). These systems will typically provide significantly different numbers of documents when confronted with queries where the grammatical relations within nominal expressions are inverse. Furthermore, the number of retrieved documents will also be significantly different with queries containing expanded forms of the same asymmetrical relation. In contrast, the integration of asymmetry-based facilities in information processing systems improves their performance. The presence of more words in the query reduces the scope of the search by more precisely circumscribing the searched referent.

References

1. Anderson, S. (1992) A-Morphous Morphology. Cambridge: Cambridge University Press.
2. Arampatzis, A.T., T. Tsoris and C.H.A. Koster, 1997. IRENA: Information Retrieval Engine Based on Natural Language Analysis. RIAO 97 Proceedings, McGill University.
3. Berwick, R. 1991. Principles of Principle-Based Parsing. In R. Berwick, S. Abney & C. Tenny (eds.) Principle-Based Parsing. Dordrecht: Kluwer.
4. Boguraev, B. & J. Pustejovsky (eds.) 1996. Corpus Processing for Lexical Acquisition. Cambridge, Mass.: MIT Press.
5. Chomsky, N. 1981. Lectures on Government and Binding. Dordrecht: Foris.

6. Chomsky, N. 1986. Barriers. Cambridge, Mass.: The MIT Press.

7. Chomsky, N. 1995. The Minimalist Program. Cambridge, Mass.: The MIT Press.

8. Chomsky, N. 1998. Minimalist Inquiries. Ms. MIT.

9. Church, K.1988. Stochastic Parts Program and NP Parser for Unrestricted Text. Proceedings of the Second Association of Computational Linguistics Conference on Applied Natural Language Processing.

10. Cinque, G. 1997. Adverbs and Functional Heads. A Cross-linguistic Perspective. Oxford University Press.

11. Copestake, A., & T. Briscoe. 1996. Semi-productive Polysemy and Sense Extension. In J. Pustejovsky & B. Boguraev (eds.) Lexical Semantics. The Problem of Polysemy. Oxford University Press.

12. Derose, S. J. 1988. Grammatical Category Disambiguation by Statistical Optimization. Computational Linguistics, 14.1.

13. Di Sciullo, A.M. 1995. X-bar Selection. In Johan Roorick and Laurie Zaring eds, Phrase Structure and the Lexicon. Dordrecht: Kluwer. pp. 77-107.

14. Di Sciullo, A.M. 1996. Modularity and Xo/XP Asymmetries. Linguistic Analysis 26.

15. Di Sciullo, A.M.. 1997a. Prefixed verbs and Adjunct Identification. In A.M. Di Sciullo (ed.) Projections and Interface Conditions. Oxford University Press.

16. Di Sciullo, A.M. 1997b. Argument Structure Parsing. In A. Ralli, M. Grigoriadou, G. Philokyprou, D. Christodoulakis and E. Galiotou eds. Papers in Natural Language Processing.

17. Di Sciullo, A.M. 1998. Features and Asymmetrical Relations in Morphological Objects. GLOW 1998 Newsletter.

18. Di Sciullo, A.M. 1999a.The Local Asymmetry Connection. MIT Working Papers in Linguistics. Cambridge, Mass. MIT.

19. Di Sciullo, A.M. 1999b. Formal Context and Morphological Analysis. In P. Bouquet, L. Serafini, P. Brézillon, M. Benerecetti, F. Castellani (eds.) Modelling and Using Context. CONTEXT'99. Springler.

20. Di Sciullo, A.M. 1999c. An Integrated Competence-Performance Model. VEXTAL. Venice. Italy.

21. Di Sciullo, A.M. 1999d.Conceptual Knowledge and Interpretation. ICCS/JICCS. Chukyo. Japan.

22. Di Sciullo, A.M. & S. Fong. 1999. Morphological Complexity. Ms. UQAM.

23. Di Sciullo, A.M. & C. Tenny. 1997. Modification, Event Structure and the Word/Phrase Asymmetry. NELS 18.

24. Di Sciullo, A.M. and E. Williams, 1987. On the Definition of Word. Cambridge, Mass.: The MIT Press.

25. Door, B. 1991. Principle-Based Parsing for Machine Translation. In R. Berwick, S. Abney & C. Tenny (eds.) Principle-Based Parsing. Dordrecht: Kluwer.

26. Epstein, S. 1995. The Derivation of Syntactic Relations. Ms. Harvard University

27. Fong, S. 1991. The Computational Implementation of Principled-Based Parsers. In R. Berwick, S. Abney & C. Tenny (eds.) Principle-Based Parsing. Dordrecht: Kluwer.

28. Halle, M. and A. Marantz, 1993. Distributed Morphology and the Pieces of Inflection. In K. Hale and J. Keyser (eds), The View from Building 20. Cambridge, MA: MIT Press

29. Kashket, M. 1991. Parsing Walpiri. A Free Word Order Language. In R. Berwick, S. Abney & C. Tenny (eds.) Principle-Based Parsing. Dordrecht: Kluwer.

30. Kayne, R. 1994. The Antisymmetry of Syntax. Cambridge, Mass.: MIT Press.

31. Marken, C.G. 1990. Parsing the LOB Corpus. Association of Computational Linguistics Annual Meeting.

32. Pohlmann R, and W. Kraaij, 1997. The Effect of Syntactic Phrase Indexing on Retrieval Performance for Dutch Texts. RIAO 97 Proceedings. McGill University.

33. Porter, M.F. 1980. An Algorithm for Suffix Stripping Program, 14.3.

34. Pustejovsky, J., B. Boguraev, M. Verhagen, P. Buitelaar, M. Johnston, 1997. Semantic Indexing and Typed Hyperlinking. In Natural Language Processing for the World Wide Web. Papers from the 1977 AAAI Spring Symposium. AAAI Press.

35. Robert, F. & K. Vijayashankar, 1995. C-command and Grammatical Primitives. GLOW 1995 Newsletter.

36. Reuland, E. 1998. Deriving C-command in Binding. NELS 18.

37. Savoy, J. 1993. Stemming of French Words Based on Grammatical Categories. Journal of the American Society for Information Sciences, 44.1.

38. Uszkoreit, H. 1990. Unification in Linguistics. Class Lectures, 2nd European Summer School in Language, Logic and Information. Leuven.

Universal Segmentation of Text with the Sumo Formalism

Julien Quint[1,2]

[1] GETA-CLIPS-IMAG, Université Joseph Fourier
BP 53, 38041 Grenoble Cedex 9, France
[2] Xerox Research Centre Europe
6, chemin de Maupertuis, 38240 Meylan, France
julien.quint@imag.fr

Abstract. We propose a universal formalism for the segmentation of text documents called Sumo. Its main purpose is to help creating segmentation systems for documents in any language. Because the processing is independent of the language, any level of segmentation (be it character, word, sentence, paragraph, etc.) can be considered. We will argue about the usefulness of such a formalism, describe the framework for segmentation on which Sumo relies, and give detailed examples to demonstrate some of its features.

Introduction

Tokenization, or word segmentation, is a fundamental task of almost all NLP systems. In languages that use word separators in their writing, tokenization seems easy: every sequence of characters between two whitespaces or punctuation marks is a word. This works reasonably well, but exceptions are handled in a cumbersome way. On the other hand, there are languages that do not use word separators. A much more complicated processing is needed, closer to morphological analysis or part-of-speech tagging. Tokenizers designed for those languages are generally very tied to a given system and language.

However, the gap becomes smaller when we look at sentence segmentation: a simplistic approach would not be sufficient because of the ambiguity of punctuation signs. And if we consider the segmentation of a document into higher-level units such as paragraphs, sections, and so on, we can notice that language becomes less relevant.

These observations lead to the definition of our formalism for segmentation (not just tokenization) that considers the process independently from the language. By describing a segmentation system formally, a clean distinction can be made between the processing itself and the linguistic data it uses. This entails the ability to develop a truly multilingual system by using a common segmentation engine for the various languages of the system; conversely, one can imagine evaluating several segmentation methods by using the same set of data with different strategies.

D.N. Christodoulakis (Ed.): NLP 2000, LNCS 1835, pp. 16–26, 2000.

Sumo is the name of the proposed formalism, evolving from initial work by [1]. Some theoretical works from the literature also support this approach: [2] shows that some segmentation techniques can be generalized to any language, regardless of their writing system. The sentence segmenter of [3] and the issues raised by [4] prove that even in English or French, segmentation is not so trivial. Lastly, [5] handles all kinds of presyntactic processing in one step, arguing that there are strong interactions between segmentation and morphology.

1   A Framework for Segmentation

1.1   Overview

Sumo stores a document as a layered structure. Each layer of the structure is a view of the document at a given level of segmentation; the number and exact nature of each level of segmentation are not fixed by Sumo but defined by the author of the segmentation system. The example in section 3.1 uses a two-layer structure (figure 3) corresponding to two levels of segmentation, characters and words. A third level, for sentences, would be added to make a sentence segmenter.

The levels of segmentation do not necessarily have any linguistic or structural meaning, so that artificial levels can be introduced when needed. It is also interesting to note that several layers can belong to the same level. In the example of section 3.3 the result structure can have an indefinite number of levels, and all levels are of the same kind.

We call *item* the segmentation unit of a document at a given segmentation level (e.g. items of the word level are words). The document is then represented at every segmentation level in terms of its items; because segmentation is usually ambiguous, *item graphs* are used to factorize all the possible segmentations. Ambiguity issues are further addressed in section 2.2.

The main processing paradigms of Sumo are *identification* and *transformation*. With identification, new item graphs are built by identifying items from a source graph using a *segmentation resource*. These graphs are then modified by transformation processes. Section 2 gives the details about both identification and transformation.

1.2   Item Graphs

The item graphs are directed acyclic graphs; they are similar to the word graphs of [6] or the string graphs of [7]. They are actually represented by means of weighted finite-state automata [8]. In order to facilitate their manipulations, two additional properties are also enforced: these automata always have a single finite-state and no dangling arcs (this can be enforced by pruning the automata after every modification). The examples of section 3 show various item graphs.

An item is an arc in the automaton, which is a complex structure containing a label (generally the surface form of the item), a weight, named attributes and relations. Attributes are used to hold information on the item, like part of speech tags (see section 3.2).

As is the case with finite-state automata, nodes do not carry information *per se*, but the order of the outgoing arc is important as it allows to rank paths in the graph.

1.3   Relations

Relations are links between levels. Items from a given graph are linked to items of the graph from which they were identified. We call the first graph the *lower* graph and the graph that was the source for the identification the *upper* graph. Relations exist between a path in the upper graph and either a path or a subgraph in the lower graph.

Figure 1 illustrates the first kind of relation, called *path relation*. This example in French is a relation between the two characters of the word "du" which is really a contraction of "de le".

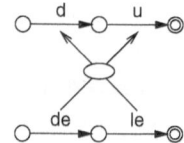

Fig. 1. A path relation.

Figure 2 illustrates the other kind of relation called *subgraph relation*. In this example the sentence "ABCDEFG." (we can imagine that A through G are Chinese characters) is related to several possible segmentations.

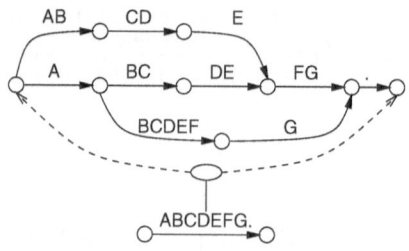

Fig. 2. A graph relation.

The interested reader may refer to [9] for a comparable structure (multiple layers of a document and relations) used in translation memory.

2   Processing a Document

2.1   Identification

Identification is the process of identifying new items from a source graph. Using the source graph and a segmentation resource, new items are built to form a new graph. A segmentation resource, or simply resource, describes the vocabulary of the language, by defining a mapping between the source and the target level of segmentation. Finite-state transducers are used to store segmentation resources; identification is performed by applying the transducer to the source automaton to produce the target automaton.

Segmentation resources are a collection of identification rules, an example of which is shown in section 3.3. The left hand side of the rule is a path in the source graph. The right hand side describes the associated path in the upper graph. A relation is created between these two paths; it is either a path relation or a graph relation. In this paper, we will only see path relations; graph relations are created using rules with a slightly different syntax.

Since resources are represented as transducers, they can be combined to create new resources. Sumo uses the usual operators from finite-state calculus (e.g. union, intersection, composition, etc). Two more operators are added: the cascade operator that applies a sequence of transducers in order until one of them matches (this is similar to the union of several transducers, except that *all* transducers are applied in this case). The "star" or "iteration" operator, inspired from [10], applies the same transducer iteratively until a fixed point is reached (an application of this operation is found in the example of section 3.3). Another benefit of using transducers for segmentation resources is that resources can then be created from segmentation graphs during the processing of the document, as [1] details.

Another extension to the finite-state model is the introduction of variables in the identification rules to allow for backreferences. Consider the following rule:

```
$A $B -> $B $A / $A = a+, $B = b+ ;
```

This identifies a string of a's followed by a string of b's in the source graph and writes the identified string of b's followed by the identified string of a's in the target graph. Backreferences are handled by the rule engine using special symbols in the rule transducer.

A special kind of identification is the automatic segmentation that takes place at the entry point of the process. A character graph can be created automatically by segmenting an input text document, knowing its encoding. This text document can be in raw text or XML format. Another possibility for input is to use a graph of items that was created previously, either by Sumo, or converted to the format recognized by Sumo.

2.2   Transformation

Ambiguity is a central issue when talking about segmentation. The absence or ambiguity of word separators can lead to multiple segmentations, and more than one of them can have a meaning. As [11] testify, several native Chinese speakers do not always agree on one unique tokenization for a given sentence.

Thanks to the use of item graphs, Sumo can handle ambiguity efficiently. Why try to fully disambiguate a tokenization when there is no agreement on a single best solution? Moreover, segmentation is usually just a basic step of processing in an NLP system, and some decisions may need more information than what a segmenter is able to provide. An uninformed choice at this stage can affect the next stages in a negative way. Transformations are a way to modify the item graphs so that the "good" paths (segmentations) can be kept and the "bad" ones discarded. We can also of course provide full disambiguation (see section 3.1 for instance) by means of transformations.

In Sumo transformations are handled by transformation functions that manipulate the objects of the formalism: graphs, nodes, items, paths (a special kind of graph), etc. These functions are written using an imperative language illustrated in section 3.1. They can also be written in the same way than identification rule, with the difference that source and target levels are now the same, the target items replacing the source items.

A transformation can either be applied directly to a graph or attached to a graph relation. In the latter case, the original graph is not modified, and its transformed counterpart is only accessible through the relation.

3 Examples of Use

3.1 Maximum Tokenization

Some classic heuristics for tokenization are classified by [2] under the collective moniker of *maximum tokenization*. This section describes how to implement a "maximum tokenizer" that tokenizes raw text documents in a given language and character encoding (e.g. English in ASCII, French in Iso-Latin-1, Chinese in Big5 or GB).

Common Set-Up. Our tokenizer is built with two levels: the input level is the character level, automatically segmented using the encoding information. The token level is built from these characters, first by an exhaustive identification of the tokens, then by reducing the number of paths to the one considered the best by the Maximum Tokenization heuristic.

The system works in three steps, with complete code shown below. First, the character level is created by automatic segmentation (lines 1-5, `input level` being the special graph that is automatically created from a raw file through stdin). The second step is to create the word graph by identifying words from character using a dictionary. A resource called `ABCdic` is created from a transducer file (lines 6-8), then the graph `words` is created by identifying items from the source level `characters` using the resource `ABCdic` (lines 9-12). The third step is the disambiguation of the word level by applying a Maximum Tokenization heuristic (line 13).

```
1   characters: input level {
2     encoding: <ASCII, UTF-8, Big5...>
3     type: raw;
4     from: stdin;
5   }
6   ABCdic: resource {
7     file: \"ABCdic.fst\";
8   }
9   words: graph <- identify {
10    source: characters;
11    resource: ABCdic;
12  }
13  words <- ft(words.start-node);
```

Figure 3 illustrates the situation for the input string "ABCDEFG" where A through G are characters and A, AB, B, BC, BCDEF, C, CD, D, DE, E, F, FG and G are words found in the resource ABCdic. The situation shown is after line 12 and before line 13.

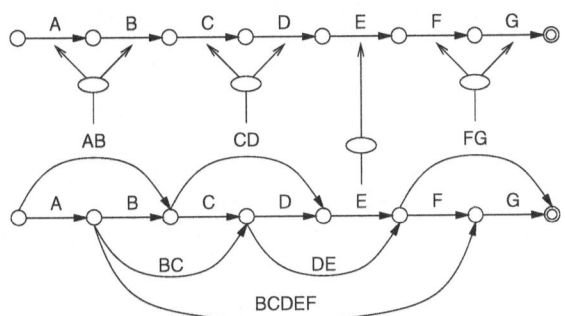

Fig. 3. Exhaustive tokenization of the string ABCDEFG.

We will see in the next three subsections the different heuristics and their implementations in Sumo.

Forward Maximum Tokenization. Forward Maximum Tokenization consists of scanning the string from left to right and selecting the token of maximum length any time an ambiguity occurs. On the example of figure 3, the result tokenization of the input string would be AB/CD/E/FG.

Shown below is a function called ft that builds a path recursively by traversing the token graph, appending the longest item to the path at each node. ft takes a node as input and returns a path (line 1). If the node is final, the empty path is returned (lines 2-3), otherwise the array of items of the nodes (n.items) is searched and the longest item stored in longest (lines 4-10). The returned path consists of this longest item prepended to the longest path starting from the destination node of this item (line 11).

```
1  function ft (n: node) -> path {
2    if final(n) {
3      return ();
4    } else {
5      longest: item <- n.items[1];
6      foreach it in n.items[2..] {
7        if it.length > longest.length {
8          longest <- it;
9        }
10     }
11     return (longest # ft(longest.dest));
12   }
13 }
```

Backward Maximum Tokenization. Backward Maximum Tokenization is the same as Forward Maximum Tokenization except that the string is scanned from right to left, instead of left to right. On the example of figure 3, the tokenization of the input string would yield A/BC/DE/FG under Backward Maximum Tokenization.

Below is shown a function called bt that is very similar to ft, except that it works backward by looking at incoming arcs of the considered node. bt is called on the final state of the graph and stops when a node with no incoming arcs is found (lines 2-3), which can only be the start node. Another implementation of this function would be to apply ft on the reversed graph and then reversing the path obtained.

```
1  function bt (n: node) -> path {
2    if n.incoming.length = 0 {
3      return ();
4    } else {
5      longest: item <- n.incoming[1];
6      foreach it in n.incoming[2..] {
7        if it.length > longest.length {
8          longest <- it;
9        }
10     }
11     return (bt(longest.src) # longest);
12   }
13 }
```

Shortest Tokenization. Shortest Tokenization is concerned with minimizing the overall number of tokens in the text. On the example of figure 3, the tokenization of the input string would yield A/BCDEF/G under shortest tokenization.

Below is shown a function called st that finds the shortest path in the graph. It works in a very similar way to ft, except that for each item starting from this node, we are not interested in the longest one but in the one leading to the path of minimum length (lines 4-14).

```
1   function st (n: node) -> path {
2     if final(n) {
3       return ();
4     } else {
5       p, mp: path;
6       i, mi: item;
7       mp <- st(n.items[1].dest)
8       foreach i in n.items[2..] {
9         p <- st(i.dest);
10        if p.length < mp.length {
11          mp <- p;
12          mi <- i;
13        }
14      }
15      return (mi # mp);
16    }
17  }
```

Combination of Maximum Tokenization Techniques. One of the features of Sumo is to allow the comparison of different segmentation strategies using the same set of data. As we have just seen, the three strategies described above can indeed be compared efficiently by modifying only part of the third step of the processing. Letting the system run three times on the same set of input documents can then give three different sets of results to be compared by the author of the system (against each other and against a reference tokenization, for instance).

And yet a different set-up for our "maximum tokenizer" would be to select not just the optimal path according to one of the heuristics, but the paths selected by the three of them, combining the three paths into a graph. We would then obtain the output graph shown in figure 4, by changing line 13 of the general program to:

```
words <- ft(words.start-node) |
         bt(words.end-node) |
         st(words.start-node);
```

3.2   Statistical Tokenization and Part of Speech Tagging

This example shows a more complicated tokenization system, using the same set-up as the one from section 3.1, with a disambiguation process using statistics.

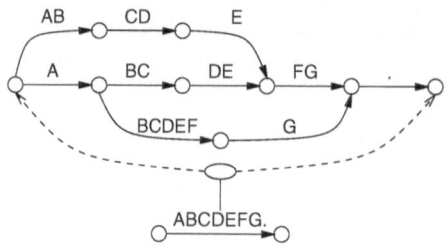

Fig. 4. Three maximum tokenizations.

Our reference for this model is the Chasen Japanese tokenizer and part of speech tagger documented in [12]. Our example is a high-level description of how to implement a similar system with Sumo.

The basic set-up is the same as the one used previously: a level for the characters, from which a level for words is built by identification using dictionaries, then this level is disambiguated.

Exhaustive Segmentation. All possible segmentations are derived from the character level to create the word level. The resource used for this is a dictionary of the language that maps the surface form of the words (in terms of their characters) to their base form, part of speech, and a cost (Chasen also adds pronunciation, conjugation type, and semantic information). All this information is stored in the item as attributes, the surface form being used as the label for the item; the only exception is the cost, which is stored as a weight on an epsilon arc. Figure 5 shows the identification of the word "cats" which is identified as the noun "cat", with cost 200.

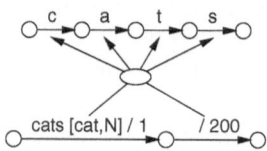

Fig. 5. Identification of the word "cats".

Statistical Disambiguation. The disambiguation method relies on a bigram model: each pair of successive items has a "connectivity cost". These costs are encoded with an epsilon arc between two successive items with a weight reflecting the connectivity cost and the cost of the morpheme itself (figure 6). Since Sumo manipulates weighted finite-state automata, it provides functions for computing the cost of a path and can rank all the possible paths according to their cost.

Disambiguating the output is choosing the path with optimal cost, but we may rather want to select all solutions above a given threshold, or the n best ones.

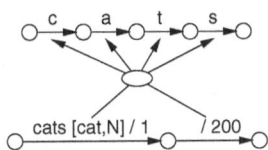

Fig. 6. Connectivity costs.

3.3 A Formal Example

This last example is more formal and serves as an illustration of some powerful features of Sumo. [7] has a similar example implemented using Q systems. In both cases the goal is to transform an input string of the form $a^n b^n c^n, n \geq 0$ into a single item S (assuming that the input alphabet does not contain S), meaning that the input string is a word of this language.

The set-up here is once again to start with a lower level automatically created from the input, then to build intermediate levels until a final level containing only the item S is produced (at which point the input is recognized), or until the process can no longer carry on (at which point the input is rejected).

The building of intermediate levels is handled by the identification rule below:

```
# _ (S) a $a b $b c $c _ #  ->  S $a $b $c /
   $a = a*, $b = b*, $c = c* ;
```

The left-hand side of the rule is the path to be matched in the lower graph, described by a regular expression. The # symbol indicates the beginning or the end of the lower graph. The _ symbol is used to distinguish the sequence of items being identified from its context. The right-hand side of the rule is the path created in the lower graph whenever a path in the lower graph is recognized. The last part of the rule describes the variables used in the rule.

This rule works by eating up the first a, b and c of a sequence of the form $a^*b^*c^*$ (with an optional trailing S), producing a new S and copying the rest of the string after the S. Figure 7 illustrates the first application of this rule to input $aabbcc$, creating the first intermediate level.

This rule is then applied again to this level to create a new intermediate level, and so on until it cannot be applied anymore, using our "star" operator on this resource.

Conclusion

We have described the main features of Sumo, a dedicated formalism for segmentation of text. A document is represented by item graphs at different levels of

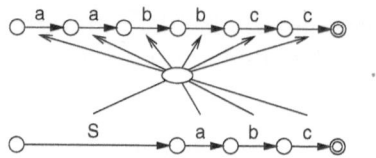

Fig. 7. First application of the rule.

segmentation, which allows multiple segmentations of the same document at the same time. Detailed examples illustrated some features of Sumo discussed here. For the sake of simplicity some aspects could not be evoked in this paper, they include: management of the segmentation resources, efficiency of the systems written in Sumo, larger applications, evaluation of segmentation systems.

Sumo is currently being implemented by the author.

References

1. Quint, J.: Towards a formalism for language-independent text segmentation. Proceedings of NLPRS'99 (1999) 404-408.
2. Guo, J.: Critical Tokenization and its Properties. Computational Linguistics 23:4 (1997) 569-596.
3. Palmer, D., Hearst, M.: Adaptative Multilingual Sentence Boundary Disambiguation. Computational Linguistics 23:2 (1997) 241-267.
4. Habert, B., Adda, G., Adda-Decker, M., Boula de Marëuil, P., Ferrari, S., Ferret, O., Illouz, G., Paroubek, P.: Towards Tokenization Evaluation. Proceedings of LREC-98 (1998) 427-431.
5. Aït-Mokhtar, S.: Du texte ASCII au texte lemmatisé : la présyntaxe en une seule étape. Proceedings of TALN-97 (1997) 60-69.
6. Amtrup, J., Heine, H., Jost, U.: What's in a Word Graph. Evaluation and Enhancement of Word Lattices. Verbmobil report 186 (1997). Universität Hamburg, Germany. http://www.dfki.de/.
7. Colmerauer, A.: Les systèmes Q ou un formalisme pour analyser et synthétiser des phrases sur ordinateur. Publication interne numéro 43 (1970). Universitè de Montréal.
8. Mohri, M., Pereira, F., Riley, M.: Weighted Automata in Text and Speech Processing. Proceedings of the ECAI 96 Workshop (1996) 46-50.
9. Planas, E.: TELA. Structures et algorithmes pour la Traduction Fondée sur la Mémoire. Thèse d'Informatique (1998). Université Joseph Fourier, Grenoble, France.
10. Roche, E.: Two Parsing Algorithms by Means of Finite-State Transducers. Proceedings of COLING-94 (1994) 431-435.
11. Sproat, R., Shih, C., Gale, W., Chang, N.: A Stochastic Finite-State Word-Segmentation Algorithm for Chinese. Computational Linguistics 22:3 (1996) 377-404.
12. Matsumoto, Y., Kitauchi, A., Yamashita, T., Hirano, Y.: Japanese Morphological Analysis System ChaSen version 2.0 Manual. Technical Report NAIST-IS-TR99009 (1999). Nara Institute of Science and Technology. Nara, Japan.

Functional Decomposition and Lazy Word-Parsing in Modern Greek

Evangelos Papakitsos[1], Maria Gregoriadou[1], and Angella Ralli[2]

[1]University of Athens, Department of Informatics Panepistimiopolis
TYPA Buildings, 157 71 Athens, Greece
[2]University of Patras, Department of Philology, Patra, Greece

Abstract. Word recognition and generation is a fundamental part of the processing of natural language, especially for languages with rich morphology such as Modern Greek, and it requires computationally effective morphological processors. Various models have been proposed for developing computerized systems to accomplish the task of recognition of morphosyntactic features of words. In this paper there is a description of extending and adapting the model of functional decomposition in order to cover a number of morphological phenomena that are encountered in Modern Greek. To achieve a more efficient word recognition modifications on the original model were introduced, the lazy word-parsing approach been adopted. The proposed system was used for processing a large scale corpus and the results are presented and discussed as well.

1   Introduction

Morphological analysis is a fundamental part of processing for languages having rich morphology, like Modern Greek (henceforth simply Greek). The target of this research was to evaluate the model of functional decomposition in order to support real scale applications for Greek. Functional decomposition was used as the parsing mechanism of the DECOMP system, the well known morphological analysis systems, which owes much to the theory of Generative Grammar. The framework of Generative Grammar is used as it is adapted to Greek [14], [17], [18], [19].

The goal of parser is to provide both accuracy of parsing and computationally safer solutions. In the latter case it is claimed that simpler algorithms should be prefered. Regarding the simplicity of the design, the selection of algorithms requiring less steps to do the job offer computationally safer solutions [3]. In the lazy word-parsing approach, the parser works as simply as possible, provided the lexicon is large enough to be relied upon. Such an approach is followed in SYL [8] where the Lazy Word-Parsing is supported by a Lexical database containing around 60,000 described lemmata. For every lemma there exists information about morphosyntactic and semantic relations, features, derivation, compounding, syllabification, pronounciation, style, domain, and others. The parser follows a

D.N. Christodoulakis (Ed.): NLP 2000, LNCS 1835, pp. 27-36, 2000.

decomposition process which is invoked only if there is a lack of match in the lexicon (hence *Lazy Parsing*). SYL was developed for Swedish and it is implemented in Ingres database using SQL for database access and Windows 4GL for the parsing procedures.

Combinations of the two above approaches were tested here for the computational treatment of Greek morphology. Especially for the tagging process, only inflection and derivation (prefixation and suffixation) were covered.

2   The Domain

Greek is a language of concatenative morphology, where morphemes constitute the basic units of morphological processes. The three major morphological processes are inflection, derivation and compounding. Following the Strong Lexicalist Hypothesis , they can be studied independently of any syntactic operations [14], [15], [16]. According to the framework of Generative Lexical Morphology, as it was adapted for Greek [13], [15], [16], [17], [18], words are analyzed and generated by a set of context-free rewritting rules. The inflectional morphology of Greek is rich as in Latin or in Slavic languages. An Infl.Affix is generally added to a bound morpheme (stem) in order to form a word. This process (inflection) is very productive since computationally more than 60 declension categories can be described, the accurate number of them depending on the approach (linguistically though it has been claimed that these categories are much less than 60- [19]). Derivation is quite productive. Generally, suffixation can change category and gender, and the result is predictable unlike prefixation where the result of the process cannot be predicted in the same way. Compounding is an important part of Greek morphology where it is traditionally defined as an association of two or more stems which always occur as one unit. In most cases the linking vowel 'o' connects the two (or more) stems together, thus a word may have the structure:

$$\{prefix/...\}stem\{suffix/...\}Infl.Affix .   \tag{1}$$

Finally it should be noted that stress is orthographically marked in Greek and plays a very important role in the morphological and phonological systems of the language and alters its semantics as well.

2.1   Related Work

Until today, several attempts have been made to develop morphological processing systems for Greek. One of the earliest attempts dates back to the seventies [12]. A variety of systems were developed to support specific applications or to test theoretical models, dealing mainly with inflection [4], [5], [6], [7], [10], [24], [25], [26]. The addressed subjects are spelling checking, lexicography, information retrieval, language statistics. One such system was used in the

EUROTRA project [2], [14], etc. There is at least one system dealing with suffixation for information retrieval purposes [9] and few systems that perform full morphological processing. Two of the later use the two-level morphology model [11], [22] and finally the last one to be mentioned is the processor ATHINA [20], [21]. This processor has been implemented in Turbo-Prolog and has a morpheme-based lexicon, grammatical rules and a finite-state automaton (FSA) and can perform both analysis and generation. It should be viewed as a prototyping test of how the Generative Grammar is adapted to Greek.

3   The Development

DECOMP was realized at MIT in order to support a text-to-speech system of English. It is composed of a lexicon containing 12,000 morphemes divided in 5 classes. A weight number is assigned to each class of morpheme. The weight is added to the weight-numbers of the other morphemes which are gradually discovered during word-parsing. The version having the lowest total weight is regarded as the correct one. The method of functional decomposition is used for word parsing, trying a longer matching first. If the search fails then the number of characters is decreased by one and the search continues. The method will only give all the probable analysis' versions of a word. DECOMP parses the word from right to left using a depth-first searching strategy. It is working as an augmented transition network (ATN) and it cannot handle long-distance dependencies. DECOMP also looks for two classes of morphemes simultaneously in a recursive manner, thus significantly decreases backtracking. DECOMP can parse 120,000 words with a success rate of 95% . It can not however perform generation [1], [23], but it can provide part-of-speech information that can be used for syntactic analysis.

Our objective was to develop modifications of the original algorithm and to evaluate their performance regarding the following points:
(a) covering inflection, derivation, compounding and long-distance dependencies,
(b) improving simplicity both of usage and of the design,
(c) examine how the size of the lexicon affects the above.

In general our processor works like MIT-Decomp having firstly the following modifications:
(d) There is no spelling change part, because text-to-speech conversion was not a research target,
(e) the sequence of search during decomposition is adapted according to Greek morphotactics, i.e. the Infl.Affix is recognized first and at the right-end of   the input string and then the rest of the input string is processed.

Then, six versions of our tagger were developed and tested. Two of them were Recursive Transition Networks (RTN-N, RTN-O), three of them were Augmented Transition Networks (ATN-W, ATN-I, ATN-D) and one of them was a Pushdown Automaton (PDA-T, below). Finally, the lexicon was used in three configurations of size: small, medium and large. In the Small Lexicon, lexical entries are morphemes of the following categories: prefixes (eg. κατα- παρα-,υπο-,etc), suffixes (eg. -ιζ-, -ικ-, etc), roots (eg. γραφ-, λογ-, etc), Infl.Affixes (eg. -ω, -ος, -ομαι etc) and free-morphemes (eg. και, οπως, ισως etc). In the Medium Lexicon all the stems containing {prefixes-root} were inserted as unified entries (eg. παρα-γραφ-, κατα-λογ-, υπο-κατα-λογ-, etc) increasing the size of Small Lexicon by 85% (6800 more entries). In the Large Lexicon all the stems containing {prefixes-root-suffix} were also added as unified entries (eg. κατα-λογ-ιζ-, λογ-ικ-, γραφ-ικ-, etc), increasing the size of Small Lexicon by 191% (15300 more entries). From the above versions of our tagger only ATN-W was tested with all the three sizes of lexicon, the rest were tested with the Small Lexicon only. The corresponding results are presented in the next section. These versions were tested on a large scale corpus, the Greek part of the ECI (European Corpus Initiative) a joint project of the Universities of Edinburgh and Geneva for ACL. The criteria of the evaluation were the accuracy and the average speed of recognition, the size of the lexical database and the complexity (measured according to McCabe's software metrics, Fig. 1).

Initially the corpus had to be prepared for parsing since the size of the corpus (initial corpus) is more than 2,145,000 words including proper names, headings, figures, mathematical expressions, tables, yes-no queries, blanks, numbers, etc. This preprocessing is responsible for filtering the initial corpus and for removing data that our tagger can not handle. A large part of this treatment was commenced manually, including the removal of spelling errors. The final size of the corpus (filtered corpus) to be parsed was 87.6% of the initial (1,879,308 words), having a spelling error rate of approximately 0.5% Our tagger was tested on the filtered corpus, containing over 1,879,000 words which is actually composed of only 88,974 different words. These different words are produced by 32,629 lexemes, consisting of 1669 free morphemes, 1542 root-Infl.Affix lexemes and 25,202 derivatives and compounds. From the above figures, approximately 7800 entries (1669 free-morphemes, 5758 roots, 149 Infl.Affixes and about 200 prefixes and suffixes) were initially extracted to make the Small Lexicon.

4   The Validation

The validation process was conducted in three stages. In the first stage, the direction of decomposition (left to right or vice-versa) was tested through the RTN-N and RTN-O using the Small Lexicon. In the second stage, the complexity and the ability of handling long-distance dependencies was tested through the ATN-I, ATN-D and PDA-T using the Small Lexicon. In the third stage, the contribution of the size of lexicon in providing accuracy in tagging and simplicity was tested through ATN-W using the Small, Medium and Large Lexicon. Each stage is separately described below.

4.1 The Direction

On the MIT-Decomp the word is parsed from right to left. The parsing direction was examined by the use of the RTN-N and the RTN-O taggers. They are both Recursive Transition Networks without any evaluation of the outcome (scoring mechanism):

RTN-N: The tagger decomposes the word form left to right (Normal direction).

RTN-O: The tagger decomposes the words from right to left (Opposite direction).

The performance of both versions was the same for words consisting of one or two morphemes. But for words having more than two morphemes, the RTN-O was up to 4 times faster with only 57% of the RTN-N's error, although it provided 37% more output than the RTN-N. The overgeneration of analysis for RTN-O reached 30% of the corpus. Giving more accurate results faster, the Opposite direction of decomposition was kept throughout the rest of the taggers. The complexity of RTN-taggers (McCabe's metrics) was used as basis, being the simpler of the designed taggers (Fig.1:L1). The taggers below were tested in a small scale data set (500 lexemes), demonstrating a potential ability to decrease the recognition error to a rate of less than 2%.

4.2 The Complexity

In this stage, the target of comparison between the three relevant taggers was both complexity (McCabe's measure) and perfomance. Two scoring-mechanisms were utilized to decrease the overgenaration output, resulting in two Augmented Transition Network taggers (ATN-I, ATN-D). An extension of them created a Pushdown Automaton tagger (PDA-T) to cover long-distance dependencies, only for derivatives. The scoring mechanism decides about the acceptability of a combination of morphemes:

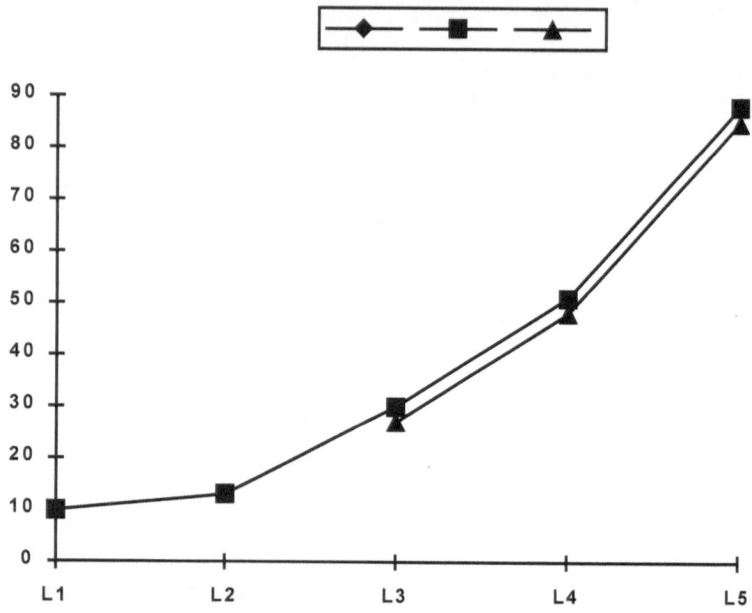

Fig. 1. The complexity of the word-parser's versions.

ATN-I: Part-of-speech (POS) and subcategory features are used to evaluate the outcome, in a way similar to SIL'S AMPLE [23]. The scoring-mechanism contains a percolation process between the set of attributes of two adjacent morphemes. It is partially based on a relevant model proposed by Steele (1992) and adapted to Greek by A.Ralli [19]. According to this model, the attributes of morphemes can be classified into three operational categories depending on their behaviour during percolation: Those remaining to a daughter-node (stem or ending), those passing to the mother-node (word) and those that remain to the daughter-nodes but are used for checking the consistency of the combination (word). This is a three stage Indirect action, where both the attributes of the two morphemes must be discovered and processed. A part of the above mechanism is used in the other taggers too, to produce the morphosyntactic attributes of the input word by the concatenation of the attributes of the stem and of the Infl.Affix. In real full scale recognition it is doubtfull if the relations between all the morphemes can be captured and encoded [23]. This scoring mechanism doubles, at least, the complexity of the tagger (Fig. 1: L3-L4).

ATN-D: Adjacent morphemes are checked Directly to evaluate the outcome: Every morpheme has a list of adjacent morphemes allowable to the left or right of it. This is a two-stage direct action where only the list of one of the two adjacent morphemes is discovered and processed. The difference of encoding between this and the previous method (ATN-I) is merely technical. Processing is more straight-forward and thus preferable, but the relation between the morphemes must be explicitly denoted. In a full-scale environment this might be not better than to enter the combination of morphemes as a single stem (see also subsection 3.3).

PDA-T: This tagger is similar to the previous one (ATN-D) but extended to cover long-distance dependencies, by the addition of a stack, in order to keep the intermediate stages of parsing. The processing time is highly increased and so is the complexity (up to 9 times more, Fig. 1: L5), just to deal with the simplest kind of long-distance dependencies and for dealing with derivatives only (compounds were excluded from testing). The effectiveness of the PDA-T is questioned below.

4.3   The Performance

In the final stage of evaluation, the ATN-W tagger was tested in the corpus, using the Weight scoring-mechanism, similar to the one of the MIT-Decomp. The complexity was increased by 28% (Fig.1: L2). The overgeneration of output decreases substantially (there are only 3 or 4 cases per million words where more than one output is produced). The weight-numbers scoring-mechanism of ATN-W is simple and robust but it has three limitations:

(f) It cannot handle long-distance dependencies.

(g) We have to wait until all the overgenerated analysis are formed before discarding them,   while it would be more preferable to discard them along the processing procedure.

(h) It is not helpfull in the case of words that cannot be dicomposed anyhow, because of their structure (these are compounds lacking the connection vowel o between the two roots, where the first one ends in εp, eg. αεp-αμυνα: air-defence but not αεp-o-πλανo: aeroplane).

In order to handle long-distance dependencies (case (f) above) a pushdown automaton is required (PDA-T). This increases the complexity of the system 9 times. In cases (g) and (h) a different scoring-mechanism is required using some kind of attributes, as in ATN-D and ATN-I of our tagger. This increases the complexity 5 times. At this point (ATN-W with Large Lexicon), the use of attributes in the scoring-mechanism can successfully diminish the parsing error to a few cases per million words (as observed in 15% of the corpus) and complexity can be kept at acceptable levels (unlike the complexity of the PDA-T).

Accordingly, the direction of modifications was shifted towards lazy parsing, in order to achieve accuracy and simplicity. The performance of ATN-W was regulated through the lexicon, by changing the form of the inserted entries towards a lazy direction, as following:

Small Lexicon: The reason for having this size of lexicon is to extract the attributes of a word by the attributes of its constituent morphemes. The above tactic is useful when the word's attributes are formed by percolating the attributes of the morphemes. This is not the case though for prefixation and for a part of compounding, where the final result is not predictable [14], [15], [23]. Moreover encoding such information is not a trivial task, even for experts users. The tagger is unable to decompose correctly 8.8% of the text.

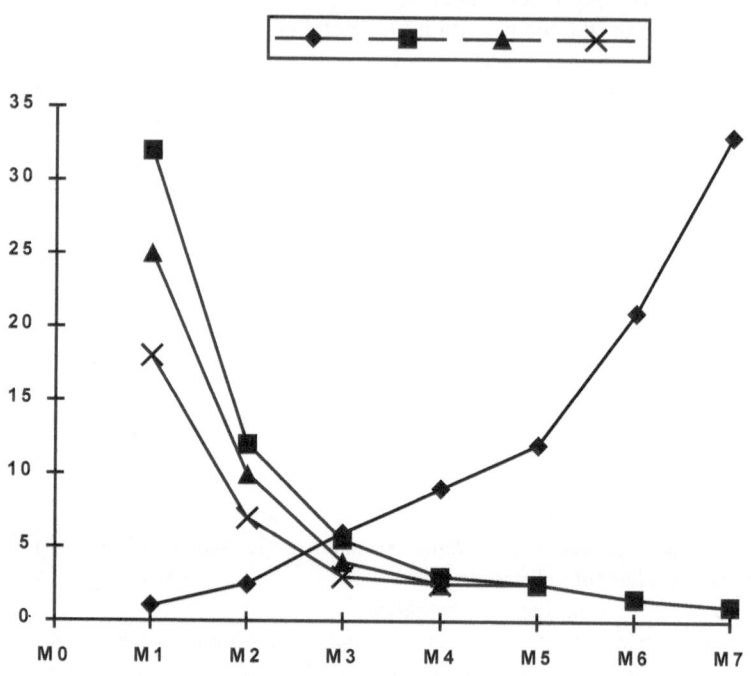

Fig. 2. Parsing-steps and processing speed per number of morphemes per word.

Medium Lexicon: The size of the lexicon is increased 85% and the performance of ATN-W is intermediate between that with the Small and the Large Lexicon.
Large Lexicon: The size of the lexicon is increased by 191% over the size of the small one but the average parsing time is increased only by 4%. The parsing error is decreased at 1.8% with less effort for the parser. The need for dealing with long-distance dependencies is practically diminished. Matching a string in the lexical database is always prior to decomposing it in the simplest possible way, thus the complexity is kept to a minimum (28% of a RTN-tagger).

The number of steps of the system is shown on Fig. 2, where Mi are the number of morphemes per input-string (word). The first diagram (rhombus marked) denotes the number of steps required to decompose a word of Mi morphemes, where one step is when retrieving a free-morpheme from the lexicon. The other three diagrams denote the proportional relation of parsing-speed to the number of morphemes per word, every time that the lexicon changes size (rectangle marked: Small Lexicon, triangle marked: Medium Lexicon, x-marked: Large Lexicon). When the number of parsing-steps increases the resolution speed decreases, as expected. An average speed of 1,132 words per second on a 486/DX machine was achieved. The Infl.Affix recognition error is 1.56%, where half of it can be corrected using only the attribute of stress. By using the paradigm of the stem, Infl.Affixes are practically fully recognized . In same cases (less than 0.5%) two analyses will be given where the correct one depends on the environment, something that a tagger can not account for. On the previous discussion compounds were parsed but not tagged because they were not fully studied. The entire treatment of compounds will even further complicate parsing.

5   Conclusions

Functional decomposition as a method of word-parsing was implemented and validated for Greek. Several modifications were tested, in order to achieve more accurate results while keeping complexity at manageable levels. In particular, the complexity (McCabe's measure) of the ATN-tagger was increased 0.25 to 5 times, while the complexity of the PDA-tagger was increased at least 9 times compared to the RTN-version. Towards that direction, it was demonstrated that the lazy parsing approach can offer the required results by developing a larger and reliable lexical database. The performance of this approach was evaluated on the Greek part of the ECI-corpus (over 1,800,000 words), achieving 98.2% accuracy in providing the morphosyntactical features of words. The rich linguistic information encoded for every lexical entry, in the form of attributes, can offer more accurate recognition, according to small scale data tests.

References

1. J. Allen, M.S. Hunnicutt and D. Klatt, From Text to Speech: The MITalk System, Cambridge University Press (1987).
2. S. Ananiadou, A. Ralli, A.Villalva, The Treatment of Derivational Morphology in a Multilingual Transfer-Based MT System-EUROTRA, Proceedings of SICONLP '90 (1990).
3. K. Church, Morphological decomposition and stress assignment for speech synthesis, ACL Proceedings, 24th Annual Meeting (1986).
4. E. Dermatas and G. Kokkinakis, Text-to-Speech Formant Synthesis of Greek and Applications, Proceedings of the Language Engineering on the Information Highway Conference, Santorini (1994).
5. E. Dermatas and G. Kokkinakis, The performance of the TTS-system and possible applications are discussed. Multilingual text-labelling and Stress Assignment, Proceedings of the Language Engineering on the information Highway Conference, Santorini (1994).
6. E. Dermatas and G. Kokkinakis, LEXITHIRAS: Multilingual Corpus based Lexicography on PCs, Proceedings of the Language Engineering on the Information Highway Conference, Santorini (1994).
7. A. Draggiotis, A parsing technique for resolving syntactic ambiguities in Greek sentences, Working Papers in NLP, Εκδόσεις Δίαυλος, Αθήνα (1997).

8. E. Dura, Lexicon and Lazy Word Parsing, Proceedings of the Language   Engineering on the Information Highway Conference, ISP Santorini (1994).
9. T. Kalaboukis, Suffix Stripping and Retrieval with   Retrieval with Modern Greek, Proceedings of the Language Engineering on the   Information Highway Conference, Santorini (1994).
10. I. Κωτσάνης, Περιγράφοντας την ομαλή κλιτική μορφολογία της Ελληνικής λέξης με ενοποιητική γραμματική, ΕΜΠ (1986).
11. G. Markopoulos, A two-level description of the Greek noun morphology with   a unification-based word grammar, Working Papers in NLP, Εκδόσεις Δίαυλος, Αθήνα (1997).
12. D. Packard, Computer-Assisted Morphological Analysis of Ancient Greek, Innovative Projects in University Instruction, University of California (1977).
13. A. Ralli, Morphologie Verbale et la Theorie du Lexique: Quelques Remarques Preliminaires, Πρακτικά της 4ης Ετήσιας Συνάντησης του Τομέα Γλωσσολογίας του ΑΠΘ (1983).
14. A. Ralli, Morphology, Prep.Phase, Volume I, Chapter 2, Eurotra-Gr (1985).
15. A. Ράλλη, ΚΛΙΣΗ ΚΑΙ ΠΑΡΑΓΩΓΗ, Πρακτικά της 7ης Ετήσιας Συνάντησης του Τομέα Γλωσσολογίας του ΑΠΘ (1986).
16. A. Ralli, Elements de la morphologie du grec moderne: la structure du verbe, PhD diss., Universite de Montreal (1988).
17. A. Ralli, Compounds in Modern Greek, Rivista di Linguistica, Special issue on Compounds, Scuola Normale Superiore, Pisa (1992).
18. A. Ράλλη, Η Θεωρία των Χαρακτηριστικών και η Δομή των Κλιτών Λέξεων της Νέας Ελληνικής, Πρακτικά της 13ης Ετήσιας Συνάντησης του Τομέα Γλωσσολογίας του ΑΠΘ (1992).
19. A. Ralli, Feature representations and feature-passing operations: the case of   Greek inflection, Proceedings of the 8th Linguistic Meeting on English and   Greek, Thessaloniki (1994).
20. A. Ralli and E. Galiotou, A Morphological Processor for Modern Greek, Proceedings of the 3rd European ACL Meeting, Copenhagen (1987).
21. A. Ralli and E. Galiotou, Affixation in Modern Greek: A Computational Treatment, Proceedings of EURISCON '91 (1991).
22. K. Sgarbas, N. Fakotakis, G. Kokkinakis, A PC-KIMMO-Based Morphological Description of Modern Greek, Literary and Linguistic Computing, Vol.10, No.3, Oxford Univ.Press (1995).
23. R.W. Sproat, Morphology and Computation, MIT, USA (1992).
24. Λ. Τουρατζίδης, Μετασχηματισμοί Φυσικής Γλώσσας και Εφαρμογές σε Διόρθωση Ορθογραφικών Λαθών και Ελληνική Στενοτυπία, Διδακτορική Διατριβή, Τμήμα Ηλ.Μηχ.-Μηχ.Υπολ/ΕΜΠ (1991).
25. L. Touratzidis and A. Ralli, A Computational Treatment of Stress in Greek   Inflected Forms, Language and Speach, 35(4):435-453 (1992).
26. Θ. Τριαντοπούλου, Χ. Τσαλίδης, Δ. Χριστοδουλάκης, InterLEX: Μία CF προσέγγιση για την μορφολογική περιγραφή της Ν.Ελληνικής, 13η Συνάντηση εργασίας του Τομέα Γλωσσολογίας του ΑΠΘ (1992).

Acknowledgements

The authors would like to thank Prof. G. Philokyprou for his comments and suggestions which improved the material presented here.

Recognition and Acquisition of Compound Names from Corpora

Goran Nenadić[1] and Irena Spasić[2]

[1] Faculty of Mathematics, University of Belgrade, Yugoslavia
goran@matf.bg.ac.yu
[2] Faculty of Economics, University of Belgrade, Yugoslavia
irenas@one.ekof.bg.ac.yu

Abstract. In this paper we will present an approach to acquisition of some classes of compound words from large corpora, as well as a method for semi-automatic generation of appropriate linguistic models, that can be further used for compound word recognition and for completion of compound word dictionaries. The approach is intended for a highly inflective language such as Serbo-Croatian. Generated linguistic models are represented by *local grammars*.

1 Introduction

The increasing availability of electronic texts (either on the Web or in local electronic libraries and archives) along with the increase of the user population and their needs for information retrieval sets the task of developing searching strategies based on compound terms.[1] It is natural to built these strategies into the systems that support information retrieval, information extraction, search on the Internet, document management, etc.

The majority of the existing search engines allow for flexible querying by combining keywords using logical operators such as disjunction, conjunction, negation, etc. This approach does not solve the problem of compound term retrieval completely, since the constituents of a compound term may occur independently in a text, and, possibly, in an entirely different context than the one in which they occur as a single lexical unit. It, hence, often results in great noise, in the sense that the retrieved set of documents contains some that are irrelevant. In order to diminish the noise, and, consequently, supply a user with more precise and efficient retrieval, the searching strategies should be based on compound terms rather than on their individual constituents.

Various natural language processing (NLP) systems have already implemented the recognition of compound terms [16,5], but mostly for the languages that are not highly inflective, such as English. In this paper, we will discuss an approach to the description of compound term structure for a highly inflective

---

[1] In this paper we will consider any multiword lexical unit as compound term, if it acts as an individual constituent in a broader syntactical unit. For example, a compound term can be a noun phrase, verb phrase, or adverbial phrase.

D.N. Christodoulakis (Ed.): NLP 2000, LNCS 1835, pp. 38–48, 2000.

language, such as Serbo-Croatian. The proposed model takes into account the fact that some of the constituents and sometimes compound term as a whole may be inflected.

Among the various types of compounds, we will restrict our discussion to proper names that identify organizations, persons, geographical locations, etc. Such entities typically comprise 10% of a text in unrestricted domain [2]. On the other hand, proper names vary both in structure and vocabulary. Moreover, new classes of proper names are regularly introduced into the language. Therefore, the recognition of proper names insists upon dynamic acquisition of the corresponding linguistic knowledge and its representation. A good approach to this problem is to semi-automatically analyze large up-to-date corpora in order to obtain the linguistic knowledge, i.e. concrete lexical classes and the way in which they are combined. We will present an approach in which lexical knowledge is represented by using the system of lexicons, while correct structures are described by local grammars.

The resulting local grammars can be used for improved indexing of digital language resources, especially for indexing and information retrieval on the Internet or in textual databases. Additionally, they can be used for recognition of specific syntactic structures (e.g. containing companies' names) for querying databases using a subset of a natural language [12,13] in a specific semantic domain of business, education or government information systems.

The paper is organized as follows: First, we will give an overview of the resources used for the acquisition and recognition of compound terms. In the third and forth sections, we will present details about our approach to the problem and give a few examples and results. Section five describes possible applications, and concludes the paper.

2   Resources

The *corpus* we were working with is a newspaper corpus containing news text taken from a few Yugoslav daily newspapers presented on the Internet. [2] This way we explore up-to-date language and collect its corresponding corpus as a complement to existing corpora of Serbo-Croatian, which usually contain texts from literature, poetry, and law. Proper names exist in large number in such a corpus, which is especially important for the purpose of this research. The corpus has been used both as a source of linguistic performance and as a test area for generated models. After the collection of corpus, the very first step is to convert encoding format of texts to ASCII for the purpose of employing the system of electronic dictionaries. At the same time, this conversion resolves the problem of Serbo-Croatian dual alphabet (Cyrillic and Latin), in the sense that the stored text is independent of the alphabet it was originally recorded with. As

---

[2]   The bulk of the corpus includes text automatically collected from URLs http://www.blic.co.yu (homepage of daily newspaper "Blic") and http://www.politika.co.yu (homepage of daily newspaper "Politika").

there are other intentions for the corpus as well, it is converted to SGML/TEI Lite scheme [1] up to the sentence level.

Processing of a text in a highly inflective language needs to include thorough lexical preprocessing and lemmatization, that must take into account various inflected forms of words. The problem of lemmatization may be approached by using the system of electronic morphological dictionaries. An *electronic dictionary* (e-dictionary) is a specific database that models morphological characteristics of a specified language [3,10]. Its form is suitable for computer processing, and is not intended for human use. An entry contains morpho-syntactic information formalized as follows: It is a triple

$$(word\ form,\ lemma,\ morpho\text{-}syntactic\ code),$$

where *morpho-syntactic code* describes the relation between a *word form* and the *corresponding lemma*. More precisely, *morpho-syntactic code* represents grammatical categories that are assigned to the given word form with regard to the corresponding lemma. In particular, in e-dictionary of Serbo-Croatian [14] noun word forms are described by morpho-syntactic code that includes values for the following features: gender, number, case, and animate property. For example, the following entries

(1)   fakulteta,FAKULTET:Nmsg-;
        fakulteta,FAKULTET:Nmpg-;

denote that *fakulteta* is a word form of the noun *fakultet* 'faculty' to which two different sets of morpho-syntactic values are assigned: masculine, singular, genitive, non-animate or masculine, plural, genitive, non-animate. The assignment of potential morpho-syntactic descriptions to a textual word is called *initial tagging* or *initial lemmatization*. The process of lemmatization by means of an e-dictionary is based on the concept of lexical recognition, which is implemented by dictionary look-up. It is obvious from the previous example that there is no one-to-one correspondence between word forms and their morpho-syntactic description. According to this fact, some lexical ambiguities are likely to arise when a text is lemmatized. On the initially tagged text one can afterwards perform additional processing (e.g. disambiguation, recognition of syntactic units, etc.), what we actually did in our approach.

The existing systems of e-dictionaries [10] include dictionaries of simple words (DELAS), simple word forms (DELAF)[3], compound words (DELAC), compound word forms (DELACF), etc. DELAC and DELACF dictionaries contain morpho-syntactic descriptions of multiword lexical units. The structure of an entry in DELACF dictionary is similar to the one in DELAF. Here is an excerption from DELACF for Serbo-Croatian, which corresponds to the CN *Istrazxivacxka stanica Petnica* 'Petnica Science Center':

Istrazxivacxka stanica Petnica, Istrazxivacxka stanica Petnica:Nfsn-;
Istrazxivacxku stanicu Petnica, Istrazxivacxka stanica Petnica:Nfsa-;

---

[3] The example (1) is taken from DELAF for Serbo-Croatian.

In general, however, e-dictionaries cannot resolve lexical ambiguities resulting from dictionary look-ups. Therefore, we need some additional tools for lexical disambiguation. In our approach, we used local grammars. A *local grammar* [9] is a finite-state transducer (FST) that describes well-formed word sequences in a text and chooses the proper tags for them. It does not describe a sentence as a whole: a local grammar defines and applies lexical constraints to a local environment containing a sequence of several words. This way, local grammars can be used for reducing lexical ambiguities.

We can represent a local grammar either by a graph or, equivalently, by a regular expression. For example, the local grammar

```
pored.PREP <N:g>
```

expresses the next constraint: a noun that follows the preposition *pored* 'by' (marked as PREP) has to be in genitive case (and, hence, is marked as ¡N:g¿); other possible tags of the noun (if any) can be automatically discarded [8]. It is essential for a local grammar neither to give incorrect tags nor to remove any possible lexical interpretation that can be applied in the local environment.

As described in [6] and [7], the structure of an NP can be defined by an extended regular morpho-syntactic expression, or equivalently by a local grammar. For example, the grammar

```
<N> <ADJ:g> <N:g>
```

denotes the set of three-word noun phrases that consist of a noun and frozen forms of an adjective and noun in genitive case. This set includes phrases such as *Fakultet politicxkih nauka* 'Faculty of Political Sciences', *Fakultet primenxenih umetnosti* 'Faculty of Applied Arts', *Insitut drusxtvenih nauka* 'Institute of Social Sciences', *operacija prirodnog spajanxa* 'natuaral join operation', *jezik visokog nivoa* 'high level language', etc.

These resources are integrated into a corpus processing system INTEX [10], which is developed at the LADL (Laboratoire d'Automatique Documentaire et Linguisitque), University Paris VII, and is adjusted for Serbo-Croatian at the University of Belgrade [15]. The system provides support for storage and use of e-dictionaries, which enables automatic initial tagging of an input digital text. Additionally, the INTEX offers a framework for applying user-defined local grammars to an initially tagged text, and for generation of lemmatized concordances. The system also makes possible to store processed corpora for later use.

3   Acquisition of Compound Name Structures

As opposed to traditional way of acquiring linguistic knowledge and language resources, we have approached the problem in a different manner. Namely, we tried to collect grammatical structures that can be automatically acquired by analyzing a corpus. Such an approach results in a set of structures that occur in a corpus. An example of an algorithm for lexical constraint acquisition concerning prepositions is presented in [8]. However, we used theoretical linguistic knowledge as well, and combined it with corpus-based acquisition of grammatical models.

One of the compound word classes we have studied are noun phrases (NPs), and especially NPs that denote names of companies, institutions, countries and other proper names of this type. We will refer to this subclass of proper names as *compound names* (CN).

The very first step in our research was to define a local grammar (based on theoretical knowledge) that describes the general structure of CNs (cf. Figure General local grammar). This grammar was defined in the INTEX system and applied to a collection of initially tagged texts from the corpus in order to isolate word sequences that match the structure described by the local grammar. However, the grammar was "overfitting", that is - the resulting set contained the sequences that represented not only CNs but other classes of NPs as well.[4] This is due to the fact that grammar rules based on theoretical knowledge are too general, and are usually neither sufficient nor adequate for automatic processing of linguistic phenomena. Therefore, it was necessary to refine the local grammar in order to reduce such "noise". The strategy that we applied was based on keywords that denote the type of a CN (e.g. *fakultet* 'faculty', *institut* 'institute', *fabrika* 'factory', *preduzecye* 'enterprise', etc.). Such keywords represent the lexical and semantical core of an NP that corresponds to a CN. The list of keywords was obtained using INTEX by isolating the heading NPs (denoted on the graph as *designator*), and than by singling out the nouns. The resulting list was manually refined in order to discard nouns that do not designate entities described by the class of compound names.

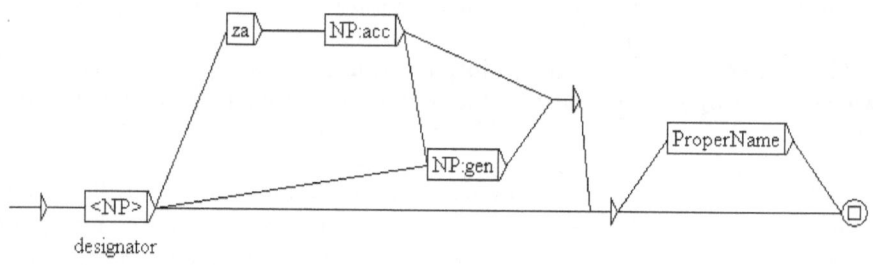

General CN local grammar

Figure 1: General local grammar for CN

---

[4] For example, the resulting set of word sequences included NPs such as *sistem za podrsxku odlucxivanju* 'decision support system', *metod za manipilasanje ljudima* 'method for people manipulation', *jezik visokog nivoa* 'high level language', *kralxevstvo za konxa* 'kingdom for a horse', etc. These NPs are not compound names in the sense that we have defined.

The next step involved concordance generation for each keyword. The concordances needed to be lemmatized, since the heading NP of a CN (i.e. designators) may appear in different inflected forms, unlike the rest of the CN, which is frozen. This task is again accomplished by using INTEX tools. The set of all concordances is then split up into distinct subsets according to keywords. The elements of each subset were then automatically clustered according to their lexical and grammatical characteristics. Namely, the concordances were first clustered on the basis of their lexical characteristics, i.e. on the set of words that appear in the right or left context of a given keyword. On the other hand, the concordances are clustered on the basis of their grammatical characteristics. The idea was to compute some kind of "intersection" of lexical and morpho-syntactic features of CNs. As the initially tagged text is ambiguous, we defined a method of extraction of a "minimal" set of lexical and morpho-syntactic features that are inherent for every CN. (Consequently, other tags can be left out so that every CN keeps at least one feature from the "minimal" set.) The method of computation of a "minimal" set is similar to that described in [8] and is implemented using *flex*. However, as opposed to the method applied for preposition phrase extraction [8], where we need to process only the right context, here we have to analyze both left and right context. The resulting set of features and constraints (both grammatical and lexical) for a keyword describes the structure of the corresponding CNs. According to this set, we generated a local grammar represented by a graph.

Afterwards, specific features of resulting graphs were examined. We noted that some of the graphs are similar with respect to their lexical constituents, especially to those that directly follow a keyword. By neglecting some of the slight differences between graphs (and, therefore, decreasing redundancy up to a certain level), we have brought together all such graphs into a generalized graph that corresponds to the union of the appropriate graphs. The details are presented in section 4.

An interesting point to notice is that the clustering of graphs using the above criterion resulted in generalized graphs that describe semantically related CNs. In the following section we present some examples of resulting graphs. Since local grammars are finite-state transducers, different versions can be designed in order to accomplish different tasks. Some of the examples are presented in sections 4 and 5.

4   Examples and Discussion

In order to illustrate the main ideas and results, we will present two examples of CN types. The first example is a local grammar related to CNs of educational and scientific organizations. The initial structure was obtained by using a few Web search engines in order to retrieve Web presentations that contain "education" keywords (e.g. *fakultet* 'faculty', *sxkola* 'school', *institut* 'institute', etc.). The initial graph is then tuned after a test against newspaper corpora. Figure 2 represents the resulting graph,[5] while Figure 3 shows a sample of a text taken from the corpus to which the graph was applied.

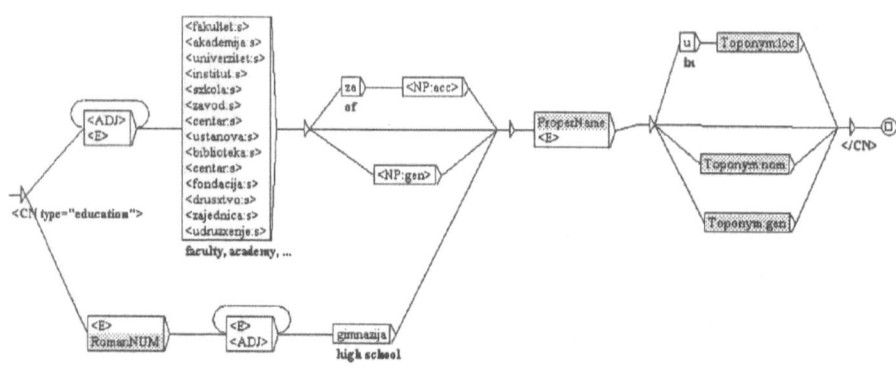

Figure 2: Local grammar for CN related to education and science

Na <CN type="education">Filolosxkom fakultetu u Beogradu</CN>
svi profesori koji nisu potpisali ugovore o radu, tridesetak
njih dobili su u petak popodne pismenu odluku dekana kojom se svi
rasporedyujemo na poslove i radne zadatke u <CN type="education">
Centru za naucxno-istrazxivacxki i publicisticxki rad</CN> u
vremenu od 7 i 30 do 15 sati. Ovakav centar je nepostojecyi na
<CN type="education">Filolosxkom fakultetu</CN>.
. . .
BEOGRAD - Suspendovani profesori <CN type="education">Pravnog
fakulteta</CN> podeljeni su u dve grupe, polovinu plate primaju
oni koji imaju izdrzxavane cxlanove porodice, a trecyinu ostali.
Postojala je inicijativa sa visxe strana da se osnuje fond
solidarnosti, ali mi za sada nismo za tu varijantu, iako ne
iskljucxujemo mogucynost da se to ucxini na nivou
<CN type="education">Univerziteta</CN> ili od strane
<CN type="education">Udruzxenja nastavnika i istrazxivacxa</CN> -
rekao je jucxe Jovica Trkulja, suspendovani profesor
<CN type="education">Pravnog fakulteta</CN>.

Figure 3: Sample of a tagged text

---

[5] The shaded box called *ProperName* represents the other graph which describes proper names structures (usually names of persons, uppercase strings or any sequence between quotation marks). During the recognition process, the graph is automatically invoked by INTEX.

It is possible to estimate the minimum number of different paths in a graph: in the presented example there are 656 possible paths, which denotes the same number of different forms of CNs. Note that the graph describes different forms of the same CN. (Consider, for example, *Filolosxkom fakultetu u Beogradu* 'Faculty of Philology in Belgrade', *Filolosxkom fakultetu* 'Faculty of Philology'.) We would like to emphasize a few more points. The first letter of a CN is capitalized except when the first character of a CN is a quotation mark. This fact was used as a heuristic rule for identification of CNs. Additionally, each keyword in the graph has to be in singular form. This fact can be used in order to reduce lexical (morpho-syntactic) ambiguity by discarding morpho-syntactic codes that indicate plural. Similar remarks apply to the graph shown in Figure 4, as well. This graph is related to another class of CNs, which describes names of factories, enterprises, and other organizations of a similar type. However, note that the structure described by the graph shown in Figure 4 differs from the one in figure 2. Similar graphs were designed for other subclasses of CNs.

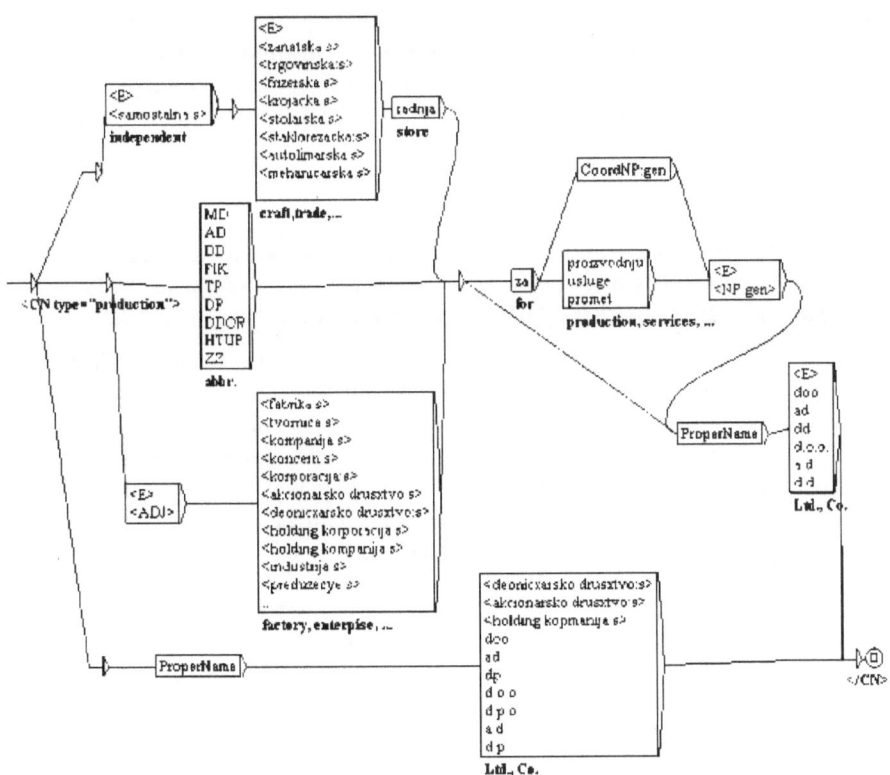

Figure 4: Local grammar for CN related to production and services

In general, substructures that are specified in a graph (e.g. <NP>, <ADJ>) cannot be replaced by an arbitrary lexical unit of the appropriate type due to the fact that sublanguage of each CN class has a restricted vocabulary. The vocabulary elements can be automatically obtained from the concordances that are generated for a specific subclass of CNs. Having collected such a vocabulary, the graphs can be improved by adding lexical details. This can prevent the graph from possible false recognition, as indicated in the following examples:

```
tuzxena je nasxa Fabrika za utaju poreza
u Centru za naucxno-istrazxivacxki i publicisticxki rad u
vremenu od 7 i 30 do 15 sati
```

The words in italic shape do not belong to specified vocabularies. This problem can also be approached by using the idea of a "negative" list, which contains the most usual words that appear in a context of a keyword, but are not part of CNs.

5 Conclusion and Further Research

The method described can be used for compound name recognition and acquisition of new compound names of a similar type. This way, the structure of compound names is obtained from a corpus, which is important for filling in the gap between the need for compound name recognition in digital language resources and the shortage of specific naming rules that can govern their extraction.

As indicated in section 4, described classes of CNs can be recognized by applying local grammars to a digital text. This way, a word sequence that represents a CN can be marked as a separate syntactical unit, for example, by using SGML-like tags:

```
<NP type='CN' class='education'>Matematicxki fakultet u Beogradu</NP>
<NP type='CN' class='education'>Visxa elektro-tehnicxka sxkola</NP>
<NP type='CN' class='production'>Fabrika automobila "Zastava"</NP>
```

These SGML-tags can be produced as an output of a corresponding local grammar transducer (as illustrated in Figures 2 and 4), and can be used for improved indexing of digital language resources, especially for indexing and information retrieval on the Internet or in textual databases. Besides, lemmatized forms of CNs, appropriate abbreviations, etc. may be produced as output, as well. Additionally, the resulting local grammars can be used for recognition of specific syntactic structures (e.g. companies' names) for querying databases using natural language interface [12,13].

A recognized CN can be stored into appropriate DELAC/DELACF subdictionaries of compound names, which may be used as cache dictionaries [9,10] for later processing of a digital text in order to recognize such entities. This way, the method can help in automated completion of e-dictionaries by new CNs obtained from corpus, and consequently, upgrade the coverage of CN recognition in further processing. Obviously, the decision to include a CN in a DELAC dictionary rather than in a local grammar may be difficult to take [4]: although cache dictionaries suppress the size of lexical ambiguities that arise during the initial tagging, the growth of a dictionary causes the problem of its maintenance. These considerations are left for further research.

We also point out that some foreign words can be found as a part of a compound name, which insists upon multilingual approach [11]. By analyzing the corpus, we noted that the list of such words is rather closed.[6] This problem can be approached by isolating left and right context of a trigger word given in the list. These contexts usually contain capitalized and/or uppercase words (e.g. *IR Info-Rad Computers, Duga Computers, Grossi Engineering*, etc.), unlike CNs that contain only Serbo-Croatian words. Further, the companies that are representatives of foreign enterprises can have an additional designator (e.g. *Ltd., Co.*) which terminates a CN, and, consequently, the CN can be isolated up to the appearance of the designator. Further research includes implementation of adequate multilingual support.

Procedures similar to the one proposed for compound name recognition can be implemented for consideration of other classes of compounds (e.g. adverbial phrases, particularly those whose lexical core are adverbs that denote some abstract and non-countable quantity such as *nesxto* 'some', *malo* 'a little', *mnogo* 'a lot of', etc.). This is a part of further research activities, as well.

As a final remark, we want to point out that the method described is efficient as it is based on finite-state tools, and that it does not make false recognition, although the percentage of successfully recognized compound names depends on the number of local grammars that are defined and applied to the text.

References

1. Burnard, L. et al: TEI Lite: An Introduction to Text Encoding for Interchange, doc. No: TEI U 5, June 1995
2. Coates-Stephands, S.: The Analysis and Acquisition of Proper Names for Robust Text Understanding, PhD Thesis, Department of Computer Science, City University London, 1992
3. Gross M., Perrin D. (eds.): Electronic Dictionaries and Automata in Computational Linguistics, Lecture Notes in Computer Science, Berlin, Springer Verlag, 110 p., 1989
4. Gross M.: A Bootstrap Method for Construction Local Grammars, in Monograph on 125th anniversary of the Faculty of Mathematics, University of Belgrade, pp. 231-249, 1998
5. Maier-Meyer P., Oesterle J.: Recognition of Noun-Phrases in German, in Actes des Premieres Journees INTEX, LADL, 1996
6. Nenadić, G., Vitas, D.: Using Local Grammars for Agreement Modeling in Highly Inflective Languages, in Proc. of First Workshop on Text, Speech, Dialogue - TSD 98, Brno, 1998
7. Nenadić, G., Vitas, D.: Formal Model of Noun Phrases in Serbo-Croatian, BULAG 23, Universite Franche-Compte, 1998

---

[6] The list includes word like *Computers, Company, Club, System, Software, Hardware, Trade, Commerce, Group, Informatique, Design, Shop, International*, etc, that reflect "modern" tendencies in naming companies in Serbo-Croatian.

8. Nenadić G., Spasić I.: The Acquisition of Some Lexical Constraints from Corpora, in Text, Speech and Dialogue - TSD '99, Lecture Notes in Artificial Intelligence 1692, Berlin, Springer Verlag, 1999
9. Silberztein, M: INTEX: a Corpus Processing System, in Proc. of COLING 94, ACL, Tokyo, 1994
10. Silberztein, M.: Dictionnaries électroniques et analyse automatique de textes: le systéme INTEX, Masson, Paris, 1993
11. Spasić I.: Automatic Foreign Words Recognition in a Serbo-Croatian Scientific and Technical Texts, in Proc. of Conference on "Terminology Standardization", Serbian Academy of Arts and Sciences, 1996 (in Serbo-Croatian)
12. Spasić I.: Natural Language Interface towards Relational Databases, MSc thesis, Faculty of Mathematics, University of Belgrade, 1999 (in Serbo-Croatian)
13. Spasić I., Pavlović-Lažetić G.: Syntactic Structures in a Sublanguage of Serbian for Querying Relational Databases, in Proc. of Third European Conference on Formal Description of Slavic Languages FDSL-3, 1999
14. Vitas, D.: Mathematical Model of Serbo-Croatian Morphology (Nominal Inflection), PhD thesis, Faculty of Mathematics, University of Belgrade, 1993 (in Serbo-Croatian)
15. Vitas D., Krstev C.: Tuning the Text with an Electronic Dictionary, in Proc. of COMPLEX 96, Budapest, Hungarian Academy of Sciences, 1996
16. Wakao T., Gaizauskas R., Wilks Y.: Evaluation of an Algorithm for the Recognition and Classification of Proper Names, in Proc. of the 16th International Conference on Computational Linguistics (COLING96), Copenhagen, pp. 418-423, 1996

Use of a Morphosyntactic Lexicon as the Basis for the Implementation of the Greek Wordnet

A. Ntoulas[1], S. Stamou[1], I. Tsakou[2], Ch. Tsalidis[1,2],
M. Tzagarakis[1,2], and A. Vagelatos[1,2]

[1] Computer Engineering & Informatics Department, University of Patras, Greece
[2] Computer Technology Institute, Kolokotroni 3
GR-26221 Patras, Greece

Abstract. Greek WordNet is a project aiming at developing a database of wordnets for the Greek language, structured along the same lines as the EuroWordNet project. This contribution presents the morphosyntactic lexicon, which will be used as the basis for the development of the whole project. This lexicon was developed within the framework of a spelling correction system. Later on, it was enhanced by adding syntactic information for each lemma and by using a relational database for the storage and management of the data.

1 Introduction

Last year, the idea of building the Greek WordNet succeeded in receiving a high grade in a GSRT[1] competition and as a consequence, in being financed by the Greek Government.

The partners for the implementation of the above idea were chosen carefully:

1. The *Computer Technology Institute*, with an active team on computational linguistics and a number of tools and resources already developed.
2. The *Linguistics Department of Patras University*, with a team of experts in linguistics who have been conducting extensive research on the Greek language, for the past years.
3. The *Informatics Department of Athens University*, with its computational linguistics team.
4. The *Computer Science Institute of the Foundation of Research and Technology Hellas*, with its experienced team on user interfaces and web based applications.

---

[1] GSRT = General Secretariat for Research and Technology is one of the Secretariats of the Ministry of Development and is responsible for the following activities in Greece: planning and execution of national policy on research and technology through the design and execution of relevant programmes, creation and activation of research and technological infrastructure, technological development, importation and exportation of technology, research and technology orientation, investigations of the consequences of research and technology on the economic, social and cultural development of the country.

D.N. Christodoulakis (Ed.): NLP 2000, LNCS 1835, pp. 49–56, 2000.

5. *Pattakis Publications*, having under development an exhaustive lexicon of the Greek language.

The above partners agreed to cooperate for the implementation of the Greek WordNet, following the same lines as the *EuroWordNet* project[2]. The role of each one is well defined: *CTI* together with the *Informatics Department of Athens University* will develop the appropriate computer infrastructure for the project, as well as provide the linguistic resources. The *Linguistics Department of Patras University* will have as its primary goal to provide the necessary expertise in semantics for building the Greek WordNet. *CSI* will develop the appropriate user interfaces as well as the Web page that will host the final outcome. Finally, *Patakis Publications* will complete its lexicon, which is presently under development, so as to be used as a linguistic resource by the linguists.

In this paper, we present the morphosyntactic lexicon that is going to be used as a linguistic resource for the implementation of the above-mentioned project. More specifically, firstly, we give a small description of the EuroWordNet project since the Greek WordNet is going to be developed following the same structure. We, then, describe the Greek Morphosyntactic lexicon developed by CTI within the framework of a spelling correction system. Later on, this lexicon was enhanced by adding syntactic information for each lemma. Next, we present the design challenges of the information infrastructure that has to be implemented. Finally, we mention our future plans and some conclusions.

2   Goals of the Project

The main goal of the Greek WordNet project is the development of a large-scale lexical resource for the Greek language containing semantic relations between words organised around the notion of synsets (one or more word senses which are considered to be similar in meaning). The Greek WordNet will be built from existing resources and then stored in a database following the methodology of the EuroWordNet project, so as to be compatible with the specific project. The aim of the Greek WordNet is to represent the Greek lexicalization patterns and language-dependent differences of the Greek language, whilst using the language-independent ontology of the EuroWordNet for the classification of the Greek major concepts and words. This will enable the merging of the Greek WordNet in the EuroWordNet multilingual database, so as to strengthen the position of Greek in Language Technology and in particular in the field of Multilingual Information Retrieval.

During the realisation of the project, the participants will gain, from their participation to the project, significant experience and knowledge in the field of Language Engineering. The Greek WordNet project will also give them the possibility to develop important technical infrastructure that can be used as the basis for building further linguistic tools and techniques.

---

[2] http://www.hum.uva.nl/~ewn.

3   The EuroWordNet Project

The EuroWordNet project is a multilingual database comprising WordNets for several European languages (Dutch, Italian, Spanish, German, French, Czech and Estonian). Each WordNet represents a unique language-internal system of lexicalizations. The individual WordNets are organised around a set of Base Concepts, extracted by each country from already existing linguistic resources such as monolingual and bilingual lexicons, corpora, etc. Then, all the sets of Base Concepts are compared and a set of Common Base Concepts (concepts selected by at least two countries) is extracted. These Common Base Concepts, plus a selection of other meanings that are important in each language, function as the starting point for the development of the local WordNets, which are built taking into account the lexicalization patterns that are relevant to the specific languages. The structure of the individual WordNets is based on the formation of synsets, ie. sets of word meanings between which basic semantic relations, such as synonymy, hyponymy, meronymy, cause, etc. are expressed. In other words, Base Concepts function as "anchors" to which other concepts are attached.

All the data is then converted into the EuroWordNet import format and loaded to the EuroWordNet database. All WordNets all linked to an Inter-Lingual-Index (an unstructured list of concepts) interconnecting the languages so as to make possible to connect word meanings in one language to similar word meanings in the other participant-languages. Furthermore, all the languages that form part of the EuroWordNet share a three-entities top ontology of 63 semantic distinctions, as well as domain ontologies, which provides a common semantic framework for the classification of word meanings, enforcing, in this way, uniformity and compatibility of the different WordNets.

Today, that the EuroWordNet project is completed, it provides a large-scale linguistic resource which is used to improve the capacities and performance of current multilingual information retrieval systems with regards to reformulation of queries, automatic indexing and other issues of text retrieval task.

4   Greek Morphosyntactic Lexicon

Within the framework of a spelling checking/correction system for Modern Greek[3] our team created a morphological lexicon. In order for this lexicon to become efficient, an in-depth morphological analysis of Modern Greek (MG) was carried out.

The main characteristics of M.G. morphology can be summarised as follows:

- A complex inflectional system. For example, for the M.G. masculine nouns ending in "-os" /os/, there are six different inflections, whereas for the present tense of the active voice of verbs ending in " $-\omega$ " /o/ there are seven different inflections.

---

[3] The spelling correction system was developed by our team at CTI, funded by Intracom S.A. and was approved and adopted by Microsoft corp. as the Greek spelling checker that will be marketed with their products.

- The existence of marked stress: Words in M.G. are stressed in either the final, penultimate or antepenultimate position.
- A "graphematic" spelling system consisting of single graphemes, compound graphemes and grapheme equivalents.
- Free-word-order: the sentence constituents (i.e. subject, verb, object) can be found in various positions. This characteristic is mainly a consequence of the inflectional system, since the syntactic role of word-forms is usually denoted by the syntactic information attached to their inflectional endings and it is not necessary for the word forms to occupy a special position within the sentence itself.
- The existence of numerous characteristics carried over from Ancient Greek. The use of old and new word forms, which gives rise to an endless linguistic debate whether both forms should continue to be used (accepted).

M.G. word classification incorporates two basic categories: The inflected and the non-inflected. Our main task was to study the inflected M.G. words in order to describe their declinations and conjugations as economically as possible.

All inflected words were given the following morphological description:

$$\text{WORD} = [\text{PREFIX}] + \text{STEM} + [\text{INFIX}] + \text{INFLECTION(S)}$$

where: STEM and INFLECTION(S) are features that are necessary for the derivation of all possible forms, PREFIX and INFIX are not always present and thus appear bracketed "[ ]" in the above description; e.g.,

```
/ksana-graf-tik-a/ = PREFIX(ksana) + STEM(graf) +
                     INFIX(tik)+INFLECTION(a)
/e-graf-a/         =PREFIX(e) + STEM(graf) +
                     INFLECTION(a)
```

This analysis led to the development of a description-language that coded both the inflectional morphology and marked stress of M.G. This language utilises 260 rules. Given the stem of every declinable word, the appropriate set of rules is attached, making possible the production of all valid forms for the particular word. Every such combination is included in the lexicon, forming a lexicon entry. This way, all words with the same stem are stored as a single lexical item along with rules regarding the allowable inflection, thus saving vast amounts of storage.

Later on, the lexicon was enhanced by extending the previously described formalism in at least 4 points:

1. The morphemes used for the formation of Greek words can incorporate sets of morphosyntactic or semantic attributes.
2. A lemma can be defined as a cluster of word-form definitions.
3. Two-dimensional information structures can accompany a lemma.

4. Syntactic or semantic relations between lemmas can be defined as typed links that are resolved during lexicon construction.

This extended formalization allows us to denote:

- Attributes: Morphological or syntactic. These attributes can accompany a morpheme or a word; e.g. %attributes = (NOUN | ARTICLE | ...).
- Infos: The name and structure of the two-dimensional tags that a lemma can use to incorporate structural or free text information; e.g. %infos = (ANTONYM: ...| MEANING: ...| ...).
- Attribute sets: Sets of attributes that can accompany a morpheme or a word; e.g. @MCSING = (MASCULINE | SINGULAR).
- Inflection: Suffixes for gender, number, case, person, etc. Inflection is denoted by inflectional rules; e.g. #MSCas$ = (as @ (NOMINATIVE) | a @GAV) @ MSCSING "masculine singular ending in -as".
- Stress: Words in M.G. are stressed on the final, penultimate or antepenultimate position while single-syllable words are not stressed. Stress is denoted by stress-rules; e.g.
  !a1 = (1). – stress in final position
  !a2 = (2). – stress in penultimate position
  a6 = (3). – stress in antepenultimate position
- Forms: Combination of infix, suffix, stress and either attributes or attribute sets, e.g. $S1 = (o-te-r #OSe !a6 @(MASCULINE
  | – o-te-r = Infix,
  | – #Ose = infl. Rule
  | – !a6 = stress rule
  | – @(MASCULINE)=attribute
  o-te-r #OSp !a6 @(MASCULINE) |
  o-te-r #THIi !a6 |
  o-te-r #ESWN !a6 @(FEMININE) |
  o-te-r #OUDOe !a6 |
  o-te-r #OUDOp !a6 |) @EPSIGR
  – @EPSIGR = attributes applied – to all morphemes.

Our morphological lexicon consists of about 80,000 entries, whereas all possible forms produced reach about one million. The primary indexing / storage mechanism used to access the words of the lexicon is the Compressed Trie. This data structure was chosen as the most appropriate for our purpose of creating a lexicon, since it makes possible efficient searching and occupies minimal disk space. The Compressed Trie is used as an index to the database records of the lemmas, and since it is relatively small (about 700Kb), compared to the size of data needed to represent the entire lexicon, it is possible to load it in the main memory as a whole. A path in the Trie, starting from the root and ending to a leaf, represents a word prefix; the leaf points to those lemma records in the database that contain the suffixes of word-forms with this prefix. Using the Compressed Trie as an index to access the lemma records, we achieved approximately one disk access per search for data located in the disk.

5 Information Infrastructure and Linguistic Problem Domains

Apart from providing the morphosyntactic lexicon for the development of the Greek wordnet, CTI is responsible for the implementation of certain linguistic tools, thus creating the appropriate information infrastructure for the linguist to work with.

The role of such infrastructure is to provide all the necessary structures and operations that will allow the linguist to operate upon them. In order to capture the linguistic problem domain better, we outline the usage of such a system and identify the paradigms and patterns on which it is based.

Information Analysis. Linguists, especially those working in the field of lexicography, do not have a clear overview or understanding of the size of the problem. Lexicographical lemmas can be very simple (e.g. a simple link to a lemma explaining the word) or complicated structures that include synonyms, example sentences, references to other entries in the lexicon etc. In order to code such entries, linguists need tools that organise their thinking with regards to what constitutes a lexicographical entry. These tools should be flexible enough to follow the incremental formalization process.

Associative Storage and Retrieval. Linguists also need tools to associate lemmata they have imported into the system. In particular, the Greek WordNet project associates lemmata, trying to create structures containing semantic information e.g. hyponyms, hyperonyms, homonyms, synonyms. Linguists create and browse such associations and in this way are able to find more information on specific lemmata by following specific associations. Furthermore, the system must support a personalized view of such associations: for example one linguist may relate with the association synonym the words dog and canine - indicating that dog and canine are synonyms - whilst others may not. The system should support such personalization. Associations among different data types should also be supported. E.g. the association of the lemma dog with a picture of a dog.

Classification. In the WordNet projects the notion of ontology is essential. Ontologies consist of synsets that contain lemmata or other synsets. As a consequence, they can be viewed as a tree with synsets as nodes. Synsets at different levels of the tree have different meanings. Linguists are therefore assigned the task of classifying synsets within a specific ontology. This classification however should be very flexible, since different linguists may classify synsets in different ways within the same ontology. The issue of personalization is eminent. Furthermore, linguist should be enabled to compare the ontologies they have created and find the differences, allowing this way a more co-operative working.

We identified the above patterns to be very important in the creation of language engineering tools. Of course, more patterns can be identified by examining the work and needs of linguists. The set of patterns is not complete: new semantic models can be discovered that outline the needs of linguists. Currently, most language engineering tools are monolithic: they support only one or a limited number of the aforementioned patterns. Such monolithic systems widen the gap between linguists and language engineering tool designers: while linguists discover new semantic models to capture and structure language entities, system designers fail to respond to their needs. Language engineering systems should be redesigned with the scope of capturing the new models of linguists and avoiding to reuse the existing architectures and systems. Our aim is to design an Open Language Engineering System (OLES): A language engineering system, that provides the framework in which more cognitive models - capturing more patterns as described above - can be developed and even imported within the architecture, in an effort to fill the gap between linguists and system designers.

6   Future - Parallel Plans

At present time, important knowledge and linguistic information exists in most European countries. Especially after the completion of the EuroWordNet project, scientific horizons of West European countries were greatly expanded. The success of EuroWordNet has determined the emergence of several projects that aim at the development of multilingual WordNets for the remaining European languages.

However, apart from the EuroWordNet project, no other effort has been made towards the combination and mapping across these languages. Moreover, all researchers using EuroWordNet to study and compare languages have little or no exposure to East European languages and thus, their conclusions are limited.

Our future aim is to form an relevant project for the development of a multilingual resource representing semantic relations among basic concepts of the following languages: Greek, Turkish, Bulgarian, Romanian, Serbo-Croatian and Czech.

Balkan languages have been less studied during the past years and little or not at all investigated, since they have not been deemed to have commercial impact in the short run. Furthermore, presently, information retrieval has been limited to West European data, whilst vast amounts of information written in Balkan languages still remain inaccessible. This project aims at filling this gap and making the less studied, nevertheless equally important, Balkan languages known to the entire Europe. It aims at the development a multilingual database compatible with the EuroWordNet database, enabling this way its extension with new data. The main goal of the project will be to expand the EuroWordNet project by adding to it WordNets structured for the Balkan languages.

7   Conclusions

The use of a morphosyntactic lexicon as the basis for the development of the Greek WordNet was presented in this report. The project follows the same lines as the EuroWordNet project. This way the outcome will comply with a "de facto" standard that has been set since the creation of Princeton's WordNet.

The construction of the Greek WordnNet is expected to reveal interesting aspects of linguistic phenomena as well as cross-linguistic patterns of lexicalisation.

Furthermore, it will demonstrate the feasibility of such a large scale relational lexicon for lesser studied languages, showing the way for similar projects for other Balkan languages.

References

1. Cole, R. et al.: Survey of The State of The Art in Human Language Technology. (1997). Cambridge University Press.
2. EAGLES project: Creating standards on Electronic Lexicons, Interim Reports. (1996).
3. Ide, N. and Greenstein, D.: EuroWordNet. Computers and the Humanities. **32** , (1998), Double Special Issue on EuroWordNet.
4. Egedi, D. and Martin, P.: A Freely Available Syntactic Lexicon for English. Proceedings of the Int. Workshop on Sharable Natural Language Resources, Nara, Japan, (1994).
5. Ferwell, D., Guthrie, L. and Wilks, Y.: Automatically Creating Lexical Entries for ULTRA, a Multilingual MT System. Machine Translation, **8** (1993) 127–145.
6. Grishman, R., Macleod, C. and Meyers, A.: Comlex Syntax: Building a Computational Lexicon. Project Report. (1994).
7. Knight, K. and Luk, S.: Building a Large-Scale Knowledge Base for Machine Translation. (1994).
8. Maly, K.: Compressed Tries. Communications of the ACM, **19** (1976).
9. Oostdijk, N. and deHaan, P. (Eds): Corpus-based research into language. Rodopi Publ. Amsterdam, (1994).
10. Stamison-Atmatzidi, M., Vagelatos, A., Triantopoulou, T. and Christodoulakis, D.: The Utilization of An Electronic Morphology Dictionary and a Spelling Correction System for the Teaching of Modern Greek. C.A.L.L. Journal **7** (1994) 37–49.
11. Tsalidis, C. and Orphanos, G. Word Description Languages. Proceedings of the first Workshop in Natural Language Processing, Athens, Greece, (1995) 239–253.
12. Vagelatos, A., Stamison-Atmatzidi, M., Triantopoulou, T, Farmaki, V. and Christodoulakis, D.: Analysis of Literary Style of Poet A. Sikelianos - A Computer Based Approach. "Consensus Ex Machina ?", Joint International Conference, ALLC-ACH, Sorbonne, Paris, (1994).
13. Vagelatos, A., Triantopoulou, T., Tsalidis, C. and Christodoulakis, D.: A Spelling Correction System for Modern Greek. International Journal on Artificial Intelligence & Tools. **8** (1995).
14. Vagelatos, A., Triantopoulou, T., Tsalidis, C. and Christodoulakis, D.: Utilization of a Lexicon for Spelling Correction in Modern Greek. 10th Annual Symposium on Applied Computing (SAC '95) - Special Track on Artificial Inteligence, ACM Computing Week, Nashville, Tenesse, U.S.A. (1995)
15. Vossen, P.: EuroWordNet: A Multilingual Database with Lexical Semantic Networks. Kluwer Academic Publishers, (1998).
16. WordNet: Five Papers on WordNet, International Journal of Lexicography, (1994).

On Verb Selectional Restrictions: Advantages and Limitations

Françoise Gayral, Nathalie Pernelle[1], and Patrick Saint-Dizier[2]

[1] LIPN, Université Paris Nord
av. JB Clément, 93430 Villetaneuse, France
fg@lipn-univ-paris13.fr
[2] IRIT-CNRS, 118, route de Narbonne
31062 Toulouse, France
stdizier@irit.fr

Abstract. This paper deals with theoretical and applied NLP considerations about the definition and the uses of selectional restrictions as a means (1) to restrict the nature of the arguments of a predicate, (2) to detect and resolve sense variations and more generally (3) to be exploited in the composition process. Via several examples, we show the advantages and the limits of such an approach.

1 Introduction

The development on a large scale of structured sets of selectional restrictions, realized either manually or via automatic acquisition procedures, has shed a new light on their status and uses. While an indeniable progress has been made, we believe it is necessary to evaluate their contributions from a theoretical and practical perspective and to explore alternative conceptions for cases where they turn out to be inadequate.

Selectional restrictions are generally associated to predicates. They indicate semantic constraints that a predicate imposes on its linguistic environment, particularly on the nature of the arguments it may be combined with. These constraints often have the form of labels (e.g. 'human', 'edible', 'physical-object', 'event') which, according to the application and its domain, can be borrowed either from a simplified and standard model of the world (termed ontologies), or from application terminology.

They are used in almost every NLP system as a restrictive principle which limits the potential combinations of terms. They can also be used more dynamically to trigger appropriate semantic composition rules for computing the meaning of an expression. But, we show a number of situations where they are not appropriate to express semantic restrictions. We then sketch out a few proposals using recent paradigms in lexical semantics among which lexical semantics relations, properties, and the Qualia system of the Generative Lexicon [14]. Finally, we show several examples where these paradigms cannot be used as such satisfactorily. We then sketch out a few solutions.

D.N. Christodoulakis (Ed.): NLP 2000, LNCS 1835, pp. 57–68, 2000.

2   Expressing Selectional Restrictions: Theoretical Means

2.1   Simple Labels Associated to Words

The most widely known technique is to label arguments by means of labels borrowed from structured sets of terms. This is the most simple technique since, considered as constants, labels are easy to handle in a program and also probably easy to grasp at intuitively by readers and developers.

These labels are often structured by different types of relations, among which the taxonomy (is-a relation) and the meronomy (part-of and its sub-relations
[18]). This hierarchical organization allows the application of subsumption mechanism, which is a simple operation when only constants are involved.

This type of representation can be used in a number of situations, among which, in NLP:

- as a complement to other linguistic knowledge such as the syntactic subcategorization frames, thematic roles, etc., specifying semantic constraints on the nature of the arguments of a predicate. All this knowledge is included into the verb descriptions in the lexicon.
- as a simple characterization of verb polysemy in the construction of lexical resources: if a verb has several selectional restrictions with no compatible labels, it is "splitted" into different senses possibly corresponding to different lexical entries for this verb. For example, in French, when contrasting *le vase fuit (the vase leaks)* and *Paul fuit (Paul is running away)*, the restriction 'recipient'+ *fuir* means 'to leak' whereas 'animate'+ *fuir* means 'to run away'.
- symmetrically, in natural language interpretation, as a set of constraints in the semantic composition process to disambiguate and to construct the meaning of verbal expressions. Checking the concordance of the labels for the arguments of the verb leads to choose its appropriate meaning. When arguments do not fit the constraints, other mechanisms have to be triggered, e.g. to account for metonymy and metaphor. Compare, for example the direct usage: *to eat chocolates* and the metonymic one: *to eat the whole box* with selectional restrictions for the verb *eat* assumed to be 'animate' *eat* 'edible'.
- as a means to restrict the application of syntactic alternations, e.g. from [13]: the dative alternation with animates as obj2 (*give something to someone*).
- as a means to express constraints, in language generation, on the different forms of lexicalization of a concept and thus as a help to produce an appropriate verb (e.g. 'eat' is lexicalized as *essen* for human agents, and as *fressen* for animals in German).

However, the use of labels as selectional restrictions raises open questions.

- Cross-domain universality: evaluating the degree of their re-usability from a domain to another is not obvious ; some subsets may indeed be more universal than others (e.g. from the EuroWordNet top ontology [5], subsets such as: 'instrument', 'container' and 'usage' may largely vary in form and contents depending on domains), therefore, adaptations and extensions, which may overlap existing labels, must be defined carefully.

- Cross-users universality: when comparing identical tasks performed by different lexicographers or when comparing manual document classifications carried out by different persons, it is quite easy to note that a number of labels, or a number of conjunctions of labels are interpreted differently. The point is that a label, since it is expressed with a word in a given language, does not escape polysemy even if its interpretation is constrained by its place in the hierarchy of labels.
- Cross-language universality: it is not easy to evaluate how re-usable ontologies are over different languages. Since ontologies reflect a certain form of cultural or social organization of the world, they may differ from one community to another.
- Tuning the granularity of labels: if labels are too generic, they introduce overgeneration since restrictions are not precise enough; if they are too fine-grained, then selectional restrictions become complex logical expressions, difficult to understand and to maintain.

From our point of view, selectional restrictions and their organization cannot be defined independently of a theory of what meaning and what a word sense are. So, relatively different approaches to define labels exist depending on the discipline.

In Artificial Intelligence, these labels come from general purpose hierarchies modeling the world and can be assimilated to concepts in ontologies. They are strongly related to the notion of inference and allow to establish a bridge between linguistic and pragmatic (domain) knowledge, useful for constructing semantic representations. In theoretical approaches, they are viewed as types and these types are the support of compositionality rules. For linguistic distributional approaches, labels (or semantic classes) are often defined from sets of nouns which occur in identical contexts and can be, to a large extent, automatically acquired from huge corpora. They are close to labels used in dictionaries, terminological databases and thesauri. Labels may be psycholinguistic markers, not directly connected to a model of the world.

These approaches have recently been fruitfully developed, merged, evaluated and compared (e.g. in the EEC Eagles project).

Besides these questions, it is worth-noting that there are many well-known verbs for which the expression of selectional restrictions by means of labels is problematic, as showed later in the paper. Constraining an argument to be tagged with a particular label in order to be acceptable with a given verb is often a too strong hypothesis.

3   Complex Information Structures for Representating Words

Rather than considering simple labels, "splitting" the meaning into multiple lexical entries and considering composition as a simple concordance check, it seems preferable to enrich on one hand the description of the lexical entries associated with nouns, verbs and adjectives, and on the other hand the mechanism associated to the composition between a verb and its arguments (or a noun and an adjective). This complexification will substitute the simple unification and allow the composition process going in more depth into the lexical entry of the argument in order to grasp appropriate informations.

It is the claim of the current trend [15] [3] [2]. The Generative Lexicon (GL) [14] is certainly the corner stone of these approaches. The lexical entries involve several levels of representation, among them:

(1) the argument structure describes, for a predicate, the list of its arguments and their types,

(2) the Qualia structure, via its four roles, describes different aspects of the entity being defined: its environment (formal role), its constitutive parts (constitutive role), its uses (telic role) and the way it has been created (agentive role).

The Qualia structure is associated with different generative devices.

Selective binding accounts for polysemic adjectives. For example, the lexical semantics for the adjective *fast* indicates that it modifies the telic role of the head noun. So, *a fast typist / a fast car*, will be interpreted by *a typist who types quickly / a car which is driven quickly* since the information *type/drive* will be found in the telic role of *typist /car*.

Coercion allows to treat metonymies of several sorts [1]. For instance, the verb *begin* is described in the lexicon to expect for an object-argument of type 'event'. In the cases where there is no direct match between the type of the argument and the expectations of the verb, the Qualia of the argument will be explored in order to seek the expected type. If values in the Qualia match this type, the complement will be coerced. So, *begin a book* will be interpretable by *begin to read a book* or *begin to write a book* since *read* will be present in the telic role of *book* and *write* in its agentive role.

4   The Qualia Structure: Improvements and Limits

Labels accompanied with such an enrichment of the description of the lexical entries and of the composition process turn out to be sufficiently expressive in a number of situations. We show below less standard cases where the existence of properties, relatively inherent, of the object determines acceptance and interpretation.

We discuss the abilities or difficulties for these cases to be treated inside the Qualia theory.

4.1   Use of the Qualia Structure

Restrictions Involving the Part-Of Relation. The part-of relation is often involved in the expression of constraints on arguments.

---

[1] Pustejovsky also proposes dotted types to account for this issue.

For a verb such as *voler* (*fly*), as in *a bird/ a plane flies*, a label such as 'flying-object' is not likely to be available. But the entities which are subject argument of *fly* share the property of having wings. We assume that *fly* may be combined with nouns possessing this information [2].

This property of 'having wing' can be expressed via a part-of relation since the part-of relation describes the parts of an entity (element-set, functional part, etc.) [18], and all what is possessed by the entity considered. This type of information can be integrated in the constitutive role of the Qualia's argument. As a matter of fact, this Qualia facet contains the parts of an object and some of its properties (texture, color, weight, shape, etc. and more abstract ones), boolean and scalar (see also the SIMPLE project).

The lexical structures associated to *fly* and *plane* can be the following:

$$\left[\begin{array}{l} \textbf{Plane: } phys - obj \\ \cdots \\ \text{QUALIA} \ : \ \left[\text{CONSTITUTIVE} \ : \ part - of(X, Y : wing) \right] \end{array} \right]$$

$$\left[\begin{array}{l} \textbf{Fly: } movement - verb \\ \text{ARGSTR} \ : \ \left[\text{ARG1} \ : \ \begin{array}{l} X : phys - obj \wedge constitutive \rightarrow part - of(X, Y : wing) \\ \cdots \end{array} \right] \end{array} \right]$$

where $X : phys - obj \wedge constitutive \rightarrow part - of(X, Y : wing)$ expresses on one hand the label of the subject (X) and the constraint for it to possess in its constitutive facet the property $part - of(X, Y : wing)$.

But notice that the mechanism which is at stake for such a semantic composition is not coercion: the bird does not change its type to become 'wings' (it is not the wings which fly).

More generally , the reference to part-of relations is straightforward for most sensorial verbs such as *see, hear, taste*. The subject argument must have a part that allows the perception (e.g. eyes, ears, tongue). The part can be incorporated into the verb's semantics as in [1].

Restrictions Involving other Properties of the Argument. There are restrictions which can only be expressed by means of other properties of the argument. Let us examine some examples.

Cognition verbs such as *concevoir* (*conceive*) have a sense where the object argument must be something which is related in some way to an intellectual

---

[2] It is worth noting that there are many other entities which can fly without having wings (*a leaf flies*) but we think theses cases are more or less metaphoric: the movement of a leave which flies is comparable to the movement of an object which would possess wings. The treatment of metaphoric use of verbs, although important, is not tackled here, neither the metonymic one as in *Paul flies to New-York*.

activity for the object to be conceived and then, possibly, created , as in *concevoir une maison, une sonate, un programme ... (conceive a house, a sonata, a program)*.

Considering the argument, the hypothesis that this information can be found in the agentive role of the Qualia structure is plausible. As a matter of fact, the agentive role deals with the coming into being of the entity being described. This is relatively expressible for concrete terms, particularly for artefacts, while much more complex for abstract ones. Predicates falling into this Agentive role can be considered as classified with the main verb classes as those expressed in WordNet terminology [5]: verbs of creation and destruction, cognition verbs, verbs of body care and verbs of consumption. So, predicates can be typed according to these classes or according to narrower classes, allowing more accurate constraints.

So, we consider that *conceive* may combine with nouns which have a verb of type 'cognition' in the agentive role of their Qualia structure:

$$\left[\begin{array}{l} \textbf{Conceive:} \; cognition \; process \\ \text{ARGSTR} \; : \; \left[\begin{array}{ll} \text{ARG1} \; : \; X \; : \; human \\ \text{ARG2} \; : \; Y \; : artefact \; \wedge \; agentive \; \rightarrow \; P \; : cognition \; \wedge \; process \\ \cdots \end{array} \right] \end{array} \right]$$

The expression: Y: $artefact \wedge agentive \rightarrow P : cognition \wedge process$ means that the agentive role of the Qualia of Y must contain a predicate P which is a process of type cognition.

Let us illustrate the composition with a noun such as *house*. The Qualia structure of *house* is partially given as:

$$\left[\begin{array}{l} \textbf{house} \\ \text{ARGSTR} \; : \; \left[\begin{array}{l} \text{ARG1} \; : \; X \; : \; artefact \\ \cdots \end{array} \right] \\ \\ \text{QUALIA} \; : \; \left[\begin{array}{l} \cdots \\ \text{AGENTIVE} \; : \; \begin{array}{l} plan(e_1, Y : human, X) : \; cognition \; process, \\ build(e_2, Y : human, X) : \; construction \; process \end{array} \end{array} \right] \end{array} \right]$$

So, *conceive a house* will be understood as make plans for the house rather than build it.

Thus, this approach, while allowing the composition, also allows for the construction of a precise representation of the meaning of the utterance. From *conceive a house*, the composition process leads to: 'make plans for the house'. From *conceive a symphony*, it deduces 'composes a symphony'. This is thus a step towards deeper understanding [3].

---

[3] Notice that while nouns such as *house* or *computer program* or *symphony* have, with no doubt, a predicate of type 'cognition' in their Agentive role, this is less obvious for a noun such as *garden* which can appear as a more "natural" object. Nevertheless, *conceive a garden* is understood as 'make plans for the organization of the garden'. We will come back to that problem in the last section.

4.2   Beyond the Qualia Structure

Other verbs can require, for their arguments, the presence of some properties which are sometimes impossible to classify inside the Qualia structure.

Let us consider some examples.

The verb *chauffer* (*heat*) requires, in its initial sense and in the unergative form, an argument that uses, produces or stores energy (e.g. the sun, an engine, a battery, a lamp, etc.).

A verb such as *couper*, studied in [7], used in the sense of 'interrupt a process' (*couper le moteur, le son, la musique, le film, l'électricité, les fonds, cut an engine, the sound, the music, a film, electricity, funds, heating*, etc. [4]) selects for objects which evoke or can be assimilated to flows. A speech, a discussion, or iterative processes, can, at a coarser-grained level, be assimilated to continuous flows, such as funds regularly obtained, which can suddenly be cut.

These properties and their characteristics might be included into NLP lexicons. But it is not, in fact, clear at all, whether they could be found in the Qualia structure of the argument unless loosening the boundaries and the interpretation of the Qualia roles. So far, this point has not received much attention, in spite of its crucial character. Although some approaches have descriptions of properties (such as in the Mikrokosmos approach, or in the Penman approach), these properties are often just listed in the lexical entry and lack a structure which allows inferences to be drawn.

Whereas Qualia must remain within linguistic boundaries, links with contextual knowledge seem necessary in most cases. This required knowledge cannot be reduced to a small number of role fillers. As underlined by several authors [11], the interpretation of a proposition cannot, in a number of cases, be reduced to a strict reference to lexical resources and simple compositional rules.

Consider the restrictions on a verb such as *pousser* with the sense 'activate, increase activity, attain a higher degree of development', as in *pousser le moteur, le feu, des études, les enchères, une enquête* (*an engine, the fire, studies, an investigation*). The object argument describes a relatively autonomous process on which the agent has an influence by a certain means or instrument, so that the intensity of the process (or a prototypical property of that process) can be increased. Therefore, to be an acceptable argument, the object must be related to a predicate (1) that describes its main uses and activity(ies) and (2) which can be subject to variations of e.g. (i) intensity for *burn* or *run* (fire or engines) or (ii) expansion in time and depth of knowledge for *push a student to make higher studies* and for *push an investigation*. It is clear that this type of information and the way the process can increase its activity, often higher-order, cannot, in general, be found in any lexical description. Forms of inferences are required, in particular to be paired with predicates in Qualia roles.

Consider the noun *crime*. To understand a sentence as *résoudre un crime* (*resolve a crime*), it is necessary to relate the term *crime* to informations such

---

[4] We are aware that the translation of our french examples is not always a good illustrations of the phenomena we are interested in.

as: a crime involves police investigations, these investigations consist in looking for the culprit, the weapon, the motives of the crime... It is clear that this cannot be found in any role of the Qualia structure.

An example which is likely more striking is the verb *surveiller* (*watch + after/over,...*) ; it has an object argument which is quite complex to characterize. In French, you can 'watch' over a swimming pool, a child, an exam, a cake, your luggage at the station, etc. These arguments are semantically very heterogeneous and do not share any property which would be useful for the composition with the verb *surveiller*. The interpretation of such sentences coincides with the restitution of one or more processes related to the object being watched: actions performed in or around a swimming pool, actions done by a child, the cooking of a cake, the fact that your luggage is still there, etc. But you don't watch over a tree or a wall, unless exceptional circumstances. The constraint on the object argument is that it is a process which may lead to a negative state: a child may have an accident, your cake may burn, your luggage may be stolen. These constraints are very difficult to characterize in a systematic way. Quite a lot of world knowledge is involved, which cannot necessarily be found even in an extended Qualia. For example, the telic role of *swimming pool* contains a predicate such as 'swim(X,Y)' but not predicates describing accidents, even if they are direct potential consequences. This type of information being quite far from the roles and uses of a swimming pool, it would be too ad'hoc to be generalized over most Qualia structures. This would even worse for the case for a child or pieces of luggage.

The only solution, still very informal, is the reference to domain knowledge, stored, for example, in scripts. The formal operations to access the information, to validate the well-formedness of the expression and to compute the semantic representation are far from clear yet. On the other hand, just stating that there is a general metonymy where the object can be taken for a process associated to it (as would do the GL) clearly overgenerates and does not lead, in this case, to the construction of any accurate representation.

5   Complexification of Composition Rules

5.1   Co-composition

Semantic composition rules must account for examples where the composition between a verb and its arguments 'reduces' or specifies, either the verb meaning or the argument meaning, without any metaphor or metonymy being involved. We illustrate in this section the mechanism of co-compositionality emphasized by Pustejovsky.

A first example is characterized by the adjunction of a property to the object, provided that it does not contradict any knowledge about that object. This property is introduced by the verb, in particular by its expectations about the argument.

Consider *lire une archive* (*read an archive*). A priori, an archive contains 'information', whatever its nature is: textual, audio, photographic... This is expressed in the constitutive role.

$$
\begin{bmatrix}
\textbf{archive} \\
\text{ARGSTR} : \begin{bmatrix} \text{ARG1} : X : phys - obj \\ \cdots \end{bmatrix} \\
\\
\text{QUALIA} : \begin{bmatrix} \cdots \\ \text{CONSTITUTIVE} : contain(X, Y : information) \end{bmatrix}
\end{bmatrix}
$$

Read constrains its object-argument to be a physical object that contains 'textual information'.

$$
\begin{bmatrix}
\textbf{Read} \\
\text{ARGSTR} : \begin{bmatrix} \text{ARG1} : X : phys - obj \wedge contain(X, Y : textual - info) \\ \cdots \end{bmatrix}
\end{bmatrix}
$$

The composition process specifies, since it is not contradictory, the archive to be textual. On the other hand, such a mechanism is blocked for *tape* since a tape has in its constitutive role the information that it contains 'audio-information' and nothing else.

It is the same for *read a story, read a work* or *drink a mixture* or *resolve a situation* where the reader will deduce that the story is written, the work is a literary work, the mixture is liquid, the situation is problematic. It is thus clear that some verbs impose an interpretation on an argument that it would otherwise not a priori carry. This mechanism can also be found in more complex examples such as *manger toute la boite* (*eat the all box*) where a metonymy is at stake. As a matter of fact, the box, which can contain a priori any type of physical object, contains, in this context, edible objects.

The reverse phenomenon, consisting for an argument to specify the verb meaning is noteworthy. Above, we saw that *conceive*, when used with *house* takes the meaning of making plans, when used with *music* means composing...

In addition, an argument is able to impoverish the semantics of a verb, illustrating the fact that semantic constraints are not one-way. For example, in *manger un chewing gum* (*eat a chewing gum*), the complete act of eating chew + ingest, is not accomplished till its term. It is only the first part which is realized, and should therefore appear alone in the semantic representation.

To go back to the verb *read*, sentence such as *Paul reads Arabic/Chinese/ Hebrew* can be pronounced if Paul is just able to decipher the characters of the given alphabet while unable to understand the meaning of what is decoded [5]. As previously, the meaning of the verb *read* can be considered as impoverished.

---

[5] What is implicit is that Paul's language possesses a different alphabet than the Arabic/Chinese/Hebrew one, or that Paul is illiterate in its own language.

This loss of a part of the verb meaning is typical of some metaphors. For instance, consider *vendre des rêves*, (*to sell dreams*). *Sell* incorporates in its semantics a transfer of money corresponding to the value of the object sold. *Sell* also basically expects an object1 of type 'physical object', which intrinsically may get a 'monetary' value. *Dream* can be typed as e.g. 'psychological', it has therefore no monetary value. *To sell dreams* is thus interpreted as a metaphor, where there is an inhibition of the transfer of money dimension due to the psychological dimension of *dream*. This is just one, but realistic, interpretation, which remains compositional, but which involves a non-monotonic operation. The loss of one of the most salient characteristic of *sell* in these sentences raises a stylistic effect.

5.2   Co-text Dependency

An important issue that has not been yet treated is that restrictions on an argument may depend on the semantics of another argument.

A verb such as *contrôler* (*to control, to check*) where a part, often a property of the object argument, is what is controlled. Therefore, restrictions on arguments are both atomic: the object argument must have something to be controlled, and relational: what is being controlled depends on the subject. The nature of the control depends both on the controller and the controllee. In *The manager controls the employees*, the manager controls the work and presence of his employees, whereas *the doctor controls the employees*, the doctor controls health and related working conditions. What is controlled is complex. It may either be a prototypical property of the object as such, or a less prototypical property of the object infered and made salient from the subject's prototypical activities. It is the case when the subject is a profession noun; a watchman, a doctor, a surgery, a policeman: all have prototypical activities which can be refered to and used in the composition process.

Until now, we have just considered the verbal phrases and the semantic constraints which operate between the verb and its arguments. Obviously, the rest of the text provides other semantic constraints which may act upon the interpretation of the verb itself [6].

Let us examine the following sentences which are all based on the same couple verb-object:

(1) *J'ai laissé l'examen de système sur ton bureau.*
   I left the system exam on your desk.

(2) *J'ai laissé l'examen de système à Paul. Il est plus compétent.*
   I left the system exam to Paul. He is more competent.

(3) *Ne laissez pas l'examen traîner.*
   Do not leave the exam lying around.

(4) *J'ai laissé l'examen de système pour le mois prochain.*
   I left the system exam for next month.

Laisser (to leave) is roughly equivalent to put in (1), to entrust in (2), to remain in (3) and to postpone in (4) while examen refers to a paper in (1) and

(3), to the process of writing the subject in (2) and to the fact to prepare the examination in (4).

These examples emphasize that a verbal phrase have various meanings depending on the sentence it is included in and that finding the appropriate interpretation for the verbal phrase depends on finding it for the words of the co-text. But, there is no reason to consider that their meaning can be determined independently. That yields inevitably to circularity and shows that the classical hypothesis of compositionality which is generally assumed [6] is not always adequate [12].

6   Conclusion and Perspectives

It is clear that the labels under the form of constants should be preferred when sufficiently expressive. Their use range from constraining the semantics of arguments and resolving ambiguities, to triggering simple semantic composition rules.

An alternative is the use of the information represented in Qualia structures. We showed some improvements and enrichments allowing the composition process to check the presence of some given properties or bring/specify a property. On the other side, we emphasized the limits of such approaches.

Although useful, lexical knowledge is often insufficient to allow the expression of semantic constraints and to construct the meaning of an expression in context: domain knowledge and common sense knowledge are often required. However, the introduction of world knowledge is very delicate. Qualia structures and more generally lexical entries cannot be too much extended: that would be a slippery slope towards bringing all word knowledge into the lexicon. That's why we think that an important issue is to develop principles to limit the world knowledge in the lexicon while connecting in some way this lexical information to scripts [17] and inferential systems. The type of inference forms needed to account for the different phenomena described above, particularly the predicate / arguments combinations, go far beyond type coercion. From a computing perspective, this remains to be further investigated in depth.

References

1. Baker, M.C, (1988) *Incorporation*, University of Chicago Press.
2. Bouillon, P. (1998), *Polymorphie et Sémantique Lexicale: le Cas des Adjectifs*, presse du septentrion, Lille.
3. Copestake, A. and Briscoe, T. (1995), Semi-productive polysemy and sense extension, *Journal of semantics*, 12, pp15-67.
4. Cruse, A., (1986) *Lexical Semantics*, Cambridge University Press.

---

[6] The compositionality hypothesis enables to elaborate the meaning of an expression from its syntactic structure and from the meaning of its parts. That leads to consider the composition process as a purely bottom-up mechanism.

5. Fellbaum, C. (1997), A Semantic Network of English Verbs, in C. Fellbaum (ed) *WordNet:An electronic Lexical Database*, Cambridge, MIT press.
6. Gayral, F., Kayser, D., Pernelle, N., (1999) In Search of the Semantic Value(s) of an Occurrence : an Example and a Framework, in *proc. IWCS*, Tilburg, pp 87-100.
7. Gayral, F., St Dizier, P., (1999) Peut-on Couper à la Polysémie Verbale, in *proc. TALN* 99, pp155-164.
8. Gruber, J., *Studies in Lexical Relations* (1976), MIT doctoral dissertation and in *Lexical Structures in Syntax and Semantics*, North Holland.
9. Jackendoff, R., (1990), *Semantic Structures*, MIT Press.
10. Jackendoff, R., (1997), *The Architecture of the Language Faculty*, MIT Press.
11. Jayez, J., (to appear), *Underspecification, Context Selection and Generativity*.
12. Kayser, D., Abir, H., (1995) A Non-Monotonic Approach to Lexical Semantics, *Computational lexical semantics*, Cambridge University Press, Cambridge UK, pp.303-318.
13. Levin, B., (1993) *English verb classes and Alternations : a Preliminary Investigation*, Chicago University Press.
14. Pustejovsky, J., (1991), The Generative Lexicon, *Computational Linguistics*, vol 17-4.
15. Pustejovsky, J., (1995), *The Generative Lexicon*, MIT Press.
16. Saint-Dizier, P., (1998), A Generative Lexicon Perspective for Adjectival Modification, in *proc. ACL-Coling*, Montreal.
17. Schank, R. (1982), Reminding and Memory Organization : an introduction to MOPs, in *Strategies for Natural Language Processing*, eds. W.Lenhert and M.Ringle, xdvi nou.dvi Lawrence Erlbaum Ass., Hillsdale.
18. Winston, M.E., Chaffin, R., Hermann, D., (1987) A Taxonomy of Part-Whole Relations, *Cognitive Science*, 11, pp 417-444.

Some Principles for Implementing Underspecification in NLP Systems

Alda Mari[1] and Patrick Saint-Dizier[2]

[1] EHESS, 9, rue de Mezieres
75006 Paris, France
Alda.Mari@ehess.fr
[2] IRIT-CNRS, 118, route de Narbonne
31062 Toulouse, France
stdizier@irit.fr

Abstract. This paper deals with theoretical and applied NLP consideration about sense variation and its representation by means of underspecification. We underline the main problematics, and show how Lexical Conceptual Structures can be used, paired with elements from the Generative Lexicon, to deal with meaning variations introduced by arguments w.r.t. the basic sense of a predicate. We develop different forms of underspecification and instantiations and show more formally an instantiation procedure based on constraint resolution.

1 Introduction

In this paper concerning underspecification, we address three main questions:

1. what are the nature and the formal principles governing underspecification in language utterances ?
2. what kind of means do we need to represent underspecification in practice ?
3. what are the main practical problems of implementing underspecification within a given semantic representation theory ?

These points are first worked out through the example of the verb *lire* (read) in section 4. We are concerned with the problem of the well-known relation between (abstract) sense and meaning in context. This is illustrated through the following examples:
Jean lit le grec (John reads Greek) lit/reads = decodes the scripts,
Jean lit l'allemand (John reads German) lit/reads = understands the language,
Jean lit Kant (John reads Kant) lit/read = understand the meaning of Kant's philosophy. In our approach all these uses of *lire* are related to the same sense. We also think that there is a kind of 'semantic' continuum between these readings.

The scope of underspecification is then studied in section 5, where we explore the nature of underspecified fields, In section 6, we show an instantiation procedure that includes subsumption and we show how it can be implemented in constraint logic programming.

D.N. Christodoulakis (Ed.): NLP 2000, LNCS 1835, pp. 69–80, 2000.

2   Postulates and Maxims Related to Underspecification

As shown in [9], [10] and [11], underspecification is concerned with the same problem than Generative Lexicons already attempted to solve: the computation of all the possible meanings a word can acquire through all the possible contexts in which it can appear. Within the current literature in the field (see e.g. [1]), underspecification presents itself as an alternative to Generative approaches [12]: these latter pretend to be able to anticipate all the semantically acceptable combinations by coding all the needed information within representation structures (e.g. the Qualia structure) and generation rules. On the contrary, the underspecification approach postulates that it is impossible to foresee all the possible interpretations for a whole proposition. In fact, it recognizes the difficulty of deductively calculating all the meanings in context for the items of a proposition. Since knowledge of a form or another is necessary to effectively determine the acceptance of a sentence and its meaning, the main difference between the two approaches is mainly at the control level: the underspecification approach makes a kind of 'lazy evaluation' while allowing inferences to be drawn on incomplete forms by making hypothesis on their potential instantiations. It is therefore a more powerful inference mechanism than coercion.

In order to solve the combinatorial explosion puzzle, underspecification relies on 2 postulates and a maxim:

- do not generate a priori all the possible interpretations for a given item in a given context (this is probably obvious),
- do generate only the interpretations you assume you need for a given context (the difficulty is to evaluate what is needed, heuristics may help at this level),
- maxim: when you have a plausible interpretation for an item in a given context, keep it as long as it is not contradicted by any further information.

Another new theoretical position underspecification assumes is that before or during the interpretation procedure it is possible to draw accurate inferences from the underspecified representations. At the representation level, this means that the coded information has to be appropriate for these tasks, e.g. hypothesis must be allowed from underspecified contents to allow inferences to be drawn. Another point is that the granularity is not fixed once for all for all the items of a language. This reflects the possibility of defining different levels of underspecification and also the possibility of being vague for terms which are almost semantically empty by themselves (e.g. some prepositions).

Each item is subject to a specific analysis taking into account the specific relationships between sense and meaning in context (precisification [9] or first-order instantiation).

An important feature that has to be stressed before going into representations is that, from our point of view, the instantiation mechanism in the treatment underspecification must be monotonic.

3 Representing Underspecification

Let us assume that a verb has one or more 'basic' or 'primitive' senses. These senses are often quite general, they correspond to relatively standard and straightforward realizations, with typical arguments expected by the verb. However, very often, the arguments encountered are not exactly those expected by the basic sense. In that case, they often slightly alter the meaning of the predicate, whereas operations such as metaphors and metonymies sometimes involve deeper structural changes.

The approach often taken in language processing is to define relatively generic representations for predicates, with appropriate fields left underspecified and with devices designed to instantiate these underspecified (or underdetermined) fields depending on the arguments found in a sentence. However, so far, the underspecification is in general represented by means of relatively general types, e.g. 'location', 'psychological attitude', which turn out, in concrete situations, to be insufficiently constrained and therefore to overgenerate. Representing underspecification is an extremely delicate task, in particular due to the large number of exceptional behaviors.

This paper aims at developing a few steps towards the definition of semantic representations and computational procedures that support and handle underspecification in a more adequate and constrained way. We show, in particular, that the Lexical Conceptual Structure (LCS) language, [90, 97] paired with some elements of the Generative Lexicon (GL) are particularly well-adapted to deal with underspecification.

It has been shown in several articles that the LCS cannot, in its current form, represent any type of predicate. Its primitive system is somewhat limited and overloaded, but we think that the LCS formalism, its links with syntax, and the approach should be kept and extended. From this enlarged perspective, it turns out, from our experiments on a number of semantic classes of verbs, that the LCS is a relatively adequate framework to deal with sense variations and underspecification (see also B. Dorr's work on LCS forms for verb classes in English). The different, hierarchically organized, elements at stake in the LCS seem (1) to correspond, in general, to the variation factors that we have identified and (2) to be sufficiently fine-grained.

Furthermore, in the LCS, the primitive constituents and some basic formulae correspond to different steps of the categorization procedure when learning a language. It is then conceivable to specialize or change autonomous, and often elementary, well-formed fragments of LCS forms by other wff forms, when representing sense variations, in a way similar that human categorization and learning procedures revise the contents of concepts (see e.g. [2] for the possession verb family).

Knowledge revision is not in general a monotonic process, however, in our approach, we have designed underspecified forms and instantiations mechanisms in a way such that only monotonic operations need to be involved, for obvious computational reasons.

The following features of the LCS are, to our opinion, particularly well-fitted to deal with underspecification:

- decompositionality: the LCS analyses linguistic concepts into a number of primitives and rules that, by their combinations and interactions, incrementally build up the representation(s) of an item. We have developed a grammar for the LCS that we have validated on a psychological basis [2], [6], [7].
- transpositionability of well-formed, underspecified fragments of representations to different conceptual fields (poss, temp, epist, psy,..). In the specification process there are instantiations ranging over conceptual fields. For example, there are partially instantiated LCS structures which can be appear within the scope of different conceptual fields, by analogy. These can be fields related to direct uses or fields related to metaphorical uses (e.g. direct: localization, metaphorical: psychological for a verb like to push).

Within the LCS framework, the following elements can be appropriately investigated and implemented:

- dealing with underspecification means to exactly identify the semantic components that bear the underspecified information. It turns out that these semantic components correspond to well-formed fragments of LCS representations.
- another problem with dealing with underspecification concerns the appropriateness of the specific information involved and elaborated during interpretation. It is necessary to describe the space of those semantic values which can specify a given information. There are different techniques for that purpose, e.g. dedicated grammars as in formal grammars (W-grammars), or via the Herbrand base in logic programs. The LCS allows the encoding, in a principled and guided way, of this required information in dedicated fields.
- Once the semantic underspecified components have been isolated into LCS structures, for computational reasons, it is possible to establish a typed lambda-calculus to allow for a simple and direct instantiation of underspecified fields.

4   A Working Example

Let us consider the example of *lire* given in the introduction. The problem is to relate the abstract description of the sense of *lire* given in the LCS representation below with meanings in context.

Let's begin with the abstract meaning of the verb.

Lire can be represented in the LCS language as follows:

$$[_{event} CAUSE([_{thing} I], [_{event} GO_{+epist}([_{thing} J : text],$$

$$[_{path} INTO_{+epist}([_{place} MIND - OF([_{thing} I])])])]$$

This formula illustrates the properties of the LCS stated in the above section.

This representation roughly says that I is the cause of an event, namely the transfer (GO) in the epistemic domain (+epist) of J of type text into I's mind. Here, text is the underspecified field, since it covers different specifications.

Coming next to the meaning in context, we observe at least three possible specifications:

1. $text_1$ = a set of characters in a certain script. In 'John reads Greek', if John is not a Greek speaker, the immediate interpretation is that he can at least decode the alphabet.
2. $text_2$ = syntactic and semantic rules governing the language. In 'John reads German', the immediate interpretation is that John has competences in German. If John is an English speaker, it is taken for granted, during the interpretation, that he can decode the German characters.
3. $text_3$ = informational contents. In 'John reads 'the critique of pure reason', the interpreter assumes that John can decode the characters, has a good command of the syntactic and semantic rules of German, and, moreover, understands Kant's philosophy.

This leads us to elaborate in the following way, the content information of the word text formally represented in the LCS as: $[_{thing} \; J : text \;]$:

1. sequence of scripts, formally represented as: $IDENTITY - OF(scripts - of(J : text))$, where identity-of is a 'basic' function related to properties of the argument, as advocated in (Jackendoff 97),
2. 1 + set of grammar and semantic composition and concordance rules:, formally represented as: $formal - rept - of(J : text)$,
3. 1 + 2 + set of interpretation rules formally represented as: $contents - of(J : text)$.

There is an 'upward' implication from 3 to 2 and 2 to 1. Moreover, assuming e.g. 1 does not exclude that 2 or 3 may be also valid interpretations.

Let us now remind how the underspecification works and how the different instantiations can be worked out during the interpretation phase. The maxim in section 1 leads us to look for the maximal interpretation coherent with the other constraints currently available in the statement (we assume monotonicity of new information to simplify). this amounts to computing the greater lower bound, in terms of denotation size, of a set of representations. For instance, if we know that John is English, the maximal interpretation is number 2 above.

If we follow up this reasoning, we have to be able to find within the utterance the proper elements that trigger a certain interpretation ([11] and his anti-random hypothesis).

Let us now look how it works in a practical way:

(1) John isn't Greek and therefore uses an alphabet which isn't the Greek one. The minimal interpretation is:
$[_{event} \; CAUSE([_{thing} \; I \;],$

$$[_{event} \; GO + epist([_{thing} \; IDENTITY - OF(scripts - of(J : text))\;],$$
$$[_{path} \; INTO_{+epist}([_{place} \; MIND - OF([_{thing} \; I \;])])])]$$

(2) John is English, he can decode the scripts of German, therefore, the minimal assumption is that he is a linguistic competence of German:

$$[_{event} \; CAUSE([_{thing} \; I \;],$$
$$[_{event} \; GO + epist([_{thing} \; formal - rept - of(J : text)\;],$$
$$[_{path} \; INTO_{+epist}([_{place} \; MIND - OF([_{thing} \; I \;])])])]$$

(3) John is a scholar, we can assume that he understands German and the philosophy of Kant.

$$[_{event} \; CAUSE([_{thing} \; I \;], \; [_{event} \; GO + epist([_{thing} \; contents - of(J : text)\;],$$

$$[_{path} \; INTO_{+epist}([_{place} \; MIND - OF([_{thing} \; I \;])])])]$$

5   Scope of Underspecification

Underspecification may take many forms and is subject to a large number of constraints, including preferences, for example some predicates in the Qualia structure of the Generative Lexicon are more prototypical than others and will be preferred. Let us now briefly present the characteristics of underspecification we have identified while studying semantic variations for verbs of different families: verbs of transfer of possession, communication verbs, cooking verbs, verbs of action and aspectual verbs and the semantic behavior of a number of evaluative adjectives (e.g. good, bad, sad, happy, lousy, terrible, noisy).

5.1   Nature of Underspecified Fields

Underspecified fields must not be gaps with which almost any type and form of information can be associated. It is of much importance to precisely define the scope of these fields, either intensionally, for example by means of a grammar (e.g. as in attribute grammars) or via the Herbrand Base approach (e.g. as in Logic programs), or extensionally, as it is e.g. often the case for systems based on type feature structures (where values are often listed explicitly).

In the present case, some elements can be defined extensionally, e.g. the list of semantic fields of the LCS language, whereas others are defined intentionally, by means of a grammar which describes e.g. the structure of LCS fragments which can fill in the different types of underspecified fields. The instances of these fragments can always be defined in a recursively enumerable way.

The first important result when representing underspecification, which can be seen in the examples above, is that sense variations can be characterized entirely by means of elements with narrow scope in the LCS. They are mainly:

- semantic fields, where variations occur between the following fields: loc (localization), poss (possession), temp (temporal), psy (psychological), epist (epistemic), comm (communication). These variations reflect the partial analogies that exist among these fields, they are extensively used in the production of metaphors. The loc → poss metaphor is well-known in the LCS, note also loc → epist (cut the news, and article, a film), or loc → comm (cut a conversation).

- low-level functions or predicates, used in 'terminal' fields of the LCS, such as AVAILABILITY-OF(X) above. Function variations occur only between functions with a comparable abstract or generic level. These functions are usually organized in ontologies describing e.g. the status of events, of resources, etc. Compared to ontologies being constructed around nouns (representing concepts) for general purpose domains (e.g. at ISI, NMSU, or within EuroWordNet and Eagles), these ontologies are much smaller, i.e. 3 to 10 nodes in general. However, except for events, and contrary to common ontologies based on nouns, they are seldom found in the literature. They must be constructed experimentally from the beginning.
- low-level well-formed LCS structures, typed by semantic domains: thing, place, etc., possibly including conceptual variables already introduced in the main representation, e.g.: $[_{thing}\ I\ ]$. They are in fact essentially things, places, paths and properties. We have, for example, the shift from thing to properties.

We have observed that, in particular, no new variable is introduced when underspecified fields are instantiated. Similarly, there is no structure change, the primitives present in the general form (either generic: GO, BE, or circumstantial: FROM, TO, etc.) are unaltered. The only change observed is the adjunction to the representation of a modifier, via an anchoring procedure. In that latter case, new variables may be added, but they remain local to the modifier.

Underspecified fields may (recursively) receive one of the following items, from the most specific ones to the most general:

- specific data associated with particular lexical entries, they are constants,
- functions from ontologies, as advocated above,
- semantic field values, functionally inferred from the type of the argument:
  cut: cut electricity (thing) versus cut conversation (comm).
  sell: sell objects (thing) versus sell dreams (psy).
- LCS elementary representations (e.g. specified by defaults rules),
- predicates essentially form the Telic roles of nouns, using an appropriate selection strategy. In particular, preferences among predicates should be stated, even if this is a risky enterprise, since preferences may vary depending on the predicate.

5.2 Instantiations from Lexical Data: The Case of Construction Verbs

The construction verb class includes verbs like *construire, bâtir, édifier, réaliser, composer,* (build, construct, realize, compose), etc. Let us concentrate on the

verb *construire*, which includes usages such as:
construire une maison / un cercle / un projet / une relation.
(to build a house / a circle / a project/ a relation).
The sense variation goes from a central meaning with a concrete, physical object
to an abstract object (of type psy or epist in the LCS). The general representation
of this verb is, for example:

$$\lambda J, I, [_{event} CAUSE([_{thing} I],$$
$$[_{event} GO_A([_{thing} J], [_{path} TOWARD_A([_{state/prop} EXIST]$$
$$FROM_A(part - of(J)),$$
$$VIA_A(definition - constitutive(J))])])].$$

which describes the coming into being of J.

A is a variable, whose value is functionally determined from the object argument:

J : physical object : A = +loc,
J : psychological relation : A = +psy,
J : intellectual construction : A = +epist, etc.

Two functions, related to lexical data, are used: part-of(J) which gets the
parts of J from its lexical entry (or from other sources of knowledge), and
definition-constitutive(J) which gets the definition of J (e.g. a circle is a set
of points equidistant from a particular point: the center). If this definition is
not available or instantiated in the lexical entry corresponding to the lexeme
J, then the function remains as it is, just stating that J has a certain constitutive definition. We may, in fact, consider that this type of information is
domain-dependent and not linguistic data. Note also that GO denotes a change
of state, which is made more precise by means of semantic fields such as +loc,
+poss or +char,+ident. In fact, GO gets its major meaning from those fields.
It is contrasted with BE, which denotes a state, with identical semantic field
specializations.

Construire is probably the generic element of the class. If we consider the
following sense of the verb *composer*, which is more specific, as in: *composer
une sonate* (to compose a sonata), which is basically restricted to musical pieces
(imposed by constraints proper to the verb), we get exactly the same phenomena
and restrictions, modulo inherent restrictions proper to that verb. Note that this
verb has closely related uses such as *composer un menu / une salade* (to compose
a menu, a salad) where the property outlined is that the menu or the salad is
nicely designed and is going to look like a piece of art. Note that *construire*
would be less appropriate here because of the connotation included in *composer*,
but would still be acceptable for a menu. These extensions are treated exactly as
above. There is no changes in the semantic fields of the LCS form, the variations
being handled by instantiations from lexical data.

The form *se composer un visage* (to compose one's face = to hide one's
opinions/feelings) is metaphorically derived from the sense considered here, but
is rather a semi-fixed form since it is quite remote from the original sense and
weakly compositional.

6   Instantiation Procedures of Underspecified Fields

One of our main observations is that instantiations of underspecified fields can be modeled as a monotonic operation, similarly to unification. We need first to characterize the subsumption relation among LCS forms, where LCS forms are viewed as (recursive) types. This means that representations do not undergo any revisions for structures already instantiated. Given that relation, we briefly present the operations that realize the instantiations. The main operation is unification via β-reduction, a well-known operation, it is paired here with two types of mechanisms: default reasoning and constraint-based reasoning.

6.1   LCS and Subsumption

We have observed that there is no structural change besides the instantiation of underspecified fields when the underspecified semantic representation of a predicate is used in the semantic representation of a sentence. These representations become instantiated step by step, depending on the arguments, via semantic composition rules. Different arguments affect different underspecified elements: there is no conflict and the order arguments are considered in semantic composition rules does not seem to be relevant. Therefore, the instantiation of an underspecified form is monotone increasing. All valid instances of an underspecified form are in a subsumption relation with that generic form.

Subsumption is defined as follows in the LCS. The LCS language is composed of conceptual domains (D), subdivided into conceptual types (T) such as event, state and thing and semantic fields (S) such as loc, temp or poss (see above). The LCS introduces a small number of primitives (P). A primitive is a partial function:

P: $D_1 \times D_2 \times .... D_n \rightarrow D_0$

where the D_i are element of D. D_0 is the type of the primitive P. We have, for example:

GO: thing $\times$ path $\rightarrow$ event,

TO: thing $\vee$ place $\rightarrow$ path,

GO_{+loc}: thing $\times$ (path $\wedge$ loc) $\rightarrow$ event.

Primitives are stable under semantic field restrictions and argument instantiations. An LCS form is a composition of primitives and fields, the latter corresponding to the arguments. Modifiers have the same form and are adjoined or anchored. The general syntax of an LCS expression is defined recursively as follows:

1. p $\in$ P, v $\in$ Var, $p_{+semanticfield}$ are wff LCS expressions,
2. $p(C_1, C_2, ..., C_n)$ is a wff LCS if p $\in$ P and the C_i are wff LCS,
3. $[_e C_1, C_2, ..., C_n]$ is a wff LCS if e is a conceptual type of T and the C_i are defined as above in 2.

An LCS expression, in particular when it is underspecified, can be viewed as a type. Let L and L' be two wff LCS expressions. We say that L subsumes L' iff the following two conditions are met:

Let L be of the form: $[_e\ C_1, C_2, ..., C_m\ ]$ and L': $[_{e'}\ C'_1, C'_2, ..., C'_n\ ]$, then:

1. $[_e\ C_1, C_2, ..., C_m\ ]$ subsumes $[_{e'}\ C'_1, C'_2, ..., C'_n\ ]$ iff:
   - e subsumes e' in the hierarchy associated with T [1],
   - $\forall\ i \in [1,m]$, $\exists\ j \in [1,n]$, such that C_i subsumes C'_j, n $\geq$ m $\geq$ 0 and at least one C'_j is not a variable,
   - [ ], the universal type, subsumes any structure.
2. $p(C_1, C_2, ..., C_n)$ subsumes $p'(C'_1, C'_2, ..., C'_n)$, iff:
   - p subsumes p' in the hierarchy associated with P or, if the two primitives are identical, the semantic field associated with p subsumes or is identical to the semantic field of p',
   - $\forall\ i \in [1,m]$, $\exists\ j \in [1,n]$, such that C_i subsumes C'_j, n $\geq$ m $\geq$ 0 and at least one C'_j is not a variable.

A type lattice of LCS forms can then be defined, with top being the universal LCS form [ ], and all fully instantiated LCS forms being linked to the bottom: the contradiction. Note that this type lattice may be very large, but it is *a priori* finite since the depth of LCS forms, in terms of embedded structures, is, in practice, relatively limited (i.e. a maximum of 5 to 6 levels is usually observed).

6.2   Instantiation Mechanisms

Instantiation of underspecified fields is realized in a classical way by means of λ-abstractions and reduction operations. This is characterized by the instantiation of variables, as exemplified above.

This instantiation is however not so straightforward for cases where:

1. the type of an argument is ambiguous (e.g. between a metaphorical use and a direct one) and its disambiguation requires knowledge from other constituents in the sentence or text. For example: *cut the film* may be the cutting of the object 'film' or the interruption of the event of showing (or even producing) a film. Only contextual elements may help disambiguate.
2. other elements in the sentence may contradict initial (i.e. preferred) choices. For example, a knife has the typical function of cutting in its telic role, but if we say:
   [[a good knife] [to carve]]
   then, it is necessary to postpone the determination of the function of the knife until all relevant information in the sentence is found (see many examples in [8]).
3. the variable occurs in different predicates in a sentence or a text.

---

[1] if any, since LCS types are very much coarse-grained, but more specific ones may be added to the language

From a computational perspective, we think that programming languages based on unification and the generate and test strategy (e.g. Prolog) may be too weak to handle the problem of sense variation in general. We indeed need languages which can handle sets (disjunctions) of potential solutions and can postpone computations (i.e. resolutions) instantiations until all constraints on the combination predicate + argument(s) have been identified. Constraint-based approaches precisely handle domains of potential assignments for variables; domains become restricted as soon as constraints are formulated on them, via dedicated constraint resolution mechanisms.

Constraint logic programming is one such paradigm where logical implication has been paired with other mechanisms (interpretation mechanisms for operations on particular domains) for handling various forms of constraints, in particular on finite domains. In that case, more or less complex algorithms have been developed and integrated into logic programs. These algorithms basically handle classical operations on sets (e.g. intersection), which is precisely what we need, be these sets atomic elements or LCS structures.

Let us now briefly explain the type of constraint resolution mechanism we have specified. Given a lexicon of word-senses, it is *a priori* possible to define for each predicate its generative expansion (the projection space defined in the GL). This generative expansion can be specified by a fixed-point semantics. From a constraint programming point of view, domains are wff LCS expressions (restricted to those defined above). Operations combine unification, subsumption and set operations. Other resources used are the ontologies and their taxonomies.

Independently of the strategy implementing the parsing procedure, when a compound 'predicate + argument' is found, if there are several assignments for a given variable in an underspecified field of the predicate, then all these assignments are kept, with their triggering context (e.g. constraints on the type of the head noun of the argument). When there is no more constraints to add, for each underspecified position, the constraint resolution mechanism proceeds as follows, for each variable with multiple assignments:

1. simplify conjunctions of constraints associated with that variable if appropriate (redundancies, overlap, etc),
2. if there is a single solution, assign it directly,
3. if there are several solutions, there are two situations:
    - either there is a unique greater lower bound (except the contradiction), then it is assigned,
    - or there is no such greater lower bound, then the least upper bound in the lattice of all the possible solutions is assigned. This is equivalent to the most general unifier in Logic Programs.
    - however, if that least upper bound is too general, a disjunction of assignments can be kept, reflecting the ambiguity of the statement.

7   Perspectives

The following points are currently under investigation. Although we have already been working extensively on the primitive system of the LCS, quite remains a lot to be done to attain a sufficiently comprehensive, abstract and expressive set of primitives. The goal is to represent in a way as natural as possible the semantics of the predicative forms of a language.

The above example has shown the difficulty of the identification and the ad'hoc character of the triggering semantic elements. We are currently investigating the nature, the formal status, and the representation of these elements in concrete NLP systems. We think that we can borrow several elements from several paradigms developed e.g. in WordNet [3] and EuroWordNet and other systems based on ontologies (e.g. Mikrokosmos).

Another major question is the identification of convergence points and the useful cross-fertilization between systems dealing with underspecification and the Generative Lexicon theory.

References

1. von Deemter, K. and Peters, S. (eds), (1996), *Semantic ambiguity and underspecification*, CSLI Lecture Notes, nb. 55.
2. Dubois, D., Mari, A., Saint-Dizier, P. (1997). Quelques principes psycholinguistiques et formels pour la mise en oeuvre de la générativité en sémantique lexicale. Genève AIDRI'97.
3. Fellbaum, C. (1997), A Semantic Network of English Verbs, in C. Fellbaum (ed) *Wordnet: An electronic Lexical Database*, Cambridge, MIT press.
4. Jackendoff, R., (1990), *Semantic Structures*, MIT Press.
5. Jackendoff, R., (1997), *The Architecture of the Language Faculty*, MIT Press.
6. Mari, A. (1997). Générativité en sémantique lexicale. Proposition d'un modèle utilisant la structure lexicale conceptuelle. Rapport de Recherche IRIT no. 97-23.
7. Mari, A., Saint-Dizier, P. (1997). Générativité: au delà d'une théorie des types. Grenoble, TALN'97.
8. Pernelle, N., (1998), *Traitement automatique des polysémies relationnelles: utilisation et contrôle des règles d'extension de sens*, PhD dissertation, LIPN, Paris13.
9. Pinkal, M. (1985). Logic and Lexicon. Oxford: Oxford University Press.
10. Pinkal, M. (1983). Towards a Semantics of Precization. In T. T. Ballmer et M. Pinkal (eds.), Approaching Vagueness. Amsterdam : Elsevier Science Publisher.
11. Poesio, M. (1996). Semantic Ambiguity and Perceived Ambiguity. In K. van Deemter, S. Peters, (eds.), Semantic Ambiguity and Underspecification. Stanford: CSLI Lecture Notes.
12. Pustejovsky, J., (1995), The Generative Lexicon, MIT Press.

HYPERTAGS: Beyond POS Tagging

Alexandra Kinyon

TALANA
Université Paris 7, UFRL case 7003
2 pl Jussieu, 75251 Paris Cedex 05
Alexandra.Kinyon@linguist.jussieu.fr

Abstract. Traditional part of speech tagging assigns very limited information to lexical items, thus providing only limited help for parsing. To solve this problem, [14] extends the notion of POS by introducing Supertags, within the framework of Lexicalized Tree Adjoining Grammars (LTAGs). Unfortunately, words are assigned on average a much higher number of Supertags than traditional POS. In this paper, we introduce the notion of Hypertag, which allows to factor the information contained in several Supertags, so that a single structure can be assigned to each word. We also discuss why this approach is useful within frameworks other than LTAGs

1   Introduction

Traditional part of speech tagging assigns very limited information (i.e. morphological and local) to lexical items, thus providing limited help for parsing. [14] proposes to extend the notion of POS by introducing Supertags, within the framework of Lexicalized Tree Adjoining Grammars (LTAGs). The idea behind Supertags is to assign to each word in a sentence an "elementary tree" (i.e. a primitive syntactic structure within LTAGs) [11].

Unfortunately, words are assigned a much higher number of Supertags than traditional POS, even when no lexical ambiguity occurs : on average for English a word has 9 supertags, but only 1.5 POS [10]. This high number of supertags / word is especially problematic for words which can be verbs: [4] find that French verbs anchor on average 71 supertags. One solution is to retain only the "best" supertag, or eventually the 3 best supertags, for each word. This affects the quality of parsing if the wrong supertag(s) have been kept : one typically obtains between 75% and 91% accuracy when keeping only one supertag / item, depending on the kind of text being supertagged [7]. So, at worst, every word in 4 will be assigned a wrong supertag, which will inevitably degrade the quality of parsing. (whereas typical POS taggers achieve an accuracy above 95%.).

In this paper, we present the notion of hypertags. A hypertag contains the same information as a set of supertags and thus allows to associate one unique structure to each word.

First, we briefly introduce the LTAG framework, including examples of supertags. Then we briefly recapitulate what has been attempted in the past to underspecify supertags. Finally, we present hypertags, building up on the notion of MetaGrammar

D.N. Christodoulakis (Ed.): NLP 2000, LNCS 1835, pp. 81-90, 2000.
© Springer-Verlag Berlin Heidelberg 2000

introduced by [5] and [6] and discuss how this can be used in practice, and why it is interesting for formalisms other than LTAGs.

2   Brief Overview of LTAGs

A LTAG consists of a finite set of **elementary trees** of finite depth. Each elementary tree must "anchor" one or more lexical item(s). The principal anchor is called "head", other anchors are called "co-heads". All leaves in elementary trees are either "anchor", "foot node" (noted *) or "substitution node" (noted). These trees are of 2 types : **auxiliary** or **initial**[1]. A tree has at most 1 foot-node, such a tree is an auxiliary tree. Trees that are not auxiliary are initial. Elementary trees combine with 2 operations : **substitution** and **adjunction**, but we won't develop this point since it is orthogonal to our concern and refer to [9] for more details. Morphosyntactic features are encoded in atomic feature structures associated to nodes in elementary trees, in order to handle phenomena such as agreement.

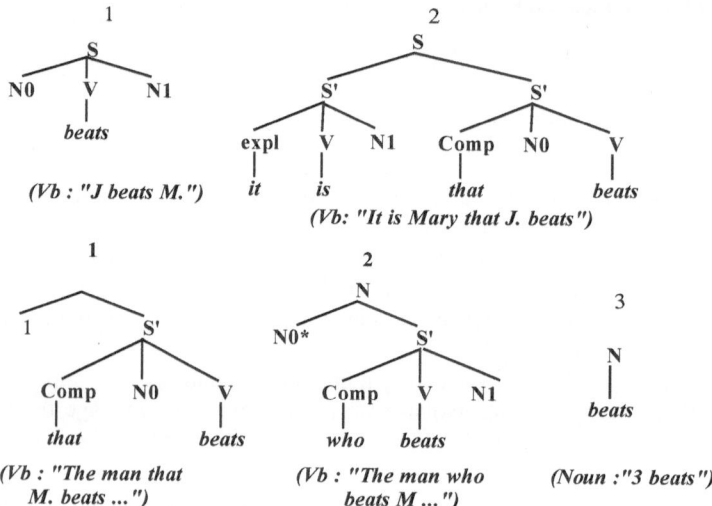

Fig. 1. Examples of Supertags for "beats"

Supertagging consists in assigning to lexical items one or more elementary trees. Therefore, in addition of providing traditional POS information, supertags allow to encode the syntactic behavior of a given word such as subcategorization information, order of realization of arguments, possible syntactic operations (e.g. passivization, relativization ...).

---

[1] Traditionnaly, initial trees are called , and auxiliary trees .

Figure 1 shows a non exhaustive set of Supertags which can be assigned to "beats"[2], which is a verb in trees   1,   2,   1 and   3 and a noun in tree   3.

3   Underspecifying Supertags

The idea of underspecifying constituent trees (and thus elementary trees) is not new. Several solutions have been proposed in the past. We will now recapitulate how these solutions could potentially be used to encode a set of supertags in a compact manner, and show why these solutions are unsatisfactory, essentially because they only rely on "mathematical" properties of supertags (i.e. tree structures) without taking into account linguistic aspects (see[13] for more details)

3.1   Parse Forest

Since elementary trees are constituent structures, one could represent a set of elementary trees with a graph instead of a tree [16]. This approach is not particularly interesting though. For example, if one considers the trees   1 and   1 from figure 1, it is obvious that they hardly have any structural information in common, not even the category of their root. Therefore, representing these 2 structures in a graph would not help. Moreover, packed structures are notoriously difficult to manipulate and yield an unreadable output.

3.2   Logical Formulae

With this approach, developed for instance in [12] a tree can be represented by a logical formula, where each pair of nodes is either in relation of dominance, or in relation of precedence. This allows to resort to 1st order logic to represent a set of trees by underspecifying dominance and/or precedance relations . Unfortunately, this yields an unreadable output. Also, it relies only on mathematical properties of trees (i.e. no linguistic motivations)

3.3   Linear Types of Trees

This approach, introduced in [14], used in other work (for example in [8]) is more specific to TAGs. The idea is to relax constraints on the order of nodes in a tree as well as on internal nodes. A linear type consists in a 7-tuple <A,B,C,D,E,F,G> where A is the root of the tree, B is the category of the anchor, C is the lexical anchor, D is a set of nodes which can receive an adjunction, E is a set of co-anchors, F a set of nodes marked for substitution, and G a potential foot node (or nil in case the tree is initial). In addition, elements of E and F are marked + if they are to the left of the anchor, - if they are to the right.

---

[2] For sake of readability, morpohological features are not shown.

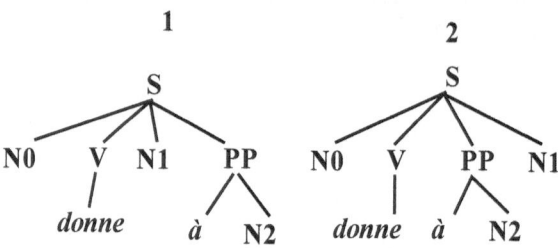

Fig. 2. Two trees with the same linear type

For example, the tree *N0donneN1àN2* for "Jean donne une pomme à Marie" (John gives an apple to Mary) and the tree *N0donneàN2N1* for "J donne à Marie une pomme" (Jean gives Mary an apple) which are shown on Figure 2, yield the unique linear type (a)

(a) <S,V,donne,{S,V,PP}, {à+}, {N0-,N1+,N2+} ,nil>

This approach is robust, but not really linguistic : it will allow to refer to trees that are not initially in the grammar.

(b) <S,V,gives,{S,V,PP}, {to+}, {N0-,N1+,N2+} ,nil>

(c) <S,V,gives,{S,V}, {}, {N0-,N1+,N2+} ,nil>

For instance, the linear type (b) will correctly allow the sentence "John gives an apple to Mary", but also incorrectly allow "*John gives to Mary an apple". Moreover, linear types are not easily readable[3]. Finally, trees that have more structural differences than just the ordering of branches will yield different linear types. So, the tree *N0giveN1toN2* (J. gives an apple to M.) yields the linear type (b), whereas the tree *N0giveN2N1* (J. gives M. an apple) yields a different linear type (c), and thus both linear types should label "gives". Therefore, it is impossible to label "gives" with one unique linear type.

4   Exploiting a MetaGrammar

[5] & [6] has developed a tool to generate semi-automatically elementary trees She use an additional layer of linguistic description, called the metagrammar (MG), which imposes a general organization for syntactic information in a 3 dimensional hierarchy:

- **Dimension 1:** initial subcategorization
- **Dimension 2:** redistribution of functions and transitivity alternations
- **Dimension 3:** surface realization of arguments, clause type and word order

Each terminal class in dimension 1 describes a possible initial subcategorization (i.e. tree family in the TAG terminology). Each terminal class in dimension 2 describes a list of ordered redistributions of functions (e.g. it allows to add an

---

[3] This type of format was considered as a step towards creating a treebank for French (cf [2]), but unfortunately proved impossible to annotate manually.

argument for causatives). Finally, each terminal class in dimension 3 represents the surface realization of a (final) function (e.g. cliticized, extracted ...).

Each class in the hierarchy corresponds to the partial description of a tree [15]. An elementary tree is generated by inheriting from one terminal class in dimension 1, from one terminal class in dimension 2 and from n terminal classes in dimension 3 (were n is the number of arguments of the elementary tree). The hierarchy is partially handwritten. Then crossing of linguistic phenomena (e.g. passive + extraction), terminal classes and from there elementary trees are generated automatically off line. This allows to obtain a wide-coverage grammar which can be used to parse online [1]. Currently, the wide-coverage grammar for French contains approximately 5000 elementary trees [3]. When the grammar is generated, it is straight forward to keep track of the terminal classes each elementary tree inherited from : Figure 3 shows seven elementary trees which can supertag "donne" (gives), as well as the inheritance patterns[4] associated to each of these supertags. All the examples below will refer to this figure.

The key idea then is to represent a set of elementary trees by a disjunction for each dimension of the hierarchy. Therefore, a hypertag consists in 3 disjunctions (one for dimension 1, one for dimension 2 and one for dimension 3). The crossing of the disjunctions can then be done automatically and from there, the set of elementary trees referred to by the hypertag will be automatically retrieved We will now illustrate this, first by showing how hypertags are built, and then by explaining how a set of trees (and thus of supertags) is retrieved from the information contained in a hypertag.

4.1   Building Hypertags: A Detailed Example

Suppose we want "donner" to be assigned the supertags   1 (*J. donne une pomme à M.*) and   2 (*J donne à M. une pomme*). On figure 3, one notices that these 2 trees inherited exactly from the same classes : the relative order of the two complements is left unspecified in the hierarchy, thus one same description will yield both trees. In this case, the hypertag will thus simply be identical to the inheritance pattern of these 2 trees :

Let's now add tree   3 (*J. donne des soucis / J. gives concerns*) to this hypertag. This tree had its second object declared empty in dimension 2 (thus it inherits only two terminal classes from dimension 3, since it has only 2 arguments realized). The hypertag now becomes[5] :

---

[4] We call inheritance patterns the structure used to store all the terminal classes a tree has inherited from.

[5] What has been added to a supertag is shown in bold characters.

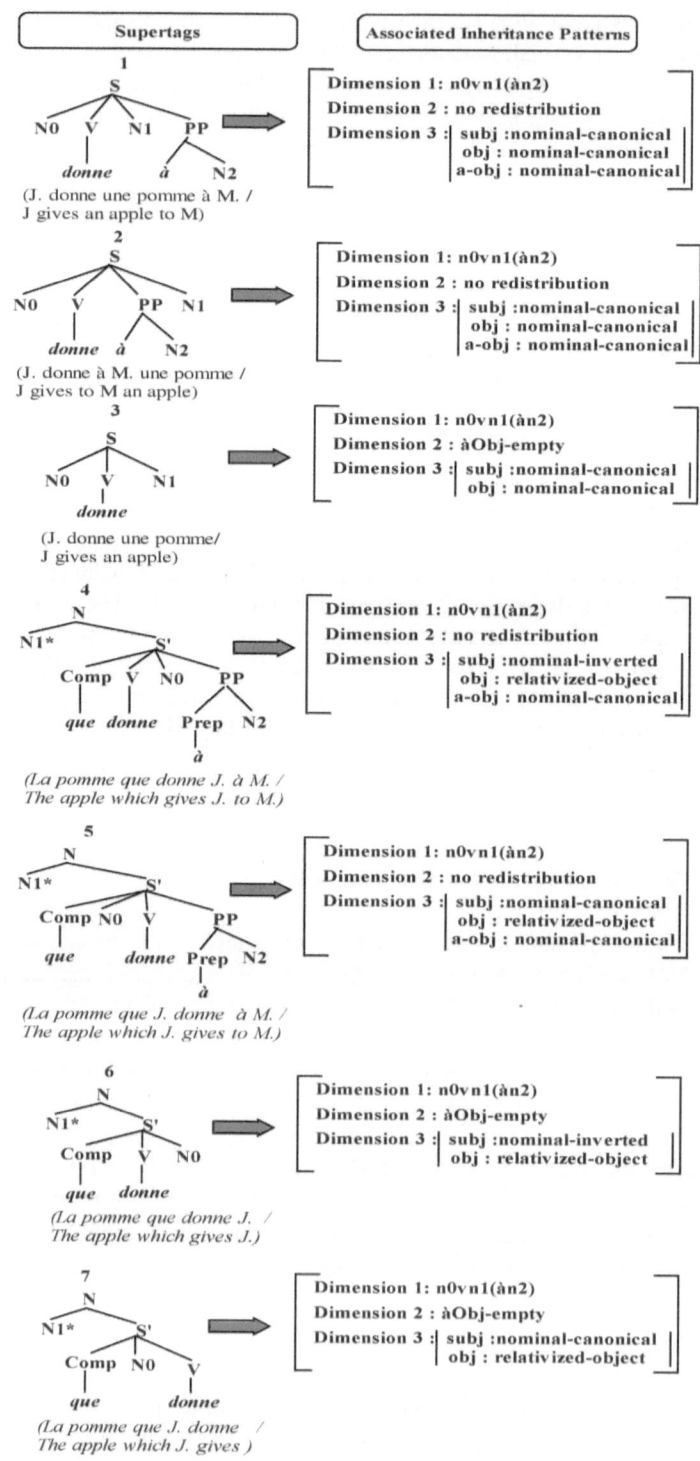

Fig. 3. SuperTags and Corresponding inheritance patterns

Let's now add the tree 4 for the object relative to this hypertag. This tree has been generated by inheriting in dimension 3 from the terminal class "nominal inverted" for its subject and from the class "relativized object" for its object. This information is simply added in the hypertag, which now becomes :

Also note that for this last example the structural properties of 4 were quite different than those of 1, 2 and 3 (for instance, it has a root of category N and not S). But this has little importance since a generalization is made in linguistic terms without explicitly relying on the shape of trees.

$$
\begin{bmatrix}
\text{Dimension 1: n0vn1(àn2)} \\
\text{Dimension 2 : no redistribution} \\
\text{Dimension 3} \begin{vmatrix} \text{subj :nominal-canonical} \\ \text{obj : nominal-canonical} \\ \text{a-obj: nominal-canonical} \end{vmatrix}
\end{bmatrix}
$$

It is also clear that hypertags are built in a simple, monotonic fashion : each supertag added to a hypertag just adds information. Also, hypertags allow to label each word with a unique structure[6], contain rich syntactic information about lexical items (For our example, the word "donner"), are linguistically motivated, and yield a readable output.

$$
\begin{bmatrix}
\text{Dim. 1: n0vn1(àn2)} \\
\text{Dim. 2 : no redistribution \textbf{OR àObj- empty}} \\
\text{Dim. 3} \begin{vmatrix} \text{subj :nominal-canonical} \\ \text{obj : nominal-canonical} \\ \text{a-obj: nominal-canonical} \end{vmatrix}
\end{bmatrix}
$$

4.2   Retrieving Information from Hypertags

Retrieving information from hypertags is straightforward. For example, recovering the set of supertags contained in a hypertag is done by crossing between the 3 dimensions of the hypertag, as shown on figure 4, in order to

$$
\begin{bmatrix}
\text{Dim. : n0vn1(àn2)} \\
\text{Dim. 2 : no redistribution OR àObj- empty} \\
\text{Dim. 3} \begin{vmatrix} \text{subj :nominal-canonical \textbf{OR nominal-inverted}} \\ \text{obj : nominal-canonical \textbf{OR relativized-object}} \\ \text{a-obj: nominal-canonical} \end{vmatrix}
\end{bmatrix}
$$

obtain all inheritance patterns. These inheritance patterns are then matched with the inheritence patterns in the grammar (i.e. the right column in Figure 3)

---

[6] We presented a simple example for sake of clarity, but traditional POS ambiguity is handled in the same way, except that disjuncts are then added in dimension 1 as well.

to recover all the appropriate supertags. Also, since the same MG is used both to generate the grammar (i.e. trees + corresponding inheritance patterns) and to expand hypertags, it is therefore impossible for a hypertag to refer to a tree which is not actually in the grammar i.e. no unintended trees are generated : Inheritance patterns which are generated but don't match any existing trees in the grammar are simply discarded.

We observe that the 4 supertags 1, 2 and 3 and 4 which we had explicitly added to the hypertag in 4.1 are correctly retrieved. But also, the supertags 5, 6 and 7 are retrieved, which we did not explicitly intend since we never added them to the hypertag. But this is not a problem, since if a word can anchor the 4 first trees, then it will also necessarily anchor the three last ones. In fact, the automatic crossing of disjunctions in the hypertag insures consistency.

Also note that no particular mechanism is needed for dimension 3 to handle arguments which are not realized : if àObj-empty is inherited from dimension 2, then only subject and object will inherit from dimension three (since only arguments that are realized inherit from that dimension when the grammar is generated).

Information can also be modified at runtime in a hypertag, depending on the context of lexical items. For example "relativized" can be supressed in dimension 2 from the hypertag shown on Figure 4, in case no Wh element is encountered in a sentence. Then, the   correct set of supertags will still be retrieved from the hypertag by automatic crossing (that is, trees 1, 2 and 3), since the other inheritance patterns generated won't refer to any tree in the grammar (here, no tree inherits in dimension 3 "subject:inverted-nominal", without inheriting also "object: relativized-object") .

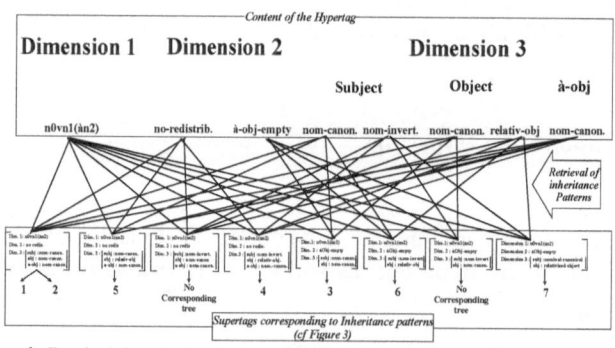

Fig. 4. Retireving Inheritance Patterns and SuperTags from a Hypertag

4.3   Practical Use

An LTAG can be seen as a dictionary, in which each lexical entry is associated to a set of elementary trees. But with hypertags, each lexical entry is now paired with one unique structure. Therefore, automatically hypertagging a text is easy (i.e. simple dictionary lookup). The equivalent of finding the "right" supertag for each lexical item in a text (i.e. reducing ambiguity) then consists in dynamically removing information from hypertags (i.e. suppressing elements in disjunctions). This can be achieved by specific rules, which we do not develop here because of space constraints. It is important to note though that the resulting output can easily be manually annotated in order to build a gold-standard corpus : manually removing linguistically relevant pieces of information in a disjunction from a single structure is simpler than dealing with a set of trees. In addition of obvious advantages in terms of display (tree structures are often unreadable), the task becomes easier because topological problems are solved automatically: annotators need just answer questions such as "*does this verb have an extracted object ?*", "*is the subject of this verb inverted ?*" to decide which terminal classe(s) must be kept[7] .We believe that these questions are easier to answer than "*Which of these trees have a node N1 marked wh+ at address 1.1 ?*" (for an extracted object) [2].

Moreover, supertagged texts are difficult to use outside of an LTAG framework, contrary to hypertagged texts, which contain general linguistic information. An example would be searching and extracting syntactic data on a large scale : suppose one wants to extract all the occurrences where a given verb V has a relativized object. To do so on a hypertagged text simply involves performing a "grep" on all lines containing a V whose hypertag contains "*dimension 3 : objet:relativized*", without knowing anything about the LTAG framework. Performing the same task with a supertagged text involves knowing how LTAGs encode relativized objects in elementary trees, scanning potential trees associated with V ... Another example would be using a hypertagged text as an input to a parser based on a framework other than LTAGs : for instance, information in hypertags could be used by an LFG parser to constrain the construction of an F-structure, whereas it's unclear how this could be achieved with supertags.

5   Conclusion

We have introduced the notion of hypertag. Hypertags allow to assign one unique structure to lexical items. Moreover this structure is readable, linguistically and computationally motivated, and contains much richer syntactic information than traditional POS, thus a hypertagger would be a good candidate as the front end of a parser. It allows in practice to build large annotated resources which are useful for extracting syntactic information on a large scale, without being dependant on a given grammatical formalism.

We have shown how hypertags are built, how information can be retrieved from them. Further work will investigate how hypertags combine directly.

---

[7] This of course implies that one must be very careful in choosing evocative names for terminal classes.

References

1. Abeillé A, Candito M.H., Kinyon A. 1999. FTAG: current status and parsing scheme. Vextal '99. Venice.
2. Abeillé A., Clément L., Kinyon A. 2000. Building a treebank for French. Proc. LREC'2000. Athens.
3. Abeillé A, Candito M.H., Kinyon A. 1999. Current status of FTAG. Proc. TAG+5. Paris
4. Barrier N, Barrier S., Kinyon A. 2000. Lexik: A maintenance tool for FTAG. Proc. TAG+5. Paris.
5. Candito M-H. 1996. A principle-based hierarchical representation of LTAGs, COLING'96 Kopenhagen.
6. Candito M.-H, 1998. Représentation modulaire et paramétrable de grammaires électroniques lexicalisées. Application au français et à l'italien. PhD dissertation. University Paris 7.
7. Chen J., Srinivas B., Vijay-Shanker K .1999: New models for Improving Supertags disambiguation. Proc. EACL'99. Pp. 188-195. Bergen
8. Halber A. 1999. Stratégie d'analyse pour la compréhension de la parole : vers une approche à base de Grammaires d'Arbres Adjoints Lexicalisées. PhD thesis. ENST. Paris
9. Joshi A.: 1987. *An introduction to Tree Adjoining Grammars.* In Mathematics of Language. A. Manaster-Ramer (eds). John Benjamins. pp. 87-114.
10. Joshi A. 1999. Explorations of a domain of locality. CLIN'99. Utrecht.
11. Joshi A. Srinivas B. 1994. Disambiguation of Super Parts of Speech (or Supertags) : Almost parsing. COLING'94. Kyoto.
12. Kallmeyer L, 1999, Tree Description Grammars and Underspecified Representations. PhD thesis, Universität Tübingen.
13. Kinyon A. 2000. Even better than Supertags Introducing Hypertags ! Proc. TAG+5. Paris.
14. Srinivas B., 1997. Complexity of lexical descriptions and its relevance for partial parsing, PhD thesis, Univ. of Pennsylvania.
15. Rogers J., Vijay-Shanker K. 1994. Obtaining trees from their descriptions: An application to TAGs. Computational Intelligence, 10:4 pp 401-421.
16. Tomita M.: 1991. *Generalized LR Parsing.* Masaru Tomita (eds). Kluwer academic publishers. Boston.

A Theory of Stochastic Grammars

Christer Samuelsson

Xerox Research Centre Europe
6, chemin de Maupertuis, 38240 Meylan, France
Christer.Samuelsson@xrce.xerox.com
http://www.xrce.xerox.com/people/samuelsson/samuelsson.html

Abstract. A novel theoretical framework for describing stochastic grammars is proposed based on a small set of basic random variables that generate tree structures and relate them to surface strings. A number of prominent statistical language models are formulated as stochastic processes over these basic random variables.

1 Introduction

The availability of large corpora and treebanks has sparked renewed interest in parsing using stochastic grammars, e.g., [1,2,3], etc. Many of these seemingly divergent approaches are in fact quite similar and we here try to provide a unified view of them by proposing a novel theoretical framework for describing and analyzing a wide class of stochastic grammars.

Since tree structures are central objects in most contemporary models of natural-language syntax, our strategy will be to define a small set of basic random variables that generate tree structures and formulate stochastic grammars as stochastic processes over these basic random variables.

The bulk part of the article consists of case studies, where the method is applied to a number of prominent statistical language models, namely stochastic context-free grammars (SCFGs), stochastic tree-substitution grammars, stochastic versions of projective and non-projective dependency grammar, Alshawi's head automata, and Collins' ACL'97 scheme. The progression will be from simpler to more complex models; key ideas will be introduced in each case and reused in subsequent ones. In particular, the important relationship between tree structure and surface string will evolve throughout the case studies. We briefly discusses extensions to richer probabilistic models and more general graphs, and the tightness of the studied grammars.

Traditional approaches to stochastic grammars typically view each parse tree as generated by a sequence $x_1, \ldots, x_N$ of derivation steps, e.g., string rewrites or parser actions. A random variable $\mathcal{X}_j$ is associated with the jth derivation step, and the probability of the generated tree $\mathcal{T}$ is defined as the probability of the outcome of a stochastic process:

$$P(\mathcal{T}) = P(\mathcal{X}_1 = x_1, \ldots, \mathcal{X}_N = x_N) = \tag{1}$$
$$= P(\mathcal{X}_N = x_N \mid \mathcal{X}_1 = x_1, \ldots, \mathcal{X}_{N-1} = x_{N-1}) \cdot P(\mathcal{X}_1 = x_1, \ldots, \mathcal{X}_{N-1} = x_{N-1})$$

D.N. Christodoulakis (Ed.): NLP 2000, LNCS 1835, pp. 92–105, 2000.
© Springer-Verlag Berlin Heidelberg 2000

$$= \prod_{j=1}^{N} P(\mathcal{X}_j = x_j \mid \mathcal{X}_1 = x_1, \ldots, \mathcal{X}_{j-1} = x_{j-1})$$

Since one cannot accurately estimate the probabilities

$$P(\mathcal{X}_j = x_j \mid \mathcal{X}_1 = x_1, \ldots, \mathcal{X}_{j-1} = x_{j-1})$$

for each possible derivation history $x_1, \ldots, x_{j-1}$ from frequency counts, one resorts to defining equivalence classes $g(x_1, \ldots, x_{j-1})$ over the derivation histories

$$P(\mathcal{X}_j = x_j \mid \mathcal{X}_1 = x_1, \ldots, \mathcal{X}_{j-1} = x_{j-1}) = \qquad (2)$$
$$= P(\mathcal{X}_j = x_j \mid g(\mathcal{X}_1 = x_1, \ldots, \mathcal{X}_{j-1} = x_{j-1}))$$

through the use of an extraction function g. For a stochastic context-free grammar, the extraction function would construct a sentential form from the string rewrites $x_1, \ldots, x_{j-1}$ and extract its leftmost nonterminal symbol. For an LR parser, it might extract the state on top of the stack after parser actions $x_1, \ldots, x_{j-1}$.

This approach, however, actually defines probability distributions over derivations, which can only be interpreted as probability distributions over parse trees if there is a one-to-one correspondence between derivations and parse trees. This is the case for, e.g., stochastic context-free grammars [4], probabilistic LR parsing [5], and some instantiations of IBM-style history-based parsing [6,1], but not for, e.g., stochastic tree-substitution grammars, such as the data-oriented parsing model [7], or stochastic lexicalized tree-adjoining grammars [8]. For the latter grammar types, the parse probability is typically defined as the sum of the derivation probabilities over all derivations that yield that parse tree. Unfortunately, this makes finding the most probable parse of a given input string NP-complete [9].

2   Notation, Random Variables, and Theoretical Issues

To describe a tree structure $\mathcal{T}$, we will use a string notation, introduced in [10], for the nodes $\mathcal{N}$ of the tree, where the node name specifies the path from the root node ϵ to the node in question.

> **If** ϕj is a node of the tree $\mathcal{T}$, with $j \in N_+$ and $\phi \in N_+^*$,
> **then** ϕ is also a node of the tree $\mathcal{T}$ **and** ϕj is a child of ϕ.
> **If** $\phi i, \phi j : i < j$ are both nodes of $\mathcal{T}$, **then** ϕi and ϕj are distinct
> **and if** $\mathcal{T}$ is an ordered tree, **then** ϕi precedes ϕj.

N_+ denotes the set of positive integers and N_+^* the set of strings over N_+. Figure 1 shows a parse tree for the sentence *John ate beans* using this notation.

We introduce three basic random variables that generate the tree structure:

- $\mathcal{L}(\phi) = l$ assigns the label l to node ϕ.
- $\mathcal{V}(\phi) = v$ indicates that node ϕ has exactly v child nodes.
- $\mathcal{D}(\phi j) = d$, used for dependency grammars, indicates the dependency type d linking the label of node ϕj to its regent, the label of node ϕ.

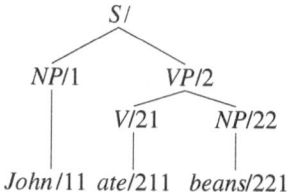

Fig. 1. Phrase-structure tree for *John ate beans*.

Note the use of $\mathcal{V}(\phi) = 0$, rather than a partitioning of the labels into terminal and nonterminal symbols, to indicate that ϕ is a leaf node. Figure 2 encodes the parse tree of Figure 1 using this notation. Ignore the last two columns for now.

$\mathcal{N}$	$\mathcal{L}$	$\mathcal{V}$	$\mathcal{R}$	$\mathcal{S}$
ϵ	S	2	$S \rightarrow NP\ VP$	$s(1)\ s(2) = John\ ate\ beans$
1	NP	1	$NP \rightarrow John$	$s(11) = John$
11	$John$	0	$John$	$John$
2	VP	2	$VP \rightarrow V\ NP$	$s(21)\ s(22) = ate\ beans$
21	V	1	$V \rightarrow ate$	$s(211) = ate$
211	ate	0	ate	ate
22	NP	1	$NP \rightarrow beans$	$s(221) = beans$
221	$beans$	0	$beans$	$beans$

Fig. 2. Phrase-structure encoding of *John ate beans*.

We will use a fourth fundamental variable $\mathcal{S}(\phi)$ denoting the string associated with node ϕ, not to be confused with the node label $\mathcal{L}(\phi)$. For phrase-structure grammars, this string is simply the yield of the node, whereas for other grammars, the string may not be uniquely determined by the tree structure. We will use a fifth fundamental variable $\mathcal{M}(\phi)$ to handle long-distance dependencies.

We must ensure that that the random variables generate a tree structure where all necessary information is present. Gorn's notation enforces most of this; we only need to ensure that the outcomes of the $\mathcal{L}$ and $\mathcal{V}$ variables, and for dependency grammars, also the $\mathcal{D}$ variables, are specified for each node, together with the outcome of any extra random variables motivated by the stochastic model. A simple way of doing this is to first define local completeness at a node ϕ and then require each node to be locally complete:

A coherent set of random-variable outcomes is *locally complete at node* ϕ iff $\mathcal{V}(\phi) = v$ is specified, as are the outcomes of $\mathcal{L}(\phi), \mathcal{L}(\phi 1), \ldots, \mathcal{L}(\phi v)$ — and for dependency grammars, also $\mathcal{D}(\phi 1), \ldots, \mathcal{D}(\phi v)$ — and any extra random variables at nodes $\phi, \phi 1, \ldots, \phi v$ from the stochastic model.

We want is a specification rooted in ϵ that is locally complete at each node:

A coherent set of random-variable outcomes over a set of nodes $\mathcal{N}$ containing the node ϵ, which is locally complete at each node, specifies a proper tree structure with all the necessary information.

We must also ensure that the stochastic model allows breaking down the tree probability into a product of conditional probabilities as is done in Eq. (1). To this end we require that there exist some ordering of the random-variable outcomes where the probability of the material conditioned on is already known. This is to avoid a Catch-22 situation where, say, $P(A \mid B)$ and $P(B \mid A)$ are given, but not $P(A)$ or $P(B)$, when trying to calculate $P(A, B)$.

We will use an extraction function as in Eq. (2) which must be transparent in the sense that it captures all relevant conditioning material, and, in particular, does not obscure redundant or incoherent specifications.

The extraction function is *transparent* iff it is logically possible that the probability distributions with and without it are identical.

For example, $\mathcal{L}(\phi 1) = V$ (trivially) implies $\mathcal{L}(\phi 1) = V$ and contradicts $\mathcal{V}(\phi) = 0$. The extraction function is not transparent if it fails to condition on $\mathcal{L}(\phi 1) = V$, despite this being in the conditioning material, when calculating the probability of (events including) $\mathcal{L}(\phi 1) = V$ or $\mathcal{V}(\phi) = 0$. This was the problem with the generative probabilistic LR-parsing model of [5]; here the lookahead symbols were multiply specified (after each reduction), but conditioning on this fact was masked by the implicit extraction function.

3   Case Studies

3.1   Stochastic Context-Free Grammars

Stochastic context-free grammars extend context-free grammars $\langle V_N, V_T, S, P \rangle$ with one set of probabilities over the productions P for each (nonterminal) symbol in V_N, indicating the probability of the production given its left-hand-side symbol. We let $\mathcal{L}$ range over the grammar symbols $V = V_N \cup V_T$, and introduce composite variables $\mathcal{R}$ ranging over $P \cup V_T$:

$$\mathcal{R}(\phi) = l \to l_1 \ldots l_v \in P \Leftrightarrow \begin{cases} \mathcal{L}(\phi) = l \in V_N \\ \mathcal{V}(\phi) = v \\ \forall_{j \in \{1, \ldots, v\}} \mathcal{L}(\phi j) = l_j \end{cases}$$

$$\mathcal{R}(\phi) = l \in V_T \Leftrightarrow \begin{cases} \mathcal{L}(\phi) = l \in V_T \\ \mathcal{V}(\phi) = 0 \end{cases}$$

The outcomes of the string variables $\mathcal{S}$ are determined by the outcomes of the production variables $\mathcal{R}$ and the string variables of the child nodes

$$\mathcal{S}(\phi) = \begin{cases} s(\phi 1) \ldots s(\phi v) & \text{if } \mathcal{R}(\phi) = l \to l_1 \ldots l_v \in P \\ l & \text{if } \mathcal{R}(\phi) = l \in V_T \end{cases}$$

where $s(\phi j)$ is the outcome of $\mathcal{S}(\phi j)$. This equation specifies the unique outcomes of the $\mathcal{S}$ variables; in a probabilistic interpretation of the $\mathcal{S}$ variables we write

$$P(\mathcal{S}(\phi) = s(\phi 1) \ldots s(\phi v) \mid \mathcal{R}(\phi) = l \to l_1 \ldots l_v \in P) = 1$$
$$P(\mathcal{S}(\phi) = l \mid \mathcal{R}(\phi) = l \in V_T) = 1$$

We introduce the probability

$$P_{\mathcal{R}}(\phi) = P(\mathcal{R}(\phi) = r \mid \mathcal{L}(\phi) = l)$$

If $r \in P$, this is one of the production probabilities of the SCFG; it equals one when $r \in V_T$, since nodes with children cannot be labeled by terminal symbols. We define the joint probability of the tree $\mathcal{T}$ and the node strings $\mathcal{S}$

$$P(\mathcal{T}, \mathcal{S}) = P(\mathcal{T}) = P(\mathcal{L}(\epsilon) = S) \cdot \prod_{\phi \in \mathcal{N}} P_{\mathcal{R}}(\phi)$$

We define a stochastic process that generates the tree-structure variables $\mathcal{R}$ top-down. Then, the probability of the conditioning material of $P_{\mathcal{R}}(\phi j)$, i.e, $\mathcal{L}(\phi j)$, is known from $P_{\mathcal{R}}(\phi)$, and that of $P_{\mathcal{R}}(\epsilon)$ known from $P(\mathcal{L}(\epsilon) = S) = 1$, the latter since ϵ is the root node and S is the top symbol. We then deterministically generate the string variables $\mathcal{S}$ bottom-up, as $\mathcal{S}(\phi)$ is determined by $\mathcal{R}(\phi)$ and $\mathcal{S}(\phi j)$. The use of the $\mathcal{R}$ variables guarantees the internal coherence and local completeness at each node. Generating $\mathcal{R}$ for all nodes ensures global completeness. The only multiple specifications are $\mathcal{L}(\phi j)$ in $\mathcal{R}(\phi j) = r'$ following $\mathcal{R}(\phi) = r$, but here, $\mathcal{L}(\phi j)$ is explicitly conditioned on, which ensures transparency and global coherence.

Figure 2 also shows the $\mathcal{R}$ and $\mathcal{S}$ processes for the tree of Figure 1. The third column should be read downwards: $\mathcal{L}(\epsilon) = S$, $\mathcal{R}(\epsilon) = S \to NP\ VP$, $\mathcal{R}(1) = NP \to John$, etc.; the fourth one upwards: $\mathcal{S}(221) = beans$, $\mathcal{S}(22) = s(221)$, etc.

A stochastic tree-substitution grammar is very similar to an SCFG. Instead of a set of productions and probability distributions over them conditioned on the LHS symbol, we have a set of elementary trees and probability distributions over them conditioned on the root label; instead of expanding a node in the partial tree using a production, we expand it using an elementary tree. If we alter the scheme used for SCFGs to instead let $\mathcal{R}(\phi)$ generate an elementary tree rooted in ϕ, and instead sum $P_{\mathcal{R}}$ only over the root node ϵ and the leaf nodes of all elementary trees, we arrive at a formalization of stochastic tree-substitution grammars, e.g., Bod's instantiation [7] of the data-oriented parsing (DOP) framework. The resulting stochastic processes assign probabilities to derivations, not parse trees, cp. the discussion at the end of Section 1.

3.2 Projective Dependency Grammars

A dependency description segments the input string into nuclei and establishes a tree structure where each node is labeled by a nucleus. A nucleus can be a word, a part of a word, or a sequence of words and subwords, and these need not appear contiguously in the input string. Figure 3 shows a dependency tree for the sentence *John ate beans*. In classical dependency grammar [11], only the dependency structure, not the order of the dependents, is represented by a dependency tree; its surface-string realization is handled separately. This means that variants in local precedence are equivalent, and we factor out $\mathcal{P}$ by generating the child nodes either all at once, or in some otherwise specified order.

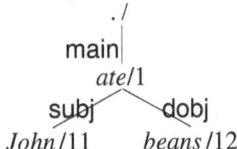

Fig. 3. Dependency tree for *John ate beans*.

We let $\mathcal{L}$ range over nuclei in Σ^*, where Σ is the vocabulary, and introduce the composite variables $\mathcal{F}(\phi)$ ranging over the power bag[1] N^D, where D is a finite set of dependency types, indicating the bag of dependency types of ϕ's children:

$$\mathcal{F}(\phi) = f = [d_1, \ldots, d_v] \Leftrightarrow \mathcal{V}(\phi) = v \ \wedge \ \forall_{j \in \{1,\ldots,v\}} \ \mathcal{D}(\phi j) = d_j$$

Figure 4 encodes the dependency tree of Figure 3 accordingly.

$\mathcal{N}$	$\mathcal{L}$	$\mathcal{F}$	$\mathcal{S}$
ϵ	.	[main]	$s(1)$.
1	*ate*	[subj,dobj]	$s(11)$ *ate* $s(12)$
11	*John*	$\emptyset$	*John*
12	*beans*	$\emptyset$	*beans*

Fig. 4. Dependency encoding of *John ate beans*.

We introduce the probabilities

$$P_{\mathcal{L}}(\epsilon) = P(\mathcal{L}(\epsilon) = l)$$
$$P_{\mathcal{L}}(\phi j) = P(\mathcal{L}(\phi j) = l_j \mid \mathcal{L}(\phi) = l, \mathcal{D}(\phi j) = d_j)$$

---

[1] A bag (multiset) can contain several tokens of the same type. We denote sets $\{\ldots\}$, bags $[\ldots]$ and ordered tuples $\langle\ldots\rangle$, but overload $\cup, \subseteq$, etc.

$$P_{\mathcal{F}}(\epsilon) = P(\mathcal{F}(\epsilon) = f \mid \mathcal{L}(\epsilon) = l)$$
$$P_{\mathcal{F}}(\phi) = \{ \text{ for } \phi \neq \epsilon \} \; P(\mathcal{F}(\phi) = f \mid \mathcal{L}(\phi) = l, \mathcal{D}(\phi) = d)$$

$$P_{\mathcal{S}}(\epsilon) = P(\mathcal{S}(\epsilon) = s(\epsilon) \mid \mathcal{L}(\epsilon), \mathcal{F}(\epsilon), C(\epsilon))$$
$$P_{\mathcal{S}}(\phi) = \{ \text{ for } \phi \neq \epsilon \} \; P(\mathcal{S}(\phi) = s(\phi) \mid \mathcal{D}(\phi), \mathcal{L}(\phi), \mathcal{F}(\phi), C(\phi))$$

where

$$C(\phi) = \bigcup_{j=1}^{v} [s(\phi j)]$$
$$\mathcal{S}(\phi) = \mathrm{adjoin}(C(\phi), l(\phi))$$
$$\mathrm{adjoin}(A, \beta) = \mathrm{concat}(\mathrm{permute}(A \cup [\beta]))$$

These probabilities are either model parameters or decomposed into such:

- $P_{\mathcal{L}}(\phi j)$ is the probability of $\mathcal{L}(\phi j)$ given its regent $\mathcal{L}(\phi)$ and the dependency type $\mathcal{D}(\phi j)$ linking them, reflecting lexical-functional collocation statistics.
- $P_{\mathcal{F}}(\phi)$ is the probability of the bag of dependency types $\mathcal{F}(\phi)$ given the label $\mathcal{L}(\phi)$ and its relation $\mathcal{D}(\phi)$ to its regent, reflecting the situated probability of the label's valency (lexical-functional complement) and optional adjuncts.
- $P_{\mathcal{S}}(\phi)$ is the surface-string-realization probability, defining the likelihood of each permutation of the regent and its dependent strings. We postpone handling discontinuous nuclei until Section 3.4.

We define the tree probability

$$P(\mathcal{T}, \mathcal{S}) = P(\mathcal{T}) \cdot P(\mathcal{S} \mid \mathcal{T}) = \left(\prod_{\phi \in \mathcal{N}} P_{\mathcal{L}}(\phi) \cdot P_{\mathcal{F}}(\phi) \right) \cdot \left(\prod_{\phi \in \mathcal{N}} P_{\mathcal{S}}(\phi) \right)$$

We first generate the tree-structure variables $\mathcal{L}$ and $\mathcal{F}$ using a top-down stochastic process, where $\mathcal{L}(\phi)$ is generated before $\mathcal{F}(\phi)$. The probability of the conditioning material of $P_{\mathcal{L}}(\phi j)$ is then known from $P_{\mathcal{L}}(\phi)$ and $P_{\mathcal{F}}(\phi)$, and that of $P_{\mathcal{F}}(\phi j)$ is known from $P_{\mathcal{L}}(\phi j)$ and $P_{\mathcal{F}}(\phi)$. We then generate the string variables $\mathcal{S}$ using a bottom-up stochastic process. The probability of the conditioning material of $P_{\mathcal{S}}(\phi)$ is then known either from the top-down process or from $P_{\mathcal{S}}(\phi j)$. The use of the $\mathcal{F}$ variables guarantees the internal coherence and local completeness at each node. Generating $\mathcal{F}$ and $\mathcal{L}$ for all nodes ensures global completeness. There are no multiple specifications here that could potentially jeopardize transparency or global coherence.

Figure 4 shows the two processes generating the dependency tree of Figure 3 and the surface string *John ate beans*; first the $\mathcal{L}$ and $\mathcal{F}$ columns are read downwards in parallel, $\mathcal{L}$ before $\mathcal{F}$: $\mathcal{L}(\epsilon) = .$, $\mathcal{F}(\epsilon) = $ [main], $\mathcal{L}(1) = ate$, $\mathcal{F}(1) = $ [subj,dobj], etc., then the $\mathcal{S}$ column is read upwards.

3.3   Alshawi's Head Automata

Head automata [2] constitute a variant of dependency grammar which first generates the regent (head), and then repeatedly generates dependents with adjacent string realizations. The $\mathcal{F}$ and $\mathcal{S}$ variables are thus intertwined, but can be separated using directional random variables $\mathcal{U}(\phi j)$ ranging over $\{+, -\}$. Let $\phi 1, \ldots, \phi v$ be the order in which the dependents of ϕ are generated. We break down $\mathcal{S}(\phi) = \mathcal{Z}(\phi v)$ into the subprocess $\mathcal{Z}(\phi 0), \ldots, \mathcal{Z}(\phi v)$, where[2]

$$P(\mathcal{Z}(\phi j) = z(\phi j\text{-}1)\ s(\phi j) \mid j > 0, \mathcal{U}(\phi j) = +) = 1$$
$$P(\mathcal{Z}(\phi j) = s(\phi j)\ z(\phi j\text{-}1) \mid j > 0, \mathcal{U}(\phi j) = -) = 1$$
$$P(\mathcal{Z}(\phi 0) = l(\phi)) = 1$$

We also break down $\mathcal{F}(\phi)$ and merge it with $\mathcal{U}(\phi j)$

$$\mathcal{F}(\phi) = f = \langle d_1, u_1, \ldots, d_v, u_v \rangle \Leftrightarrow$$
$$\Leftrightarrow \mathcal{D}(\phi 1) = d_1, \mathcal{U}(\phi 1) = u_1, \ldots, \mathcal{D}(\phi v) = d_v, \mathcal{U}(\phi v) = u_v, \mathcal{V}(\phi) = v$$

and realize it as a subprocess specified by first selecting an automaton a with initial state $\mathcal{Q}(\phi 0) = q_0^a$ mediating the conditioning on $\mathcal{L}(\phi)$ and $\mathcal{D}(\phi)$:

$$P_{\mathcal{F}}(\phi) = P(\mathcal{F}(\phi) = \{ \text{ for } \phi \neq \epsilon \}\ f \mid \mathcal{L}(\phi) = l, \mathcal{D}(\phi) = d) =$$
$$= P(\mathcal{F}(\phi) = f \mid \mathcal{Q}(\phi 0) = q_0^a) \cdot P(\mathcal{Q}(\phi 0) = q_0^a \mid \mathcal{L}(\phi) = l, \mathcal{D}(\phi) = d)$$

$P_{\mathcal{L}}$ remains the same as before, save at the root, where it is combined with $P_{\mathcal{F}}$:

$$P_{\mathcal{L}}(\phi j) = P(\mathcal{L}(\phi j) = l_j \mid \mathcal{L}(\phi) = l, \mathcal{D}(\phi j) = d_j)$$
$$P_{\mathcal{L},\mathcal{F}}(\epsilon) = P(\mathcal{L}(\epsilon) = l, \mathcal{Q}(0) = q_0^a) \cdot P(\mathcal{F}(\epsilon) = f \mid \mathcal{Q}(0) = q_0^a)$$

At the core of the scheme we find

$$P(\mathcal{F}(\phi) = f \mid \mathcal{Q}(\phi 0) = q_0^a) = \left(\prod_{j=1}^{v} P_{\mathcal{D}\mathcal{Q}\mathcal{U}}(\phi j) \right) \cdot P(\mathcal{V}(\phi) = v \mid \mathcal{Q}(\phi v) = q_v^a)$$

where the stop probability $P(\mathcal{V}(\phi) = v \mid \mathcal{Q}(\phi v) = q_v^a)$ and

$$P_{\mathcal{D}\mathcal{Q}\mathcal{U}}(\phi j) = P(\mathcal{D}(\phi j) = d_j, \mathcal{Q}(\phi j) = q_j^a, \mathcal{U}(\phi j) = u_j \mid \mathcal{Q}(\phi j\text{-}1) = q_{j-1}^a)$$

are model parameters of automaton a. The tree probability is basically as before

$$P(\mathcal{T}, \mathcal{S}) = P_{\mathcal{L},\mathcal{F}}(\epsilon) \cdot \prod_{\phi j \in \mathcal{N}} P_{\mathcal{L}}(\phi j) \cdot P_{\mathcal{F}}(\phi j)$$

and we use the same top-down tree-generating process and bottom-up string-realization process, the latter which is now deterministic. The subprocess generating $\mathcal{F}$ ensures the internal coherence and local completeness at each node. The rest is as before, ensuring transparency and global completeness and coherence.

If q_j^a is uniquely determined by u_j, d_j and q_{j-1}^a, then the automaton a simply implements an extraction function over the sequence $d_1, u_1, \ldots, d_j, u_j$. If not, this results in approximating the parse probability with a derivation probability, cp. the discussion at the end of Section 1.

---

[2] Here $j = 0$ is a technical construction to break the recursion; there is no node $\phi 0$.

3.4 Non-projective Dependency Grammars

To accommodate long-distance dependencies, we allow a dependent to be realized adjacent to the label of any node that dominates it, immediately or not. For example, consider the dependency tree of Figure 5 for the sentence *What beans did Mary say that John ate?* as encoded in Figure 6. Here, *What beans* is a dependent of *that ate*, which in turn is a dependent of *did say*, and *What beans* is realized before *did*. This phenomenon is called movement in conjunction with phrase-structure grammars; when drawing dependency trees, it creates crossing dependencies if the trees also depict the word order.

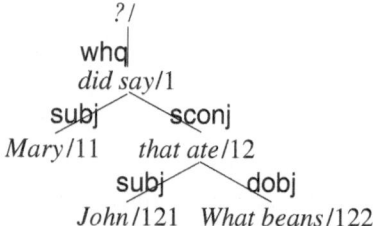

Fig. 5. Dependency tree for *What beans did Mary say that John ate?*

We introduce variables $\mathcal{M}(\phi)$ that randomly select from $C(\phi)$ a subbag $C_M(\phi)$ of strings passed up to ϕ's regent:

$$C(\phi) = \bigcup_{j=1}^{v} ([s(\phi j)] \cup C_M(\phi j))$$
$$C_M(\phi) \subseteq C(\phi)$$
$$P_\mathcal{M}(\phi) = P(\mathcal{M}(\phi) = C_M(\phi) \mid \mathcal{D}(\phi), \mathcal{L}(\phi), \mathcal{F}(\phi), C(\phi))$$

The rest of the strings, $C_S(\phi)$, are realized here:

$$C_S(\phi) = C(\phi) \setminus C_M(\phi)$$
$$P_S(\phi) = P(\mathcal{S}(\phi) = s(\phi) \mid \mathcal{D}(\phi), \mathcal{L}(\phi), \mathcal{F}(\phi), C_S(\phi))$$
$$\mathcal{S}(\phi) = \text{adjoin}(C_S(\phi), l(\phi))$$

We generalize the scheme to discontinuous nuclei by allowing $\mathcal{S}(\phi)$ to insert the strings of $C_S(\phi)$ anywhere in $l(\phi)$: [3]

$$\text{adjoin}(A, b_1 \ldots b_m) = \text{concat}(\text{permute}_{i<j \Rightarrow b_i \prec b_j}(A \cup \bigcup_{j=1}^{m} [b_j]))$$

This means that strings can only be inserted into ancestor labels, not into other strings, which enforces a type of reverse island constraint. In Figure 6 *John* is inserted between *that* and *ate* to form the subordinate clause *that John ate*.

---

[3] $x \prec y$ indicates that x precedes y in the resulting permutation.

$\mathcal{N}$	$\mathcal{L}$	$\mathcal{F}$	$\mathcal{M}$	$\mathcal{S}$
ϵ	?	[whq]	$\emptyset$	$s(1)$?
1	*did say*	[subj,sconj]	$\emptyset$	$C_M(12)(s(122))$ *did* $s(11)$ *say* $s(12)$
11	*Mary*	$\emptyset$	$\emptyset$	*Mary*
12	*that ate*	[subj,dobj]	$[s(122)]$	*that* $s(121)$ *ate*
121	*John*	$\emptyset$	$\emptyset$	*John*
122	*What beans*	$\emptyset$	$\emptyset$	*What beans*

Fig. 6. Dependency encoding of *What beans did Mary say that John ate?*

The adjoin operation can be further refined to allow handling an even wider range of phenomena, such as negation in French. Here, the dependent string is effectively merged with the label of the regent, as *ne ... pas* is wrapped around portions of the verb phrase, e.g., *ne me quitte pas*, see [12]. In addition to this, the node labels may be linguistic abstractions, e.g. "negation", calling on the $\mathcal{S}$ variables also for their surface-string realization.

We define the tree probability

$$P(\mathcal{T}, \mathcal{S}) = P(\mathcal{T}) \cdot P(\mathcal{S} \mid \mathcal{T}) = \left(\prod_{\phi \in \mathcal{N}} P_{\mathcal{L}}(\phi) \cdot P_{\mathcal{F}}(\phi) \right) \cdot \left(\prod_{\phi \in \mathcal{N}} P_{\mathcal{M}}(\phi) \cdot P_{\mathcal{S}}(\phi) \right)$$

To avoid derivational ambiguity when generating a tree-string pair, cp. the discussion at the end of Section 1, we require that no string be realized adjacent to the string of any node it was passed up through. This introduces a practical problem that we here merrily sweep under the carpet, namely that of ensuring that zero probability mass is assigned to all derivations violating this constraint.

The tree-structure variables $\mathcal{L}$ and $\mathcal{F}$ are generated just as before. We then generate the string variables $\mathcal{S}$ and $\mathcal{M}$ using a bottom-up stochastic process, where $\mathcal{M}(\phi)$ is generated before $\mathcal{S}(\phi)$. The probability of the conditioning material of $P_{\mathcal{M}}(\phi)$ is then known either from the top-down process or from $P_{\mathcal{M}}(\phi j)$ and $P_{\mathcal{S}}(\phi j)$, and that of $P_{\mathcal{S}}(\phi)$ is known either from the top-down process, or from $P_{\mathcal{M}}(\phi)$, $P_{\mathcal{M}}(\phi j)$ and $P_{\mathcal{S}}(\phi j)$. The coherence of $\mathcal{S}(\phi)$ and $\mathcal{M}(\phi)$ is enforced by explicit conditioning, and they are specified only once each.

Figure 6 shows a top-down process generating the dependency tree of Figure 5; the columns $\mathcal{L}$ and $\mathcal{F}$ should be read downwards in parallel, $\mathcal{L}$ before $\mathcal{F}$. It also shows a bottom-up process generating the surface string; the columns $\mathcal{M}$ and $\mathcal{S}$ should be read upwards in parallel, $\mathcal{M}$ before $\mathcal{S}$.

3.5   Collins' ACL'97 Models

We finally turn to the three models of [3], warming up with a 0th model. First, we extend Gorn's notation to strings over integers, interpreting ϕj as

- the jth sibling to the right of the head node if $j > 0$,
- the $-j$th sibling to the left of the head node if $j < 0$,
- the head node itself if $j = 0$.

The head node is a distinguished node defined by the underlying syntactic theory. Intuitively, it is the child node most similar to its parent; in a dependency grammar, it would be the regent of its current siblings. In Collins' scheme, the underlying SCFG is lexicalized by projecting each word up its head chain.

Model 0. We reuse the $\mathcal{R}$ variables, but split $\mathcal{V}(\phi) = v$ into $\mathcal{V}^{\pm}(\phi) = v^{\pm}$ and $\mathcal{V}^0(\phi) = v^0$, where $v = v^+ + v^0 - v^-$.

$$\mathcal{R}(\phi) = r = l \rightarrow l_{v^-} \ldots l_0 \ldots l_{v^+} \in P \Leftrightarrow \begin{cases} \mathcal{L}(\phi) = l \in V_N \\ \mathcal{V}^{\pm}(\phi) = v^{\pm} \\ \mathcal{V}^0(\phi) = v^0 \\ \forall_{j \in \{v^-, \ldots, v^+\}} \mathcal{L}(\phi j) = l_j \in V \end{cases}$$

$$\mathcal{R}(\phi) = l \in V_T \Leftrightarrow \begin{cases} \mathcal{L}(\phi) = l \in V_T \\ \mathcal{V}^{\pm}(\phi) = \mathcal{V}^0(\phi) = 0 \end{cases}$$

We again define the probabilities

$$P_{\mathcal{R}}(\phi) = P(\mathcal{R}(\phi) = r \mid \mathcal{L}(\phi) = l)$$
$$P(\mathcal{T}, \mathcal{S}) = P(\mathcal{L}(\epsilon) = l(\epsilon)) \cdot \prod_{\phi \in \mathcal{N}} P_{\mathcal{R}}(\phi)$$

Since the grammar is lexicalized, $P(\mathcal{L}(\epsilon) = l(\epsilon))$ does typically not equal one.

$\mathcal{R}$ is broken down into first generating the head $\phi 0$, and then its right and left siblings as subprocesses:

$$P_{\mathcal{R}}(\phi) = P_{\mathcal{R}}^0(\phi) \cdot P_{\mathcal{R}}^+(\phi) \cdot P_{\mathcal{R}}^-(\phi)$$
$$P_{\mathcal{R}}^0(\phi) = P(\mathcal{L}(\phi 0) = l_0 \mid \mathcal{L}(\phi) = l)$$
$$P_{\mathcal{R}}^{\pm}(\phi) = \left(\prod_{j=\pm 1}^{v^{\pm}} P_{\mathcal{L}}^{\pm}(\phi j) \right) \cdot P_{\mathcal{V}}^{\pm}(\phi)$$

$P_{\mathcal{R}}^-$ mirrors $P_{\mathcal{R}}^+$ exactly; we thus treat only the latter:

$$P_{\mathcal{L}}^+(\phi j) = P(\mathcal{L}(\phi j) = l_j \mid \mathcal{L}(\phi) = l, \mathcal{L}(\phi 0) = l_0)$$
$$P_{\mathcal{V}}^+(\phi) = P(\mathcal{V}^+(\phi) = v^+ \mid \mathcal{L}(\phi) = l, \mathcal{L}(\phi 0) = l_0)$$

The process generating the $\mathcal{R}$ variables ensures internal coherence and local completeness at each node. The rest is as in the SCFG case, which guarantees transparency and global completeness and coherence.

Model 1. We refine Model 0 by adding to the conditioning of $P_{\mathcal{L}}^{\pm}(\phi j)$ a distance h over strings, e.g., measuring their lengths and counting the number of verbs and punctuation marks in them:

$$P_{\mathcal{L}}^+(\phi j) = P(\mathcal{L}(\phi j) = l_j \mid \mathcal{L}(\phi), \mathcal{L}(\phi 0), h(\mathcal{S}^+(\phi 0) \ldots \mathcal{S}(\phi j-1)))$$

$\mathcal{S}(\phi)$ is the yield of ϕ, and $\mathcal{S}^+(\phi)$ is the part of it following the head word. This forces us to interleave generating the $\mathcal{L}$ and $\mathcal{S}$ variables by first generating the head subtree, given the parent label, and then recursively generate the left and right siblings increasingly removed from the head. The resulting depth-first, head-corner process ensures that the probability of the conditioning material is already known. The conditioning on h does not affect completeness or coherence.

Model 2. We add lexical complements to Model 1 by partitioning the set of grammar symbols V into complements V_C and adjuncts V_A, see [3], and reviving the $\mathcal{F}$ variables to range over bags of complement labels drawn from V_C. Having generated the head label, we let $\mathcal{F}^\pm$ generate its left and right complements:

$$P_{\mathcal{R}}^0(\phi) =$$
$$= P(\mathcal{L}(\phi 0) = l_0 \mid \mathcal{L}(\phi) = l) \cdot P(\mathcal{F}^+(\phi) = f^+(\phi) \mid \mathcal{L}(\phi 0) = l_0, \mathcal{L}(\phi) = l) \cdot$$
$$\cdot P(\mathcal{F}^-(\phi) = f^-(\phi) \mid \mathcal{L}(\phi 0) = l_0, \mathcal{L}(\phi) = l)$$

Following Alshawi, we encode each complement $f^\pm$ as the initial state $q_0^\mp$ of an automaton, where each state is a bag of complement labels. We add the state variables $\mathcal{Q}^+$ to the subprocesses generating $P_{\mathcal{R}}^+$:

$$P_{\mathcal{L}}^+(\phi j) = P(\mathcal{Q}^+(\phi j) = q_j^+, \mathcal{L}(\phi j) = l_j \mid \mathcal{Q}^+(\phi j\text{--}1), \mathcal{L}(\phi), \mathcal{L}(\phi 0), h(\ldots))$$
$$P_{\mathcal{V}}^+(\phi) = P(\mathcal{V}^+(\phi) = v^+ \mid \mathcal{Q}^+(\phi v^+) = q_{v+}^+, \mathcal{L}(\phi) = l, \mathcal{L}(\phi 0) = l_0)$$

Note that the stop probability $P_{\mathcal{V}}^+(\phi)$ equals 0 if $q_{v+}^+ \neq \emptyset$. The state transitions are defined by

$$q_j^+ = \begin{cases} q_{j-1}^+ & \text{if } l_j \in V_A \\ q_{j-1}^+ \setminus [l_j] & \text{if } l_j \in q_{j-1}^+ \end{cases}$$

and $P_{\mathcal{L}}^+(\phi j)$ equals 0 if $l_j \in V_C$ but $l_j \notin q_{j-1}^+$. The process generating the $\mathcal{R}$ variables again ensure internal coherence and local completeness at each node.

Model 3. We add movement to Model 2 by reintroducing the variables $\mathcal{M}(\phi)$, now indicating the bag of complement labels $C_M(\phi)$ inherited from ϕ's parent. Given $C_M(\phi)$ and $f^\pm(\phi)$, we let $\mathcal{L}^\pm(\phi j)$ randomly generate the bag of child-node labels $C(\phi) = C_C(\phi) \cup C_A(\phi)$, where

$$C_C(\phi) = \bigcup_{\phi j \,:\, l(\phi j) \in V_C} [l(\phi j)] \quad \text{and} \quad C_A(\phi) = \bigcup_{\phi j \,:\, l(\phi j) \in V_A} [l(\phi j)]$$

and let $\mathcal{M}(\phi j)$ randomly generate $C_M(\phi j)$, in both cases constrained by the complement-label conservation-law

$$C_M(\phi) \cup C_C(\phi) = f^+(\phi) \cup f^-(\phi) \cup \bigcup_{\phi j} C_M(\phi j)$$

We must merge generating the $\mathcal{M}$ variables with the head-corner process generating the tree structure. Collins limits the range of $\mathcal{M}$ to $\{\emptyset, [NP_C]\}$ and merges generating $\mathcal{M}(\phi j)$ with the $P_{\mathcal{R}}^\pm(\phi)$ processes, the details of which we omit.

4   Discussion

The novel contribution of this article is to propose a theoretical framework for describing stochastic grammars based on having a small set of basic random variables generate tree structures and relate them to surface strings as two separate stochastic processes. In particular, viewing surface-string generating as a stochastic process conditioned on tree structure, and formalizing it using the S and M variables constitutes an important novel idea. Collins' treatment of movement is the converse of that proposed for dependency grammars; Collins passes labels down the tree, the latter passes strings up the tree. Both approaches are reminiscent of the "slash" feature of GPSG, see [13], pp. 137–168.

Despite the limitations of being able to refer only to immediate dominance and local precedence, we managed to capture all schemes, which suggests a tendency towards locality in grammatical descriptions. Nothing prevents conditioning the random variables on arbitrary portions of the partial tree generated this far, using, e.g., maximum-entropy or decision-tree models to extract relevant features of it; there is no difference in principle between this and history-based parsing, apart from the partial trees mediating the derivation history.

Nor does anything prevent us from letting our basic variables generate more general graphs, e.g., allowing multiple parents in dependency descriptions or reentrance in feature-logic terms, e.g., in *Mary let John eat beans*, where *John* is clearly both the object of *let* and the subject of *eat*. However, extending Gorn's notation to allow equating nodes introduces aliasing, and thus effectively graph unification when checking the specifications for coherence. It might be worth salvaging by enforcing further constraints on the stochastic processes, but it may be better to abandon it altogether. We stress the possibility of associating an S variable with each node of any graph, thus establishing a direct stochastic relationship between, say, feature-logic terms and their surface-string realizations.

Both Alshawi and Collins first generate the regent, or the head, and then generate the $\mathcal{F}$ variable, or the rest of the $\mathcal{R}$ variable, as subprocesses, employing automata as subprocess memory devices, although Collins does so only implicitly. We appreciate Collins' strategy of simultaneously generating the entire lexical complement according to the valency of the head, or of the regent, but then adding optional adjuncts incrementally. This strategy would be a sensible instantiation of the described dependency-grammar scheme.

We finally note the recurring theme, which really only Collins defies, of a top-down process generating the tree structure and a bottom-up process generating the surface string given the tree structure:

$$P(\mathcal{T}, S) \;=\; P(\mathcal{T}) \cdot P(S \mid \mathcal{T})$$

This is a variant of Shannon's noisy channel model, consisting of a language model of tree descriptions and a signal model converting trees to surface strings. It should be straight-forward to apply the methodology of [14] to prove that all the studied stochastic grammars are tight. A stochastic grammar is *tight* or *consistent* if the probabilities sum to one over the set of finite derivations. Chi proves that any SCFG is tight if the model parameters are extracted from frequency counts in any reasonable way. Since word order is immaterial for tightness, it should suffice to simply map the model under consideration to an SCFG, where the tightness of one implies the tightness of the other. This approach should work also for models like Collins', since these are top-down models, and what conditioning on the surface string there is is irrelevant to tightness.

References

1. David Magerman. Statistical decision-tree models for parsing. *Procs. 33rd Annual Meeting of the Association for Computational Linguistics*, pages 276–283, 1995.
2. Hiyan Alshawi. Head automata and bilingual tiling: Translation with minimal representations. *Procs. 34th Annual Meeting of the Association for Computational Linguistics*, pages 167–176, 1996.
3. Michael Collins. Three generative, lexicalized models for statistical parsing. *Procs. 35th Annual Meeting of the Association for Computational Linguistics*, pages 16–23, 1997.
4. T. L. Booth and R. A. Thompson. Applying probability measures to abstract languages. *IEEE Transactions on Computers, C-22(5)*, pages 442–450, 1973.
5. Ted Briscoe and John Carroll. Generalized probabilistic lr parsing of natural language (corpora) with unification-based grammars. *Computational Linguistics*, 19(1):25–59, 1993.
6. Ezra Black, Fred Jelinek, John Lafferty, David Magerman, Robert Mercer, and Salim Roukos. Towards history-based grammars: Using richer models for probabilistic parsing. *Procs. 28th Annual Meeting of the Association for Computational Linguistics*, pages 31–37, 1993.
7. Rens Bod. *Enriching Linguistics with Statistics: Performance Models of Natural Language*. ILLC Dissertation Series 1995-14, Amsterdam, 1995.
8. Yves Schabes. Stochastic lexicalized tree-adjoining grammars. *Proc. 14th International Conference on Computational Linguistics*, pages 426–432, 1992.
9. Khalil Sima'an. Computational complexity of probabilistic disambiguations by means of tree-grammars. *Procs. 16th International Conference on Computational Linguistics*, page at the very end, 1996.
10. Saul Gorn. Processors for infinite codes of shannon-fano type. *Symp. Math. Theory of Automata*, pages ??–??, 1962.
11. Lucien Tesnière. *Éléments de Syntaxe Structurale*. Libraire C. Klincksieck, Paris, 1959.
12. Jacques Brel. Ne me quitte pas. *La Valse à Mille Temps (PHI 6325.205)*, 1959.
13. Gerald Gazdar, Ewan Klein, Geoffrey K. Pullum, and Ivan A. Sag. *Generalized Phrase Structure Grammar*. Basil Blackwell Publishing, Oxford, England, 1985. Also published by Harvard University Press, Cambridge, MA.
14. Zhiyi Chi. Statistical properties of probabilistic context-free grammars. *Computational Linguistics*, 25(1):131–160, 1999.

Monte-Carlo Sampling for NP-Hard Maximization Problems in the Framework of Weighted Parsing

Jean-Cédric Chappelier and Martin Rajman

DI-LIA – EPFL – CH-1015 Lausanne – Switzerland
{chaps,rajman}@lia.di.epfl.ch

Abstract. The purpose of this paper is (1) to provide a theoretical justification for the use of Monte-Carlo sampling for approximate resolution of NP-hard maximization problems in the framework of weighted parsing, and (2) to show how such sampling techniques can be efficiently implemented with an explicit control of the error probability. We provide an algorithm to compute the local sampling probability distribution that guarantee that the global sampling probability indeed corresponds to the aimed theoretical score. The proposed sampling strategy significantly differs from existing methods, showing by the same way the bias induced by these methods.

1 Motivations

In the framework of Speech Recognition and Natural Language Processing, it is a very common task to search for elements (e.g. sentences, parse trees) a score that depends on the process that was used to produce them. Examples of such tasks include searching a word graph for the most-probable sentence (MPS) according to a Stochastic Context-Free Grammar (SCFG) [11] or finding, for a given sentence, the most probable parse tree (MPP) according to a Stochastic Lexicalized Tree Adjoining Grammar (SLTAG) [16] or a Data-Oriented Parsing (DOP) model [5].

The problem with such maximisation tasks is that they often correspond to an instance of an NP-hard problem [17] and, as such, cannot be solved exactly in an effective way. In such cases, heuristics and/or approximations need to be used instead. Monte-Carlo sampling is an example of an approach that approximates the exact maximization by a search over a reduced random sample that can be generated at reasonable (i.e. polynomial) algorithmic cost [4].

The purpose of the present paper is to provide theoretical justification for the use of Monte-Carlo sampling for such NP-hard maximization problems in the framework of parsing, and to show how such sampling techniques can be efficiently implemented and controlled; i.e. guarantee, with some *a priori* fixed probability error, that the approximate solution indeed corresponds to an exact solution of the problem.

D.N. Christodoulakis (Ed.): NLP 2000, LNCS 1835, pp. 106–117, 2000.

The paper first provides a short overview of some NP-hard maximization problems in the general framework of *"weighted parsing"* (as defined in section 2.1). It then presents a generic implementation for an approximate solution based on Monte-Carlo sampling. The problem of the control of the probability error during sampling is finally discussed.

2   General Framework

2.1   Weighted Parsing

Weighted parsing can be defined as parsing with a phrase-structure grammar, the productions of which (i.e. rules) are scored, i.e. mapped on a subset of the positive real numbers $[0, +\infty)$. Such scores often consist of probabilities, but this is by no means mandatory for the approach described here.

The mapping (denoted by σ) is extended by definition to any derivation as the product of the scores associated with the productions in the derivation.[1] More precisely, the score $\sigma(d)$ associated with a derivation $d = r_1 \circ ... \circ r_q$ [2] is

$$\sigma(d) = \prod_{r \in d} \sigma(r) = \prod_{i=1}^{q} \sigma(r_i).$$

Moreover, if some equivalence classes are defined over the derivations (for instance the equivalence classes induced by sentences: two derivations are in the same class if they produce the same sentence), the scores can be extended to derivation classes $(\bar{d})$ as the sum of the scores of all the derivations that belong to a given class, finally leading a sum of products: $\sigma(\bar{d}) = \sum_{d \in \bar{d}} \sigma(d) = \sum_{d \in \bar{d}} \prod_{r \in d} \sigma(r).$

2.2   Some NP-Hard Maximization Problems in the Framework of Weighted Parsing

When only one single class of derivation is considered (for instance the parsing of a unique input sentence with a SCFG), weighted parsing may be achieve in polynomial time using standard parsing techniques [13,18,9].

But parsing may also be used in situations where *several different* classes of derivations are mixed together (i.e. share some components). Examples of such situations include finding the MPS in a word-graph using a SCFG as a language model (speech recognition), or looking for the most-probable parse of a sentence according to a Stochastic Tree Substitution Grammar (STSG, as in DOP for instance [7]), where several derivations may lead to the same parse tree[3].

---

[1] This is in fact a morphism between the (partial) semi-ring of the derivations in the grammar and the natural semi-ring $\mathbb{R}^+$. Readers interested by this formal aspect are referred to [15].

[2] where $\circ$ denotes the sequential composition of production rules. $r \in d$ will denote the fact that production r occurs in derivation d.

[3] in that case the derivations classes are defined as the set of derivations that lead to the same tree

Let us summarize what are the derivations, the classes and the score to be maximized in two specific cases: SCFG-MPS and DOP-MPP:

	SCFG-MPS	DOP-MPP
input	a word-graph	a sentence
derivations	all the derivations of all sentences in the word-graph	all the derivations of the input sentence
classes	all the derivations of a single sentence	all the derivations leading to the same parse tree
class score	sentence probability	DOP probability of a parse tree

For these two cases, finding the class that maximizes the score σ is an NP-hard problem [17]. This means that finding the (exact) optimal class cannot be achieved in polynomial time (in general).

Parsing usually consists in two phases:

analysis i.e. building a compact representation of all the possible derivations of the input;

extraction of results from the former representation: e.g. displaying all the parse trees or extracting the best parse tree.

The analysis can always be achieved in a time cubic with respect to the input size. However, the extraction, i.e. the "unfolding" of the compact representation produced by analysis, may lead to the NP-hard problem mentioned above.

2.3   Parsing Analysis and Notations

In our case, the analysis phase of the parsing consists in a bottom-up filling of a parse chart with items that represent all the possible subderivations of all possible substrings of the input, a sentence in the DOP-MPP case [9] and a word-graph in the SCFG-MPS case [10].

More precisely, the parse chart consists of a set of *items* $[X, i, j]$ each representing the fact that the substring $w_i...w_j$ of the input can be derived from the non-terminal X (this will be noted $X \Rightarrow^* w_i...w_j$). In the case of DOP-MPP, where the input consists of a single sentence, $w_i...w_j$ is simply the substring from the i-th to the j-th word of that sentence. In the case of SCFG-MPS, where the input is a time-indexed word-graph, $w_i...w_j$ represents the subsequence of words going from time-step i to time-step j. In the latter case, notice that the actual number of words in $w_i...w_j$ may be any value between 1 and $j - i + 1$.

For an item $[X, i, j]$, a *decomposition* of that item is defined as a set of items that explicit the first step in the derivation $X \Rightarrow^* w_i...w_j$. For instance in the case of a binary grammar[4], a decomposition of $[X, i, j]$ is a couple consisting of:

1. a production r of the form $X \rightarrow Y\,Z$ [5] or $X \rightarrow w$ and that is the first step of some $X \Rightarrow^* w_i...w_j$,

---

[4] i.e. Chomsky Normal Form for SCFG and binary trees grammar for DOP

[5] In the case of DOP, the production $r = X \rightarrow Y\,Z$ is indeed an elementary tree, the root of which is X, the left-most non terminal leave is Y and the other is Z. Notice that the points discussed here are independent of the internal structure of the

2. and a position k where to "split" the production r, i.e. defining the substrings $w_i...w_k$ and $w_{k+1}...w_j$ such that $Y \Rightarrow^* w_i...w_k$ and $Z \Rightarrow^* w_{k+1}...w_j$. By convention $k = 0$ if r is a terminal production $X \to w$.

In the case of a non binary grammar, the above definition can be generalized by replacing k by a tuple of indices (see [8] for details.)

A decomposition ξ of $[X, i, j]$ can either be denoted by $\langle r, k \rangle$ defined above or, in a equivalent manner, by the two[6] corresponding items $\xi = \ll [Y, i, k], [Z, k+1, j] \gg$ (or $\xi = \ll w_i...w_j \gg$ when the production r is terminal: $X \to w_i...w_j$).

In order to simplify the notation, the score σ will be extended to decompositions of items by $\sigma(\langle r, k \rangle) = \sigma(r)$.

Finally, for a decomposition ξ, let $\mathcal{D}(\xi)$ denote the set of all possible decompositions of the item of which ξ is itself a decomposition. This notation is generalized to items: $\mathcal{D}([X, i, j])$ is the set of all possible decompositions of the item $[X, i, j]$.

Example: As illustration, let us consider the very simple case of parsing the input sequence "a a a" with the following CFG: S $\to$ S S | a where a is the only terminal and S the only non-terminal. In that case, 6 items will be present in the chart and have the following decompositions:

item	number of decompositions	$\langle r, k \rangle$ representation of decompositions	$\ll [Y, i, k], [Z, k+1, j] \gg$ representation
$[S, 1, 1]$	1	$\langle$S $\to$ a, $0\rangle$	$\ll$a$\gg$
$[S, 2, 2]$	1	$\langle$S $\to$ a, $0\rangle$	$\ll$a$\gg$
$[S, 3, 3]$	1	$\langle$S $\to$ a, $0\rangle$	$\ll$a$\gg$
$[S, 1, 2]$	1	$\langle$S $\to$ S S, $1\rangle$	$\ll[S, 1, 1], [S, 2, 2]\gg$
$[S, 2, 3]$	1	$\langle$S $\to$ S S, $2\rangle$	$\ll[S, 2, 2], [S, 3, 3]\gg$
$[S, 1, 3]$	2	$\langle$S $\to$ S S, $1\rangle$, $\langle$S $\to$ S S, $2\rangle$	$\ll[S, 1, 2], [S, 3, 3]\gg$, $\ll[S, 1, 1], [S, 2, 3]\gg$

If ξ is the decomposition $\ll[S, 1, 2], [S, 3, 3]\gg$ of item $[S, 1, 3]$, then $\mathcal{D}(\xi) = \mathcal{D}([S, 1, 3]) = \{\ll[S, 1, 2], [S, 3, 3]\gg, \ll[S, 1, 1], [S, 2, 3]\gg\}$.

2.4   Monte-Carlo Estimation

The purpose of Monte-Carlo estimation in the above described framework is to approximate the extraction of the best class by a search limited to a sample of derivations randomly extracted [4]. This approximated search is controlled by an arbitrary small probability of error a priori fixed ("control error"). Such an approach is possible and interesting only if:

1. the approximated score of the sampled classes may be computed from samples;

---

elementary trees. The internal structure of elementary tree (which are in general of depth greater than 1) is therefore kept apart in another representation not addressed here and that is only used for the final display of the whole result.

[6] g in the general case of non-binary grammars, with g the arity of the production r.

Sample $[X, i, j]$:

choose at random a decomposition $\xi = \langle r, k \rangle$ of $[X, i, j]$
<u>if</u> ξ is terminal (i.e $k = 0$ and $r = X \rightarrow w_i$)
    <u>return</u> r
<u>else</u>
    (here $\xi = \langle r, k \rangle = \ll [Y, i, k], [Z, k+1, j] \gg$)
    <u>return</u> r, **Sample** $[Y, i, k]$, **Sample** $[Z, k+1, j]$

Table 1. A simple version of the sampling algorithm in the case of a binary grammar. This algorithm is applied top-down from $[S, 1, m]$ to words on a filled parse chart.

2. the best class (according to the <u>real</u> score) can be found on the basis of the approximated scores;
3. the sampling of classes may be achieved efficiently (polynomial time).

For the sake of simplicity, let us first explain on a simple binary grammar what the sampling method consist of, although it may easily be generalized to any chart parser and any SCFG/STSG [8]. As detailed in table 1, the sampling algorithm (that takes place once the analysis step described in the previous section has been performed) consists in recursively choosing at random, from top $[S, 1, m]$ to bottom (words), a possible decomposition of the current item.

As choosing a decomposition of an item may be $\mathcal{O}(m)$ if not carefully implemented (see also [12] page 177), this sampling technique might be of cost $\mathcal{O}(m^2)$ [7] but can easily be improved to $\mathcal{O}(m)$ if the storage of an item in the parse chart directly points to its decomposition [8].

The main problem of Monte-Carlo estimation however is not the sampling function itself but how to correctly implement the action *"choose at random a decomposition"*, so that the three above mentioned conditions are fulfilled (and especially so as to ensure that the sampling probability converges to the appropriate score).

The two following sections detail the different sampling strategies that are possible for general item-based chart parsers:

rescored sampling: the sampling probability for choosing the items in the parse chart is a simple, *a priori* defined, value. The probability of the sampled classes then needs to be rescored *a posteriori* so as to get the proper (theoretical) value for its score;

exact sampling: the sampling probability of items ensures that the overall sampling probability of a class is the normalized score of that class, i.e. the (theoretical) score of the class divided by the sum of the scores of all classes.

The advantages of the first approach consist in its simplicity and its generality while the advantages of the second one lies in a faster convergence as well as the

---

[7] where m is the input size

possibility of an *a priori* control over the error probability (and hence over the accuracy of the method).

3 Rescored Sampling

3.1 General Method

Let $d_i, i = 1...N$ be all the possible derivations that can be sampled (i.e. all the derivations of all the classes for the considered problem) and n_i the corresponding number of occurrences in a given sample of size n.[8] Notice that some n_i may be null. Let us define the estimated rescoring $W^{(n)}(\overline{d})$ of a class $\overline{d}$ by: $W^{(n)}(\overline{d}) = \sum_{d_i \in \overline{d}} \frac{n_i}{n} W_i$, where W_i is some rescoring factor for the derivation d_i. The interest of such a definition lies in the fact that, by the law of large numbers (i.e. when n grows to infinity), the rescored estimation $W^{(n)}(\overline{d})$ converges to $W^{(\infty)}(\overline{d}) = \sum_{d_i \in \overline{d}} P_{si} W_i$, where P_{si} the <u>sampling</u> probability of derivation d_i.

This convergence property makes the link between local random choices (P_{si}) and the global score obtained for the sampled classes. Provided that it is possible to compute both W_i and P_{si} for each sampled derivation d_i, this allows to estimate $W^{(\infty)}(\overline{d})$ by the sampled value $W^{(n)}(\overline{d})$. This is of course particularly useful when $W^{(\infty)}(\overline{d}) = \sigma(\overline{d})$, the original score to be maximized.

A first way of sampling, which will be called "*naive sampling*", consists of randomly choosing among the decompositions of an item with a uniform distribution. This corresponds to $P_{si} = \prod_{\xi \in d_i} \frac{1}{|\mathcal{D}(\xi)|}$.[9] Without rescoring (i.e. choosing $W_i = 1$), naive sampling leads, for every class $\overline{d}$, to a score $W^{(\infty)}(\overline{d})$ of the form $\sum_{d_i \in \overline{d}} \prod_{\xi \in d_i} \frac{1}{|\mathcal{D}(\xi)|}$, which is <u>not</u> the score $\sigma(\overline{d})$ to be estimate. Naive sampling can however be corrected, introducing rescoring factors $W_i = \frac{\sigma(d_i)}{\prod_{\xi \in d_i} \frac{1}{|\mathcal{D}(\xi)|}}$, which lead to $W^{(\infty)}(\overline{d}) = \sigma(\overline{d})$. It is important to notice that these rescoring factors are easily computable during sampling. Indeed, as $W_i = \frac{\sigma(d_i)}{\prod_{\xi \in d_i} \frac{1}{|\mathcal{D}(\xi)|}} = \frac{\prod_{\xi \in d_i} \sigma(\xi)}{\prod_{\xi \in d_i} \frac{1}{|\mathcal{D}(\xi)|}} = \prod_{\xi \in d_i} \frac{\sigma(\xi)}{|\mathcal{D}(\xi)|}$, it can be computed during the top-down extraction of each sampled derivation by iterative multiplications of the $\frac{\sigma(\xi)}{|\mathcal{D}(\xi)|}$ scores. Naive sampling may therefore be implemented anyway, therefore providing a very easy estimation method for the class that maximizes $\sigma(\overline{d})$.

---

[8] $\sum_{i=1}^{N} n_i = n$

[9] with the notation $\xi \in d_i$ as a subscript of a sum or product meaning "*for all decompositions of items chosen during the sampling of derivation d_i*".

However a better way for finding the best class by sampling is to choose $W_i = 1$ for all derivations and $P_{si} = \sigma(d_i)$,[10] leading to $W(\overline{d}) = \sum\limits_{d \in \overline{d}} P_{si} = \sigma(\overline{d})$.

Whether $P_{si} = \sigma(d_i)$ can actually be implemented is studied in section 4.

3.2   R. Bod Sampling Method for DOP

We now have all the theoretical tools to study the sampling method used by R. Bod for DOP [4,5,7,6]. His sampling technique is exactly the one described above but without the correct rescoring. Bod chooses as local random choice a probability such that "*a subderivation[11] that has n times as large a [DOP] probability as another subderivation should also have n times as large a chance to be chosen as this other subderivation*" [5] i.e. the sampling probability of a decomposition ξ of $[X, i, j]$ is $P_s(\xi) = \dfrac{\sigma(\xi)}{\sum_{\xi' \in \mathcal{D}(\xi)} \sigma(\xi')} = \dfrac{P_{\mathrm{DOP}}(\xi)}{\sum_{\xi'} P_{\mathrm{DOP}}(\xi')}$,[12] leading therefore to a P_{si} for a derivation d_i of the form $P_{si} = \prod\limits_{\xi \in d_i} \dfrac{P_{\mathrm{DOP}}(\xi)}{\sum_{\xi' \in \mathcal{D}(\xi)} P_{\mathrm{DOP}}(\xi')} =$

$P_{\mathrm{DOP}}(d_i) \cdot \dfrac{1}{\prod_{\xi \in d_i} \sum_{\xi' \in \mathcal{D}(\xi)} P_{\mathrm{DOP}}(\xi')}$. The resulting score for classes[13] is therefore

$\sum\limits_{d \in \overline{d}} \dfrac{P_{\mathrm{DOP}}(d)}{\prod_{\xi \in d} \sum_{\xi' \in \mathcal{D}(\xi)} P_{\mathrm{DOP}}(\xi')}$ which is <u>not</u> the DOP-probability of that tree in the general case. This shows that Bod's sampling does not at all lead to the right (i.e. DOP) probability, therefore imposing on parse trees a score that as nothing to do with the DOP theory. To have his sampling correct, R. Bod should have rescored the sampled derivations by $W_i = \prod\limits_{\xi \in d_i} \sum\limits_{\xi' \in \mathcal{D}(\xi)} P_{\mathrm{DOP}}(\xi')$, which is indeed computable during sampling (and is not 1 in the general case). Notice also that $P_s(\xi)$ has to be a probability over $\mathcal{D}(\xi)$, i.e. that $\sum_{\mathcal{D}(\xi)} P_s(\xi') = 1$. Therefore $P_s(\xi) = P_{\mathrm{DOP}}(\xi)$ is not a possible choice.

Table 2 resume the three sampling rescoring seen so far.

4   Exact (Controlled) Sampling

The purpose of exact sampling techniques is to sample decompositions so as to get a sampling probability for each class that is equal to the (theoretical) score of the class divided by the sum of the scores of all possible classes without any rescoring. Such sampling techniques ensure that the best class has the best sampling probability. Then, due to the law of large numbers (the sampling frequency

---

[10] more precisely: a renormalized version of σ in case where σ in not a probability.

[11] i.e. decomposition

[12] $P_{\mathrm{DOP}}(\xi)$ is the product of the probabilities of elementary trees constituting this subderivation.

[13] i.e. parse trees in this case.

method	$P_s(\xi)$	rescoring factor W_i
R. Bod for DOP	$\dfrac{\sigma(\xi)}{\sum_{\xi' \in \mathcal{D}(\xi)} \sigma(\xi')}$	used: 1 correct: $\displaystyle\prod_{\xi \in d_i} \sum_{\xi' \in \mathcal{D}(\xi)} \sigma(\xi')$
naive	$\dfrac{1}{|\mathcal{D}(\xi)|}$	$\dfrac{\sigma(d_i)}{\prod_{\xi \in d_i} \frac{1}{|\mathcal{D}(\xi)|}}$

Table 2. Rescoring factors for non exact sampling methods.

converging towards the sampling probability) the most frequent class in a sample is the best class. One important advantage of exact sampling is the fact that it allows a control of the number of samples to be drawn.

4.1 Computation of the Decomposition Sampling Probability

We here derive the exact form for the sampling probability of the decomposition elements so that the final sampling probability of a class is directly the correct score (divided by the sum of scores) without any rescoring.

The explanation is once again given in the simpler case of binary grammars but still generalizes, using significantly much more notations, to any SCFG/STSG grammar as detailed in [8].

For each decomposition, an intermediate score σ_0 is introduced. For $\xi = \langle r, k \neq 0 \rangle = \ll [Y, i, k], [Z, k+1, j] \gg$, σ_0 is defined by

$$\sigma(r) \cdot \sum_{\xi_Y \in \mathcal{D}([Y,i,k])} \sigma_0(\xi_Y) \cdot \sum_{\xi_Z \in \mathcal{D}([Z,k+1,j])} \sigma_0(\xi_Z) \ ,$$

and by $\sigma(r)$ for terminal decomposition $\xi = \langle r, 0 \rangle$.

Then for any decomposition ξ, the sampling probability is set to $P_s(\xi) = \dfrac{\sigma_0(\xi)}{\sum_{\xi' \in \mathcal{D}(\xi)} \sigma_0(\xi')}$ which actually is a probability over all the possible choices at a given point of the derivation extraction (i.e. on $\mathcal{D}(\xi)$). In the case of DOP, notice how this differs from Bod's sampling explained in the former section: σ_0 is indeed the inside probability of a subderivation whereas, in Bod's case, it is replaced by P_{DOP}, the probability of the subderivation *in the corresponding derivation currently being extracted* (which, in the most general case, is different from its inside probability). Rephrasing what R Bod said, the correct sentence would have been "*a subderivation that has n times as large an* <u>inside</u> *probability as another subderivation should also have n times as large a chance to be chosen as this other subderivation*".

Coming back to the general case, what is the sampling probability of a given derivation d? Each decomposition being chosen independently (cf the sampling algorithm given in table 1), the sampling probability of a derivation is the product of the sampling probabilities of the chosen decomposition: $P_s(d) = \displaystyle\prod_{\xi \in d} P_s(\xi)$.

It can be shown by induction [8] that $P_s(d)$ is equal to $\dfrac{1}{\sum_{\bar{d}}\sigma(\bar{d})}\prod_{r_j\in d}\sigma(r_j)$ which

actually is $\dfrac{\sigma(d)}{\sum_{\bar{d}}\sigma(\bar{d})}$.

The sampling probability of a class $\bar{d}'$, being the sum of sampling probabilities

of its derivations, is then $P_s(\bar{d}') = \displaystyle\sum_{d\in\bar{d}'}\dfrac{\sigma(d)}{\sum_{\bar{d}}\sigma(\bar{d})} = \dfrac{1}{\sum_{\bar{d}}\sigma(\bar{d})}\sigma(\bar{d}')$, i.e. the score

of the class over the sum of all scores of all classes.

This sampling method therefore behaves as a multinomial random variable with K modalities (K being the number of possible classes) whose parameters

are $\dfrac{\sigma(\bar{d})}{\sum_{\bar{d}'}\sigma(\bar{d}')}$. This is precisely the reason why the method can furthermore be

controlled.

4.2   Control for Exact Sampling Method

The whole story consist in *controlling* the convergence of the sampling, i.e. determining the number of samples so as to **ensure** that the most frequent class in the sample actually is the best one.[14] This is a classical problem of statistical ordering for this problem is exactly the same as finding the most probable modality in a K-modal binomial law.

The control method proposed by R. Bod for his sampling in the DOP-MPP framework is an illustration of such a mechanism. However (and regardless of the fact that the sampling probability he used does not converge to the right score) the estimation of sampling probabilities themselves is wrong, estimating the error $\sum_{i>1}(1 - (\sqrt{p_{[1]}} - \sqrt{p_{[i]}})^2)^n$ by $\sum_{i>1}(1 - (\sqrt{f_{[1]}} - \sqrt{f_{[i]}})^2)^n$.[15] It is very difficult to evaluate the impact of such an error on the results obtained. Moreover the purely sequential aspect of his methods does not permit to *a priori* compute the size of the sample needed for right estimation.

For all the reasons, it is important to use more sophisticated methods as, for instance, the ones existing in the statistic literature. We will explain only one of these, the most powerful: the Bechhofer-Kiefel-Sobel truncated methods (BKST) [2] which is a sequential truncated sampling method that combines two other methods: BEM and BKS sampling.

BEM Sampling. It is known that for any multinomial random variable with K modalities (as it is the case for classes of derivations) such as $p_{[1]} \geq \theta\, p_{[2]}$

---

[14] even if P_s corresponds to the correct score, this does not ensure that for a given sample the most frequent class in that sample is actually the best one since for a given sample the most probable (with respect to P_s) class in not necessary the most frequent in that sample.

[15] where n is the number of samples, $f_{[i]}$ is the frequency in the sample of the i-th most frequent class (in that sample) and $p_{[i]}$ its theoretical probability to be sampled.

with $\theta > 1$,[16] the probability that the most frequent modality in a sample if effectively the most probable one is always bigger than the probability P_{min} of selecting the best one in the case where all but this best one are equal [14]. This lower bound P_{min} can more be *a priori* computed as a function of K,[17] θ and n [1].

The non-sequential BEM controlled sampling method is then as simple as:

1. choose *a priori* some value for $\theta = \frac{p_{[1]}}{p_{[2]}}$ and a control error probability P,
2. compute (from tables) the smallest sample size n so that $P \leq P_{min}(K, \theta, n)$,
3. determine the best class as the most frequent one on a sample of n classes.

BKS Sampling. BKS is a sequential sampling method that relies on the following result: for any multinomial random variable with K modalities such as $p_{[1]} \geq \theta p_{[2]}$ with $\theta > 1$, the probability that the most frequent modality in a sample if effectively the most probable one is always bigger than $\frac{1}{1+Z}$ with

$$Z = \sum_{i=2}^{K} (\frac{1}{\theta})^{(n_{[1]} - n_{[i]})} \ [3].^{18} \text{ The BKS method is then:}$$

1. choose *a priori* some value for $\theta = \frac{p_{[1]}}{p_{[2]}}$ and a control error probability P,
2. keep on sampling, updating the $n_{[i]}$'s[19] and Z, as long as $\frac{1}{1+Z} < P$,
3. determine the best class as the most frequent one.

BKST. BKST is a sequential truncated sampling method that combine BEM and BKS: BEM is included in BKS, adding to the stopping condition of BKS the BEM criterion on the maximal (precomputed) sample size. BKST is therefore guaranteed to stop at the minimal stopping time of BEM and BKS.

If we really have $p_{[1]} \geq \theta p_{[2]}$ then the class chosen with any of these methods is really the best one (with a error probability P).

4.3   Convergence of Sampling Methods

In addition to the fact that exact sampling allows perfect control, another advantage of this method is its much faster convergence to the correct distribution of classes. This can be illustrated by the simple simulation results given in figure 4.3 where 20 runs of 5000 sample of a single random variable have been produced using either the rescored sampling method or the exact one. It clearly appears on that figure that the variance (resp. the convergence rate) of the first one is much bigger (resp. smaller) than for the exact (not rescored) one.

---

[16] $p_{[1]}, ..., p_{[K]}$ being the K parameters of the multinomial in decreasing order: $p_{[1]} \geq ... \geq p_{[K]}$ (with $p_{[1]} + ... + p_{[K]} = 1$).
[17] If K is not known *a priori*, it can be replaced without restriction by some upper bound.
[18] $n_{[i]}$ being the i-th number of occurrence of a class in the sample, in decreasing order.
[19] not only the values but also the order.

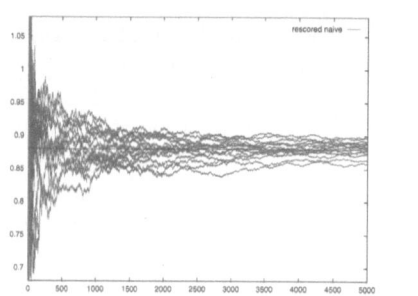 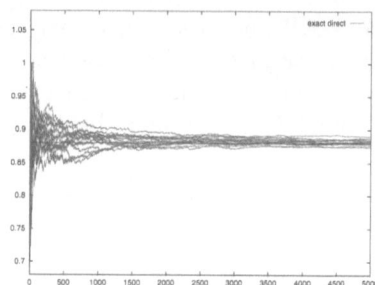

Fig. 1. (score .vs. sample size) Comparison of convergence of the rescored sampling method (left) and the exact method (right) on 20 runs of 5000 samples converging to the known score of 0.88: exact method converges much faster.

This fact is easy to understand intuitively: rescoring is needed when the sampling probability does not lead to the correct score, which means that the most frequent samples are not the correct ones. Therfore, in the case where rescoring is needed, the good exemples are less frequent than they should be (if the sampling probability would have been correct). Therefore more samples are needed to have a good approximation of the (correct) best class.

5   Conclusion

This paper presents three important results for the approximation of solutions of NP-hard maximization problems in the framework of weighted parsing:

1. We have shown that Monte-Carlo sampling techniques can actually be implemented in such cases. We furthermore derive the relationship between (local) sampling probability and the score of a class;
2. We have computed what the sampling probability of a decomposition has to be so that the sampling probability of a class exactly is the score of that class (among the sum of the scores). This sampling strategy significantly differs from the former existing ones, showing by the same way the bias induced by such methods.
3. Finally we have presented a method that allow to control the sample quality so as to be sure (with some *a priori* known control error) that the most frequent class in the sample is the best one.

These results allow experiments on and practical use of, for instance, SCFG-MPS word-graph extraction (useful in speech recognition) or STSG-MPP extraction (useful for the DOP model), grounded on a more robust and theoretically grounded basis.

References

1. R.E. Bechhofer, S. Elmaghraby, and N. Morse. A single-sample multiple-decision procedure for selecting the multinomial event which has the largest probability. *Ann. Math. Statist.*, 30:102–119, 1959.
2. R.E. Bechhofer and D.M. Goldsman. Truncation of the Bechhofer-Kiefer-Sobel sequential procedure for selecting the multinomial event which has the largest probability. *Communications in Statistics: simulation and computation*, 14(2):283–315, 1985.
3. R.E. Bechhofer, J. Kiefer, and M. Sobel. *Sequential Identification and Ranking Procedures*. University of Chicago Press, Chicago, 1968.
4. R. Bod. Applying Monte Carlo techniques to Data Oriented Parsing. In *Proceedings Computational Linguistics in the Netherlands*, Tilburg (The Netherlands), 1992.
5. R. Bod. *Enriching Linguistics with Statistics: Performance Models of Natural Language*. Academische Pers, Amsterdam (The Netherlands), 1995.
6. R. Bod. *Beyond Grammar, An Experience-Based Theory of Language*. Number 88 in CSLI Lecture Notes. CSLI Publications, Standford (CA), 1998.
7. R. Bod and R. Scha. Data-Oriented language processing: An overview. Technical Report LP-96-13, Departement of Computational Linguistics, University of Amsterdam, 1996. cmp-lg/9611003.
8. J.-C. Chappelier and M. Rajman. Extraction stochastique d'arbres d'analyse pour le modèle DOP. In *Proc. of 5ème conférence sur le Traitement Automatique du Langage Naturel (TALN98)*, pages 52–61, Paris (France), June 1998.
9. J.-C. Chappelier and M. Rajman. A generalized CYK algorithm for parsing stochastic CFG. In *TAPD'98 Workshop*, pages 133–137, Paris (France), 1998.
10. J.-C. Chappelier, M. Rajman, R. Aragues, and A. Rozenknop. Lattice parsing for speech recognition. In *Proc. of 6ème conférence sur le Traitement Automatique du Langage Naturel (TALN'99)*, pages 95–104, July 1999.
11. A. Corazza, R. Demori, R. Gretter, and G. Satta. Optimal probabilistic evaluation functions for search controlled by stochastic context-free grammars. *IEEE Trans. on Pattern Analysis and Machine Intelligence*, 16(10):1018–1027, October 1994.
12. J. Goodman. *Parsing Inside-Out*. PhD thesis, Harvard University, May 1998. cmp-lg/9805007.
13. F. Jelinek, J. D. Lafferty, and R. L. Mercer. Basic methods of probabilistic context-free grammars. In P. Laface and R. De Mori, editors, *Speech Recognition and Understanding: Recent Advances, Trends and Applications*, volume 75 of *F: Computer and System Science*. Springer, 1992.
14. H. Kesten and N. Morse. A property of the multinomial distribution. *Ann. Math. Statist.*, 30:120–127, 1959.
15. W. Kuich. Semirings and formal power series: Their relevance to formal languages and automata. In G. Rozenberg and A. Salomaa, editors, *Handbook of formal languages*, volume 1, chapter 9, pages 609–677. Springer-Verlag, 1997.
16. Yves Schabes. Stochastic lexicalized tree-adjoining grammars. In *Proc. 14th Int. Conf. of Computationnal Linguistics (COLING)*, pages 426–432, Nantes (France), August 1992.
17. K. Sima'an. Computational complexity of probabilistic disambiguation by means of tree grammars. In *Proceedings of COLING'96*, Copenhagen (Denmark), 1996. cmp-lg/9606019.
18. A. Stolcke. An efficient probabilistic context-free parsing algorithm that computes prefix probabilities. *Computational Linguistics*, 21(2):165–201, 1995.

Preprocessing for Unification Parsing of Spoken Language

Mark-Jan Nederhof

DFKI, Stuhlsatzenhausweg 3, D-66123 Saarbrücken, Germany
nederhof@dfki.de

Abstract. Wordgraphs are structures that may be output by speech recognisers. We discuss various methods for turning wordgraphs into smaller structures. One of these methods is novel; this method relies on a new kind of determinization of acyclic weighted finite automata that is language-preserving but not fully weight-preserving, and results in smaller automata than in the case of traditional determinization of weighted finite automata. We present empirical data comparing the respective methods.

The methods are relevant for systems in which wordgraphs form the input to kinds of syntactic analysis that are very time consuming, such as unification parsing.

1   Introduction

Wordgraphs are weighted, labelled, directed, acyclic graphs that form the output of a certain type of speech recogniser [2]; they are also called word lattices. The nodes in a wordgraph roughly correspond to points in time during an utterance from the user. An edge connecting two nodes is labelled by a word which the speech recogniser proposes may have been uttered between the corresponding points in time.

The weight attached to an edge indicates a measure of confidence that the edge and its label participate in a path in the graph that corresponds to the string of words that were actually uttered. For many speech recognisers, this weight is the negative logarithm of the probability, according to some appropriate probabilistic model. This means that for combining edges into paths (see below), one should apply addition on the weights of the constituent edges in order to determine the weights of the paths. Further, lower weights indicate higher levels of confidence.

An edge may also be labelled by a symbol indicating that *no* word may have been uttered between the corresponding points in time. This symbol we will write as ε.

The wordgraphs involved in our experiments are connected and have exactly one initial node, i.e. a node without incoming edges, and exactly one final node, i.e. a node without outgoing edges. The initial and final nodes correspond to the points in time at the beginning and end, respectively, of the utterance. We will refer to a path from the initial node to the final node as a *complete path*.

D.N. Christodoulakis (Ed.): NLP 2000, LNCS 1835, pp. 118–129, 2000.
© Springer-Verlag Berlin Heidelberg 2000

Wordgraphs may serve as input to syntactic analysis. In the VERBMOBIL project, deep syntactic analysis is performed on the basis of the grammatical formalism HPSG, which requires expensive unification [11]. Parsing is tabulated, which allows sharing of the computation for a parse of a subpath in the graph when the subpath is extended to several larger paths, or when the parse is extended to several larger parses. Furthermore, when between two nodes several parses are found that are similar, in some appropriate sense, then the parses may be packed together, in order to save duplicated efforts when the parses are further extended to cover larger paths in the wordgraph. (The issues of "sharing" and "packing" are discussed by [5]. For packing in the context of unification, we refer to the literature on "subsumption" [14,4].)

Since a wordgraph may consist of many nodes and many edges connecting them, the number of complete paths may be quite large. To some extent, tabulation in the parser may prevent duplicated effort for subpaths, avoiding treatment for each complete path individually. However, in practice many subpaths in the wordgraph involving distinct nodes have identical labels attached to the edges, and in such a case, tabulation cannot avoid duplicated effort, since sharing and packing are only effective with regard to parses between an identical pair of nodes.

In this paper we will discuss methods to turn wordgraphs into simpler structures, in which fewer distinct subpaths have identical labels, so that tabular parsing will lead to less duplicated effort. None of these methods eliminate any string of labels, contrary to some well-known techniques as described for example in [13]. The motivation is that the weights of edges should merely direct the search for grammatical phrases, in the sense that the lowest-weighted paths are to be investigated first, but high weights should not lead to a path being taken out of consideration; a path with a relatively high weight is still considered to be preferable if the HPSG parser is less successful in finding grammatical phrases for all alternative paths with lower weights.

The theory of parsing of wordgraphs is well-developed, for simple formalisms such as context-free grammars (cf. [3]) as well as for unification grammars. Yet in practice, it is often too expensive to apply unification parsing to spoken language. This research is intended to reduce the gap between theory and practice.

2 Investigated Methods

For all of the five investigated methods, the resulting structure does not satisfy the restriction that there should be a unique final node in the wordgraph. This is related to the elimination of edges labelled by ε, following the first method. This first method is also an implicit first phase of the remaining four methods. In the fifth method furthermore, a different concept for edges is introduced.

2.1 Elimination of Epsilon Edges

Edges labelled by ε, henceforth called *epsilon edges*, represent intervals when no word may have been uttered. In our parsers, such edges themselves are not treated as meaningful for the purpose of e.g. segmentation (i.e. dividing an utterance into consecutive sentences or phrases), and therefore they may be safely eliminated from the wordgraph without affecting the functionality of the system as a whole. Also edges labelled by interjections indicating hesitation (e.g. "h'm") can be treated in this way.

Elimination of epsilon transitions as known in the area of finite automata can be straightforwardly applied here (see e.g. [12,15]). Our implementation investigates paths consisting of zero or more epsilon edges followed by an edge labelled $a \neq \varepsilon$. Such a path in the old wordgraph is replaced in the new wordgraph by an edge labelled a connecting the two nodes at the beginning and end of the old path. The weight of the new edge is the sum of those of the old edges.

For paths in the old wordgraph that consist of epsilon edges and that end on the former final node, we need an extension of the concept of wordgraph. In the new data structure, nodes are themselves labelled by weights. A finite weight attached to a node indicates that the node is final, and the utterance of the user may end there with a level of confidence indicated by the weight. There may be one or more of such final nodes, and a final node may have outgoing edges. For a complete path through the wordgraph starting from the (still unique) initial node and ending in a final node n, the total weight is given by the sum of the weights of the edges plus the weight of n. For a related type of finite automaton, see [12].

During epsilon edge elimination, the weight of a path consisting of epsilon edges starting in node n in the old wordgraph and ending in the old final node is translated to a weight for n in the new wordgraph. If more than one such weight is found for n, we choose the lowest.

Elimination of epsilon edges preserves strings of labels and their weights. For example, if we choose a path in the old wordgraph such that its weight is minimal, and do the same for the new wordgraph, then the corresponding weights will be identical, and the strings of (non-epsilon) labels of the paths are identical.[1]

In some cases, for a given pair of nodes n_1 and n_2 and a label a, the new wordgraph contains more than one edge between n_1 and n_2 labelled by a. Then, only the one with the lowest weight needs to be preserved. However, such edges are found too seldom in the cases we have investigated to warrant the computational overhead of finding them.

2.2   Automaton Minimisation

Apart from the weights, a wordgraph can be seen as a nondeterministic finite automaton accepting a set of strings. Finding an alternative automaton for the

---

[1] For the minimal weight (modulo a small factor to allow for inaccuracies coming from floating-point operations), there may be more than one path. In this case, in the two wordgraphs two corresponding *sets* of strings of labels are found to be identical. In the experiments reported in Sect. 3, we determined a unique lowest-weighted string of labels by means of the lexicographical ordering.

same set of strings having a minimal number of nodes is prohibitively expensive [10], but we can effectively compute a new automaton for the same language that is deterministic and minimal in the number of nodes. One such method for computing minimal deterministic automata was proposed by [6]: the source automaton is made deterministic, first from right to left, considering the reversed automaton, then from left to right. For each pass of determinization, the powerset construction can be applied. This can be generalised to weighted automata, as demonstrated in [12].

In the two applications of determinization, subsets of states from the input automaton are turned into states of the determinized automaton. In order to preserve the weights that the automata assign to strings, one needs to associate the states in a subset with "residual weights" that need to be taken into account at a later transition or at the weight of a final node. When we encounter several subsets with identical states, but distinct associated weights, then most published determinization algorithms (e.g. [12]) would produce distinct states in the determinized automaton, one for each occurrence of the subset with a distinct assignment of residual weights, or at least for each assignment of which the distance to any other assignment for the same subset exceeds a certain fixed number ϵ, as was made explicit in [8]. This means the resulting automaton may have significantly more states than in the unweighted case. (It has been demonstrated by [7] in the case of wordgraphs that it may be the assignment of weights, rather than the topology of the automaton, that is mostly responsible for growth of the determinized and minimised automaton.) Since our objective is to obtain small wordgraphs, this kind of determinization may be undesirable.

We have therefore investigated an alternative kind of determinization for (acyclic) weighted automata, which is presented in Fig. 1, combined with reversal of the automaton. For an edge e labelled a, leading from node n_1 to n_2, and with weight w, we write $label(e) = a$, $from(e) = n_1$, $to(e) = n_2$, and $weight(e) = w$. For a final node n, $weight(n)$ denotes its weight. We assume there is a topological sort that assigns a number $number(n)$ to each node n [9]; commonly, the output of a speech recogniser already incorporates a topological sort of the nodes.

The algorithm uses an agenda Q of nodes of the new graph that are as yet unprocessed; nodes of the new graph are, as before, sets of nodes of the old graph. The initial node of the new graph is the set of final nodes in the old graph (lines 1 and 3). Line 6 selects a node q to be processed. The topological sort and the condition in line 7 ensure that after processing of q, no nodes will be processed from which edges ensue that lead to q. The reason this needs to be ensured is that, upon processing of q, we need access to the value $Ws(q)$, which is the set of all assignments of residual weights to nodes in q, which means we do not want any assignments to be added to $Ws(q)$ after q is processed. (By indexing elements q in Q by the nodes $n \in q$ that are maximal with regard to the topological sort, lines 6 and 7 can be realized with low costs.)

The first value of the form $Ws(q)$ is determined in line 2, where the residual weights of nodes are their weights as final nodes in the old graph; where this is

(0) initialize the new graph to be empty;
(1) **let** $q_0 = \{n \mid weight(n) < \infty\}$;
(2) **let** $Ws(q_0) = \{\{(n, w) \mid n \in q_0 \wedge w = weight(n)\}\}$;
(3) make q_0 to be the initial node in the new graph;
(4) **let** $Q = \{q_0\}$;
(5) **while** $Q \neq \emptyset$
(6) **do** remove an element q from Q which is such that
(7) $\quad\quad\quad\quad \neg \exists q' \in Q[\max_{n' \in q'} number(n') > \max_{n \in q} number(n)]$;
(8) $\quad$ **let** $W = \{(n, w) \mid n \in q \wedge w = \frac{\Sigma_{W' \in Ws(q)} W'(n)}{|Ws(q)|}\}$;
(9) $\quad$ **let** $E = \{e \mid to(e) \in q\}$;
(10) $\quad$ **let** $A = \{a \mid \exists e \in E[label(e) = a]\}$;
(11) $\quad$ **foreach** $a \in A$
(12) $\quad$ **do let** $E' = \{e \in E \mid label(e) = a\}$;
(13) $\quad\quad$ **let** $q' = \{n \mid \exists e \in E'[from(e) = n]\}$;
(14) $\quad\quad$ **let** $W' = \{(n, w) \mid n \in q' \wedge w = \min_{e \in E' \text{ s.t. } from(e) = n} weight(e) + W(to(e))\}$;
(15) $\quad\quad$ **let** $z = \frac{\Sigma_{n \in q'} W'(n)}{|q'|}$;
(16) $\quad\quad$ **let** $W'' = \{(n, w - z) \mid (n, w) \in W'\}$;
(17) $\quad\quad$ create an edge e' in the new graph with
(18) $\quad\quad\quad\quad from(e') = q,\ to(e') = q',\ label(e') = a,\ weight(e') = z$;
(19) $\quad\quad$ **if** set q' had not yet been seen
(20) $\quad\quad$ **then** add q' as node in the new graph;
(21) $\quad\quad\quad\quad$ **let** $Q = Q \cup \{q'\}$; **let** $Ws(q') = \{W''\}$
(22) $\quad\quad$ **else let** $Ws(q') = Ws(q') \cup \{W''\}$
(23) $\quad\quad$ **end**
(24) $\quad$ **end**;
(25) $\quad$ **if** q contains initial node n_0 in old graph
(26) $\quad$ **then** make q to be a final node with $weight(q) = W(n_0)$
(27) $\quad$ **end**
(28) **end**

Fig. 1. Reversal and determinization of a wordgraph.

more convenient, we represent functions from nodes to residual weights as pairs of nodes and weights.

In line 8 we see that if $Ws(q)$ for some node q contains several assignments, then to each node $n \in q$ we assign the average weight. To an edge e' in the new graph that leads from q to node q', line 15 assigns the weight z, which is chosen such that the residual weights in W'' that we compute for q' average to 0. This will allow a fair combination, in line 8 for a future iteration of the loop, of W'' with assignments in $Ws(q')$ that originate in some other (past or future) iteration.

The algorithm differs from traditional determinization of weighted automata in that only one node is created for each set q, as opposed to one node for each q and each assignment of residual weights separately. Note further that our algorithm cannot guarantee that $weight(q) \geq 0$ for all newly created final nodes q, nor that $weight(e') \geq 0$ for all newly created edges e'. If this would pose a problem to algorithms that process wordgraphs (e.g. the syntactic analysis), then the idea of "pushing" [12] can be used to remove the negative weights.

This method preserves the set of strings of labels for complete paths, but unlike epsilon edge elimination, there is a loss of accuracy of the associated weights, due to the treatment of the $Ws(q)$ that contain more than one element. In the sequel, we will refer to this method as the fa-method, and to the more traditional determinization and minimisation of weighted finite automata, by means of two non-approximating passes of reversal/determinization, as the wfa-method. We did however not implement the minimisation proposed in Section 3.7 of [12], which gives the same end result as the wfa-method, but may be faster in some practical cases.

2.3   Node Merging

The wordgraphs found in practice contain many edges with identical labels that overlap in the time interval they cover. A simple heuristics to simplify a word-graph is to merge a pair of nodes if they are both at the beginning or at the end of a pair of such overlapping edges. A node n_2 is merged into node n_1 by changing the incoming and outgoing edges of n_2 to be new incoming and outgoing edges of n_1, respectively; node n_2 is thereafter eliminated from the graph. If this leads to two edges with the same label and between the same pair of nodes, one of them is eliminated. (Some kind of merging of nodes is often already performed by speech recognisers, before they output the wordgraphs that are the subject of this paper.)

That our realization of this heuristics cannot introduce cycles is ensured by abstaining from merging a node n_2 into a node n_1 if a fixed topological sort '$number$' of nodes in the graph would be violated afterwards; that the topological sort is preserved is a sufficient, though not necessary, condition for the graph to remain free of cycles. Specifically, for the case that $number(n_1) < number(n_2)$, we check whether all the begin nodes of incoming edges of n_2 precede n_1:

$$\forall n[\exists e[from(e) = n \wedge to(e) = n_2] \Rightarrow number(n) < number(n_1)]$$

If this holds, then n_2 can be safely merged into n_1. In the case that $number(n_2) < number(n_1)$, we check whether:

$$\forall n[\exists e[from(e) = n_2 \wedge to(e) = n] \Rightarrow number(n_1) < number(n)]$$

If this holds, then n_2 can be safely merged into n_1.

In more detail, the method can be described as follows. We treat nodes one by one starting at the initial node, following the topological sort. For each node n, we investigate the set of outgoing edges twice. In the first phase, for each edge e_1 we try to find an overlapping edge e_2 with the same label seen before (when there is more than one such edge, we take the one most recently seen), and we consider $n_1 = to(e_1)$ and $n_2 = to(e_2)$. Provided the topological sort can be preserved, we merge n_1 into n_2, or otherwise, provided the topological sort can be preserved in this alternative way, we merge n_2 into n_1. If in neither case the topological sort can be preserved, the nodes are not merged.

If a node n' is merged into n'', this means that each edge e with $from(e) = n'$ is changed such that $from(e) = n''$; if there already is an edge e' such that $from(e') = n''$ and furthermore $to(e') = to(e)$ and $label(e') = label(e)$, then only the edge that has the better weight of the two is retained (see below for what it means for an edge to have a better weight). Similarly, each edge e with $to(e) = n'$ is changed such that $to(e) = n''$; again, if this leads to a pair of edges that are identical in '$from$', 'to', and '$label$', then the one with the better weight is retained.

In the second phase, we do the same for each outgoing edge of the current node n, except that now the begin nodes of the overlapping edges may be merged.

When a node n_1 is merged into a node n_2, then the edges connected to n_1 are made longer or shorter in terms of the time interval they cover. We should adjust the weight of such an edge in proportion to the change in the amount of time that is covered, under the assumption that for the speech recogniser the average weight assigned to an edge is linear to the time interval that is covered. We further assume that the speech recogniser provides an assignment from nodes n to discrete points in time denoted as $time(n)$. This assignment may or may not be equal to the topological sort '$number$'.

To simplify the algorithm, we first replace each weight w of an edge e by $\frac{w}{time(to(e))-time(from(e))}$, the "weight per time unit". This new value determines which edge to preserve if two edges result that are identical in '$from$', 'to' and '$label$'; the lower value indicates the better edge. After nodes have been merged where possible, each "weight per time unit" for an edge e is translated back to an actual weight by multiplying by $time(to(e)) - time(from(e))$. Similar readjustments of weights for another method are discussed in the following section.

2.4 Hypergraphs

The use of hypergraphs for representing the result of simplifying wordgraphs has been proposed by [1]. As in the method of node merging above, edges overlapping in time and with identical labels are merged. Here however, the data structure differs substantially from the wordgraphs we have discussed in previous sections. In hypergraphs, edges can have several begin nodes and several end nodes. For example, for a pair of overlapping edges in the original wordgraph, the resulting hypergraph may contain a single edge, with two begin nodes and two end nodes.

Some degree of accuracy is lost when transforming a wordgraph into a hypergraph. First, for a certain edge in the hypergraph (henceforth called a *hyperedge*), the information which individual begin node connects to which individual end node in the original wordgraph is no longer available. Thereby, new strings of labels for complete paths may be introduced. Secondly, weights from the original wordgraph are preserved in a merely simplified form in the hypergraph by attaching a single weight to each hyperedge. This weight is the lowest weight per time unit for each of the corresponding edges in the original wordgraph, much as in the previous section.

Finding paths in a hypergraph involves combining pairs of adjacent hyperedges, where a pair of hyperedges is defined to be adjacent if at least one end node of the first hyperedge is also a begin node of the second. The structure representing the combination of adjacent hyperedges can itself be seen as a hyperedge, of which the begin nodes are the begin nodes of the first hyperedge in the pair, and the end node are those in the second hyperedge. Henceforth we will refer to a hyperedge constructed from hyperedges in the hypergraph as a *parse edge*.

The weight of a parse edge is computed from the weights of the two hyperedges it is constructed from, according to somewhat involved formulae presented by [1]; weights for parse edges, like weights for hyperedges in the hypergraph, represent weights per time unit with respect to the paths that would be found in the original wordgraph.

In the experiments to be discussed shortly, we assume that paths are constructed strictly from left to right, as follows. First we consider hyperedges that have the initial node among the begin nodes. These edges are then combined to the right with edges from the hypergraph. This is repeated until no more new parse edges can be found. That paths are formed in this way is a reasonable assumption, although for an actual parsing algorithm this may lead to a slightly different computation of paths and consequently to different weights.

For the weight of a complete path we select a parse edge that has the initial node among the begin nodes and a final node among the end nodes; we multiply its value, which is a "weight per time unit", with the number of time units between this pair of nodes and add to this the weight of the final node. (In case there are several final nodes among the end nodes we take the one resulting in the lowest weight.)

3   Empirical Results

The effectiveness of hypergraphs in reducing the number of edges and thereby the decrease in time and space requirements for exhaustive parsing has been shown by [1]. From our perspective however, the data presented there does not show unequivocally that hypergraphs are suitable in general for spoken-language systems, for a number of reasons. First, the average size of the investigated wordgraphs is very large, viz. 1828 edges per graph. Such large wordgraphs are untypical for the speech recognisers available to us.

Secondly, the quality of the paths in the hypergraphs was not discussed. In particular, it is unclear how many strings of labels with low weights may be introduced in the hypergraphs that were not in the original wordgraphs. Such strings may increase the frequency that a spoken-language system misinterprets an utterance from the user.

Thirdly, the number of parse edges constructed by exhaustive parsing may far exceed the number that is investigated in practice. Often parsers stop investigating the search space once an acceptable parse for some path has been found, making use of a strategy of first investigating paths with lowest weights.

Furthermore, for unification parsing, often only a few paths can be investigated before a time-out is reached. Therefore, what one is interested in is foremost how many distinct strings of labels can be investigated in a given amount of time, rather than how much time is consumed by investigating all paths.

We conclude that an appropriate wordgraph would offer many *different* strings of labels among the lowest-weighted paths, and these strings should be close to the actual utterance. In light of the discussion in Sect. 1, we would also prefer wordgraphs in which paths that share substrings in their strings of labels often also share corresponding subpaths, which improves sharing of computation. Further, small numbers of nodes benefit packing of subparses.

In this section, we present the results of a new set of experiments that investigate the appropriateness for our purposes of the five methods for reducing the size of wordgraphs. The experiments were performed on a set of 1717 wordgraphs, with an average of 74 edges per graph. The average width, i.e. the number of edges divided by the length in words of the manually transcribed utterance, was 4.5. On the average, 21 % of all edges were epsilon edges, and the number of non-epsilon edges divided by the number of *distinct* non-epsilon labels was 1.9, which means that each label occurred almost twice, on the average.

We will first consider a property that is independent from any particular parsing algorithm, viz. the *word accuracy* of the string for the best complete path through a preprocessed wordgraph with respect to that in the original wordgraph.

Commonly, word accuracy is defined as follows. For a pair of strings, we defined the *distance* as the minimum number of substitutions, insertions and deletions needed to turn one string into the other. This quantity can be effectively computed along the lines of [16]. The *word accuracy* of a string x with regard to a string y is defined to be $1 - \frac{d}{n}$, where d is the distance between x and y and n is the length of y. This implies that the accuracy is undefined when y is the empty string, and therefore excluded from consideration would be wordgraphs that contain a path from the initial node to the final node consisting of epsilon edges. We therefore redefine the accuracy for a pair of strings x and y as 1 if both x and y are the empty string, and otherwise as $1 - \frac{d}{n}$, where n is now the average of the lengths of x and y.

Apart from epsilon edge elimination and **wfa**, which by nature do not affect word accuracy, accuracy decreases for all methods of preprocessing, as shown in the second column of Tab. 1. The strongest decrease of accuracy is observed for hypergraphs, and the weakest decrease for **fa**. The word accuracy of the best path relative to the manually transcribed utterance was also measured, but this did not result in any significant differences between the respective methods; it seems that the original wordgraphs were of too poor quality to reliably measure the impact of the methods on the word accuracy relative to the transcribed utterance, which was around 0.41 for the **epsilon** method.

Further, we counted the number of nodes in a wordgraph and the number of edges, which correlate roughly to the amount of packing and sharing, respectively, that can be applied in the case of tabular parsing. As can be seen in the

method	accuracy	factor increase # nodes	factor increase # edges	time (msec)	# parses	# distinct strings
epsilon	1.00	0.90	0.89	357	15.3	9.4
fa	0.98	0.78	0.76	817	30.2	11.0
wfa	1.00	0.94	1.12	1839	14.5	9.0
merge	0.92	0.72	0.67	480	15.1	9.3
hyper	0.74	1.05	0.51	418	-	-

Table 1. Behaviour of the respective methods.

third column of Tab. 1, the number of nodes decreases by 10 % after elimination of epsilon edges. A further reduction is achieved by **fa** and **merge**, but a subsequent increase results from **wfa**. (Remember that **epsilon** is an implicit first phase of the other methods.) In terms of the number of nodes, the size of a hypergraph is by nature identical to that of the wordgraph from which it is constructed, which is in this case the wordgraph as it results from elimination of epsilon edges. For parsing a hypergraph however, we are more interested in the number of sets of nodes that may occur as the set of begin nodes or the set of end nodes at hyperedges, since each parse edge is associated with a pair of such sets, rather than a pair of nodes as in the case of conventional wordgraphs. For hypergraphs, this number of distinct sets is the quantity that is indicated in the table. We see that it is higher than the number of nodes for the other methods.

A different situation is found with regard to the number of edges, in the fourth column. Here, the smallest average size resulted in the case of hypergraphs, and the largest in the case of **wfa**, which far exceeded even the size of the original graph, on the average.

We also measured the average time needed for applying the methods to the wordgraphs. The results are given in the fifth column, in msec. The time consumption in relation to the size of a wordgraph (rounded off to the nearest multiple of 10) is presented in Fig. 2. That the time consumption for all of the methods seems rather high is due to the fact that the implementation is merely a prototype, and the load on the machine was particularly high at the time the experiments were performed. However, since the implementations of **wfa** and **fa** share almost all of their code, we can be confident that the comparison between at least these two methods is fair, and this comparison shows that **wfa** is much more sensitive to an increase in the size of wordgraphs than **fa**.

For the first 500 of the 1717 wordgraphs, we have performed experiments on an HPSG parser [11], with a grammar for German. The parser is driven by an agenda that gives priority to paths with low weights. A realistic time-bound is set. When this bound is reached, the (partial) parses that have been found are retrieved.

Each of the 500 wordgraphs was processed by means of each of the first four methods. We had to leave the method **hyper** out of consideration, since the HPSG parser itself would have had to be altered in order to handle hypergraphs, which was not within our reach. We measured the number of parses that were

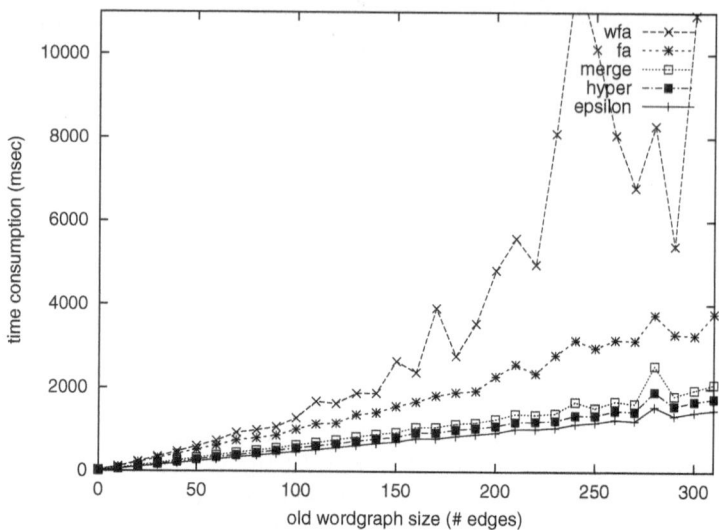

Fig. 2. Time consumption, against the size of wordgraphs.

found, and the number of *distinct* strings of labels that corresponded to these parses. The results are reported in the two right-most columns of Tab. 1.

Regrettably, the results do not match our expectations that more distinct strings of labels would be found among the computed parses in the case of more compact wordgraphs. Although we do find more distinct strings for **fa** than for **wfa**, the ratio to the total number of computed parses is much smaller. Furthermore, although the size of wordgraphs in the case of **merge** is much smaller than in the case of **wfa**, about the same number of parses is found, and these correspond to a comparable number of distinct strings. At this point it is difficult to provide an explanation. This is partly due to the fact that the HPSG parser consists of a number of distinct components that cooperate in a subtle way to divide the available time over the different tasks that have to be performed. Further investigation is needed to determine e.g. what properties of the wordgraphs in the case of **fa** interact with which components from the parser to cause the substantial increase in the number of computed parses.

Acknowledgements

Bernd Kiefer provided much help in performing the experiments with the HPSG parser. I gratefully acknowledge fruitful discussions with Hans-Ulrich Krieger, Mehryar Mohri, Jakub Piskorski, Michael Riley, and Thomas Schaaf.

This work was funded by the German Federal Ministry of Education, Science, Research and Technology (BMBF) in the framework of the VERBMOBIL Project under Grant 01 IV 701 V0. The author was employed at AT&T Shannon Laboratory during a part of the period this paper was written.

References

1. J.W. Amtrup and V. Weber. Time mapping with hypergraphs. In *36th Annual Meeting of the Association for Computational Linguistics and 17th International Conference on Computational Linguistics*, volume 1, pages 55–61, Montreal, Quebec, Canada, August 1998.

2. H. Aust, M. Oerder, F. Seide, and V. Steinbiss. The Philips automatic train timetable information system. *Speech Communication*, 17:249–262, 1995.

3. Y. Bar-Hillel, M. Perles, and E. Shamir. On formal properties of simple phrase structure grammars. In Y. Bar-Hillel, editor, *Language and Information: Selected Essays on their Theory and Application*, chapter 9, pages 116–150. Addison-Wesley, 1964.

4. F. Barthélemy and E. Villemonte de la Clergerie. Subsumption-oriented push-down automata. In *Programming Language Implementation and Logic Programming, 4th International Symposium*, volume 631 of *Lecture Notes in Computer Science*, pages 100–114, Leuven, Belgium, August 1992. Springer-Verlag.

5. S. Billot and B. Lang. The structure of shared forests in ambiguous parsing. In *27th Annual Meeting of the Association for Computational Linguistics, Proceedings of the Conference*, pages 143–151, Vancouver, British Columbia, Canada, June 1989.

6. J.A. Brzozowski. Canonical regular expressions and minimal state graphs for definite events. *Mathematical Theory of Automata*, 12:529–561, 1962.

7. A.L. Buchsbaum, R. Giancarlo, and J.R. Westbrook. On the determinization of weighted finite automata. In *Automata, Languages and Programming, 25th International Colloquium*, volume 1443 of *Lecture Notes in Computer Science*, pages 482–493, Aalborg, Denmark, 1998. Springer-Verlag.

8. A.L. Buchsbaum, R. Giancarlo, and J.R. Westbrook. Shrinking language models by robust approximation. In *ICASSP '98*, volume II, pages 685–688, 1998.

9. T.H. Cormen, C.E. Leiserson, and R.L. Rivest. *Introduction to Algorithms*. The MIT Press, 1990.

10. T. Jiang and B. Ravikumar. Minimal NFA problems are hard. *SIAM Journal on Computing*, 22(6):1117–1141, 1993.

11. B. Kiefer, H.-U. Krieger, J. Carroll, and R. Malouf. A bag of useful techniques for efficient and robust parsing. In *37th Annual Meeting of the Association for Computational Linguistics, Proceedings of the Conference*, Maryland, June 1999.

12. M. Mohri. Finite-state transducers in language and speech processing. *Computational Linguistics*, 23(2):269–311, 1997.

13. H. Murveit et al. Large-vocabulary dictation using SRI's DECIPHER™ speech recognition system: progressive search techniques. In *ICASSP-93*, volume II, pages 319–322, 1993.

14. S.M. Shieber. Using restriction to extend parsing algorithms for complex-feature-based formalisms. In *23rd Annual Meeting of the Association for Computational Linguistics, Proceedings of the Conference*, pages 145–152, Chicago, Illinois, USA, July 1985.

15. G. van Noord. Treatment of ε-moves in subset construction. In *Proceedings of the International Workshop on Finite State Methods in Natural Language Processing*, pages 57–68, Ankara, Turkey, June–July 1998.

16. R.A. Wagner and M.J. Fischer. The string-to-string correction problem. *Journal of the ACM*, 21(1):168–173, 1974.

A Semantic Based Approach for Spontaneous Spoken Dialogue Understanding

Mohamed Zakaria Kurdi

Groupe d'Etude pour l'Oral et le Dialogue
Laboratoire CLIPS – IMAG, BP. 53
380401, Grenoble cedex 09, France
email: zakaria.kurdi@imag
URL: http://www-geod.imag.fr/kurdi

Abstract. In this paper we present a semantic based partial parsing system for spontaneous dialogue processing. The processing is done following three main steps: at the first a pre-processing module normalizes spoken utterances from errors and extragrammaticalities. The second step consists of parsing the input utterances. Parsing is done on Semantic Tree Unification Grammar STUG. We propose this formalism as an extended version of traditional semantic grammar. The key features of this formalism are linguistic and cognitive motivation, robustness and efficiency in processing spoken language extragrammaticalities. The partial aspect of the parser is achieved via a selective strategy allowing the system to detect and process relevant islands in the utterance.Finally, the parsed utterances are associated with a semantic interpretation by a frame module.
Keywords: semantic grammar, partial parsing, spontaneous dialogue, spoken language extragrammaticalities.

1 Introduction

Interactive spoken language provides many challenges for speech processing. These systems are faced with many problems like imperfect accuracy of speech recognizers and spoken language extragrammaticalies (ellipsis, incomplete sentences, repetition, false start, etc.). In order to overcome these problems, the most common solution consists in extracting semantic information directly from speech by means of semantic based grammars, [4], [11], [12], [17], [18], [21]. Despite its real efficiency, this formalism has no real linguistic and cognitive basis. In general, the choice of semantic units is arbitrary and depends only on implementation constraints.

In this paper, we propose a partial semantic based approach. The key features of this approach are both effectiveness in real applications and cognitive and linguistic relevance.

The outline of this paper is as follow: in section one we present the hotel reservation corpus on which our system is constructed. In section two, we describe the system architecture and how it works. Finally, evaluation results and summary follow.

D.N. Christodoulakis (Ed.): NLP 2000, LNCS 1835, pp. 130-138, 2000.

2 System Architecture

As shown in Figure 1, our system contains three main components. The first one serves as a preprocessing step for allowing the parser to analyze the utterance correctly. Then parsing module associates a shallow syntactic-semantic representation (a parse tree) with the utterance and finally the *frames* module associates a deep semantic representation to the parsed utterance.

We are using the hotel reservation corpus [7] which is obtained by simulating conversations between hotel agent and client. This corpus contains 184 dialogues (385 KB of words). The training was achieved on 130 dialogues.

2.1 Speech Recognition

We are using the RAPHAEL recognition system. RAPHAEL was adapted to French on the JANUS–CMU platform by Mohammad AKBAR and Dominique Vaufreydaz [2]. It achieves a recognition rate of 96% on the C-STAR project task (touristical information seeking).

2.2 Preprocessing and Normalization

The main function of this component is the correction of Lexical Extragrammaticalities like unknown and amalgamated words and supralexical extragrammaticalities like simple repetitions, self-corrections, etc. [8].

2.3 The Semantic Tree Unification Grammar (STUG)

We propose STUG as a hybrid (syntactic-semantic) tree based formalism. The main difference between STUG and Tree Adjoining Grammar is that only substitution operation is used and the trees nodes are labeled by both syntactic and semantic labels. STUG allows a direct linearization of the semantic structure. This is possible by the reduction of the *amount* of syntactic information which becomes limited to the order's (topological) information of constituents.

Formally, STUG is equivalent to a Context Free Grammar (CFG). It can be represented by a four-tuple: (, NT, S, L_t) where:

1.   is a final set of terminal symbols;
2.   NT is final a set of non terminal symbols. Non-terminal symbols can be semantic or syntactic categories;
3.   P is a distinguished non terminal symbol (S   NT),
4. L_t is a final set of elementary trees.

Furthermore the grammar was doted by a phonetic confusion model for avoiding some recognition errors.

If we consider the functional (practical) point of view, a grammar like STUG can be defined following three factors: (1) output representation, (2) the basic unit of representation, (3) combination operation.

2.3.1   The Output of the Grammar

The grammar output is a logical representation which encodes utterance's analysis. This representation will be produced as a set of labeled trees, where the labels are primitive (syntactic or semantic) symbols.

2.3.2   Basic Units

The basic units are the elementary structures used in the processing. These structures are subtrees. The elementary trees can be divided into two parts according to semantic and syntactic criteria:

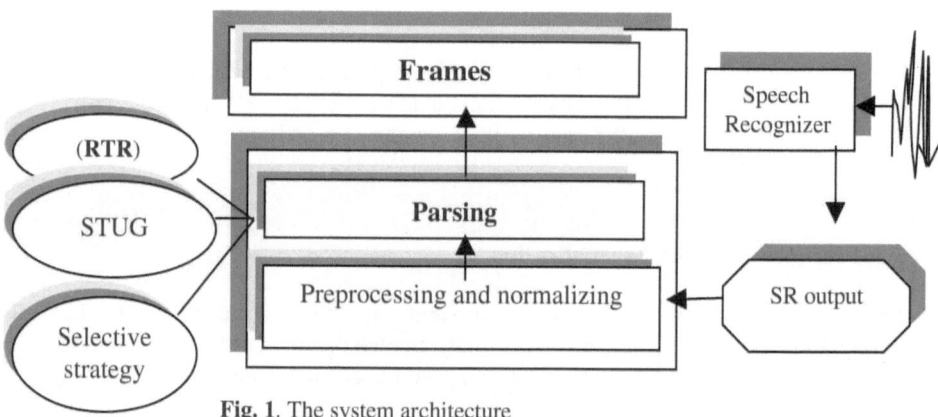

Fig. 1. The system architecture

Local Trees: In each local tree the root is labeled by a semantic non-terminal symbol. The nodes on the frontiers are labeled with terminal and non terminal symbols. The depth of these trees are limited to 2. Local trees are constructed following two cognitive and linguistic (semantic/pragmatic) well formedness principles.

Principle of Semantic consistence: each local tree has to be associated to a non-empty semantic representation.

Principle of Semantic Non-compositionnality: each local tree corresponds to a unique conceptual unit. A conceptual unit is a set (chunk) of words playing a particular semantic/pragmatic role in the utterance. These roles involve a great variety of cognitive and linguistic considerations [3] such that:

Topicality of the Utterance: in topic comment articulation, some chunks play usually the role of the topic, which indicates what the utterance is about. The comment, which is the remainder of the sentence, provides information about the topic. This factor is used both in the choice of the elementary trees as well as the representation of their relations.

Given vs. Non-given: What the system is presumed to know *a priori* (via the task model: frames) vs. what it doesn't know.

Importance: what is forwarded as important vs. what is backwarded as secondary.

Specificity: whether the speaker is referring to a particular instance of an entity or to this entity in itself.

Global Trees: In each global tree the root nodes and leaf nodes are labeled by non terminal symbols. The global trees serve to combine local trees into derivation trees. A sample of one local and two global trees is presented in figure 2.

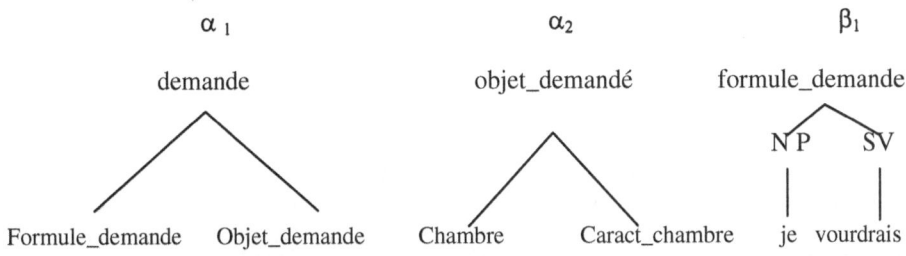

Fig. 2. A sample of local and global trees in STUG

2.3.3   Combination Operation

(henceforth unification) operation is the only composition operation in STUG. Unification is a partial function on pairs of labeled trees. The composition of tree a and tree b, written as $a \dots b$, is defined iff. the label on the root node of b is identical to the label on the leftmost non-terminal leaf node of a.

2.4 Parsing Algorithm

For parsing STUG, we are using a Recursive Transition Network RTN such a top-down parser allows to predict the possible alternatives that may occur at a given point. Furthermore, the algorithm we proposed is a partial one (in the sense that only the relevant elements of an utterance are processed). In spoken dialogue systems, it is necessary to carry out partial parsing for many (theoretical and practical) motivations:

1. Cognitive motivations: due to limitations of their capacities of attention and memory, humans don't consider the whole utterance in their interpretation process. They interpret only the more relevant elements.
2. Linguistic motivations: spoken utterances are usually '*ill-formed*' (compared to written-grammar rules) and traditional parsers are in the most cases unable to find a complete and correct parse of an utterance.

Parsing is done as the following: at first, the system tries to find a complete parse of the utterance. If complete parse fails, the system tries to find as big chunks as possible in the utterance. The provided partial parses are then combined following purely semantic and pragmatic considerations by frames (C.f. section 2.5).

Partial parsing is achieved by way of a selective heuristics. Selective heuristics are noise models based on the two factors:

a. The top down aspect of the parser,
b. The lexicon frontier of local trees.

The Lexical Frontier LF is a lexical item able to be the first word in the linear form of the tree. For example, in the tree ₁ (Figure 2), the word *je* is a lexical frontier but *voudrais* is not). When the system predicts a local tree, the selective heuristics take the LF of this tree as reference and compare each word in the input to it. If the word doesn't fit with the lexical units of the LF of current tree, it is directly skipped. If not, the system begins the parsing.

2.5 Task Model and Frames

The application task of our system is hotel reservation. Usually, a dialogue consists of a negotiation between a client and a hotel worker about room reservation, its price, its location, stay duration, etc. The task is represented as a set of structured feature frames. Each frame concerns a special aspect of the task like information asking, room reservation etc.

Features are organized into slots following subtasks. A subtask can be arrival date, room, clients, etc. A simplified frame is presented in figure 3.

{ Service = room reservation:
       Room   [Number_of_rooms = X1, Room_number = X2, Price = X3,
       Number_of_Beds = X4, Bathroom = X5, Television = X6, etc.)]
       Clients [Adult (Number = X1, Name = X2, tel. = X3, address = X4)
               Children (Number = X)   ]
       Date [Arrival (Year = X1, Month = X2, Day = X3, Hour, X5),
               Departure(Year = X1, Month = X2, Day = X3, Hour = X4),
               Stay duration (X)] }

Fig. 3. A simplified frame of room reservation

2.6 A Sample of Sentence Analysis

The processing of the utterance *je voudrais euh je voudrais réserver une chambre pour deux personnes* (I want euh I want to reserve a room for two persons) is done as the following:
1. The product of the speech recognizer is the following: *je voudrais je voudrais réserver une chambre pour de personne*. The speech recognizer produces the utterance except of the hesitation *euh* and creates two errors. The first one consists of replacing *deux* (two) by *de* (of) (*de* and *deux* are quasi homophones in French). And it doesn't write the plural mark *s* at the end of *personne*.
2. The preprocessing module detects and corrects the repetition *je voudrais*.
3. The parsing module process the corrected utterance *je voudrais réserver une chambre pour de personne* which still contains two grammatical errors. The system corrects *de* to *deux* with the phonetic confusion model and parses the

Nb_person tree without considering the number coordination problem between *deux* and *personnes*.

The output of the system is a derivation tree which is the product of the combination of the elementary trees presented in figure 2 with some others. This derivation tree is presented in figure 4.

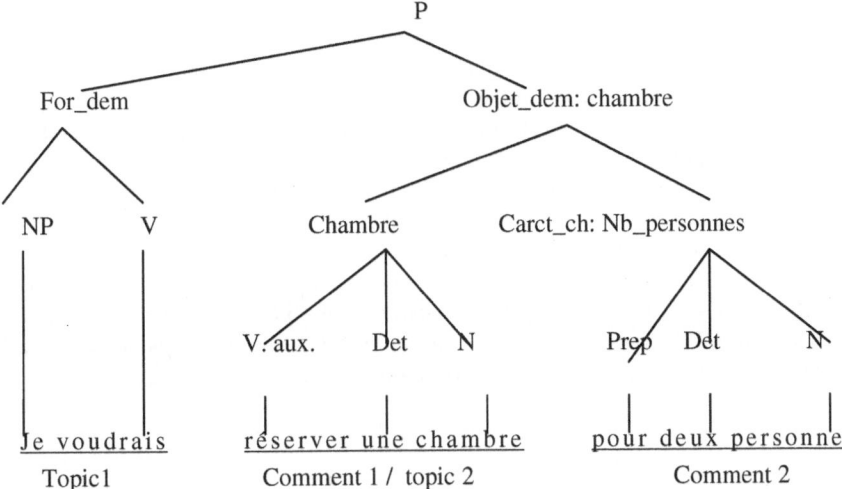

Fig. 4. A sample derivation tree.

3   Evaluation and Results

The system was tested on a corpus of 320 utterances (2705 words extracted from 54 dialogues). The test's results are presented in table 1.

Table 1. The system results

	% Parsed words	% Parsed trees
Recall	78,8	86,8
Precision	88,3	84,2

Our recall rate shows a good coverage rate of the grammar and the robustness of the parser even in cases of ill-formed utterances. The good precision rate of our results shows the efficiency of global trees (used for the context modeling) in parsing disambiguation. At the word level, our system achieves a good coverage rate (approximately 80%).

The main reasons of parsing errors are under-generativity of the grammar (incompleteness of rules corresponding to some concepts), speech recognition errors, and deletion of some trees by selective strategy.

In comparison[1] to the other results that have been reported in the literature like L'ATIS system [13] [15] which gives a recall rate of 85,6% of correct parsing and the OVIS system of [20] which gives a recall rate of 82 % of correct parsing, our results show the efficiency and the robustness of our approach.

4   Conclusion

In this paper, we presented a linguistically and cognitively motivated semantic based formalism used in the context of spoken language systems.

The general approach followed is to exploit as much information as possible from both lexical and topological levels for extracting a semantic representation from spoken utterances. The reduction of *the amount* of syntactic information allows a more flexible parsing of speech recognition output which contains usually many syntactic errors.

Another aspect of our work is the consideration of the spoken language extragrammaticalities by way of the normalization module.

Our results show the efficiency of our system to recognize and parse the relevant parts of an utterance even in cases of extragrammaticalities and speech recognition errors. Further more, compared to other selective approaches, our system shows a good coverage at the word level.

We are studying the use of STUG in systems with larger tasks like touristical information seeking. An extended version of this formalism is also under study. We are particularly interested in extending STUG for enabling it to represent complex syntactic phenomena like relative and negative utterances.

---

[1] The comparison with other systems results is approximative because their dialogue tasks and their test conditions are not identical to ours.

Acknowledgements

We wish to thank Alain Lecomte and Jean Caelen for their helpful comments about this work. We thank also Dominique Vaufreydaz for his assistance in speech recognition. Errors are mine.

References

1. Abney, Steven, Parsing by chunks, in Robert BREWICK, Steven ABNEY, Carol Tenny(eds.), *Principle-based parsing*, Kluwer Academic Publishers (1991)
2. Akbar, M., Caelen, J., Parole et traduction automatique le module de reconnaissance RAPHAEL, COLING98 (1998)
3. Andrews, A., The major functions of the noun phrase, in T. SHOPEN (editor), *Language typology and syntactic description*, Vol. 1 Cambridge university press (1985)
4. Aust, H., et al., The Philips train timetable information system, Speech Communication 17 (1995) pp. 249 – 262
5. Bod, R., Data oriented language processing, in S. Young and G. Bloothshooft (eds.) corpus-based methods in language and speech processing, Kluwer academic publishers, Boston (1997)
6. De Mori, R., Apprentissage automatique pour l'interprétation sémantique, Trégastel, XXèmes JEP, Juin (1994)
7. Hollard, S., L'organisation des connaissance dans le dialogue orienté par la tâche, rapport technique 1-97, GEOD CLIPS-IMAG, Grenoble (1997)
8. Kurdi, M. Z., A chunk based partial parsing strategy for reranking and normalizing Nbest speech recognition hypothesis, ESSLLI'99 student session, Utrecht, Netherlands, 6 - 18 August (1999)
9. Kurdi, M. Z., SAFIR: un analyseur conceptuel de la parole spontanée, CJSC III, Soulac-Bordeaux, 26 – 28 april (1999)
10. Langacker, Ronald W., Structural syntax: the view from cognitive grammar, Colloque international Lucien Tesnière aujourd'hui, Mont-Saint-Aignant, 19 - 21 november (1992)
11. Matrouf, A. et al, Système de dialogue orienté par la tâche: une application en avionique, 16e jounée d'études sur la parole, Hammamet, 5-9 october (1987)
12. Mayfield, L., *et al,* Concept based speech translation, Detroit: in proceedings of ICASSP-95 (1995)
13. Minker, W., An english version of the LIMSI L'ATIS system, Rapport technique LIMSI No. 95-12 (1995)
14. Minker, W., BENNACEF, S., Compréhension et évaluation dans le domaine ATIS, JEP'96 Juin (1996)
15. Minker, W., *et al.*, A Stochastic case frame approach for natural language understanding, Philadelphia, ICSLP 1996 October (1996)
16. Nash-Webber, B., The rol of semantics in automatic speech understanding, in Daniel Bobrow and Allan Collins (editors), *representation and understanding*: studies in cognitive science, Academic Press (1975)
17. Perennou, G., Compréhension du dialogue oral: Rôle du lexique dans le décodage conceptuel, Séminaire GDR-PRC CHM lexique et communication parlée, October (1996)
18. Pieraccini, R., Levin, E., Stochastic Representation of Semantic Structure for Speech Understanding, Proc. EUROSPEECH 91, September 1991, Genova, Italy, Speech Communication, Vol.11 pp. 283-288 (1992)

19. Sowa, J., Using a lexicon of canonical graphs in a semantic interpreter, in Walton Evens, M., *Relational model of the lexicon*: representing knowledge in semantic networks, Cambridge: Cambridge university press (1982)
20. Van Noorda, G., *et al.,* Robust grammatical analysis for spoken dialogue systems, Natural language engineering, Vol. 1, pp. 1 – 48 (1998)
21. Ward, W., Understanding spontaneous speech: the phoenix system, in proceedings of the international conference on acoustics, speech and signal processing, pages 365-367, May (1991)
22. Woszczyna, M., et al, A Modular Approach to Spoken Language Translation for Large Domains, In Proceedings of the 3rd Conference of the Association for Machine Translation in the Americas (AMTA-1998), Langhorne, Pennsylvania, U.S.A., October (1998)
23. Zechner, C., Waibel A., Using chunk based partial parsing of spontaneous speech in unrestricted domains for reducing word error rate in speech recognition, COLING-ACL, Montréal (1998)

A Practical Chunker for Unrestricted Text

E. Stamatatos, N. Fakotakis, and G. Kokkinakis

Dept. of Electrical and Computer Engineering
University of Patras
26500 Rio, Greece
stamatatos@wcl.ee.upatras.gr

Abstract In this paper we present a practical approach to text chunking for unrestricted Modern Greek text that is based on multiple-pass parsing. Two versions of this chunker are proposed: one based on a large lexicon and one based on minimal resources. In the latter case the morphological analysis is performed using exclusively two small lexicons containing closed-class words and common suffixes of the Modern Greek words. We give comparative performance results on the basis of a corpus of unrestricted text and show that very good results can be obtained by omitting the large and complicate resources. Moreover, the considerable time cost introduced by the use of the large lexicon indicates that the minimal-resources chunker is the best solution regarding a practical application that requires rapid response and less than perfect parsing results.

1 Introduction

Nowadays, there is a wealth of texts available in electronic form, in large databases. These databases include unrestricted texts of any length and complexity. Such texts usually contain headlines and other non-sentential fragments, dialects and colloquial forms, and plenty of words that are not part even of the largest machine-readable lexicon. On the other hand, they may be ill-formed, especially in the case of databases including electronic texts taken from optical character recognition tools.

In general, the goal of a parser is to assign appropriate labels to input texts. Many Natural Language Processing (NLP) applications (e.g., information extraction, information retrieval, etc.) require fast and robust parsing of large volumes of unrestricted text. In such applications obtaining less than perfect parsing results but rapidly is very important.

Special attention has to be paid on low-level tasks such as text segmentation, sentence boundary detection, and *text chunking* (or intrasentential phrase boundaries detection). A closer look to these tasks, that are prerequisite for the vast majority of NLP applications, proves that their insufficient solution may cause considerable losses of accuracy of a consequent, more complicate task, especially in the case of dealing with unrestricted text. A sufficient solution of a low-level problem has the following desiderata:

D.N. Christodoulakis (Ed.): NLP 2000, LNCS 1835, pp. 139-150, 2000.
© Springer-Verlag Berlin Heidelberg 2000

- *Minimal computational cost*: It is not efficient for a low-level task to demand excessive computational cost, or to be based on complicated, time-consuming and hard-to-build resources such as large lexicons containing at least thousands of lexical entries and large grammars consisting of hundreds of thousands of rules, etc. [1].
- *Use of non-specialized information*: A system performing a low-level task has to be based on easily available resources rather than specialized information that is not necessary to subsequent tasks.
- *Robustness*: The unknown word problem is substantial to parsers based on large lexicons. Some approaches use heuristics (e.g. the recognition of certain suffixes or the case of the first letter in order to identify proper names) or simply ignore all the unknown words and try to parse the remaining part of the text [2]. Recently, several systems utilize statistical methods in order to assign the most likely morpho-syntactic information to the words not found in the lexicon [3, 4].

In this paper we present a practical approach to text chunking for unrestricted Modern Greek text that is based on multiple-pass parsing, an alternative technique to the traditional left-to-right parsing. This technique has been applied mainly to statistical parsers in order to improve parsing results [5] as well as in speech processing as a way to reduce computation substantially, without an increase in error rate [6]. Specifically, two versions of the proposed chunker are presented regarding the morphological analysis of the words that compose the text:

- The first one is based on a large lexicon together with a keyword lexicon and unknown word guessing techniques (called hereafter the lexicon-based chunker), and
- The second one is based exclusively on a keyword lexicon and word-guessing techniques, in other words the large lexicon is omitted (called hereafter the minimal-resources chunker).

The next section deals with relevant work in text chunking. Section 3 describes the proposed approach in detail. Then, some comparative performance results of the two versions are given in section 4. Finally, the conclusions drawn by this study are given in section 5.

2   Relevant Work

The term *text chunking* refers to techniques used for dividing sentences into relatively simple syntactic structures, such as noun phrases and prepositional phrases. It has been proposed by Abney [7] as a useful precursor to full parsing.

A parser for Modern Greek texts is presented in [8]. This parser is able to mark the type of clauses contained in long sentences as well as to identify the phrases included in these clauses, based on a set of keywords and a set of heuristic rules. An accuracy of 84% is reported (this percentage increases to 96% after the use of some enhanced heuristics). This approach requires complete morphological analysis of every word included in the text. Moreover, when the text contains unknown words or extremely complicated syntax it fails to return any useful information.

A language-independent system for parsing unrestricted text based on Constraint Grammar formalism is presented in [1]. It is able to accurately disambiguate morphologically and syntactically any piece of text. However, it requires a very large master lexicon and some domain-specific lexicons used during morphological analysis as well as a large grammar containing thousands of rules.

On the other hand, shallow parsers provide analyses that are less complete than the output of conventional parsers. A shallow parser typically identifies some phrasal constitutes, such as noun phrases, without indicating their internal structure and their function in the sentence [9].

A text chunker using transformation-based learning is described by Rashaw and Marcus [10]. This approach has achieved recall and precision rates of roughly 92% for simple noun phrase chunks and 88% for somewhat more complex chunks that partition the sentence. Moreover, a stochastic approach to text chunking using Markov models is described by Skut and Brants [11]. However, both of these approaches require a part-of-speech tagger of high accuracy.

LEXTER [12] is a surface-syntactic analyzer that extracts maximal-length noun phrases from French texts for terminology applications. It is claimed that 95% of all maximal length noun phrases is recognized correctly, but no precision results are mentioned. Another maximal-length noun phrase extractor is *NPTool* [13]. This tool is based on a handcrafted lexicon and two finite state parsers, one noun phrase hostile and one noun phrase friendly. The combination of these parsers produces a list of acceptable noun phrases that can be used for terminological purposes. The reported recall and precision results are 98.5-100% and 95-98% respectively, evaluated against a 20,000-word corpus including texts from different domains. An efficient partial parser that combines enhanced part-of-speech tags, called *supertags*, with a lightweight dependency analyzer is presented by Srinivas [14]. The reported recall and precision rates for noun chunking are 93% and 91.8% respectively.

Last but not least, *FASTUS* described in [2], is a system for extracting information from English texts which works as a cascaded, non-deterministic automaton. This system initially tries to recognize basic noun and verb phrases, by using a finite-state grammar, and then identifies complex phrases by combining the simple ones. Unknown or otherwise unanalyzed words are ignored in subsequent processing unless they occur in a context that indicates they could be names. The comparison of *FASTUS* to more sophisticated systems show that one can go a long way with simple techniques and achieve very good parsing results very fast [15].

3   System Description

Our solution attempts to take advantage of some linguistic characteristics of Modern Greek in order to minimize the required resources. Particularly:

- Modern Greek is a quasi-free word order language. Thus, the sequence of the chunks may be changed without affecting the meaning of the sentence.

- Its morphology is extremely rich including a wealth of inflectional categories identified generally by word suffixes. It is worth noting that Sgarbas and his colleagues [16] propose 99 inflectional categories in order to cover the nouns of Modern Greek.
- Modern Greek verbs usually have characteristic endings different from all other inflectional parts-of-speech.
- The use of articles and particles usually indicating the start of noun and verb phrases respectively is very common, even in front of proper names. The identification of the beginning of simple phrases is therefore relatively easy.

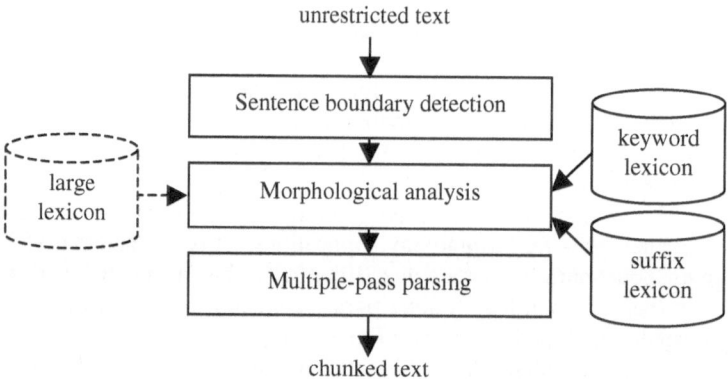

Fig. 1. Overview of the proposed text chunker. The large lexicon may be included (lexicon-based chunker) or omitted (minimal-resources chunker).

An overview of the proposed system is given in figure 1. Initially, the input text is segmented into sentences using a sentence boundary detector trained for Modern Greek [17]. Then, each word of the sentence is analysed morphologically as described in the next subsection. The chunk boundaries are identified by applying multiple passes to the input text as described in subsection 3.2.

3.1   Morphological Analysis

The morphological analysis of the words is performed based on a hierarchical procedure. Initially, in both versions of the chunker (i.e., minimal resources and lexicon-based) the keyword lexicon is used to identify the most common words. In more detail, this lexicon contains 432 keywords (or closed-class words) including articles, particles, prepositions, pronouns, numerals, and some special adverbs. The entries in this lexicon are of the following format (i.e., Prolog predicates):

keyword(WORD, INITIAL, DESCRIPTIONS)

where *WORD* is the keyword, *INITIAL* indicates whether it indicates the beginning of a noun phrase, a verb phrase or a prepositional phrase, and *DESCRIPTIONS* is a list of morphological descriptions. The keyword lexicon was constructed manually.

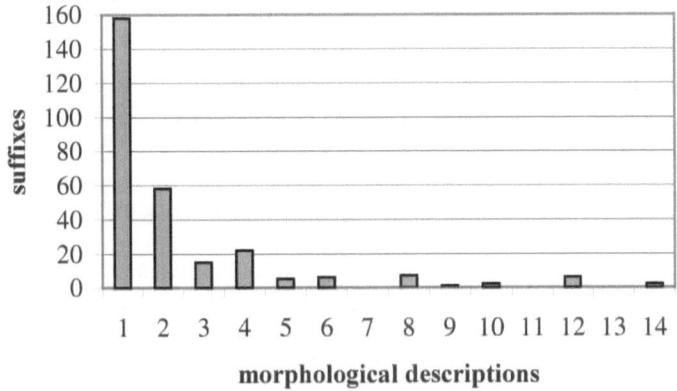

Fig. 2. Number of suffixes per morphological descriptions to which they correspond.

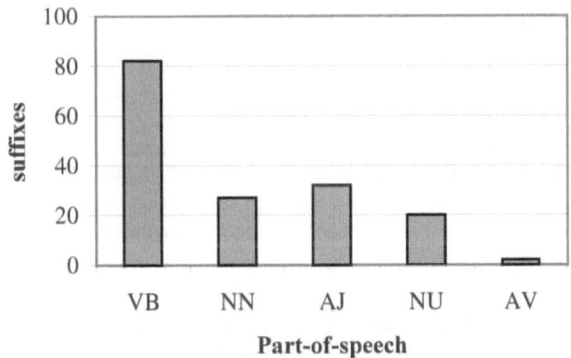

Fig. 3. Suffixes with one morphological description per part-of-speech. The abbreviations *VB*, *NN*, *AJ*, *NU*, and *AV* stand for verbs, nouns, adjectives, numerals, and adverbs, respectively.

However, any large lexicon that covers closed-class words can be used for the extraction of a keyword lexicon.

For the words not found in the keyword lexicon, the lexicon-based chunker uses a large lemma lexicon. This already existing lexicon was developed in the framework of a PC-KIMMO-based morphological analyzer for Modern Greek [16] and contains 30,000 lemmas covering nouns, adjectives, verbs, and adverbs. The combination of the PC-KIMMO-based analyzer and the lemma lexicon is able to give non-deterministic morphological descriptions for any word-form of the covered lemmas.

In the case of the lexicon-based chunker, the words not covered by this lexicon are analyzed using a guessing procedure based on the word suffixes. In the case of the minimal-resources chunker the words not found in the keyword lexicon are analyzed by this guessing procedure. Specifically, the suffix lexicon contains 282 suffixes that cover the vast majority of Modern Greek words. These suffixes were taken mainly from the already existing PC-KIMMO-based morphological description of Modern Greek [16]. The entries in this lexicon are of the following format (i.e., Prolog predicates):

suffix(SUFFIX, DESCRIPTIONS)

where *DESCRIPTIONS* is a list of morphological descriptions assigned to each word according to its *SUFFIX*. The maximal length suffix that matches the input word is selected.

Figure 2 shows the number of suffixes (vertical axis) in connection to the number of morphological descriptions that they assign (horizontal axis). Over 56% (158 out of 282) of the total suffixes assign only one morphological description to the words they match. Approximately 52% (82 out of 158) of these deterministic suffixes correspond to verbs as depicted in figure 3.

If a word suffix does not match to any of the entries of the suffix lexicon (usually foreign names or archaic words) then no morphological description is assigned, and this word is marked as a special word. However, it is not ignored in subsequent analysis. Additionally, a flag that indicates a possible proper name is assigned to every word based on the case of its first letter.

3.2 Multiple-Pass Parsing

The goal of our chunker is the identification of the boundaries of the main phrases (i.e., chunks) included in each sentence without analyzing their internal structure or their function in the sentence. Nevertheless, simple morphological disambiguation is performed, by applying selectional restrictions (e.g., number, case and gender agreement within noun phrases).

In particular, the detected chunks may be noun phrases (NPs), prepositional phrases (PPs), verb phrases (VPs), and adverbial phrases (APs). In addition, two chunks are usually connected by a sequence of conjunctions (CONs).

The identification of chunk boundaries is performed via multiple-passes on the input sentence. Each pass analyzes a part of the sentence, based on the results of the previous passes, and the remaining part is kept for subsequent passes. In general, the first passes try to detect simple cases that are easily recognizable, while the last passes deal with more complicated ones. Moreover, the last passes are less accurate than the initial ones due to the high degree of ambiguity they have to resolve. Cases that are not covered by the disambiguation rules remain unanalyzed. The presented approach utilizes five passes. The function of each one is described below.

- **Pass 1:** Simple NPs, PPs, and VPs are detected based on the recognition of phrase initial keywords, and the application of simple, empirically derived rules. For instance, this pass may detect the following chunks:

Example	Detected chunk
<u>Example</u>	<u>Detected chunk</u>
την αναγκαία γνώση και ευαισθησία	*NP*
(the necessary knowledge and sensitivity)	

ο 20ος αιώνας (the 20th century)	*NP*
της κ. Ελένης Παπαδοπούλου	*NP*
(of Mrs. Heleni Papadopoulou)	
οι αραιοκατηκημένες και γεωλογικά σχεδόν	
απομονωμένες περιοχές	*NP*
(the thinly populated and geologically	
almost isolated areas)	
με πολλή δύναμη (with great power)	*PP*
με συγκριτικά ελάχιστο κόστος	*PP*
(with comparetively minimum cost)	
δεν έχουν περάσει (they haven't passed)	*VP*
αναρωτήθηκα (I wondered)	*VP*
να δώσεις (to give)	*VP*

- **Pass 2:** Simple NPs at genitive case that usually follow other NPs as well as simple PPs are detected. Thus, this pass may detect the following chunks:

Example	Detected chunk
NP[*την χρήση*] *δορυφορικών συστημάτων*	*NP*
(NP[the usage] of satellite systems)	
με NP[*τον κ. Μπιλ Σμιθ*] (with NP[Mr. Bill Smith])	*PP*
από NP[*το περιπολικό*] (from NP[the cruiser])	*PP*
για NP[*τον μηχανικό*] (for NP[the engineer])	*PP*

Note, that in the above examples the chunks included in brackets (NP[*την χρήση*], NP[*τον μηχανικό*]) have been detected by the previous pass.

- **Pass 3:** Remaining pronouns either are appended to adjacent NPs or forming new NPs, and verbal predicates are detected. For example, this pass may detect the following chunks:

Example	Detected chunk
VP[*είναι*] *σημαντικά αλλά περίπλοκα*	*VP*
(VP[they are] important but complicated)	
όλα NP[*τα κλειδιά*] (all NP[the keys])	*NP*
NP[*η μητέρα*] *μας* (our NP[mother])	*NP*
αυτό (this)	*NP*

Note that the chunks included in brackets have been detected by previous passes.

- **Pass 4:** CONs, APs, as well as NPs with no initial keywords are detected in the remaining words. Moreover, PPs are formed based on NPs that have been detected in pass 3. For instance, this pass may detect the following chunks:

Example	Detected chunk
αν και (although)	*CON*
σχεδόν τελείως (almost completely)	*AP*
εθνικό έργο (national project)	*NP*

ζωή και ελπίδα (life and hope)   *NP*
σε NP[όλες τις περιπτώσεις] (in NP[all the instances])   *PP*

- **Pass 5:** In this pass, the simple phrases are combined in order to form more complex ones. Moreover, complex APs are detected. Thus, this pass is able to detect chunks like the following:

Example	Detected chunk
NP[η ανάπτυξη] NP[της νέας τεχνολογίας]	*NP*
(NP[the development] NP[of the new technology])	
PP[με τα μάτια] NP[της καρδιάς]	*PP*
PP[with the eyes] NP[of the heart]	
πολύ AP[προσεκτικά] (very AP[carefully])	*AP*
VP[τρέχει] VP[να σωθεί]	*VP*
(VP[he runs] VP[to be saved])	

Note that punctuation marks are included in the parsing procedure and treated as special symbols. It must be stressed that we tried to separate the identification of simple phrases from more complex ones since many applications require the identification of simple rather than complex phrases. An example analysis of the analysis of a sample text is given in the appendix at the end of the document.

4   Performance

The presented text chunker has been tested using a corpus of roughly 200,000 words which includes texts downloaded from the website of the Modern Greek newspaper entitled "TO BHMA" (the tribune).[1] These texts cover the majority of the genres found in a newspaper including news reportage, editorials, articles, letters to the editor, sports review, etc.

The entire corpus was analyzed using both the lexicon-based and the minimal-resources chunker and then one human judge manually evaluated its output. Comparative results in terms of recall and precision are given in table 1. As regards the minimal-resources chunker, the low recall of APs is caused by the similarity of the suffixes of the majority of Modern Greek adverbs to the suffixes of adjectives. The low precision of NPs is caused mainly by the analysis of remaining words that took place in the fourth pass.

On the average, the recall of the lexicon-based approach is considerably higher, especially in the case of NPs and APs. On the other hand, the precision results are lower. This is due to the fact that the lexicon is not able to provide all the possible morphological descriptions for some words. Additionally, the words remained unanalyzed using the lexicon-based system are 20% less in comparison with the minimal-resources chunker (i.e., 2.9% and 3.6% of the total words respectively).

---

[1] http://tovima.dolnet.gr

However, the parsing time cost of the lexicon-based approach is approximately 50% higher than the corresponding one of the minimal resources approach and this is very crucial for an application that requires analysis of large volumes of text very fast.

Table 1. Comparative performance of the two chunkers.

Chunk	Lexicon-based		Minimal-resources	
	Recall (%)	Precision (%)	Recall (%)	Precision (%)
NPs	94.46	85.58	91.18	88.72
PPs	93.96	99.12	93.35	99.36
VPs	93.63	97.57	91.32	98.19
Aps	85.28	96.90	72.47	96.27
Overall	*93.05*	*92.35*	*89.55*	*94.45*
Time cost (words / sec)	238		514	
Unanalyzed words (%)	2.9		3.6	

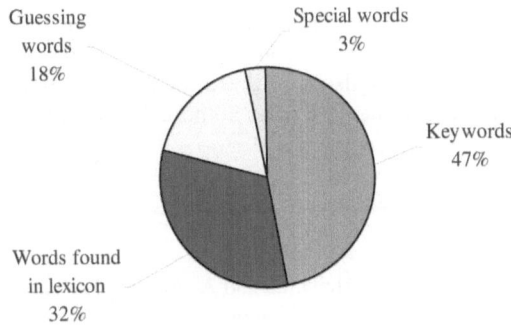

Fig. 4. The analysis of the test corpus by the lexicon-based approach.

An overview of the morphological analysis results of the entire corpus using the lexicon-based parser is given in figure 4. Approximately 47% of the total words were included in the keyword lexicon. The lexicon succeeded to provide information for 32% of the total words. It has also to be noted that the lexicon provided an average of 1.9 morphological descriptions per word. On the other hand, the application of the guessing procedure to these very same words (i.e., 32% of the total words) for comparative purposes provided an average of 3.6 morphological descriptions per word. The guessing procedure was applied to 18% of the total words while 3% of the total words did not match any of the entries of the suffix lexicon (i.e., special words).

5   Conclusion

We presented a text chunker for unrestricted Modern Greek text. We proposed two versions of this chunker: one based on a large lexicon and one based on minimal resources. In the latter case the morphological analysis is performed using exclusively two small lexicons containing closed-class words and common suffixes of the Modern

Greek words. The comparison of these two systems shows that very good results can be obtained by omitting the large and complicate resources. Moreover, the considerable time cost introduced by the use of complicate resources indicates that the minimal-resources chunker is the best solution regarding a practical NLP application that requires rapid response and less than perfect parsing results.

The presented text chunker takes advantage of some characteristics of Modern Greek that facilitate the recognition of simple phrases. Nevertheless, we strongly believe that similar methods can be applied to other natural languages with similar characteristics (i.e., morphological complexty, mandatory use of articles, particles, etc.). For example, Italian and Spanish are most likely to benefit by our approach.

The proposed system is currently modified in order to be adopted to the specific requirements of three national research projects: (i) MITOS[2], a system for information retrieval and extraction from financial spot news, (ii) DILOS[3], a bilingual electronic dictionary of economic terms with references to frequencies and terms in text corpora, and (iii) DIKTIS[4], a dialogue system for information extraction from medical text corpora. In each of these cases, we attempt to take advantage of the special characteristics of the domain-specific text corpora (e.g., financial spot news, medical prescriptions, etc.) that have to be analyzed for improving the performance. The minimal-resources chunker has also be utilized for the extraction of stylistic measures that have been used in the framework of an authorship attribution system [18].

References

1. Karlsson, F., A. Voutilainen, J. Heikkila, and A. Anttila (1995). *A Language-Independent System for Parsing Unrestricted Text.* Mouton de Gruyter.
2. Hobbs, J., D. Appelt, J. Bear, D. Israel, M. Kameyama, M. Stickel, and M. Tyson (1996). FASTUS: a Cascaded Finite-State Transducer for Extracting Information from Natural-Language Text. In E. Roche and Y. Schabes (eds) *Finite State Devices for Natural Language Processing.* Cambridge MA: MIT Press.
3. Dermatas, E. and G. Kokkinakis (1995). Automatic Stochastic Tagging of Natural Language Texts. *Computational Linguistics*, 21(2), pp. 137-164.
4. Mikheev, A. (1997). Automatic Rule Induction for Unknown Word Guessing. *Computational Linguistics*, 23(3), pp. 405-423.
5. Goodman, J. (1997). Global Thresholding and Multiple-Pass Parsing. In *Proc. of the Second Conference on Empirical Methods in Natural Language Processing*, pp. 11-25.
6. Schwartz, R, L. Nguyen, and J. Makhoul (1996). Multiple-Pass Search Strategies. In C. Lee, F. Soong, and K. Paliwal (eds) *Automatic Speech and Speaker Recognition: Advanced Topics*, Kluwer Academic Publishers, pp. 429-456.
7. Abney, S. (1991). Parsing by Chunks. In Berwick, Abney, and Tenny (eds), *Principle-based Parsing.* Kluwer Academic Publishers.
8. Michos S., F. Fakotakis, and G. Kokkinakis (1995). A Novel and Efficient Method for Parsing Unrestricted Texts of Quasi-Free Word Order Languages. *Int. Journal on Artificial Intelligence Tools*, 4(3). World Scientific, pp. 301-321.

---

[2] EPET II – 2-1.3-102

[3] EPET II – 98LE-12

[4] EPET II – 98LE-24

9. Church, K. (1988). A Stochastic Parts Program and Noun Phrase Parser for Unrestricted Text. In *Proc. of Second Conference on Applied Natural Language Processing*, pp. 136-143.
10. Ramshaw, L. and Marcus M. (1995). Text Chunking Using Transformation-based Learning. In *Proc. of ACL Third Workshop on Very Large Corpora.* pp. 82-94.
11. Skut, W. and Brants T. (1998). Chunk Tagger: Statistical Recognition of Noun Phrases. In *ESSLLI-98 Workshop on Automated Acquisition of Syntax and Parsing.*
12. Bourigault, D. (1992). Surface Grammatical Analysis for the Extraction of Terminological Noun Phrases. In *Proc. of the Fifteenth Int. Conference on Computational Linguistics*, 3, pp. 977-981.
13. Voutilainen, A. (1993). NPtool, a Detector of English Noun Phrases. In *Proc. of the Workshop on Very Large Corpora: Academic and Industrial Perspectives,* Ohio State University, pp. 48-57.
14. Srinivas, B. (1997). Performance Evaluation of Supertagging for Partial Parsing. In *Proc. of the Fifth International Workshop on Parsing Technologies.*
15. Sundheim, B. (ed.) (1995). *Proceedings of the 6th Message Understanding Conference (MUC-6).* Columbia, Advanced Research Projects Agency, Information Technology Office, Maryland.
16. Sgarbas, K., N. Fakotakis and G. Kokkinakis (1995). A PC-KIMMO-based Morphological Description of Modern Greek. *Literary and Linguistic Computing*, 10(3), Oxford University Press, New York, pp. 189-201.
17. Stamatatos, E., N. Fakotakis, and G. Kokkinakis (1999). Automatic Extraction of Rules for Sentence Boundary Disambiguation. In *Proc. of the Workshop in Machine Learning in Human Language Technology, Advance Course on Artificial Intelligence (ACAI'99)*, pp. 88-92.
18. Stamatatos, E., N. Fakotakis, and G. Kokkinakis (1999). Automatic Authorship Attribution. In *Proc. of the 9th Conf. of the European Chapter of the Association for Computational Linguistics (EACL'99)*, pp. 158-164.

Appendix: Analysis of a Sample Text

In order to illustrate the parsing procedure using the multiple passes, we give an analysis example of a sample text The chunks detected in each pass are shown in boldface. The sentence boundaries are indicated by the symbol #. Note that the word *Σύμφωνα* (i.e., according) remains unanalyzed since its suffix may indicate a noun, an adjective, or an adverb and the context do not solve this ambiguity. The minimal-resources chunker was used to analyze this sample text. Note also that the rough English translation aims mostly at helping the reader to understand the syntactic complexities of the text.

Sample text (and rough English translation):
Το άλλο, τραγικό θύμα (the other tragic victim) αυτής της ιστορίας (of this story), η 25άχρονη (the 25-years-old) Αμαλία Παπαδοπούλου (Amalia Papadopoulou), συνεχίζει (keeps) να δίνει (on giving) από την εντατική μονάδα (from the emergency unit) του Ερυθρού Σταυρού (of the Red Cross), τον αγώνα της (her fight) να κρατηθεί στη ζωή (for staying alive). Σύμφωνα με το σημερινό ιατρικό ανακοινωθέν (according to today's medical bulletin), οι θεράποντες ιατροί (the attendant doctors), διαπιστώνουν (ascertain) μικρή βελτίωση (slight improvement) της κατάστασης (of

the situation), η οποία (which) ωστόσο (however) παραμένει (remains) ιδιαιτέρως κρίσιμη (particularly crucial).

Pass 1:
NP[Το άλλο , τραγικό θύμα] αυτής **NP[της ιστορίας]** , **NP[η 25άχρονη Αμαλία]** Παπαδοπούλου , **VP[συνεχίζει] VP[να** δίνει] από **NP[την εντατική μονάδα] NP[του Ερυθρού Σταυρού]** , **NP[τον αγώνα]** της **VP[να κρατηθεί]** σε **NP[τη ζωή]** . *# Σύμφωνα με* **NP[το σημερινό ιατρικό ανακοινωθέν]** , **NP[οι θεράποντες ιατροί]** , **VP[διαπιστώνουν]** μικρή βελτίωση **NP[της κατάστασης]** , **NP[η οποία]** ωστόσο **VP[παραμένει]** ιδιαιτέρως κρίσιμη . #

Pass 2:
NP[Το άλλο , τραγικό θύμα] αυτής NP[της ιστορίας] , NP[η 25άχρονη Αμαλία] **NP[Παπαδοπούλου]** , VP[συνεχίζει] VP[να δίνει] **PP[από την εντατική μονάδα]** NP[του Ερυθρού Σταυρού] , NP[τον αγώνα] της VP[να κρατηθεί] **PP[στη ζωή]** . *# Σύμφωνα* **PP[με το σημερινό ιατρικό ανακοινωθέν]** , NP[οι θεράποντες ιατροί] , VP[διαπιστώνουν] μικρή βελτίωση NP[της κατάστασης] , NP[η οποία] ωστόσο VP[παραμένει] ιδιαιτέρως κρίσιμη . #

Pass 3:
NP[Το άλλο , τραγικό θύμα] **NP[αυτής της ιστορίας]** , NP[η 25άχρονη Αμαλία] NP[Παπαδοπούλου] , VP[συνεχίζει] VP[να δίνει] PP[από την εντατική μονάδα] NP[του Ερυθρού Σταυρού] , **NP[τον αγώνα της]** VP[να κρατηθεί] PP[στη ζωή] . *# Σύμφωνα PP[με το σημερινό ιατρικό ανακοινωθέν]* , NP[οι θεράποντες ιατροί] , VP[διαπιστώνουν] μικρή βελτίωση NP[της κατάστασης] , NP[η οποία] ωστόσο **VP[παραμένει ιδιαιτέρως κρίσιμη]** . #

Pass 4:
NP[Το άλλο , τραγικό θύμα] NP[αυτής της ιστορίας] , NP[η 25άχρονη Αμαλία] NP[Παπαδοπούλου] , VP[συνεχίζει] VP[να δίνει] PP[από την εντατική μονάδα] NP[του Ερυθρού Σταυρού] , NP[τον αγώνα της] VP[να κρατηθεί] PP[στη ζωή] . *# Σύμφωνα PP[με το σημερινό ιατρικό ανακοινωθέν]* , NP[οι θεράποντες ιατροί] , VP[διαπιστώνουν] **NP[μικρή βελτίωση]** NP[της κατάστασης] , NP[η οποία] **CON[ωστόσο]** VP[παραμένει ιδιαιτέρως κρίσιμη] . #

Pass 5:
NP[Το άλλο , τραγικό θύμα αυτής της ιστορίας] , **NP[η 25άχρονη Αμαλία Παπαδοπούλου]** , **VP[συνεχίζει να δίνει] PP[από την εντατική μονάδα του Ερυθρού Σταυρού]** , NP[τον αγώνα της] VP[να κρατηθεί] PP[στη ζωή] . *# Σύμφωνα PP[με το σημερινό ιατρικό ανακοινωθέν]* , NP[οι θεράποντες ιατροί] , VP[διαπιστώνουν] **NP[μικρή βελτίωση της κατάστασης]** , NP[η οποία] CON[ωστόσο] VP[παραμένει ιδιαιτέρως κρίσιμη] . #

A Distributed Approach for a Robust and Evolving NLP System

João Balsa[1] and Gabriel Lopes[2]

[1] Dep. Informática, Fac. Ciências de Lisboa
Campo Grande, Lisboa, Portugal
jbalsa@di.fc.ul.pt
[2] Dep. Informática, Fac. Ciências e Tecnologia da Universidade Nova de Lisboa
Monte da Caparica, Portugal
gpl@di.fc.unl.pt

Abstract. We present in this paper some aspects concerning the design and implementation of an architecture that is the basis for the development of a natural language processing system that, besides the obvious goal of building some computational representation (at a desired level) of the input, has two main objectives: to be robust and to evolve. To be robust in the sense that the non recognition of some input should not block the system but, instead, should lead the system to an automatic recovery process. To evolve, so that when some incompleteness/incorrectness is detected (or suspected) during a recovery process, the component responsible for the mistake should be updated accordingly, so that in future analogous situations the system can perform better. In order to achieve this goal we propose the definition of a distributed architecture.

1 Introduction

We present in this paper some aspects concerning the development of a distributed architecture for evolving and robust natural language processing (NLP) systems. Athough the focus of our work is in the integration of two properties (robustness and evolving capability) we consider fundamental in the NLP systems we are working with, in this paper we will detail more on the robustness property. We will be primarily concerned with how the achievment of robustness may conduct to system evolution.

1.1 Motivation

Virtually every natural language processing (NLP) system is in some (or in many) ways incomplete and/or incorrect. So, there is a concrete need for automatic improvement (augmentation, correction, validation) of the linguistic resources of every research group, namely the lexicons used. These were two key aspects that motivated us to adopt as one of the main goals of our work the design and implementation of an architecture that could be the basis for the development of an NLP system that, besides the obvious goal of building some

D.N. Christodoulakis (Ed.): NLP 2000, LNCS 1835, pp. 151–161, 2000.

computational representation (at a desired level) of the input, has two main objectives: to be robust and to evolve. To be robust in the sense that the non recognition of some input should not block the system but, instead, should lead the system to an automatic recovery process. To evolve, so that when some incompleteness/incorrectness is detected (or suspected) during a recovery process, the component responsible for the mistake should be updated accordingly, so that in future analogous situations the system can perform better.

The architecture we propose and present here is a distributed one. The need to face a large number of diversified potential problems and the necessity of integrating tools very different in nature, motivated us to conceive our system's architecture as a multi-agent one. On one hand this is a way to improve efficiency, on the other it allows for more design simplicity.

1.2 Related Work

The complexity of the natural language understanding task has for a long time (according to [2], since the 70s) motivated researchers to try to somehow distribute both its execution and the knowledge involved in order to improve system performance. From the implementation of parallel chart-parsers, to the development of multi-agent systems where the agents cooperate to produce an interpretation for a sentence, lots of proposals have been made in order to try to obtain acceptable performance results for NLP systems. This work is in a line of research related to the use of the multi-agent metaphor in the development of NLP systems.

Our work can be distinguished from related work following the Multi-Agent Systems approach [12,14], mainly due to the following aspects:

1. The used methodology. Although the use of multi-agent systems for natural language processing is not, by itself, original, the focus of our work is not so much on the linguistic analysis (like in [12]) but rather on the recovery process. We assume the existence of a subsystem (the parser [9]) that provides a set of partial parses. The goal of the system we're designing is to try to reduce the number of partial parses of every given input. This is done by performing a diagnosis process after a previous normal parsing phase has been done. During the diagnosis phase some possible faults should be pinpointed and repaired, if possible.
2. The interconnection of parsers, and lexicons, with learning components. During the diagnosis process mentioned in the previous item, some component of the system (for instance, a lexicon entry) can be found to be somehow incorrect. This will trigger the communication with a learning component that will adequately incorporate the information provided by the sentence being analysed - for instance information related to the verb properties (see example in section 1).
3. The hybrid character of the approach. Some components are symbolic in nature (the parsers and some learning components), others are subsymbolic (the used POS-tagger [7]), others are statistically based (bringing with them statistical inference).

4. The generality of the approach. Although we are working with the Portuguese language, our approach is language independent. To use our approach with other languages it is enough to take an initial grammar, an initial lexicon, and a POS-tagger for the desired language and text genre.

5. The flexibility of the architecture. Besides having some components that can evolve, the architecture of the system is an open one, in the sense that new agents, devoted to deal with some specific problem or phenomenon can be added without having to change the others' structure.

In the following sections we will first present the strategies we are using to deal with the robustness problem (section 2). In section 3 we focus on the evolution perspectives we're interested in. In section 4 we detail on the system's architecture and finally (section 5) we present some conclusions.

2   Strategies for Robustness

We are currently working on three types of strategies to solve the robustness problem: the parallel distribution approach, the break analysis approach and the third is a combination of the previous two. Let's see each one in more detail.

2.1   Parallel Distribution

This strategy is motivated by the intuition that when some input is not recognised as a sentence or a phrase that is not due to many diverse causes but, instead, to very few concrete problems. So, instead of designing a robust system that will, in a centralized manner, incorporate the treatment of all possible causes, we distribute the problem to many simple components working in parallel, each specialized in some particular type of problem - the types of problems can be related both to the input or to some component of the system. This way an adequate component will find solutions very quickly and deliver them. By adequate component we mean one that is specialized in the particular problem that was the cause of a particular failure. In some cases there might be the need for some communication of results between components.

The materialization of this strategy was made through the definition of a hierarchical multi-agent architecture as described in section 4.1.

2.2   The Break Analysis Approach

This approach is motivated by taking into account what would a human do to solve the problem of finding what prevented two contiguous partial parses of some input to become a single parse. That is, to find why there is a break in a particular point between two constituents.

For instance, consider the following sentence[1]:

$$_0 \text{He} \ _1 \text{fell} \ _2 \text{asleep} \ _3$$

It is possible to recognise a sentence between points 0 and 2. Supposing the parser is unable to integrate the third word in a single parse for the sentence, we may ask what caused that break in point 2. In this example (and in our lexicon we have lots of verbs with similar error patterns) it is plausible to assume that the problem is with the lexicon - it does not have complete information for the verb *to fall* (it is unable to recognize *fall asleep* as a phrasal verb). So we can design components that use heuristic rules representing solutions for particular break patterns. To cover the problem in this example we could have a rule stating that a sentence ending with a verb form (*fell* or any other) but with some particular constituent after it should lead to the revision of the verbal information for the specific verb: either it subcategorizes an adjective phrase (and that can be automatically extracted from corpora [6]) or there is a multi-word lexical unit (*fall asleep*) which can also be automatically extracted from corpora [13] that fits perfectly in.

2.3   Combination of Strategies

A combination of the previous two strategies consists in incorporating the knowledge related to break occurrence in the parallel distribution process. Instead of blindly distributing the problem amongst the several components, this distribution can be made using some criteria preventing some components that, for a specific problem, are unlikely to produce a solution, to waste time trying to find one.

3   Perspectives on Evolution

We see the evolution of our system in two different perspectives: development perspective and application perspective. In the development perspective of evolution we are concerned with the improvement of particular components of the system. Presently our group is concerned primarily with the lexicon that we have. It has some incompletenesses and incorrections that have to be surpassed in order to improve the performance of the applications. In this perspective, data from text corpora is used and statistical strategies have been implemented to extract relevant information from the corpora that will enable the appropriate update of the lexicon. We will not detail this perspective in this paper. We are more concerned here with the application perspective.

---

[1] This is just a motivating example. Our work and experiments are with the Portuguese language.

3.1   The Application Perspective

Whereas in the development perspective the focus is in the evolution and the robustness property is accessory, in the application perspective it is the reverse. The focus is in the robustness of the system and in exceptional cases a recovery process may lead to the update of one of its components. This is a consequence of the fact that when the system is connected to a specific application execution time is even more important. The system must be trusted to be as reliable as possible. Otherwise too much effort could be spent on evolving processes. An update of some system component should occur rarely when interacting with a client application.

3.2   Evolving Possibilities

Considering the application perspective, we are once again primarily concerned with the update of the lexicon. For instance, when faced with a situation like the one exemplified in 1, the system should send the information obtained during the recovery process to the learning component in order to update (or not) the information relative to the verb *to fall* or to create a new lexicon entry with *fall asleep*. In our case this process will also involve statistical validation of the hypothesis formulated before the definite inclusion of the new information.

4   General Architecture

The global architecture of the system, considering the application perspective mentioned above, is sketched in figure 1. As shown in this figure each component of the system has a facilitator agent associated with it. Each facilitator agent serves as an interface between the corresponding component and the other system components. Since each component of the system is completely independent of the others (and they may be used in other contexts) the use of facilitator agents is a way to achieve component integration more easily and in an elegant manner. Let's see each one of them in more detail.

4.1   The System Components

Normal Parsing. This is one of the nuclear components of the system. It is responsible for the normal parsing of the input. The parsing facilitator serves as an interface between the application and the NLP system. It receives a request from the application, sends it to the component and collects the result. In case of success it sends the result to the application. In case of failure (only a partial parse obtained for the input) it contacts the parsing diagnosis facilitator.

Parsing is done using a cascade chart parsing technique [11], that involves three steps: pre-processing, main chart parsing, and constituent movement analysis.

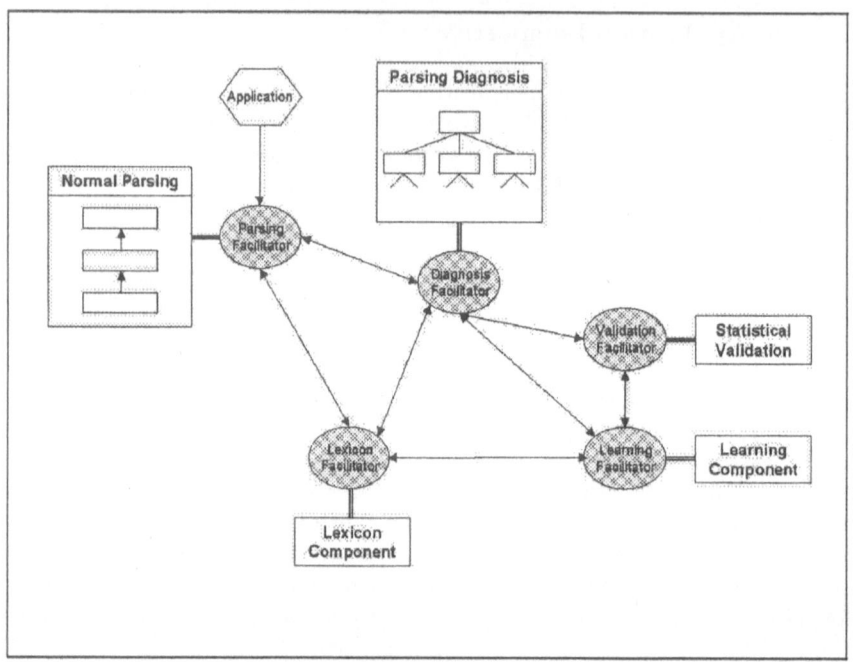

Fig. 1. General Architecture

Parsing Diagnosis. An architecture for this component incorporating the first strategy mentioned in section 2.1 (parallel distribution) was first introduced in [1]. In this architecture there is a three layer agent hierarchy (figure 2) where the bottom-layer agents implement the specialist components that will have very narrow perspectives on the problem but will produce candidate solutions very quickly.

Basically what happens in this component is the following. As the top layer agent receives a request (to improve a partial parse of some input), it distributes it to its descendants (intermediate level agents), that will independently work on it. Each of these will redistribute the problem amongst their descendents (typically a bottom-layer agent). Each of these bottom-layer agents are chart-parsers working on the same grammar [10]. As chart parsers they have a chart (where the analysis already done is kept), an agenda (where the tasks they still must perform are updated, and an engine that picks up a task from an agenda, acts as it always acts, according to the grammar used, and ends up updating the chart and the agenda [10]. The only difference that each of these chart parsers have, regarding their companions, is related to the way how they initiate their own agenda, that depends on the specific diagnosis capabilities that the chart parser has. Even the initial chart parser is identical to their companions but differs from them in the way how it initiates its agenda.

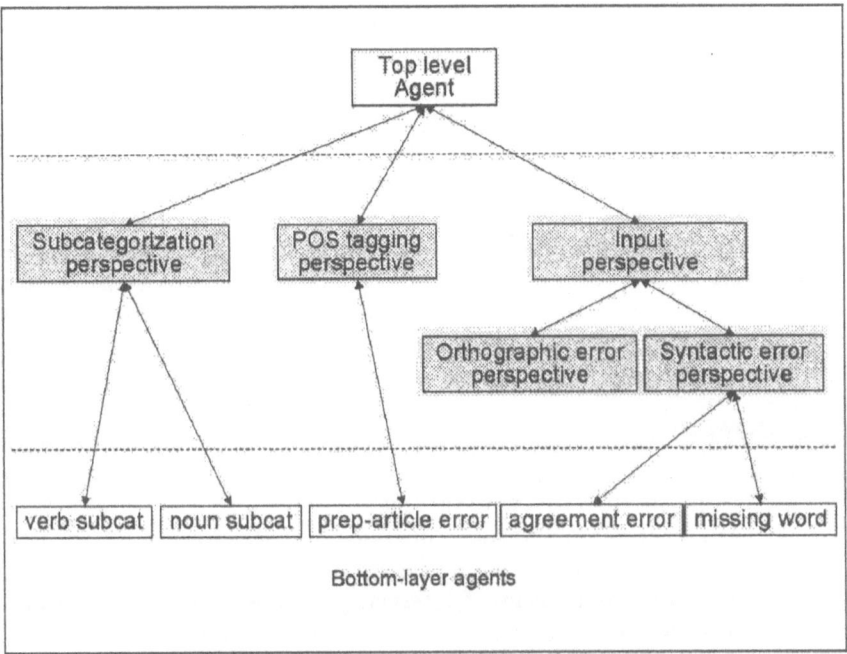

Fig. 2. Parsing Diagnosis Architecutre

As it was shown in [10], these chart parsers differ from traditional chart parsers as the edges, both in the agenda and in the chart, do include a description of the faults they have assumed together with the possible repair for that fault. If initially possible repairs for observed faults, signaled by the above mentioned "break points", are accepted by the grammar used then the edges separated by those "break points" are bridged and a chart with a smaller number of edges spanningover the input is obtained. This means that they have achieved a resolution state for the problem they have received that is better (with a smaller number of edges spanning over the input (i.e., with a lower granularity[2]) than the resolution state of the problem they worked out. Once a diagnosis chart parser exhausts its agenda and gets a chart with lower granularity than the chart it has originally received, it sends out the chart it has obtained. This chart is sent together with the parsers own signature that adds up to the signatures of all parsers that worked out previously on the problem it has worked out and contributed to the resolution state it has originally received. If a diagnosis parser does not obtain a chart with lower granularity than the one it has received, it just gives up, and picks a new problem that meanwhile it may have received for improvement (i.e., for lowering the granularity of the received chart).

---

[2] The granularity of a chart is the minimum of the number of edges spanning over the input divided by the number of words in the input.

Acting this way, we are pruning a lot the number of resolution states that that might be produced. Our chart parsers act as reactive agents that apply different strategies for improving the resolution state of the problems they receive, according to their specialization.

At the intermediate layer, agents work in a higher abstraction level relative to the types of problems that may occur. Specifically, it is at this level that the solutions obtained by lower level chart parsers are broadcasted to bottom layer chart parsers while a minimum for the granularity of a given input has not been achieved (1/n, i.e. one edge divided by to number 'n' of words in the input) and there are chart parsers that did not work on an evolving solution of a given initial problem. But at this level, partial solutions may also be sent to the upper layer agent so that those solutions may be validated or used to start a learning process.

The top layer agent is the ultimate responsible for the diagnosis process. Some details concerning one part of this hierarchy (the one related to the verb subcategorization perspective) were presented in [3].

The parsing diagnosis facilitator is, in some sense, the heart of the robustness of the system we're presenting. Besides being responsible for the interface with the parsing diagnosis component, it interacts with the validation and learning facilitators in order to improve the response that must be sent back to the application. In section 4.2 we present a more detailed example.

Statistical Validation. The statistical validation component is used to validate new proposals. As a way to filter candidate solutions, a statistical validation may be applied in order to ensure that a new proposal is plausible with respect to the corpus that was used to build this component. In what respects the validation of subcategorization classes for some verbs this component uses the techniques presented in [7,6,5].

Learning Component. Although this component was built with the development perspective in mind, it is also useful here, but with a different focus. Besides the possibility of contributing to the learning of new verb subcategorization classes [7,6,5] (as it does in the development perspective), in this context it is also designed to incorporate a learning mechanism that will allow the parsing diagnosis component to perform better, in the following sense. This component collects information on every problem that is solved by the parsing diagnosis, in order to try to establish links between the patterns of partial parses and the way the best solution for it was found. This will be important information for the upper layers of the diagnosis hierarchy, since it will enable them to manage the redistribution of messages and the evaluation of the results in a more intelligent/optimized way.

Lexicon Component. Besides the common type of dictionary that most NLP system uses, we also use special types of dictionaries, namely ones with the representation of multi-word lexical units (terms) [13], that are useful in early stages of the analysis and that allow for lots of saving in later stages. For instance "natural language" is surely a relevant expression if one considers the corpus of all papers in natural language processing conferences. Our group works in two approaches for this problem, as described in [13].

4.2   The System at Work

Since our work is for the Portuguese language, only for illustration purposes consider again the analysis of the sentence

$$_0 \text{He} \ _1 \text{fell} \ _2 \text{asleep} \ _3$$

If some application requests the analysis of this sentence the system will proceed in the following way:

1. The parsing facilitator receives the request and sends it to the normal parsing component.
2. Assuming the the normal parsing does not succeed in obtaining a full parse for the sentence, obtaining only a partial parse with two arcs: *He fell* and *asleep*. The parsing facilitator sends this analysis to the diagnosis facilitator so that the associated component can propose a correction for the problem.
3. On receiving this request the top level agent of the parsing diagnosis component distributes it to its subordinates, i.e., it requests them to try to improve the partial parse of the sentence.
4. In this particular example it is unlikely that an error in the input would be found. A more plausible one (that corresponds to what we're trying to illustrate) would be an error detected by the verb subcategorization agent. This will propose a change in the subcategorization class for the verb, so that the word *asleep* can be included in the verbal phrase.
5. At this stage the parsing facilitator does two things:
   (a) It takes this proposal and sends it (through the corresponding facilitator) to the statistical validation component. This component will verify the statistical plausibility of the new proposal and, according to result obtained, propose to the learning component the adoption of the new subcategorization class.
   (b) Simultaneously the diagnosis facilitator can send the result received from its component to the learning facilitator so that it can process the information on how the proposal is obtained (namely, the mentioned signatures if the agents that contributed to the solution). This way it is possible to learn which agents are more useful in solving certain types of problems (patterns of partial parses).
6. Finally the response is sent back. Assuming the proposal was successfully validated the sentence would be parsed correctly.

5   Conclusions

Although some more experimentation is still needed to fully evaluate the system, the approach we presented here has two main advantages: the flexibility of the architecture and the robustness capability. The full implementation of the system is currently under way, but some partial aspects of the sub-systems are already implemented and have been subject to some experiments [4]. Namely, some tests with the hierarchical diagnosis have provided good results related to the improvement of the quality of the solutions. For instance, for the parsing diagnosis component, the communication between the subcategorization agents led to an improvement of 87% of the sentences tested. If we take into account that the total number or arcs generated by the chart parsers is similar this is a very good result. Besides, the sentences that serve as the basis for our experiments are automatically extracted from a news agency corpus. This means that due to formatting issues some of the sentences are not really meaningful. So, the application of our methodology to a set of "cleaner" sentences could only present even better results.

The components of the system more closely related to the parsing process are implemented in Prolog (namely the normal parsing and parsing diagnosis components). DyaLog [15], a tabling system for parsing, is also used for specific chart parsing tasks. This results in a considerable improvement in efficiency relatively to the use of Prolog (see [9] for detailed results). So that we can virtually or actually parallelize the system we are currently using the PVM platform with the Prolog extension developed by [8].

Acknowledgements. We would like to thank our collegues from our research group (GLiNt*) specially Vitor Rocio and Alexandre Agustini for useful comments and discussions and for colaborating with us in some experiments. Thanks are also due to Luis Antunes for his comments on the paper.

This work is partially supported by the projects DIXIT (funded by Praxis XXI, under contract 2/2.1/1670/95), and PGR (funded by "Fundação para a Ciência e Tecnologia", under contract LO59-P31B-02/97).

References

1. João Balsa. A hierarchical multi-agent system for natural language diagnosis. In Henri Prade, editor, *Proceedings of the 13th European Conference on Artificial Intelligence (ECAI)*, pages 195–196. John Wiley & Sons, 1998.
2. Udo Hahn and Geert Adriaens. Parallel natural language processing: Background and overview. In Geert Adriaens and Udo Hahn, editors, *Parallel Natural Language Processing*, pages 1–134. Ablex Publishing, 1994.
3. J. G. Pereira Lopes and João Balsa. Overcoming incomplete information in NLP systems - verb sub-categorization. In Fausto Giunchiglia, editor, *AIMSA '98 - Proceedings of the 8th International Conference*, volume 1480 of *LNAI*, pages 331–340. Springer-Verlag, 1998.

4. José Gariel Lopes, Vitor Rocio, and João Balsa. Superando a incompletude da informação lexical. In Palmira Marrafa and Maria Antónia Mota, editors, *Linguística Computacional - Investigação Fundamental e Aplicações*, pages 121–149. Edições Colibri / Associação Portuguesa de Linguística, 1999.
5. Nuno Marques, J. G. Pereira Lopes, and Carlos A. Coelho. Using loglinear clustering for subcategorization identification. In M. Quafafou and J. Zytkov, editors, *Proceedings of the 2nd European Symposium on Principles of Data Mining and Knowledge Discovery (PKDD '98)*, LNCS 1510, pages 379–387. Springer Verlag, 1998.
6. Nuno M. Marques, J. G. P. Lopes, and Carlos A. Coelho. Learning verbal transitivity using loglinear models. In C. Nedellec and C. Rouveirol, editors, *Machine Learning: ECML-98*, pages 19–24. Springer Verlag, 1998.
7. Nuno Miguel Cavalheiro Marques. *A Methodology for the Statistical Modelling of Verb Subcategorization*. PhD thesis, Universidade Nova de Lisboa, 1999. (in portuguese).
8. Rui Filipe Pereira Marques. Um modelo de programação paralela e distribuída para o prolog. Master's thesis, Universidade Nova de Lisboa, 1996. (in Portuguese).
9. Vitor Rocio and J. G. Pereira Lopes. Partial parsing, deduction and tabling. In *Proceedings of the First Workshop on Tabulation in Parsing and Deduction (TAPD '98)*, pages 52–61, 1998.
10. Vitor Rocio and J. G. Pereira Lopes. An infra-structure for diagnosing causes for partially parsed natural language input. In *Proceedings of the Sixth International Symposium on Social Communication*, pages 550–554, 1999.
11. Vitor Rocio and José Gabriel P. Lopes. Análise sintáctica parcial em cascata. In Palmira Marrafa and Maria Antónia Mota, editors, *Linguística Computacional - Investigação Fundamental e Aplicações*, pages 235–251. Edições Colibri / Associação Portuguesa de Linguística, 1999.
12. João L. T. Da Silva, Paulo R. C. Abrahão, and Vera L. S. de Lima. Integrating morphological, syntactical and semantic aspects through multi-agent cooperation. In *Proceedings of SBIA '98*, pages 83–92. Springer Verlag, 1998.
13. Joaquim Ferreira Da Silva, Gaël Dias, Sylvie Guilloré, and José Gabriel P. Lopes. Using LocalMaxs algorithm for the extraction of contiguos and non-contiguous multiword lexical units. In Pedro Barahona and José Alferes, editors, *Progress in Artificial Intelligence (Proceedings of the 9th EPIA Conference)*, pages 113–132. Springer Verlag, 1999.
14. Marie-Hélène Stefanini and Yves Demazeau. TALISMAN: A multi-agent system for natural language processing. In *Proceedings of SBIA '95*, pages 312–322. Springer Verlag, 1995.
15. Eric Villemonte de la Clergerie. *Automates à Piles et Programmation Dynamique. DyALog : Une application à la programmation en Logique*. PhD thesis, Université Paris 7, 1993.

An Incremental Discourse Parser Architecture

Dan Cristea

"Alexandru Ioan Cuza" University of Iasi
Faculty of Computer Science
16, Berthelot St., 6600 – Iasi, Romania
dcristea@infoiasi.ro

Abstract. We present a discourse parsing architecture based on an incremental approach and aimed at building a rhetorical structure of a free text. Vein expressions computed on the developing structure help to restrict the domains of referential accessibility on which resolution of anaphora is performed. The parsing process is guided by cohesion and coherence constraints.

1   Introduction

Incremental discourse parsing is particularly challenging to systems aimed at doing automatic text processing because of its resemblance with the linear processing of texts done by humans. Although humans process texts linearly, there are strong reasons to believe that they build structures which are not linear but hierarchical and that they use these structures to further resolve co-references and to build interpretations. Theories like Attentional State Theory [7], and Rhetorical Structure Theory [8] argued in favour of a hierarchical structure of discourse. There is debate whether the discourse structure must resonate with the resolution of anaphora (see for instance [13]). We believe there is tight relationship between discourse structure and references. In [12] a system that integrates the expertise of several modules (syntactic, semantic, common sense inference, discourse planning, anaphora resolution, cue-words and temporal) in order to build incrementally the meaning of free texts was presented. The behaviour is based on the assumption that the performance of the system could be affected but is not vitally dependent on any of the contributing expert modules. The more one knows the more accurate the representation could be. If less is known, less is obtained, but the system can still survive.

In this paper we describe a configuration that integrates a part of speech tagger, a cue-expert module, a discourse parser and a reference resolution module. Section 2 presents the theoretical clues the approach is anchored in: Veins Theory and expectation-based incremental parsing, section 3 explains in detail the behaviour of the system on a particular fragment of English text and section 4 compares the proposed architecture with other work.

D.N. Christodoulakis (Ed.): NLP 2000, LNCS 1835, pp. 162-174, 2000.
© Springer-Verlag Berlin Heidelberg 2000

2   Veins Theory

Veins Theory [3] uses a representation of the discourse structure as a binary tree, close to the representation in Rhetorical Structure Theory (RST) [8]. Terminal nodes in the tree represent *discourse units* and non-terminal nodes represent continuous text spans and are labelled with *rhetorical relations.* Usually a label uniquely identifies a unit. A polarity is established among the children of a relation, which identifies at least one node, the *nucleus,* considered essential for the writer's purpose; non-nuclear nodes, which include spans of text that increase understanding but are not essential to the writer's purpose are called *satellites.* VT operates with two concepts: *head* and *vein,* which are expressions of terminal labels (discourse unit labels) attached to each node in the discourse structure. Head expressions (equivalent to Marcu's promotion sets [9]) are computed bottom-up: the head of a terminal node is its label; the head of a non-terminal node is the concatenation of the heads of its nuclear children.

Veins expressions are sub-sequences of the sequence of unit labels making up the discourse and are computed top-down:

the vein expression of the root is its head expression;

for each nuclear node whose parent node has vein v, the vein expression is:

- if the node has a left non-nuclear sibling with head h, then $seq(mark(h), v)$, where $mark(x)$ is a function that takes a string of symbols x and returns each symbol in x marked in some way (e.g. with parentheses) and $seq(x, y)$ is a sequencing function that computes that permutation of x concatenated with y given by the left to right reading of the sequence of labels in x and y on the terminal frontier of the tree
- otherwise (if the node has no left sibling or its left sibling is nuclear), v;

for each non-nuclear node of head h whose parent node has vein v, the vein expression is:

- if the node is the left child of its parent, then $seq(h,v)$
- otherwise, $seq(h, simpl(v))$, where $simpl(x)$ is a function that eliminates all marked symbols from its argument, if they exist.

The definition for the vein expression of a node is intended to put in evidence a list of units of the discourse that make up a comprehensible context for the span of text covered by the node. In particular, the vein expression of the root node gives a summary of the whole discourse, while the vein expression of a terminal node – a unit of the discourse, reveals the minimum context around that unit that makes the unit understandable. The particular interest given to left satellites resides from empirical observations that they are accessible to their immediate to the right nuclei, but inaccessible to subsequent satellites.

The *domain of referential accessibility* (DRA) of a unit is defined as the string of unit labels appearing in its vein expression and prefixing that unit label itself.

Ex. 1

1. *John sold his bicycle*
2. *although Bill would have wanted it.*
3. *He obtained a good price for it,*
4. *which Bill could have not afforded.*
5. *Therefore he decided to use the money for going in a trip.*

The RST structure of Ex. 1, as put in evidence by the cue-words *although, which, therefore,* must be one of those evidenced in Fig. 1. VT makes two important claims. The first regards discourse cohesion, the second discourse coherence.

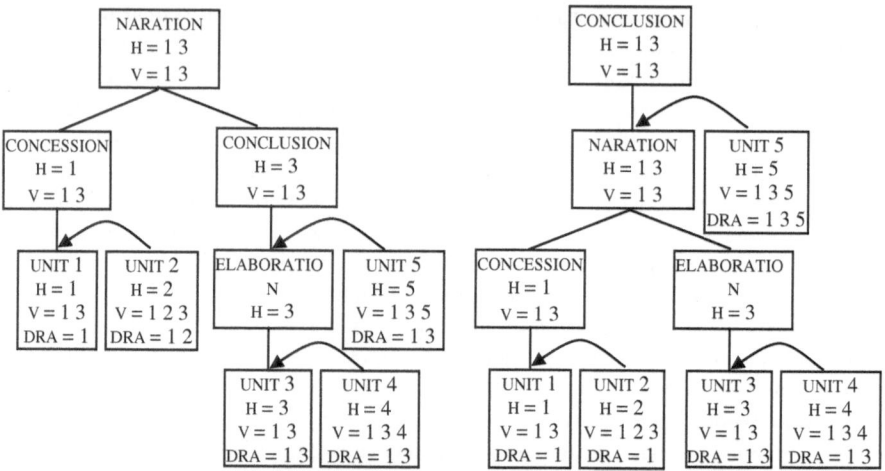

Fig. 1. Possible RST structures for Ex. 1

2.1   VT and Discourse Cohesion

Veins Theory claims that references from a given unit are possible mainly in its domain of referential accessibility. By restraining the domains the antecedents of anaphors are to be looked for, VT makes the existing anaphora resolution techniques [10] more effective and more efficient. The model we have studied for experimenting VT-driven anaphora resolution is based on a three tiered representation and a two steps process.

The first layer is that of the *surface text*. Referring expressions (REs) belong to this layer. The second layer is the one of the *morpho-semantic restrictions*. This layer is populated with feature structures that display sets of morphological and semantic feature-value pairs. To each RE on the textual layer correspond one or more representations on the morpho-semantic layer. We say that the morpho-semantic signs are *projected* there from the textual layer. The third layer is the *situational layer*, also populated with feature structures, but where all references are resolved. There is only one representation for each discourse entity on this layer. We say that the entities on the situational layer are *evoked* there from the restrictions layer (

Fig. **2** displays the three layers for two co-referencing REs). Let's notice that the composition of the *projects* and *evokes* relations yields the *realises* relation of centering [6]. As such, the world of REs can be seen as a simplification of the overall dynamic model of language interpretation, where we retain only REs and representations emerged from them.

Different theories of anaphora resolution use specific evoking mechanisms. For instance, the resolution of pronominal anaphors could impose the agreement in person, number, gender and a semantic feature (human or non-human). The evoking mechanism of noun phrase anaphors could be more complicated, as they could involve also synonymy and hipernymy relations as well as navigation processes in a WordNet-like conceptual hierarchy.

VT sees references in conjunction with discourse structure. The following types of references are put in evidence:

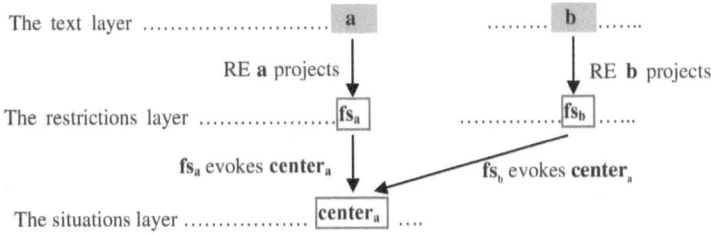

Fig. 2. The three-layer representation for two co-referencing REs

Direct References. If *A* and *B* are units in this textual order, *A* belongs to the DRA of *B* and *a* ⊂ *A* is linearly the most recent (to *B*) RE that realizes that same center as *b* ⊂ *B*, we say that *b* *directly co-refers* the center evoked by *a* (see Fig. 3).

If *A* and *B* are units in this order, *A* belongs in the DRA of *B* and *a* ⊂ *A* is linearly the most recent RE (to *B*) that realises a role of *b* ⊂ *B*, we say that *b* *functionally directly co-refers* the center realised by *a*. To put in evidence the DRAs of units, in the following graphical representations the units and the veins they belong to are drawn above REs. Also, to simplify notation, only the first and the second layers are shown.

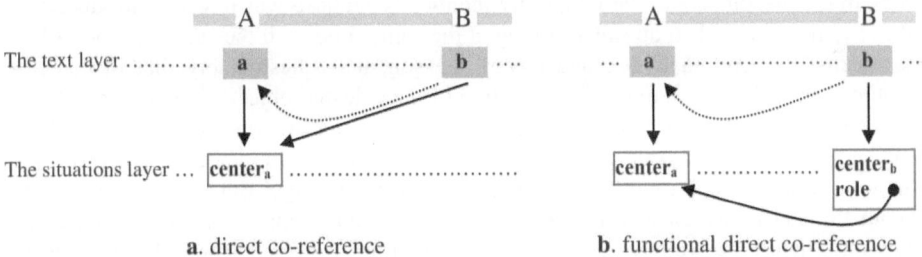

a. direct co-reference   b. functional direct co-reference

Fig. 3. Direct co-reference: the linearly most recent RE that realises the same center of an RE is shown by a dashed arrow and the realisation relation by a full arrow

Indirect References. If *A*, *B* and *C* are units in this order, *b* ⊂ *B* is linearly the most recent (to *C*) RE that realises the same center as *c* ⊂ *C*, *B* is not on the DRA of *C*, *A* is linearly the most recent (to *B*) unit that is both on the DRA of *B* and of *C*, and it contains a RE *a* ⊂ *A* such that *b* ⊂ *B* realises the same center as *a*, we say that *c* indirectly co-refers the center realised by *a* (see). A similar definition applies for indirect functional references.

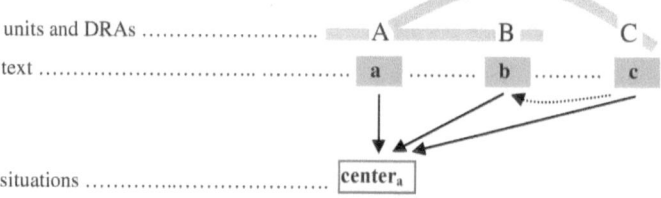

Fig. 4. Indirect co-reference

In other words, an indirect reference occurs when the DRA expression of the anaphor's unit intersects the one of the most recent antecedent, there is a unit on this common segment that realises the same center as the one referred by the anaphor and this unit is not linearly the most recent to the anaphor. In still another words, an indirect reference occurs when the chain of units of backward looking co-references intersects the DRA of anaphor's unit in a unit that is not the most recent to the anaphor's unit.

Anything that does not obey the direct or indirect references are *inferential references*. This happens when there is no intersection between the backward looking chain of co-references' units and the DRA of the anaphor's unit.

A particular category of inference references is something that we would call *pragmatic references*, or *pseudo references*. These are REs that practically do not refer back in the discourse although an entity identically realised was already introduced. If she says that she waked up this morning at the same time with the sun and, after a few sentences, she says that no cloud covers the sun, it is questionably that in this last sentence she refers back to her first mention of the celestial object. One can understand the last sentence without making the connection with the first one. We all know about sun and anytime we are said about it we know what the concept is because it is outside the text, it is the same to all of us, it is pragmatic knowledge. But if we make a story about the sun in which it is passing through different events, from its raising to its dawning, than here we have references. Although everybody knows what the sun is, one can understand the story only linking the textual entities mentioned in sequence to the same situational entity. Because they are told about in the same story, doing things or participating in connected events, it is important that one has the same mental representation about all the mentioned suns, and not only knowing them as having identical functionality.

The difference between cases as the ones mentioned could be reflected, although not necessarily, by considering the references in connection with the veins structure. It is most plausible that references in the first example could appear as inferential references, while references in the second example could be recovered as direct or indirect references.

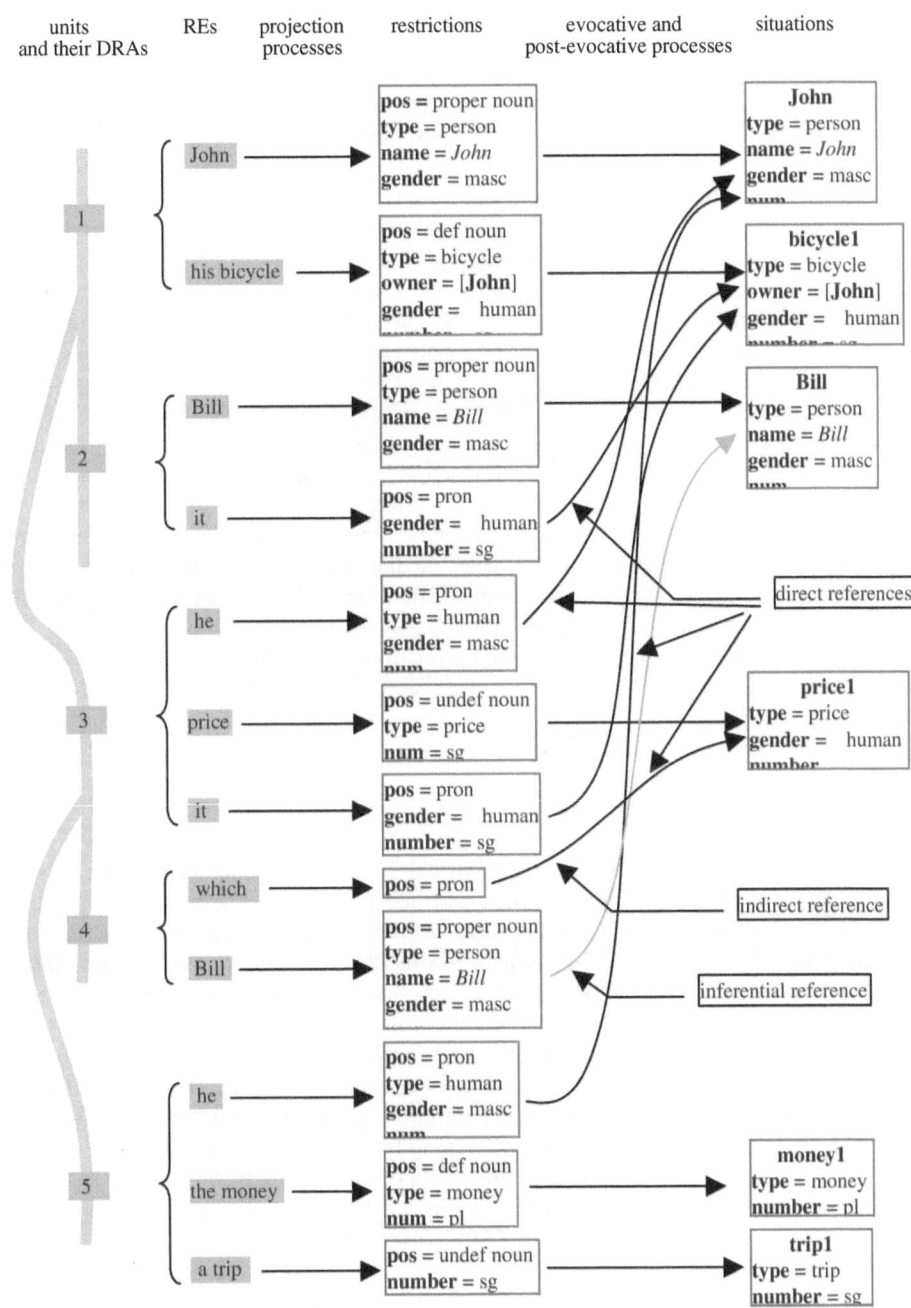

Fig. 5. Anaphoric relations in connection with discourse structure on Ex. 1

Inferential references seem to minimize the importance of the domain of referential accessibility, as defined in VT, because references can now "escape" from the domain. Does anymore the domain of accessibility have any significance? Is it an artificial invention or it is defended by a natural characteristic of the manner humans process texts? We claim that there are two significantly distinct types of anaphora resolution processes: *evocative* (or *associative*) and *post-evocative* (or *inferential*).

The evocative resolution processes are due to direct and indirect references. They are based on associations, which are processes of pattern-matching on feature structures decorated with morpho-semantic attributes. They are performed between a feature structure projected by the anaphor RE and a center that exists already in the DRA of the unit the anaphor belongs to. As such, they are performed between layer two and layer three feature structures. These are fast processes, direct ones being faster and more frequent than indirect ones.

On the other hand, the post-evocative processes are inferential processes that are developed in memory, based on the knowledge accumulated by the preceding discourse, or based on the cultural knowledge the subject owns. We believe these inferences swings the semantic space in an order that is also dictated by discourse structure. Eventually, the target entity can be found based on a pattern-matching process between the projected structure of the anaphor and the center of the antecedent. They are slow (compel to more inference load), necessitate more powerful referencing means (like proper nouns) and are less frequent processes.

Fig. 5 shows different types of anaphoric relations for the discourse of Ex. 1.

2.2   VT and Discourse Coherence

The second claim of VT extends the classical Centering Theory (CT) [6] at global level. As defined, centering is a theory of local coherence. CT defines a set of transition types for discourse [6], [1]: CONTINUATION which is easier to process than RETAINING, which is easier than SMOOTH SHIFTING, which is easier than ABRUPT SHIFTING. In [3] a *smoothness index* was introduced to compare different discourse structures and interpretations. The smoothness index for a transition is based on the CT natural rating of transitions: CONTINUATION = 4, RETAINING = 3, SMOOTH SHIFTING = 2, ABRUPT SHIFTING =1, no backward-looking center (Cb) = 0. Then the scores for each transition in the entire segment are summed up, and the result is divided by the number of transitions in the segment. An index of the overall coherence of the segment, called *global smoothness score*, is such obtained. VT claims that the global smoothness score of a discourse when computed following the neighbouring metric given by vein expressions, following VT, is at least as high as the score computed following the adjacency metric recommended by CT, when extended to the whole discourse. By this, VT claims that long-distance transitions computed over return-pops, using vein expressions, are systematically smoother than accidental transitions at segment boundaries. We use the global smoothness score as criteria of acceptability of a discourse structure.

Table 1 and Table 2 exemplify transitions and global scores in CT and, respectively, VT for Ex. 1. A comparison between the two tables clearly show the better global score obtained in the hierarchical case. The three sequences of units form coherent argumentation lines:

1. *John sold his bicycle*
2. *although Bill would have wanted it.*

1. *John sold his bicycle*
3. *He obtained a good price for it,*
4. *which Bill could have not afforded.*

1. *John sold his bicycle*
3. *He obtained a good price for it,*
5. *Therefore he decided to use the money for going in a trip.*

and, on each of them, the discourse is smoother then in the original overall discourse.

Table 1. Transitions and scores on a linear adjacency metric (**J** = [**John**], **b** = [**John's bicycle**], **B** = [**Bill**], **p** = [**price**], **m** = [**the money**], **t** = [**a trip**])

	1	2	3	4	5
CF	**J, b**	**B, b**	**J, p, b**	**p, B**	**J, m, t**
CB	**J**	**b**	**b**	**p**	**-**
Trans		ASH	RET	SSH	no Cb
Score		1	3	2	0
Global					6/4 = 1.5

Table 2. Transitions and scores on a hierarchical adjacency metric (same notations as in Table 1). Only one transition is computed for each unit (excepting the first)

	1	2
CF	**J, b**	**B, b**
CB	**J**	**b**
Trans		ASH
Score		1
Global		

	1	3	4
CF	**J, b**	**J, p, b**	**p, B**
CB	**J**	**J**	**p**
Trans		CON	SSH
Score		4	2
Global			

	1	3	5
CF	**J, b**	**J, p**	**J, m, t**
CB	**J**	**J**	**J**
Trans		CON	CON
Score			4
Global			11/4 = 2.75

2.3   Incremental Discourse Parsing

Expectation-driven incremental discourse parsing [4] applies to the processing of discourse an idea of incremental parsing developed initially for syntactic analysis within the LTAG framework [11]. Two operations on trees, *adjunction* and *substitution*, add at each step a small piece of structure to the current developed tree (CDT). Adjoining adds an auxiliary tree with at least one material (discourse unit) node. Substitution unifies the root of a substitution structure with an empty node (denoting an expectation) of a CDT. These operations can be performed only on the generalised right frontier of the CDT, equal to the right frontier if CDT is expectation nodes free, or the right frontier of the subtree rooted by the left sibling of the inner-most expectation node, otherwise.

3   A Mixed Approach in Discourse Parsing

Using VT as a guiding theory in an incremental discourse parsing approach is based on the assumption that the tree resulted after the parsing process, among the family of all possible RST-like discourse trees composed with rhetorical relations induced by cue-words of the text, is the one which manifests the more natural overall references over the discourse structure and the smoothest overall CT transitions on veins. The computation of centering transitions is based heavily on the resolution of anaphoric expressions which are looked for within the domains of accessibility given by the vein expressions in the developing tree.

In what follows we investigate the behaviour of a system with a more restricted architecture than the one presented in [12]. From the set of optional knowledge sources we retain only four: a *part-of-speech tagger (PosTag)* – which provides morphological markers for each word, a *cue-words expert (CueExp)* – which splits the text in discourse units[1] and provides hints with respect to identification of rhetorical relations and their place of insertion based on a collection of cue-words heuristics, a *reference resolution expert (RefExp)* – aiming to solve inter-unit pronominal and functional anaphora, and an incremental *discourse parser (DiscPar)* – which builds the associated discourse tree(s).

On the text in Ex. 1 the incremental parser performs as shown in Fig. 6[2]. The first step builds the trivial tree made of only one unit. As this unit initialises the discourse, *RefExp* will introduce two semantic entities (centers) corresponding to *John* and *his bicycle*, as in Fig. 5.

Based on the cue-word *although*, *CueExp* proposes for the auxiliary tree of the second unit a CONCESSION relation and the discourse parser adjoins it in the unique node of the right frontier – unit 1 (in Fig. 6 nodes of the right frontier are numbered in sequence bottom-up - 0 being the lowest right one). *RefExp* will find that the projected FS of *Bill* doesn't match any of the centers [**John**] and [**bicycle1**], both placed on the vein of unit 2, the only existing FS on the semantic layer at the moment, and this will result in introducing a new entity, [**Bill**]. As for *it*, it will match [**bicycle1**].

---

[1] Minimally a clause, maximally a dot-to-dot compound sentence.
[2] To make the text shorter, some details are skipped.

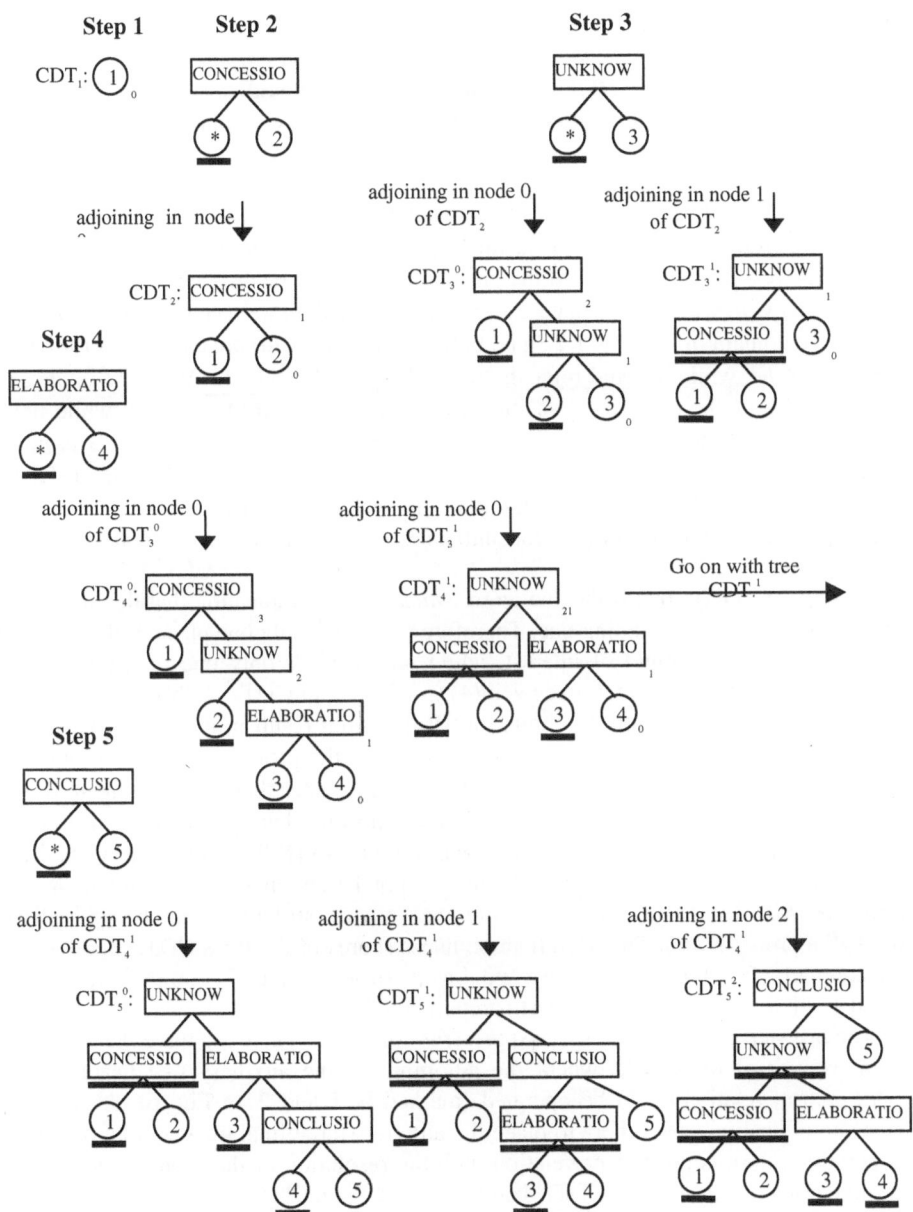

Fig. 6. Incremental tree building for the discourse in Ex. 1.

There is no cue word in unit 3 that could hint on the type of relation, so *CueExp* proposes an UNKNOWN relation as root of the auxiliary tree. At step 3 there are two places (marked 0 and 1) on the right frontier of the CDT_2 where this auxiliary tree could be adjoined by *DiscPar*. Adjoining at node 0 would raise CDT_3^0 such that vein(3) = 1 2 3, while adjoining at node 1 yields CDT_3^1 where vein(3) = 1 3. *RefExp* is trying to resolve the anaphors using the DRAs given by VT on the already developed tree. As the domain of unit 3 on CDT_3^1 is 1 3, the REs *he, price* and *it* of this unit will be matched against semantic entities introduced by REs of units 3 and 1 (in this order) and will, therefore, be found to be [**John**], [**price1**] (no match, newly introduced) and [**bicycle1**], respectively. Note that the pronoun *he* will not be erroneously linked to the entity [**Bill**] with whom it resonate and which is linearly more recent. In the variant of CDT_3^0 the domain of unit 3 is 1 2 3 and both [**John**] and [**Bill**] are candidates for being referents of *he*, while *it* could refer the same [**bicycle1**] as before. When *he* is chosen to evoke [**John**] the centering transition from 2 to 3 is ABRUPT SHIFTING while if *he* would be [**Bill**], the transition is CONTINUING. Therefore on CDT_3^0 *he* in 3 is more plausible to be [**Bill**] than [**John**] (obviously an erroneous choice), while in CDT_3^1 *he* is unequivocally [**John**]. At this moment the parser has two structures that will continue to be developed in parallel until one is significantly better scored than the other.

At step 4 *CueExp* founds the cue word *which* to be an indication that this unit is an ELABORATION of the preceding one. Therefore on CDT_3^0 only one place of the three on the right frontier is found of interest, while on CDT_3^1 – only one of the two. The resulting trees are CDT_4^0 that gives vein(4) = 1 2 3 4 and CDT_4^1 with vein(4) = 1 3 4. The variant when *he* in unit 3 is bound to [**Bill**] would result in the case of CDT_4^0 to the extremely low probable reference (see [5]) from the proper noun *Bill* in unit 4 to the entity [**Bill**] realised by a pronoun in unit 3. This makes that at this moment, of the two possible variants of CDT_4^0, to be retained the one that indicated *he* in 3 being bound to [**John**] and *Bill* in 4 referring back in unit 2 to [**Bill**]. On the tree CDT_4^1 the same links are found, although now unit 2, not being on the vein of unit 4, the reference *Bill* from 4 to 2 is of an inference nature, still plausible (being realised through a proper noun). The overall smoothness scores of the trees CDT_4^0 and CDT_4^1, are compared (6 – on the sequence 1 2 3 4 as in Table 1, versus 7 – on the sequences 1 2 and 1 3 4 as in Table 2) and the best is retained: CDT_4^1.

The last step exploits the cue-word *therefore* of unit 5. There are three places on the right frontier of the CDT_4^1 where the adjoining of the auxiliary tree headed by a CONCLUSION relation could be operated (marked 0, 1 and 2 on Fig. 6). As *CueExp* gives no indication as to where to place the aux tree, three final trees will be obtained. A possible rating is done in correlation with the resolution of the pronoun *he* and the definite noun *the money*. On CDT_5^0 vein(5) = 1 3 4 5, on CDT_5^1 vein(5) = 1 3 5 and on CDT_5^2 vein(5) = 1 5.

CDT_5^0 where *he* in 5 is [**Bill**] is a rather strange interpretation where *the money* are those Bill intended to give for buying John's bike, and because they were not enough he decided to use them for going in a trip. CDT_5^1 gives an interpretation where the decision of John to use the money for going in a trip came as a result of John obtaining a good price for his bike, and is inferable that the money are the money John obtained for the bike. CDT_5^2 evokes the interpretation in which the decision to go in a trip is only a result of John selling the bike. The money are again those obtained for the bike. The CT transitions rates for the three interpretations are given in the following tables:

Table 3. Transitions corresponding to CDT_5^0 and *he* in 5 = [**Bill**]

	1	2	1	3	4	5
CF	J, b	B, b	J, b	J, p, b	p, B	B, m, t
CB	J	b	J	J	p	B
Trans		ASH		CON	SSH	SSH
Score		1		4	2	2
Global						9/4 = 2.25

Table 4. Transitions corresponding to CDT_5^0 and *he* in 5 = [**John**]

	1	2	1	3	4	5
CF	J, b	B, b	J, b	J, p, b	p, B	J, m, t
CB	J	b	J	J	p	-
Trans		ASH		CON	SSH	no Cb
Score		1		4	2	0
Global						7/4 = 1.75

Table 5. Transitions corresponding to CDT_5^1 and *he* in 5 = [**John**]

	1	2	1	3	4	1	3	5
CF	J, b	B, b	J, b	J, p, b	p, B	J, b	J, p, b	J, m, t
CB	J	b	J	J	p	J	J	J
Trans		ASH		CON	SSH		CON	CON
Score		1		4	2			4
Global								11/4 = 2.75

Table 6. Transitions corresponding to CDT_5^2 and *he* in 5 = [**John**]

	1	2	1	3	4	1	5
CF	J, b	B, b	J, b	J, p, b	p, B	J, b	J, m, t
CB	J	b	J	J	P	J	J
Trans		ASH		CON	SSH		CON
Score		1		4	2		4
Total							11/5 = 2.75

The scores given in these tables are used to rate the trees obtained. The final trees of the analysis are thus CDT_5^1 and CDT_5^2, very close to the ones in Fig. 1.

4   Conclusions

In this paper we revise Veins Theory – a theory of discourse cohesion and coherence and show how it can be used in an architecture aimed at building discourse structure simultaneously with resolving anaphorae. The discourse units are revealed from raw text by a collection of heuristics that rely on cue words. Units are incrementally attached to the developing tree on the right frontier. By computing the vein expression and the domain of referential accessibility of the current unit, the search for antecedents of anaphorae belonging to this unit is restricted. The resolution of anaphorae permits determination of centering transitions using the hierarchical adjacency metric given by veins. Transitions are then used to restrain the exponential explosion of the obtained trees by sorting the trees in the descending order of a global smoothness score and retaining only the most relevant ones for further processing.

Further work is necessary in order to establish the generosity of this approach compared to others (as the one in [9], for instance, that is very well suited for learning parser's moves from a corpus). Automatic learning of heuristics for splitting the discourse in units from an annotated corpus is equally possible in our approach. It remains to establish the feasibility of applying learning techniques for acquiring heuristics that would indicate shapes of auxiliary trees and the places of their adjunction on the developing tree.

References

1. Brennan, S.E., Walker Friedman, M., Pollard, C.J.: A centering approach to pronouns. Proc. of the 25th Annual Meeting of ACL, Stanford (1987)
2. Cristea, D., Ide, N., Marcu, D., Tablan, M.V.: Discourse structure and Co-Reference: An Empirical Study. In: Proceedings of the Workshop Relations Between Discourse Structure and Reference, ACL Maryland (1999)
3. Cristea, D., Ide, N., Romary, L.: Veins Theory - A Model of Global Discourse Cohesion and Coherence. In: Proc. of Coling/ACL'98, Montreal (1998)
4. Cristea, D. Webber, B.L.: Incremental expectations in discourse parsing. In: Proc. of ACL/EACL, Madrid (1997)
5. Gordon P.C., Hendrick R.: The representation and processing of coreference in discourse. In: Cognitive Science, 22 (1998)
6. Grosz, B.J.; Joshi, A., Weinstein, S.: Centering – a framework for modelling the local coherence of discourse. In: Computation Linguistics, 12(2), June (1995)
7. Grosz, B., Sidner, C.: Attention, intention and the structure of discourse. In: Computational Linguistics, 12 (1986)
8. Mann, W.C., Thompson S.A.: Rhetorical structure theory: A theory of text organization. In: Text 8:3 (1988)
9. Marcu, D.: A Decision-Based Approach to Rhetorical Parsing. In: Proceedings of the ACL'99 (1999)
10. Mitkov, R.: Robust Pronoun Resolution with Limited Knowledge. In: Proceedings of COLING-ACL'98, Montreal (1998)
11. Shabes, Y.: Mathematical and Computational Aspects of Lexicalized Grammars, Technical Report MS-CIS-90-48, LINC LAB 179 (1990)
12. Tablan, M.V., Barbu, C., Popescu, H., Hamza, R.O., Ciobanu, C., Nita, I.C., Bocaniala, C.D., Georgescul, M., Cristea D.: Co-opertion and Detachement in Discourse Understanding. In: Proc. of the Workshop on Lexical Semantics and Discourse, ESSLLI'98, Saarbruecken (1988)
13. Walker M.A.: Centering, Anaphora Resolution and Discourse Structure. In Walker, M.A.; Joshi, A.K.; Prince, E.F. (eds.): Centering in Discourse, Oxford University Press (1997)

A Spatio-temporal Model for the Representation of Situations Described in Narrative Texts

S. Gerard and J.P. Sansonnet

LIMSI-CNRS, BP 133, F-91403
Orsay Cedex (France)
{gerard,jps}@limsi.fr

http://www.limsi.fr/Individu/jps/interviews/

Abstract. Situation models have been developed to answer to the general problem of understanding and reasoning about texts.. The model we propose aims to represent the spatio-temporal information contained in a text. We propose the use of 2-D holophrastic matrixes to represent space, and of 1-D holophrastic matrixes to represent time. Then, the analysis of a text starts from a void scene. Each time a new object appears into the text, the system uses a prototype to create the object's representation and then places it at the proper position (time and place) into the scene. This representation is called dynamical in that a prototype is not only a spatial extension of a given object but it also contains the behaviours associated to the object. The representation of an explicit action of the text is the application of these behaviours to the corresponding objects. Finally, the representation of a feature is the modification of an object's extension and behaviour by the application of an operator.

1. Background

Researches led during the last ten years in the field of comprehension and memorisation of sentences have largely confirmed the model proposed by [3]. Far from being only an interpretative activity (strict application of grammar rules), the comprehension is the product of three interdependent processes [2]: **a) an integration process** - the subject builds a coherent semantical representation from semantically linked but not necessarily concomitant data. **b) a construction process** - the semantical representation is enhanced with the results of the inferences, either deductions or induction, made by the subject **c) an elaboration process** - the personal subject knowledge is finally added to the semantical representation.

The model developed by Kintsch [11] in the context of his researches on processes in reading, actualises these different processes at the text level. According to it, the comprehension is not only considered as a local process, but also as holistic. Indeed, the representation is supposed to be built by a succession of construction-integration cycles applied to small successive fragments of the text. Kintsch used this model to simulate the arithmetic problems comprehension and seems to meet good results. Nevertheless, according to [10], the third step of the construction phase, where the

D.N. Christodoulakis (Ed.): NLP 2000, LNCS 1835, pp. 176-184, 2000.
© Springer-Verlag Berlin Heidelberg 2000

system has to operate the inferences necessary to the comprehension itself, is probably more difficult to realise, in the particular case of *narrative texts*, which are addressed in this paper.

The study presented here has been developed with the intent of being integrated to the MoHa (an hybrid machine learning model) project [1]. This project aims to propose a model for natural language comprehension and machine learning by a permanent confrontation with experience. The system has thus to be able to learn new knowledge from *concrete experiences*, and reciprocally to use this knowledge to understand new experiences. The model proposed by MoHa relies on the decomposition of knowledge into four different levels. One of these levels, the episodic one, represents the history of simulated "experiences" [7].

2. The Spatio-temporal Model

Our claim is that, in the general context of the stable text comprehension model proposed by Kintsch, the logical mode of representation is not fully adapted to the particular problem of automatic narrative texts comprehension. De Vega and Rodrigo [6] conducted some experiments concerning the mental models build by subjects during the processing of narrative texts. They especially showed the way these models are used by the readers to *operate inferences on spatial implicit relations* in the particular case of movement descriptions in some environment. They also measured that mental models *preserve the spatial perspective*. On our opinion, it is not only a human cognitive limitation, but also a justification of the use of homomorphic representations of the world to develop a natural language comprehension, at least in the field of narrative texts.

To integrate this point of view into a natural language processing system, we based it on a **physical model** of the situation in order to support the semantical representation of the text [4], [8]. By "physical models", we mean that these models are:

Extensional representations: that is, based on a description of the objects of the world, and not on abstract concepts; they are homomorphic representations of the world.

Dynamical representations: since their content evolves with the situation they represent.

Constructive representations: they are produced by the integration of different objects and general knowledge about the world. In particular, a models does not correspond to an *a priori* schema instantiation like Scripts [12].

The comprehension that this representation brings, comes from the fact that it is used to make inferences from compiled knowledge about the environment and that it acts back over the model itself. Some examples extracted from [4] are:

Common sense: "if X includes Y and that Y is removed then Y is removed."
Domain: "if A is composed of thyroidal cells then A fixes iodine."

This way, one can build a large number of inferences from the interaction of independent knowledge sources, *without having to explicit all the a priori possible inferences*.

For this work, we focused on the extraction of spatio-temporal features from narrative texts. To give an optimal answer to the need for a homomorphic representation, we propose a model where representations are *distributed over time and space*. The objects representation in our model will obviously seem less complete than in the Cavazza and Zweigenbaum model, but we think it worth the effort since we do not want to be restrained to a particular domain.

3. Model Definition

The proposed model has three fundamental characteristics:

- Our model makes use of a spatio-temporal representation.

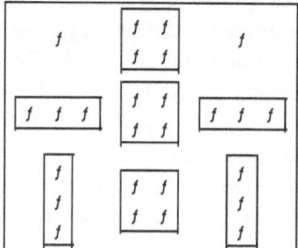 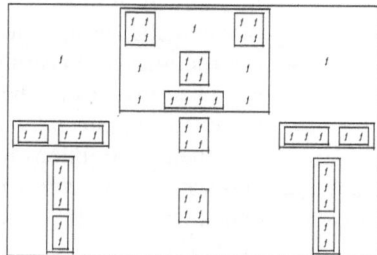

Fig. 1. Two different levels of representation for a human being. The one on the right hand side is a further decomposition of the one on the left hand side.

Objects, scenes and global situation of a particular text correspond to an extension. Time and Space are discrete. Nevertheless, to allow some flexibility of the model, a time or space unit can be either *terminal* (written as a small square when representing solid space: , otherwise considered as empty and therefor which can contain other objects, written with braces: {}) or *decomposed* by refinements into other extensions. This is expressed by the following syntax:

$$extension \; ::= \; \mathbf{Space} \, [\, (\, M_{i,j,k} \,) \,] \mid \mathbf{Time} \, [\, (\, M_i \,) \,] \, ; \qquad (1)$$

$$\mathbf{i, j, k} \; M_{i,j,k}{}^1, M_i \; ::= \quad \mid \{ \, object... \, \} \mid extension \, ; \qquad (2)$$

We will say that this representation is based on *holophrastic matrixes* i.e. matrixes that can be embedded, within each other, in order to implement a variable granularity

---

[1] The testbed that we have developed (Cf. *§4*) is restricted to the handling of two-dimensional space, for the convenience of displaying the scenes.

for the objects, depending on their degree of description within the narrative texts (Cf. *Fig. 1*).

- Our model is based on prototypes.

We defined a library of prototypes (with a hierarchical structure) which are associated with an ontology of classes corresponding to objects occurring in the described world. When we effectively build the situation from the narrative text, prototypes of occurring objets are instantiated, with regard to their specific attributes in the text. In *Fig. 2*, an example of prototype is given for a human being: thus we obtain the spatio-temporal representation of a prototypal human built from human parts: head, body, legs...

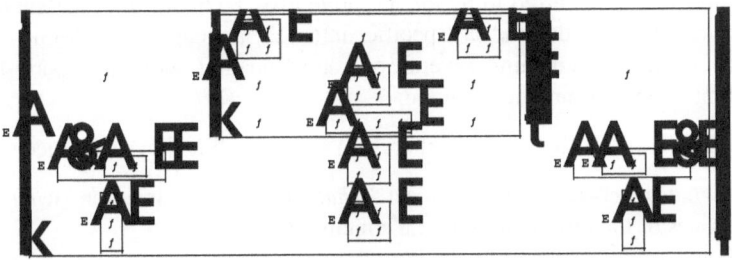

Fig. 2. Internal representation of a prototypal human being. A particular part, say the head, is in turn decomposed into subparts: two eyes, a nose, a mouth... When the granularity of a part is finer, the display of its representation is enlarged.

- Our model is based on dynamical processes.

In order to represent a situation, we did not simply represent the results of actions, but we made the choice of an effective simulation of them, as they are described within the text. Therefore, in our model, to each object is attached a process which determines its default movement in the world (when it is not explicited in the text). As we have mentioned earlier, our claim is to provide a "physics" simulating the real world in a quite precise way. This commitment requires that some of the basic physical laws were integrated in the model (basics of Newtonian physics, of Thermodynamic...). Instead of implementing global laws, we choose to link to each dynamical object a process describing its own behaviour, e.g. law of displacement for its internal parts. The formal definition for a physical object (or for a prototype) is given by:

$$object, \ prototype \ : : = \ \{ \ extension, \ movement, \ law \} ; \qquad (3)$$

$$movement, \ law \ : : = \ \{ \ displacement, \ forbidden\text{-}objects, \qquad (4)$$

$$mandatory\text{-}objects \ \} ;$$

$$forbidden\text{-}objects, \ mandatory\text{-}objects \ : : = \ \{ \ object... \} ; \qquad (5)$$

An example of dynamical scene is given in the appendix.

4. Implementation and Experiments

In order to make an evaluation of the relevance of our model, it has been implemented and applied [9] to a newspaper text which describes an assassination attempt on the person of Martin Luther-King and which has been used as a benchmark (called MLK bench) in the MoHa project.

The software system that has been developed[2] cannot be considered as a complete natural language processing system: in fact, in order to build the representation of a situation we start from the intermediate language already in use in MoHa. The situation described in the narrative text is built within an "experiment arena" which is formally defined as the initially empty objet { } and which will include all the scenes and physical objects referred to by the narrative text. To build the representation of a particular scene, we defined a specific internal language: the Arena Building Language (**ABL**). It contains several operators dealing with the spatio-temporal localisation of objects, among them are:

ClearArena: resets the experiment arena, i.e. clears all its physical objects.

Place[*what, where*]: places an object (*what*) at a precise location (*where*), using coordinates or the representation of a containing object.

FindInto[*where, what*]: searches for the location of all the occurrences of a particular object (*what*) within a specified object (*where*).

PlaceInto[*what, within_what, where*]: places a given set of objects (*what*) within a specified object (*within_what*), while specifying an optional location (*where*).

DistributeInto[*what, within_what, filter*]: executes a random dispatch of the set of objects (*what*) within the specified object (*within_what*), while specifying an optional location *filter*.

Below, is given the translation into the **ABL** for the first sentence of the MLK Bench: "Some years ago, I was in a big department store in Harlem, among several dozens of people":

ClearArena[ ]
Place[{some, years}, ARENA]
Place[{1, town}, {1, 1}]
PlaceInto[ARENA, {town}, {1, big, store}]
DistributeInto[{big, store}, {1, speaker, and, some, 12, human}]

Fig. 3 shows, on the left hand side, the whole scene resulting from the execution of these ABL instructions. On the right hand side is an enlarged display of this scene zooming in the department store. As the sentence is essentially a static description, the scene has no dynamical object. The appendix gives in the same way the display of a dynamical scene built from another sentence of the MLK bench.

---

[2] Using the Mathematica 3.0.1 environment from Wolfram Research.

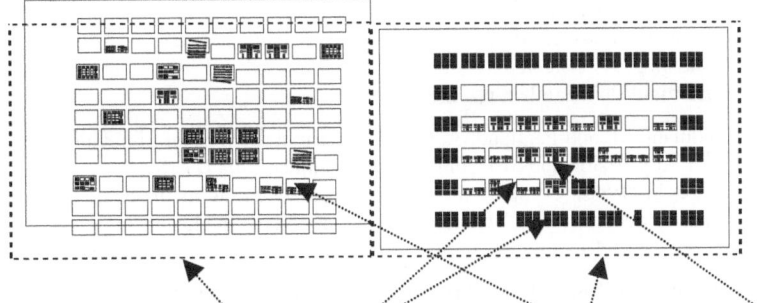

Fig. 3. the representation of **Harlem** seen from upside, the **big department store** with **Martin Luther King** among several dozens of **people**.

5. Conclusion and Further Work

We proposed a model that associates spatio-temporal representation features with situation and dynamical processes for the automatic comprehension of narrative texts, and we applied it to a restrained but real narrative text corpus coming from the AFP (French Press Agency).

We define two complementary axes for future work. First, we have to ameliorate the spatio-temporal representation of objects and scenes to allow a refinement of the prototypes descriptions and to develop the construction of the ABL situation language, more particularly concerning dynamic aspects. Second, we have to define reasoning tools that operate on the effective representation builds into the arena. These tools should allow an effective explicitation of the implicit (determination of the tacit) contents of narrative texts, which is the underlying aim for our model.

References

1. Bordeaux, F., Forest, F., and Grau B. (1993). *MoHA, un modele hybride d'apprentissage*. Notes et documents LIMSI n. 93-10, Orsay.

2. Bransford, J.D. (1979). *Human Cognition : Learning, Understanding and Remembering*. Belmont, Wadsworth Publishing Company.

3. Bransford, J.D. and Franks, J.J. (1972). The abstraction of linguistic ideas : A review. *Cognition*, **1**, pp. 211-249.

4. Cavazza, M. and Zweigenbaum, P. (1992). Comprehension automatique du langage naturel par construction de modeles, *TSI*, **11**, 4.

5. Cohen P. and Oates T. (1998). A Dynamical Basis for the Semantic Content of Verbs. *AAAI 1998 Workshop The Grounding of Word Meaning: Data and Models*.

6. De Vega, M. and Rodrigo, M.J (1997). - Les representations topologiques dans le traitement des descriptions spatiales. In M. Denis (Ed.), *Langage et cognition spatiale*, Masson, Paris, pp. 51-68.

7.   Ferret, O. and Grau, B. (1997) - An episodic memory for understanding and learning. In Ruslan Mitkov et Nicolas Nicolov (Ed.), *Recent Advances in Natural Languages Processing : Selected Papers from RANLP'95*, John Benjamins, Amsterdam/Philadelphia, pp. 173-184.

8.   Friedmann M. and Pentland, A. (1992), Distributed Physical Simulation. MIT Media Laboratory Vision and Modeling Group Technical Report #189.

9.   Gerard, S. (1998). Etude d'un modele de representation distribuee de textes narratifs. Memoire de D.E.A. de Sciences Cognitives, Notes et documents LIMSI n. 99-17, Orsay.

10. Guha A. and Rossi J.P. (1996). Theoretical aspects of the "construction-integration" model, LIMSI-CNRS, Universite Paris-Sud.

11. Kintsch, W. (1988). The role of knowledge in discourse comprehension : A construction-integration model. *Psychological review, 95*, pp. 163-182.

12. Schank R. (1977). SAM A story understander, Yale University Press, 43.

13. Winkler F.-G. (1995). Meaningful Representations? A Dynamical Systems Approach and Some Implications for Cognitive Science. In O'Nuallain S. and McKevitt P.(eds.), *AISB-95 Workshop on Reaching for Mind: Foundations of Cognitive Science*, Society for the Study of Artificial Intelligence and Simulation of Behaviour.

Appendix

To show how the dynamic is simulated in our model, we present here the visualisation (in our system, it is a real movie animation, represented here by successive pictures, to be read from top to bottom, and left to right) constructed for the fifth sentence of the MLK bench : "I was driven in emergency to Harlem's hospital where I stayed long hours while thousands of preparative were done to extract the weapon out of my body".

The first part of the sentence, "I was driven in emergency to Harlem's hospital", produces:

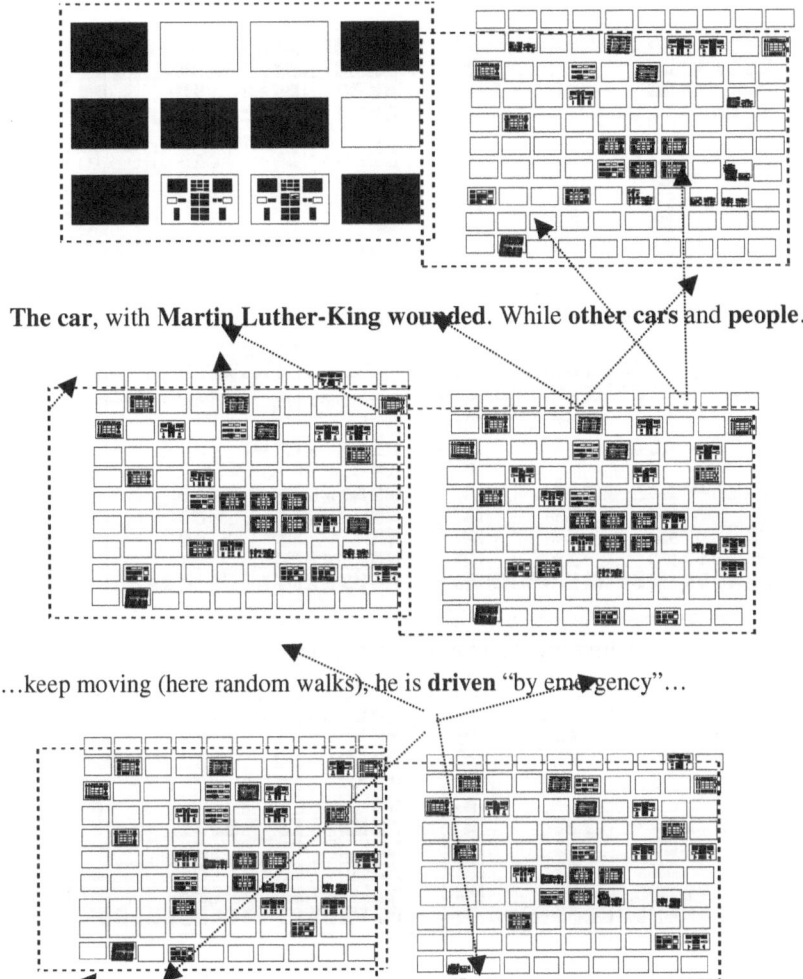

The car, with **Martin Luther-King wounded**. While **other cars** and **people**…

…keep moving (here random walks), he is **driven** "by emergency"…

…(twice the speed of other cars) to the **hospital.**

The second part, "where I stayed long hours while thousands of preparative were done to extract the weapon out of my body", produces:

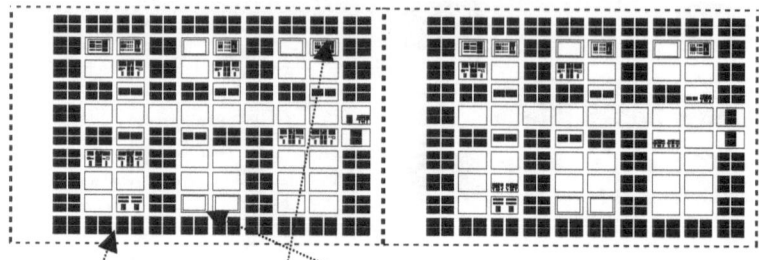

In the **hospital**, there are **patients** (on **beds**, they don't move),...

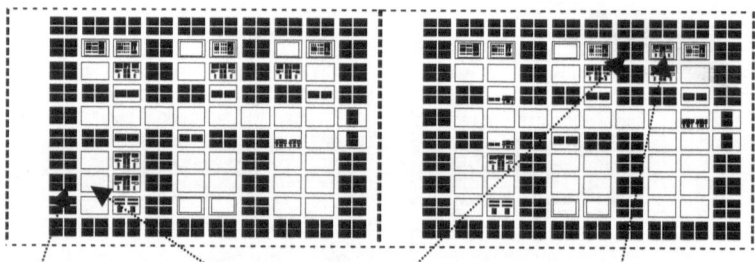

...**doctors** (they have a **bistoury**) and **nurses** (they have a **suringe**).

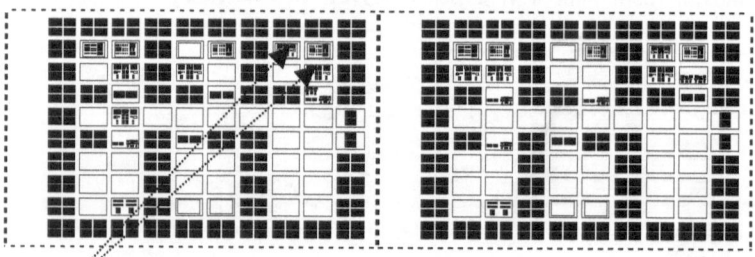

Some of them are doing thousands (not all represented here) of preparatives.

Enhancing Preference-Based Anaphora Resolution with Genetic Algorithms

Constantin Orăsan, Richard Evans, and Ruslan Mitkov

School of Humanities, Languages and Social Sciences
University of Wolverhampton, Stafford Street
Wolverhampton, WV1 1SB, UK.
{in6093,in6087,r.mitkov}@wlv.ac.uk
http://www.wlv.ac.uk/sles/compling/

Abstract. The paper argues that a promising way to improve the success rate of preference-based anaphora resolution algorithms is the use of machine learning. The paper outlines MARS - a program for automatic resolution of pronominal anaphors and describes an experiment which we have conducted to optimise the success rate of MARS with the help of a genetic algorithm. After the optimisation we noted an improvement up to 8% for some files. The results obtained after optimisation are discussed.

1 Introduction

Anaphors are words or groups of words which point back to preceding words, groups of words or larger fragments of text called antecedents and which take the meaning of the antecedents for their own. Anaphora resolution is the task of tracking down the antecedent of a specific anaphor.[1] The resolution rules based on different sources of knowledge and used in the resolution process (and which constitute the anaphora resolution algorithm) can be *preferential* giving more preference to certain candidates over others, such as salience (center of attention), parallelism or proximity. Alternatively, rules can be *eliminating* i.e. discarding certain noun phrases from the set of possible candidates, such as in the case of gender and number constraints, c-command constraints and selectional restrictions. The *preference-based* strategies which compute the antecedent from a set of candidates on the basis of various preferences have been particularly popular in recent years.

In [6], Mitkov (1998) described a knowledge-poor preference-based approach[2] to anaphora resolution (the current implementation of which will be referred to as MARS) and reported its high success rate in a restricted genre. The evaluation of that approach was carried out as the algorithm was applied to texts manually

---

[1] In NLP the best understood and investigated task is the resolution of nominal anaphors (anaphoric pronouns and noun phrases) whose antecedents are NPs. Our project addresses the automatic resolution of pronominal anaphors.
[2] We term the preferences used in our algorithm 'antecedent indicators'.

D.N. Christodoulakis (Ed.): NLP 2000, LNCS 1835, pp. 185–195, 2000.
© Springer-Verlag Berlin Heidelberg 2000

annotated with the correct marking of the lexical categories of words and NP boundaries. Therefore, the evaluation addressed the accuracy of the resolution algorithm and did not take into account possible pre-processing errors.

Our project deals with fully automatic pronoun resolution whose antecedents are NPs. We do not rely on any pre-processed corpora, (manual) selection of anaphors whose antecedents are NPs only, or preliminary (manual) filtering of instances which are difficult to resolve - as is often done with implemented systems.

Given the limitations of pre-processing and the drop in performance that inevitably results, ways of improving the accuracy of anaphora resolution systems should be sought. One important factor is to use, if possible, high-quality pre-processing tools. We have chosen for MARS one of the best available "super-taggers" in English - Conexor's FDG Parser [7]. This super-tagger provides information on the dependency relations between words which allows the extraction of complex NPs. It also gives morphological information and the syntactic roles of words.

For preference-based algorithms, in addition to the traditional intuitive and corpus-based amendments of the preferences employed and their numerical values, one more promising way of improving the accuracy is to make use of genetic algorithms for optimisation.

This paper discusses the experiment we embarked upon to improve the performance of the fully automatic anaphora resolution performed by MARS. It will be shown that optimising preference-based anaphora resolution algorithms with genetic algorithms will improve the success rate.

The paper is structured as follows. Section 2 presents the original statement of our anaphora resolution algorithm. In section 3 we show that this algorithm can be improved and optimised by adding new indicators and by using a genetic algorithm to find the optimal set of values for indicator outcomes. In sections 4 and 5 we present our evaluation and conclusions.

2   MARS: The Pronoun Resolution Algorithm

[6] was proposed for resolving anaphors in the domain of technical manuals. It is a three step process which requires accurate identification of pronouns and preceding NPs in a window of two sentences prior to each pronoun. Considered by some researchers to be a straightforward task, the identification of NPs can be problematic due to the occurrence of complex embedded constituents and prepositional phrase attachment ambiguity. For this reason, that task is quite error-prone. In section 4, we show that this imposes limits on the maximum possible success rate of our system. In some cases, the correct antecedent is not considered as a possible candidate.

In step one, an agreement filter is applied so that no NP may be considered a suitable candidate for antecedent of a pronoun if it does not agree with the pronoun in terms of number and gender.

In step two, a set of boosting and impeding indicators are applied to each candidate NP. The boosting ones apply a positive score to a NP, reflecting a positive likelihood that it is the antecedent of the current pronoun. In contrast, the impeding indicators apply a negative score to a NP, reflecting a lack of confidence that it is the antecedent of the current pronoun. In this paper, we will refer to the different scores applied by an indicator to a pronoun's candidates as *indicator outcome values*. It should be noted that steps one and two have not been implemented with perfect accuracy and there are several differences between this original statement of the algorithm and MARS itself.

For the English language, the *boosting indicators* are:

- *First Noun Phrases* (FNP): A score of +1 is assigned to the first NP in a sentence.
- *Indicating Verbs* (IV): A score of +1 is assigned to those NPs immediately following a verb which is a member of a predefined set.
- *Indicating Noun Phrases* (IN): A score of +1 is assigned to those NPs that follow a verb where the head of the NP preceding the verb is a member of the set {chapter, section, table, ...}.
- *Lexical Reiteration* (Rei): A score of +2 is assigned to those NPs repeated twice or more in the paragraph in which the pronoun appears, a score of +1 is assigned to those NPs repeated once in that paragraph.
- *Section Heading Preference* (SH): A score of +1 is assigned to those NPs that also occur in the heading of the section in which the pronoun appears.
- *Collocation Pattern Preference* (CPP): A score of +2 is assigned to those NPs that have an identical collocation pattern to the pronoun.
- *Immediate Reference* (IR): A score of +2 is assigned to those NPs appearing in constructions of the form "... *(You) V_1 NP ... con (you) V_2 it (con (you) V_3 it)*" where con ϵ {after, and, before, or, ...}.
- *Sequential Instructions* (SI): A score of +2 is applied to NPs in the NP_1 position of constructions of the form: "To V_1 NP_1, V_2 NP_2. (sentence). To V_3 it, V_4 NP_4".
- *Term Preference* (TP): A score of +1 is applied to those NPs identified as representing terms in the genre of the text.

The *impeding indicators* are:

- *Definiteness* (Def): Indefinite NPs are assigned a score of -1.
- *Non-prepositional Noun Phrases* (NPN): NPs appearing in prepositional phrases are assigned a score of -1.

One indicator, *Referential Distance* (RD), may impede or boost a candidate's chances of being selected as the antecedent of a pronoun depending on that NP's distance in terms of clause and sentence boundaries from the pronoun. NPs in the previous clause to the pronoun are assigned a score of +2, those in the previous sentence to the pronoun are assigned a score of +1, those in the sentence prior to *that* are assigned a score of 0 and more distant candidates are assigned a score of -1.

In step three, the total score of each candidate is computed by adding the scores of each of its indicators and the candidate with the highest score is selected as the antecedent of the current pronoun. When a number of candidates jointly have the highest score, a number of heuristics are applied to distinguish one as the antecedent. In future work, we intend to further examine the operations and ordering of these heuristics. A more detailed description of each stage of the approach is provided in [6].

3   Improvement and Optimisation

In this section we show how we can improve and optimise the performance of the method described previously. One way of improving it was to change the existing indicators and propose new ones, presented in the next subsection. Another way of improving the system is by recognising non-nominal *it*. (see section 3.2 or [2] which appears in this volume, for a more detailed account).

All the scores for the indicator outcomes were determined by observation of the characteristics of texts from the domain of technical manuals. In section 3.3, we propose an automatic method for finding the optimal set of scores.

3.1   Addition of New Indicators

The new indicators that we proposed are:

- *Penalise Pronoun* (PP): Given that previous pronouns may enter the list of candidates of the current pronoun, we found it useful to impede their chances of being marked as the antecedents of that pronoun. The consideration of pronouns serves simply as an occasional bridge from the current pronoun to candidates that lie beyond the edge of the 2 prior sentences considered by the algorithm. In the rare cases when one pronoun is marked to be the antecedent of another, the antecedent of that pronoun is put forward as the true antecedent.
- *Syntactic Parallelism* (SP): The preprocessing software (FDG-Parser, [7]) used by MARS also provides the syntactic role of the NP complements of the verbs. This indicator increases the chances that a NP with the same syntactic role as the current pronoun will be its antecedent.

3.2   Identification of Non-nominal *It* for Anaphora Resolution

A separate program was implemented to identify only those instances of the pronoun *it* that were linked anaphorically to NPs in the text. This was accomplished by recognising and filtering out pleonastic, idiomatic, cataphoric, pro-action [3], clause referential and discourse segment referential uses of the pronoun. By incorporating this program it is expected that the system's overall performance will increase given that it does not attempt to resolve pronouns which are not anaphoric.

3.3   Optimisation Using a Genetic Algorithm

As we mentioned in section 2, the score of a candidate is computed by adding the scores of each of its indicators. Therefore, we can represent the algorithm as a function with 14 parameters, each being one of the indicators:

$$score_k = \sum_{i=1}^{i=14} x_{k_i} \tag{1}$$

where, $score_k$ is the score of the candidate k and x_{k_i} is the score given by the indicator i for the candidate k. This formula suggests that one way of improving the results of the anaphora resolution system is to find the set of indicator outcome values for which the score is maximum for the antecedents and lower for the rest of the candidates. The current literature identifies three main types of traditional search methods: calculus-based, enumerative and random. The calculus-based search methods have extensively been studied and try to find local extrema. These methods are not very successful in cases where the search space is very noisy because the methods tend to stop in local extrema instead of finding the global one. The enumerative methods try to evaluate the function which is to be optimised for every point in the search space. The method is very simple, but impossible to implement for large search spaces. Random searches have to be discounted for the same reasons as enumerative search. An alternative solution is offered by genetic algorithms, search methods developed in the field of artificial intelligence.

Genetic algorithms (GA) are search algorithms that imitate the principles of natural evolution as a method to solve parameter optimisation problems where the problem space is large, complex and contains possible difficulties like high dimensionality and noise. First proposed by [4], they mimic reproduction and selection of natural populations to achieve efficient and robust optimisation. These algorithms can be viewed as a mathematical representation of Darwin's observations and of the recent synthesis in the theory of evolution. One of the most important aspects of the GA is robustness, meaning a good balance between the exploration of new regions in the solution space and exploitation of those good regions that have already been discovered.

The genetic algorithm maintains a population of candidate solutions to a fitness function represented in the form of *chromosomes*. The *chromosomes* are strings defined over some alphabet that encode the properties of the individual and are specific to each problem. The most widely used codification is the binary codification where the alphabet consists only of 0 and 1.

The algorithm starts with a randomly generated population and with each iteration, using selection, crossover and mutation a new population is created. The algorithm may be terminated when a satisfying solution has been obtained or after a predefined number of generations.

Given that in our case it is necessary to determine the set of indicator outcome values which maximises the success rate of our anaphora resolution system, we tried a number of optimisation techniques including memory-based learning

Table 1. The characteristics of the texts used for evaluation

Text	#Words	#Anaphoric pronouns	#Non-nominal *it*	Classification accuracy for *it*
ACC	9753	158	23	80.15%
CDR	10453	83	7	89.28%
BEO	7493	67	25	77.36%
MAC	15131	148	17	89.65%
PSW	6475	77	2	96.61%
WIN	2882	51	3	-
Total	52187	484	77	-

and the perceptron method, both of which performed poorly with success rates lower than the base. We found GA to be more suitable.

In our case the fitness function, F(X), is the number of anaphors correctly resolved by MARS when the original indicator outcome values are replaced by those generated by the GA.

$$F(X) = \sum_{p \in Pron} \delta(X, p) \tag{2}$$

where $\delta(X, p)$ is 1 if the system selects the correct candidate as an antecedent for the pronoun p, using the set of indicators outcome values X and 0 otherwise. Our aim is to find the set of outcome values for which this function is maximised. Each chromosome, representing a set of indicators, is a string of 31 real numbers, each value representing the outcome of an indicator application and the alphabet is the set of real numbers. We start the process with a randomly generated population in the interval [-3, 3], but we noticed after optimisation that the values obtained are in the interval [-1, 1]. For selection we used the proportional roulette wheel method, where each chromosome has a chance to be selected according to its fitness. On the selected set of chromosomes we apply crossover and mutation operators. We found the best results are obtained using immediate recombination and uniform mutation [1].

4   Evaluation

MARS was evaluated with respect to 6 technical manuals, with the characteristics shown in table 1. The correct classification of *it* as anaphoric or non-anaphoric imposes some limits on the success rate of the system. The accuracy of this classification is presented in the final column of the table.

4.1   Evaluation Measures and Analysis of the Indicators

- *Success Rate*: the ratio of the total number of anaphoric pronouns successfully resolved by MARS and the total number of pronouns in the text identified as being anaphoric by the system.

Table 2. Relative Importance of the set of indicators for different texts (non-optimised version)

Inds	PSW	MAC	WIN	ACC	BEO	CDR
Def	5.26%	5.9%	7.04%	4.61%	2.94%	9.25%
FNP	3.5%	0.99%	13.04%	12.30%	14.70%	11.11%
IV	0%	0%	0%	0%	0%	0%
IN	0%	0%	0%	0%	0%	0%
Rei	-3.5%	1.98%	-13.04%	0%	-14.70%	11.11%
SH	0%	-2.97%	0%	3.07%	0%	5.55%
NPN	-1.75%	-6.93%	4.34%	7.69%	8.82%	0%
CPP	0%	1.98%	0%	-3.07%	0%	0%
IR	0%	5.9%	13.04%	1.53%	5.88%	3.70%
SI	0%	0%	0%	0%	0%	0%
RD	19.26%	10.89%	30.43%	15.38%	14.70%	1.85%
TP	5.26%	-1.98%	4.34%	-9.23%	2.94%	1.85%
SP	0%	0%	0%	0%	-2.94%	1.85%
PP	10.52%	14.85%	30.43%	8.47%	0%	12.96%

– *Relative Importance*: This measure shows how much the system's performance is degraded when an indicator is removed from the algorithm. It is defined as the ratio of the normal success rate - the success rate obtained if a specific indicator is removed to the normal success rate.

Tables 2 and 3 present the *Relative Importance* of each indicator for each file, both before and after optimisation. Negative values in the table reflect the fact that in some cases, removing one of the indicators actually improves the performance of MARS. Inspection of the non-optimised table shows that the most important indicators are RD and PP in most of the cases. The finding that *referential distance* makes a very great relative contribution coincides with that reported in [5]. For the WIN, ACC, BEO and CDR files, FNP is also an important indicator. In all cases, the importance of IV, IN, SI and CPP is negligible. One reason for this might be the characteristics of the texts used for evaluation. Those indicators all look for very specific patterns which do not appear in our texts. A similar observation can be made for the optimised version of the algorithm, but the importance of RD, PP and FNP decreases slightly and the importance of less important indicators increases. Therefore, we can argue that the genetic algorithm makes use of all the indicators proposed by the original method. This is very important, demonstrating that as long the indicators do not contradict each other, more indicators can better select the antecedent.

We carried out a very thorough evaluation on our six files. In addition we merged 2 different files, PSW and MAC, to see the behaviour of the optimisation on files by 2 different authors. The results of this evaluation are summarised in table 4.

Table 3. Relative Importance of the set of indicators for different texts (optimised version)

Inds	PSW	MAC	WIN	ACC	BEO	CDR
Def	4.76%	6.4%	3.44%	-5.55%	0%	-3.38%
FNP	1.58%	3.6%	0%	1.38%	7.14%	3.38%
IV	3.17%	0%	3.44%	-2.77%	-2.38%	1.69%
IN	3.17%	-0.91%	-3.44%	-5.55%	0%	3.38%
Rei	1.5%	-1.8%	0%	2.77%	-2.38%	3.38%
SH	3.17%	-1.8%	-3.44%	0%	4.76%	3.38%
NPN	3.17%	-0.91%	0%	0%	-2.38%	5.08%
CPP	3.13%	0.91%	0%	0%	-2.38%	0%
IR	4.76%	1.83%	0%	-1.38%	7.14%	1.69%
SI	4.76%	1.83%	3.44%	-2.77%	0%	3.38%
RD	14.28%	9.17%	20.68%	4.10%	16.66%	8.47%
TP	1.50%	-2.75%	10.34%	-6.94%	2.38%	1.69%
SP	4.76%	-1.80%	3.44%	-2.77%	-2.38%	1.69%
PP	6.34%	5.5%	20.68%	-1.38%	4.76%	8.47%

On this table, the *MARS* column presents the success rate of both the optimised and non-optimised versions when it is run in its full version (*Default*) and a version in which non-nominal *it* has been identified (*w/o it*). The *MAX* column shows the upper-bound for the success rate. There are two columns in the table because it is possible to have two ways to consider that an anaphor has been correctly resolved. The column *Sct* represents the maximum possible success rate if partial matching is not permitted during the evaluation. As can be seen, this figure does not exceed 91%. Cases where only a part of the antecedent was identified as the correct antecedent were considered successfully resolved, provided the identified part included the head of the NP. In this way, the maximum possible success rate increased to 97%, as shown in the *Ptl* column of the same table. Two baseline models, presented in the *Baseline* column, were evaluated, one in which the most recent candidate was selected as the antecedent and one in which a candidate was selected at random. The success rates are reported here.

In Table 4, it is noticeable that in all the cases when the genetic algorithm was used the success rate of the system increased. The greatest increase was in the case of the PSW file, by almost 8%. This result was expected since PSW was one of the files used for developing the original heuristics.

Initially we considered imposing some constraints for the indicator outcome values to make sure that they behave as they were proposed (impeding or boosting). This can be done by adding another term to the fitness function which penalises it whenever the indicator outcome values do not behave as expected. In the end we decided not to implement this, but to proceed with the GA regardless and to examine whether or not the indicators behave in the manner originally proposed.

Table 4. The results of our experiment

	MARS				MAX		Baseline	
	Non-optimised		Optimised					
Files	Default	w/o it	Default	w/o it	Sct	Ptl	Recent	Random
PSW	72.15	72.00	79.74	80.00	90.91	96.10	12.65	21.51
MAC	61.21	65.33	66.06	70.00	85.13	95.27	23.63	26.06
WIN	45.09	-	56.86	-	82.35	88.23	7.84	21.56
ACC	36.11	38.80	40.00	41.87	77.85	90.51	17.77	20.00
CDR	59.34	62.20	64.83	68.30	72.29	91.57	16.48	20.87
BEO	36.55	44.20	45.16	53.20	85.07	97.01	9.10	18.27
PSW+MAC	64.75	67.60	68.44	71.10	87.05	95.54	20.08	27.86

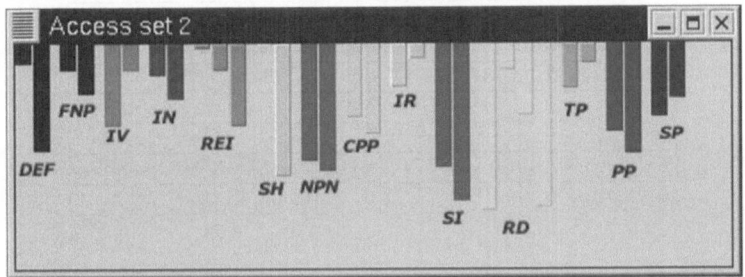

Fig. 1. The normalised indicator outcome values for ACC file

We investigated the characteristics of the indicator outcome values after the optimisation and to this end we designed a program which takes these values, normalises them and then displays their histogram. The results for two files are presented in figures 1 and 2 which enable us to compare different indicator outcome values and look for patterns. Our investigation led to interesting results. In particular, the behaviour of the RD indicator was different from what we expected. In the original method the scores for referential distance are +2 for the candidates in the same sentence, +1 for the ones in the previous sentence, 0 for candidates situated two sentences further back and -1 for more distant candidates. The optimised algorithm proposed other preferences based on the evaluation files. In all of the cases but one, the candidates which are in the same sentence get the highest score (the exception being the file CDR where the highest score was given to candidates which are 3 or more sentences away). More interestingly, in all the studied cases but one (the CDR file), the second highest score was always proposed for the candidate which was 3 or more sentences away. Finally, the results suggested that in some cases the candidates which were 2 sentences away should get a better score than the ones which are only one sentence away. These results point to the fact that unless a very large amount of statistically representative data is analysed, it is difficult to form a conclusive opinion as to the role of referential distance.

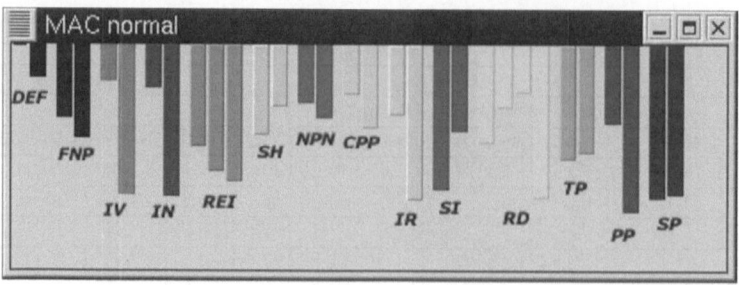

Fig. 2. The normalised indicator outcome values for MAC file

Table 5. The results of cross-evaluation

Text	PSW	MAC	WIN	ACC	CDR	BEO
Indicators from PSW	79.75	62.42	49.02	36.11	60.44	39.78
Indicators from MAC	67.09	66.06	50.98	31.11	52.75	38.71
Indicators from WIN	70.89	59.39	56.86	35.00	53.85	39.78
Indicators from ACC	68.35	63.64	39.22	40.00	58.24	39.63
Indicators from CDR	67.09	63.03	27.45	36.11	64.84	36.56
Indicators from BEO	77.22	61.82	49.02	36.11	52.75	45.16

The behaviour of some of the other indicators did not coincide fully with our expectations either. However, most of these deviations did not seem to have a significant impact and were probably caused by noise in the training data.

Given that the values of the indicator outcomes are real numbers and not integers as proposed in the original method, the cases in which a tie between two candidates with the same aggregate final score are rare. Therefore we replaced the final tie-breaking heuristics with selection of the most recent high scoring candidate.

Having used the GA to obtain the optimal sets of indicator outcome values, we applied the values from data on one text to a different text, in the hope that the optimisation was more generally useful. We show the results of cross-evaluation in table 5. In 50% of the cases, applying the optimal indicator outcome values from one file induces a success rate greater than the base algorithm for another file.

5   Conclusions

In this paper we showed how the results of a pronominal anaphora resolution method can be improved using genetic algorithms. The genetic algorithm views the resolution algorithm as a function depending on 14 parameters, which are the indicators proposed by the method. Using common operators from the field of genetic algorithms (selection, mutation and crossover), we obtained sets of indicator outcome values which optimise the performance of the algorithm. We found that the optimal set of indicator outcome values is different for every text and that in most of the cases the optimal set produced better results than the original method.

The analysis of the optimal set of indicator outcome values showed that the behaviour of some of the indicators did not fully coincide with our expectations. More evaluation will be needed to reach more conclusive results on the role and impact of each indicator.

The original method was also tested for languages other than English [6]. Therefore, it would be interesting to see if the genetic algorithms will improve the success rates of the non-English versions of MARS too.

References

1. Dumitrescu, D., Lazzerini, B., Jain, L. and Dumitrescu, A. (forthcoming) *Evolutionary Computation*, CRC Press
2. Evans, R. (2000) A Comparison of Rule-Based and Machine Learning Methods for Identifying Non-nominal *It*, in *Proceedings of NLP 2000 Conference*, Patras, Greece.
   http://www.muc.saic.com/proceedings/co_task.pdf
3. Hirst, G. (1981) *Anaphora in Natural Language Understanding*, Springer Verlag, Germany
4. Holland, J.H. (1975) *Adaptation in Natural and Artificial Systems*, University of Michigan Press, US.
5. Lappin, S. and Leass, H.J. (1994) An Algorithm for Pronominal Anaphora Resolution, in *Computational Linguistics* Volume 20, Number 4
6. Mitkov, R., Belguith, L. and Stys, M. (1998) Multilingual Robust Anaphora Resolution, in Proceedings of *The Third International Conference on Empirical Methods in Natural Language Processing*, Granada, Spain.
7. Tapanainen, P. and Järvinen, T. (1997) A Non-Projective Dependency Parser, in The Proceedings of The *5th Conference of Applied Natural Language Processing*, pages 64-71, ACL, US.

Anaphora Resolution through Dialogue Adjacency Pairs and Topics

M. Palomar and P. Martínez-Barco

Departmento de Lenguajes y Sistemas Informáticos
Universidad de Alicante
Carretera de San Vicente del Raspeig - Alicante - Spain
Tel. +34965903653 Fax. +34965909326
{mpalomar,patricio}@dlsi.ua.es

Abstract. This paper shows an algorithm to relate noun phrase antecedents to 3rd person personal pronouns, possessive pronouns, demonstrative pronouns, and adjectival anaphora. This algorithm is based on the annotation scheme of dialogue structure within the combination of several kinds of knowledge (including lexical, morphological and syntactic knowledge). The algorithm has been applied to Spanish dialogues and its evaluation was carried out on a dialogue corpus. This corpus consist of 40 transcribed dialogues that are conversations between the telephone operator of a railway company and a user of the company. After this experiment a success rate of 73.8% was obtained in pronominal anaphora and 78.9% in adjectival anaphora. The implementation was performed using LPA Prolog.

1   Introduction

Anaphora resolution is one of the most active areas of research in Natural Language Processing (NLP). The comprehension of anaphora is an important process in any NLP system, and it is among the toughest problems to solve in Computational Linguistics and NLP. Anaphora could be classified in many different ways, depending on the particular criteria one chooses to employ. Regarding the element that carries out the reference (or anaphor) for example, clear distinctions should be made between pronominal anaphora, adjectival anaphora, definite descriptions, one-anaphora, surface-count anaphora, verbal-phrase anaphora and time and/or location references. This paper focuses on the resolution of pronominal (3rd person personal pronouns, possessive pronouns and demonstrative pronouns) and adjectival anaphora[1].

At this stage, it is widely agreed that the process of resolving anaphora, in natural language texts, is supported by a variety of strategies that employ different kinds of knowledge. By different kinds of knowledge we mean the various

---

[1] We deal exclusively with such anaphora as they are the ones that appeared most frequently in the dialogues we evaluated, but our algorithm can easily be extended to resolving of other kinds of anaphora.

D.N. Christodoulakis (Ed.): NLP 2000, LNCS 1835, pp. 196–203, 2000.

types of information usually employed for anaphora resolution. In other words, information such as morphological agreement, syntactic parallelism, semantic information, discourse structure, topical knowledge, and so on.

The efforts made so far towards resolving anaphora have focused on several points of view: on one hand, there are works depending on linguistic knowledge, and, on the other hand, there are works depending on dialogue structure. We consider the combination of both approaches is needed in order to solve the anaphora. Thus, linguistic knowledge (lexical, morphological and syntactical information), as well as knowledge on dialogue structure (including topical information) will be proposed to the resolution of anaphora.

Moreover, anaphora as a phenomenon that occurs during discourse, can be found in different kinds of texts (news, interviews, dialogues, etc.). In this paper we focus exclusively on anaphora resolution in dialogues.

Dahlbäck [5] proposes a dialogue taxonomy from different dimensions: from the means of communication, a dialogue can be written (typed) if the interaction between the speakers is carried out through a computer, (e.g. man-machine dialogues, or man-man dialogues in the form of a *chat*), or spoken if it corresponds to a transcribed spoken conversation. In this paper, we focus on spoken dialogues.

To summarize, we propose an algorithm for the resolution of Spanish pronominal and adjectival anaphora that occur in spoken dialogues. This algorithm is based on the combination of linguistic knowledge and dialogue structure knowledge. It has been evaluated on a corpus of dialogues provided by the project *Basurde*[2]. These dialogues are conversations between the telephone operator of a railway company and a user of the company. The evaluation was carried out on 40 different dialogues. Five of them were randomly selected for the training of the algorithm and the remaining 35 were reserved in order to carry out the final evaluation. On this evaluation, several experiments have been performed in order to define the adequate combination of different kinds of knowledge. Besides, the kappa statistic [4] has been obtained guaranteeing the reliability of the dialogue structure annotation.

2   A Survey of Related Work on Anaphora Resolution in Dialogues

For anaphora resolution in dialogues, there has been a proliferation of methods based on dialogue structure, (discourse-oriented approaches), among which we should like to make a special mention of the Grosz's works [9,10] in which the influence of dialogue structure in anaphora resolution is justified. These works focus specifically on task-oriented dialogues. Other studies, such as those published by Grosz *et al.* [11,12], present a centering framework as a model that explains the coherence of the local discourse. They relate the speaker's focus of

---

[2] BASURDE: Spontaneous-Speech Dialogue System in Limited Domains. CICYT (TIC98-423-C06).

attention to reference expressions. This model has achieved successful results in anaphora resolution in monologues, but would require certain adaptations to be successfully applied to dialogues. In that line, Byron and Stent [2] present extensions of the centering method for its application to dialogues, and concludes that centering is as consistent in dialogues as it is in monologues.

Nevertheless, according to Strube and Hahn [16], the crucial point in centering model is the ranking of the candidate list. [12] state that this list may be ordered using different factors, but they only use information about grammatical roles. However, it is difficult to define grammatical roles in free-word-order languages like German or Spanish without using semantic information.

On the other hand, we must comment on the work carried out by Eckert and Strube [6], who details a method for resolving pronominal anaphora in dialogues with a precision of 66.2% and a recall rate of 68.2%. This method is based on the use of dialogue acts annotation as an alternative to centering method.

Furthermore, the work published by Martínez-Barco et al. [13] emphasizes the importance of discourse-topic knowledge as a complementary method for anaphora resolution in dialogues in which certain topical knowledge is necessary for long-distance anaphora resolution. The best way of combining this knowledge is shown by the authors in [14].

3   Anaphora Resolution Algorithm to Spoken Dialogues Systems

In this section, the intuitive algorithm for anaphora resolution in spoken dialogues systems is presented. This algorithm uses and combines two kinds of knowledge from dialogue texts: a) linguistic knowledge such as lexical, morphological and syntactic knowledge; b) knowledge from the dialogue's structure itself, which is based on the annotation of adjacency pairs [3], and knowledge taken from the topic of the dialogue (manually annotated).

The proposed algorithm is based, intuitively, on the following three steps:

1. To obtain all possible antecedents from structure and topic of dialogue texts, following these directives:
   (a) To take those NPs that are included in the same adjacency pair (AP) as the anaphor and,
   (b) To take those NPs that are included in the previous AP to the anaphor and,
   (c) To take those NPs that are included in the last unclosed AP and,
   (d) To take the topic of the dialog.
2. Linguistic constraints are applied on the previously selected antecedents, with the aim of discarding incompatible antecedents:
   (a) For pronominal anaphora

---

[3] The use of adjacency pairs as a dialogue unit for anaphora resolution is based on the work by Sacks et al. [15]. According to them, one form of anaphora which appears to be very common in dialogues is the reference within an adjacency pair.

      i. Morphological constraints: to discard those antecedents that do not agree in gender, number and person.

     ii. Syntactic constraints: c-command constraints [7].

(b) For adjective anaphora

      i. Morphological constraints: to discard those antecedents that do not agree in gender, number and person for pronominal anaphora, and to discard those antecedents that do not agree in gender and person.

     ii. Syntactic constraints: to accept only antecedents which head noun has lexical category equal to "COMMON".

3. If there are more than one antecedent left after applying the previous constraints, then the following preferences are applied, in the order that they are presented next. These preferences have been obtained from the empirical study shown in section 5, and from the structure of the dialogue itself:

(a) For pronominal and adjetival anaphora

      i. Preference for those antecedents that are in the same AP as the anaphor.

     ii. Preference for those antecedents that are in the previous AP to the anaphor.

    iii. Preference for those antecedents that are in the previous unclosed AP.

    iv. Preference for antecedents included in the topic of the text.

(b) For pronominal anaphora

     v. Preference for those antecedents in the same position with reference to the verb as the anaphor (before or after).

    vi. Preference for those antecedents in the same syntactic position as the anaphor.

   vii. Preference for the nearest antecedent to the anaphor.

(c) For adjective anaphora

     v. Preference for those antecedents that share the same kind of modifiers (e.g. a prepositional phrase, and/or adjective and so on).

    vi. Preference for those antecedents with exactly the same modifiers (e.g. the same adjective 'red').

   vii. Preference for the nearest antecedent to the anaphor.

4   Evaluation of the Algorithm

In order to carry out the evaluation of the algorithm, we had 200 transcribed spoken dialogues at our disposal, afforded us by the project *Basurde* from which we selected and POS-tagged 40. The tagging provides us with lexical and morphological knowledge for each word of the text. From the 40 POS-tagged dialogues, 5 were randomly selected to train the annotators and the remaining 35 were reserved in order to carry out the test. Afterwards, the structure of the dialogue is manually annotated, according to the following directives:

Firstly, turns were classified by two annotators according to the work carried by Gallardo [8], who applies to Spanish dialogues the theories put forward by

Sacks *et al.* [15]. According to this proposal, turns may be **Initiative Interventions (IT$_I$)** when they formulate invitations, requirements, offers, reports, etc., or **Reaction Interventions (IT$_R$)** when they answer or evaluate the previous speaker's Initiative Intervention. They may also be **Initiative/Reaction Interventions (IT$_{R/I}$)**, meaning a reaction that begins as a response to the previous speaker's intervention, and ends as an introduction of new information. Finally, a **Continuing Turn (CT)** represents an empty turn, which is quite typical of a listener whose aim is the formal reinforcement and ratification of the cast of conversational roles. Such turns lack information.

In order to guarantee the results of this classification, a reliability test was performed (see works by Carletta [3] and Carletta *et al.* [4]). The reliability test use the k (kappa) statistic that measures the affinity between the annotators. After the annotation process, a k measurement of 0.91 was obtained, meaning the total reliability between the results of both annotators.

Therefore, **Adjacency Pairs** or **Exchanges (AP)** could be annotated as groups of turns headed by an initiation intervention turn (IT$_I$) and ended by its reaction intervention turn (IT$_R$).

Finally, the label **TOPIC** was also manually annotated including information about the main topic of this dialogue. An example of this annotation is shown in table 1.

According to the above-mentioned structure, the following set of tags is considered necessary for dialogue structure annotation: IT$_I$, IT$_R$, IT$_{R/I}$, CT, AP and TOPIC. AP and TOPIC tags will be used to define the anaphoric accessibility space and the remaining will be used to obtain the adjacency pairs.

To perform the evaluation, a Natural Language Processing System that focuses on anaphora resolution in dialogues was employed. This system consists of a POS tagger, a partial parser and several modules for resolution of linguistic problems. The partial parser obtains noun and prepositional phrases, and verbal chunks that are stored in a structure, in which lexical, morphological and syntactic knowledge is also stored.

For the proper evaluation of the algorithm, several experiments have been carried out in an attempt to demonstrate the importance of combining dialogue structure knowledge with other kinds of knowledge for anaphora resolution. These experiments, performed with the above mentioned spoken dialogues, are shown in table 2.

Our baseline was the constraint and preference system defined in [7] where results of 82.3% precision for pronominal anaphora resolution were obtained when the system was applied to a monologue text. This system used only lexical, morphological and syntactic knowledge lacking dialogue structure information. However, when this system was applied to our test dialogues, a precision of 59% for pronominal anaphora resolution and 23.7% for adjectival anaphora resolution were obtained. Next, better results were obtained when this constraint and preference set based on linguistic knowledge was replaced with a new set based on dialogue structure information. But the optimum results were achieved when a constraint and preference set based on linguistic knowledge plus dialogue

TOPIC			tren *(train)*
AP_1	$\mathbf{IT}_I$	**(OP)**:	información de Renfe, buenos días
			(Renfe information, good morning)
	$\mathbf{IT}_R$	**(US)**:	hola, buenos días *(hello, good morning)*
	CT	**(OP)**:	hola *(hello)*
AP_2	$\mathbf{IT}_I$	**(US)**:	me podéis decir algún tren que salga mañana
			por la tarde para ir a Monzón
			(could you tell me about some train that leaves
			tomorrow evening for Monzon)
	$\mathbf{IT}_R$	**(OP)**:	si, vamos, mira hay un talgo a las tres y media de la tarde
			(let me see, there is a talgo at half past three)
AP_3	$\mathbf{IT}_I$	**(US)**:	si tiene que ser más tarde *(it has to be later)*
	$\mathbf{IT}_R$	**(OP)**:	más tarde. Pues entonces, hay por ejemplo un intercity
			a las cinco y media, un expreso a las seis y media
			(later. There is, for instance, an intercity at half
			past five, an expreso at half past six)
AP_4	$\mathbf{IT}_I$	**(US)**:	el de las seis y media ¿llega a Monzón?
			(the half past six one, does it go to Monzon?)
$AP_5{}^a$	$\mathbf{IT}_I$	**(OP)**:	a ver. El de las seis y media me ha preguntado
			¿verdad?
			(let me see. You have asked about the half
			past six one, haven't you?)
	$\mathbf{IT}_R$	**(US)**:	si *(yes)*
	$\mathbf{IT}_R$	**(OP)**:	a las nueve y veinticinco *(at twenty-five past nine)*
AP_6	$\mathbf{IT}_I$	**(US)**:	a las nueve y veinticinco está en Monzón
			(at twenty-five past nine is at Monzon)
	$\mathbf{IT}_R$	**(OP)**:	si *(yes)*
	CT	**(US)**:	vale, pues ya está. Esto ya es suficiente.
			(ok, that's all. That's enough.)
	CT	**(OP)**:	hum, hum
AP_7	$\mathbf{IT}_I$	**(US)**:	gracias, ¿eh? *(thank you, ok?)*
	$\mathbf{IT}_R$	**(OP)**:	muy bien a usted. Hasta luego *(thanks. Bye)*

[a] Notice that AP_5 is included in AP_4

Table 1. Example of an annotated dialogue

Experiments	pronominal anaphora	adjectival anaphora
Linguistic knowledge (baseline)	59.0%	23.7%
Dialogue structure	62.3%	65.8%
Linguistic knowledge + Dialogue structure	73.8%	78.9%

Table 2. Evaluation

structure properly combined was developed. After this experiment, a precision of 73.8% for pronominal anaphora resolution and 78.9% for adjectival anaphora resolution were shown.

5   Conclusions

In this paper, the need for knowledge of dialogue structure and topic to resolve pronominal and adjectival anaphora in dialogues has been demonstrated. These two kinds of knowledge are used in conjunction with linguistic knowledge such as lexical, morphological and syntactic information, in a novel way of combining several kinds of knowledge.

The algorithm we propose in this paper has been evaluated on 35 spoken dialogues and the results obtained are quite good, (73.8% for pronominal anaphora and 78.9% for adjetival anaphora resolution). We should emphasize, however, the difficulty of achieving such a knowledge combination, in addition to the lack of suitable resources, such as anaphorically tagged corpora and with structure knowledge (e.g. topic of the text).

References

1. *36th Annual Meeting of the Association for Computational Linguistics and 17th International Conference on Computational Linguistics (COLING-ACL'98)*, Montreal (Canada), August 1998.
2. D.K. Byron and A. Stent. A Preliminary Model of Centering in Dialog. In *Proceedings of the 36th Annual Meeting of the Association for Computational Linguistics and 17th International Conference on Computational Linguistics (COLING-ACL'98)* [1].
3. J. Carletta. Assessing agreement on classification task: the kappa statistic. *Computational Linguistics*, 22(2):249–254, 1996.
4. J. Carletta, A. Isard, S. Isard, J.C. Kowtko, G. Doherty-Sneddon, and A.H. Anderson. The Reliability of a Dialogue Structure Coding Scheme. *Computational Linguistics*, 23(1):13–32, March 1997.
5. N. Dahlbäck. Towards a dialogue taxonomy. In Elisabeth Maier, Marion Mast, and Susann LuperFoy, editors, *Dialogue Processing in Spoken Language Systems*, LNAI-Lecture Notes in Artificial Intelligence. Springer Verlag, 1997.
6. M. Eckert and M. Strube. Dialogue Acts, Synchronising Units and Anaphora Resolution. In *Proceedings of Amsterdam Workshop on the Semantics and Pragmatics of Dialogue (AMSTELOGUE'99)*, University of Amsterdam, Holland, May 1999.
7. A. Ferrández, M. Palomar, and L. Moreno. Anaphor resolution in unrestricted texts with partial parsing. In *Proceedings of the 36th Annual Meeting of the Association for Computational Linguistics and 17th International Conference on Computational Linguistics (COLING-ACL'98)* [1], pages 385–391.
8. B. Gallardo. *Análisis conversacional y pragmática del receptor*. Colección Sinapsis. Ediciones Episteme, S.L., Valencia, 1996.
9. B. Grosz. The representation and use of focus in a system for understanding dialogs. In *Proceedings of Fifth International Joint Conference on Artificial Intelligence (IJCAI'77)*, Cambridge, MA., 1977.
10. B. Grosz. Focusing and description in natural language dialogues. In *Elements of Discourse Understanding*. Cambridge University Press, Cambridge, 1981.
11. B. Grosz, A. Joshi, and S. Weinstein. Providing a unified account of definite noun phrases in discourse. In *Proceedings of the 21st Annual Meeting of the Association for Computational Linguistics*, pages 44–50, 1983.

12. B. Grosz, A. Joshi, and S. Weinstein. Centering: a framework for modeling the local coherence of discourse. *Computational Linguistics*, 21:203–225, 1995.
13. P. Martínez-Barco, R. Muñoz, S. Azzam, M. Palomar, and A. Ferrández. Evaluation of pronoun resolution algorithm for Spanish dialogues. In *Proceedings of the Venezia per il Trattamento Automatico delle Lingue (VEXTAL'99)*, pages 325–332, Venice (Italy), November 1999.
14. P. Martínez-Barco and M. Palomar. Dialogue structure influence over anaphora resolution. In *Lecture Notes in Artificial Intelligence*, Acapulco, México, April 2000. Springer-Verlag Berlin Heidelberg New York. To appear.
15. H. Sacks, E. Schegloff, and G. Jefferson. A simplest systematics for the organization of turn taking for conversation. *Language*, 50(4):696–735, 1974.
16. M. Strube and U. Hahn. Functional Centering - Grounding Referential Coherence in Information Structure. *Computational Linguistics*, 25(5):309–344, 1999.

Semantic Knowledge-Driven Method to Solve Pronominal Anaphora in Spanish Texts

Maximiliano Saiz-Noeda and Manuel Palomar

Departamento de Lenguajes y Sistemas Informáticos
Tfno: +34 96 590 37 72 Fax: +34 96 590 93 26
Universidad de Alicante, Apdo. 99, 03080 Alicante, Spain
{max,mpalomar}@dlsi.ua.es

Abstract. Tendencies in *Natural Language Processing (NLP)* systems go towards the study of the semantic knowledge that can be extracted from the words within a context. For this reason, semantic information addition is necessary for the definition of new NLP strategies.

In this paper, a method oriented to pronominal anaphora resolution in Spanish is presented. This method is based on two ontologies, O_n and O_v, that define semantic concept branches for nouns and verbs respectively. Also, the method uses two relation sets in order to solve the anaphora. These sets are formed by semantic patterns that define the compatibility between a subject and its verb and verb and its complement, using the ontological concepts of their heads.

The semantic behaviour provided by these patterns allows the identification of the noun phrase antecedents of a Spanish personal pronoun. This antecedent has the best compatibility ratio among all proposed antecedents of the anaphoric pronoun. This compatibility ratio is measured using the relation level between concepts in the ontological branch of each pair member.

1 Introduction

Tendencies in *Natural Language Processing (NLP)* systems go towards the study of the semantic knowledge that can be extracted from the words within a context. For this reason, semantic information addition is necessary for the definition of new NLP strategies.

Some tasks like information search on the Web –that according to Clark in [2] is like "looking for a needle in a haystack"–, have their critical feature in the use of indexing systems and word joining, without considering the information that provides word meaning in a context. In the specific case of the anaphora resolution, the main limitation comes from the lack of semantic knowledge in the mechanisms of traditional methods.

Therefore, a semantic knowledge-driven method should provide conceptual characteristics of the senses taken by each word in a text. These concepts can be classified in an ontological structure as well as in a semantic network where each word is connected with others through semantic relations (synonymy, hypernymy, meronymy...).

D.N. Christodoulakis (Ed.): NLP 2000, LNCS 1835, pp. 204–211, 2000.

An example of resource that provides these kinds of relations is WordNet in its Spanish version (see [11]). The well-known problem of this resource is that its big size makes it difficult to use in NLP tasks. In this line, some approaches like in [13] treat to reduce the size of WordNet towards its application in restricted domains.

All kinds of information sources are useful for the treatment of anaphora resolution for knowledge-based approaches. Morphological information establishes gender, number and person parallelism between an anaphoric expression and its antecedents. Lexical information provides word roots for comparing and relating them to each other. Syntactic information establishes syntactic parallelism between anaphoric expression and antecedent. Nevertheless, criteria obtained from these sources are not always enough to solve the anaphora. It is necessary to extend resolution methods with semantic information in order to achieve better results.

Section 2 shows some work related to anaphora resolution tasks and systems. Some aspects of the pronominal anaphora in Spanish are shown in section 3. The need of semantic knowledge is illustrated in this section with the use of different examples. Section 4 describes all the elements involved in the method and the anaphora resolution mechanism itself. Finally, conclusions and a brief description of the work in progress is given.

2   Related Work

Theories and formalisms used in the anaphora resolution-oriented work have different natures. Our approach is based on the use of semantic information sources for identifying the antecedent of the pronoun. Thus, use of semantic information will be the main criterion in studying related works.

Hobbs in [5] proposed one of the first approaches to anaphora resolution using only syntactic restrictions for selecting the correct antecedent of a pronominal anaphora. Lappin and Leass in [8] defined an algorithm based also on syntactic information, and Kennedy and Boguraev in [7], on the basis of this work, used enriched restrictions and morpho-syntactic preferences with information relative to the context of certain pronouns. Mitkov and Stys in [9] proposed a pronominal anaphora resolution system based on morpho-syntactic restrictions and a series of preferences (antecedent indicators) that vary according to the text type. Baldwin in [1] presented *CogNIAC*, a pronominal anaphora resolution system. He also used morpho-syntactic restrictions (gender and number agreement and c-command) and a series of heuristic preferences. These approaches (summarized in Table 1) do not make use of semantic information sources as an additional resource for pronominal anaphora resolution. For this reason, they are called knowledge-poor systems.

On the other hand, Ferrández *et al.* in [3] included a pronominal and adjective anaphora resolution module from a partial or full parsing in a NLP system. It uses a grammatical formalism based on restrictions and morpho-syntactic preferences. Moreover, this method proposes the addition of semantic information

N°	Author	Year	ref	Algorithm features
1	Hobbs	1977	[5]	One of the first approaches. Syntactic restrictions for the pronominal references. 81.6% precision
2	Lappin & Leass	1994	[8]	Resolution based on syntactic restrictions from a complete analysis. 85% success in computer science manuals.
3	Kennedy & Boguraev	1996	[7]	Adds information according to the context of certain pronouns (*it*) and uses weight-based preference system. 75% success in varied and less formal texts.
4	Mitkov & Stys	1997	[9]	Morpho-syntactic restrictions and preferences for the pronominal anaphora. Adds information based on the verb with the antecedent. 95.8% and 92.1% success in technical manuals in English and Polish.
5	Baldwin	1997	[1]	*CogNIAC*. Pronominal anaphora. Only treats pronouns without ambiguity. Morpho-syntactic constraints and heuristic preferences - 90% precision and 60% recall

Table 1. Some poor knowledge algorithms for anaphora resolution

for restricted domain texts with *IRSAS*, a system developed by Moreno *et al.* in [10]. In this line, another approach to use semantic information to help the anaphora resolution tasks is shown by Saiz-Noeda *et al.* in [12]. Moreover, LaSIE system presented by Gaizauskas *et al.* in [4] and by Humphreys *et al.* in [6] was designed as a general purpose information extraction (IE) system where a discourse model based on a predefined domain model is built, using the semantic analysis supplied by the parser. The domain model represents a hierarchy of domain-relevant concept nodes, together with associated properties.

3 Scope: Pronominal Anaphora

Pronominal anaphora is one of the most frequent type of anaphora in Spanish and it will be the fundamental object of this study. Specifically, it will deal with the personal pronoun anaphora. It will be classified according to the role carried out by the pronoun: pronominal anaphora of subject and pronominal anaphora of complement. Each type of anaphora is accompanied by two examples. The first could be solved with the systems based on morpho-syntactic criteria (knowledge-poor) mentioned previously. The second presents a situation in which the relation between the anaphora and its antecedent is based on semantic features. Therefore, its resolution implies the use of semantic criteria. This means that, even supposing that these knowledge-poor systems provide the correct solution for this examples, it is only due to a coincidence.

In the following classification, the traditional difference between personal pronouns of subject and complement is assumed.

3.1 Personal Pronoun: Subject

In (2), there is a complete morphological agreement between the anaphoric personal pronoun *él* (*he*), usually omitted in Spanish, and the three noun phrases in the previous sentence (they are all masculine, singular and third person). Nevertheless, only *un plátano* (*a banana*) can be related to the anaphora because it is the only one than can be associated with the characteristic of *estar maduro* (*to be ripe*).

(1) *Andrés* sabe la combinación de la caja fuerte. **Él** está hoy de viaje.
     Andrés *knows the combination for the safe.* **He** *is away today*

(2) El mono subió al árbol a coger *un plátano* cuando el sol salía. (**Él**) estaba maduro.
     The monkey climbed the tree to get a banana *when the sun was rising.* **It** *was ripe*

3.2 Personal Pronoun: Complement

Following the previous example, there are in (4) three possible antecedents (noun phrases) of the anaphoric pronoun *la* (*it*), but only *la televisión* (*the TV set*) can be *apagada* (*switched off*).

(3) No tengo noticias de *Pedro*. No **lo** veo desde octubre.
     I haven't heard from Pedro. *I haven't seen* **him** *since October*

(4) *La televisión* está encendida cuando Luisa llega a la cocina. Ella **la** apaga cuando se acuesta.
     The TV set is switched on when Luisa arrives at the kitchen. She switch **it** *off when she goes to bed*

4 Semantic Knowledge-Driven Method

4.1 Elements

The proposed method is characterized by the use of four main elements:

Firstly, an ontology of noun semantic characteristics, On, is defined, whose graphical representation is shown in Figure 1. Each noun is in a leaf of the tree. This way, all the elements in the same ascending branch of a noun, Sn_{noun}, define its semantic features (from the most concrete to the most general): $Sn_{plátano}$ =[*fruta, comida, sustancia, objeto*].

Moreover, it is defined an ontology of verb semantic characteristics, Ov (also represented in Figure 1). It has similar structural characteristics than On and defines ascending branches associated to each verbal form: Sv_{apagar}=[*apagar,desconexión, contacto, acción*].

In order to establish links between nouns and verbs, it is defined a set of subject-verb compatibility relations, Rsv, formed by pairs [$n_{subj}, verb$] where

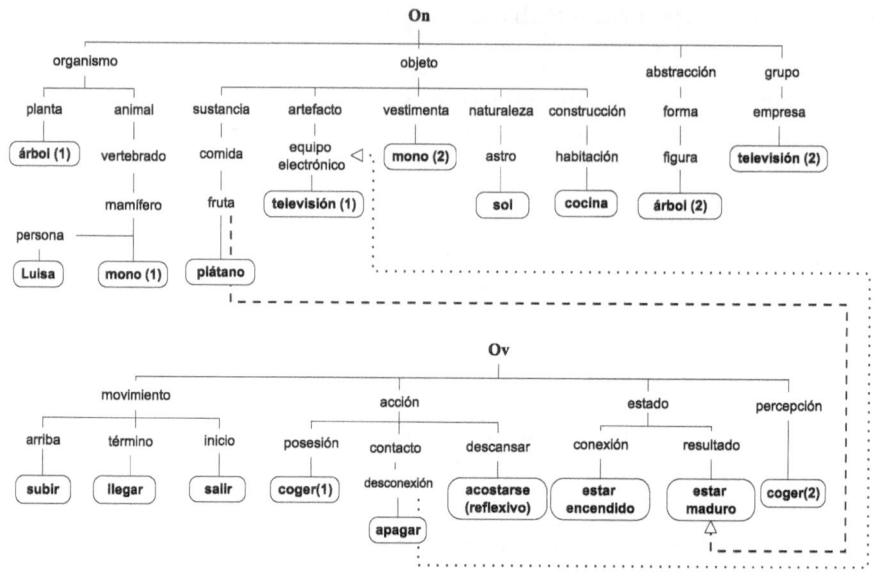

Fig. 1. *On and Ov ontologies*

$n_{subj} \in On$ is a noun or a semantic characteristic of a noun with a subject role and $v \in Ov$ is a verb or a verb semantic characteristic compatible with n_{subj}. Figure 1 shows an example of this type of compatibility relations in *[fruta,estar maduro]* (*[fruit,be ripe]*).

Moreover, another set of verb-complement compatibility relations is defined, *Rvo*. It is formed by pairs $[v, n_{obj}]$ where $v \in Ov$ is a verb or a semantic characteristic of a verb and $n_{comp} \in On$ is a noun or a semantic characteristic of a noun with a complement of v role. In Figure 1, *[apagar, equipo electrónico]* (*[switch off, electronic equipment]*) is an example of these kind of relations.

The reflexive feature of a verb is marked in *Ov* (see the verb *acostarse* in Figure 1). This is due to the difference between the behaviors of reflexive and non-reflexive verbs (the subject type of *acostarse* –go to bed– does not have to agree with the subject type of its non-reflexive form *acostar* –put to bed–).

In addition, different meanings of names and verbs are represented in both ontologies as different entries. Next section describes the way the method tries to choose between several senses of the same word.

4.2   Co-reference Resolution

The proposed method constitutes a helpful tool for choosing the correct antecedent of an anaphoric expression. For this reason, it can be applied with other resolution methods based on morpho-syntactic criteria. This method provides compatibility criteria between the verb that appears with the anaphoric expression and its antecedent. This antecedent can play the role of subject or complement.

Once a pronoun is detected, the method begins extracting the head nouns of the noun phrases stored into the list of possible antecedents. The method uses this list of head nouns Ln as input.

As above mentioned, different meanings of nouns and verbs have different entries in On and Ov. Figure 1 shows two different entries for the Spanish word *mono* relating to its meanings of animal (*monkey*) and work clothes (*overalls*). Moreover, the verb **coger** (*to catch*) have also a double meaning of possession and perception. Because of the lack of a word sense disambiguation or a semantic labeling tools, our method will try to provide the compatibility between the possible senses of each word and the verb appearing in the same sentence as the anaphoric expression. This compatibility is extracted from the relation sets Rsv or Rvo.

Every noun of Ln is represented using its list of ontological concepts Sn_{noun}. Also, the verb associated to the anaphoric expression is represented by Sv_{verb}. The proposed method establishes two concepts of compatibility: the verb and its subject compatibility and the verb and its complement compatibility.

(d1) The verb v is compatible with the noun n being the subject of v $\iff$
$\exists cn \in Sn_n$, $\exists cv \in Sv_v \mid [cn, cv] \in Rsv$

(d2) The verb v is compatible with the noun n being the complement of v $\iff$
$\exists cn \in Sn_n$, $\exists cv \in Sv_v \mid [cv, cn,] \in Rvo$

According to (d1) and (d2) premises, the compatibility between the verb and each noun is verified. Thus, this compatibility is provided in an absolute way (a verb is or is not compatible with a noun). Nevertheless, different heuristics can be applied in order to determine a compatibility degree between nouns and verbs. This compatibility can be based on the type of ontological concepts (more or less concrete) in Sn_{noun} and Sv_{verb} that are related in Rsv or Rvo.

Let us see the application of this method in example (2). When the pronoun *él* (*he*) is detected (omitted in this situation), its verb **está maduro** (*be ripe*) is taken and a list of head nouns $Ln=[mono, árbol, plátano, sol]$ is extracted from the list of antecedent noun phrases.

From the verb and the list of nouns, the possible pairs formed by the ontological concepts associated to each noun in Ln and the concepts of the verb v are established.

The existence of some of the pairs in the subject-complement compatibility set (Rsv) is checked in the construction process of the pair according to the definition given in (d1). Thus, it can be shown:

$\exists cn \in Sn_{plátano} \mid cn = \{fruta\},$
$\exists cv \in Sv_{estar\ maduro} \mid cv = \{estar\ maduro\}$
$\mid [cn, cv] \in Rsv$

For this reason, it is possible to deduce a compatibility relation between *plátano* (*banana*) and **estar maduro** (*to be ripe*) and not between the rest of the candidates.

Now let us see the method applied on example (4). In this situation, the object pronoun *la* (*it*) is detected. the list of nouns *[televisión, Luisa, cocina]* is extracted from the antecedent list of the anaphoric expression. The association process between the ontologic concepts for the verb and each name produces:

$\exists cn \in Sn_{televisión}|cn = \{equipo\ electrónico\},$
$\exists cv \in Sv_{apagar}|cv = \{desconexión\}$
$|\ [cn, cv] \in Rvo$

Following this, the first meaning of *televisión* (*TV set*) and *apagar* (*to switch off*) have a compatibility relation that the rest of the antecedents have not.

5   Conclusion and Work in Progress

In this paper, a semantic information adding method oriented to anaphora resolution has been presented. For this purpose, two conceptual ontologies for nouns and verbs have been defined in order to describe the semantic concepts associated to each word. Moreover, two relation sets establish the compatibility between nouns and verbs, it means, between a subject and its verb and between a verb and its complement.

We have treated to demonstrate that semantic information extracted from these kinds of ontologies helps to anaphora resolution tasks. This information can be applied with other information sources in order to improve their results.

From this proposal, our targets are focused on the construction of a anaphora resolution prototype based on a tagged corpus and an ontology extracted from a lexical resource like Spanish WordNet. The study of the corpus and the evaluation of the method will allow the improvement of the method from both linguistic and computational points of view.

Furthermore, the use of other lexical databases, ontologies or semantic resources, the treatment of other types of pronouns, the extension of this method to other types of anaphora are opened research line.

References

1. B. Baldwin. CogNIAC: high precision coreference with limited knowledge and linguistic resources. In *ACL/EACL workshop on Operational factors in practical, robust anaphor resolution*, 1997.
2. D. Clark. Natural Language, relevancy ranking and common sense. *IEEE Intelligent Systems*, 14(4):17–19, 1999.
3. A. Ferrández, M. Palomar, and L. Moreno. Anaphora resolution in unrestricted texts with partial parsing. In *36th Annual Meeting of the Association for Computational Linguistics and 17th International Conference on Computational Lingustics*, pages 385–391, 1998.
4. R. Gaizauskas, T. Wakao, K. Humphreys, H. Cunningham, and Y. Wilks. Description of the LaSIE system as used for MUC-6. In *Sixth Message Understanding Conference*, pages 207–220, 1995.
5. J. Hobbs. Resolving pronoun references. *Lingua*, 44:311–338, 1997.

6. K. Humphreys, R. Gaizauskas, S. Azzam, C. Huyck, B. Mitchell, H. Cunningham, and Y. Wilks. Description of the LaSIE-II System as Used for MUC-7. In *Seventh Message Understanding Conference*, 1998.

7. C. Kennedy and B. Boguraev. Anaphora for everyone: pronominal anaphora resolution without a parser. In *16th International Conference on Computational Linguistics*, volume I, pages 113–118, 1996.

8. S. Lappin and H. Leass. An algorithm for pronominal anaphora resolution. *Computational Linguistics*, 20(4):535–561, 1994.

9. R. Mitkov and M. Stys. Robust reference resolution with limited knowledge: high precision genre-specific approach for English and Polish. In *Recent Advances in Natural Language Resolution*, 1997.

10. L. Moreno, F. Andrés, and M. Palomar. Incorporar Restricciones Semánticas en el Análisis Sintáctico: IRSAS. *Procesamiento del Lenguaje Natural*, 12, 1992.

11. P.Vossen. EuroWordNet: Building a Multilingual Database with WordNets for European Languages. *The ELRA Newwsletter. K.Choukri, D.Fry, M. Nilsson (des). ISSN:1026-8200*, 3(1), 1998.

12. M. Saiz-Noeda, J. Peral, and A. Suárez. Semantic Compatibility Techniques for Anaphora Resolution. In *International Conference on Artificial and Computational Intelligence for Decision, Control and Automation in Engineering and Industrial Applications*, March 2000.

13. A. Suárez, M. Saiz-Noeda, and M. Palomar. A method of restricted knowledge acquisition from WordNet. In *Third international conference on knowledge-based intelligent information engineering systems*, August 1999.

Processing of Spanish Definite Descriptions with the Same Head

Rafael Muñoz and Manuel Palomar

Grupo de investigación en Procesamiento del Lenguaje y Sistemas de Información
Departamento de Lenguajes y Sistemas de Informáticos
Universidad de Alicante
Apartado 99, 03080 Alicante, Spain
{rafael,mpalomar}@dlsi.ua.es

Abstract. In this paper, an algorithm in order to solve definite descriptions in Spanish texts with the same head noun as their antecedent is presented. This algorithm is based on the relationships between pre and post-modifier of both noun phrase (antecedent and anaphoric expression). This algorithm only considers as an antecedent all kinds of noun phrase, but do not considers other kinds of antecedents like sentences or full text. This algorithm has achieved an average precision score of 83.6%.

1 Introduction

Anaphora resolution algorithm is a fundamental component in any natural language processing system. In order to solve this linguistic phenomenon, this anaphora resolution component can provide information that does not explicitly appear in texts. There are several grammatical categories with referential properties such as pronouns, adjectives, adverbial adjuncts and definite descriptions (DD) (Definite description is defined as a noun phrase headed by the definite article -*el, la, los, las*- or a demonstrative -*este, esta, estos, estas, ese, esa, esos, esas, aquel, aquella, aquellos, aquellas*-, such as *el perro (the dog)* or *este perro (this dog)*). Our research efforts are focused on resolving definite descriptions. In the following example we can see different kinds of DD.

> *[Juan López]₁ es [un aficionado de [los automóviles]₂]₃ y se compró [un coche de competición]₄ y [un coche utilitario]₅. [El coche de competición]₆ fue [un capricho]₇ y [la cilindrada de 3000 cc]₈ no fue [un impedimento]₉ para él. [El coche utilitario]₁₀ lo utilizaba para desplazarse a [su empresa]₁₁. [Los motores de ambos]₁₂ eran fabricados por [Porsche]₁₃. [El presidente de [la empresa]₁₄]₁₅ sigue siendo [un aficionado]₁₅ a [la velocidad]₁₆. [Los vehículos]₁₇ requieren [un cuidado especial]₁₈.*

In the above example, there are DD with the same head noun -(6,4),(10,5), (14,11)-, DD of kind of Part-of -(12,2)-, DD of kind of proper nouns that need

D.N. Christodoulakis (Ed.): NLP 2000, LNCS 1835, pp. 212–220, 2000.

in order to solve world-Knowledge -(15,1)-, DD with semantic relation -(17,2)- and non-anaphoric DD -2,8,16-. This paper is focused in the DD with same head noun resolution.

2   Relevant Related Works in DD

Main works in DD resolution are focused in English texts. We emphasize those by Kameyama [5] and Viera and Poesio [12,11].

2.1   Kameyama Algorithm [5]

Kameyama described a definite description processing algorithm. This algorithm is applied to the information extraction system FASTUS [4]. This algorithm only solves *identity co-reference* without evaluating others co-reference types as *parts of, set - subset and set - member*. The algorithm is based on three factors:

1. *Accessible Text Region.* This algorithm uses a searching window (accessible text region) for each anaphoric expression type. The window size was arbitrarily set to ten sentences for definite descriptions and three sentences for pronouns.
2. *Semantic Consistency.* Semantic consistencies between anaphoric expression and its potential antecedent are based on:
   - *number consistency*, i.e., anaphoric expression and antecedent must be consistent in number, singular or plural.
   - *sort consistency*, i.e. anaphoric expression sort must be either equal or subsume antecedent sort.
   - *modifier consistency*.
3. *Dynamic Syntactic Preference.* Dynamic syntactic preferences are the last factor that this algorithm uses. There are three dynamic syntactic preferences:
   - The preceding part of the same sentence in the left-right order.
   - The immediately preceding sentence in left-right order.
   - Other preceding sentences within the searching window in the right-left order.

Also, alias and acronym references are solved by the algorithm, although results are not shown.

Table 1 shows the algorithm's performance in solving three kind of anaphoric expressions (pronoun, definite description, proper name). This algorithm achieved 46% recall[1] for definite descriptions, 62% recall for pronouns and 69% recall for proper nouns. In general, the performance of this system achieved a recall of 59% and precision[2] of 72% in the evaluation of 30 newspaper articles.

---

[1] Recall is the quotient between correctly solved and number of occurrences.

[2] Precision is the quotient between number of correctly solved and number of processed occurrences.

Type	Precision	Recall
definite description		46%
pronoun		62%
proper names		69%
general performance	59%	72%

Table 1. Kameyama's algorithm results

2.2   Vieira and Poesio Algorithm [12,11]

Viera and Poesio [12,11] described an algorithm focused on the resolution of definite descriptions. This system solves references between definite descriptions and antecedents with either the same head noun or a semantic relationship (synonym, hyperonym, hyponym). Clark, in [2], named *bridging references* the uses of definite descriptions whose antecedents have a different head noun.

Vieira and Poesio algorithm is based on several test in order to classify the definite description as non-anaphoric expression or to provide the correct antecedent. The algorithm executes the following test:

- four tests for identifying new discourse descriptions before trying to find out an antecedent.
- If these tests fail, the system will look for an antecedent with same head as the anaphoric expression (direct anaphora).
- Finally, the system applies several heuristic rules in order to look for semantic relations (*synonym, hyponym* and *meronym*) between both head nouns (indirect anaphora).

Type	Precision	Recall
direct anaphora	83%	62%
indirect anaphora		30%

Table 2. Vieira and Poesio's algorithm results

Table 2 shows the algorithm's performance in solving definite description's references. This algorithm achieved 62% recall and 83% precision in solving direct anaphora (same head noun). Bridging descriptions (indirect anaphora) were evaluated by hand, and 61 relations of 204 in the corpus were achieved.

2.3   Star Point of Muñoz and Palomar Algorithm

Algorithms above presented are focused on solving references in English texts. Several taxonomies as Cristopherson [1], Hawkins [3], Prince [10] and Poesio and Vieira [9] have been carried out for definite descriptions in the English language. These taxonomies are usually based on relations between the anaphoric expression (definite descriptions) and the antecedent.

This paper are focused exclusively on definite description in Spanish texts. For this reason, the classification of definite descriptions (Figure 1) for Spanish texts developed by Muñoz [7] is used as start point to carry out a co-reference resolution module. This module are made up by several algorithm focused on solving every kind of definite description. Next section present an algorithm to solve references produced by definite descriptions with the same head noun as their antecedent.

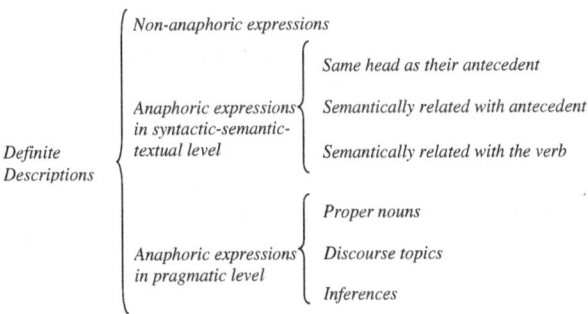

Fig. 1. *Definite description's classification [7]*

3   DD with Same Head Noun Resolution

There are several kind of definite description, as Figure 1 has shown. This algorithm treat only definite description with the same head noun as their antecedent. In order to solve this kind of definite description syntactic and semantic information is needed. This algorithm processes the texts sentence by sentence adding every noun phrase into a list of antecedent (LA). Noun phrases are provided for SUPP parser [8].

The steps of the algorithm are the following:

- The detection of the definite description in the text
- Search for candidate antecedents with the same head noun
- Choice of the correct antecedent

Next, each step of the algorithm is going to be described in full detail.

3.1   The Detection of the Definite Description in the Text

The algorithm for the resolution of definite descriptions starts searching these definite descriptions in sentences. This algorithm considers definite descriptions as noun phrases that begin with a definite or demonstrative article. Otherwise, if the algorithm detects others noun phrase types are introduced in the list of antecedents, they are considered as *new discourse entities*.

Once the noun phrase has been obtained, the algorithm checks its first sub-constituent. If this sub-constituent is a definite article or a demonstrative, then the noun phrase is classified as a definite description and the algorithm goes on. Otherwise, it is stored into the list of antecedents (LA).

3.2   Search for Candidate Antecedents with the Same Head Noun

Once the definite description is detected, their head noun is extracted. This head noun is compared with every head noun of elements from list of antecedents. This list of antecedents stores all noun phrases from all previous sentences. If there is not one antecedent from the list of antecedents satisfying this rule then the definite description will be classified as a *non-anaphoric expression*. In this case, the definite description is stored into the list of antecedents. Otherwise the definite description will be classified as an *anaphoric expression*. Every antecedent that satisfies at least one heuristic rule is stored into a list of candidate antecedents (LC) being processed in the next step.

3.3   Choice of the Correct Antecedent

If there are more than one antecedent into the list of candidate antecedents (LC), then heuristic rules are applied. Otherwise, if there is only one antecedent, then it is considered as the solution of the definite description adding to the *LA*.

Type	Percentage
identical	44%
included	40%
semantic relation	16%

Table 3. Distribution of antecedents with the same head as their anaphoric expression

A deep study of a fragment of LEXESP[3] corpus shows us (table 3) that a 44% of the definite description is identical to the antecedent, a 40% of the definite description is included into their antecedent and a 16% of definite description has a semantic relation between their pre-modifiers and post-modifiers. From this study the following heuristic rules are extracted:

---

[3] LEXESP is a Spanish corpus. This corpus has about 5 million of tagged words developed by Psychology Department from University of Oviedo, Computational Linguistic Group of University of Barcelona and Language Treatment Group from Technical University of Cataluña.

- **Heuristic H1: (Repetition)**. Antecedents with the same pre-modifiers and post-modifiers are preferred.
- **Heuristic H2: (Included)**. Some pre-modifiers or post-modifiers of antecedent are as pre-modifiers or post-modifiers of definite descriptions, i.e. definite description is included into its antecedent.
- **Heuristic H3: (Modifiers Relation)**. Antecedents with semantic relations between pre-modifiers and post-modifiers of antecedents and definite description.
- **Heuristic H4: (Genre and Number Concordance)**. Antecedents with number and gender concordance are preferred.
- **Heuristic H5: (Frequency)**. Most appeared antecedents the text are preferred.
- **Heuristic H6: (Closest)**. Nearest antecedent is preferred.

The scheme to apply heuristic rules is the following. The first heuristic rule (H1) is applied to the LC list. If there are more than one antecedent that satisfies this heuristic rule, then the second heuristic rule (H2) is applied to these antecedents. And so on with the remaining heuristic rules (H3..H6). This process is stopped when there is only one antecedent that satisfies a heuristic rule. In this case, this antecedent is considered the solution of the definite description. Those heuristic rules that are not satisfied by any antecedent are ignored, and the process continues with the following heuristic rule.

Example: *[El coche de [competición]$_1$]$_2$ que [Juan López]$_3$ se compró le costó [diez millones de [pesetas]$_4$]$_5$. [Este coche]$_6$ había sido usado por [corredores profesionales]$_7$. [El coche de [competición]$_8$]$_9$ quedó destrozado en [un accidente]$_{10}$ en [el circuito del [Jarama]$_{11}$]$_{12}$. [El coche de [carrera]$_{13}$]$_{14}$ fue vendido como [chatarra]$_{15}$. [Los coches de [competición]$_{16}$]$_{17}$ para poder competir en [carreras del [campeonato del [mundo]$_{18}$]$_{19}$]$_{20}$ tienen que cumplir [unas normas muy estrictas]$_{21}$. [Estos coches]$_{22}$ son revisados continuamente para que [ningún piloto]$_{23}$ pueda aprovecharse de [ciertas ventajas mecánicas]$_{24}$ que le proporcione [algunos segundos de [ventaja]$_{25}$]$_{26}$ frente a [otros pilotos]$_{27}$. [La mayoría de [fabricantes de [coches de [competición]$_{28}$]$_{29}$]$_{30}$]$_{31}$ lo son también de [coches utilitarios]$_{32}$. [Estos coches]$_{33}$ no pueden ser comprados por [cualquier persona]$_{34}$. [Carlos Sainz]$_{35}$ es [un piloto de [rallies]$_{36}$]$_{37}$ que ha ganado [el campeonato del [mundo de [rallies]$_{38}$]$_{39}$]$_{40}$. [Marc Gené]$_{41}$ y [Pedro de la Rosa]$_{42}$ son [pilotos de [Formula I]$_{43}$]$_{44}$. [Estos pilotos]$_{45}$ no han ganado [ningún campeonato]$_{46}$.*

Table 4 shows antecedents that satisfy each heuristic for each definite description. The H0 heuristic is the antecedents before heuristics (antecedents with the same head). If a defined description does not have modifiers H1 heuristic is no applied.

In the example above, definite description indexed by *6* (El coche) is included into the noun phrase indexed by *2* (El coche de competición). For this reason, the correct antecedent is chosen after applying the heuristic H2. The

N.	H0	H1	H2	H3	H4	H5	H6	Solution
6	2		2					2
9	2,6	2						2
14	2,6,9			2,9	2,9	2,9	9	2
22	2,6,9,14,17		2,6,9,14,17	17				17
33	2,6,9,14,17		2,6,9,14,17	17,29	17,29	29		29
45	23,27,37,44		23,27,37,44	44				44

Table 4. Heuristics applied

definite description indexed by *9* must choose between two noun phrases with the same head (noun phrases indexed by *2* and *6*) in order to solve its reference. Noun phrase indexed by *2* is chosen after applying the heuristic H1. Heuristics H3, H4, H5 and H6 are applied in order to solve the reference produced by the noun phrase indexed by *14*. Last heuristic (H6) provides us the noun phrase indexed by *9* as solution. The heuristic H3 stores noun phrases indexed by *2* and *9* into the candidate list because there is a semantic relation between *competición* and *carrera* modifiers. The heuristic H4 is applied to provide the correct antecedent (*17*) to definite description indexed by *22*. Noun phrase indexed by *45* prefers the noun phrase *44* as antecedent instead of *37* because they have gender and number agreement (heuristic H4).

4   Evaluation

This algorithm has been checked on two different corpus. The first corpus is a different fragment from LEXESP corpus used as was training corpus. And, the second one is formed by several deed. In order to check the last corpus the algorithm has been introduced into the information extraction system EXIT [6].

Corpus	DD Total	Failure	Precision
LEXESP	245	35	85.7%
DEED	195	36	81.5%

Table 5. Results obtained with our algorithm.

Table 5 shows the results achieved by the algorithm: In LEXESP corpus a precision[4] of 85.7% in co-reference task for definite description with the same head noun as their antecedent. In deed corpus, a precision of 81.5% produced by the same head.

---

[4] Precision is the quotient between number of correctly solved and number of processed definite descriptions.

In the first step, all definite descriptions are considered as *anaphoric expressions*, i.e. the algorithm tries to find out its antecedent. If the algorithm cannot find a suitable solution, then this definite description is considered as an expression that introduces a *new discourse entity (non-anaphoric expressions)*.

Moreover, we have compared our algorithm with Kameyama algorithm and Viera and Poesio algorithm in table 6. The problem of this comparison is that these algorithms neither used the same corpus nor the same language.

Algorithm	Precision	Recall
Kameyama algorithm	72%	46%
Viera and Poesio algorithm	83%	62%
Muñoz and Palomar algorithm	83.6%	73%

Table 6. Comparison with related work.

5   Conclusion

Main contribution of this work is the definition of a set of heuristic extracted from an unrestricted corpus (LEXESP) that can be applied as restrictions or preferences in order to solve and classify definite descriptions. These heuristics were checked in an information extraction system that works on deed texts and an unrestricted text.

Our future algorithm aims will use other semantic tools such as Spanish WordNet that will provide us with more detailed semantic knowledge. Moreover, in order to solve the problem of the best searching window (number of sentences in which the solution of an anaphora is scanned), the algorithm will scan a lower number of sentences, and if there is no solution, then a higher number of sentences will be scanned. Then, a study of the best searching window will be carried out. Furthermore, this algorithm will be applied on English texts, in order to compare it with other methods.

References

1. P. Christopherson. *The Articles: A study of their theory and use in English*. E. Munksgaard, Copenhagen, 1939.
2. H. H. Clark. Bridging. In P. Johnson-Laird and P Wason, editors, *Thinking: readings in cognitive science*, pages 411–420. Cambridge: CUP, 1977.
3. J. A. Hawkins. *Definiteness and indefiniteness*. Humanities Press, Atlantic Highlands, NJ, 1978.
4. J. R. Hobbs, D. E. Appelt, J. Bear, D. Israel, M. Kameyama, M. Stickel, and M. Tyson. FASTUS: A cascaded finite-state transducer for extracting information from natural-language text. *In E. Roche and Y. Schabes, eds. Finite State Devices for natural Language Processing. MIT Press, Cambridge, Massachussetts*, 1996.

5. M. Kameyama. Recognizing Referential Links: An Information Extraction Perspective. In R. In Mitkov and eds. B. Boguraev, editors, *Proceedings of ACL / EACL Workshop on Operational Factors in Practical, Robust Anaphora Resolution for Unrestricted Texts*, pages 46–53, Madrid, Spain, July 1997.
6. F. Llopis, R. Muñoz, A. Suárez, and A. Montoyo. EXIT: Propuesta de un sistema de extracción de información de textos notariales. *Revista Nováatica*, 133:26–30, 1998.
7. R. Muñoz, M. Palomar, and A. Ferrández. Processing of Spanish Definite Descriptions. In *Proceeding of Mexican International Conference on Artificial Intelligence*, Lectures Notes in Artificial Intelligence, Acapulco, Mexico, April 2000. Springer-Verlag. (To appear).
8. M. Palomar, A. Ferrández, L. Moreno, M. Saiz-Noeda, R. Muñoz, P. Martínez-Barco, J. Peral, and B. Navarro. A Robust Partial Parsing Strategy based on the Slot Unification Grammars. In *Proceeding of 6e Conférence annuelle sur le Traitement Automatique des Langues Naturelles. TALN'99*, pages 263–272, Cargèse, Corse, July 1999.
9. M. Poesio and R. Vieira. A Corpus-Based Investigation of Definite Description Use. *Computational Linguistics. MIT Press*, 24:183–216, 1998.
10. E. Prince. Toward a taxonomy of given-newinformation. *In P.Cole, editor, Radical Pragmatics. Academic Press, New York*, pages 223–256, 1981.
11. R. Vieira. Co-reference resolution of definite descriptions. In *Proceedings of VI Simposio Internacional de comunicación Social*, pages 497–503, Santiago de Cuba, Cuba, January 1999.
12. R. Vieira and M. Poesio. *Corpus-based and computational aproach to anaphora*, chapter Processing definite descriptions in corpora. S.Botley and T. McEnery eds. UCL Press, London, 1998.

Constraints, Linguistic Theories, and Natural Language Processing

Philippe Blache

LPL, Université de Provence
29 Avenue Robert Schuman
13621 Aix-en-Provence, France
pb@lpl.univ-aix.fr
http://www.lpl.univ-aix.fr/~blache

1 Introduction

The notion of constraints is generally used in modern linguistics (in particular in syntax and phonology) for representing properties that an object must satisfy (see [4], [15]). Constraints can be general (or universal), valid for different languages, or at the opposite very specific, representing for example the variability of a given language. In all cases, the idea consists of stipulating properties ruling out structures which don't belong to the language.

Most linguistic theories now integrate this notion, in particular constraint-based approaches (HPSG being the theory making the most intensive use of this notion), but also in the principle and parameters paradigm (in particular Optimality Theory, see[1]). Even dependency grammars propose a constraint-based version called Constraint Dependency Grammars (see [11]). However, the interpretation of this notion can be very different from one approach to another.

It is interesting to note that constraints are also used in computer science (see [10], [17]), and logic programming in particular. The question addressed here concerns precisely the adequation of the notion of constraints in linguistics and in computer science (see [8], [13], [14]). We want to show that, while a superposition of both points of view is possible, the linguistic interpretation doesn't exploit all the properties of a constraint system. Concretely, several approaches in parsing try to interpret the parsing process as a constraint satisfaction problem. However, in most cases, constraints are used in a passive sense.

We show here that this problem comes in particular from the generative interpretation of the relation between grammar and language. More precisely, the derivation relation entails a conception of the parsing process consisting in building first a local structure (usually a tree) and then in verifying some properties over it. Then, the information allowing to build trees doesn't have the same status as the other linguistic knowledge. In such a perspective, constraints are relegated to a secondary role. We propose an approach representing all the information by means of constraints, at the same level and allowing to consider the parsing process as one of constraint satisfaction.

In a first section, we detail some examples illustrating different interpretations (and different uses) of constraints in linguistics. We then describe more

D.N. Christodoulakis (Ed.): NLP 2000, LNCS 1835, pp. 221–232, 2000.
© Springer-Verlag Berlin Heidelberg 2000

precisely how constraints generally work within linguistic theories. Concretely several characteristics inhibit constraints from playing the same role as in computer science. The second section describes these limits and presents some properties that should be present in the definition of a constraint-based formalism. The third section proposes such a formalism, called *Property Grammars*, illustrating how constraints can form a system, useful both in a descriptive perspective and for parsing. The last section shows how such a system can be used for implementation.

2   Constraints in Linguistics

The following examples show different uses of constraints. They illustrate the variability of the representation level of constraints which can be used at a low level in order to verify properties or more generally, as part of the theory itself, the analysis mechanism becoming one of resolution.

2.1   *Constraint Grammars*

The notion of constraints as used in *Constraint Grammars* (see [9]) is close to *if-then* rules. In this approach, constraints are applied to categories and express contextual dependencies. They are particularly useful to restrict the categorization mechanism.

1. (@w = 0 "REP" (-1 DET))
2. (@w = 0 VFIN (-1 TO))
3. ("that" =! "⟨ Rel ⟩" (-1 NOMHEAD) (1VFIN))

Example (1) indicates that if a word can be interpreted as a preposition and the preceding one (at position -1) is a determiner, then the "PREP" interpretation is ruled out. The same kind of constraint is represented in example (2) which stipulates that a word cannot be a finite verb before "TO". Such constraints express cooccurrence restrictions on the right and left contexts, as in the third example which indicates that "that" is a relative if it immediately follows a nominal head and precedes a finite verb.

One interesting aspect of these constraints is then the possibility of representing properties over objects with different granularities: objects can be specified as categories or subset of features (see [16]). This kind of technique is very efficient for POS tagging or text chunking. But representing linguistic information with such an approach can become difficult, in particular for the expression of generalizations.

2.2   *Constraint Dependency Grammar*

The use of constraints in dependency grammars was first proposed in [11]. Dependency grammars build relations between words. CDG proposed some constraints over these relations.

1. $word(pos(x))=PP \Rightarrow (word(mod(x)) \in \{PP, NP, V\}, mod(x) \prec pos(x))$
2. $mod(x) \prec pos(y) \prec pos(x) \Rightarrow mod(x) \preceq mod(y) \preceq pos(x)$

In the first example, the constraint stipulates that if a word at position x is a PP, it can modify a PP, a NP or a V, these modified elements preceding the word in x. The second constraint implements projectivity and indicates that no crossing relations are allowed for modifications.

In this approach, constraints are not directly expressed over linguistic objects, but over relations. This entails a passive use of constraints in the sense that the parsing process consists in building first these relations and then verifying that they satisfy the constraints.

Some recent implementations of CDG control the satisfaction process by introducing a notion of weight over constraints (see [12], [18]) which, in a certain respect, comes to ranking constraints, like Optimality Theory. But this doesn't modify the fact that parsing is a two-stage process: determining relations, then satisfying constraints.

2.3 HPSG

In HPSG, principles, grammar rules and lexical entries are considered as constraints which interact in order to specify a syntactic structure. The theory relies explicitly on the notion of constraint satisfaction (cf. [15]): "*A phrase structure is well formed just in case each local subtree within it either : (1) satisfies a lexical entry or (2) satisfies some grammar rule and all grammatical principles.*"

The following example presents a constraint on head-complement phrases. It stipulates that if a word takes complements (values of the COMPS feature), then the corresponding categories must appear as non-head daughters of the phrase headed by the word.

$$
\begin{bmatrix}
\text{SYNSEM} & \begin{bmatrix} \text{SYN} & \begin{bmatrix} \text{COMPS} \langle\rangle \end{bmatrix} \end{bmatrix} \\
\text{HD-DTR} & \begin{bmatrix} word \\ \text{SS} & \begin{bmatrix} \text{SYN} & \begin{bmatrix} \text{COMPS} \langle \boxed{1}, ..., \boxed{n} \rangle \end{bmatrix} \end{bmatrix} \end{bmatrix} \\
\text{NHD-DTRS} & \left\langle \begin{bmatrix} \text{SS} \boxed{1} \end{bmatrix}, ..., \begin{bmatrix} \text{SS} \boxed{n} \end{bmatrix} \right\rangle
\end{bmatrix}
$$

In such a view, there is no particular order for the verification of the information and the grammatical information is considered as a set of constraints. But, as explicit in the description of the grammaticality given above, this is also a two-stage mechanism which consists in first building a local tree (using tree schemas) and then verifying the other constraints.

3   Constraints in Linguistic Theories

As shown in the previous section, the use of constraints is of deep interest both from a descriptive and a formal point of view. However, in these examples, coming from three different formal paradigms, we can notice that constraints are passive in the sense that a structure has first to be built before verifying its properties. Practically, this has an impact on the scope of the constraint which can only be local and applied to a given structure. In other words, it is difficult to stipulate constraints over general variables, they have to be linked to a given structure. In constraint dependency grammars for example, relations have to be known before verifying constraints. The same is true in HPSG which requires a local structure (a local tree) before applying the principles.

In the case of constraint-based theories, this point comes from the generative interpretation of the relation between grammars and languages. Indeed, in this paradigm, a language is generated by a grammar and this relation is implemented by the derivation process. Even without explicit phrase-structure rules like in HPSG, this relation remains the core of the process: building a local tree (e.g. selecting a rule schema) is equivalent to deriving a non-terminal in classical PS grammars. This point is crucial because it is in a certain sense contradictory with an actual constraint-based view of the parsing process.

Now let us examine the computer science side. In constraint programming, the set of constraints forms a system which has to be verified at each step of the process (in constraint logic programming, for example, constraint resolution replaces unification). As soon as a variable needs to be instantiated, the coherence of the constraint system is verified before actually applying the instantiation. This means in particular that in constraint satisfaction problems, variables are accessible at each step (they have a global scope) in order to allow the coherence verification of the system and to control the evaluation all along the resolution: constraints in this sense are active and specify properties over the constrained objects during the process. Generally speaking, a constraint satisfaction process requires the possibility of expressing constraints over objects independently from the way to accessing them. Such an approach has interesting properties, in particular concerning declarativity: the description of the problem relies on the description of constraints, its resolution makes use of these constraints. Thus, describing a problem is equivalent to its resolution. This is one of the most important characteristics of constraint logic programming.

Concerning the particular problem of parsing, this means that constraints have to be specified directly over variables, independently from complex structures. In the examples described above, we encounter two different situations. Constraint grammars express constraints directly over words. However, it is difficult to figure out how these local contextual constraints can constitute a grammar. In the other example, constraints are not expressed directly over objects, but according to their situation within a structure (or a relation). In this case, we cannot consider that the set of constraints forms a system whose consistency can be checked globally: constraints form subsets (or subsystems) each being relevant to a substructure. The general process cannot then be considered as a constraint satisfaction one[1]. In this sense, we can consider that constraints have a local use in the process. This limitation doesn't come from a particular restricted interpretation but from the theory itself.

Moreover, we can say that such a conception of constraints illustrates a particular conception of the role of grammars in linguistic analysis (this is particularly clear in natural language processing). The classical consideration consists in using grammatical information in order to separate the well-formed structures from the others. In this approach, constraints are imperative and used to implement the notion of grammaticality. However, it is important to notice that one of the arguments for using constraints in computer science is the possibility of building approximate solutions: the constraint system at the end of the process, even when it cannot be simplified to a unique solution, contains a lot of information. In other words, we can consider that the state of the constraint system constitutes in itself a solution, whatever its form. Concerning natural language processing, this means the possibility of associating information to an input, whatever its grammaticality status.

4   What an Constraint-Based Approach Should Be

We have seen in the previous section that even if constraints play a crucial role in modern linguistic theories, we cannot totally conceive the parsing problem as one of constraint satisfaction. The main consequence is that a grammar cannot be viewed as a set of constraints containing all the information. As shown before, a parsing process in these approaches consists first in applying a derivation (i.e. building a local structure) and then verifying some constraints. We present in the following a set of characteristics that should be present in a constraint-based approach.

Constrained Objects: The objects affected by a constraint have to be accessible independently from structural information. In other words, it is necessary to express constraints over every kind of object (whatever its level) without needing the knowledge of a local structure for accessing its value. This condition is necessary to interpret the grammatical information as a constraint system and the parsing process as a constraint satisfaction problem. Otherwise, constraint resolution only constitutes a subpart of the entire mechanism, which is contradictory with the goals of a constraint-based theory.

In the same perspective, the constraints have to be expressed independently from the form of the objects and reciprocally, the structure of an object should not depend on the constraint that can affect it.

Constraint System: All the information has to be represented by means of constraints, for the same reasons as for the accessibility of values described above. A

---

[1] It is then false to consider that Maruyama and CDG allows the interpretation of parsing as a constraint satisfaction problem.

grammar must form a system of constraints which contains all the information required for a linguistic
    analysis. This is imperative if one want to interpret parsing as a CSP.

A Constraint System Is a Set: All the constraints are represented and treated at the same level. There is no hierarchization nor sequencing of the constraints. The reason is that, again, the mechanism of constraint resolution must only rely on information contained by constraints[2] . With this property, a parsing mechanism can make use exclusively of constraints.

Encapsulation: Same information should not be disseminated through different representations. This means that the information represented in a constraint must be homogeneous and reciprocally that this information be linguistically motivated.

Grammaticality vs. Characterization: As shown in the previous section, constraints are used for the verification of the well formedness of a local structure. Reciprocally, when no local structure can be built, constraints cannot be checked. The analysis problem is then restricted to the grammaticality question. It seems however interesting to take advantage of the notion of constraints in order to allow approximate solutions. In this case, the main goal of the analysis is the characterization of an input by means of linguistic properties rather than the verification of its grammaticality and the construction of an associated syntactic representation.

5   Property Grammars

We propose a formalism, called *Property Grammars*, implementing the advantages of using constraints. In this approach, all the information is represented by means of properties (see [2]) which form a system of constraints. The properties are expressed over categories, which can be hierarchized. However, properties do not depend on a particular local structure. In this sense, the grammar forms an actual set of constraints. This also means that this approach is equational rather than generative: there is no derivation between the grammar and the described language.

    In property grammars (as should be the case for actual constraint-based theories), the notion of grammaticality is not crucial. More precisely, grammaticality is replaced with a more general notion: *characterization*. Concretely, the characterization of an input corresponds to the state of the constraint system at the end of the parse. We will see in the following that such a result can be interpreted as a unique structure (which can for example be represented as a

---

[2] Constraint ranking as used in OT contains in fact implicit information. Moreover, it can be reduced in certain cases to a simple default mechanism more than an actual parsing process.

tree), but not necessarily: some inputs can be characterized with several disconnected structures. The main consequence is that parsing is not restricted to grammatical inputs.

5.1 Properties

In this approach, properties (which are synonyms to constraints) express relations between categories. A category is, classically in a constraint-based approach, a set of hierarchized features. The propagation of feature values from one category to another is explicit in the constraints.

We propose a limited set of relations corresponding to different types of properties: linearity, dependency, obligation, exclusion, exigency, constituency, unicity. This set constitutes the basic syntactic relations represented in *Property Grammars*. As said before, a property is expressed independently from any local structure, but directly between categories. Obviously, for clarity, it is interesting to group properties according to the described syntactic unit, but such a presentation has no operational consequences.

We give in the following a presentation of the properties (together with their notations). A predicative representation is given for these constraints, indicating the concerned syntactic unit. Again, this is not a limitation to a particular local structure, but used only for clarity[3].

- **Constituency** (*const*): Defines the maximal set of categories constituting a syntactic unit. This property allows the determination the non lexical categories that will appear in the characterization of a given input.

  Example: *const(NP)* = {*Det, AP, N, Sup, PP, Pro*}

  The corresponding categories (in which *Sup* stands for superlative) can be dominated in the hierarchy by a *NP*.
- **Obligation** (*oblig*): Specifies the set of compulsory, unique categories. Such categories correspond to the heads.

  Example: *oblig(VP)* = {*V*}
- **Unicity** (*uniq*): Set of categories which cannot be repeated in a phrase.

  Example: *unic(NP)* = {*Det, N, AP, PP, Sup, Pro*}
- **Requirement** ($\Rightarrow$): Cooccurrence between sets of categories.

  Example: {*le être*$_{[N,P]}$} $\overset{VP}{\Rightarrow}$ *ClR*$_{[N,P]}$ (*Je me le suis dit/I told that to myself*)
  If the clitic *le* and a finite verb *être* (with agreement features N and P) cooccur (characterizing a *VP*), then a reflexive clitic (which agrees with the verb) is needed.
- **Exclusion** ($\nRightarrow$): Restriction of cooccurrence between sets of categories.

---

[3] Examples are in French.

Example: $Clit[Ref] \overset{VP}{\not\leadsto} lui$ (*Je me lui dis / *I told him myself)
In a *VP*, a reflexive clitic cannot cooccur with the clitic *lui*.

– **Linearity** ($\prec$): Linear precedence constraints.

   Example: $Det \prec AP$ $\quad\quad\quad AP \prec N$

– **Dependency** ($\leadsto$): Dependency relations between categories.

   Example: $Det \leadsto N$ $\quad\quad\quad AP \leadsto N$

These properties contain the basic syntactic information. Other properties can be added if necessary, in particular for the integration of knowledge coming from other linguistic domains or for particular devices, for example long distance dependencies.

One can note the use of a dependency property which, as in dependency grammars, concerns a syntactico-semantic relation. It is then possible to express a dependency grammar using the formalism of property grammar. However, several deep differences, among them the use of a hierarchical structure organizing the categories, distinguish these approaches.

A property grammar is formed by a set of (unordered) properties which define constraints over categories.

In an analysis perspective, all the subsets of categories involved in the description of a given input can be characterized by the constraint system (i.e. the grammar). The problem with the use of a hierarchical structure representation is the accessibility of the objects values: we need to know the set of categories associated to an input. We have shown that building a local structure before verifying constraints has negative consequences on the use of constraints. However, constituency property contains such an information: each category can be associated to another which dominates it in the hierarchy. This means that all the possible categories forming part of the syntactic structure can be deduced from the set of lexical categories associated to a given input[4]. The characterization of this input is calculated from this maximal set of categories.

Building this set of categories doesn't amount to building a local structure: first, this information is directly accessible from the constituency property, for each category and secondly the hierarchical information between a particular category and an upper-level indicated by such a property is not used in the satisfaction process, as we will see it in the next section.

The satisfiability process consists then of the following mechanism: knowing the set of categories that can be associated with an input, a characterization is the state of the constraint system formed by the relevant constraints (i.e. the constraints that can be evaluated) for this set of categories. The interest of such a conception is that no notion of well-formedness is used. It can be the case that all constraints are satisfied, but this is not an imperative condition. All kind of input can consequently receive a characterization.

---

[4] The knowledge of the entire set of categories actually depends on the syntactic structuration. Preferring flat structures allows an immediate access to this set of categories.

5.2   An Example

We give in this section an example of description of the *NP* in French (including the superlative). This grammar (see figure (1)) illustrates the use of the different properties. As mentioned in the previous section, the properties are grouped according to the syntactic unit they describe, but this is merely for readability. All constraints are at the same level, not hierarchized and the entire grammar has to be considered as a constraint system in which constraints can be verified independently from each other. In the same order of idea, the indexation doesn't play a particular role, but is used in the following to refer to the constraints.

Properties of the *AP*

(1) $Const = \{Adj, Adv\}$
(2) $Oblig = \{Adj\}$
(3) $Adv \prec Adj$
(4) $Adv \leadsto Adj$

Properties of the *NP*

(1) $Const = \{Det, N, AP, Sup\}$
(2) $Oblig = \{N, AP\}$
(3) $N[com] \Rightarrow Det$
(4) $Det \prec N$
(5) $Det \prec AP$
(6) $Det \prec Sup$
(8) $N \prec Sup$
(9) $AP \not\prec Sup$
(10) $Det \leadsto N$
(11) $AP \leadsto N$
(12) $Sup \leadsto N$

Properties of the *Sup*

(1) $Const = \{Det, Adv, Adj\}$
(2) $Oblig = \{Adj\}$
(3) $Adj \Rightarrow Det$
(4) $Adj \Rightarrow Adv$
(5) $Det \prec Adv$
(6) $Det \prec Adv$
(7) $Adv \prec Adj$
(8) $Det \leadsto Adj$
(9) $Adv \leadsto Adj$

Fig. 1. A property grammar for the *NP*

Let's give some precisions on this grammar. Constraint (3) of the *NP* stipulates that a common noun requires a determiner. This is the classical subcategorization information for which syntactic aspects are represented separately from semantic ones (using exigency and dependency constraints). Concerning the dependency relation, we can also notice that all kinds of category (not necessarily the head) can be the target of the relation. In constraint (2), we can see that an *AP* can be the head of the *NP* which can be the case in examples such as *"donne-moi la rouge (give me the red)"*. In this case, we would need another dependency constraint (not represented here) indicating that *Det* depends on the *AP*. Constraint (9) stipulates that an *AP* cannot cooccur with a superlative as shown in the examples:

(1)   a. le vieux livre. (*the old book*)
       b. le livre le plus vieux. (*the oldest book*)
       c. * le vieux livre le plus cher.

Finally, concerning the superlative, the property (4) indicates that an adverb necessarily belongs to this unit without being a possible head.

5.3 Parsing

We describe in this section the general parsing mechanism. Let's take an example relying on the grammar of the *NP* described in the previous section:

(2) a. *le livre le plus vieux. (the oldest book)*

Step 1 (Categorization): The first stage consists in finding the categories associated with the words of the input. We don't need to disambiguate this operation, the goal being to build all the possible characterizations of the input. Each category is associated with the position of the corresponding word, we obtain a set of pairs of the form $\langle cat, pos \rangle$. For clarity, we note these pairs as cat_{pos}. For our example, we build :

$$\Sigma_1 = \{ Det_1, Pro_1, N_2, V_2, Det_3, Pro_3, Adv_4, Adj_5 \}$$

Step 2 (Determining All the Objects): The second operation consists in building the set of all the relevant categories for the input. This amounts to defining a set of variables in which the constraints will be applied. This operation consists in finding for each category the *constituency* property to which it belongs. These properties indicate the dominating syntactic unit which will then belong to the set of possible objects. We build this new set from the first set Σ_1:

$$\Sigma_2 = \{ Det_1, Pro_1, NP_1, Sup_1, N_2, NP_2, V_2, Det_3, Pro_3, NP_3, Sup_3, Adv_4,$$
$$AP_4, Sup_4, Adj_5, AP_5, Sup_5, \}$$

Step 3 (Building Characterizations): Characterizing an input consists in building the set of all subsets of Σ_2 and verifying constraints for each subset. Concretely, it is possible to associate to these subsets the state of the relevant constraints described by P^+ (the set of satisfied constraints) and P^- (the set of unsatisfied constraints). Figure (2) presents some characterization sets (i.e. characterizations associated to some subsets of Σ_2).

- Det_1/N_2 :	$P^+(NP) = \{1, 2, 3, 4, 10\}$	$P^-(NP) = \emptyset$
- Sup_1/N_2 :	$P^+(NP) = \{1, 2, 12\}$	$P^-(NP) = \{6,3\}$
- Det_3/Sup_4 :	$P^+(NP) = \{1, 6\}$	$P^-(NP) = \{2\}$
- Det_3/AP_4 :	$P^+(NP) = \{1, 5\}$	$P^-(NP) = \{2\}$
- Sup_3/AP_4 :	$P^+(NP) = \{1\}$	$P^-(NP) = \{2, 9\}$
- Adv_4/Adj_5 :	$P^+(AP) = \{1, 2, 3, 4\}$	$P^-(AP) = \emptyset$
	$P^+(Sup) = \{1, 2, 4, 9\}$	$P^-(Sup) = \{3\}$
- $Det_1/N_2/Sup_3$:	$P^+(NP) = \{1\text{-}4, 6, 8, 9, 10, 12\}$	$P^-(NP) = \emptyset$
- $Sup_1/N_2/Det_3$:	$P^+(NP) = \{1, 2, 3, 9, 10, 12\}$	$P^-(NP) = \{4, 6, 8\}$
- $Det_3/Adv_4/Adj_5$:	$P^+(Sup) = \{1, 2, 3, 4, 5, 6, 8, 9\}$	$P^-(NP) = \emptyset$
- $Det_3/AP_4/Sup_5$:	$P^+(Sup) = \{1, 4, 5, 6\}$	$P^-(NP) = \{2, 9\}$
- $Det_1/N_2/Sup_3/AP_4$:	$P^+(NP) = \{1\text{-}8, 10, 11, 12\}$	$P^-(NP) = \{9\}$

Fig. 2. Characterization sets

We can remark that all subsets can be characterized, some of them having an empty set P^-. In all cases, whatever the form of the input, a precise description can be given in terms of satisfied and unsatisfied properties. Some subsets can have different characterizations: the subset Adv_4/Adj_5 can be characterized using relevant properties of AP and Sup.

If characterizations are restricted to that receiving an empty P^-, then only grammatical constructions are analyzed. In our example, the positively characterized subsets are: $\{Det_1/N_2,\ Adv_4/Adj_5,\ Det_1/N_2/Sup_3,\ Det_3/Adv_4/Adj_5\}$. Finding a sequence covering the total input leads to a syntactic structure formed by the last two subsets.

6   Conclusion

Property grammars rely entirely on constraints, both from the linguistic and the computational point of view: all the syntactic information is represented by means of properties, the parsing process being one of constraint satisfaction. The main characteristics of this approach is that constraints can be expressed generally, independently from the form of the syntactic representation. In other words, it is not necessary in this approach to build a local structure and then verify constraints. All the objects being available before the parsing process itself, a grammar can play the role of an actual constraint system and linguistic properties can be verified independently.

One of the main interests of this approach is the possibility of using the general notion of *characterization* in place of that of *grammaticality*. It is then possible to analyze any kind of input, well-formed or not. This is of great importance for real-life natural language processing applications such as dialogue systems. In fact, such an approach proposes a more realistic view for the study of language in which a syntactic structure is not necessarily a homogeneous structure but can be constituted by several (possibly disconnected) pieces of information.

References

1. Archangeli D. & D.T. Langendoen eds. (1997) *Optimality Theory*, Blackwell.
2. Bès G. & P. Blache (1999) *Propriétés et analyse d'un langage*, in actes de TALN'99.
3. Blache P. (1999) *Filtering and Fusion: A Technique for Parsing with Properties*, in proceedings of NLPRS'99.
4. Borsley R. (1996), *Modern Phrase Structure Grammars*, Blackwell.
5. Carpenter B. & Penn G. (1995) "Compiling Typed Attribute-Value Logic Grammars", in H. Bunt and M. Tomita (eds.), *Current Issues in Parsing Technologies*, Kluwer.
6. Duchier D. & Thater S. (1999) "Parsing with Tree Descriptions: a constraint based approach", in proceedings of *NLULP'99*.
7. Götz T., D. Meurers & D. Gerdemann (1997), *The ConTroll Manual*, SFS Report.
8. Guenthner F. (1988) "Features and Values 1988", *CIS-Bericht-90-2*, Universität München.

9. Karlsson F. (1990), "Constraint Grammar as a Framework for Parsing Running Text", in Proceedings of *COLING'90*.
10. Marriott, K. & Stuckey, P. J. (1998) *Programming with Constraints*, MIT Press.
11. Maruyama H. (1990), "Structural Disambiguation with Constraint Propagation", in proceedings of *COLING-ACL'98 workshop on Dependency-based Grammars*.
12. Menzel W. & I. Schröder (1998), "Decision Procedures for Dependency Parsing Using Graded Constraints", in proceedings of *ACL'90*.
13. Meurers D. & Minnen G. (1998) "Off-line Constraint Propagation for Efficient HPSG Processing", in G. Webelhuth, J.-P. Koenig, A. Kathol (eds.): *Lexical and Constructional Aspects of Linguistic Explanation*, CSLI.
14. Morawietz F. & Cornell T. (1997) "Representing Constraints with Automata", in proceedings of the ACL/EACL.
15. Sag I. & T. Wasow (1999), *Syntactic Theory. A Formal Introduction*, CSLI.
16. Samuelsson C., P. Tapainen & A. Voutilainen (1996), "Inducing Constraint Grammars", *CLAUS Report 79*.
17. Saraswat V. (1993), *Concurrent Constraint Programming*, MIT Press.
18. I. Schröder, W. Menzel, K. Foth & M. Schulz (2000), "Modeling Dependency Grammars with Restricted Constraints", submitted to the journal *TAL*.
19. Shieber S. (1992) *Constraint-Based Grammar Formalisms*, MIT Press.

A Comparison of Rule-Based and Machine Learning Methods for Identifying Non-nominal *It*

Richard Evans

School of Humanities, Languages and Social Sciences, University of Wolverhampton
Stafford Street, Wolverhampton, WV1 1SB, UK
in6087@wlv.ac.uk
http://www.wlv.ac.uk/sles/compling/

Abstract. The pronoun *it* is noted to be used in a variety of non-nominal ways. The identification of non-nominal pronouns is important in information retrieval, machine translation and automatic summarisation. Given that previous work has only tackled a subset of those non-nominal uses, a machine learning method for identification of all instances of non-nominal *it* is presented. The machine learning method is compared with a rule-based approach. The performance of each implementation is evaluated. The construction of an annotated corpus and training data are also described.

1   Introduction

The pronoun *it* has a variety of uses in English. Attention is directed toward six of them for the purposes of this paper. It is used most commonly in an anaphoric relationship with some noun phrase (NP) in a text (1). However, in a significant minority of cases it may have a clausal (2) or a discourse segmental (3) antecedent. The pronoun may have an antecedent in the text, but the relation of the pronoun to that antecedent is cataphoric rather than anaphoric (4). In addition to this, there are the *pleonastic* uses of *it* where the pronoun is non-referential and appears due to some requirement in the grammar of the language (5). Finally, *it* is used in idiomatic constructions (6) as well as combining with *do* to form *proactions* [6]. Such uses are termed *non-nominal* in this paper.

(1) *Do not sweep* the dust$_i$ *when dry, you will only recirculate* it$_i$.

(2) *One day in 1970 fifty thousand women marched down fifth Avenue in New York.* It *is said to have been the biggest women's gathering since suffrage days.*

(3) *Always use a tool for the job it was designed to do. Always use tools correctly. If* it *feels very awkward, stop.*

(4) *When* it$_i$ *fell, the glass$_i$ broke.*

D.N. Christodoulakis (Ed.): NLP 2000, LNCS 1835, pp. 233–240, 2000.

(5) It *is worth having more than one size or a good-quality set with interchangeable bits.*

(6) *I take* it *you're going now.*

The paper is structured as follows: Section 2 motivates recognition of non-nominal *it*. Section 3 surveys previous work, examining the phenomenon with respect to its grammatical characteristics and inspecting previous approaches to its recognition. The application of machine learning to a similar task in NLP is reviewed. In section 4, the development of a novel corpus for use in training and evaluation of the systems is described. A rule-based and a machine learning approach to recognition of non-nominal *it* is described in sections 5 and 6 respectively. Evaluation and comparison of those approaches is presented in section 7 and in section 8, conclusions are drawn and future research considered.

2   Motivation

One task that has formed part of previous Message Understanding Conferences is the coreference task [5]). Here, systems are required to tag portions of a text with identity labels conveying the fact that they represent the first mention of some entity in the text. Subsequent mentions of the same entity are tagged with their own identity label and a reference to the first mention. The systems are evaluated with respect to a human-annotated corpus.

When a number of phrases all refer to the same discourse entity, they are said to *corefer* and can be put into a set known as a *coreferential chain*. The accurate construction of coreferential chains by systems is impossible unless non-nominal uses of pronouns such as *it* are recognised. Systems should not assign non-nominal pronouns to coreferential chains.

The accurate recognition of non-nominal *it* thus contributes to all fields in which coreference resolution is a concern, whether it be information retrieval, information extraction [5], machine translation or text summarisation [4]. It must further be recognised that these non-nominal uses are quite common. Lappin and Leass found that 8% of all the pronouns in their corpus were pleonastic [7]. The present author found that almost a third of the appearances of *it* in the corpus used here were non-nominal. Further motivation for the present work derived from the fact that the previous work to be detailed in section 3.2 has only addressed recognition of pleonastic *it* and not the identification of all occurrences of non-nominal *it*.

3   Previous Work

3.1   A Grammatical Description of the Phenomenon

Most volumes on English usage; [13], [15], [16]; devote some attention to the pronoun, *it*, usually in the roles exemplified by case (5) in section 1. In such works, it is referred to as "impersonal," "dummy," "empty," "preparatory subject," "clause subject" and "preparatory" *it*. There has thus been some description of those constructs that contain "structural" and "idiomatic" uses.

In [15], Sinclair et al. identified five categories of usage of non-nominal *it*. These were in the description of places and situations, in comments about time and the weather, in reference to whole situations or facts, in making requests or passing on instructions, and in commenting on actions, activities or experiences. The constructs associated with these uses include cleft-sentences; *it* as an object complement with a *to*-infinitive; as the subject of passive reporting verbs and verbs with a *that*-clause; and a variety of miscellaneous constructions.

3.2   Automatic Identification of Pleonastic *It*

Paice and Husk identified nine different pleonastic (referred to in [11] as *structural*) uses of *it*. They identified these uses by means of constructs that afforded a greater degree of coverage than those proposed by subsequent researchers such as Denber [3] and Lappin and Leass [7]. Although there are relatively few constructs; given in (1) - (6) below; each one was derived following a thorough examination of the data and reflects a generalisation of several patterns. In addition, various individual rules were used to handle idiomatic expressions. Due to their scarcity in the corpus data, expressions relating to time and ambience were not covered by any constructs. Supporting this, no such expressions were associated with the first 200 non-nominal uses of *it* in the data used for training and testing in this paper.

(1) The *It...to* Construct: [*it*..."Status" *word*...Infinitival *to*].
e.g. *If you are planning to give a particularly large sum*, it *is always more* advantageous to *give out of income by covenant than to give a capital sum.*

(2) The *It...that* Construct: [*it...that*].
e.g. *A newsletter in 1964 complains that* it *is clear* that *the requested 10 per annum is more than one group can manage.*

(3) Constructions Expressing Uncertainty: [*it*..."State of Knowledge" Expression + *whether/if/what/how/why/etc.*].
e.g. it *is not* known whether *such an exchange was in fact performed...*

(4) The *It...which* Constructs: [*it...which*].
e.g. it *was his Manchester period* which *produced the most important results...*

(5) *It* with a Gerund: [*it...worth...*a Gerund].
e.g. it *is now* worth considering...*other aspects...*

(6) Parenthetical *It*: [, *it* ...Less Than 4 Words... ,].
e.g. *Each of the 72 d has*, it *is now clear* , *a twin d'...*

As well as proposing a set of patterns for identification, [11] also set out some general properties of the patterns. Firstly, they may include negatives, adverbs and other material. The size of a pattern is not permitted to exceed 27 words. There are constraints on the intervening punctuation permissible in the patterns. Finally, in most cases, when *it* immediately follows any of a predefined subset of prepositions, *it* is referential, not pleonastic. Much of the novelty and effectiveness of this system over those of [3] and [7] comes from the enforcement of these properties.

Identification of the patterns relies in part on recognition of particular words (the "Status" words, "State-of-Knowledge" expressions and prepositions which may not immediately precede pleonastic *it*) held in separate open-ended files that may be updated in light of new data [11].

Paice and Husk noted that the lack of a part-of-speech tagger caused some problems in their implementation. Incorporating such a tool into the program would allow more accurate identification of the elements in the proposed patterns. As reported in section 5, part-of-speech information *was* incorporated into our implementation of the rule-based method.

Evaluating their procedure over a substantial corpus, the method in [11] obtained a success rate of 93.9% for the general classification of *it* as either referential or not.

Other researchers have proposed methods based on pattern recognition [7] and [3], but in the case of [7], the identification method was not formally evaluated and in the case of [3], it had not been implemented.

3.3   Machine Learning Applied to a Comparable Task

Machine learning has been used for various tasks in NLP. In [8], Litman used a methodology similar to that used in this work for a different application. In that paper, a classification was sought for words and phrases that may convey *either* structural or semantic information to the discourse. As in this work, a human annotated corpus was used to supervise the learning methods (CGRENDEL and C4.5 in [8]). That system was evaluated using ten-fold cross-validation and was found to out-perform manually derived models.

4   Annotating a Corpus

A corpus was constructed by random selection of 12 texts from the BNC [1] and 65 plain texts obtained by removing mark-up from the Susanne corpus [14]. In total, the data contained 368830 words, with 3171 occurrences of *it* and 1025 non-nominal uses of *it*. As hinted at in section 2, in 32% of its appearances, the impersonal pronoun was not used NP-anaphorically.

A program was implemented to facilitate the mark-up of non-nominal uses of *it*. On detecting an instance, the program would display the paragraph in which the pronoun appeared and ask for a decision from the human annotator about whether *it* was NP-anaphoric or not. Instances judged to be non-nominal are tagged and other instances are left unmarked. Once the entire corpus has been annotated in this way and written to an SGML file, it is tokenised using the SGML aware LT-Chunker [9]. The tokenised text is used by another program to produce a key file with the paragraph, word and sentence positions for all the non-nominal instances in the corpus.

5   A Rule-Based Approach

A system was implemented based on the approach used by [11]. In the first step, texts are tagged using the FDG-Parser [17] which also returns the stems of words and generally eases the lexical comparison aspects of the implementation. The tagged text is then converted to an SGML format and passed to the main program. The program itself accesses 3 small data files containing word lists for the "prepositional", "Status" and "State of Knowledge" words defined in [11]. Broadly speaking, it attempts to apply 10 rules to each instance of *it*. When a rule applies and no constraints (also expressed as rule applications) are breached, the instance is classified as pleonastic.

6   A Machine Learning Approach

The Tilburg Memory Based Learner (TiMBL) [2] was used to execute the machine learning approach. TiMBL is a memory-based learning method; a training set is held in memory and new data is classified according to its similarity to instances in that set. Each training instance is represented by a feature-value vector and a field explicitly stating the classification of that vector. A distance metric is computed for query vectors. The k-nearest neighbours are determined using that metric. The new vector is then classified based on the most frequent classification of the k nearest neighbours. TiMBL allows the use of different metrics and different values of k on which to base the classification.

The vectors of the training set consist of 35 features that express information about the position of the instance of *it* in the text, the stems of proximal words such as adjectives and verbs, the parts of speech of words in an 8-token window, and the distance of other elements such as complementisers, prepositions, gerunds, infinitival-*to* and NPs. In some cases, information relating to the sequencing of elements in the text was found to be effective in classifying vectors. For example, the sequence of an adjective and then a full NP assisted recognition of certain patterns, whereas a sequence involving a complementiser preceding a full NP after the instance was effective in recognition of other expressions.

In general, the vector can be regarded as the synthesis of the information in section 3 noted to be useful in identifying pleonastic instances of *it*. The FDG-Parser [17] was involved in the implementation due to the advantages mentioned in section 5 as well as the fact that by returning the dependency relations between words in the input, it allows the identification of complex constituents such as NPs.

Mitkov [10] noted that a pronoun's antecedent is usually found in the same paragraph as the pronoun. Anaphoric nominal pronouns are not therefore expected to be the first NPs in the paragraph. Expressing the information about whether or not the instance is the first NP in the paragraph was not found to be useful, nor was a feature expressing the location of the instance in terms of the paragraph position rather than the sentence position. A number of other features were tried but rejected as they caused a deterioration in the performance of the system.

7   Evaluation and Comparison

Manual classification of vectors for the training set is potentially the most labour intensive aspect of methods based on memory based learning. That process was facilitated by consultation of the corpus-derived key file. Having classified the training instances, the accuracy of the machine learning method was measured using ten-fold cross-validation. It was found that optimal performance was obtained when TiMBL considered 19 nearest neighbours and as many values as possible were treated numerically, using Gain Ratio feature weighting [12]).

Both approaches were evaluated with respect to the key described in section 4. The figures are given in the table below.

Table 1. A Comparative Evaluation of the Rule-Based and Machine Learning Approaches

Approach	Rule-Based	Machine Learning
#TP	615	592
#TN	1881	1903
#FP	265	243
CA	0.7871	0.7868
NDR	0.6000	0.5776

True Positives (TP) are those instances correctly classified by the system as being non-nominal. *True Negatives* (TN) are the cases where the system correctly classifies an instance as being NP anaphoric. *False Positives* (FP) are cases where the system has falsely classified an instance as being non-nominal.

The classification accuracy (CA) is given by (1), and the non-nominal detection rate (NDR) by (2)

$$CA = \frac{TP + TN}{TNI} \tag{1}$$

$$NDR = \frac{TP}{TNP}. \tag{2}$$

TNI and TNP are the total number of instances of *it* presented to the system and the number of non-nominal instances of *it* presented to the system, respectively.

A number of the false positives were caused by anomalies in the training data. In some cases, the classification derived from the key failed because of a mismatch in tokenisation between the FDG-Parser [17] and the LT-Chunker [9] which was used to construct the key.

One problem for the rule-based approaches was noted because various expressions were seen to be analogous to constructs identified in [11], but the item normally triggering recognition of the pattern was not reflected in the surface form of the sentence. If input sentences were analysed and given structural tags by a syntactic parser, rather than a part of speech tagger, it would be possible to use structural information as triggers for pattern recognition. Of course, such an approach would depend on the use of a reliable syntactic parser, and these are not readily available.

Due to the scarcity of those expressions in the corpus, neither system identifies "weather" or "time" *it* as being non-nominal.

The results were somewhat inconclusive. Although the two methods differ with respect to classification accuracy and the number of false positives returned, there is some question as to the significance of this difference. If the difference *is* considered significant then it may be said that the rule-based method was slightly more accurate in terms of both the classification of *it* and the detection of non-nominal uses. However, if users wish to avoid false positives, then the machine learning method is better. Given that the method is intended to be incorporated into an anaphora resolution system, priority is given to the avoidance of false positives.

8   Conclusions and Future Work

The machine learning based method was incorporated into an approach for anaphora resolution. Filtering non-nominal instances of *it* induced small improvements to the success rate of the system (+2.86%). Further, such filtration made the system more amenable to genetic optimisation (+7.04% without filtering versus +8.00% with filtering).

With respect to the rule-based system, work still needs to be done towards the identification of the complex phrasal expressions that are used in constructs that contain pleonastic *it*.

The reader will note that the corpus used for training by the machine learning approach needs to be extended, quantitatively and qualitatively.

Given the high dimensionality of the vectors and the complex combination of features that the classifications are based on, 3171 instances cannot be considered adequate in terms of the size of the training set used for the memory-based learning method. The training set should be increased in size. It will also be interesting to extend the classification used in the training set. At the present time, a binary classification is being used (*non-nominal* or *not*). The training vectors may become more useful if they are classified more specifically, in line with the six uses given in section 1.

Of course, English is not the only language in which non-nominal pronouns occur. It will be a matter for future research to investigate the multilingual application of the machine learning method shown in this paper.

References

1. Burnard, L. (1995) *Users Reference Guide British National Corpus Version 1.0*, Oxford University Computing Services, UK.
2. Daelemans, W. (1999) *TiMBL: Tilburg Memory Based Learner version 2 Reference Guide*, ILK Technical Report - ILK 99-01, Tilburg University, The Netherlands
3. Denber, M. (1998) *Automatic Resolution of Anaphora in English* Eastman Kodak Co., Imaging Science Division
4. Harabagiu, S.M. and Maiorano, S.J. (1999) Knowledge-Lean Coreference Resolution and its Relation to Textual Cohesion and Coherence, in Proceedings of the Workshop *The Relation of Discourse / Dialogue Structure and Reference, ACL '99*, Maryland, US.
5. Hirschmann, L (1997) *MUC-7 Coreference Task Definition* at http://www.muc.saic.com/proceedings/co_task.pdf
6. Hirst, G. (1981) *Anaphora in Natural Language Understanding*, Springer Verlag, Germany
7. Lappin, S. and Leass, H.J. (1994) An Algorithm for Pronominal Anaphora Resolution, in *Computational Linguistics* Volume 20, Number 4
8. Litman, D.J. (1996) Cue Phrase Classification Using Machine Learning, in *Journal of Artificial Intelligence Research*, vol 5, pp.53-94
9. Mikheev, A. (1996) *LT_CHUNK V 2.1*, Language Technology Group, University of Edinburgh, available from http://www.ltg.ed.ac.uk/software/chunk/index.html
10. Mitkov, R., Belguith, L. and Stys, M. (1998) Multilingual Robust Anaphora Resolution, in Proceedings of *The Third International Conference on Empirical Methods in Natural Language Processing*, Granada, Spain.
11. Paice, C.D. And Husk, G.D. (1987) Towards the automatic recognition of anaphoric features in English text: the impersonal pronoun 'it,' in *Computer Speech and Language*, 2 p.109-132, Academic Press, US.
12. Quinlan, J.R. (1993) *C4.5: Programs for Machine Learning*, Morgan Kaufmann, US.
13. Quirk, R. et al. (1985) *A Comprehensive Grammar of the English Language*, Longman, UK.
14. Sampson, G. (1995) *English for the Computer: The SUSANNE Corpus and analytic scheme*, Oxford Univerity Press, UK.
15. Sinclair, J. et al. (1995) *English Grammar*, Harper Collins Publishers, UK.
16. Swan, M. (1995) *Practical English Usage*, Oxford University Press, UK.
17. Tapanainen, P. and Järvinen, T. (1997) A Non-Projective Dependency Parser, in The Proceedings of The *5th Conference of Applied Natural Language Processing*, pages 64-71, ACL, US.

Constitution and exploitation of an annotation system of electronic corpora: Toward automatic generation of understandable pronouns in French language

Catherine CLOUZOT, Georges ANTONIADIS, Agnès TUTIN

Équipe CRISTAL-GRESEC, Université Stendhal
B.P. 25, 38040 Grenoble cedex 9, France
Tél.: (+33 / 0) 4 76 82 43 97 Fax: (+33 / 0) 4 76 82 41 26
c.clouzot@wanadoo.fr Georges.Antoniadis@u-grenoble3.fr
Agnes.Tutin@u-grenoble3.fr

1 Introduction

The aim of automatic text generation is the creation of texts addressed to human beings. One of the major characteristics of generated texts is the fact that they must be understandable for humans, i.e. be able to convey all the desired informative contents without ambiguities. The production of such texts requires the knowledge and the control of the "mechanisms" which govern the human texts. This must be valid for each phenomenon used in NLG, and particularly, for anaphoric processes[1], which, in our opinion, is a major phenomenon at the time of text elaboration.

In order to be able to describe and to model the mechanisms of this phenomenon, we chose to study it in corpora, and for this reason, to build an annotation system of electronic corpora, which easily allows the study of anaphoric process. The aim of this paper is to present this annotation system and the first results of its exploitation.

Some systems of anaphoric and coreferential encoding in written texts and spoken texts have been already constituted, primarily by the Anglo-Saxon linguistic community, then also in the French community. We'll mention, for example, the project of MUC-7 (Message Understanding Conference) [9], the corpus of Lancaster [13], the work of LORIA at Nancy [7], and also the studies about dialogues in the MATE project [12]. These researches focused on English or French languages. However, these encoding systems encode few information about the different linguistic levels such as morphology, syntax, semantic. This fact limits their further exploitations. We propose, in the following paragraphs, a new annotation system for the pronominal anaphora phenomena in written French texts, system which fills this lack. This encoding scheme was created, firstly, to study linguistic constraints of pronominal anaphora. This system, based on SGML, adopts the TEI Light recommendations [8].

---

[1] The terminology of "anaphoric process", here, must be understanding for anaphoric and cataphoric relationships, and ana-cataphoric relationship following the Kesik's meaning [Kesik 89]

D.N.Christodoulakis (Ed.): NLP 2000, LNCS 1835, pp. 242-251, 2000.
Springer-Verlag Berlin Heidelberg 2000

Besides, this encoding system is partly used for annotating electronic corpora in a research project funded by ELRA[2]. This project aims at annotating the grammatical anaphora for French electronic corpora, and we are working in partnership with researchers of XRCE (Xerox Research Centre Europe, MLTT team) and LORIA laboratory (Nancy, France).

2 Objectives of the encoding system

This encoding system aims at annotating anaphoric and cataphoric expressions, but only grammatical expressions, and it aims at annotating referential expressions involved in an anaphoric or cataphoric relation (like noun phrases, textual segments, clauses) and the annotation of the relationships between antecedent and anaphoric segments. Beside these linguistic elements, various attributes, with linguistic values, are inserted in the marks. This annotation system enables one to observe morphologic, syntactic, semantic constraints, some discursive factors, the distance between source and anaphoric segments, and textual organisation process.

The annotated corpus is a tool by means of which we can extract and study the strategies of grammatical anaphora. This study is facilitated by the numerous information that the annotator includes into the corpus. Then the results could be used for creating unambiguous anaphora generation algorithms.

3 Annotation system

In the following paragraph, we explain our markup method. Firstly, we specify the different elements that we want to annotate, then we present the attributes we associate to some elements. We cannot detail here the set of values for each attribute. So we refer the reader to our work [11].We end by an illustration of this annotation system in reporting a sample of annotated text.

3.1 Global markup scheme

We start by displaying the different levels of isolated elements in the text, then we provide with the list of attributes that we associate on certain elements.

3.1.1   Elements in text

Texts are divided into numbered paragraphs. Within every paragraph, sentences are also marked. The sentence is defined according to the typographical marks. These operations are automatically performed, then revised by hand. The tag for paragraph is <P></P>, and the tag for sentence is <SEG></SEG>. These two marks enable one to study inter or intra sentential relationships and the case of paragraph changes.

---

[2] ELRA: European Language Resources Association

Within the segments <SEG></SEG>, the referential expressions and anaphoric expressions are treated as elements, whether they are noun phrases, pronouns or clauses. Each element receives the tag <RS></RS> and a numerical identifier.

At the end of each paragraph including one or several anaphoric relations, one or more elements, marked <LINK></LINK>, are inserted. These elements isolate the attributes and the values appropriate to the characteristics of the relation itself. Several linguistic attributes are associated with the elements <RS></RS> and <LINK></LINK>.

3.1.2   Attributes of element <RS>

We have chosen the names of the attributes and their values so as that they could not be confused with the textual segments. The attributes describe:

a) Part of speech: with values like noun phrases (definite or indefinite), clitic pronouns, disjunctive pronouns, clauses etc. The attribute of part of speech is "CAT". In the following samples, its value is, in the first example 'GND' i.e. definite noun phrase, and, in the second example, 'PPV' i.e. clitic pronoun:

1. Original text: *the managers*

```
<RS ID="21.10" CAT="GND" MORPGR="MAS" MORPNB="PLU"
SYNT1="C0" SYNT2="PH1" TYPE="HUM"> Les dirigeants </RS>
```

2. Original text: *he*

```
<RS ID="2.2" CAT="PPV" MORPGR="MAS" MORPNB="SING"
SYNT1="C0" SYNT2="PH2" TYPE="HUMCOLL">il</RS>
```

b) Morphology: the morphological values of gender and number are declared whenever it is possible. Two attributes are distinguished: one attribute, named 'MORPGR', and one attribute named 'MORPNB'. In the previous example 1), the value "MAS" is used for the masculine gender, and the value "PLU" is used for the plural number.

c) Syntax: two attributes are used, one for the syntactic position and one for the type of clause. The first attribute, named 'SYNT1': with values denoting the syntactic position of the element (subject, object, or indefinite etc.). In the previous example 2), the clitic pronoun *il* is subject of the verb: its attribute 'SYNT1' receives the value "C0". We have adopted the usual classification about the verbal complementation of pre-verbal pronouns in French language (C0, C1, C2, C3, C4)[3] [6]. For example, the value "C1" is given to the pronouns *le, la, les and l'*, and to the noun phrases that occur in object position.

However, this classification being inadequate to describe the syntactic positions of the disjunctive pronouns or the noun phrases, we have created a sizeable set of tags in order to account for the different configurations.

In the following sample, example 3), the case is complex. The element included in the tags <RS> </RS> is a noun phrase inserted in a large phrase, the value of the attribute 'SYNT1' is "CNOM", which means that the syntactic position of the element is noun complement.

3. Original text: *he does not recognize the existence of a Brussels' region*

---

[3] C2 is used for dative pronoun, C3 is used for *y*, C4 is used for *en*.

```
...il ne reconnaît pas l'existence d' <RS ID="24.12"
CAT="GNI" MORPGR="FEM" MORPNB="SING" SYNT1="CNOM"
SYNT2="PH2" TYPE="HUMCOLL">une région bruxelloise
</RS>...
```

The following example 4) shows the case of a dislocation segment which is the antecedent of a clitic pronoun:

4. Original text: *About the government, it gathers different partners...*

```
<SEG> Quant <RS ID="20.1" CAT="GND" MORPGR="MAS"
MORPNB="SING" SYNT1="TP" SYNT2="PH1" TYPE="HUMCOLL"> au
gouvernement </RS>, <RS ID="20.2" CAT="PPV"
MORPGR="MAS" MORPNB="SING" SYNT1="C0" SYNT2="PH1"
TYPE="HUMCOLL"> il </RS> rassemble des partenaires
différents...
```

In this example, the noun phrase *au gouvernement* receives the attribute 'SYNT1' with the value "TP", value established for the cases of cleft sentences or dislocation structures.

The second syntactic attribute denotes the type of clause where the isolated element occurs. This attribute is named 'SYNT2', and two values are used to characterise the clauses. The value "PH1" notifies the independent clauses, the main clauses and the utterances without verb. The value "PH2" is used for the subordinate clauses. The example 5) illustrates these two values:

5. Original text: *the party is intending to fight a spectacular mediatic campaign and to stand for the elections with leading candidates of whom however it is refusing to cite the names.*

```
<RS ID="26.1" CAT="GND" MORPGR="MAS" MORPNB="SING"
SYNT1="C0" SYNT2="PH1" TYPE="HUMCOLL">le parti </RS>
entend mener une campagne médiatique spectaculaire et
se présenter aux élections avec des candidats-vedettes
dont <RS ID="26.2" CAT="PPV" MORPGR="MAS" MORPNB="SING"
SYNT1="C0" SYNT2="PH2" TYPE="HUMCOLL">il </RS> se
refuse cependant à citer les noms.
```

d) Semantic: some values describe the semantic category of the isolated element (e.g. human, human collective, locative, action etc.). In the previous example 5), the noun phrase *parti* and the clitic pronoun *il* both are categorized as a human collective.

3.1.3 Attributes of elements <LINK>

Each relationship between one or several antecedent segments and anaphoric segment is isolated with an element <LINK></LINK>.

The first attribute is composed of the list of numerical identifiers, which distinguish each antecedent and anaphoric expression. This attribute is named 'ARGS'. In the following example 5), we can read that the element numbered "48.1" is the antecedent segment of the anaphoric segment numbered "48.2". If the relationship is a cataphoric link, the order of identifiers is reversed.

6.

```
<LINK ARGS='"48.1""48.2"' TYPE="IDSEM" TYPANA="AG">
```

The second attribute, named 'TYPE', specifies if the relationship is a co-referential link, or an semantic identity or a link such as "element of". In the following example 7), we can observe a case of semantic identity :

7.

```
<SEG>On est ici à mille lieues <RS ID="15.1" CAT="GND"
MORPGR="FEM" MORPNB="PLU" SYNT1="CNOM" SYNT2="PH1"
TYPE="EVEN">des petites querelles </RS> qui opposent
les Etats-Unis et l'Europe sur des sujets tels que le
veau aux hormones, les droits d'atterrissage ou même
Airbus. </SEG><SEG> <RS ID="15.2" CAT="PPV"
MORPGR="FEM" MORPNB="PLU" SYNT1="C0" SYNT2="PH1"
TYPE="EVEN">Elles</RS> s'exacerbent et s'apaisent dans
un contexte de complémentarité à long terme,
d'équilibre des échanges et d'interpénétration mutuelle
via les investissements directs à l'étranger. </SEG>

<LINK ARGS='"15.1" "15.2"' TYPE="IDSEM" TYPANA="AG">
```

The third and last attribute, named 'TYPANA' indicates the type of the relationship. Two values distinguish the anaphoric and cataphoric links. The value "AG" indicates a grammatical anaphora, and the value "CG" indicates a grammatical cataphora.

3.2 Illustration of the encoding system

In the following paragraph, we present an example of annotation. This text is an excerpt of the study about pronominal anaphora in automatic text generation [11].

Original text

```
Son piano et son sourire, Estrella l'humaniste continue
ainsi de les offrir aux plus démunis, aux exclus des
prisons autant qu'aux oubliés des villages les plus
reculés des Andes ou encore aux victimes de Tchernobyl.
A chacun, il rend la confiance et l'idée que "la
justice et la dignité sont possibles pour tous".

His piano and his smile, Estrella the humanist, in this
way, is going on giving them to the most destitutes, to
the captive excluding persons as well as to the missing
humans from the most distant villages of Andes or again
to the victims of Tchernobyl. To each one, he is giving
back confidence and the idea that "justice and dignity
are possible for everyone."
```

Annotated text

```
<P ID="7">
<SEG><RS ID="7.1" CAT="GND" MORPGR="MAS" MORPNB="SING"
SYNT1="TP" SYNT2="PH1" TYPE="OBJET">Son piano</RS> et
<RS ID="7.2" CAT="GND" MORPGR="MAS" MORPNB="SING"
SYNT1="TP" SYNT2="PH1" TYPE="ACTION">son sourire </RS>,
<RS ID="7.3" CAT="GND" MORPGR="MAS" MORPNB="SING"
```

```
SYNT1="C0" SYNT2="PH1" TYPE="HUM">Estrella</RS>
l'humaniste continue ainsi de
<RS ID="7.4" CAT="PPV" MORPNB="PLU" SYNT1="C1"
SYNT2="PH1" TYPE="IND">les</RS> offrir aux plus
démunis, aux exclus des prisons autant qu'aux oubliés
des villages les plus reculés des Andes ou encore aux
victimes de Tchernobyl. </SEG> <SEG> A chacun,
<RS ID="7.5" CAT="PPV" MORPGR="MAS" MORPNB="SING"
SYNT1="C0" SYNT2="PH1" TYPE="HUM">il</RS> rend la
confiance et l'idée que "la justice et la dignité sont
possibles pour tous". </SEG>

<LINK ARGS='"7.1" "7.2" "7.4"' TYPE="COREF"
TYPANA="AG">
<LINK ARGS='"7.3" "7.5"' TYPE="COREF" TYPANA="AG">
```

In this sample, we met two cases of pronominal anaphora which refer back to two noun phrases, with clitic pronouns (*les* and *il*). The first relation is an intra-sentential link (included in the same mark <SEG></SEG>), and it is a coreferential anaphora linking two definite nouns phrases coordinated, in position of dislocation, to the accusative pronoun *les*. The second relation is an inter sentential link, it is also a co-referential anaphora linking the proper name *Estrella* to the clitic subject *il*.

4   The first results of the exploitation of the annotated corpus

This annotation system was tested on a corpus of newspaper texts (extracted from *Le Monde Diplomatique* electronic corpora 1998). This corpus is composed of 92 articles. The size was about 95000 words. The specific objective of this study was the evaluation of different pronominal anaphora which refer back to noun phrases by clitic or disjunctive pronouns, and textual segments different from noun phrases. We also wanted to evaluate the anaphoric versus cataphoric frequency and to underline syntactic and discursive constraints which could be exploited in the perspective of automatic generation [11].

All in all, 1316 anaphoric or cataphoric relations were found. Among these 1316 relations, 97% are anaphoric while only 3% are cataphoric. The distribution of pronouns is: 90% clitic pronouns and 10% disjunctive pronouns. The anaphoric substitution of noun phrases by disjunctive pronouns must not be too recurring in automatically generated text, in so far as the proportion of clitic and disjunctive pronouns is steady in the texts produced by scripters[4].

The analysis shows that the disjunctive pronoun behaviour, at the levels of morphology and syntax, but also at the discursive level, is different from the clitic pronoun behaviour. The disjunctive pronouns are often inserted in apposition, or in prepositional phrases. The constraints of production, in automatic generation, are thus not similar.

Within the clitic pronoun class, 91% pronouns are linked to noun phrases and, only 9% clitic pronouns are linked to clauses or other textual segments. We have to underline the difficulty sometimes in recognising and isolating the real textual

---

[4] See [Clouzot 98]

segment which is detected as antecedent. The antecedent can be ambiguous when it is formed of several noun phrases, and we cannot retrieve the right segment when its boundaries are uncertain in the case of clauses.

The predominance of anaphoric and cataphoric relations between noun phrases and clitic pronouns shows that, in the French system of pronominal substitution, there are gradations, in the variation of frequency depending on substitution types.

Generally, the anaphoric relation mainly affects the noun phrases which are in position of subjects or objects. However, we have to consider that the substitution is carried out by a clitic pronoun in 90% cases. The results of this study underline the fact that the pronominal substitution, beside their prototypic features, offers large possibilities for the anaphora of noun phrases which are neither subjects nor objects.

On the one hand, however, the analysis of noun phrases of which the syntactical position is a nominal complementation shows the necessity of cross-level studies, i.e. morphological, syntactic, semantic and pragmatic studies, because the study of the complex noun phrases requires some notions like the world knowledge, or the definition of referring expressions.

On the other hand, certain phenomena such as the clause anaphora are infrequent. They probably are less important in the perspective of automatic generation. Nevertheless they should be studied on large corpora, because, in order to extract as much knowledge as possible, it is necessary to analyse many samples.

The anaphoric links are mainly intra sentential relations or they occur in consecutive sentences (about 85%), but some rare cases show more important distances. This fact involves that the notion of distance between source expressions and anaphoric expressions is not really established, and in automatic generation, other studies could be interesting.

Obviously, these first results must be considered according to the type of texts. We recall that in this case the texts are newspaper extracts. However, we could consider that this is standard language, contrasting with specific languages, and so we would use these results for an attempt at modelising the anaphoric process.

5 Toward the model of automatic understandable anaphora generation

Automatic text generation achieves its goal when the reading of produced texts by the addressee, i.e. by human reader, enables to convey him the accurate informative content, without ambiguities, the intended content which the implementation used by the generation system forecast. In this way, the generated text must be able to transmit to the reader all the intended informative content and only this content. However, the main cause of ambiguities at the time of reading and understanding of texts originates from ambiguous anaphora which give the reader a wrong understanding or even prevent the reader from understanding the text.

According to this fact, the system of anaphora production implemented into a text generator has to satisfy two requirements:

1. An anaphora could be produced only if the system is able to compute the linguistic and pragmatic knowledge needed to its resolution. These sources of knowledge, extracted from the co-text of the anaphora, are assumed to be known by the reader.

2. Each generated anaphora must be unambiguous for the reader. The process resolution the reader will resort to (exploiting his abilities as well as the knowledge carried out by the anaphora co-text), must lead him to an unique solution. This solution, preferably, will be the one wanted by the system.

We have been able to meet the first requirement by paying attention to the knowledge (included in the text) carried out by the anaphoric expressions. We have drawn a typology of these knowledge sources and for each of them, we attempted to determine their contribution and their impact in relation to the expected result (the determination of the antecedent) [Antoniadis & *alii* 1997]. Such an approach allows the production of anaphora which require, for their resolution, only some knowledge sources contained in the generated text. It is, nevertheless, incomplete in so far as it does not take the human mechanisms into account in the anaphoric resolution process.

Taking the second constraint into account requires knowledge about the human process involved in anaphoric resolution, knowledge that would be modelisable. However this knowledge is currently only partial and for the majority not yet formalized. We adopted for our generation system a more empirical approach aiming at simulating the strategies of anaphoric process observed in texts which are considered *a priori* to be understandable. The annotation system, previously described, aims at enriching texts in order to underline these strategies of anaphoric process, to model them and to implement them at the time of text generation in the field of kernel generation[5]. In this context, the strategy of anaphoric process is a parameter (a constraint) of the generation system. This strategy enables to determine the choice of the anaphora which will be produced, choice that, we hope, would allow the production of "natural" anaphora, closer to human anaphoric process and, in this way, easily understandable for the reader. Such an approach will be validated only by experimentation on the human understanding of generated texts.

6   Conclusion

In future, we wish we could apply this encoding system on various textual corpora, in order to compare our first results with new data. A comparative study with technical or literary texts could enable us to evaluate the variability of different anaphoric process, according to the genres of texts. This aspect seems of the utmost importance to us, because, in the generation process, the choice among the different elements, grammatical or lexical anaphora, is not devoid of repercussions for the final generated text.

This annotation system can be easily improved with the addition of new parameters, and it also can be used for lexical anaphora investigations. Our investigation method of anaphoric elements allows the studies of textual productions whatever discursive kind they belong to, on a large scale, and the researches of knowledge for natural language processing or and also for information retrieval, in so far as anaphoric resolution in texts remains a crucial question.

---

[5] The kernel generation and the system of kernel generation are explained in detail in [Ponton 96] and [Antoniadis & Ponton 96].

References

1. ANTONIADIS G., BALICCO L., CHEVROT J.P., EYMARD G. (1997), *Proposition pour la génération automatique d'anaphores compréhensibles: vers une approche systématique.*, in Actes de *GAT' 97*, 2-3 octobre 1997, Grenoble, France.
2. ANTONIADIS G., BALICCO L., PONTON C., STEFANINI M.H., WARREN K. (1996), *Vers une approche distribuée pour la génération automatique de textes* , TALN'96 , Marseille, France
3. ANTONIADIS G., PONTON C. (1996) *A kernel generation system.* ECAI'96, Workshop " Gaps and Bridges ": New Directions in Planning and Natural Language Generation, 12-16 Août 1996, Budapest (Hongrie)
4. APOTHELOZ D. (1995), Rôle et fonctionnement de l'anaphore dans la dynamique textuelle, Librairie Droz, Genève.
5. BIBER D. (1992), Using computer-based text corpora to analyze the referential strategies of spoken and written texts , in Directions in corpus linguistics, Mouton de Guyter, J. Svartwik ed., BERLIN NY.
6. BLANK I. (1987), Etude des constructions syntaxiques du verbe en vue d'un traitement automatique, in *Les cahiers du CRISS*, n° 11, Grenoble.
7. BRUNESEAUX F., ROMARY L. (1997), Codage des références et des coréférences dans les DHM , Actes de ACH-ACLL.
8. BURNARD L., SPERBERG-McQUEEN C.M. (1996), La TEI simplifiée : une introduction au codage des textes électroniques en vue de leur échange (traduction française) , in Cahiers Gutenberg, 24 juin 1996.
9. CHINCHOR N., HIRSCHMANN L. (1997), MUC-7 Coreference Task definition, Version 3.0, Proceedings of MUC-7.
10. CLOUZOT C., (1998), *La génération automatique d'anaphores pronominales compréhensibles (non ambiguës)* , Mémoire de Maîtrise de Sciences du Langage - Mention Industries de la Langue, Université Stendhal, Grenoble.
11. CLOUZOT C. (1999), Autour de la notion d'anaphore pronominale, constitution et étude d'un corpus électronique annoté dans une perspective de génération automatique de textes , Mémoire de DEA de Sciences du Langage - Option Traitement Automatique de la Langue Ecrite, Université Stendhal, Grenoble.
12. DAVIES S., POESIO M., BRUNESEAUX F., ROMARY L. (1998), Annotating Coreference in Dialogues : Proposal for a Scheme for MATE (First Draft), document HTML.
13. GARSIDE R., FLIGESTONE S., BOTLEY S. (1997), *Discourse annotation : anaphorics relations in corpora*, in R. Garside, G. Leech & A. McEnery (eds), Corpus annotation : Linguistic Information from Text Corpora, Longmann, London.
14. HABERT B., FABRE C., ISSAC, F. (1998), De l'écrit au numérique - Constituer, normaliser et exploiter les corpus électroniques, InterEditions, Masson, Paris.
15. KESIK M, (1989), *La cataphore*, PUF, Paris.
16. KLEIBER G. (1994), *Anaphores et pronoms*, Duculot, Paris.
17. NOT E., ZANCANARO M. (1996), Exploiting the Discourse Structure for Anaphora Generation, in Proceedings of the Discourse Anaphor and Resolution Colloquium (DAARC96), Lancaster, p.223-234.
18. PONTON C. (1996), *Formalisme et architecture d'un système ouvert multi-applications*, Thèse de doctorat, Université Stendhal, Grenoble.
19. SILBERZTEIN M. (1993), Dictionnaires électroniques et analyse automatique de textes : le système INTEX, Masson, Paris.
20. TUTIN A. (1992), *Etude des anaphores grammaticales et lexicales pour la génération automatique de textes de procédures.* Thèse de Ph.D. en linguistique, option intelligence artificielle, Université de Montréal, Canada.

21. TUTIN A., ANTONIADIS G., CLOUZOT C. (1999), *Annoter des corpus pour le traitement des anaphores*, in Actes de l'atelier Corpus et TAL : Pour une réflexion méthodologique, TALN, Cargèse, 12-17 juillet 1999.
22. VAN HERWIJNEN E. (1995), *SGML PRATIQUE*, International Thomson Publishing France, Paris.

Generation of Spanish Zero-Pronouns into English

Jesús Peral and Antonio Ferrández

Grupo de Procesamiento del Lenguaje y Sistemas de Información
Departamento de Lenguajes y Sistemas Informáticos
Tfno: +34 96 590 37 72 Fax: +34 96 590 93 26
Universidad de Alicante, Apdo. 99, 03080 Alicante, Spain
{jperal,antonio}@dlsi.ua.es

Abstract. It is widely agreed that anaphora and ellipsis resolution is an important problem that is still to be solved in Natural Language Processing systems, such as Machine Translation and Information Extraction applications. Zero-pronouns are a special kind of anaphora, whose resolution also lies in ellipsis phenomenon since they do not appear explicitly in the text. They must first be detected (ellipsis), and then resolved just like any other pronoun (anaphora). This kind of pronoun occurs in Spanish texts when they occupy the grammatical position of the subject. In this paper, we propose an approach that resolves zero-pronouns in Spanish texts and subsequently generates them into English. A success rate of 75% has been obtained in the generation of Spanish zero-pronouns into English.

1 Introduction

In this paper we focus specially on the generation of Spanish zero-pronouns into English. While in other languages zero-pronouns may appear in either the subject's or the object's grammatical position, in Spanish texts zero-pronouns only appear in the position of the subject.

Zero-pronouns have already been studied in other languages, such as Japanese, (e.g. [7]). They have not yet been studied in Spanish texts, however. Among the work done for their resolution in different languages, nevertheless, there are several points that are common for Spanish. The first point is that they must first be located in the text (ellipsis detection), and then resolved (anaphora resolution). At the ellipsis detection stage, information about the zero-pronoun (e.g. person, gender, and number) must first be obtained and then used to identify the antecedent of the zero-pronoun. The detection process depends knowledge about the structure of the language itself, which gives us clues to the use of each type of zero-pronoun.

In order to generate Spanish zero-pronouns into English, the Interlingua system presented in [8] has been used. The Interlingua system takes as input a structure that stores both the Spanish zero-pronoun and its antecedent (after

D.N. Christodoulakis (Ed.): NLP 2000, LNCS 1835, pp. 252–260, 2000.

the zero-pronoun has been detected and resolved). From this structure, the corresponding English pronoun will be generated.

With this approach the translation is carried out in two stages: from the source language to the interlingua, and from the interlingua into the target language. Modules for analysis are independent from modules for generation. Similar approaches have been used in two Dutch projects: the DLT system at Utrecht based on a modification of Esperanto [9] and the Rosetta system at Phillips (Eindhoven) which is experimenting with Montague semantics as the basis for an interlingua [1].

Other approaches are based on transfer systems [3][6][2]. In these systems the translation is carried out in three stages: the first stage convert texts into intermediate representations in which ambiguities have been resolved irrespective of any other language. In the second stage these are converted into equivalent representations of the target language; and in the third stage, the final target texts are generated.

The main difference between our approach and transfer approaches consists of intermediate representations. In transfer systems the representations remain language-specific: they typically have source and target language words in them, and they reflect the structure, whether superficially or in more depth, of the respective source and target languages. By contrast, our system provides representations which are language-independent both in lexicon and in structure.

In the following section, we present a description of the process for the detection and resolution of zero-pronouns. Following this, we describe the generation of zero-pronouns into English. Finally, we present an evaluation of the results we have obtained with this approach.

2   Zero-Pronoun Resolution

The resolution of zero-pronouns has been implemented in the computational system called *Slot Unification Parser for Anaphora resolution (SUPAR)*. This system, which was presented in [5], resolves anaphora in both English and Spanish texts with an accuracy of 87% and 84% respectively. It is a modular system and it can be used for different applications, e.g. Information Retrieval or Information Extraction.

The first stage of zero-pronoun resolution consists of the detection of zero-pronouns. As we may work on unrestricted texts to which partial parsing is applied, zero-pronouns must also be detected when we do not dispose of full syntactic information. In [4], a partial parsing strategy that provides all the necessary information for resolving anaphora is presented. That study shows that only the following constituents were necessary for anaphora resolution: coordinated prepositional and noun phrases, pronouns, conjunctions and verbs, regardless of the order in which they appear in the text. The *free words* consist of constituents that are not covered by this partial parsing (e.g. adverbs).

When partial parsing is carried out, one problem that arises is the detection the different clauses of a sentence. Another problem is how to detect the omission of the subject from each clause.

With regard to the first problem, the following heuristic is applied to identify a new clause:

H1: *Let us assume that the beginning of a new clause has been found when a verb is parsed and a free conjunction is subsequently parsed.*

In this particular case, a *free conjunction* does not imply conjunctions that join co-ordinated noun and prepositional phrases. It refers, here, to conjunctions that are parsed in our partial parsing scheme. For instance, in the following sentence:

(1) *John and Jane were late for work because they over-slept.*

the following sequence of constituents is parsed: *np(John and Jane), verb(were), freeWord(late), pp(for work), conj(because), pron(they), verb(over-slept).*

Since the free conjunction *because* has been parsed after the verb *were*, the new clause with a new verb *over-slept* can be detected.

Regarding the problem of how to detect the omission of the subject from each clause with partial parsing, we can establish the following heuristic:

H2: *After the sentence has been divided into clauses, a noun phrase or a pronoun is sought, for each clause, through the clause constituents on the left-hand side of the verb, unless it is imperative or impersonal. Such a noun phrase or pronoun must agree in person and number with the verb of the clause.*

In (1), for example, we can verify that neither of these verbs have their subject omitted since there appears a *np(John and Jane)* and a *pron(they)* before them.

In addition, we must verify whether the verb is impersonal or imperative, as it would have no subject in either case, in Spanish. For example, in: *Llueve (it is raining)*, as the verb *llueve (rains)* is impersonal, we do not have to search for its antecedent. In the command: *Haz un nudo en el pañuelo (tie a knot in the handkerchief)*, the verb "*haz*" (*tie*)[1] is imperative.

Sometimes, gender information of the pronoun can be obtained when the verb is copulative. For example, in[2]:

(2) *Pedro$_j$ vio a Ana$_k$ en el parque. $\emptyset_k$ Estaba muy guapa.*
    (Peter$_j$ saw Ann$_k$ in the park. She$_k$ was very beautiful.)

---

[1] In this case, we are equating the verbs, *haz* and *tie*, and although we accept that the translation is not precise, the sense of the imperative is implicit.

[2] In this example, the symbol $\emptyset$ indicates the place where the pronoun *ella (she)* has been omitted

In (2), the verb *estaba* (*was*) is copulative, so that its subject must agree in gender and number with its object whenever the object can have either a masculine or a feminine linguistic form (*guapo: masc, guapa: fem*). We can therefore get information about its gender from the object, *guapa* (*"beautiful" in its feminine form*) which automatically assigns it to the feminine gender so the omitted pronoun would have to be *she* rather than *he*.

Gender information can be obtained from the object of the verb with partial parsing as we simply have to search for a noun phrase on the right of the verb. Since we are working on the output of a POS-tagger, it does not provide us with information about whether the object could have both a masculine and a feminine linguistic form. Our computational system, therefore, will always add gender information to a zero-pronoun, although it will be used only as a preference. (Number and person, however, will be considered restrictions).

After the zero-pronoun has been detected, *SUPAR* inserts the pronoun in the position in which it has been omitted. This pronoun will be detected and resolved in the following module of anaphora resolution.

The final result of this process is a structure (interlingua structure) that contains both the zero-pronoun and the chosen antecedent. It stores the following information for each one of them: morphologic, semantic and syntactic information; discourse marker (identifier of the entity or discourse object) and the interlingua structures of its subconstituents.

3   Zero-Pronoun Generation

The generation phase is split into two modules: syntactic generation and morphological generation. The basic task of syntactic generation is to order constituents in the correct sequence for the target language. In this paper, we have only focused on the generation of zero-pronouns, then this module have not been taken into account.

In the morphological generation, the differences in the translation of pronouns from the source language into the target language are taken into account. These differences are what we have called *discrepancies*. The Spanish-English-Spanish discrepancies and their resolution have been explained in detail in [8]. Basically, we have to treat and solve number and gender discrepancies.

a) **Number Discrepancies**: This discrepancy is produced by words of different languages that express the same concept. These words can be referred to a singular pronoun in the source language and to a plural pronoun in the target language.

For example, in Spanish the concept *people* is singular, whereas in English is plural.

(3) *El estadio estaba lleno de gente$_i$. Ésta$_i$ estaba muy enfadada con el árbitro.*

(4) *The stadium was full of people$_i$. They$_i$ were very angry with the referee.*

In (3), it can be observed that the name *gente* in Spanish has been replaced with the singular pronoun *ésta* (*it*), whereas in English (4) the name *people* has been replaced with the plural pronoun *they*.

Number discrepancies also exist in the translation of other languages such as in the German-English translation.

b) **Gender Discrepancies**: English has less morphologic information than Spanish. With reference to plural personal pronouns, the pronoun *we* can be translated into *nosotros* (masculine) or *nosotras* (feminine), *you* into *vosotros* (masculine) or *vosotras* (feminine) and *they* into *ellos* or *ellas*. On the other hand, the singular personal pronoun *it* can be translated into *él/éste* (masculine) or *ella/ésta* (feminine). For example:

(5) *Las mujeres$_i$ estaban en la tienda. Ellas$_i$ estaban comprando regalos para sus maridos.*

(6) *Women$_i$ were in the shop. They$_i$ were buying gifts for their husbands.*

In Spanish the plural name *mujeres* is feminine and is replaced by the personal pronoun *ellas* (plural feminine) (5), whereas in English *they* is valid for masculine as well as for feminine (6). The solution of this problem consists of finding the correct antecedent of the anaphors in the source language. Then, the pronoun obtains its gender information from the antecedent one.

These discrepancies do not always mean that Spanish anaphors bear more information than English one. For example, Spanish possessive adjectives (*su casa*) do not carry gender information whereas English possessive adjectives do (*his/her house*).

We can find similar discrepancies among other languages. The English-German translation, like English-Spanish, supposes a translation from a language with neutral gender into a language that assigns gender grammatically.

In the process of zero-pronoun generation, the pronoun's information is extracted from the interlingua structure (intermediate representation) in the following way: number and person information are obtained from the pronoun and gender information is obtained from the chosen antecedent. With this information and the developed discrepancy analysis we will be able to generate the correct English pronoun.

4   Evaluation

Our computational system has been trained with a handmade corpus of 106 zero-pronouns. After that, we have carried out a blind evaluation on unrestricted texts. In this case, partial parsing of the text with no semantic information has been used.

With regard to unrestricted texts, our system has been run on two different Spanish corpora: a) a fragment of the Spanish version of *The Blue Book corpus* (15,571 words), which contains the handbook of the International Telecommunications Union CCITT, and b) a fragment of the *Lexesp* corpus (9,746 words), which contains ten Spanish texts from different genres and authors. These texts are taken mainly from newspapers. These corpora have been POS-tagged. Having worked with different genres and disparate authors, we feel that the applicability of our proposal to other sorts of texts is assured.

4.1   Evaluating the Detection of Zero-Pronouns

To achieve this sort of evaluation, several different tasks may be considered. Each verb must first be detected. This task is easily accomplished since both corpora have been previously tagged and manually reviewed. No errors are therefore expected on verb detection. The second task is to classify the verbs into two categories: a) verbs whose subjects have been omitted, and b) verbs whose subjects have not. The overall results on this sort of detection are presented in Figure 1 (success rate[3] of 88% on 1,599 classified verbs, with no significant differences seen between the corpora). We should also remark that a success rate of 98% has been obtained in the detection of verbs whose subjects were omitted, whereas only 80% was achieved for verbs whose subjects were not. This lower success rate is justified for several reasons. One important reason is the non-detection of impersonal verbs by the POS tagger. Two other reasons are the lack of semantic information and the inaccuracy of the grammar used.

In Figure 1 an interesting fact can be observed: 46% of the verbs in these corpora have their subjects omitted. It shows quite clearly the importance of this phenomenon in Spanish. Furthermore, it is even more important in narrative texts, as this figure shows: 61% with the *Lexesp* corpus, compared to 26% with the technical manual. We should also observe that *The Blue Book* has no verbs in either the first or the second person. This may be explained by the style of the technical manual, which usually consists of a series of isolated definitions, (i.e. many paragraphs that are not related to one another). This explanation is confirmed by the relatively small number of anaphors that are found in that corpus, as compared to the *Lexesp* corpus.

We have not considered comparing our results with those of other published works, since, (as we have already explained in the *Introduction* section), ours is the first study that has been done specifically for Spanish texts, and the designing of the detection stage depends mainly on the structure of the language in question. Any comparisons that might be made concerning other languages, therefore, would prove to be rather insignificant.

4.2   Evaluating Anaphora Resolution

As we have already shown in the previous section, (Figure 1), of the 1,599 verbs classified in these two corpora, 734 of them have zero-pronouns. Only 581 of them, however, are in third person and will be anaphorically resolved. In Figure 2, we present a classification of these third person zero-pronouns, which

---

[3] By "success rate", we mean the number of verbs successfully classified, divided by the total number of verbs in the text.

	Verbs with their subject omitted						Verbs with their subject **no**-omitted					
	First person		Second person		Third person		First person		Second person		Third person	
	Total	% Success	Total	% Success	Total	% Success	Total	% Success	Total	% Success	Total	% Success
Lexesp corpus	111	100%	42	100%	401	99%	21	81%	3	100%	328	76%
	20%		7%		73%		7%		1%		92%	
	554 (61%) (**success rate:** 99%)						352 (39%) (**success rate:** 76%)					
Blue Book corpus	0	0%	0	0%	180	96%	0	0%	0	0%	513	80%
	0%		0%		100%		0%		0%		100%	
	180 (26%) (**success rate:** 97%)						513 (74%) (**success rate:** 82%)					
Total	734 (46%) (**success rate:** 98%)						865 (54%) (**success rate:** 80%)					
	1,599 success rate: 88%											

Fig. 1. *Results obtained in the detection of zero-pronouns.*

have been conveniently divided into three categories: cataphoric, exophoric and anaphoric. The first category is comprised of those whose antecedent comes after the anaphor (i.e. the verb appears before its subject in the sentence). This kind of verb is quite common in Spanish, as can be seen in this figure (49%). This fact represents one of the main difficulties found in resolving anaphora in Spanish: The structure of a sentence is more flexible than in English, so that cataphoric zero-pronouns will not be resolved, since semantic information is needed to be able to discard all of their antecedents and *to prefer* those that appear within the same sentence and clause after the verb. The second category consists of those zero-pronouns whose antecedents do not appear, linguistically, in the text. (They refer to items in the external world rather than things referred to in the text). And finally, the third category is that of pronouns that will be resolved by our computational system, i.e., those whose antecedents come before the verb: 228 zero-pronouns.

	Cataphoric	Exophoric	Anaphoric	
			Number	Success
Lexesp corpus	171 (42%)	56 (12%)	174 (46%)	78%
The Blue Book corpus	113 (63%)	13 (7%)	54 (30%)	68%
Total	284 (49%)	69 (12%)	228 (39%)	75%

Fig. 2. *Classification of third person zero-pronouns.*

The different accuracy results are also shown in Figure 2: A success rate of 75% was attained for the 228 zero-pronouns. By "successful resolutions" we mean that the solutions offered by our system agree with the solutions offered by two human experts.

4.3 Evaluating Zero-Pronoun Generation

The generation of the 228 Spanish zero-pronouns (see Figure 2) into English has been evaluated. Although we have obtained a success rate of 75% in pronoun resolution, we will generate the 228 pronouns into English.

Due to the used corpora that do not include semantic information, these heuristics have been applied in the generation into the English pronoun: all the pronouns in third person and singular whose antecedents are proper nouns have been translated into *he* (antecedent with masculine gender) or *she* (antecedent with feminine gender); otherwise they have been translated into *it*.

The following results in the generation have been obtained: a success rate of 70% in *Lexesp* and a success rate of 89% in *The Blue Book*. In general (both corpora) a success rate of 75% has been achieved. The errors are mainly produced by the generation into the pronouns *he, she / it* because the following can occur, that the antecedents are not proper nouns and they have to be generated into the pronoun *it* (for example: "el viejo (the old man)" has to be translated into *he* and the system has translated into the pronoun *it* because the antecedent is not a proper noun).

5 Conclusions

We have proposed a complete computational system to generate Spanish zero-pronouns into English. These kinds of pronouns have never been dealt with in the Spanish language before. The generation into English has been developed by means of an Interlingua system, by using the gender and number information from their antecedent. The blind evaluation results (success rates) have been the following: 88% in detecting zero-pronouns, 75% in detecting their antecedent and 75% in its generation into English.

As a future aim, we pretend to incorporate semantic information in the whole system in order to measure its improvement.

References

1. L. Appelo and J. Landsbergen. The machine translation project Rose. In T.C. Gerhardt, editor, *Proceedings of I. International Conference on the State of the Art in Machine Translation in America, Asia and Europe, IAI-MT'86*, pages 34–51, Saarbrücken, 1986.
2. W.S. Bennett and J. Slocum. The LRC machine translation system. *Computational Linguistics*, 11:111–121, 1988.
3. C. Boitet and N. Nedobejkine. Recent developments in Russian-French machine translation at Grenoble. *Linguistics*, 19:199–271, 1981.
4. A. Ferrández, M. Palomar, and L. Moreno. Anaphora resolution in unrestricted texts with partial parsing. In *Proceedings of the 36th Annual Meeting of the Association for Computational Linguistics and 17th International Conference on Computational Linguistics, COLING-ACL'98*, pages 385–391, Montreal, Canada, 1998.

5. A. Ferrández, M. Palomar, and L. Moreno. An empirical approach to Spanish anaphora resolution. *To appear in Machine Translation*, 2000.
6. H.-D. Luckhardt. SUSY: capabilities and range of application. *Multilingua*, 1:213–220, 1982.
7. M. Okumura and K. Tamura. Zero Pronoun Resolution in Japanese Discourse Based on Centering Theory. In *Proceedings of the 16th International Conference on Computational Lingustics, COLING'96*, pages 871–876, Copenhagen, Denmark, 1996.
8. J. Peral, M. Palomar, and A. Ferrández. Coreference-oriented Interlingual Slot Structure and Machine Translation. In *Proceedings of ACL'99 Workshop on Coreference and its Applications*, pages 69–76, College Park, Maryland, USA, 1999.
9. A.P.M. Witkam. *Distributed language translation: feasibility study of multilingual facility for videotex information networks*. BSO, Utrecht, 1983.

Combining Different Translation Sources

Uwe Küssner and Dan Tidhar

Technische Universität Berlin
Fachbereich Informatik
Franklinstr. 28/29, D-10587 Berlin, Germany
{uk,dan}@cs.tu-berlin.de

Abstract. Within the machine translation project *Verbmobil*, translation is performed simultaneously along four independent translation paths, each implementing a different MT strategy. The four competing translations are combined by a selection procedure so as to form a single optimized output for each input utterance. This selection procedure relies on confidence values that are delivered together with each of the alternative translations. Since the confidence values are computed by four independent modules that are fundamentally different from one another, they are not directly comparable and need to be rescaled in order to gain comparative significance. In this paper we describe a machine learning method tailored to overcome this difficulty by using off line human feedback to determine an optimized confidence rescaling scheme.

1 Introduction

Verbmobil [23] is a speech to speech machine translation project, aimed at handling a wide range of spontaneous speech phenomena within the restricted domain of travel planning and appointment scheduling dialogues. For the language pairs English-German and German-English, *Verbmobil* applies four different translation methods that operate in parallel, according to four alternative approaches to machine translation, thus increasing the system's robustness and versatility. Since the system should always produce exactly one translation for each input utterance that it encounters, a selection procedure is necessary, which would choose the best alternative for each given utterance. In order to benefit more from this diversity of translation methods, the alternative translations are furthermore combined within the boundaries of single utterances, so as to form a new compound translation. Combining translations from different sources within a multi-thread MT system has already proved beneficial in the past [11]. Our present work differs from the work reported in there in several ways (apart from the trivial fact that we use 'four heads' rather than three). Firstly, we attempt to investigate a systematic solution to the problem of incomparability of the various confidence values, a problem which was indeed acknowledged and treated in [11], but is nevertheless not playing there a role as central as we believe it should. Another important difference is that translation in our case is speech to speech rather than text to text. As the translation modules communicate with

D.N. Christodoulakis (Ed.): NLP 2000, LNCS 1835, pp. 261–271, 2000.

the speech recognizer independently of one another, different segmentations for each given input string are allowed, which makes the segment combination process significantly more complicated. In the following sections we first describe the main problem that our learning procedure is meant to solve. We then state some of our presuppositions, with some hints as to how they can be justified. We then provide the reader with brief descriptions of the different translation paths, which construct the basic setting in which the problem, along with its proposed solution, can be understood. We then turn to describe the basic selection algorithm that we apply, assuming that learning has already taken place. Finally, we describe the learning phase itself, along with our annotation strategy and with the optimization algorithm that we apply.

2   The Incomparability Problem

Each translation module calculates a confidence value for each of the translations that it produces, to serve as a guiding criterion for the selection procedure. However, since the various translation methods are fundamentally different from one another, the resulting confidence values cannot be compared per se. Whereas we do assume a general correspondence between confidence values and translation quality within each one of the modules, there is no guaranty whatsoever that a high value delivered by a certain module would indeed signify a better translation when compared with another value, even a much lower one, which was delivered by another module. An additional step needs to be taken in order to make the confidence values comparable with one another.

3   Working Hypotheses

It should be noted that one of our working hypotheses, namely, that confidence values do generally reflect translation quality, also compensates to a certain extent for the lack of a wide range theory of translation, according to which translations of different sorts could be unanimously evaluated. The task of evaluating translation quality is non-trivial also for human annotators, since the applicable criteria are diverse, and at the absence of a comprehensive translation theory, very often lead to contradicting conclusions. This difficulty is partially dealt with in section 6.1 below, but for practical reasons we tend to accept the need to rely on human judgment, partially theory assisted and partially intuitive, as inevitable. Another presupposition that we have awarely adopted throughout the current work is that the desirable rescaling can be well approximated by means of linear polynomials. The computational benefits of this assumption are immense, as it allows us to remain within the relatively friendly realm of linear equations (albeit inconsistent). The price that we have to pay in terms of precision is not as big as one might expect, because the crucial matter to our case is the comparative behavior of the obtained confidence curves, i.e. the breakpoints in which one overtakes the other, rather than the precise details of their behavior in between.

4   The Various *Verbmobil* Translation Paths

The *Verbmobil* system includes four independent translations paths that operate in parallel. The input shared by all paths consists of sequences of annotated *Word Hypotheses Graphs (WHG)*. Each *WHG* is produced by a speaker independent voice recognition module, and is annotated with additional prosodic information and pause information by a prosody module [4]. In principle, every translation subsystem chooses independently a path through the *WHG*, and a possible segmentation according to its grammar and to the prosody module information. This implies that even though all translation paths are sharing the same input data structure, both the chosen input string and its chosen segmentation may well be different for each path. In this section we provide the reader with very brief descriptions of the different translation subsystems, along with their respective methods for calculating confidence values.

- The **ali** subsystem implements an example based translation approach. Confidence values are calculated according to the matching-level of the input string with its counterparts in the database.
- The **stattrans** [17] subsystem is a statistical translation system. Confidence values are calculated according to a statistical language model of the target language, in conjunction with a statistical translation model.
- The **syndialog** [13] subsystem is a dialogue act based translation system. Here the translation invariant consists of a recognized dialogue act, together with its extracted propositional content. The confidence value reflects the probability that the dialogue act was recognized correctly, together with the extent to which the propositional content was successfully extracted.
- The **deep** translation path in itself consists of multiple pipelined modules: linguistic analysis, semantic construction, dialogue and discourse semantics, and transfer [8] and generation [12] components. The transfer module is supported with disambiguation information by the context [14] and dialogue modules. The linguistic analysis part consists of several parsers which, in turn, also operate in parallel [19]. They include an HPSG parser, a Chunk Parser and a statistical parser, all producing data structures of the same kind, namely, the *Verbmobil Interface Terms (VITs)* [7]. Thus, within the deep processing path, a selection problem arises, similar to the larger scale problem of selecting the best translation. This internal selection process within the deep path is based on a probabilistic *VIT* model. Confidence values within the deep path are computed according to the amount of coverage of the input string by the selected parse, and are subject to modifications as a byproduct of combining and repairing rules that operate within the semantics mechanism. Another source of information which is used for calculating the 'deep' confidence values is the generation module, which estimates the percentage of each transfered *VIT* which can be successfully realized in the target language.

Although all confidence values are finally scaled to the interval $[0, 100]$ by their respective generating modules, there seems to be hardly any reason to believe that such fundamentally different calculation methods would yield magnitudes that are directly comparable with one another. As expected, our experience has shown that when confidence values are taken as such, without any further modification, their comparative significance is indeed very limited.

5   The Selection Procedure

In order to improve their comparative significance, the delivered confidence values $c(s)$, for each given segment s, are rescaled by linear functions of the form:

$$a \cdot c(s) + b \ . \tag{1}$$

Note that each input utterance is decomposed into several segments independently, and hence potentially differently, by each of the translation paths. The different segments are then combined to form a data structure which, by analogy to *Word Hypotheses Graph*, can be called *Translation Alternatives Graph (TAG)*. The size of this graph is bound by 4^n, which is reached if all translation paths happen to choose an identical partition into exactly n segments. The following vectorial notation was adopted in order to simplify the simultaneous reference to all translation paths. The linear coefficients are represented by the following four-dimensional vectors:

$$\mathbf{a} = \begin{pmatrix} a_{ali} \\ a_{syndialog} \\ a_{stattrans} \\ a_{deep} \end{pmatrix} \qquad \mathbf{b} = \begin{pmatrix} b_{ali} \\ b_{syndialog} \\ b_{stattrans} \\ b_{deep} \end{pmatrix} \ . \tag{2}$$

Single vector components can then be referred to by simple projections, if we represent the different translation paths as orthogonal unit vectors, so that $\mathbf{s}$ denotes the vector corresponding to the module by which s had been generated. The normalized confidence is then represented by:

$$(\mathbf{a} \cdot k(s) + \mathbf{b}) \cdot \mathbf{s} \ . \tag{3}$$

In order to express the desirable favoring of translations with higher input string coverage, the compared magnitudes are actually the (rescaled) confidence values integrated with respect to the time axis, rather than the (rescaled) confidence values as such. Let $\|s\|$ be the length of a segment s of the input stream, in milliseconds. Let **SEQ** be the set of all possible segment sequences within the TAG, and $Seq \in \mathbf{SEQ}$ any particular sequence.

We define the normalized confidence of Seq as follows:

$$C(Seq) = \sum_{s \in Seq} ((\mathbf{a} \cdot c(s) + \mathbf{b}) \cdot \mathbf{s}) \cdot \|s\| \ . \tag{4}$$

This induces the following order relation:

$$seq_1 \leq_C seq_2 \overset{def}{=} C(seq_1) \leq C(seq_2) \ . \tag{5}$$

Based on this relation, we define the set of best sequences as follows:

$$Best(\mathbf{SEQ}) = \{seq \in \mathbf{SEQ} \mid seq \text{ is a maximum element in } (\mathbf{SEQ}; \leq_C)\} \ . \ (6)$$

The selection procedure consists in generating the various possible sequences, computing their respective normalized confidence values, and arbitrarily choosing a member of the set of best sequences. It should be noted that not all sequences need to be actually generated and tested, due to the incorporation of Dijkstra's well known "Shortest Path" algorithm (e.g. in [6]).

6 The Learning Cycle

Learning the rescaling coefficients is performed off line, and should normally take place only once, unless new training data is assembled, or new criteria for the desirable system behavior have been formulated. The learning cycle consists of incorporating human feedback (training set annotation) and finding a set of rescaling coefficients so as to yield a selection procedure with optimal or close to optimal accord with the human annotations. The first step in the learning procedure is choosing the set of training data. This choice has a direct influence on the learning's result, and, of course, on the amount of time and resources that it requires. In the course of our work we've performed this procedure several times, with training sets of various sizes, all taken from a corpus of test dialogues, designed to provide a reasonable coverage of the desirable functionality of the current *Verbmobil* version. Since the optimization algorithm (described below) normally terminates within no more than a couple of hours, the main bottle neck in terms of time consumption have normally been the human annotators. With what appears to be, from our experience, a reasonably large training set, i.e. a set of 7 from the above mentioned test dialogues (including 240 dialogue turns and 1980 different segments), the complete learning cycle can be performed within a few days, depending on the annotators' diligence, of course. Once a training set has been determined, it is first fed through the system, while separately storing the outputs produced by the various translation modules. The system's output is then subject to two phases of annotation (see section 6.1), resulting in a uniquely determined 'best' sequence of translated segments for each input utterance. The next task is to learn the appropriate linear rescaling, that would maximize the accord between the new, rescaled confidence values, and the preferences dictated by the newly given 'best' sequences. In order to do that, we first generate a large set of inequalities as described in section 6.2 below, and then obtain their optimal, or close to optimal solution, as described in section 6.3.

6.1 Training Set Annotation

As mentioned above, evaluating alternative translations is a complex task, which sometimes appears to be difficult even for specially trained people. When one alternative seems highly appropriate and all the others are clearly wrong, a vigilant annotator would normally encounter very little difficulty. But when all options fall within the reasonable realm and differ only slightly from one another, or even more so, when all options are far from perfect, each having its uniquely combined weaknesses and advantages — which criteria should be used by the annotator to decide which advantages or disadvantages are more crucial than the others? Our human feedback cycle is twofold: first, the outputs of the alternative translations paths are annotated separately, so as to enable the calculation of the 'off line confidence values' as described below. For each dialogue turn, all possible combinations of translated segments that cover the input are then generated. For each of those possible combinations, an overall off line confidence value is calculated, in a similar way to which the 'online' confidence is calculated (see section 5), leaving out the rescaling coefficients, but keeping the time axis integration. These segment combinations are then presented to the annotators for a second round, sorted according to their respective off line confidence values. The annotator is requested at this stage merely to select the best segment combination, which would normally be one of the first to appear on the list. The first annotation stage may be described as 'theory assisted annotation', and the second is its more intuitive complement. To assist the first annotation round we have compiled a set of annotation criteria, and designed a specialized annotation tool for their application. These criteria direct the annotator's attention to 'essential information items', and refer to the number of such items that have been deleted, inserted or maintained during the translation. Other criteria are the semantic and syntactic correctness of the translated utterance as well as those of the source utterance. The separate annotation of these criteria allows us to express the 'off line confidence' as their weighted linear combination. The different weights can be seen as implicitly establishing a method of quantifying translation quality. One can determine, for instance, which is of higher importance — syntactical correctness, or the transmission of all essential information items. Using the vague notion of 'translation quality' as a single criterion would have definitely caused a great divergence in personal annotation style and preferences, as can be very well exemplified by the case of the dialogue act based translation: some people find word by word correctness of a translation much more important than the dialogue act invariance, while others argue exactly the opposite [20,21].

6.2   Generating Inequalities

Once the best segment sequences for each utterance have been determined by the completed annotation procedure, a set of inequalities is created using the linear rescaling coefficients as variables. This is done simply by stating the requirement that the normalized confidence value of the best segment sequence should be better than the normalized confidence values of each one of the other possible sequences. For each utterance with n possible segment sequences, this requirement is expressed by $(n-1)$ inequalities. It is worth mentioning at this point that it sometimes occurs during the second annotation phase, that numerous sequences relating to the same utterance are considered 'equally best' by the annotator. In such cases, when not *all* sequences are concerned but only a subset of all possible sequences, we have allowed the annotator to select multiple sequences as 'best', correspondingly multiplying the number of inequalities that are introduced by the utterance in question. These multiple sets are known in advance to be inconsistent, as they in fact formulate contradictory requirements. Since the optimization procedure attempts to satisfy the largest possible subset of inequalities, the logical relation between such contradicting sets can be seen as disjunction rather than conjunction, and they do seem to contribute to the learning process, because the different 'equally best' sequences are still favored in comparison to all other sequences relating to the same utterance. The overall resulting set of inequalities is normally very large, and can be expected to be consistent only in a very idealized world, even in the absence of 'equally best' annotations. The inconsistencies reflect many imperfections that characterize both the problem at hand and the long way to its solution, most outstanding of which is the fact that the original confidence values, as useful as they may be, are nevertheless far from reflecting the human annotation and evaluation results, which are, furthermore, not always consistent among themselves. The rest of the learning process consists in trying to satisfy as many inequalities as possible without reaching a contradiction.

6.3 Optimization Heuristics

The problem of finding the best rescaling coefficients reduces itself, under the above mentioned presuppositions, to that of finding the maximal consistent subset of inequalities within a larger, most likely inconsistent, set of linear inequalities, and solving it. In [3], the problem of extracting close-to-maximum consistent subsystems from an inconsistent linear system (MAX CS) is treated as part of a strategy for solving the problem of partitioning an inconsistent linear system into a minimal number of consistent subsystems (MIN PCS). Both problems are NP-hard, but through a thermal variation of previous work by [2] and [18], a greedy algorithm is formulated by [3], which can serve as an effective heuristic for obtaining optimal or near to optimal solutions for MAX CS. Implementing this algorithm in the C language enabled us to complete the learning cycle by finding a set of coefficients that maximizes, or at least nearly maximizes, the accord of the rescaled confidence values with the judgment provided by human annotators.

7 Additional Knowledge Sources

Independently of the confidence rescaling process, we have made several attempts to incorporate additional knowledge sources in order to refine the selection procedure. Some of these attempts, such as using probabilistic language model information, or inferring from the logical relation between the approximated propositional contents of neighboring utterances (e.g. trying to eliminate contradiction), have sofar not been fruitful enough to be worth full description in the present work. Two other attempts do seem to be worth mentioning in further detail, namely, using dialogue act information, and using disambiguation information, which are described in the following two sections.

7.1   Dialogue Act Information

Our experience shows that the translation quality that is accomplished by the different modules varies, among the rest, according to the dialogue act at hand. This seems to be particularly true for **syndialog**, the dialogue act based translation path. Those dialogue acts that normally transmit very little propositional content, or those that transmit no propositional content at all, are normally handled better by **syndialog** compared to dialogue acts that transmit more information (such as INFORM, which can in principle transmit any proposition). The dialogue act recognition algorithm used by **syndialog** does not compute the single most likely dialog act, but rather a probability distribution of all possible dialogue acts[1] We represent the dialogue act probability distribution for a given segment s by the vector $da(s)$, where each component denotes the conditional probability of a certain dialogue act, given the segment s:

$$da(s) = \begin{pmatrix} P(suggest|s) \\ P(reject|s) \\ P(greet|s) \\ \vdots \end{pmatrix} . \tag{7}$$

The vectors a and b from section 5 above are replaced by the matrices A and B which are simply a concatenation of the respective dialogue act vectors. Let $A^s = A \cdot da(s)$, and $B^s = B \cdot da(s)$.
The normalized confidence value, with incorporated dialogue act information can then be expressed as:

$$C(Seq) = \sum_{s \in Seq} ((A^s \cdot c(s) + B^s) \cdot s) \cdot \|s\| . \tag{8}$$

7.2   Disambiguation Information

Within the **deep** translation path, several types of underspecification are used for representing ambiguities [15,16,9]. Whenever an ambiguity has to be resolved in order for the translation to succeed, resolution is triggered on demand [5]. Several types of disambiguation are performed by the context module [14]. Within this module, several knowledge sources are used in conjunction for resolving anaphora and lexical ambiguities. Examples for such knowledge sources are world knowledge, knowledge about the dialogue state, as well as various sorts of morphological, syntactic and semantic information. Additionally, dialogue act recognition is performed, and a representation of the main dialogue turn content is

---

[1] For more information about dialogue acts in *Verbmobil*, see [1]

constructed. Of considerable importance to the *Verbmobil* scenario are the representations and reasoning on date and time expressions [22,10]. All these different tasks are strongly interdependent. For example, in order to distinguish between certain dialogue acts it is necessary to compare date expressions. Dialogue act information is, in its turn, very important for the disambiguation process. This kind of knowledge based disambiguation is only integrated in the **deep** translation path. The German word "Essen", for example, can be translated into English as either "dinner" or "lunch", depending of the relevant time of day. Another German example is "vorziehen", which has two alternative readings, namely, "move" and "prefer". In order to use disambiguation as an additional information source for the selection procedure, we have assembled a set of ambiguities which are normally dealt with incorrectly by all translation paths except for **deep** (which is the only one that performs the above mentioned disambiguation procedures). When such ambiguities occur, the confidence value for **deep** is artificially increased.

8   Conclusion

We have described certain difficulties that arise during the attempt to integrate multiple alternative translation paths and to choose their optimal combination into one 'best' translation. Using confidence values that originate from different translation modules as our basic selection criteria, we have introduced a learning method which enables us to perform the selection in close to maximal accord with decisions taken by human annotators. Along the way, we have also tackled the problematic aspects of translation evaluation as such, and described some additional sources of information that are used within our selection module. The extent to which this module succeeds in creating higher quality compound translations is of course highly dependent on the appropriate assignment of confidence values, which is performed by the various translation modules themselves. Despite the relative simplicity of the methods that are currently being used by these modules for confidence calculation as such, applying our approach within the *Verbmobil* system has already yielded a significant improvement. The most recent *Verbmobil* evaluation results demonstrate this improvement very clearly. The evaluation is based on annotating five alternative translations for a chosen set of dialogue-turns. The translations provided by the four single translation paths, and the combined translation delivered by the selection module, were all marked by the annotators as 'good', 'intermediate', or 'bad'. Judged by the percentage of 'good' turns from the overall number of annotated turns, the selection module shows an improvement of 27.8% compared to the best result achieved by a single module.

References

1. Alexandersson, J., Buschbeck-Wolf, B., Fujinami, T., Kipp, T., Koch, S., Maier, E., Reithinger, N., Schmitz, B., Siegel,M.: Dialogue Acts in VERBMOBIL-2 *Second Edition*. DFKI Saarbrücken, Universität Stuttgart, Technische Universität Berlin, Universität des Saarlandes, Verbmobil-Report **226** (1997)
2. S.Agmon, S.: The relaxation method for linear inequalities. Canadian Journal of Mathematics, **6** (1954) 382–392
3. Amaldi, E. Mattavelli, M.: A combinatorical optimization approach to extract piecewise linear structure from nonlinear data and an application to optical flow segmentation. **TR 97-12**, Cornell Computational Optimization Project, Cornell University, Ithaca NY, USA (1997)
4. Buckow, J., Batliner, A., Gallwitz, F., Huber, R., Nöth, E., Warnke, V., Niemann H.: Dovetailing of Acoustics and Prosody in Spontaneous Speech Recognition. Proc. Int. Conf. on Spoken Language Processing, volume **3**, Sydney, Australia (1998) 571–574
5. Buschbeck-Wolf, B.: Resolution on Demand. Universität Stuttgart. Verbmobil-Report **196** (1997)
6. Cormen, T., Leiserson, C. Rivet, L.: Introduction to Algorithms. MIT Press, Cambridge, Massachusetts (1989)
7. Dorna, M.: The ADT Package for the Verbmobil Interface Term.. Universität Stuttgart, Verbmobil-Report **104X** (1999)
8. Emele, M. Dorna, M.: Efficient Implementation of a Semantic-based Transfer Approach. Proceedings of the 12th European Conference on Artificial Intelligence (ECAI-96) (1996)
9. Emele, M., Dorna, M.: Ambiguity Preserving Machine Translation using Packed Representations. Proceedings of the 17th International Conference on Computational Linguistics (COLING-ACL '98), Montreal, Canada (1998)
10. Endriss, U.: Semantik zeitlicher Ausdrücke in Terminvereinbarungsdialogen. Technische Universität Berlin, Verbmobil-Report **227** (1998)
11. Frederking, R., Nirenburg, S.: Three Heads are Better than One. ANLP94P (1994) 95–100
12. Kilger, A., Finkler, W.: Incremental Generation for Real-Time Applications. DFKI Report **RR-95-11**, German Research Center for Artificial Intelligence - DFKI GmbH (1995)
13. Kipp, M., Alexandersson, J., Reithinger, N.: Understanding Spontaneous Negotiation Dialogue. Proceedings of the IJCAI Workshop Knowledge and Reasoning in Practical Dialogue Systems. Stockholm, Sweden (1999)
14. Koch, S., Küssner, U., Stede, M., Tidhar D.: Contextual reasoning in speech-to-speech translation. Proceedings of 2nd International Conference on Natural Language Processing (NLP2000), Springer Lecture Notes in Artificial Intelligence (2000)
15. Küssner, U.: Applying DL in Automatic Dialogue Interpreting. Proceedings of the International Workshop on Description Logics - DL-97, Gif sur Yvette, France (1997) 54–58
16. Küssner, U.: Description Logic Unplugged. Proceedings of the International Workshop on Description Logics - DL-98, Trento, Italy (1998) 142–146
17. Och, F.J., Tillmann, C., Ney, N.: Improved Alignment models for Statistical Machine Translation. Proceedings of the Joint SIGDAT Conf. on Empirical Methods in Natural Language Processing and Very Large Corpora, University of Maryland (1999)

18. Motzkin, T.S., Schoenberg, I.J.: The relaxation method for linear inequalities. Canadian Journal of Mathematics, **6** (1954) 393–404
19. Ruland, T., Rupp, C.J., Spilker, J., Weber, H., Worm C.: Making the Most of Multiplicity: A Multi-Parser Multi-Strategy Architecture for the Robust Processing of Spoken Language. Proceedings of ICSLP (1998)
20. Schmitz, B.: Pragmatikbasiertes Maschinelles Dolmetschen. Dissertation, FB Informatik, Technische Universität Berlin (1998)
21. Schmitz, B., Quantz, J.J.: Dialogue Acts in Automatic Dialogue Interpreting. Proceedings of the Sixth International Conference on Theoretical and Methodological Issues in Machine Translation (TMI-95), Leuven (1995)
22. Stede, M., Haas, S., Küssner U.: Understanding and tracking temporal descriptions in dialogue. Proceedings of KONVENS-98, Bonn (1998)
23. Wahlster, W.: Verbmobil: Translation of face-to-face dialogues. Proceedings of the Third European Conference of Speech Communication and Technology. Berlin (1993)
24. Worm, C., Rupp, C.J.: Towards Robust Understanding of Speech by Combination of Partial Analyses. Proceedings of ECAI (1998)

Parsing and Collocations

Eric Wehrli*

LATL, University of Geneva
wehrli@latl.unige.ch

Abstract. Proper treatment of collocations constitutes a serious challenge for NLP systems in general. This paper describes how Fips, a "Principle and Parameters" grammar-based parser developed at LATL handles multi-word expressions. In order to get more precise and more reliable collocation data, the Fips parser is used to extract collocations from large text corpora. It will be shown that collocational information can help ranking alternative analyses computed by the parser, in order to improve the quality of its results.

1 Introduction

Scaling-up grammar-based NLP systems is known to be a challenging task. To be sure, although dozens, perhaps hundreds of prototypes have been developed, featuring the widest variety of grammar formalisms and parsing algorithms, few have matured into large-scale parsing systems. As a result, today's commercial NLP products are by and large based on surprisingly unsophisticated linguistic tools.

There is no single reason for this state of affairs. For one thing, building a full-scale NLP system requires means that are usually beyond the reach of most academic teams. There are also true scientific challenges, such as the ambiguity problem, which all too easily can lead to combinatorial explosions. With regard to grammar, one must take into consideration the difficulty of writing a coherent grammar, sufficiently rich to cover not just the set of sentences that one particular person is likely to utter, but all the sentences that very many different people, under very different circumstances, might use.

In this paper, we would like to address a small, but arguably important aspect of the scaling-up problem: the treatment of multi-word expressions. Multi-word expressions (henceforth MWE), taken here as *fixed or semi-fixed lexical or syntactic units made up of several words*, are considered as one of the most difficult tasks for NLP systems in general and for machine translation (MT) in particular (See [2], [18], among many others).

Several papers have been devoted to MWEs, both from a theoretical viewpoint [12], [13], and from a computational viewpoint [9] [1], [17], [21]. The topic

* Thanks to Paola Merlo, Luka Nerima, Juri Mengon, and Stephanie Durrleman for comments on an earlier version of this paper. This research was supported in part by a grant from the Swiss Commission for technology and innovation (CTI).

D.N. Christodoulakis (Ed.): NLP 2000, LNCS 1835, pp. 272–282, 2000.

of the present paper is the implementation of a large-scale treatment of MWEs in **Fips**, a large-scale parser based on an adaptation of Chomksy's "Principles and Parameters" theory [6], [20]. In particular, we will propose a training cycle, where the parser is used to acquire MWEs from text corpora, and in turn, MWEs are used to improve the quality of the parser. Preliminary results suggest that the acquisition of MWEs from syntactically annotated text corpora is far more precise and reliable than the ones obtained by standard statistical methods. There is no doubt that syntactic dependencies, such as the ones expressed by grammatical functions or modification relations between two terms constitute a more appropriate criterion of relatedness than simple linear proximity, such as being 2 or 3 words away. As for the improvement of the parser, it will be argued that co-occurrence data collected through the acquisition of MWEs can serve as an additional scoring function to rank alternative analyses computed by the parser.

The paper is structured as follows. The second section will present a typology of MWEs, in which we distinguish compounds, idioms and collocations, based on their categorical status (lexical vs phrasal categories), as well as on the degree of compositionality of their semantics. The third section discusses the treatment of these three subclasses of MWEs in Fips. It will be shown how the lexical vs phrasal category distinction (X^0 vs XP) and other fundamental differences between compounds, idioms and collocations lead to distinct treatments in our system. The role of Fips for the acquisition of collocations constitutes the topic of section 4, while the use of co-occurrence data to improve the parser by means of a scoring function is addressed in section 5.

2   A "Practical" Typology of Multi-word Expressions

MWEs constitute a heterogeneous class, the limits of which are difficult to establish. We shall consider that MWEs are part of a continuum spreading from free associations of words on the one hand, to frozen, idiomatic expressions, on the other hand. While keeping in mind this continuum, we will suggest, mostly for practical reasons, to partition MWEs into three distinct subclasses: compounds, idioms and collocations.

2.1   Compounds

Compounds correspond to MWEs whose elements are strictly adjacent: no other lexical materiel can intervene between them. Furthermore, compounds have the same distribution as simple words, i.e. lexical category elements, or more technically, X^0-level elements. For instance, French compounds such as *fer à cheval* (*horseshoe*), *pomme de terre* (*potato*) behave just like ordinary nouns, *peu à peu* (*little by little*) like an adverb, *tant et si bien (que)* (*so that*) like a conjunction. A third caracteristic feature of compounds is the fact that their semantics is not strictly compositional: the meaning of compounds such as *chemin de fer* (*railways*), *libre arbitre* (*free will*) or *parti pris* (*prejudice*) does not strictly correspond to the combination of the meanings of their parts.

In view of these three basic properties, we suggest a treatment of compounds similar to the treatment of simple words, that is, compounds are listed in the lexicon along with simple words, and their identification is carried out during lexical analysis (we return to that in section 3 below).

2.2   Idioms

While compounds are lexical units whose parts are strictly adjacent to each other, idioms constitute units of a higher categorical level, i.e. XP (phrasal) level – typically but not exclusively, verbal phrases. As expected from phrasal units, idioms exhibit a certain amount of freedom in terms of placement or modification, as illustrated below :

(1)a. Jean a forcé la main à Luc.
      Jean has forced the hand to Luc
      'Jean forced Luc's hand'
   b. C'est à Luc que Jean a forcé la main.
      It is to Luc that Jean has forced the hand
      'It is Luc's hand that Jean has forced'
   c. C'est à Luc que Paul prétend que Jean a voulu forcer la main.
      It is to Luc that Paul claims that Jean has wanted to force the hand
      'It is Luc's hand that Paul claims that Jean has wanted to force'
   d. La main semble lui avoir été un peu forcée.
      The hand hand seems to him to have been a little forced
      'His hand seems to have been somewhat forced'

Forcer la main à quelqu'un (*to force sb's hand*) is typical of a very large class of idioms based on a verbal head. As argued in [21], such idioms behave syntactically like verb phrases with a fixed direct object argument (*la main* in this example), while the other arguments are open. In this case (but not in all), the verb phrase is completely regular in its behaviour. For instance, it can undergo syntactic operations such as passive, raising, dislocation and adverbial modification.

The extent to which idiomatic expressions can undergo modifications and other syntactic operations can vary considerably from one expression to the next, and in the absence of a general explanation for this fact, each expression must be recorded with a detailed description of its particular properties and constraints[1]. This means that idiom entries are far more complex than entries of simple words or entries of compounds.

It will be argued in the next section that the identification of idiomatic expressions should be carried out on the basis of a normalized structure, such as the D-structure level of representation of a generative grammar[2]. Our treatment

---

[1] See [12], [13], [14] or [15] for enlightening discussions on the degree of flexibility of idioms.

[2] Roughly speaking, the D-structure level of representations, which corresponds to the old "deep-structure" level, is an abstract level of representation of a sentence, where all the lexical items occur in their canonical position.

of idiomatic expressions takes advantage of the normalization process that the Fips parser carries out.

2.3   Collocations

The term "collocation" is commonly used to refer to an *arbitrary and recurrent word combination* [4]. In addition to this broad sense, that we take to be virtually synonymous with "multi-word expression", we will suggest a somewhat narrower view of collocations, defined as the set of MWEs with the exclusion of compounds and idioms. Since compounds have been roughly defined as X^0-level units (units of lexical category) whose meaning is not compositional, and idioms partially fixed phrasal units with either (i) a non-compositional meaning or (ii) a non-standard form (e.g. in French, a bare noun as direct object), what is left for collocations in the narrow sense is: arbitrary and recurrent combinations of words, which are not necessarily contiguous and whose meaning is roughly speaking compositional. A word of warning is mandatory here. Given the fact that the various types of MWEs constitute a continuum, the boundary between them is likely to be difficult to establish. We will, therefore, only refer to clear examples, such as those in (2):

(2)

Collocation	Collocation type	Translation
haute technologie	adjective noun	high technology
dernière chance	adjective noun	last chance
part de marché	noun-prepositional phrase	market share
vent souffler	subjet-verb	wind blow
rumeur circuler	subject-verb	rumor go around
battre oeuf	verb-direct object	beat egg
fouetter crème	verb-direct object	whip cream
poser question	verb-direct object	ask question
signer accord	verb-direct object	sign agreement
brandir menace	verb-direct object	threaten
apporter soutien	verb-direct object	bring support

The collocations in (2) are given in their lemmatized form. It should be clear that they usually don't appear in this particular form, and, with the exception of the adjective-noun type, the elements which constitute the collocation are virtually never adjacent to each other.

According to the narrow interpretation that we have just suggested, collocations correspond to a conventional combination of two or more words, with transparent meaning. "Conventional combinations" means that native speakers recognize such combinations as the "correct" way of expressing a particular concept. For instance, substituting one term of a collocation with a synonym or a near-synonym is usually felt by native-speakers as being "not quite right", although perfectly understandable (e.g. *firing ambition vs burning ambition* or in French *exercer une profession* vs *pratiquer une profession* (*to practice a profession*)).

3   The Treatment of Collocations in Fips

This section briefly presents the treatment of collocations (taken here in the broad sense of multi-word expressions) in Fips.

Given the categorical distinction (X^0 vs XP) and other fundamental differences sketched above, compounds and idioms are treated very differently in our system. Compounds are simply listed in the lexicon as complex lexical units. As such, their identification belongs to the lexical analysis component. Once a compound has been recognized, its treatment in the parser does not differ in any interesting way from the treatment of simple words.

While idiomatic expressions must also be listed in the lexicon, their entries are far more complex than the ones of simple or compound words. For one thing, as we mentioned above, idiomatic expressions typically correspond to phrasal units, partially fixed phrase structures, such as VP, whose properties must be carefully listed. As for their identification, it turns out to be a rather complex operation, which cannot be reliably carried out at a superficial level of representation. As we saw in the examples (1), idiom chunks can be found far away from the (usually verbal) head with which they constitute an expression; they can also be modified in various ways, and so on. Preprocessing idioms, for instance during the lexical analysis, might therefore lead to lengthy, inefficient or unreliable treatments. We will argue that in order to simplify the task of identifying idioms, it is necessary to undo whatever syntactic operations they might have undergone. To put it differently, idioms can best be recognized on the basis of a normalized structure, a structure in which constituents occur in their canonical position. In a generative grammar framework, normalized structures correspond to the D-structure level of representation. At that level, for instance, the four sentences in (1), share the common structure in (3).

(3) ... [$_{VP}$ forcer [$_{DP}$ la main] [$_{PP}$ à X]]
litt: force the hand to X
'force so's hand'

To better illustrate the way the Fips parser identifies idioms, let us consider a complete example. Sentence (4a), which contains the famous idiom *casser sa pipe* (*kick the bucket*), is first analyzed, which yields the structure given in (4b)[3]:

(4)a. Paul a cassé sa pipe.
'Paul has kicked the bucket'

---

[3] The labels used in the syntactic representations are: TP (Tense Phrase) for sentences, VP for verb phrases, DP for Determiner Phrases, NP for Noun Phrases, and PP for Prepositional Phrases.

b. [$_{TP}$ [$_{DP}$ Paul] [$_{\overline{T}}$ a [$_{VP}$ cassé [$_{DP}$ sa [$_{NP}$ pipe]]]]]

Notice that the analysis in (4b) has nothing specific to idioms. So far, the parser has carried out a standard syntactic analysis. As we argued above, the idiom identification task is best accomplished at the abstract level of representation (D-structure), which is part of the enriched syntactic structure computed by Fips. The idiom recognition procedure is triggered by the "head of idiom" lexical feature associated with the verbal head *casser*. This feature is associated with all lexical items which are heads of idioms in the lexical database.

The task of the recognition procedure is (i) to retrieve the proper idiom, if any (*casser* might be the head of several idioms), and (ii) to verify that all the constraints associated with that idiom are satisfied. Idioms are listed in the lexical database as roughly illustrated in (5) :

(5)a. casser sa pipe
'kick the bucket'
b. 1: [$_{DP}$]   2: [$_{V}$ casser]   3: [$_{DP}$ POSS pipe]
c. 1. [+human]
   2. [−passive]
   3. [+literal, −extraposition]

Idiom entries specify (a) the canonical form of the idiom (mostly for reference purposes), (b) the syntactic frame with an ordered list of constituents, and (c) the list of constraints associated with each of the constituents.

In our (rather simple) example, the lexical constraints associated with the idiom (5) state that the verbal head is a transitive lexeme whose direct object has the fixed form "POSS *pipe*", where POSS stands for a possessive determiner coreferential with the external argument of the head (i.e. the subject). Furthermore, the subject constituent bears the feature [+human], the head is marked as [-passive], meaning that this particular idiom cannot be passivized. Finally, the object is also marked [+literal, -extraposition], which means that the direct object constituent cannot be modified in any way (not even pluralized), and cannot be extraposed.

The structure in (4b) satisfies all those constraints, provided that the possessive *sa* refers uniquely to *Paul*[4]. It should be noticed that even though an idiom has been recognized in sentence (4a), it also has a semantically well-formed literal meaning[5].

As we can see from this example, the identification of idioms in Fips is not a matter of syntactic analysis, but rather a matter of how such structures are interpreted, based on lexical specifications.

---

[4] Given a proper context, the sentence could be construed with *sa* referring to some other person, say Bill.

[5] In general, the idiom reading takes precedence over the literal interpretation. Such a heuristic seems to correspond to normal usage, which would avoid formulation (4a) to state that 'Paul has broken someone's pipe'.

As for the treatment of collocation (in the narrow sense), it roughly corresponds to a much lighter version of the idiom treatment. Like idioms, collocations are listed in the lexical database. Their presence in the lexicon is fully justified, for instance, because they can serve as units for lexical transfer in a translation application. However, their lexical representation is much simpler than the representation of idioms, specifying (i) the lexemes involved in the collocation and (ii) the type of the collocation (e.g. subject-verb, verb-object, adjective-noun, etc.).

4   Extracting Collocations with Fips

As mentioned in the introduction, one of the problems in connection with the treatment of MWEs is the acquisition of collocational knowledge, in general or for restricted domains. This issue has been much addressed in the literature mostly since the work of [7], and several statistical packages have been designed for this purpose (See, for instance, the Xtract system, [16]). Although very effective, those system suffer from the fundamental weakness that the measure of relatedness they use is essentially the linear proximity of two or more words. There is no doubt that syntactic dependencies, such as the ones expressed by grammatical functions or modification relations between two constituents provide a finer criterion of relatedness than say being 2 or 3 words away.

To illustrate this point, consider the following examples of the collocation *éprouver - difficulté (experience problems)* taken in the corpus of the French newspaper "Libération":

(6)a. **éprouvent** les **difficultés**
  b. **éprouve** des **difficultés**
  c. **éprouvant** de très sérieuses **difficultés**
  d. **éprouvaient** d'extrêmes **difficultés**
  e. **éprouve** la même **difficulté**
  f. n'**éprouvent** aujourd'hui aucune **difficulté**
  g. ont **éprouvé** au premier semestre des **difficulté**
  h. **éprouvent** toujours les plus grandes **difficultés**
  i. **éprouver**, comme pour d'autres entités plus grandes, ou moins européennes dans leurs caractéristiques, de grandes **difficultés**
  j. **difficultés** qu'**éprouve**
  k. des **difficultés** que peuvent **éprouver**
  l. Les **difficultés** de gestion gouvernementale qu'**éprouve**
  m. l'extrême **difficulté** qu'**éprouve**

Such examples show the variety of contexts in which such a simple "verb-direct object" collocation can be found. The distance between the two lexemes can be important. In fact, an arbitrary number of words can separate them, as illustrated in (6i). Furthermore, since direct objects can undergo various grammatical operations, such as passivization, extraposition (interrogation, relativization, topicalization, etc.), the canonical order verb-object cannot even be assumed, as illustrated in examples (6j-m), where they occur in the reverse order.

Notice that in order to correctly handle such cases, superficial syntactic tagging would not suffice. What is needed is a more comprehensive analysis, capable of interpreting extraposed elements, such as relativized phrases. As illustrated in the (simplified) example (7a) below, a noun phrase such as *the difficulties that he might have experienced* must be recognized as an occurrence of the verb-object collocation *experience-difficulty*. Specifically, this means that the parser must be able (i) to recognize the presence of a relative clause, (ii) to identify the antecedent of the relative pronoun, and (iii) to establish a link between this antecedent and the verb with which the relative pronoun is syntactically dependent. As illustrated in (7b), Fips does exactly that. A chain is established, first, between the canonical direct object position (represented by the empty element $[_{DP}$ e], which stands for the trace of the extraposed element) of the verb *éprouver* and the relative pronoun *que*, and then between this pronoun and its antecedent *difficulté*. In the structures returned by Fips, chains are expressed by means of coindexation. The double chain connecting *difficultés* and the trace of the relative pronoun is represented in the structure (7b) by the index $\mathbf{i}$[6].

(7)a. Les difficultés qu'il aurait pu éprouver...
   'the difficulties that he might have experienced...
   b. $[_{DP}$ les $[_{NP}$ difficultés$]_i$ $[_{CP}$ $[_{DP}$ qu'$]_i$ $[_{TP}$ $[_{DP}$ il$]_j$ aurait $[_{VP}$ pu
   $[_{TP}$ $[_{DP}$ e$]_j$ $[_{VP}$ éprouver $[_{DP}$ e$]_i$]]]]]]

The need for syntactic normalization in order to identify particular types of collocations is not restricted to the case of relative clauses. Similar arguments can be made for all cases of extraposed elements, including passives, topicalization, raising, disloction, etc.

Given the high frequency of such constructions in text corpora, it is clear that the use of syntactically analyzed texts as the basis for the acquisition of collocations yields more precise results than the ones obtained by standard statistical methods. With the development of robust parsers, such as Fips, text corpora can be relatively easily turned into syntactically annotated corpora, opening the way for a wide-scope treatment of collocations. Of course, syntactic analyses computed by current parsers are not always correct. One of the most common errors lies with attachment ambiguities, particularly in the case of attachment of prepositional phrases. We will show in the next section, that collocation data can be used to help improving the parser, particularly in the case of attachment ambiguities.

An additional advantage of using syntactically parsed text corpora to extract collocations is the possibility of representing co-occurrences at a more ab-

---

[6] The reason why the link between the antecedent of a relative pronoun and the trace of the pronoun is presented here as a double link, although represented by the same index, lies with technical details of the theory, which are not directly relevant here (wh-chain vs predication).

stract level than simple orthographic words. In our experiment, we are using
the level of lexemes, i.e. a particular reading associated with simple words or of
multi-words expressions. For instance, when Fips extracts the verb-object collocation *réserver-droit* (*to reserve the right*), the lexeme *réserver* is specifically
the pronominal reading (*se réserver*). Similarly, we get subject-verb collocations
with verbal lexemes corresponding to idioms, such as *tribunal-donner raison
à qqn* (*court-prove someone right*) or *rencontre-avoir lieu* (*meeting-take place*)
or with compound, such as *donner-feu vert* (*to give the green light*), and not
rencontre-avoir (*meeting-have*) or *donner-feu* (*give-fire*), which would be irrelevant. The selection of the proper lexeme associated with an orthographic word or
compound is an important aspect of the disambiguation process that a full-scale
parser must carry out.

5   Collocation Frequencies as Parsing Heuristics

The problem of ranking competing analyses produced by a grammar-based
parser becomes more acute as the coverage of the parser increases. Enriching
the lexicon with additional word senses (lexemes), adding new rules (or extending old ones) to extend the grammatical coverage lead to increasingly large
numbers of alternatives. For that reason, large-scale grammar-based parsers implement scoring functions, whose purpose is to rank alternatives according to
various types of preferences (See [3], [5], [10], [11], [20]). Typically, those preferences are based on intuition, sometimes backed by psycholinguistic results.
Alshawi et al. and Hindle et al. [3], [8] have shown the potential of collocation
information as one possible basis for the scoring function. In both cases, they
mostly take into consideration the problem of prepositional phrase attachment.
In our experiment, we would like to extend this proposal to a much wider class
of collocations, in order to capture intuitions about the relative ranking of lexicalized versus non-lexicalized MWEs. In other words, we expect co-occurrence
information to be helpful not just in the case of prepositional phrase attachment
ambiguities but for any type of ambiguity for which co-occurence information is
available[7].

Exactly how collocation data will be used in the scoring function in Fips
is still a research topic, but the general idea is to rank analyses according to
their co-occurrence score, that is, to give preference to an analysis involving a
collocation (in the broad sense) over alternatives devoid of collocations. More
generally, a collocation score could be computed for each alternative, based on
the presence of collocations and on their frequency.

Consider the problem of the prepositional phrase attachment illustrated in
the following example :

(8)a. Il parle au chef de l'état-major [$_{pp}$ de l'armée]...

    'He talked to the chief of staff [$_{pp}$ of the army]...'

---

[7] See [5] for a detailed analysis of the effectiveness of co-occurrence information for
  subcategorization ambiguity resolution for the English version of Fips.

b. Il parle au chef de l'état-major [$_{PP}$ du problème]...

   'He talked to the chief of staff [$_{PP}$ of the problem]...'

Leaving aside other possible ambiguities in these sentences, the prepositional phrase *de l'armée* (*of the army*) in (8a) and *du problème* (*of the problem*) in (8b) can attach either as complement of the verb or as complement of the compound *chef de l'état-major* (*chief of staff*). Native speakers show a strong preference for an attachment to the noun phrase in the first example and for an attachment to the verb phrase in the second example. It turns out that co-occurrence data would support the same decision : given the fairly frequent co-occurrence of the collocation [$_{NP}$ *état-major* [$_{PP}$ *de l'armée*]], Fips would favor the analysis involving such a collocation over the alternative which does not feature any collocation. However, preference for the attachment to the verb phrase in the second example would follow from the fact that such an attachment satisfies an argument slot of the verb (*to talk to someone of/about sth*).

If such a treatment turns out to be on the right track, the use of collocation data to rank alternatives could easily be generalized to a much wider range of ambiguities, including the fixed vs "free association" readings of compounds and idioms.

6   Conclusion

Proper treatment of collocations is one aspect of the scaling-up problem in NLP systems. In this paper, we have described how this particular problem is handled in Fips, a robust parser based on the "Principles and Parameters" theory. We have first argued for a three-way partition of MWEs, distinguishing compounds, idioms and collocations (in the narrow sense of that term) on the basis of their distributonal and categorial properties, as well as their degree of semantic compositionality. Although the three subclasses of MWEs are somehow listed in the lexicon, we have shown that the precise way in which they are recorded is quite different, a difference which is also reflected in the manner they are identified during the parsing process.

With respect to the problem of the acquisition of collocations (now in the broad sense), it has been argued that syntactically annotated corpora provide a much better basis (i) because in such corpora lexical units are disambiguated and lemmatized, and (ii) because syntactic configurations constitute the proper criterion to select collocation (much better, in any case, than linear proximity).

In our research, the Fips parser has been used to annotate text corpora. Although a significant percentage of the parses are not completely correct, the results are very encouraging. Given the fact that the collocation data can be used to improve the quality of the parser, through a scoring function based on co-occurrence frequencies, a training loop can be initiated, in which the improvement of the parser based on collocations in turn improves the quality of the collocation acquisition.

References

1. Abeillé, A. & Schabes, Y.: "Parsing Idioms in lexicalized TAGs", *Proceedings of EACL-89*, Manchester, (1989) 1-9.
2. Arnold, D., Balkan, L., Lee Humphrey, R., Meijer, S., Sadler, L.: *Machine Translation: An Introductory Guide*, HTML document (`http://clwww.essex.ac.uk`), (1995).
3. Alshawi, H. & Carter, D.: "Training and scaling preference functions for disambiguation" *Computational Linguistics* 20:4, (1994) 635-648.
4. Benson, M.: "Collocations and general-purpose dictionaries" *Internation Journal of Lexicography* 3:1, (1990) 23-35.
5. Berthouzoz, C. & Merlo, P.: "Statistical Ambiguity Resolution for Grammar-based Parsing", *Recent Advances i Natural Language processing: Selected Papers form RANLP97, Current Issues in Linguistc Theory*, Nicolas Nicolov et Ruslan Mitkov (eds.), John Benjamins, Amsterdam/Philadelphia, (1998).
6. Chomsky, N. & Lasnik, H.: "The Theory of Pinciples and Parameters" in Chomsky, N. *The Minimalist Program*, Cambridge, MIT Press, (1995) 13-127.
7. Church, K., Gale, W., Hanks, P., Hindle, D.: "Using Statistics in Lexical Analysis", in Zernick, U. (ed.) *Lexical Acquisition: Exploiting On-Line Resources to Build a Lexicon*, Lawrence Erlbaum Associates, (1991) 115-164.
8. Hindle, D. & Roots, M.: "Structural Ambiguity and Lexical Relations" *Computational Linguistics* 19:1, (1993) 103-120.
9. Laporte, E.: "Reconnaissance des expressions figées lors de l'analyse automatique", *Langages* 90, Larousse, Paris, (1988).
10. Lin, D.: "Extracting Collocations from Text Corpora", *First Workshop on Computational Terminology*, Montreal, (1998).
11. McCord, M.C.: "Heuristics for broad-coverage natural language parsing", *Proceedings ARPA Human Technology Workshop*, Los Altos, Morgan Kaufmann, (1993) 127-132.
12. Nunberg, G., Sag, I., Wasow, T.: "Idioms", *Language*, 70:3, (1994) 491-538.
13. Ruwet, N.: "Du bon Usage des Expressions Idiomatiques dans l'argumentation en syntaxe générative". In *Revue québécoise de linguistique*. 13:1, (1983).
14. Schenk, A.: 'The Syntactic Behavior of Idioms'. In Everaert M., van der Linden E., Schenk, A., Schreuder, R. *Idioms: Structural and Psychological Perspectives*, Lawrence Erlbaum Associates, Hove, (1995).
15. Segond, D. & Breidt, E.:"IDAREX : description formelle des expressions à mots multiples en français et en allemand" in A. Clas, Ph. Thoiron and H. Béjoint (eds.) *Lexicomatique et dictionnairiques*, Montreal, Aupelf-Uref, (1996).
16. Smadja, F.: "Reitrieving collocations form text : X-tract", *Computational Linguistics* 19:1, (1993) 143-177.
17. Stock, O.: "Parsing with Flexibility, Dynamic Strategies, and Idioms in Mind", *Computational Linguistics*, 15.1., (1989) 1-18.
18. Volk, M.: "The Automatic Translation of Idioms : Machine Translation vs Translation Memory Systems" in Nico Weber (ed.) *Machine Translation: Theory, Applications, and Evaluation, An Assessment of the State-of-the-art*, St. Augustin, Gardez Verlag, (1998).
19. Wanner, L.: "On the representation of collocations in a multilingual computational lexicon", *TAL* 40:1, (1999) 55-86.
20. Wehrli, E.: *L'analyse syntaxique des langues naturelles : problèmes et méthodes*, Paris, Masson, (1997).
21. Wehrli, E.: "Translating Idioms", COLING-98, Montreal, (1998) 1388-1392.

Contextual Reasoning
in Speech-to-Speech Translation

Stephan Koch*, Uwe Küssner, Manfred Stede, and Dan Tidhar

Technische Universität Berlin, FB Informatik, Projektgruppe KIT
Franklinstr. 28/29, 10587 Berlin/Germany
{skoch,uk,stede,dan}@cs.tu-berlin.de

Abstract. In a speech-to-speech translation system, contextual reasoning for purposes of disambiguation has to respect the specific conditions arising from speech input; on the one hand, it is part of a real-time system, on the other hand, it needs to take errors in the speech recognition phase into account and hence be particular robust. This paper describes the context evaluation module of the Verbmobil translation system: What are the linguistic phenomena that require contextual reasoning, what does the context representation look like, how is it constructed during utterance interpretation, and how is it used for disambiguation and reasoning.

1 Introduction

The 'Verbmobil' project [13] develops a domain-specific speech-to-speech translation system that processes dialogues concerned with travel planning and appointment scheduling. The system consists of about 40 individual modules, and our group is building the Context Evaluation (ConEval) module. In line with the efficiency-oriented "resolution on demand" strategy in Verbmobil [4], contextual evaluation is triggered by the transfer module only when an ambiguity cannot be preserved in the target utterance. In this case, transfer sends a request to context, which builds up a representation of the discourse history in parallel with the other modules and thus affects the translation time only when a specific request is to be answered.

In the following, we first briefly describe the position of the context module in the Verbmobil system architecture, characterize the specific context evaluation tasks arising in the application scenario, and then outline our approach to representing the discourse context on three different levels of abstraction, up to symbolic representations linked to domain knowledge, which facilitates performing the necessary disambiguations.

2 The Context Evaluation Module in Verbmobil

The overall processing in the Verbmobil system can be roughly sketched as follows. The speech input is first converted into a word lattice, which represents

---

* Authors listed in alphabetical order.

D.N. Christodoulakis (Ed.): NLP 2000, LNCS 1835, pp. 283–292, 2000.

possible sequences of words making up the complete string. From this graph, various modules concerned with syntactic and semantic analysis derive the most likely sequence of utterance segments and for each segment construct a syntactic-semantic structure, the source language VIT (Verbmobil Interface Term, [3]). Both the transfer module and the context evaluation module take this VIT as input. Transfer maps the source language VIT to a target language VIT [5], which is handed over to the English generation module. Thus, the format of the VIT plays a crucial role in the overall system. Figure 1 shows the excerpt of the system architecture just described.

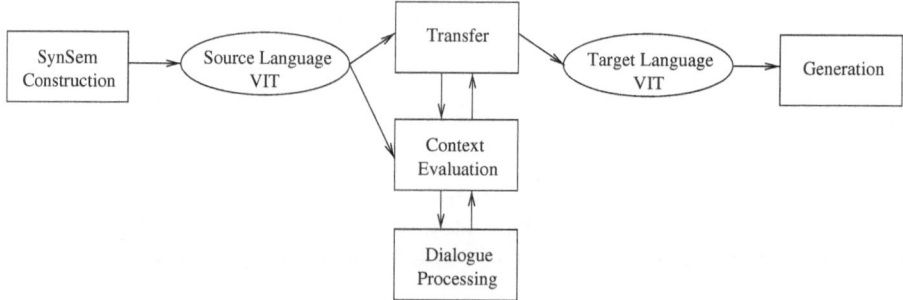

Fig. 1. Excerpt from the Verbmobil system architecture

Importantly, parts of the VIT can be left *underspecified*. This concerns scope ambiguities and lexical ambiguities, which thus need not be resolved by syntactic and semantic analysis in order to produce a well-formed representation. The transfer module decides whether a disambiguation is necessary, and if it cannot perform it itself on the basis of information about the immediate context, as represented in the VIT, transfer asks ConEval to do so.

3   Context Evaluation Tasks

3.1   Referential Ambiguities

When translating from German to English, the gender of pronouns often needs to be modified. Consider the example *Der Zug fährt um drei Uhr ab, aber er hat oft Verspätung*, which translates to *The train departs at three o'clock, but it is often delayed*; the German *er* is masculin, but since it refers to an inanimate entity (the train), its translation is not the literal equivalent *he*, but *it*. Getting this right presupposes anaphora resolution and thus a context representation (and therefore commercial MT systems regularly produce bad translations for such examples).

Other prominent cases of referential ambiguity are German demonstrative pronouns such as *da, dann, es* and *das*. For example, *da* can be used to refer both to a location (corresponding to *there*) or to a point in time (*then*); in addition, it can be a causal subordinator or merely a discourse particle that does not refer at all. Similarly, *dann* can refer to a point in time (*then*), signal a causal relation (*therefore*), or act as a discourse particle. *Es* and *das* are personal pronouns that in dialogues are very often used as event anaphors — but sometimes refer to objects as well, which needs to be reflected in the translation. In short, resolving anaphoric pronouns is one of the key contextual reasoning tasks. One of the semantic analysis modules (prior to ConEval) first tries to perform the resolution solely on the basis of syntactic feature agreement; but whenever this does not lead to a unique antecedent, ConEval makes the decision.

Besides pronouns, the referents of certain definite NPs are resolved. While this is not necessary for their translation, it serves to keep the context model up to date, which records what speakers are talking about and what commitments they make. To give an example, when a speaker asks *Can we meet in Hamburg on Tuesday* and the partner responds *Yes, I arrive in the city on Monday*, we infer that *the city* and *Hamburg* refer to the same entity (of the type GEO-LOCATION).

3.2   Lexical Ambiguities

Even in the limited domain of arranging travel and appointments, there are many verbs and nouns requiring lexical disambiguation. In some cases, the syntactic environment and the lexical sorts provide sufficient information to detect the reading — these are handled directly by the transfer module, which can inspect the syntactic representation of the utterance. Other verbs require semantic knowledge and sometimes reference resolution. The German *annehmen*, for example, translates to *to assume* if it occurs with a complement clause (*Ich nehme an, dass X = I assume that X*). When it has a direct object, it usually means *to accept*; however, if the object is a pronoun (e.g., *ich nehme es an*), we need to know the referent: If it is a proposition, we have the *assume* case, and if it is an entity, the reading is very likely to be *accept*, but some additional sort checking is necessary.

Inferences in the knowledge base can enter the disambiguation process in the case of the German noun *Essen*, which covers both the English *lunch* and *dinner*. If the time is known, as in *Das Essen soll um 19 Uhr sein* ('Dinner should be at 7 p.m.'), it can be used to decide on the translation. Alternatively, world knowledge is employed to decide that the most likely reading in *das Essen vor dem Theaterbesuch* is *dinner*, since it takes place before the theater play.

An important class of ambiguities arises from discourse particles, which are especially abundant in spoken German. Many of them are ambiguous, and quite a few do not have any straightforward English translation at all — instead, their function in discourse needs to be signalled by different means. Furthermore, in many cases a particle is best dropped from the translation process altogether, if its existence is due merely to certain conventions in spoken German, which do not carry over to English.

Consider, for example, the particle *doch*. As the sole response to an utterance, *Doch!* denies what the other participant has just said and at the same time reaffirms the (opposite) opinion of the speaker. In English, one would say something like *Yes it is!* (or use the more specific verb in question). However, when *doch* is used within a sentence, it has (at least) the following two functions. In *Das ist doch klar*, *doch* signals that the proposition is assumed to be shared knowledge, or self-evident. Probably the closest English rendering is *That's clear anyway*. But in a sentence like *Lassen Sie uns doch einen Termin ausmachen*, *doch* merely smoothens the utterance and should not be translated at all, since English does not offer a corresponding word. Thus, the translation is "Let us arrange an appointment".

In order to deal with particles of this kind (on the German side, there are about 30 of them), we have devised a taxonomy of *discourse functions* indicating the type of pragmatic impact a particle has in a specific context. By inspecting the context, we assign a discourse function to each particle, and transfer employs this information when deciding how to translate the particle, or whether to drop it. Our discourse function taxonomy is explained in [12].

3.3 Dialogue Act Recognition

The third task of ConEval is to determine the *dialogue act* (DA) underlying the utterance — a pragmatic label somewhat more specific than a traditional speech act, but still general enough to be useful across domains of interaction. Examples are GREET, INIT, SUGGEST, REJECT, GIVE_REASON, CLARIFY; the complete list of DAs currently used, including definitions, is given in [2]. To identify the DA underlying the current utterance, we use a set of symbolic rules testing for prosodic, syntactic, and semantic features, the DA of the preceding utterance or turn, and certain domain-specific inferences. Very few of these rules are strict implications; rather, combinations of features in general merely indicate the presence of a certain DA. To model this uncertainty, we use a mechanism of weighted default rules that determines the most likely DA for the utterance. This scheme is described in [10].

3.4 Propositional Content

The DA represents the illocutionary force of an utterance independent of the specific propositional content; this content, however, is an equally important source of information for many disambiguation tasks (e.g., a verb reading can depend on the topic, or semantic field, of the previous utterance). Following Levinson [8], who states that "the illocutionary force and the propositional content of utterances are detachable elements of meaning," we treat the combination of DA and propositional content as the most abstract utterance representation in our context model. It is used for disambiguations in the following utterances as well as for purposes of generating a dialogue protocol [1]. The propositional content is represented as a (domain-specific) concept–role configuration. For illustration, when the dialogue partners negotiate the means of transportation and the system is given the utterance *Maybe we should fly*, we construct this representation, which is also represented in a description logic, see Section 4.

```
dialogue-act:suggest
topic: travelling
prop_cont: has_action:move_by_plane
           has_agent: speaker_hearer
```

3.5 Temporal Reasoning

Interesting questions arise in dealing with the temporal descriptions that are negotiated between dialogue partners searching for an appointment slot. The vast majority of temporal descriptions used is heavily underspecified (e.g., *on Monday / on the fourth / at half past*), and the full description of the date is clear only in the context. Although in many cases knowing the full description is not necessary for a correct translation, there are several situations in which that knowledge is needed. In addition, ConEval performs a *consistency check* with all the temporal descriptions, in order to detect errors made by the users as well as errors that occurred in the system's speech recognition phase. Therefore, it is necessary that the system keeps track of the precise dates that are being negotiated in the course of the dialogue, and thus every temporal description is internally 'completed' by the system (e.g., *on Monday* is automatically enriched with the information on week, month, and year).

To this end, we have developed a two-step mapping procedure. First, expressions in a 'shallow' representation language TEL are constructed for temporal expressions [6]. TEL expressions on the one hand abstract from variant linguistic realizations of the same temporal entity (e.g., *ten fifteen, quarter past ten, fifteen minutes past ten, ...*) but on the other hand are still "close enough" to the linguistic surface so that they can be efficiently computed from the linguistic predicates in the VIT. In the example, the common TEL expression is `tod:10:15`. In order to keep track of temporal referents and to reason about them, TEL expressions are in turn mapped to more abstract *interval expressions*: feature structures that allow for easy computation. These representation levels and the mapping between them are described in [11].

3.6 Context Evaluation Tasks Interact

Having described the various tasks that ConEval has to fulfill, we now illustrate that these tasks can interact heavily, and thus no straightforward "serialization" is possible. Furthermore, as already mentioned when discussing dialogue acts, a framework of strictly monotonic deduction rules is not suitable for dealing with the many cases of vague information. Thus, for DA recognition and disambiguation, we use a mix of strict implications and weighted default rules, as described below in Section 5.

Regarding the interactions, consider the utterance *Da kann ich nicht* and recall that the pronoun *da* can refer to a location or to a point in time ('There/Then I can't make it.'). While the DA in this case can be determined (REJECT) without knowing the referent of *da*, we need this information in order to complete the propositional content, and of course in order to allow for the correct translation: *there / then*. With an utterance such as *das passt mir* ('that's OK for me'), however, we need to disambiguate *passen* and resolve the anaphor *das* before the dialogue act can be identified. In *Ich würde es vorziehen*, the referent of the pronoun *es* is required to disambiguate *vorziehen* between *prefer* and *move forward*.

Due to complications of this kind, we do not employ a strict sequence of lexical disambigation, anaphora resolution, DA recognition. Rather, we try to perform disambiguations as soon as enough information is available, which can be the case at different steps in the overall utterance interpretation procedure; see Section 5.

4   Modelling the Context

As the previous section has made clear, we need contextual knowledge for many disambiguation tasks. In this section, we describe how we build up a context model of the unfolding dialogue. For this purpose, we use the description logic LOOM [9]. We first characterize the terminological knowledge (TBox), i.e., our ontology and domain model, and then the assertional knowledge (Abox), i.e., the representations of specific utterances.

4.1   Ontology and Domain Model

The ontology and domain model are partitioned into a *linguistic* part and a *conceptual* part. The former consists of the language-specific lexicons (content words), which are subsumed by a common ontology of *sorts*. The sort hierarchy is used by several modules in the "deep analysis" line of Verbmobil; from the ConEval perspective, it is an interface to the transfer module, which often asks about the sort of an anaphoric expression (i.e., its antecedent, which ConEval needs to find).

The conceptual part of the domain model is meant to be inter-lingual and holds configurations of abstract situations underlying the conversations in the domain, as well as some world knowledge that supports disambiguation, such as the tendency that theater plays take place in the evening, which is sometimes needed to disambiguate *Essen*, an example mentioned above.

4.2   Flat and Deep Abox Representations

The terminological knowledge is *instantiated* when an utterance is processed by ConEval, represented in Loom, and integrated into the context model. This two-step process makes use of two distinct, but linked Abox representations, which correspond to the two parts of the ontology/domain model:

1. A syntactic/semantic utterance representation passed to the context module is mapped to a "flat Abox" (FAbox) representation that largely mirrors the syntactic structure. The FAbox instantiates only concepts from the linguistic portion of the ontology/domain model.
2. The FAbox is then mapped to a "deep Abox" (DAbox) which abstracts over a range of linguistic realizations and forms a conceptual representation. At the beginning of a dialogue, the DAbox is built from the first utterance (i.e., its FAbox); further segments update the existing DAbox. A subset of the DAbox for an utterance forms the propositional content (see Section 3.4).

For illustration, Figure 2 shows the slightly abridged FAboxes of three utterances and their common DAbox. The first utterance by speaker 1, *Können wir uns um 14 Uhr in Berlin im Hotel Adlon treffen?* ('Can we meet at two p.m. in Berlin at the Adlon hotel?') gives rise to the shown FAbox and to the upper part of the DAbox (`meeting` and associated case roles, whose names are omitted for brevity). The response by speaker 2, *Ja, dann bin ich gerade in der Stadt angekommen* ('Yes, at that time I will just have arrived in the city'), creates the `arrive` instance in the DAbox with the `agent` role pointing to `sp2` and the `location` role pointing to the already existing `city1` representing 'Berlin', so the anaphoric definite noun phrase *the city* has been resolved. Finally, speaker 2 adds *Das liegt auch sehr zentral* ('It also is centrally located'), creating the `located` instance in the lower portion of the DBox, which points to `hotel1` since the pronoun *das* was resolved to *hotel*.

Several additional roles have been omitted from the figure to enhance readability. Notably, every 'root' instance of a segment network in the FAbox is linked to the root instance of the preceding segment as well as to the root instance of the previous utterance. Thus, the context representation as a whole consists of the sequence of individual utterance segment representations in the FAbox and the referential-level DAbox. The linguistic objects in the FAbox are linked to their referents in the DAbox. Thus, when transfer requires the sort of a pronoun's referent, we follow the link from the pronoun–instance in the FAbox to its corresponding DAbox object and read off the sort information.

5 Constructing the Representations

Here is a brief overview of our procedure for building the FAbox and the DAbox, which also includes the various disambiguation tasks. The algorithm processes each individual segment in turn and consists of seven steps.

Step 1: Local disambiguation rules operate directly on the incoming syntactic representation. Some are strict rules yielding definite results, others only assign weights to the different results and leave the matter open.

Step 2: Mapping the syntactic representation to the FAbox. Mostly, the structure is identical, with an important exception being the pieces of information on dates and times; these are assembled into a single TEL expression (cf. Section 3.5) to enable reasoning with them. Besides, several types of ambiguities

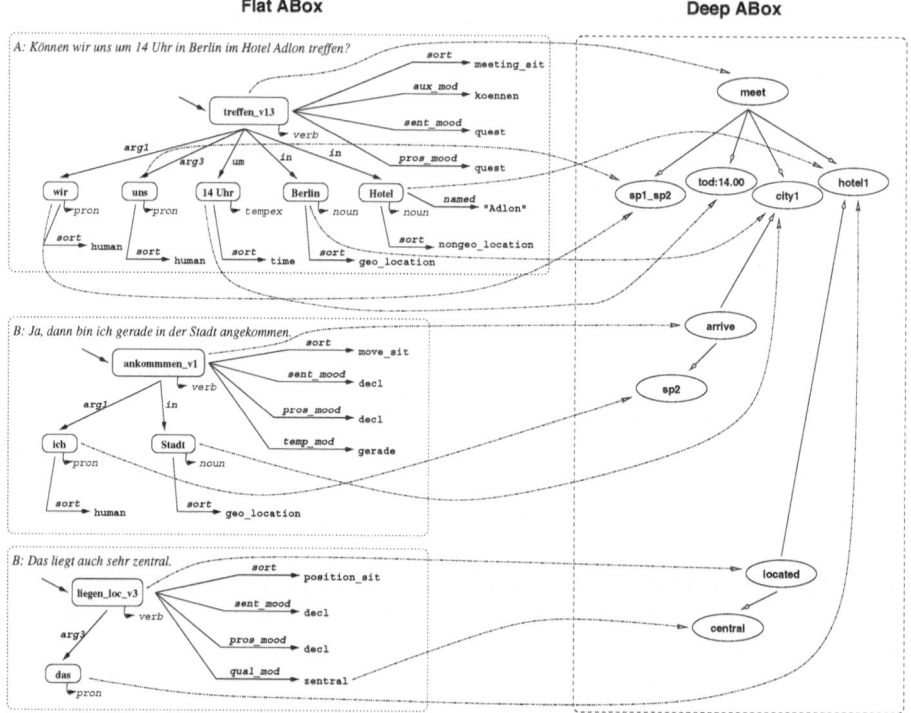

Fig. 2. Flat and Deep Abox covering 3 utterances

are preserved in the FAbox. ([7] describes the different forms of underspecification on the VIT level and the way they can be handled with description logic.)

Step 3: In a first step of abstraction, concepts like PROPOSING, SUITING
are inferred from the verb and its case frame. Also, the polarity of the utterance
is computed from the predicates and the negations (if any) with their scopes; for
example, *Monday sounds not bad* is mapped to POSITIVE, but *Monday is not
very good for me* to NEGATIVE. These concepts are represented as additional
types of the FAbox instance.

Step 4: Using a mechanism of weighted default rules (see [10]), the most
likely *dialogue act* is computed from the FAbox and the intermediate concepts
determined in step 3. The dialogue act, too, becomes an additional type of the
FAbox instance.

Step 5: Using object-oriented programming techniques (i.e., *methods*) in
LOOM, the FAbox is mapped to the DAbox. By employing anaphora resolution
techniques, for each FAbox instance representing a noun phrase, it is being decided whether it refers to an already existing DAbox object; if not, a new one is
created. The verb and its case frame are mapped to a more abstract configuration
of concept and roles, as illustrated above.

Step 6: On the basis of the dialogue act and the anaphor antecedents, the propositional content is determined; it forms a subset of the DAbox representation.

Step 7: For the remaining lexical and scope ambiguities, disambiguation rules relying on sorts, dialogue act, or anaphor antecedents fire and modify the weights that have (possibly) already been attached in Step 1. The answers with largest weights are taken to be the final disambiguation results.

To illustrate the role of the different steps, we discuss the disambiguation of the German noun *Bereich*, which can refer to either a local *area* or to a temporal *range*.

In some cases, the local context is sufficient to decide on the reading. In *der weite Bereich*, the adjective *weit* ('wide') can only modify a local description. When a prepositional phrase modifies *Bereich*, the internal argument can indicate the correct reading: In *der Bereich um 17 Uhr passt gut*, it is a temporal reading ('the range around 5 o'clock is fine'), as *17 Uhr* denotes a point in time. On the other hand, a location is referred to in *der Bereich um den Bahnhof*, as *um den Bahnhof* means 'around the station'. This kind of reasoning applies not only to the proposition *um* but also to *vor*, *nach* and a few others.

In more difficult cases, the dialogue act and propositional content of the previous utterance have to be inspected. Consider the exchange *Wie wäre es am 17. Mai? – Ja, dieser Bereich ist günstig* ('How about the 17th of May? – Yes, this range is possible'). In order to disambiguate *Bereich*, we check that the propositional content of the question (whose dialogue act is SUGGEST) is a temporal entity (which can be read off the DAbox). Alternatively, in *Wie wäre es in der Nähe vom Bahnhof? – Ja, dieser Bereich ist günstig* ('How about close to the station? – Yes, this area is good') the propositional content of the question is a location and thus *Bereich* is assigned the appropriate reading.

Finally, here is an example for a temporal inference supporting the disambiguation. The German word *außer* corresponds to the English phrases *in addition to* and *except for*. The two readings are present in the largely parallel sentences *Außer Montag geht auch Dienstag* and *Außer Montag geht es um 17 Uhr*, both of which contain two temporal expressions (Monday/Tuesday, and Monday/5pm, respectively). The fact that the types of 'Monday' and 'Tuesday' cannot be unified leads to the in-addition-to reading of *außer* in the first sentence, whereas in the second, the types of 'Monday' and '5pm' can unify, which triggers the except-for reading.

6   Conclusions: Gaining Efficiency and Robustness

Translating spontaneous speech poses more difficulties to contextual reasoning than typed text: Due to the properties of spontaneous speech, the real-time requirements, and the likelihood of speech recognition errors, efficiency and robustness are of paramount importance. We have described the context evaluation of the Verbmobil system, which is triggered by the transfer module in accordance with the 'resolution on demand' strategy: Only when transfer identifies an ambiguity as relevant with respect to the target language is a request sent to the evaluation module. This is the first means of increasing efficiency, as the relatively expensive contextual reasoning need not be waited for when "simple" utterances are processed by the system. Nonetheless, the context model constructed by our module needs to be kept up-to-date, and therefore each utterance is being processed by the module; but when no request from transfer arrives, this happens in parallel with the late stages of the translation process and does not affect it them.

We have described the five taks that the context module tackles in Verbmobil, and the three levels of representation used in this module. Progressively richer representations are constructed sequentially, but when a disambiguation request can be answered on a lower level, the response is sent right away, and the move to the next level in our module again happens in parallel to the remaining translation work.

References

1. Alexandersson, J., Poller, P.: Towards Multilingual Protocol Generation For Spontaneous Speech Dialogues. Proc. of the Ninth International Workshop on Natural Language Generation (INLG-98), Niagara-On-The-Lake, Canada (1998)
2. Alexandersson, J., Buschbeck-Wolf, B., Fujinami, T., Kipp, M., Koch, S., Maier, E., Reithinger, N., Schmitz, B., Siegel, M.: Dialogue Acts in VERBMOBIL-2 – Second Edition. Verbmobil Report 226, DFKI GmbH, Saarbrücken (1998)
3. Bos, J., Rupp, C.J., Buschbeck-Wolf, B., Dorna, M.: Managing Information at Linguistic Interfaces. Proceedings of COLING-ACL'98, Montreal (1998)
4. Buscbeck-Wolf, B.: Resolution on Demand. Verbmobil Report 196, Universität Stuttgart (1997)
5. Dorna, M., Emele, M.: Semantic-based transfer. Proceedings of the 16th International Conference on Computational Linguistics (COLING 96), Copenhagen (1996)
6. Endriss, U.: Semantik zeitlicher Ausdrücke in Terminvereinbarungsdialogen. Verbmobil Report 227, TU Berlin (1998)
7. Küssner, U.: Applying DL in Automatic Dialogue Interpreting. Proc. of the International Workshop on Description Logics (DL'97), Gif sur Yvette/Paris (1997)
8. Levinson, S.: Pragmatics. Cambridge University Press, Cambridge/UK (1983)
9. MacGregor, R., Bates, R.: The loom knowledge representation language. Technical Report ISI/RS-87-188, USC Information Sciences Institute, Marina del Rey (1987)
10. Schmitz, B., Quantz, J.: Dialogue-Act Type Recognition in Automatic Dialogue Interpreting. Proc. of the The Sixth International Conference on Theoretical and Methodological Issues in Machine Translation (TMI), Leuven (1995)
11. Stede, M., Haas, S., Küssner, U.: Understanding and tracking temporal descriptions in dialogue. In: Schröder, B., Lenders, W., Hess, W., Portele, T. (eds.): Computers, Linguistics, and Phonetics between Language and Speech. (Proc. of the 4th Conference on Natural Language Processing - KONVENS '98), Verlag Peter Lang, Frankfurt (1998)
12. Stede, M., Schmitz, B.: Discourse particles and discourse functions. To appear in: Machine Translation.
13. Wahlster, W.: Verbmobil: Translation of face-to-face dialogues. Proc. of the Third European Conference on Speech Communication and Technology, Berlin (1993)

Improving the Accuracy of Speech Recognition Systems for Professional Translators

Yevgeny Ludovik and Ron Zacharski

Computing Research Laboratory
New Mexico State University
Las Cruces, New Mexico USA
{eugene,raz}@crl.nmsu.edu

Abstract. Our principal objective was to reduce the error rate of speech recognition systems used by professional translators. Our work concentrated on Spanish-to-English translation. In a baseline study we estimated the speech recognition error rate of an off-the-shelf recognizer to be 9.98% We describe two independent methods of improving speech recognition systems for translators: a word-for-word translation method and a topic-based method. The topic-based approach performed the best, reducing the error rate significantly, to 5.07%.[1]

1 Introduction

Frequently, professional translators view the source document on a computer and type their translation of that document in a word processor running on that same computer. Our goal is to improve the throughput of these translators by using speech recognition. The problem with using current off-the-shelf speech recognition systems is that such systems have high error rates for similar tasks. For example, Ringger in [5] reports an average error rate of 30% for recognizing spontaneous speech on a specific topic. However, the error rate of careful, paced, speech can be as low as 5% if the vocabulary is severely limited or if the text is highly predictable and the system is tuned to that particular genre.[2] Unfortunately, the speech of expert translators producing spoken

---

[1] This material is based upon work supported by the National Science Foundation under award number DMI-9860308 to Onyx Consulting, Inc. Any opinions, findings, and conclusions or recommendations expressed in this publication are those of the authors and do not necessarily reflect the views of the National Science Foundation.

[2] The error rate of large vocabulary research systems (20,000-60,000 word vocabularies), on average, around 10% (as reported by various researchers at the International Conferences on Acoustics, Speech, and Signal Processing and the ARPA Spoken Language Systems Technology Workshops (see, for example, [7], [4], [1], [8]). The popular press has reported slightly lower results for commercial systems. For example, PC Magazine [3] compared Dragon's NaturallySpeaking and IBM's ViaVoice (both continuous speech recognition systems with approximately 20,000 word vocabularies). They evaluated these systems by having

D.N. Christodoulakis (Ed.): NLP 2000, LNCS 1835, pp. 293-303, 2000.
© Springer-Verlag Berlin Heidelberg 2000

translations does not fall into any of these "easy to recognize" categories. In the translation task described above, an obvious question to ask is if an analysis of the source document could lead to a reduction of the speech recognition error rate. For example, suppose we have a robust machine translation system and use it to generate all the possible translations of a given source text. We could then use this set of translations to help predict what the translator is saying. We describe this approach in §2 below. A simpler approach is to identify the topic of the source text and use that topic to aid in speech recognition. Such an approach is described in §3.

2   Using Machine Translation

One general approach is to analyze the on-line source text using a machine translation (MT) component. Hopefully, this analysis will help the speech recognition program cut down on perplexity by having the recognition program make choices only from the set of possible renderings in the target language of the words in the source language. In this section we describe the MT subsystem in detail. The function of the subsystem is to take Spanish sentences as input and produce a set of English words that are likely to occur in translations of these sentences. For example, if the Spanish text is

Butros Ghali propone vía diplomática para solucionar crisis haitiana.

we would expect the translation set to include the words (among others):

{*Boutros, Ghali, proposes, nominates, suggests, diplomatic, solution, route, to, settle, Haitian, crisis*}

Hopefully, this translation set will be a good predictor of what the translator actually said.

2.1 Subsystem Components

The MT subsystem consists of 4 components:
*   morphological analysis
*   dictionary lookup
*   lexical transfer
*   morphological generation

The morphology analyzer takes Spanish words as input and outputs a set of possible morphological analyses for those words. Each analysis consists of the root word and a

---

five speakers read a 350 word text at a slow pace (1.2 words/second) after completing a half hour training session with each system. The average recognition error rate was 11.5% (about 40 errors in the 350 word text). An evaluation of the same two systems without training resulted in a recognition error rate of 34% [2].

set of feature structures representing the information in the inflectional morphology. Examples are given in table 1.

Table 1. Examples of morphological analysis

Word	Feature structure
Cafés	((root café) (cat n) (number plural))
Veces	((root vez)(cat n)(number plural))
Pequeña	((root pequeño)(cat adj)(gender f))
pronuncio	((root pronunciar)(cat v) (tense preterit indicative) (person 3)(number singular))
Podría	((root podrir) (cat v) (tense imperfect indicative) (person 3)(number singular))

The dictionary lookup component takes a feature structure produced by the morphological analyzer, looks up the root-word/part-of-speech pair in the dictionary, and adds information to the existing feature structure. During the course of the project we used two dictionaries: a hand built one and one based on the Collins Spanish-English Dictionary. The words in the hand built one were derived from performing a corpus analysis of a set of 20 Spanish test documents. All the unique words in this corpus, including proper nouns, were included in the dictionary (approximately 1,500 words). A few examples are shown in table 2.

Table 2. Examples of morphological analysis and lookup

Word	Dictionary entry
actividad	((root actividad) (cat n) (sem activity energy) (gender f))
comenzar	((root comenzar)(cat v) (sem begin start) (verbtype irregular 129))
cuestion	((root cuestion)(cat n) (sem question dispute problem issue)(gender f))
obligar	((root obligar)(cat v)(sem compel enforce obligate oblige)(verbtype irregular 7))

The feature, verbtype irregular, identifies a particular verb inflectional paradigm and was used to filter the output of the morphological analyzer. That is, if the morphological analyzer labeled a verb as (verbtype irregular 129) and the dictionary entry did not include this feature value pair, the feature structure representing this verb would be removed from the candidate set of morphological analyses.

The second dictionary we constructed was derived from an electronic version of the Collins Spanish-English dictionary. This second dictionary contained 44,000 entries. The format of each entry was similar to the entries shown above except that it contained no information about inflectional paradigms. When evaluating the complete natural language component, we compared the results of using these two dictionaries. These results will be discussed in a later section.

Transfer

At the end of the dictionary lookup phase, for each word in the Spanish sentence we have a feature structure containing the information in the dictionary entry along with the parameter values that were gained from morphological analysis. One feature, sem, contains the possible English translations of that Spanish word. In the transfer stage this Spanish feature structure is converted to one or more English feature structures; one feature structure is created for each value in the sem field. For example, in the sample dictionary entries shown above, the feature structure associated with an instance of *actividad* encountered in some text will be 'transferred' to two English feature structures: one for *activity* and one for *energy*. Similarly, encountering an instance of *cuestion* in some text, will result in the creation of four feature structures; those representing the English words *question, dispute, problem,* and *issue* and encountering an instance of one of the inflected forms of *obligar* will result in the creation of four English structures representing the words *compel, enforce, obligate,* and *oblige*. In addition, the transfer component converts other features in the Spanish feature structure to features recognizable to the English morphological generator.

English Morphological Generator

The morphological generator takes feature structures as input and produces correctly inflected English words. Examples of the feature structures used as input and their associated output are illustrated below:

Table 3. Examples of generation

Feature structure	English words
(root run) (cat v) (form progressive))	are running
((root man) (cat n) (number plural))	men

2.2 Evaluation

Suppose we wish to have a user dictate an English translation of a Spanish sentence that appears on a computer screen. This Spanish sentence is input to the natural language subsystem and the output is a set of English words. In the ideal case, the words in the English sentence the translator dictates are contained in this set. If one could offer a sort of guarantee that the words of any reasonable translation of the Spanish sentence are contained within this set, then incorporating the natural language subsystem into a speech recognition system would be relatively straight forward; the vocabulary at any given moment would be restricted to this word set. If, on the other hand, such a guarantee cannot be made then such an approach would not work. The evaluation of the natural language subsystem is designed to test whether reasonable translations are contained within this set of words.

The test material consisted of 10 Spanish newspaper articles. The articles were translated into English by two independent translators. (These translations were not used in any way during the construction of the dictionaries.) Table 4 shows the results using the 1,500 word hand built dictionary (T1 and T2 are the two different English translations).

Table 4. Percent of words in translation that are not in word set:
1,500 word dictionary

Document number	T1	T2
1	30.4	26.78
2	30.08	33.16
3	37.88	32.66
4	32.03	39.21
5	27.69	23.79
6	31.3	27.79
7	32.85	30.25
8	34.84	31.32
9	43.8	40.05
10	34.95	34.5

Average: 32.77

The table shows that roughly $1/3$ of the words in the translations the professional translators produced are not in the set of words produced by the natural language subsystem. The experiment was replicated using the 44,000 word dictionary. These results are shown in table 5.

Table 5. Percent of words in translation that are not in word set:
44,000 word dictionary

Document number	T1	T2
1	66.87	68.85
2	63.84	64.03
3	69.64	69.91
4	71.09	72.63
5	71.79	70.08
6	69.57	69.79
7	71.22	71.43
8	75.28	69.54
9	76.2	73.9
10	67.31	67.09

Average: 70.00

In this case over $^2/_3$ of the words in the English translations were not in the associated word sets constructed by the natural language subsystem. Most of the differences between the two dictionaries could perhaps be due to the lack of proper noun coverage in the 44,000 word dictionary. Recall that the smaller dictionary contained proper nouns. To test whether this was the case, the 44,000 word dictionary was augmented to include words from the 1,500 word dictionary that were missing from the 44,000 word one. The results of using this dictionary are shown in table 6.

Table 6. Percent of words in translation that are not in word set:
augmented dictionary

Document number	T1	T2
1	33.08	34.15
2	32.72	36.22
3	39.55	36.68
4	35.67	40.0
5	35.38	31.46
6	37.39	33.53
7	41.57	37.82
8	42.7	38.51
9	51.14	48.58
10	40.45	40.89

Average: 38.57

As these results show this augmented dictionary still did not perform as well as the initial 1,500 word dictionary. One possible explanation for this discrepancy is that perhaps the 1,500 word dictionary produced a larger set of words; that is, it contained more possible translations per Spanish word. This conjecture was evaluated by comparing the size of the set of words produced per Spanish sentence per dictionary. An analysis showed that this was indeed the case. The 44,000 word dictionary generated, after transfer, an average of 1.55 English words per original Spanish word while the

1,500 word dictionary generated an average of 2.14 English words. Summarizing the results so far, we have seen the importance of having proper nouns in the dictionary. In a production version of our natural language subsystem having an onomasticon (a proper noun dictionary) would be crucial. We have also seen the importance of having many potential translations of a Spanish word. This illustrates the importance of tuning a dictionary to a specific task. For example, if our task was automatic Spanish to English translation then the number of English translations in the Collins dictionary would be adequate. However, for our application the more English translations per word in the dictionary the better. Even the 1,500 word dictionary did not have adequate coverage of potential translations of words. For example, *diplomática* was translated as "diplomatic means" by one translator and as "diplomatic route" by the other but both dictionaries lists it only as an adjective meaning "diplomatic" and as a noun meaning "diplomat". *Pronunció* was translated as "said" by one translator but the dictionaries list the meaning as "pronounce", "declare", and "utter".

The next experiment looked at a totally different approach to determining which words to put in the word set. This approach added frequent English words to the set of words derived using the morphological approach described above. To construct this set of frequent words, we analyzed a hand collected 2 million word corpus of English newspaper articles (gathered for the topic recognition component of this project) to determine word frequency information. We used the 800 most frequent words as the recognition word set. The results are illustrated in table 7.

Table 7. Percent of words in translation that are not in word set: frequent wordlist & morphological analysis

Document number	T1	T2
1	12.7	14.21
2	16.89	15.05
3	19.22	18.62
4	10.68	16.05
5	13.85	12.53
6	13.33	12.39
7	15.41	14.01
8	19.1	16.38
9	17.47	15.25
10	19.42	16.61

Average: 15.46%

The reason this combined method was tested was that often English open class lexical items are added to the translation. For example in one document, the phrase *solucionar crisis haitiana* is translated as "resolution of Haitian crisis", and the English *of* does not have a direct correlate in the Spanish phrase. While this combined method appears to work moderately well, it still does not have sufficient coverage to function as a method for generating the complete recognition vocabulary. That is, it cannot guarantee that the words of any reasonable translation of a Spanish sentence would be contained in the set of English words generated from that sentence. Since we cannot use these results to constrain the recognition vocabulary we evaluated a different method — one that uses topic recognition.

3   Topic Recognition Method

The basic idea behind the topic recognition approach is to identify the topic of the source language text and then use that topic to alter the language model for speech recognition.

3.1   Topic Recognition of Source Text

We used a naïve Bayes classifier to identify the topic of Spanish online newspaper texts. We eliminated the common words in the text under the rubric that these words are unlikely to serve as cues to the topic of the text. For example in English, *the*, *of*, *with*, and *a* provide little information as to the topic of the text. We constructed this common word list by computing the most frequent words in a one million word corpus of Spanish newspaper text. We edited this list to remove potential topic cues. For example, *Pinochet* was the 46th most frequent word and *Clinton* was the 65th most frequent, but they serve as potential topic cues. We evaluated this topic identification technique by examining its performance on identifying four topics: Pinochet, the crisis in Paraguay, the crisis in Kosovo, and Clinton's impeachment. For each topic we had a 500k training corpus (roughly 60,000-75,000 words). The test data for each topic consisted of 20 articles from web-based newspapers. The average size of these articles was 335 words. The recognition results are shown in the following table:

Table 8. Topic recognition results

words used in recognition	Pinochet	Paraguay	Kosovo	Clinton
all	100	100	100	100
100	100	100	95	100
50	95	100	95	100
25	90	95	90	95

We also evaluated an enhanced version of the algorithm on a corpus of 20 newsgroups[3]. For this evaluation we used a different method of creating a common word list. For each word encountered in any training document we computed the entropy of the distribution of a topic given the word, and picked up 100 words having the highest

---

[3]   The   corpus   was   obtained   from   Tom   M.   Mitchell's   website (http://www.cs.cmu.edu/afs/cs.cmu.edu/user/mitchell/ftp/ml-examples.html).

entropy. So no manual editing of the list was involved: high entropy for a given word meant that this word could not be a good topic cue. In this evaluation for each value of the number of words used in recognition we carried out two sets of experiments. In the first one, the first 500 documents of each topic were used as training data, and the last 500 - as test data; in the second set the last 500 documents were used for training, and the first 500 - as test data. The recognition results are presented in the following table.

Table 9. Topic recognition results for 20 newsgroups, 100 common words excluded

words used in recognition	Recognition rate, %
all	76.76
100	53.15
50	48.41
25	44.23

If a common word list contained just one word and all other words were used in recognition, the recognition rate was 76.89%.

3.2 Using Topic Language Models

In the previous section we have described a robust topic recognition system and how the system performed in identifying the topic of Spanish texts. Once we have identified the topic of the text to be translated we use that topic to identify which language models we wish to use in recognizing the text. We have constructed topic language models by processing manually collected half million word corpora for both the crisis in Kosovo and Clinton's impeachment.[4] These corpora were collected from a variety of online news sites including CNN, the Washington Post, the New York Times, the New York Daily News, and the Milwaukee Journal Sentinel. One significant question is whether a language model as small as a half a million words will have any impact on the error rate for speech recognition. We evaluated this approach by comparing the error rate in dictating 8 texts using IBM's ViaVoice dictation system. The results are shown in the table below. The 'without' row is using the recognizer without our topic system and the 'with' row uses it with topic identification.

---

[4] These topic models were constructed using the IBM ViaVoice Topic Factory. The topic language models augment the general language model.

Table 10. Dictation error rates

text #	without	with
1	8.59	5.62
2	8.67	6.15
3	10.16	4.46
4	8.88	4.75
5	12.07	5.26
6	13.47	6.15
7	8.17	4.93
8	9.8	3.27
average	9.98	5.07

4   Conclusion

We investigated two different approaches to reducing the error rate of speech recognition systems used by professional translators. The first approach used a word-for-word machine translation system to constrain recognition vocabulary. An evaluation of this approach showed that we cannot guarantee that the words of any reasonable translation of a Spanish sentence will be contained in the set of English words generated from that sentence. Thus, we cannot constrain our recognition vocabulary to just those words produced by the machine translation system. How to use the 'less than ideal' results of a machine translation system for speech recognition remains the subject of future work. Our second approach identified the topic of the source language text and then used that topic to alter the speech recognition language model. Our results suggest that topic-based methods are particularly effective for reducing the error rate of speech recognizers for translators: in our study the error rate was reduced from 9.98 to 5.07%.

References

1. Hochberg, M, Renals, S., Robinson, A., Cook, G.: Recent Improvements to the Abbot Large Vocabulary CSR System. Proceedings of the International Conference on Acoustics, Speech, and Signal Processing (1995) 69-72.
2. Keizer, G.: The Gift of Gab: CNET Compares the Top Speech Recognition Apps. (1998) (http:// 204.162.80.182/Content/Reviews/Compare/Speech/).
3. Poor, R.: Speech Recognition: Watch What You Say. PC Magazine on-line (1998) (http:// home.zdnet.com/pcmag/features/speech/index.html).
4. Renals, S., Hochberg, M.: Efficient Evaluation of the LVCSR Search Space Using the NOWAY Decoder. Proceedings of the International Conference on Speech and Language Processing (1996) 149-152.

5. Ringger, E.K.: A Robust Loose Coupling for Speech Recognition and Natural Language Understanding. Technical Report 592. University of Rochester Computer Science Department (1995).
6. Ringger, E.K., Allen, J.F.: A Fertility Channel Model for Post-correction of Continuous Speech Recognition. Proceedings of the Fourth International Conference on Speech and Language Processing (ICSLP'96) (1996).
7. Robinson, T.,, Christie, J.: Time-first Search for Large Vocabulary Speech Recognition. Proceedings of the International Conference on Acoustics, Speech and Signal Processing (1998).
8. Siegler, M.A., Stern. R.M.: On the Effects of Speech Rate in Large Vocabulary Speech Recognition Systems. Proceedings of the International Conference on Acoustics, Speech, and Signal Processing (1995).

Generic Parsing and Hybrid Transfer in Automatic Translation

Christopher Laenzlinger, Sébastien L'haire, and Juri Mengon

Laboratoire d'analyse et de technologie du langage (LATL)
Département de Linguistique
Université de Genève
{laenzlinger,lhaire,mengon}@latl.unige.ch
http://latl.unige.ch

Abstract. In this paper, we describe an automatic translation system involving French, Italian, English and German. The technique used in this project consists of the classical steps parsing-transfer-generation. Input sentences are parsed by a generic, multilingual parser based on the Principles & Parameters Theory of Chomsky's Generative Grammar. The transfer mechanism acts on hybrid structures that mix lexical items with abstract semantic information. Finally, a principle-based generator produces correct output sentences.

1 Introduction

The ITS-3 project (LATL, University of Geneva) aims at developing an automatic translation system involving French, Italian, English and German. The translation system relies on the classical architecture parsing-transfer-generation. Parsing of the source language is done by the IPS system, which is based on the Principles & Parameters Theory of Chomsky's Generative Grammar [7]. The parser produces rich syntactic structures containing lexical, phrasal, grammatical and thematic information, and focuses on (i) robustness, (ii) genericity, and (iii) deep linguistic analyses. These properties are essential for a system to be efficient in multilingual large-scale applications. The transfer mechanism acts on hybrid structures, called pseudo-semantic structures (PSS), that mix lexical items with abstract semantic information. On the basis of these PSS, the generation module produces correct output sentences. We will illustrate how the translation works with German as the source language and French as the target language.

In section 2, we distinguish the principle-based approach used in our parsing and translation systems from traditional rule-based approaches. We will underline the claim that principle-based approaches are well-suited for multilingual applications. Section 3 presents an overview of the IPS parsing system. We will discuss its modular architecture and its most important characteristics. In section 4, we address some issues of semantic representation within machine translation applications. Different transfer mechanisms will be taken into account and we will situate our hybrid structures among them.

D.N. Christodoulakis (Ed.): NLP 2000, LNCS 1835, pp. 304–314, 2000.

2   A Principle-Based Approach to Machine Translation

Rule-based grammars, such as the context-free backbone of GPSG (Generalized Phrase Structure Grammar, [12]) or LFG (Lexical Functional Grammar, [5]), mainly use context-free phrase structure rules to describe the surface pattern of a language. Parsers relying on these architectures have undeniable advantages due to their well-known mathematical and computational properties. These lead to a uniform description of the grammar and therefore make it easier to calculate their run-time complexity. Furthermore, there are several efficient parsing algorithms available for grammars expressed with phrase structure rules. Despite these advantages, rule-based grammars often also have to face serious shortcomings. The most important ones concern the construction specific property and language dependent nature of these grammars. Thus, moving towards a multilingual application normally implies a radical increase of the number of phrase structure rules.

To cope with the problem of the construction specific and language dependent nature of phrase structure rules, other formalisms favor the use of constraints to restrict the surface pattern of input sentences. A constraint-based approach using unification is realised in the HPSG formalism (Head-driven Phrase Structure Grammar, [15]).

The Principles & Parameters Theory follows a different approach [6], [7]. Within this framework, grammar is conceived as a set of interactive well-formedness principles, which hold cross-linguistically, and as a set of language specific parameters. One of the widely discussed issues within principle-based approaches is the way of applying the principles efficiently. Since these are expressed declaratively within the theory, their procedural use in a natural language processing system needs to be defined (see also [3]). There is a naive approach which consist of two steps: First, candidate structures are generated. Second, the structures that violate at least one principle are filtered out. This approach has two main shortcomings: it acts in an inefficient, *generate and test* manner and tends to overgenerate. This is the reason why a considerable effort is made for finding solutions to these problems. Fong [11] proposes an optimal ordering for the application of the various principles, whereas Dorr's parser [8] presents a co-routine design, consisting mainly of two interacting modules: one module builds skeletal syntactic structures and the other module modifies these structures according to principles and constraints of Government & Binding Theory [6]. In the PRINCI-PAR system [14], a distinction is made between constituents and their compact description. The costly operation of going through the syntactic structures for the application of the principles is replaced by a simpler test on the compact descriptions. Thus, new structures are only generated if their descriptions satisfy all the principles.

In the parsing system (IPS) presented in this paper, the problem of overgeneration is handled by a particular component: the attachment module. We will discuss this component in further detail in section 3.1 (see also [21]). As we will see in the following sections, the principle-based framework has proven to be a useful model for the implementation of a large-scale, multilingual translation system (see also [8]).

3   IPS: The Parsing System

3.1   The Modularity of the IPS System

IPS is a principle-based parsing system which differs from rule-based parsers in its modular architecture. The principles of the grammar are implemented as generic modules which dispense with phrase structure rules. These modules hold for all languages. Other modules realize language specific properties, corresponding to the values of the parameters.

The core generative module is the phrasal $\overline{X}$ module that rules the general geometry of syntactic structures. All constituents are formed according to the $\overline{X}$ format in 1.

(1) $[\text{Specifier}_{list} \ X^0 \ \text{Complement}_{list}]_{XP}$

For reasons of simplicity, the bar-level is not represented, while Specifier and Complement are implemented as (eventually empty) lists of maximal projections. X^0 stands either for a lexical head (Adv, Adj, N, V, P) or for functional category (C, I, D, F)[1], which all project a maximal projection (XP). The uniformity of phrasal projections is obtained by the category-independency of the $\overline{X}$ schema implemented in the IPS parser. Consider the position of verbal complements in German. Objects can either precede or follow the verb depending on their category (nominal/prepositional vs. sentential). Hence, they can occur either in the Complement list on the right of the verbal head or in the Specifier list on the left of this head[2]. Actually, the attachment module specifies which type of constituents can be attached in the Complement or the Specifier list of a specific head. The attachment procedure builds configurations determined by properties of selection from heads and filtered by agreement relations. Further relationships between constituents are construed through the chain-building module. Formally, the parser inserts traces into a syntactic structure and tries to bind them to their potential antecedents. As general devices, the $\overline{X}$ schema and the attachment module act as generating operations. To avoid overgeneration and ungrammatical parses, the IPS parser makes use of top-down filtering constraints, such as the thematic module, establishing thematic/semantic relations between a predicate and their arguments (agent, theme, goal, etc.), and the case assignment module, which requires that each lexical nominal phrase be

---

[1] The following abbreviations are used to represent the constituents: Adj(ective), Adv(erb), N(oun), V(erb), P(reposition), D(eterminer), C(omplementizer), I(nflection) and F(unctional).

[2] In this sense, the Specifier and Complement lists do not have an interpretative function as such. Thus, a true verb complement can occur in a Specifier list, while an adjunct (i.e. a specifier-like element) can occur in a Complement list.

associated with a morphological or abstract case (nominative, accusative, dative, etc.).

Among language specific modules for German, the IPS parser applies the verb second (V2) constraint, the Object-Verb (OV) vs. Verb-Object (VO) ordering conditions, the constituent reordering rules ('scrambling'), and some other constraints on Germanic specific constructions (extraposition of relatives, infinitivus pro participio, co-ordination possibilities, etc.).

3.2   A Parsing Example

We will illustrate how the parsing mechanism works with the following example.

(2) Dann hatte Hans es · dieser Frau   geschenkt.
     Then   had   Hans it   this   woman offered
     'Then John had offered it to this woman'

The IPS parser first undertakes a lexical analysis by segmenting the input sentence into lexical units and inserting them as edges for all their possible readings into a chart (Table 1, step 1). For every lexical unit in the chart, a maximal projection is provided and lexical features are transferred to the syntactic level (XP) in accordance with the Projection Principle (Table 1, step 2). Then, the attachment module checks all possible attachments to the Spec and Compl positions of the various XPs[3] according to selectional rules and thematic relations. The backbone of the clause structure is CP $\prec$ IP $\prec$ VP, as shown in Table 1, step 3. IP functions as the right complement of CP, while VP is the right complement of IP. In main clauses, the first constituent, here the AdvP *dann* ('then'), occupies the Spec-CP position. The tensed verb is raised to C^0, the second position of the clause. This is a simple way of applying the V2 constraint. Since tensed auxiliaries are base-generated in I^0, the chain formation module links the raised auxiliary in C^0 with its trace in I^0 (Table 1, step 4). In our analysis, the DP subject *Hans*, is attached in Spec-VP. The OV configuration of German results from the attachment of the DP[4] complements *es* ('it') and *seiner Frau* ('to his wife') in Spec-VP. The past participle *geschenkt* ('offered') occupies the V^0 position. At this point, the filtering interpretative modules verify that each argument of the clause is assigned a thematic role from the verb (thematic module), while every nominal phrase is in the right configuration to receive a case (case module, Table 1, step 5). The whole syntactic structure of the input sentence is given in Fig. 1, step 3.

---

[3] The IPS parser is a bottom-up licensing parser that pursues all alternatives in parallel. Its parsing strategy is called 'right-corner attachment' [21]. A more detailed description of the parsing algorithm used in IPS can be found in [21].

[4] We follow Abney's DP-hypothesis [1] according to which the determiner is the head of nominal expressions and takes an NP as its complement.

Steps	Process
1	Lexical analysis: [*dann*_{Adv}] [*hatte*_I] [*Hans*_D] [*es*_D] [*dieser*_D] [*Frau*_N] [*geschenkt*_V]
2	Projection: Project a maximal projection XP for every element in the lexical analysis chart 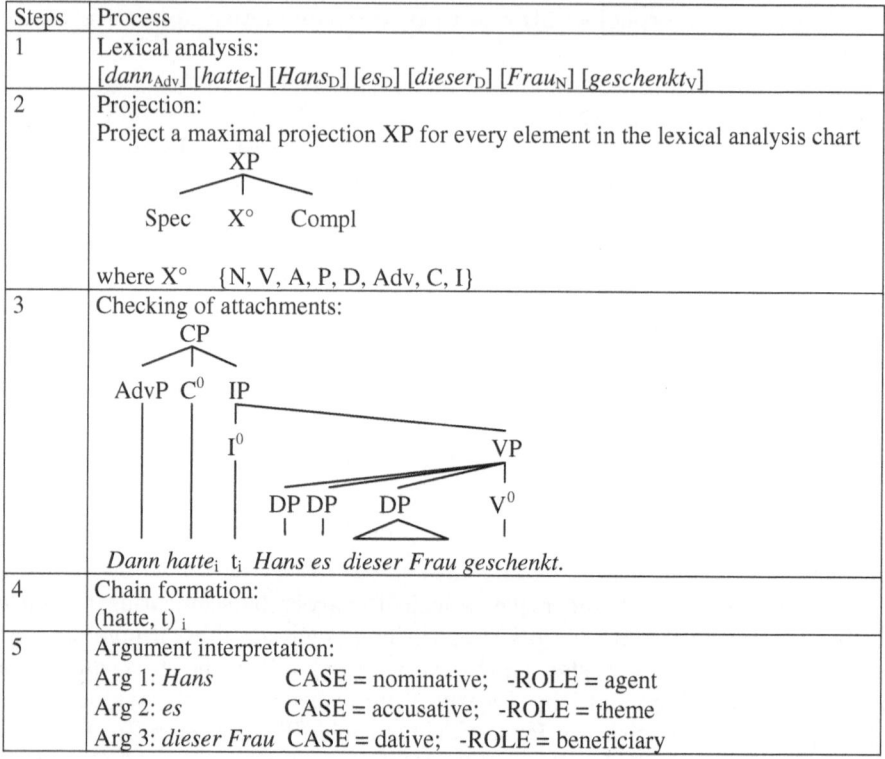 where $X°$ {N, V, A, P, D, Adv, C, I}
3	Checking of attachments: *Dann hatte*_i t_i *Hans es dieser Frau geschenkt.*
4	Chain formation: (hatte, t) _i
5	Argument interpretation: Arg 1: *Hans* CASE = nominative; -ROLE = agent Arg 2: *es* CASE = accusative; -ROLE = theme Arg 3: *dieser Frau* CASE = dative; -ROLE = beneficiary

Fig. 1. Parsing process consists of five major steps: lexical analysis, projection to the syntactic level, checking of attachments, chain building and argument interpretation

3.3   Characteristics of the IPS System

In addition to modularity and genericity, the IPS system is characterized by two other important properties: robustness and the use of rich and deep linguistic analyses. Robustness is required for any system to be efficient in large-scale, domain independent applications. For this aim, the IPS parser can treat unknown words and includes so-called micro-grammars to recognize idioms, parentheticals, temporal expressions, etc. Robustness is increased by the 'no-failure' parsing strategy according to which incomplete analyses are still exploitable through partial parsing results. In addition, the use of rich and deep linguistic information allows the parser to be involved in a large number of multilingual, domain independent applications, notably in automatic translation. This approach to language processing contrasts with the quite wide-spread approach adopted by shallow parsers or NP-identifiers which consists of using some kind of linguistic pre-processing adapted to specific applications.

4   The ITS-3 Translation Project

The ITS-3 project (Interactive Translation System) aims at developing a translation tool using abstract interface structures. Before presenting the system, we will first address the question of transfer techniques in automatic translation.

4.1   Automatic Translation and Transfer Techniques

The lexical and syntactic transfer is the most often used technique nowadays in the field of automatic translation. Among the well-known systems using this technique, we can mention Systran [18] and Ariane [4]. The lexico-structural transfer is situated halfway between word-to-word translation and the interlingua technique, as represented in Fig. 2 (see also [13]). The translation procedure goes as follows: In a first step, a given input sentence from the source language is analyzed by a parser. A functional structure is then derived from this analysis, with a various abstraction level. Such an intermediate structure is also called 'interface structure'. In a further step, the transfer component provides a corresponding functional structure for the target language via the lexical transfer and some structural adaptations [19]. In a final step, the generator produces a grammatical output sentence in the target language on the basis of this interface structure.

The lexico-structural transfer technique shows three major drawbacks, which we have already experienced in a former version of our translator, the ITS-2 system [16]. First, it requires a very large lexicon providing multiple lexical correspondences associated with syntactic, semantic and contextual information. Then, the use of semantic and pragmatic analysis beyond the sentence is needed to obtain satisfactory translation results. If the context is not restricted to a limited domain, the system has to make use of huge knowledge and context representations. At this stage, such structures are far from being conceivable for a large-scale application in automatic translation. Finally, the lexico-structural transfer technique is language dependent to a large extent. Thus, a multilingual translation system treating, for instance, 9 languages would need one transfer module for each pair of languages, which means 72 modules in total. Such a system will rapidly become unmanageable.

The interlingua approach is situated on the opposite edge of the transfer methodology schematized in Fig. 2 (see also [13]). The interlingua constitutes abstract representations of linguistic entities and functions as a third language connecting the source language to the target language. The main advantage of the interlingua is that it is not language dependent. Thus, it can be used in a multilingual system treating pairs of typologically distinct languages. In addition, the interlingua can encode contextual, extra-linguistic information (inference, anaphora, presupposition, etc.). Nevertheless, the interlingua method presents a serious disadvantage: the complexity and abstractness of its linguistic representations. So far, it is not feasible to give a set of universal abstract representations for all nouns (notations) and verbs (events), which should hold across languages. Due to the complexity and heaviness of totally abstract linguistic and contextual

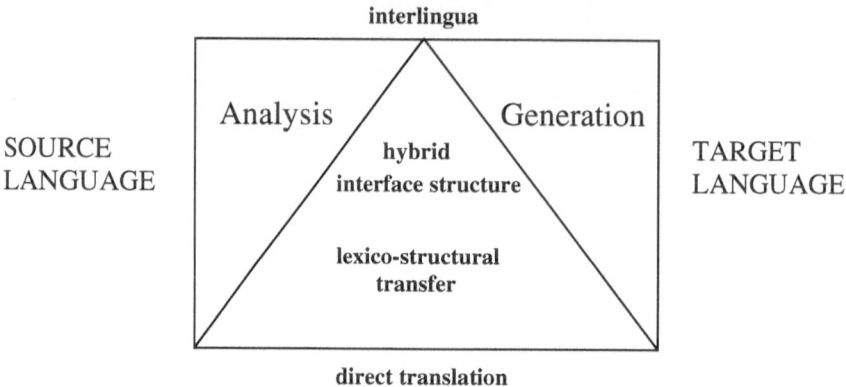

Fig. 2. Pyramid representing the level of abstractness of the different translation techniques

representations, this type of approach to automatic translation is very difficult, if not impossible, to be used in a large-scale, domain independent application.

As a solution, one can appeal to hybrid interface structures, mixing restrictive lexical transfer with abstract semantic representations. This kind of interface component has already been used in various forms in the field of automatic translation. We can mention, among others, the interface structures used in the Core Language Engine [2], which translates English sentences into formal representations called quasi-logical forms. These structures constitute context-sensitive logical forms capable of extra-linguistic interpretation (inference, anaphora, presupposition, etc) and adapted to a cross-linguistic application in automatic translation.

In the following section, we will present another form of hybrid interface structures called *pseudo-semantic structures*. They constitute language independent representations that contain as much abstract (non-lexical) linguistic information as possible for an efficient translation task.

4.2   Translating with *Pseudo-semantic Structures*

The ITS-3 system is a translation tool, that uses abstract interface structures called *pseudo-semantic structures* (PSS) [10]. The PSS present a hybrid nature combining abstract semantic representations with lexical items, and constitute the entries to the syntactic generator GBGen [9].

To understand how the entire translation procedure works, we will pursue the translation into French of the German example given in 2. The first step following the syntactic analysis consists in transferring the parse results (Table 1, step 3) to the interface PSS. A PSS contains information about the clause, namely its mood ('real' or 'unreal'), its tense and aspect specifications. The continuum relationship between Reichenbach's [17] Event time (E) and Speech time (S) values[5], intermingled with aspectual specifications (progressive, perfective, imperfective), are used to determine the tense information in the PSS. Further information about the voice, negation and the utterance type of the clause is specified. Since the PSS involve lexical transfer, which is restricted to open class lexical categories such as verb, noun, adjectives and adverbs[6], the predicate is specified as a lexical entry. Every PSS can have a certain number of 'satellites' that depend on it. Thus, non-clausal arguments are represented as DP-structures (DPS) of operator-property type, corresponding to the syntactic determiner-noun relation. AdvPs are represented in so-called characteristic structures (CHS). Thus, for sentence 2, a PSS like 3 is derived.

(3) Pseudo-Semantic Structure:[7]

```
Information about the clause
    Mood              : real      (= indicative)
    Tense             : E<S       (= past)
    Aspect            : (non progressive, perfective)
    Voice             : active
    Negation          : not negated
    Utterance type : declaration
    Predicate         : schenken/offrir
    Satellites        : {1, 2, 3, 4}

Information about the satellites
  1.) DPS                        2.) DPS
      Theta role : agent             Theta role : theme
      Property   : Hans              Property   : delta
      Operator   : delta            Operator   : delta
                                     Gender     : neutral
                                     Person     : 3rd person
                                     Number     : singular


  3.) DPS                        4.) CHS
      Theta role : beneficiary       Value      : when
      Property   : Frau/femme        Scope      : sentential
      Operator   : demonstrative     Characteristic : dann/ensuite
      Number     : singular
```

The semantic representation given in 3 constitutes the entry to the GB-Gen generator. According to this information, the output sentence will be a

---

[5] The possible values are E<S, E=S, E>S.

[6] The use of lexical transfer seems at present unavoidable in automatic translation, provided that the assignment of abstract, lexically independent, values to open lexical categories is too complex, often inconceivable, to be computed efficiently (see also [20])

[7] 'delta' indicates that the values assigned here are left un(der)specified.

declarative, active, non negated clause. The tense will correspond to the French 'indicatif plus-que-parfait' (indicative past perfect). The verbal predicate *offrir* ('to offer') takes three arguments and a sentential temporal modifier. Since the external argument ('agent') is generated as the subject of the clause, it will be realized as a DP attached in Spec-IP. The second argument is a direct object personal pronoun, which will have to be cliticized to the auxiliary in I^0 and will be linked to a trace in its base position, Compl-VP. The third argument will be realized as a 'dative' indirect object with the subcategorized preposition *à*, and will be expressed as the PP *à cette femme* ('to this woman'). This prepositional complement will be attached to Compl-VP. Finally, the fourth satellite will be syntactically generated as a AdvP attached to Spec-VP. The resulting sentence and structure are given in Fig. 3.

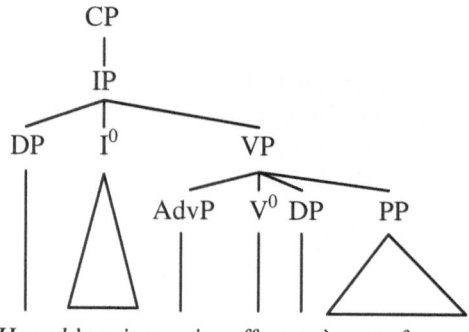

Hans l_i'avait ensuite offert t_i *à cette femme.*
'Then John had offered it to this woman.'

Fig. 3. Syntactic structure of the sentence in the target language generated by the GBGen generation system

5   Conclusion

We have described an automatic translation system based on the classical architecture parsing-transfer-generation. We have illustrated the way in which the system works with German as the source language and French as the target language. On the basis of the Principles & Parameters Theory, a generic and modular parser has been developed for multilingual NLP applications. The parser provides rich syntactic structures. From the parse results, the transfer component derives hybrid lexico-semantic representations, called pseudo-semantic structures (PSS), which combine lexical transfer with abstract functional and semantic information. This mixed transfer technique takes advantage of both the simplicity of the lexical transfer procedure and the abstractness of the interlingua approach. Furthermore, the PSS are specially adapted to the linguistic information contained in the deep syntactic structures provided by the parser. As a last step, the generation module takes the PSS as input and gives back correct output sentences.

Acknowledgements

We would like to thank Eric Wehrli, Paola Merlo and Thierry Etchegoyhen for their valuable comments and fruitful discussions on this paper. We would also like to thank Stephanie Durrelman for having gone over the English. This research is supported by a grant from the Swiss National Science Foundation (n⁰ 1214-053792.98/1)

References

1. Abney, S.: The English Noun Phrase in its Sentential Aspect. Ph. D. Thesis. MIT Press, Cambridge, Mass. (1987)
2. Alshawi, H.: The Core Language Engine. MIT Press, Cambridge, Mass. (1991)
3. Berwick, R.: Principles of Principle-based Parsing. In: Berwick, R., Abney, S., Tenny, C. (eds.): Principle-Based Parsing: Computation and Psycholinguistics. Kluwer Academic Press, Dordrecht (1991) 1–37
4. Boitet, C.: GETA Project. In: Nagao, M. et al. (eds.): Machine Translation Summit. Ohmsha, Ltd., Tokyo (1989) 54–65
5. Bresnan, J. (ed.): The Mental Representation of Grammatical Relations. MIT Press, Cambridge, Mass. (1982)
6. Chomsky, N.: Lectures on Government and Binding. Foris Publications, Dordrecht (1981)
7. Chomsky, N., Lasnik, H.: The Theory of Principles and Parameters. In: Chomsky, N. (ed.): The Minimalist Program. MIT Press, Cambridge, Mass. (1995) 13–127
8. Dorr, B.: Principle-based Parsing for Matchine Translation. In: Berwick, R., Abney, S., Tenny, C. (eds.): Principle-Based Parsing: Computation and Psycholinguistics. Kluwer Academic Press, Dordrecht (1991) 153–183
9. Etchegoyhen, T., Wehrle, T.: Overview of GBGen: A Large-Scale, Domain Independent Syntactic Generator. In: Proceedings of the 9th International Workshop on Natural Language Generation. Niagara Falls (1998) 288–291
10. Etchegoyhen, T., Wehrli, E.: Traduction automatique et structures d'interface. In: Actes de TALN'98. Paris (1998) 2–11
11. Fong, S.: Computational Properties of Principle-based Grammatical Theories. Ph. D. Thesis. MIT Press, Cambridge, Mass. (1990)
12. Gazdar, G., Klein, E., Pullum, G., Sag, I.: Generalized Phrase Structure Grammar. Blackwell, Oxford (1985)
13. Hutchins, W. J., Somers, H. L.: An Introduction to Machine Translation. Academic Press Ltd., Cambridge (1992)
14. Lin, D.: Principle-based Parsing without Overgeneration. In: Proceedings of ACL-93 (1993) 112–120
15. Pollard, C.; Sag, I.: Head-Driven Phrase Structure Grammar. University Press of Chicago, Chicago (1994)

16. Ramluckun, M., Wehrli, E.: ITS-2: An Interactive Personal Translation System. Proceedings of EACL, (1993) 446–477.
17. Reichenbach, H.: Elements of Symbolic Logic. Free Press, New York (1947)
18. Ryan, J. P.: SYSTRAN: A Machine Translation System to Meet User Needs. In: Nagao, M. et al. (eds.): Machine Translation Summit. Ohmsha, Ltd., Tokyo (1989) 116–121.
19. Tucker, A. B.: Current Strategies in Machine Translation Research and Development. In: Nirenburg, S. (ed.): Machine Translation. Theoretical and Methodological Issues. Cambridge University Press, Cambridge (1987) 22–41.
20. Vauquois, B., Boitet, Ch.: Automated Translation at Grenoble University. In: Slocum, J.: Machine Translation Systems. Cambridge University Press, Cambridge (1988)
21. Wehrli, E.: L'analyse syntaxique des langues naturelles. Problèmes et méthodes. Masson, Paris (1997)

Two Applications for a Non-context French Generator

Laurence Balicco, Salaheddine Ben-Ali, Claude Ponton, and Stéphanie Pouchot

Equipe CRISTAL-GRESEC
ICM - Université Stendhal,
BP 25, 38040 Grenoble Cedex 09, France
Phone: 33 (0) 4 76 82 68 33 / 33 (0) 4 76 82 68 62
{Laurence.Balicco,Salaheddine.Ben-ali, Claude.Ponton,
Stephanie.Pouchot}@u-grenoble3.fr

Abstract. Thanks to our researches on Natural Language Generation in French; a non context French generator has been implemented. It is based on a linguistic model which allows it to produce several versions of the same content and is adaptable to several domains and applications. We have already associated a first application to the generator. It concerns the description of abstract geometrical figures. We are still working on another application which is the integration of our generator into a information retrieval system.

1 Introduction

In the classical communication diagram, somebody sends a message to someone using a channel and a code. In order to transmit the message content, the code must be common to both interlocutors. In other words, they must speak the same language. In the Man-Machine communication context when the message is produced by a computer, it must provide human users correct and appropriate texts if it is meant to be understood. Automatically generated texts must reproduce natural language characteristics [1].

Our team has brought its research in natural language generation (NLG) in French to a non contextual generator. The following step of this work was to link the generator with some applications. We chose two applications among all possible ones. On one hand, the first one is current and consists in reproducing a corpus of texts written by human subjects. On the other hand, the second will be the integration of our generator into a information retrieval system. Our work on this field is beginning and, in this paper, we only set out a discussion about it.

This article begins with a natural generation process general presentation. Then we present our own generator. In the second and third parts, we talk about these two applications for this generator. We conclude with some perspectives.

D.N. Christodoulakis (Ed.): NLP 2000, LNCS 1835, pp. 315-327, 2000.

2   Natural Language Generation

The aim of natural language generation is to make a computer produce texts, so as to automatically express a content in natural language. This part presents the primary notions of NLG and the generator implemented in our team.

2. 1   Generalities

Classically the generation process is divided into two parts: the "what to say?" and the "how to say it?" [2], [3]. The first of these two steps corresponds to the content determination, the second one to its expression in natural language. The goal is to generate correct texts from a linguistic point of view, moreover these texts must be understandable by a human reader. Actually, the writing of a text, whatever the employed method, must be conceived while thinking of its reading and understanding [4]. Even in a generation context, it is important to take the reader into account.

The quality and the comprehension of the automatically generated texts depend on the pieces of information given to the generation system. This first category of information varies according to the elements to transmit to the readers, that is to say about the context and the application. Formally represented (using graphs, concept...), these data constitute the generator input also called the "what to say?". To go from this step to the "how to say it?", other pieces of information are necessary. They are both given and calculated during the data treatment in order to guide the generator all along the process, while expressing the content in natural language.

Thus, these data are quite diverse:

general: also called universal knowledge, shared by several interlocutors.

about the application: this might be explicit or tacit knowledge, more or less detailed.

linguistic: morphological, syntactic and also semantic.

about the message reader: a model describing him could be elaborated.

2. 2   Our French Generator

Part of our team works on Natural Language Generation in French. A non context French generator has been implemented [5], [6]. It is application independent. It functions on the "how to say it?" level. Our system is basically a surface generator, translating a given meaning into a linguistic form. This being so, the planning of the linguistic structure is a very important component. Thus, it is based on a linguistic model which allows it to produce several versions of the same content. All the versions are elaborated thanks to linguistic operations. We consider two kinds of linguistic operations: grouping operations (like coordination) and referential operations (pronominalisation, for example) [7], [8], [9], [10]. We use grouping operations in order to produce structural modifications when grouping of elements are considered necessary (this approach is already used in [9]) during the realisation phase. A referential linguistic operation replaces textual elements by anaphora like pronouns or ellipsis. For example, we replace noun phrases with personal pronouns, which is a problem that has been dealt with in generation system like [2], [3].

These two kinds of operations are applied on the input of the system (which is a predicative form) to produce variable texts in fluent language. The system uses rules in order to detect the linguistic operations which can be produced simultaneously without changing the text meaning neither creating ambiguous forms. Then, other rules allow or not the implementation of the linguistic operations.

The planning of the surface structure requires choosing words (a message couched in formal terms is mapped onto words) the determination of syntactic structure, morphological operations and surface processing (upper case letters, elisions, etc.). The realisation of linguistic operations is produced when the text is written. We use transformational rules, which are applied to the formal representation of the text. The generator uses general linguistic resources (a lexicon and a grammar which are application independent) and a lexicon which is specifically put together for each application.

The generation process is decomposed into several tasks which are defined in distinct modules (they can be modified without changing the working of the system). It has been implemented in Prolog.

3   First Application: Abstract Networks Descriptions

It was important to test and ·validate our tool by associating applications to it. A possible one for this software is to generate the same types of texts as in a corpus.

3.1   The Context

Human descriptive texts production is a very complex cognitive problem. Actually, whether it is written or not, the description of an object requires the change from a multidimensional structure (the described object) to a single dimension form (the written or oral descriptive utterance). The objective is to linearise something that is not linear [11].

A research has been carried out at the INRIA (French National Institute for Research in Computer Science and Control) in order to study linearisation in text production [12], [13]. The main purpose was to identify strategies used by people who had to describe abstract figures (geometrical networks)[1]. It was also to study the passage from a two dimensions abstract figure to a natural language text.

In that way, a corpus of descriptive texts has been constituted from an experimentation we are going to quickly describe. The material given to the subjects was composed of 16 figures made of colour circles (1.5 cm diameter) linked up to each other by black 1.5 cm segments. There were four types of more or less complex networks: linear structure, hierarchical structure and loop structure.

---

[1] These figures are those used by Levelt [14] for his research on linearisation in oral description.

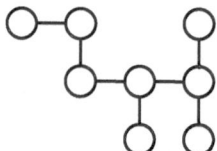

Fig. 1. One of the sixteen Levelt networks

Thirty nine subjects had to describe the 16 figures so that someone else can draw them from their description. The instructions given by the experimenter were: "You will find a booklet containing the figures to be described. Describe each figure so that someone else will be able to redraw it from your description. Note that the person redrawing the figure will be acquainted with the type of figures it contains". There were several experimental conditions: for example, the starting point of the description was either free or indicated by an arrow pointing at the circle from where the subject had to start the description. Thus 624 texts were collected. Then, these texts were captured on a word processing software respecting as far as possible their original form. Spelling and grammar mistakes were not corrected; abbreviations were kept; layout proceedings and presentation (paragraphs, indented paragraphs, etc.) were retranscribed as accurately as possible. Moreover, every text has been retained even if it does not allow to draw the described figure correctly.

In this way, a 108 pages corpus, font 12, 46 525 words, has been gathered. An example of a corpus text is:

« *Une longue ligne joint de gauche à droite: un cercle orange ensuite un cercle vert, un cercle jaune, un cercle rouge, un cercle violet. La ligne est complétée par trois lignes verticales. Le cercle rouge est relié vers le bas à un cercle marron. Le cercle violet est relié vers le bas à un cercle noir et vers le haut à un cercle rose.* »

(A long line linking from left to write: an orange circle then a green circle, a yellow circle, a red circle, a purple circle. The line is completed with three vertical lines. The red circle is connected downwards to a brown circle. The purple circle is connected downwards to a black circle and upwards to a pink circle.)

3. 2   To Simulate a Corpus

An application for our generator is to produce the same kind of texts as described above [15]. This application is very interesting because it includes the two traditional levels of generation: the determination of the text content and its expression in natural language. The process is complete. We have chosen this corpus for several reasons.

First of all because it has been collected to study the linearisation process and description strategies in descriptive texts production. Our aim is to generate texts that are similar to human productions. To reach this goal, knowing the mechanisms that organise these productions seems evident.

Then, the involved world is quite small and so more controllable. The texts are short (from 2 to 15 lines) but nevertheless rich and extremely varied in terms of vocabulary, logical structures and layout. Moreover, manipulated objects are simple (lines and circles) and could easily be studied from a semantic point of view.

All these data could be analysed and then integrated to the generator process with the intention of improving the produced texts quality and to bring them nearer to the natural ones. Finally, we can compare our results (automatically generated texts) to the corpus texts.

When we started to link together the generator and this application, the first produced texts were understandable. However they were poor from a linguistic and structural point of view. That is why several studies [16] in different fields have been realised on this set of 624 texts: cognitive (linearisation strategies), semantic (implicit or explicit knowledge and pieces of information), structural (formatting). We also analysed the corpus in order to obtain the basic vocabulary of spatial configuration descriptions. The aim of these studies was first to extract quantitative data and to consider the importance of these data on the uses of the language [17]. We wanted to establish rules and/or criteria able to guide our generating process [18].

3.3   Studies

The cognitive study [12] consisted in analysing each text of the corpus so as to classify them according to the method chosen by the subjects. Thus, three main strategies have been revealed: the tour strategy, the partitioning strategy and the squaring strategy. The tour strategy is based on the principle of connectivity: to go on into the description, the subject chooses as the following node one that has a direct connection to the current one. The partitioning strategy corresponds to a hierarchical division of the figure into a set of subparts, which are themselves formed by basic elements (circles and lines). For the global view of the figure, the subjects talk about squares, T, or more complex forms (reversed 4, deckchair, stairs, etc.). Using the third strategy, the squaring one, the subjects enumerate the circles line by line and/or column by column regardless of their links, that are mentioned afterwards. Descriptions by tour strategy form the majority of the corpus texts

A first study about the content concerned the knowledge that exists inside the texts and the separation of this knowledge into implicit or explicit information used into descriptions. The aim of this study was to determine the common knowledge of the two persons: the writer of the text and the person who must draw the figure thanks to the description. This knowledge can concern the application or be general and, in this two cases, can be explicit or implicit. This study has shown the knowledge necessary to understand easily the texts which facilitate the drawing of the figure. It has underscored the difficulty of determination and classification of this knowledge [19].

In a second study about the content, we searched information elements used to describe a figure, independently of the figure and the used strategy. There are some basic elements: elements from which the content of descriptions is expressed.

The purpose of the first linguistic study was to determine the vocabulary used by the writers. We sorted the terms according to their frequency. So, we know which term is more frequently used to express a given meaning. The vocabulary is made of about 400 canonical forms.

Then, we studied the corpus to know which linguistic operations the writers use. In the corpus there is a lot of coordinations, often by "et" (and) and anaphora: "à sa gauche" (on its left), "le premier" (the first one), "celui-ci" (this)... and some other operations used to describe a figure (for instance the relative pronouns).

The corpus contains a great diversity of layouts. Therefore, we have done a study on the different formatting processes (identifying and inventory) to implement the obtained data in our generator. Some descriptions are composed of a single block of text, without any line feed, but most of the descriptions are segmented in several parts, with more or less visible typographic indicators, from a simple line feed to a numbering list.

The last current study is more general. It does not concern only the generation context. The results will be used in cognitive applications of spatial descriptions. The starting hypothesis is that when someone describes an object, whatever it is, he uses a quite small specific vocabulary to locate the different constituting items of the object the ones in relation to the others. The aim of this study is to determine this specific vocabulary.

3.4   Assessment

As we said earlier, the first produced texts are understandable but poor, and these studies gave some results usable into the generator in order to ameliorate the texts. For example it was difficult to structure texts in paragraphs, and mainly to manage the consequences of the structure on the internal organisation and on their understanding. Some rules are about to be written and used inside the generator.

We have now to complete the studies. Some additional studies are in progress, others become necessary and will soon begin. For instance, we have not drawn up any inventory of the punctuation of the corpus [20]. We are interested in this aspect, especially since studies on punctuation have been done inside our research team [21].

We also have to generalise the vocabulary study to test the existence of a "general vocabulary" of spatial descriptions in French, which can be used in several corpora.

The different kinds of information extracted from the descriptions confirm, if necessary, the relevance use of the texts set. We have identified data that are:

contextual cognitive, linguistic, structural and semantic.

linguistic and that can generally be applied to end up in the creation of models. These models must represent linguistic operations.

experimental with the vocabulary which can be extended to other corpora.

Models are necessary to generate utterances as natural as possible. In the application these models have been developed from the different described studies. The use of a corpus in natural language seems to be essential for carrying out improvements in the automatic production of texts.

4   NLG: A Help to the Information Retrieval

Thanks to the Levelt application we have both validated and integrated some data in our generator. Moreover, it showed us that the user, here a reader, must be taken into account. At the same time, some projects lead in our team deal with Information Retrieval (IR). A new application could concern the improvement of IR. The key idea is to facilitate the search by the user in associating our system to an IR one. So, we will present the problems met during the user-system interaction and how the NLG can improve this.

4.1   The User-System Interaction Problematic

The information retrieval process (Cf. Fig. 2) involves the following actors: the user, the Information Retrieval Engine (IRE) and the database. Three steps must be taken into account and a non well-adapted use, or a miss-understanding of these levels, ends in a more or less important number of responses which are not suitable for the user. The user requests (1) the IRE to resolve a Real Information Need (RIN) [22] corresponding to a set (eventually empty) of Relevant Information (RI) in the database. In order to realise this, he builds a Perceived Information Need (PIN) which is a mental representation of his RIN. Then he expresses his PIN through a request in natural language. After the processing of this request (2) by the IRE, a set of responses (eventually empty) defined here as Request Results (RR) is sent to the user (3). These responses (relevant or not) depend on many factors. Moreover these responses will be appreciated by the user.

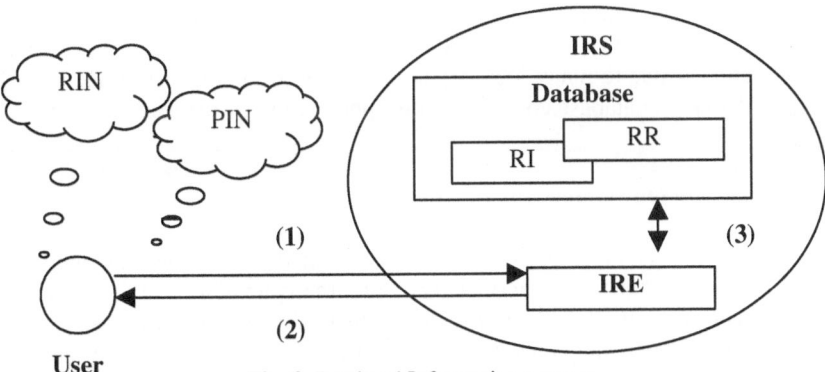

Fig. 2. Retrieval Information process

One of the information retrieval problems consists in obtaining the best matching between the relevant information set (RI) and the request results set (RR). It may be divided into two parts:

The passage from the RIN to the PIN. This operation is not so simple as it seems to be. This passage is very difficult since the user is seeking for something for which he has an anomalous state of knowledge [23] and so he cannot have a correct perception of his RIN. Thus an initial request can be expressed with some information lacks on a particular subject to find all its topics in the database.

The passage from the PIN to the request. Except the case RI = RR, it consists in reducing the production of "noise" (irrelevant information) and of "silence" (relevant information missing). In order to solve this part of the matching problem, the user request must be adapted to both IRE and database. In this particular case, only the user can change deeply the initial request. However, the information system can propose him different ways or helps to perform this change. For example, some systems like Ask Jeeves[2] purpose to the user different reformulations of his initial request. Others, like DigOut4U[3] use a lexicon (synonyms) to reformulate the request.

A second problem concerns the system responses. Indeed, they must be adapted to both request and user. For example, too many non well-presented responses could easily lead to a complex lecture for the user. Another example is the production of responses under a list form when the user request requires a single text. The results presentation ways are taken into account by several information systems. Some of them, like Copernic[4] or BullsEye[5] allow various sorts of result lists. Some others, like DigOut4U or Inforian Quest[6], can realise a short abstract of each result.

A third complex problem to solve is due to the appreciation of the responses by the user. Indeed, only the user is able to appreciate their relevance but he has no criteria to appreciate their number. In the best way, the system proposes some responses but the user does not know if they are exhaustive. In the worst way, the system does not give anything:

relevant information exists in the database but the user request is not well-adapted to the IRE

no relevant information exists in the database

In these two cases, the user generally does not know why his interrogation failed. He needs more information to appreciate this non result. In fact, the relative failure of an interrogation is due to many factors (formalisation of the request by the user, IRE internal functioning, database content, results appreciation by the user...).

4.2   Associating Our Generator to an IRS

We consider here that the IR system is constituted of four tools, the information retrieval engine, a database, a query analyser and the generator. The tools are shared into two kinds of treatment: an informational treatment (engine and database) and a linguistic one (analyser and generator). Between the user and the IRS, an interface is present in order to send all data from one part to the other. The complete process interaction could be divided into two steps: from the user to the system and from the

---

[2] An intelligent agent [24] for the Web Information Retrieval (http://www.askjeeves.com)

[3] Idem (http:// www.arisem.com)

[4] Ibidem (http://www.copernic.com)

[5] Ibidem (http://www.intelliseek.com)

[6] Ibidem (http://www.inforian.com)

system to the user. We are going to study the way our generator could take place into these two steps and the consequences on both user and IRS.

4.2.1 From the User to the System: Query Formulation.
As we said earlier, an initial request can be non adapted to both PIN and IRE. In such a situation, the system can process either in an intelligent way (transparent IR process) or in a co-operative one (interaction with the user) to contribute to the query formulation and reformulation to obtain better results.

Generating paraphrases of such user query will have an important impact on user perception, expression and formulation of his request since he has all possible texts of his RIN browsed.

In this step, we talk about a non classical NLG approach. The message is aimed at a system and not at a human. The first hypothesis we admit concerns the interrogation mode. Actually, if the system does not understand interrogation in natural language, there is no interest for us to generate something for the system. The aim here is to automatically produce user request paraphrases.

The second hypothesis is that all the requests are paraphrased [25] thanks to the generator whatever the initial query is, even if it is understandable and if it allows to obtain correct results. The generator is based on syntactic criteria (syntax correction, query modification or simplification for example). It also uses some IRE knowledge such as the application keywords. These paraphrases must respect the need expressed by the user. For this reason, we think that the best way to preserve the user expressed need is to delimit the paraphrastic transformations into two kinds: a syntactic one and a lexicon one.

Syntactic Transformation. One of the forms of a query reformulation is the transformation of its whole syntactic structure. Indeed a request can be restructured in a new one which has a very different syntax, while preserving the functions of its components and consequently the informative contents, by insertion or erasure of non-significant words as it sounds to be in the following examples: *"Consult this book is very recommended", "It is recommended to consult this book"* and *"This book is very recommended to be consulted".* These transformations are sufficiently effective if the added or erased words are indexed in the consulted database.

A particular case of these syntactic transformations is the sentence voice change. This requires, more than others, the use of a generator. In fact, a passive voice request (PR) may have its identical in the document, but only its equivalent formulated in the active voice (AR). In this case, the only and the most relevant textual passage in the document answering the request, must be the one that contains AR. It seems judicious in matching process that no sentence of the document must be nearest to request PR, more than the sentence AR. Otherwise, it is possible to have no query answer.

Lexical Transformation. Transformation can also be held on lexical bases. As above, the syntactic transformations are more effective if the used words are indexed in the database. An index file, and better a semantic network are some of the tools able to be beneficial for reformulating queries. These lexical resources can be modelised in a conceptual lexicon of the generator. Once done, it is possible to use appropriate words in query transformations especially when it deals with synonyms or nearest sense words. In this way we are sure that no anomalous sense will be carried by the new generated queries. Thus, logically the obtained results will be effective as shown in the following examples: *"Consult this book is very recommended"*, *"It is recommended to consult this monograph"* and *"This book is worth to be consulted"*.

Before submitting anything to the IRE, the generator proposes all the possibilities to the user who chooses the ones that correspond to his need. He can select one or several paraphrase(s) and his initial request. This selection is then sent to the IRE.

This step is represented by this diagram:

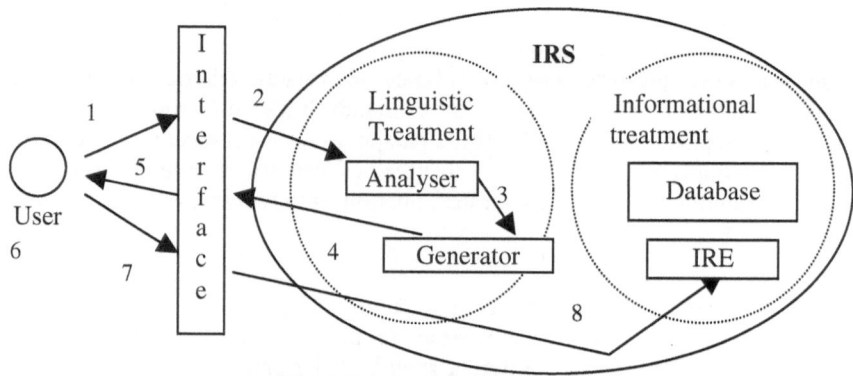

Fig. 3. Request formulation

This process is composed eight steps:
1. The user expresses his information need in natural language to the system interface
2. The interface sends the request to the analyser
3. This query is analysed, its content is given to the generator
4. The generator produces paraphrases of the query and sends them to the interface
5. The interface proposes the paraphrases to the user
6. The user selects one or more solutions, including or not his initial query
7. The selection is sent to the interface
8. The interface submits the selection to the IRE.

4.2.2 From the System to the User: Giving Some Results.
In this second step, the generation approach becomes more classical. The aim is to transmit the found pieces of information to the user. As in the first step, we consider that the whole information flow passes through the generator before being presented to the final user. In our application, there are two kinds of information.

First of all, it seems interesting to provide some ways an explanation of the IRS process to the user. By knowing this process, the user should be able to more appropriately express his query. The interest is also to give the user better answers than "no document found". For instance, it could be possible to explain to the user that the database does not contain information about the query domain. For example, if someone searches for some information about stars in a medical database, our generator could express that the base is not appropriated to his query.

Moreover, if the IRS contains a thesaurus or a hierarchical keywords organisation, it is possible to furnish some ways of widening the search. The generator work is here based on the research processes follow-up which constitutes its input for the natural language production.

Subsequently, we can deal with the given results which are often listed. The generator can improve this presentation by structuring, sorting or even summing up the IRS answers. The user can choose the more appropriate display. In this context we have set up a feasibility study on bibliographic results commentary generation [26].

The supplies of our generator to the machine-man part is represented in this diagram:

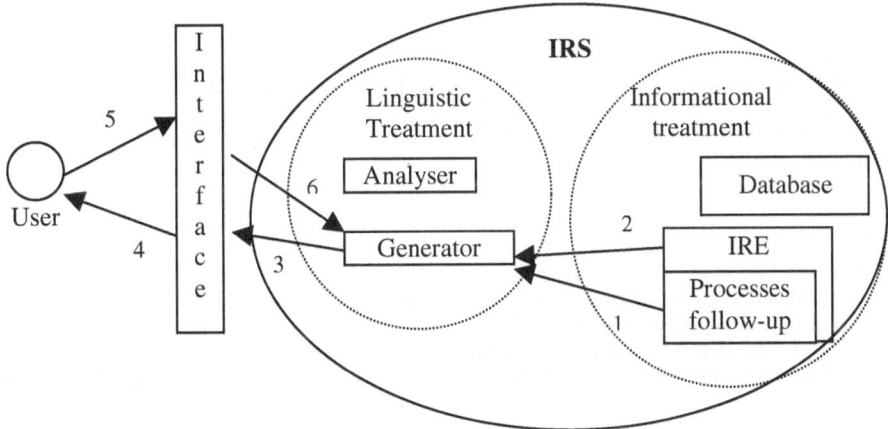

Fig. 4. IRS results

The six steps are:
1. The processes follow-up is given in input to the generation task
2. At the same time, the query results are also furnished to the generator
3. After treatment, the generator transmits these data (expressed in natural language) to the interface
4. The interface sends the results to the user
5. The user can ask the interface for other displays
6. The interface asks the generator according to the user need.

Fifth, sixth, third and fourth steps are repeated as long as the user wants different displays.

5   Conclusion

Our team generator has been elaborated in order to be linked with any kind of application. In this paper we have presented two of them. We wanted them to be very different to test the adaptability of our tool. We have worked deeply on the first application because it was well adapted to our aim. Actually, on the one hand the involved world is small enough and on the other hand the corpus is rich and varied. It was a good context to test the generator and to improve all its production rules. The second application is still less developed. This work has recently begun in order to associate several research themes of our team (NLG, IR and analysis). Its goal is to facilitate the man machine interaction during an information retrieval task. Even if the first application showed us our system limits, it also showed that the produced texts are understandable. Thus, the generator can be used to support the humans in his IR process if it can be associated to an IRS which furnishes its input data.

The improvement of our generator depends on both our current studies (linguistic in particular) and the future associated applications.

References

1. Fuchs, C., Danlos, L., Lacheret-Dujour, A., Luzzati, D., Victorri, B.: Linguistique et traitements automatiques des langues. Hachette Ed. (1993)
2. Danlos, L., Génération automatique de textes en langue naturelle. Ann. Télécommun. 44, n° 1-2 (1989)
3. Nogier, J.F.: Génération automatique de langage et graphes conceptuels. Hermès Ed., Paris (1991)
4. Sfez, L.: La communication. 5th ed., Collection "Que sais-je ?", PUF, Paris (1999)
5. Balicco, L.: Génération de répliques en français dans une interface Homme-Machine en langue naturelle. PhD Thesis, University of Grenoble 2, France (1993)
6. Ponton, C.: Génération automatique de textes – Essai de définition d'un système noyau. PhD thesis, University of Grenoble 3, France (1996)
7. Dale, R.: Generating referring expressions in a domain of objects and processes. PhD Thesis, Edinburg (1989)
8. Mann, W., Moore, J.: Computer generation of multiparagraph English text. AJCL 7:1 (1981) 27-29
9. Horacek, H.: An integrated view of text planning, aspects of automated natural language generation. 6th International Workshop on NLG, Trento (1992)
10. Hovy, E.: Unresolved issues in paragraph planning. In Currents Issues in NLG, Academic Press (1990) 17-45
11. Ehrich, V., Koster, C.: Discourse Organization and Sentence Form: The structure of Room Description in Dutch. Discourse Processes 6 (1983)
12. Bisseret, A., Montarnal, C.: Linearization in spatial descriptions: Tour or hierarchical structures?. CPC, 15:5 (1996) 487-512
13. Montarnal, C.: L'activité de linéarisation lors de la production de textes descriptifs. PhD thesis, Institut National Polytechnique de Grenoble, France (1997)
14. Levelt, W.J.M.: Linearisation in describing spatial networks. In Processes, beliefs, and questions, Reidel, Dordrecht (1982) 199-220
15. Balicco, L.: Génération automatique de descriptions textuelles de figures à deux dimensions. GAT'97, Grenoble (1997)

16. Balicco, L., Pouchot, S.: Analyses d'un corpus en langue naturelle pour la génération automatique de textes descriptifs. Workshop Corpus et TAL, TALN'99, Cargèse, (1999)
17. Biber, D., Conrad, S, Reppen, R.: Corpus linguistics: Investigating language structure and use. Cambridge University Press (1998)
18. Balicco, L. Pouchot, S.: Extraction de données d'un corpus en langue naturelle en vue de l'amélioration d'un système de génération automatique de textes. GAT'99 Grenoble, (1999)
19. Le Boëdec, L.: Connaissances supposées et connaissances posées dans la compréhension automatique d'un discours en langue naturelle. DEA report, University of Grenoble 3, France (1993)
20. Catach, N.: La ponctuation. collection "Que sais-je ?" n°2818, PUF (1993)
21. Mounier, E.: *Etude expérimentale de la segmentation d'un texte en paragraphes.* PhD thesis, University of Grenoble 3, France (1996)
22. Mizzaro, S.: How many relevances in information retrieval?. Interacting with computers, 10:3 (1998) 305-322
23. Belkin, N.J., Oddy, R.N., Brooks ,H.M.: Ask for information retrieval: Part I Background and theory. Journal of documentation, 38:2 (1982). 61-71.
24. Revelli, C.: Intelligence stratégique sur Internet. Dunod Ed., Paris (2000, to be published)
25. Ben Ali, S., Timimi, I.: De la paraphrase à la recherche d'information. CISI'99 ISD of Tunis, (1999)
26. Ben Ali, S.: Reformulation de réponses de systèmes documentaires bibliographiques. DEA report, University of Grenoble 3 (1997)

From Language to Motion, and Back: Generating and Using Route Descriptions

Gérard Ligozat

LIMSI/CNRS & Université Paris-Sud
P.O. Box 133, 91403 Orsay, France
ligozat@limsi.fr

1 Introduction: Toward a Cognitive Approach to Route Descriptions

Route descriptions are natural language productions in response to the question: How do I get from A to B?

How do people produce and use route descriptions? Trying to answer this question is a the main motivation for a long-range and long term research activity which involves various disciplines, including cognitive psychology (studying the cognitive processes involved in the elaboration and use of route descriptions), linguistics (studying route descriptions as texts/discourse), computer science (modeling and simulating the cognitive processes), biology (studying the biological bases of spatial cognition), and robotics.

This paper will describe two typical examples of ongoing work at the LIMSI Laboratory, by Lidia Fraczak [4] and Jacek Marciniak [13] on the subject of route descriptions. It elaborates on previous work by Agnés Gryl [5]. Their work is part of a more general research on the acquisition, memorization and use of spatial information in various cognitive tasks. Specifically, we will focus on two types of contexts: The first one is about generating natural language descriptions in a network-like environment: The main emphasis is on the way pragmatic parameters constrain the production of a natural-language text. The second one involves guiding a virtual robot in an office-like environment. The main focus there is on the integration of the three kinds of information arising from language, perception, and action.

2 How Do I Get from A to B: Generation

2.1 Cognitive and Discursive Processes in Route Descriptions

Fraczak aims at integrating three points of view on route descriptions, inside the general framework of cognitive science. She argues that the study of RDs is relevant to three disciplines at least: Cognitive psychology, where it fits into the domain of studying the ways humans produce and understand discourse, of how they deal with spatial information, storing it and reasoning with it, and includes the study of the evaluation of RDs as exemplified in Denis's work [2,3]. Artificial

D.N. Christodoulakis (Ed.): NLP 2000, LNCS 1835, pp. 328–345, 2000.

Intelligence, where it implies both theoretical work on the representation of and reasoning about space and movement, and applications in various fields such as the development of navigational aids. Linguistics, since RDs are ultimately natural language outputs, and specialized types of discourse, hence should be related to the work on discourse analysis [15],specialized sublanguages [8], and since they are concerned with a well-defined, restricted type of context, should prove useful in understanding how discourse functions as a process rather than as a mere production.

Fraczak characterizes her approach as cognitive and discursive in nature. Cognitive means that it intends to build a plausible plausible model of the way humans process actual route descriptions. As a corollary, it uses empirical data (mainly data collected by Gryl [5] and Corpinot [1], together with additional data related to the specific application it considers (RD in a subway environment). Discursive means that it considers the RD as a discourse with its specific properties, including traces of the cognitive processes involved in its elaboration.

She proposes to distinguish between two sub-processes, which she calls the *route determination process*, a non-discursive process, and the *route description process*, which is a discursive process using discursive knowledge (Fig. 1).

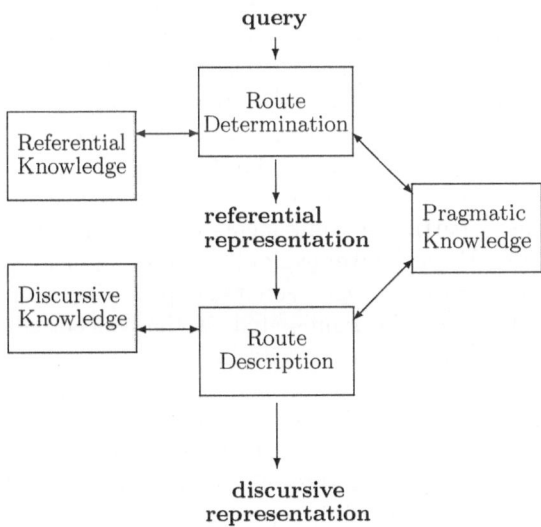

Fig. 1. The architecture of the generating system

2.2   The Model

The global model, then, comprises two basic components:

- The route determination component.
- The route description component proper.

The route determination component generates a *referential representation* by activating and organizing referential knowledge, as well as pragmatic knowledge. This intermediate representation is an abstract, mental representation, which is considered as mostly spatio-visual in character.

The route description component takes this intermediate representation as input. Using discursive and pragmatic knowledge, it generates a discourse representation which is basically linguistic in nature.

Fraczak, hence, makes a distinction between three types of knowledge. **Referential knowledge** refers to knowledge about the world of reference, the actual environment. **Pragmatic knowledge** is understood as knowledge about the context of the discourse (it will include e.g. information about what the description is used for, about the informant / addressee's knowledge). **Discursive knowledge** is concerned with the general laws structuring discourse and their particular instantiation in the actual situation considered.

A distinctive feature of her approach is the introduction of an intermediate level, the *conceptual level*, between the level of reference (objects in the real world) and the linguistic level (the text itself). This allows her to assign a specific structure to each individual level, and clarifies the roles of elements such as e.g. landmarks (are they objects from the real world, linguistic objects, or other?).

Since the structure of the route is related to the conceptual level, whereas the structure of the description itself relates to the textual level, both structures may differ: For instance, particular components of the route structure may remain implicit in the text. Fraczak gives examples as the fragment "you turn left, then right", where an action of progression takes places between the two changes of directions, hence must be represented at the conceptual level, although it corresponds to no marker in the text itself.

The textual structure is obtained as a result of the action of a set of global and local constraints on the discourse. A further assumption is the fact that describing the principles governing the textual structure presupposes having described the principles governing the conceptual structure itself.

Because of the two levels of elaboration, the segmentation of the route can appear both at the determination stage and at the description stage.

2.3   Route Determination

The initial process of route determination is activated in response to the needs expressed by the user. Apart from knowledge about the point of departure and the point of destination, pragmatic knowledge about the preferences, specific needs, particular choices of the user can be used at this stage in order to organize part of the referential knowledge into a referential representation of the route.

A frequently used strategy consists in splitting the process of route determination into two subprocesses: In the first stage, a "rough" path (this is the term used by Maass [12]) is determined. Then, in a second pass, this path is elaborated in terms of segments. Similar ideas are used by Klein [9] who distinguishes between primary and a secondary plan, and Gryl and Ligozat [6], where a first path which does not take the environment into account is refined so as to include it, using cognitive principles such as "minimizing the number of turns".

In the subway application used by Fraczak, the environment is a network of subway lines, and the determination of the path is based on a shortest path algorithm.

2.4   The Referential Representation

This representation is elaborated using knowledge on the spatial properties of the problem (referential knowledge) and possibly temporal aspects (pragmatic knowledge about the projected travel). Fraczak argues that this first representation cannot be assimilated to a cognitive map, for at least three reasons: Firstly, the cognitive map is a source of knowledge, rather than a representation. Second, the referential representation includes temporal, or procedural elements, which have no reason to be part of a cognitive map, the latter being neutral with respect to the use which is made of it. The dynamic component relates to pragmatic elements about the intended action of the user. A third reason is the fact that the referential representation may not be purely "mental": In the particular case of navigational aids, or in the case of robot guiding we discuss below, this representation is described by Fraczak as a "mental restriction" on the environment and its perception.

Once the referential representation is obtained, it can act as input to the process of route description. It determines "what to describe". It has now to be conceptualized, determining in this way "what to transmit", which may differ from "what to express", since part of the information may be left implicit.

2.5   The Route Description Process

As mentioned before, the referential representation has to undergo two types of structuring: A conceptual one, and a discursive one. Both are based on the use of pragmatic and discursive knowledge. Fraczak does not discuss the question of the temporal relationship between the two processes (sequential or parallel).

Conceptual Structuring. This process comprises a global and a local aspect. Globally, at the conceptual level, a route is made of a sequence of **segments** and **relays**. In the simplest case, a route is made of just one segment.

It is important to stress that segments and relays are spatio-temporal units *at the conceptual level*. Hence, they do not necessarily correspond in a simple way to referential units (objects in the real world) or to linguistic units, although they can be correlated to them. In first approximation, a segment is defined as a fragment of the route perceived as continuous, while a relay corresponds to a rupture in the environment. This definition is based on the way the referential environment is conceived, not on objective features. In particular, the same environment may result in different analyzes in terms of conceptual units. For instance, compare two texts referring to the same fragment of route:

Text # 1 *Walk down the walkway,* (segment # 1) *proceed straight on.* (segment# 2)

Text# 2 *Take on your left and get out through the door in front of you,* (segment# 3)*take the walkway on your left* (segment# 4)*down to its extremity,* (relay# 1)*take on your right, then straight on* (segment # 5) *until you get to the intersection,* (relay# 2) *then follow the road along the buildings.* (segment# 6)

The same portion of route which is associated to two segments in text # 1 is associated to four segments in text # 2. In particular, to segment # 2 correspond two segments (# 4 and # 5), although the direction does not change. The intersection which defines a rupture (relay # 2) is not present in the conceptual structure of text # 1.

At the local level, segments and relays are composed of subelements called stages: for a segment, they are segment beginnings, segment transfers, segment ends, and relay transfers for relays.

The second main class of components of the conceptual structure is the class of **landmarks**. Landmarks are classified as path landmarks, simple landmarks, frame landmarks, and auxiliary landmarks. A path landmark is associated to a segment, a simple landmark to a relay. A frame landmark is associated to more than a single global unit (segment or relay). An auxiliary landmark is associated to a single stage.

Examples:

- Path landmarks: *Proceed along* the footpath, *take* the walkway, *cross* the campus.
- Simple landmarks: *You arrive at* building B, *you come upon* an intersection, *cross* the intersection, *you arrive on* Champs Elysees avenue.
- Frame landmarks: *You arrive upon* the campus; *there, you take the road in front of you, you walk until you see the street signs, and you turn left.*
- Auxiliary landmarks: *There, you have to take on your right, following* the buildings on your right, *and crossing* the football stadium, *and the library is the big building.*

In this last example, two auxiliary landmarks are associated to the same transfer segment (whose path landmark corresponds to the direction "on your right").

Finally, *actions* are defined as relations linking a stage and a landmark associated to the same global unit (segment or relay). Fraczak contrasts actions to non-actions which link stages and landmarks associated to different global units. For instance, in Take *the street parallel to this one. At the end, you will* come upon *the intersection of Avenue Foch and Avenue Malakoff,* "take" corresponds to an action, whereas "come upon" corresponds to a non-action. She also notes that verbs denoting actions may appear in the imperative, while verbs denoting non-actions do not. Conversely, only the last type appears with future forms of the verb.

Textual Structuring. According to the usual practice in text generation, the process of textual structuring involves two stages: One is to decide "what to say", i.e. the **textual content**, and the other "how to say it", the **textual expression**. The *textual content* is based on the conceptual content, but it differs from it in the sense that components of the conceptual contents may be left implicit in the text, as long as they can be recovered by the addressee using discursive or pragmatic knowledge. Different choices in this respect will result in different textual structures for the same conceptual structure. For instance, a segment might be represented by its initial phase only (begin segment): "take street A", or contain also the transfer segment ("take street A, follow it"), or by directly mentioning the end segment ("take street A, you get to an intersection").

The *textual expression* is concerned with the textual units contained in the route description. It is composed of two types of textual units: **Sequences** and **connections**. A sequence expresses a list of pieces of information at the conceptual level. A connection connects two sequences or two blocks of sequences together.

A sequence is formed of a **kernel** and of **adjuncts**. For instance, in the fragment of description: *Turn left and walk to the restaurant which is situated at the corner of the street,* there are two sequences connected by the connection "and". The first sequence is formed of a kernel with no adjunct. In the second sequence, the kernel is "walk to the restaurant", and an adjunct is " which is situated at the corner of the street". According to their functions with respect to the conceptual structure, the kernels are further divided into three categories. The first category contains kernels referring to actions. The second category comprises the kernels linked to non-actions. The last category corresponds to expressions introducing landmarks, such as "you can see X", "there is X", or other similar expressions.

2.6   Application to Route Descriptions in a Subway Environment

This general framework is applied to the problem of describing a route in a subway system.

The application to the subway system uses a limited amount of referential knowledge, so that Fraczak stresses the discursive component of her work. The limitation imposed on the referential universe results in limitations on the lexicon and language used, but she argues that all general properties of route descriptions are present all the same.

A Corpus Based Approach. In order to test the validity of the general approach in this particular application, three corpora were collected and analyzed, in terms of their pragmatic, referential and discursive knowledge.

The pragmatic knowledge constrains both the determination process and the description process: The needs, intentions, goals of the traveler impart on the first aspect, while his or her expertize, familiarity with the subway system, and cognitive capabilities influence decisions made in the second.

The referential knowledge, as already mentioned, is of a limited, simple nature. Fraczak notes that it could also include knowledge of a higher granularity, such as for instance information about the layouts of the subway stations, the lengths of the corridors, the conditions of transfer, the train schedules, and so on. The knowledge used in the actual application only uses information about the network as could be retrieved from a subway map.

Finally, a detailed analysis of the discourse knowledge is presented. According to the general distinctions, this is concerned with three aspects: The conceptual content (what is conceptually present), the textual content (what is actually expressed, based on part of the former), and the textual expression.

For the conceptual content, Fraczak identifies the various components of her theoretical constructs: segments, relays, stages, on the one hand; different kinds of landmarks, on the other hand. Each type of landmark has a set of features with a status (compulsory vs optional), and various strategies can be described according to the uses which are made of the optional features.

The textual content results from further choices made about the incorporation of elements from the conceptual content. For instance, a general phenomenon is the fact that only the beginning stages of the segments are usually expressed.

The textual expression is analyzed in terms of sequences (containing a kernel and optional adjuncts) and connections between them. Fraczak describes their links with the conceptual structures, and their morpho-syntactic realizations. She also describes differents strategies of the use of the connections.

The Implemented System. The system has been implemented in Lisp. The knowledge base is represented in terms of A-lists and the system itself consists in two main modules: a referential module and a discursive module.

Given a query, the referential module builds a referential representation in terms of lists of pairs (station, end-station), using a shortest-path algorithm. The result is input to the discursive module, which determines the segments, relays and stages of the route to be described, and the linguistic material which is used for generating the actual description.

A noticeable feature of the system consists in its ability to generate conceptual as well as stylistic variants in response to the same query. Part of the variation is controlled by parameters expressing the importance given to pragmatic choices such as expressing the length of a segment or not, naming the lines or not, and so on. In that sense, the system is a first step toward a route description system parametrized by pragmatic parameters.

As a means of validating the system, its productions have been systematically compared with human productions corresponding to the same queries. The results show a close similarity, such that computer-generated descriptions are not recognizable from human ones.

3   Guiding a Robot Using Natural Language

Whereas a route description is the end-product of Fraczak's system, it is the initial input to the system which is developed by Marciniak: A natural language text is provided to a robot entering a room. The robot has to understand the description (language), relate it to the input of its visual system (perception), and use its motor system (action) in order to follow the path described in the text. This work, hence, is a study in the interaction of language, perception, and action.

3.1   General Features

The purpose of Marciniak was to show the feasibility of guiding a robot using natural language texts as input. The option was not to limit oneself to a sub-language, or a command language using natural language elements, but to be able to process genuine route descriptions, of the kind humans would generate spontaneously in the kind of context considered.

Since little was known to begin with about the kind of production which could be expected, a preliminary experiment was conducted, using a Wizard of Oz methodology [11]. That is, subjects were presented with a screen animation showing a robot in an office, which follows a prescribed path in the room. They were able to have multiple presentations of the same video, and could also visualize the room from the point of view of the robot. After getting familiar with the general setup, the subjects were told that a similar robot with natural language capabilities was the object of the experiment, that is, it was to be tested for its ability to follow correctly a path expressed in natural language. So they were asked to write a route description which would be used by this second robot to follow the same path which had been followed by the first. Actually, the real aim of the experiment was to collect a corpus of route descriptions, in order to analyze it, in particular in terms of linguistic complexity and lexical coverage. We do not discuss this particular aspect of the project here; it is described in [11].

The robot moves is a semi-open environment: Like free space, and contrarily to the network environment in the subway application, it does not constrain the motion to follow predefined trajectories. It is not totally free because of the presence of obstacles. But there is enough free space around the objects for the robot to be able in all cases to walk around an obstacle or to walk between two objects.

Route descriptions are generated off-line, before the experiment takes place. Then, they are interpreted in a dynamic way. Because of the limited field of vision of the robot, and because of occlusions caused by the presence of obstacles, some of the objets may not be perceived. Some are perceived but not recognized. The robot has to move suitably in order to change its perception, and try to achieve goals specified in the route description.

3.2   The Conceptual Level

In Marciniak's framework, a route description refers to a conceptual level. The basic elements at the conceptual level are of three kinds:

- Segments.
- Changes of direction.
- Static descriptions of space.

Segments are entities which are analogous to segments in Fraczak's work. Since motion in the environment considered here needs a more detailed analysis than in a simple network environment, the granularity of Marciniak's model is greater. Segments are built out of basic segments, which correspond to elementary motions, such as "go straight on", "go right", "go left", "proceed for N units", "go up to X", "cross X", "avoid X", "leave X on your right", "go between X and Y". Precise rules are given for building *complex* segments from basic ones.

Changes of directions (CDs) are analogous to Fraczak's connections. Again, complex changes of direction are formed from basic CDs such as "left turn", "right turn", "turn n degrees", "turn to X".

Static descriptions of space (SDSs) are associated to portions of the route where the continuity of the route breaks down. Their function consist in introducing explicitly spatial information which will allow the identification of the corresponding locations. Mostly, this is done by introducing **landmarks**, which are labeled according to their function: LOC (confirm location), ACT (used in the next conceptual item), END (assignable to the preceding conceptual item), or FAC (optional).

A sequence of conceptual elements is called a regular conceptual structure if it verifies a suitable set of constraints.

As discussed above, all the three types of conceptual elements make use of landmarks. In this model, a landmark has two classes of properties, referred to as "nature", and "location" [10]: Nature comprises type, color, dimension. Location is described by projective spatial relations, orientation, qualitative distance and quantitative distance. Hence a landmark has the format **landmark***(type, color, size)*.

A special relation, called **is**, represents the information on the location of the landmarks. It has the format:

is(landmark, projective relation, qualitative distance, quantitative distance, other landmarks).

3.3   An Example

In order to illustrate the different levels, we use the example considered in [13]. Since the language used is Polish, we give below an English equivalent. The interested reader may find the original Polish text in Annex A.

(1) There is a red chair near you on your right.
(2) Walk straight on for 4 meters,
(3) during that time,
(4) you will pass a white box on your left.
(5) Then,
(6) go up to the grey box in front of you.
(7) Once you get in front of the box, turn left.
(8) Then
(9) go toward the brown stool until you can see a red wastebasket on your right.
(10) Walk around it on the left
(11) and
(12) stop when you are in front of the big desk.

The route to be followed by the robot is shown in Fig. 2.

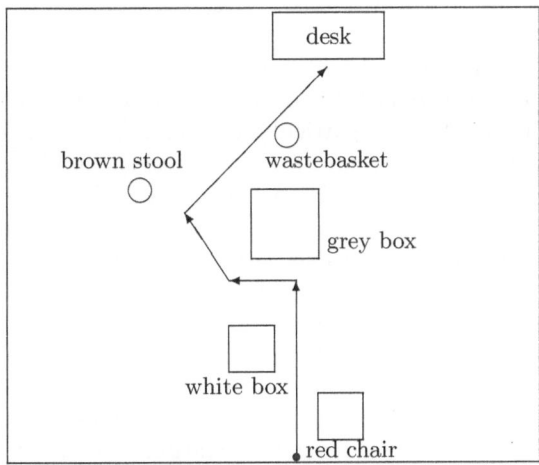

Fig. 2. The route to be followed by the robot

3.4   The Semantics of Projective Relations

Spatial expressions in natural language are assigned to one of these five categories: localization, perception, movement, rotation, end of movement.

To each category, is associated a set of attributes, namely figure, ground, projective relation, orientation, qualitative distance, quantitative distance, to expressions of localization and perception; agent, trajectory, and distance to cover, to expressions of movement; agent, direction, and angle, to expressions of rotation; agent and location, to expressions of end of movement.

A central role in the interaction of linguistic knowledge with perception is played by the interpretation of projective relations. In a projective relation in natural language, an object (figure) is localized with respect to another object (a ground). For example:

My car (figure) *is parked in front of the church.* (ground)

When such an expression is used, three types of orientation can be used:

- The intrinsic orientation of the ground.
- An orientation associated to the ground in a deictic way.
- An orientation associated to the ground in an extrinsic way.

The preceding example is an example of the first case: Presumably, the orientation of the church itself defines what has to be considered as the front of this building. An example of a deictic orientation is:

The armchair on the left of *the table.*

Here, the left of the table refers to what is on the left side according to the point of view of the speaker.

As an example of the third case, we have:

My car is parked North of *the church.*

A first basic problem in order to interpret correctly route descriptions is to determine, for each occurrence of a projective expression, the type of implicit orientation which is used in this particular instance. Marciniak makes a thorough analysis of the occurrences of projective expressions in the corpora of route descriptions collected in the experiments mentioned above. The conclusions of his study depend on a finer classification of the linguistic expressions, which he classifies into three kinds: expressions of localization (expressed by verbs such as *to stand, to lie,* etc.), expressions of perception (*to see, to perceive*), and expressions of movement (*to turn towards, to proceed to*).

A remarkable fact is the general tendency, in all the route descriptions considered, to use the point of view of the robot whenever possible. This general tendency is stronger for expressions of localization than for expressions denoting movement. Hence the preferred interpretations are based on the following principles:

- If the robot is the ground, then the spatial relation is interpreted with respect to the intrinsic orientation of the robot.
- If the robot is the figure, the interpretation uses an orientation associated to the ground object in a deictic manner, using the point of view of the robot.
- When the robot is neither the figure nor the ground, the orientation is interpreted using an orientation associated to the ground in a deictic way, using the point of view of the robot.

3.5 Interpreting the Projective Relations: The Spatial Model

The interpretation of the projective relations uses a qualitative spatial directional model inspired by Hernandez [7]. The qualitative model uses sixteen basic relations (Fig. 3), numbered from 0 to 11, which can be regrouped at three levels: Level one is the coarsest level; it only distinguishes between front (F1, that is all basic relations from 0 to 7) and back (B1), and right (R1, that is 0 to 3, and

12 to 15) and left (L1). Level two has eight relations: F2 (2-5), B2 (10-13) , R2 (0-1 and 14-15), L2 (6-9), and FL2 (4-7), FR2 (0-3),BR2 (12-15), BL2 (8-11). Finally, the third level has sixteen relations regrouping pairs of basic relations.

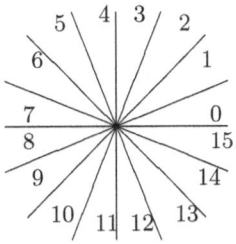

Fig. 3. The basic relations

Marciniak also introduces two notions which are useful for dealing with the problem of mapping the perceptual input of the robot to concepts in the spatial model: augmented relations and the mirror transform.

The *augmented* relation of a given relation (at any of the three levels) is obtained by adding to the relation the two neighboring basic relations (on the left and on the right). For instance, the augmented relation of relation F2 contains the basic relations from 1 to 6.

The *mirror transform* of a relation is the relation obtained by symmetry using the front-back axis. For a basic relation numbered n, $0 \le n \le 7$, the corresponding mirror image is the relation numbered $7 - n$. For the other basic relations numbered from 8 to 15, the mirror image is numbered $23 - n$.

An Example of a Conceptual Representation. Now the spatial model has been introduced, we can describe the conceptual representations. In the case of the example considered above, the first sentence is represented by:

(1) **is**(C, FR2, close, ∅, ∅): LOC
    is(B1, F1, ∅, ∅, ∅): ACT

where B1 is **landmark**(box, white, 0), and C is **landmark**(chair, red, ∅). The full representation is given in Annex B.

3.6   The System Architecture

The aim of the system developed by Marciniak is to generate from the text a representation which describes the route adequately (that is, in accordance with a regular conceptual representation), and is at the same time suitable for the robot to use it for navigation.

This aim is accomplished in two phases, as shown in Fig. 4: At a first level of representation, called the *level of spatio-temporal events*, the text is represented

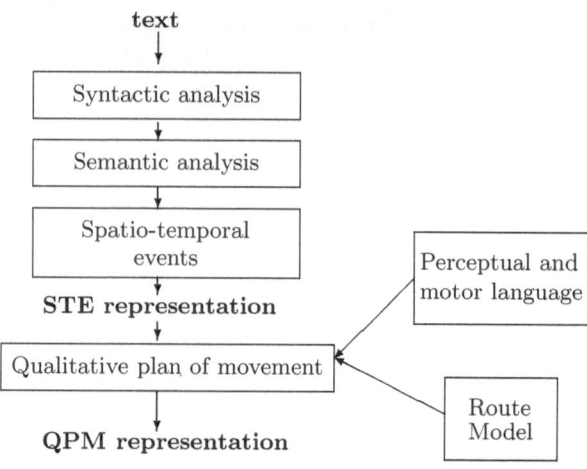

Fig. 4. The architecture of route description understanding

as a set of events. The resulting representation is further elaborated to yield a representation at the *level of the qualitative plan of movement*, which has the desired properties.

At the level of spatio-temporal events, the basic elements are events corresponding either to physical actions (movement, rotation, cessation of motion) or to perceptual events (perception of a landmark) or epistemic events (the existence of a landmark, together with some additional knowledge, is added to the robot's knowledge). Since they are events, the spatio-temporal events are temporally situated, so that they are mutually in various temporal relations (precedence, simultaneity, overlapping, containment). This level cannot be used directly by the robot as a plan for action, because of the potential complex structure of the spatio-temporal events.

At the level of the qualitative plan of movement, the representation can be used directly by the robot. It specifies the sequence of basic actions to be made, together with their conditions of completion (pre-conditions, intermediate conditions, and final conditions).

3.7   Spatio-Temporal Events

Spatio-temporal events are frame-like structures of five types: **Movement, Rotation, Stop, There-is, See.** A **Movement** has 11 slots, which can be filled by constants or structures of type MOV-i (i is an integer between 1 and 9); a **Rotation** has 4 slots, which can be filled by constants or structures of type ROT-i; a **There-is** has 6 slots, and a **See** has 4 slots.

The STE representation associated to the example is given in Annex C.

3.8   Qualitative Plan of Movement

The final representation is the qualitative plan of movement. It is composed of **go-actions** and **turn-actions**, which have starting conditions, action conditions, and ending conditions. The first action, in the case of the example, is a **go-action**:

go-action
starting-conditions
perceive(C, FR2, close, ∅, ∅, LOC)
perceive(B1, F1, ∅, ∅, ∅, ACT)
action-conditions
go-direction(straight)
go-metric(metre, 4)
pass-by(B1, left-of, ∅, ∅)
ending-conditions
perceive(B1, BLL3, ∅, ∅, ∅, END)
perceive(B2, F2, ∅, ∅, ∅, ACT)
  The full QPM representation is given in Annex D.

3.9   The Implementation

The system has been implemented by Marciniak. It is composed of three modules: A route description analyzer (RDA), a spatial reasoning module (SRM), and a virtual reality manager. The linguistic analysis uses the POLINT analyzer developed at Poznań by Vetulani [14]. The spatial reasoning module is written in C++. The virtual reality manager (VRM) is also written in C++. It uses the WTK library (WorldToolKit for Windows).

4   Conclusions

We have presented two directions of work on route descriptions: The first direction consists in starting from a request for directions, and generating a natural language output which has the right cognitive, linguistic, and communicational properties to be understandable, memorizable, and used in a successful way by a human subject. The second direction consists in modeling the actual use of such a natural language route description for navigating, where the agent is a robot rather than a human.
  Both lines of work share a common set of principles, namely:

– The concern to deal with actual, or at least realistic language productions. The goal is to be able to model, and understand, genuine human-generated route descriptions. In Fraczak's work, this point is validated by comparing the productions of the system with actual descriptions for the same requests. In Marciniak's case, a preliminary set of experiments seems to indicate that humans do not restrict their language in a substantial way for communicating with a robot, and the system was designed accordingly. It remains to be fully

tested under real conditions (using it for navigating the robot, and studying the natural language productions), which is a subject for further research.
- The careful distinction between levels of representations of the object under study, route descriptions. Part of the difficulty of formalizing route descriptions stems from the interaction of different levels at which the basic notions (actions, landmarks, events) occur.
- The conviction that, in order to be better understood and more useful, the study of route descriptions, and more generally the interaction of linguistic media with problems of spatial navigation has to be considered from the broader point of view of cognitive science, incorporating methods and results from AI, linguistics, and cognitive psychology.

References

1. K. Corpinot. Stratégies cognitives mises en oeuvre dans les descriptions d'itinéraires en milieu urbain. Rapport de DEA, Université Paris XI, LIMSI, 1993.
2. M. Denis. The Description of Routes: A Cognitive Approach to the Production of Spatial Discourse. *Cahiers de Psychologie Cognitive/Current Psychology of Cognition*, 16:409–458, 1997.
3. M. Denis, F. Pazzaglia, C. Cornoldi, and L. Bertolo. Spatial discourse and navigation: an analysis of route directions in the city of Venice. *Cahiers de Psychologie Cognitive/Current Psychology of Cognition*, 16:409–458, 1997.
4. L. Fraczak. *Descriptions d'itinéraires: de la référence au texte.* PhD thesis, Université Paris XI, 1998.
5. A. Gryl. *Analyse et modélisation des processus discursifs mis en oeuvre dans la description d'itinéraires.* PhD thesis, Université Paris XI, 1995.
6. A. Gryl and G. Ligozat. Route Descriptions: A Stratified Approach. In *Proc. of the IJCAI-95 Workshop on Spatial and Temporal Reasoning*, pages 57–64, Montreal, Canada, 1995.
7. D. Hernández. *Qualitative representation of spatial knowledge.* Number 804 in Lecture Notes in Artificial Intelligence. Springer Verlag, 1994.
8. R. I. Kittredge. Sublanguages. *American Journal of Computational Linguistics*, 8(2), 1982.
9. W. Klein. Local deixis in route directions. In R. J. Jarvella and W. Klein, editors, *Speech, place, and action*, pages 161–182. John Wiley & Sons, Ltd., 1982.
10. B. Landau and R. Jackendoff. "what" and "where" in spatial language and spatial cognition. *Behavioral and Brain Sciences*, 16:217–265, 1993.
11. G. Ligozat, J. Marciniak, J. Martinek, and Z. Vetulani. Modeling Linguistic Competence for Guiding a Robot : A Corpus-Based Approach. In *Proc. of the IJCAI-97 Workshop on Spatial and Temporal Reasoning*, pages 19–23, Nagoya, Japan, 1997.
12. Maaß. From vision to multimodal communication: Incremental route descriptions. *Artificial Intelligence Review*, 8:159–174, 1991.
13. J. Marciniak. *Langage, perception, action : raisonnement spatio-temporel dans le guidage d'un agent virtuel.* PhD thesis, Université Paris XI, 1999.
14. Z. Vetulani. Jezyk polski jako interfejs w komunikacji człowiek-komputer: system POLINT. In Z. Palka, editor, *Poznańska Szkoła Matematyczna*, pages 19–23. 1995.
15. L. R. Waugh. Reported speech in journalistic discourse: The relation of function and text. *TEXT*, 15(1):129–173, 1995.

5   Annexes

5.1   Annex A: The Polish Text

(1) Blisko po prawej stronie znajduje sie czerwone krzesło.
(2) Idź prosto 4 metry.
(3) w tym czasie
(4) z lewej strony miniesz biały karton.
(5) Nastepnie
(6) idź do szarego kartonu stojacego przed toba.
(7) Przed tym kartonem skreć w lewo.
(8) Później
(9) idź w kierunku brazowegu taboretu, tak aby po prawej stronie
     zobaczyć czerwony kosz.
(10) Omiń go z lewej strony
(11) i
(12) zatrzymaj sie przed dużym biurkem.

5.2   Annex B: The Conceptual Representation

(1) **is**(C, FR2, close, $\emptyset$, $\emptyset$): LOC
     is(B1, F1, $\emptyset$, $\emptyset$, $\emptyset$): ACT
(2) **is**(B1, -, $\emptyset$, $\emptyset$, $\emptyset$)
(3) **is**(B1, BLL3, $\emptyset$, $\emptyset$, $\emptyset$): END
     is(B2, F2, $\emptyset$, $\emptyset$, $\emptyset$): ACT
(4) **is**(B2, $\emptyset$, $\emptyset$, $\emptyset$, $\emptyset$)
(5) **is**(B2, F2, $\emptyset$, $\emptyset$, $\emptyset$): LOC
     is(S, $\emptyset$, $\emptyset$, $\emptyset$, $\emptyset$)): FAC
(6) no relation
(7) **is**(S, F1, $\emptyset$, $\emptyset$, $\emptyset$, $\emptyset$): ACT
(8) **is**(S, $\emptyset$, $\emptyset$, $\emptyset$, $\emptyset$))
(9) **is**(B, FR2, $\emptyset$, $\emptyset$, $\emptyset$)): ACT
(10) **is**(B, -, $\emptyset$, $\emptyset$, $\emptyset$)
(12) **is**(B, BRR3, $\emptyset$, $\emptyset$, $\emptyset$)): END
     is(D, FR3, $\emptyset$, $\emptyset$, $\emptyset$)): END
where:

    B1: **landmark**(box, white, 0)
    B2: **landmark**(box, grey, $\emptyset$)
    C: **landmark**(chair, red, $\emptyset$)
    S: **landmark**(stool, brown, $\emptyset$)
    B: **landmark**(basket, red, $\emptyset$)
    D: **landmark**(desk, $\emptyset$, big)

5.3   Annex C: The Spatio-Temporal Event Representation of the Example

(1)   **There-is**((chair, red, ∅), (robot, ∅, ∅), ∅, right-of, ambiguous, close)

(2)   **Movement**(straight, MOV-2(metre, 4), ∅, ∅, ∅, ∅, ∅, ∅, ∅, ∅, ∅)

(3)   SIM

(4)   **Movement**(∅, ∅, ∅, ∅, ∅, ∅, MOV-7((box, white,∅), ∅, **There-is**((box, white, ∅), (robot, ∅, ∅), ∅,right-of, ambiguous, ∅), ∅, yes), ∅, ∅, ∅, ∅)

(5)   SUC

(6)   **Movement**(∅, ∅, MOV-3((box, grey, ∅), **There-is**((box, grey,∅), (robot, ∅, ∅), ∅, in-front-of, intrinsic, ∅), ∅), ∅, ∅, ∅, ∅, ∅, ∅, ∅)

(7)   **Rotation**(left, ∅, ∅, ROT-4((box, grey, ∅), **There-is**((robot, ∅, ∅), (box, grey, ∅), ∅, in-front-of, ambiguous, ∅))

(8)   SUC

(9)   **Movement**(∅, ∅, MOV-3((stool, brown, ∅), ∅, ∅), ∅), ∅, MOV-5((basket, red, ∅), **There-is**(((basket, red, ∅), (robot, ∅, ∅), ∅, right-of, ambiguous, ∅), ∅), ∅, ∅, ∅, ∅, ∅,, ∅)

(10) **Movement**(∅, ∅, ∅, ∅, ∅, ∅, ∅, MOV-8((basket, red, ∅), ∅, **There-is**((robot, ∅, ∅), (basket, red, ∅), ∅, left-of, ambiguous, ∅), ∅, yes), ∅, ∅, ∅)

(11) SUC

(12) **Stop**(STO-1((desk, ∅, big), **There-is**((robot, ∅, ∅), (desk, ∅, big), ∅, in-front-of, ambiguous, ∅), ∅))

5.4   Annex D: The Qualitative Plan of Movement

go-action
starting-conditions
perceive(C, FR2, close, ∅, ∅, LOC)
perceive(B1, F1, ∅, ∅, ∅, ACT)
action-conditions
go-direction(straight)
go-metric(metre, 4)
pass-by(B1, left-of, ∅, ∅)
ending-conditions
perceive(B1, BLL3, ∅, ∅, ∅, END)
perceive(B2, F2, ∅, ∅, ∅, ACT)
   go-action
starting-conditions
perceive(B1, BLL3, ∅, ∅, ∅, END)
perceive(B2, F2, ∅, ∅, ∅, ACT)
action-conditions
direct-to(B2)
pass-by(B1, left-of, ∅, ∅)
ending-conditions

perceive(B2, F2, ∅, ∅, ∅, LOC)
perceive(S, ∅, ∅, ∅, ∅, FAC)

turn-action

starting-conditions
perceive(B2, F2, ∅, ∅, ∅, LOC)
perceive(S, ∅, ∅, ∅, ∅, FAC)
action-conditions
turn-direction(left)
pass-by(B1, left-of, ∅, ∅)
ending-conditions
perceive(S, F1, ∅, ∅, ∅, ACT)

go-action

starting-conditions
perceive(S, F1, ∅, ∅, ∅, ACT)
action-conditions
direct-to(S)
ending-conditions
perceive(B, FR2, ∅, ∅, ∅, ACT)

go-action

starting-conditions
perceive(B, FR2, ∅, ∅, ∅, ACT)
action-conditions
avoid(B, right-of, ∅, ∅) *ending-conditions*
perceive(B, BRR3, ∅, ∅, ∅, END)
perceive(D, F3, ∅, ∅, ∅, END)

Corpus Based Methodology in the Study and Design of Systems with Emulated Linguistic Competence

Zygmunt Vetulani and Jacek Marciniak

Department of Computer Linguistics and Artificial Intelligence
Faculty of Mathematics and Computer Science
Adam Mickiewicz University
ul. Matejki 48/49, 60-769 Poznań, Poland
Phone: +48 61 866 86 51
Fax: + 48 61 866 29 92
{vetulani,jacekmar}@amu.edu.pl

Abstract In this paper we discuss methodological issues connected with the design of computer systems communicating interactively with their human users in the human language. The methods of acquisition of the initial linguistic knowledge, necessary at the early steps of the design of NL interfaces, are being systematically implemented for Polish language at the Adam Mickiewicz University. The key point of our methodology is creation of an environment for systematic observation of the human user interaction with a "machine".

1   Introduction

1.1   ELC Systems

The problems discussed in the paper are valid and topical. With the introduction of the revolutionary Internet technology, globalisation of information is a matter of fact. A natural consequence of the progress in computer systems and robotics is that the exchange of information stops to be the exclusive domain of humans and of some animal species. Together with the growing role of information, increases also the role of the language as the most powerful medium of communication. The dream to communicate with artificial systems or devices by means of the human language in a possibly unconstrained way leaves the domain of science fiction and finds its place in the domain of science and technology. This new situation makes us extend the notion of "language communication", first reserved to human-to-human verbal communication. This extension covers NL-communication between humans and complex systems consuming, storing or/and producing information (e.g. robots, automatic information services, special systems for the disabled). As the systems we are talking about are artificial, their ability to communicate in the human language, i.e., their faculty of producing and interpreting texts in the human (natural) language, will be called Emulated Linguistic Competence (ELC) further in this paper.

D.N. Christodoulakis (Ed.): NLP 2000, LNCS 1835, pp. 346-357, 2000.

1.2   ELC and Linguistic Research

The chomskyan notion of Linguistic Competence is the main concern of classical linguistics. Allowing the situation where human languages are used as a communication medium between a human and a machine (any artificial device, software etc.) means to go beyond the classical linguistics. Communicating with machine through natural language requires at first the modelling of human linguistic competence, and then emulating it as part of machine software. The modelling of linguistic competence is a well-defined AI problem. Although this problem in a natural way addresses the linguistics, the traditional linguistics based on the investigation of natural language production (texts, recordings, observations) addressed to humans is partially inadequate in this case. This is because the traditional linguistic theories were mainly designed for the two main application areas: improvement of language teaching and enhancement of translation techniques. The required level of precision was relatively low as they were addressed to the (intelligent) human user. Descriptions of natural languages, even of those best known, are usually incomplete from the point of view of practical applications (as e.g. design of ELC systems). This remark applies in particular to the pragmatic layer. Observations and systematic descriptions of the dialogue structure, lexical quantitative structure for particular application types or most commonly used syntactic structures are usually not available to the system designer.

At the same time, at the current level of technology, insufficient number of systems emulating (fragments of) human's linguistic competence does not permit us to collect enough data in order to extend classical linguistics at these grounds. The only imaginable technique for extension of human linguistics to cover the area of human-machine language communication is through *extrapolation* from human linguistics, and through *experimental verification* involving design and implementation of artificial "speakers" or "listeners".

The insufficiency of traditional linguistics from the point of view of natural language systems design consists in the lack of precision of language descriptions and in the insufficient coverage of linguistic phenomena. *This gap between the traditional language theory and the engineering practice* was first identified by early experts of machine translation - the oldest branch of natural language processing. Some 50 years later, this gap is still persistent for practically all languages. A partial remedy to the problems related to the lack of information concerning quantitative or pragmatical aspects was the concept of sub-languages proposed in the 80ties [4]. A study of sub-languages proper for particular application classes was intended to identify the information important from language processing point of view and directly useful for system design. Let us quote after Kittredge a number of such questions.

- Are there ellipses or articles, copula, object noun phrases, etc?
- Is there frequent conjunction using "and"?
- Are there quantifier words and negation?
- Does the sub-language use long nominal compounds?
- Are there parenthetical expressions?
- ...

The sub-language approach, first considered in the field of machine translation, may be extended, with the same motivation, to the domain of systems with emulated linguistic competence. However in this case an additional problem appears. At the initial stage of research characterised by lack of implemented systems, the only way in order to gather necessary linguistic data (observations) is through different kinds of corpus generating language experiments. Further in this paper we will present how we realise this program at the Adam Mickiewicz University.

1.3   Early Research: Chapanis, Grosz

Since the seventies, after the first successful implementations of a number of experimental systems emulating various forms of linguistic competence (BASSEBALL, LUNAR, SHRDLU,...) it became clear that talking to a computer will be, sooner or later, a common way of man-machine communication and that toy systems of that time would evolve into truly utilitarian systems. This idea inspired AI researchers sensitive to the human factor in the system design to start basic research anticipating further needs. Different but complementary points of view were explicitly formulated. Alphonse Chapanis, from the Hopkins University, wrote: "If we are to know how to built computers so that they can converse with their human users in simple, human-like terms, we need to know how people naturally communicate with each other" [1]. A couple of years later Grosz (in [13]) studied dialogues collected "in situations simulating those in which a person, using a computer as a problem solving aid, interacts with a system in natural language". On this occasion she observed that "the ideal context for collection (of dialogues) would be the one in which a person is in fact interacting with a computer". These three remarks encompass three basic techniques in the ELC systems design, all of them helping to satisfy an obvious requirement that "before starting to paint a portrait one must first have a look at the model". These three techniques are:

observation of human-human interaction in the class of situations considered similar to the intended human-computer interactions,

observation of the human linguistic behaviour through the "wizard of Oz" type experiments with humans persuaded to be in communication with an ELC system,

observation of the humans interacting with an artificial system in situations possibly close to the situation of interest.

The first two techniques were intensively applied already by Chapanis, Grosz and others since the seventies. For example, Chapanis designed human-human interaction experiments in order to study how big was the impact of the communication channel type on the form of the communication act. These experiments brought about empirical data on interesting properties of voice-based communication channel in opposition to writing-based communication. Grosz, in some of her experiments aiming at dialogue generation used the "wizard of Oz" methodology in order to approach hypothetical man-machine dialogue situation. Until now, the third option, as far as we know has not been systematically explored. The reason for that was the lack of possibility of observing and recording human-computer communication acts because of quasi non-existence of strong enough, real time interactive environments with emulated linguistic competence.

1.4   Origins of the ELC Platform Program in Poznań

The first of the authors started working in the field of systems with Emulated Language Competence in 1984 already[1]. His objective was to write a Polish language module to the French-English NL system ORBIS (by Colmerauer and Kittredge) allowing the user to ask questions to a PROLOG data-base about stars and planets. This fascinating exercise resulted the first large-scale, although still relatively low efficient, language understanding system for Polish, conceptually modelled on the English and French language modules of ORBIS [9]. Further work in order to augment the language coverage and to improve efficiency drew the author's attention to the problems already mentioned above: inadequacy and insufficiency of existing linguistic descriptions that could be useful for ELC systems designers.[2] Lack of important reference points helpful to the system designers was at the origin of the idea of a long-term research program for creation of an experimental environment for gathering linguistic observation useful in system design. This program was directly inspired by the above mentioned works of Chapanis, Grosz and Kittredge. It was defined and its initial phase was implemented during the first author's fellowship at the Alexander von Humboldt Foundation in Bielefeld in years 1987-89.[3] The St. Claus Corpus was the first result of this program.

2   Methodology

The key element of our methodology is to limit arbitrariness at a possibly early stage of the system design. To achieve this objective, it is necessary to enlarge the linguistic and engineering knowledge with elements not derivable from linguistics theories but relevant for the target application (cf. [10], for our first explicit expression of this methodology). We consider that at least three independent factors are to be taken into consideration because of their importance for ergonomy of man-machine communication systems. These are:
- sub-language factor: the use of sub-language determined the domain of discourse and communication objectives,
- user factor: a human's habit to use the language channel of communication in a possibly unconstrained way (*spontaneously*),
- speech-situation factor: a human's inclination to adapt the language use to the particular speech act situation; in our case this factor may be biased by the fact of "speaking" to an artificial device.

Interaction of these three factors contributes to the "user-friendliness" of a system.

The crucial point for our methodology is to gather the necessary information from corpora in a systematic and controlled way. This pre-supposes an access to the

---

[1] As visiting research fellow at the Group of Artificial Intelligence in Marseille led by Alain Colmerauer to whom he dues his profound thanks for initiating into Computer Linguistics.

[2] With one important exception for Polish being the PhD Dissertation of Szpakowicz [8], and some contributions of Świdziński.

[3] Thanks are due to Dafydd Gibbon from Bielefeld for collaboration.

corpora which are representative of the particular class of applications. In practice, that means the necessity to design and perform experiments to generate such corpora.[4]

Linguistics and language theories of particular natural languages, as any other empirical domains, are based on observation of empirical data. Until the time of general availability of computers, the practical possibilities of processing empirical data (accessible through written texts) have been very limited. With the introduction of computers, corpus-based methodology has become one of the dominant paradigms in descriptive linguistics. Corpora are now used both to provide empirical data useful for the bottom-up development of linguistic theories as well as to verify hypotheses about language. Unfortunately, the application of corpus based methods for the development of ELC based systems is extremely difficult at the present stage of knowledge because there is shortage of corpora representative of this kind of problems. Practically, the only possibility is to generate small corpora for deliberately defined experimental setting. The small size of corpora that may be obtained in that way changes the role the text corpora may have with respect to that they play in descriptive linguistics. This may be considered as a disadvantage. On the other hand, the strong side of experiment-based corpus acquisition is a possibility to guarantee a high repetition level of observations, thus a possibility to control (and modify if necessary) important parameters of the experiment setting.

The methodology we propose presupposes the following general scheme of design and production of systems with Emulated Linguistic Competence.

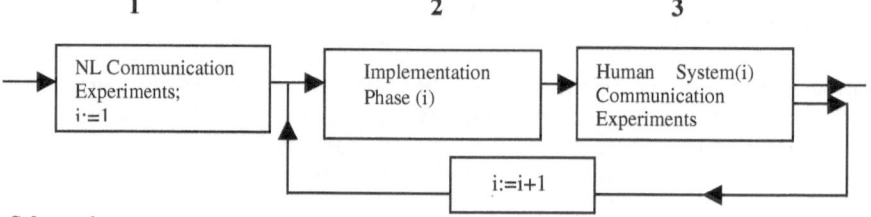

1   **2**   **3**

Scheme 1

An important element of this methodology is represented by Box 1 of the diagram in Scheme 1. This box represents the preliminary stage where the sub-language and user factors are studied in specific experimental setting(s). It is intended for planning the initial kick-off of the design procedure just before the process enters into the iterated loop represented by the sequence of Box 2 and Box 3. Box 1 corresponds to the pre-implementation stage of the design procedure. In the main loop the phases of the system design and implementation (Box 2) alternate with evaluation sessions involving end-users in the interaction with the system (Box 3). This last box involves excellence tests with appropriate *stop conditions* permitting an exit from the prototyping cycle.

Initially, Box 1 was reserved for human-to-human communication experiments as well as experiments within a "wizard of Oz" setting [10]. What we postulate now is an important methodology modification consisting in *creation of a virtual-reality-based*

---

[4] We are aware about limits of this methods which may be sometimes hard to apply correctly because of cost limitations (in time and resources), problems of representative experimental setting (with respect to the intended application), various problems of interpretation of results.

experimental platform, permitting a dialogue between the human user of the system, and a virtual device with emulated linguistic competence.

This platform should be possibly general, i.e. allowing a reasonable usage for a class of applications, rather that restricted to one application, currently under consideration. This postulate is based on the conjecture that an important amount of useful linguistic observations may be collected while experimenting with an interactive platform already at the very beginning stage of the target system design also when the relationship between the pre-implementation experiments and the target system is relatively loose. With this modification, the "NL Communication Experiments" of Box 1 includes three kinds of elements: human-to-human communication experiments, "wizard of Oz" experiments and experiments where the user interacts (in a natural language) with the Virtual ELC Platform. These experiments will constitute the main sources of empirical data in the form of recorded dialogue text corpora generated in experiments.

The collection of empirical data at the very beginning stage of system design with the help of the three kinds of tools of Box 1 *does not* exclude these kind of experiments to be applied at further steps of design and implementation. In particular, it may be very helpful to apply virtual modelling at the later stages too (why not in parallel to the real prototyping). Such a strategy may be particularly desirable where prototyping appears costly (e.g. in robotics). In that case, however, in experiments with the end user we shall use virtual prototypes of the target system constructed specifically within the project. The following diagram represents this situation more exactly than the one of Scheme1.

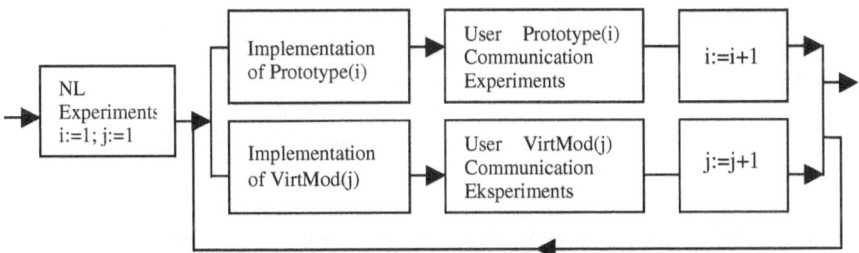

Scheme 2

One important and legitimate question about the methodological status of experiments with the Virtual Experimental Platform is the following.

Are such experiments to be considered as "disposable" tools whose role is to contribute once and for all to extend our knowledge about language use, or on the contrary, it should be considered as a quasi-obligatory element of the system design process?

We opt for the second interpretation. One of reasons is that the speech situation factor changes not only from situation to situation, but also with the evolution of the user profile and knowledge. This means that we will probably never be able to fix a "valid" model of man-machine communication, because the knowledge about the computer technology and user expectations with respect to the "intelligence" of the computer systems (in the role of "conversation partner") will evolve. We may expect that this evolution will modify the contents of the notion of "user friendliness", and, in turn, will change parameters of systems being designed. That means that once acquired observations may become outdated not because the methodology would not be valid any more, but because humans would become increasingly familiar with technology.

3   Towards Creation of Emulated Linguistic Competence Platform - Important Stages

There are four reference points on our way to the creation of the ELC Platform:
- Human-to-human language communication experiment resulting in the St. Claus Corpus.
- Implementation of the POLINT question answering system.
- Design of portable "Wizard of Oz" experiment setting, resulting with generation of the ROBOT corpus,
- Creation of the ACALA virtual platform for an autonomous virtual ELC robot.

3.1   Human-to-Human Language Communication Experiment: St. Claus Corpus

Implementation of this program (methodology) was initiated in the late 80s with a preliminary research on human-to-human interaction. Direct goal was the acquisition of practical knowledge to help improve of our first system to understand and answer questions about planets (module to the ORBIS system, cf. above). The ORBIS system was not time-effective because of a highly non-deterministic parsing algorithm and for this reason it was not suitable for human-machine experiments aiming at observation of "natural" dialogues. We decided instead to observe human-to-human dialogues in an experimental situation.

Experimental Setting. A carefully designed experimental setting was chosen in order to generate an empirical corpus of information-acquisition-oriented-dialogues. On the basis of observations made by Chapanis[5] about properties of various communicational channels, we decided to consider situations where human participants perform an information-acquisition-oriented-dialogue through exchanging questions and answers in the form of hand-written messages. We designed an experimental situation with the following features.
- There were two participants involved: an Information Seeker (IS) and an Information Provider (IP).
- Information was provided to both of them in a non-verbal way (picture), excepted names of some of individuals represented in the pictures.
- The situation the dialogue was about was chosen to be familiar and banal (St. Claus distributing Christmas presents to children under a Christmas tree).
- Time limit of 30 minutes was imposed.

---

[5] Within each of the two communication modes considered by Chapanis [1], [2] , i.e. the voice-based one and the writting-based one, variations of forms are minor (cf. also in [10]).

- Any oral form of communication between IP and IS was forbidden.
- IP was given full information in form of a picture with many details, IS was provided with partial information (the same picture with several explicit gaps).
- IS was supposed to ask questions helping him to complete necessary information, and IP was supposed to give true answers.

Some Results. This experiment resulted with a corpus of 30 dialogue sessions (582 question-answer pairs). Dialogues were described and analysed [10], [11]. The corpus was analysed from the point of view of lexicon, syntax, semantics and dialogue structure. Some of the observations seem be of particular interest for system designers. Frequency lists were built (separately for questions and for full dialogues) and a virtual vocabulary for questions (about single-picture scene) was evaluated to 1200-1500 lexemes. Syntactic structure of all questions was described and almost 130 patterns (in terms of predicate-argument structure) were observed. Finally several aspects of the discourse structure were considered, as e.g., anaphorical and elliptical links, focus structure of dialogues. Among the most interesting observations concerning questions are:

- relatively simple syntactic structure of questions (usually short questions of 6-7 words with short nominal groups of 2-3 words),
- elision of predicate-argument level components was rare in the observed dialogues,
- low number of parenthetical expressions,
- low number of relative clauses with respect to participial clauses,
- total absence of negation,
- small number of long-distance anaphora.

Some of these observations appeared useful for design and implementation of a powerful, real time ELC system POLINT for understanding and answering questions asked by a human user (in Polish) and encouraged us to further experiments within the "wizard of Oz" methodology (cf. below).

3.2 Question-Answering System POLINT

POLINT is a system for question understanding and answering easily adaptable to different application domains. The name POLINT is applied (since 1993) to the systems derived from the Polish module to ORBIS. What makes an essential difference with respect to its predecessors is that POLINT may be used as an interface in real-time systems because of substantial efficiency improvement. Natural language interfaces to the ORBIS system were written in PROLOG as standard DCG grammars where the surface order of components was explicitly reflected in grammar clauses and where syntactic and semantic information were specified together in the same grammar rules. This solution was particularly inefficient for languages with flexible word order, like Polish, because of intensive and costly backtracking. Our solution consisted in two ideas set together. These were:

- to precede application of the grammar by a pre-analysis module aiming at limiting the search space of the parser by exploring information (mainly lexical) which may be obtained from the dictionary when reading-in the sentence and in linear time,

- to postpone semantic calculations until syntactic analysis is done ("2-run sentence processing").

Consistent application of the pre-analysis technique permitted us to drastically limit non-determinism of parsing. Pre-analysis was based on the concept of "lexical witness" for syntactic phenomena and on systematic usage made of lexicon grammar dictionary as a support of the system. A lexical witness (as relative pronoun for relative clause or interrogative pronoun for interrogative sentence) may help to select appropriate grammar rule in a deterministic way. Essential efficiency improvement (cf. [3]) was the result of exploring syntactic information contained in the lexicon grammar. At the pre-analysis stage the sentence was scanned word by word for all predicative words, the syntactic requirements were read out from the dictionary and compared to properties of surrounding words. This observation usually permitted a formulation of a plausible hypothesis about syntax of the considered sentence (at the predicate-argument level) in form of "expected configuration of sentence arguments". Such configuration(s) was (or were) used as input parameter to the parsing module in order to make parsing more deterministic. This method appeared particularly efficient to sentences of medium size and complexity sentences (e.g. with relative clauses).

The parser of the POLINT system has broad linguistic coverage and allows questions and affirmative sentences of various kinds [12][6]. This parser, before having been applied within the ACALA system, was first compared with the St. Claus Corpus with (more than 80% coverage for non-elliptical and non-polypredicative questions). Than it was successfully applied as a part of NL-interface (EXPÆRT) to an expert system for Art History data and documents and as an interface to a PROLOG data-base describing an (authentic) episode of a football match. This last application was presented[7] in 1994 to the external users who were given the possibility to ask questions through a MINITEL terminal (in local mode) with generally positive user feedback.

3.3   Wizard of Oz Experiment: The ROBOT Corpus

The next essential step[8] was design and execution of a "wizard of Oz" type experiment [5], [6], [7] aiming to characterise the sub-language of route descriptions destined to a mobile robot (with NL-competence). The experiment resulted with a ROBOT corpus.

It worth noticing that the experimental setting obtained at this occasion is mobile, fully reusable and language independent (although the actual data were collected for Polish), so that it may be used to generate parallel corpora for any language. The data obtained within the experiment appeared to be very useful for the design of the ACALA system.

---

[6] Some important phenomena still remain out of the scope of POLINT: elliptical constructions, anaphora, polypredicative questions, discontinuous constructions.

[7] At the INFOSYSTEM Computer Faire, Poznań, 17-20.05.1994.

[8] This research was done partially within a Joint French-Polish Research Project (*Accès en langage naturel aux bases de connaissances spatiales*) involving UAM (Z. Vetulani, J. Marciniak) and LIMSI/CNRS (Orsay, France, G. Ligozat).

Experiment Design. The experiment was based on two video presentations of a (dummy) robot following an itinerary in a room with multiple obstacles. The first video animation shows the robot moving in the room as seen by an observer standing outside the scene. The background is immobile, and only the robot moves in the scene. The second animation presents the same itinerary seen by the robot itself. The subject can see several time both animations and may also stop the presentation and fix a picture. After getting familiar with the film, the subject is informed that another robot of the same make, which understands natural language, has to follow the same itinerary as the one presented in the film. The subject is then asked to write natural language text to be interpreted by the robot as a route description. The arrangement of objects was chosen to contain a variety of spatial relations, such that specific semantic properties of route descriptions could be tested afterwards (properties expressing the orientations of objects or dealing with indications of distance, adequacy between complexity of spatial configurations and the appropriate linguistic expressions).

ROBOT Corpus Analysis. The ROBOT corpus is composed of 60 texts generated by 60 native speakers of Polish. The length of the texts varies from 80 up to 180 words.

The first objective of the ROBOT corpus analysis was to obtain characteristics of a specific sub-language presumably used by humans to guide a robot. This communication situation was a new one and it was difficult to predict how humans would have produced a route description knowing that it would be read by a robot. Two preliminary hypotheses were possible: (1) the human user would prefer to use a simplified command-like language register (underestimating linguistic competence of the robot), or (2) he would decide to use the same language register as applied when communicating with other humans (assuming non-restricted linguistic competence of the robot). The corpus analysis has shown that the second hypothesis was correct. It is interesting to note that in the majority of texts there was no metric information at all and that the number of command-like sentences was negligible.

Lexical saturation of the corpus had been studied and interesting observations were obtained. For example, for words of movement (verbs and nouns), the corpus may be considered as saturated. Analysis of syntactical structures used in the route descriptions permitted us to specify a grammar for a (fragment of) route description sub-language.Semantic analyses of spatial expressions permitted us to observe in a systematic way how spatial concepts are expressed in the corpus. The most important part of this work concerned the semantics of linguistic expression of movement. We identified 16 different ways of expressing (in Polish) different relations between the entity in movement and other entities. This result is very important for adequate modelling the aspects of linguistic competence relevant to the movement description. Another important deal of information obtained from corpus is about the way of expressing orientation of objects: orientation of objects was systematically expressed with respect to the position of the robot. This result is important in the situation where the robot interacts with the human agent having different point of view from that of the robot.

3.4   ACALA System

ACALA (Autonomous Cognitive Agent with Linguistic Ability) is a mobile software agent placed in a virtual reality environment. It has been conceived to elaborate and verify mechanisms permitting a robot to navigate using natural language text [6].

System Characteristics. ACALA is equipped with all necessary elements that the real robot interpreting the natural language route descriptions is assumed to have. Thus, it has the motor system giving it the possibility to navigate autonomously in the environment. It is specified at two levels: metric and abstract. The metric level corresponds to motor systems of real robots. It allows the agent to move (or turn) about a metric distance (angle). The abstract level is introduced to give the agent possibility to execute some actions assuming presence of some objects (going into direction of *an object*, passing by *an object*, etc.). The abstract level actions refer to conceptualisations of actions in natural language.

The perception system can deliver the information about the objects that are perceived and recognized, as well as about the objects that are perceived, but not necessarily recognized (i.e. no information or only partial information about intrinsic features of objects is provided). The perception system provides the information about the objects situated close to the agent and about those not hidden by other objects. Three following features can be recognized by ACALA: shape, size and color.

The language understanding module processes a human-written route description and transforms it into some formal representation called the *qualitative plan of route*. This representation is directly interpretable by ACALA. The elements of this representation refer to motor and perceptual skills of the agent. It can be constructed using abstract level actions and system-recognisable perceptual facts. The parser integrated in the NL-understanding module was adapted from POLINT. Its language coverage corresponds to the grammar based on the ROBOT corpus.

The appropriate reasoning module has been introduced to equip ACALA with the aptitude to take decisions about moving according to the route description. This module uses qualitative plan of route and information from the perception system as input data. For each part of qualitative plan of route, the output from the reasoning module activates the motor system. The reasoning is based on the comparison of spatial information from the perception system and those included in the appropriate part of qualitative plan of route. It results in selection of the appropriate action allowing the agent to advance in the route according to natural language description.

ACALA as a Virtual Experimental Platform. The linguistic competence of ACALA meets the linguistic needs of the human user at the elementary level. This result has been obtained thanks to the analysis of the ROBOT corpus. However, we consider this as a preliminary stage of the system construction. We intend to further develop the linguistic competence of ACALA system through a series of experiments giving us an opportunity to test and improve the results obtained so far. Those experiments will be realised in the situation of a real human-machine communication.

The construction of an ACALA system is a key element in our research on human-machine communication. It can be used to observe the interaction in a natural language between the human user and the real computer system in very realistic situations. The virtual reality environment gives us the opportunity of a supple complexity control for spatial configurations (type and number of objects, positions of objects, etc.). This feature, together with ACALA's autonomy (resulting from its reasoning abilities), makes it invaluable from the point of view of future experiments aiming at design of systems with Emulated Linguistic Competence.

4   Conclusion

The ambition of the long-term research project presented in this paper is to partially cover a methodological gap still persisting *between theory and practice* in the area of design and implementation of ELC systems. The presented here elements converging to the *Emulated Linguistic Competence Platform Program* have already proved their utility. We believe that the whole Program, once completed, will also do.

References

1. Chapanis, A.: The communication of factual information through various channels. In: *Information storage retrieval*, vol. 9. Pergamon Press (1973) 215--331
2. Chapanis, A.: Interactive human communication. In: *American scientist* (1975) 36--42
3. Jassem, K. and Vetulani, Z.: Linguistically Based Optimisation of a TDDF Parsing Algorithm of the NL system POLINT. In Dieter W. Halwachs (ed.), Akten des 28 Linguistischen Kolloquiums, Graz - 1993 (Linguistische Arbeiten 321), Max Niemeyer Verlag, Tübingen (1994) 321--326
4. Kittredge, R. and Lehrberger, J. (eds.): Sublanguage. Studies of Language in Restricted Semantic Domains, Walter de Gruyter, Berlin, New York (1982)
5. Ligozat, G., Marciniak, J., Martinek, J. and Vetulani, Z.: Modeling Linguistic Competence For Guiding a Robot: a Corpus-Based Approach. In H. Guesgen (ed.): Spatial and Temporal Reasoning, IJCAI'97, August 23-29, 1997, Nagoya (1997) 19--23
6. Marciniak, J.: Langage, perception, action : raisonnement spatio-temporel dans le guidage d'un agent virtuel. PhD Dissertation, Paris XI University, Orsay, France (1999)
7. Marciniak, J. and Vetulani, Z.: Ontological problemes related to construction of natural language interface for a mobile robot In H. Guesgen (ed.): Workshop on Hot Topics in Spatial and Temporal Reasoning, IJCAI'99, Stockholm (1999) 31--36
8. Szpakowicz, St.: Formalny opis składniowy zdań polskich, WUW, Warszawa (1983)
9. Vetulani, Z. PROLOG Implementation of an Access in Polish to a Data Base, in: Studia z automatyki, XII, PWN (1988) 5--23
10. Vetulani, Z.: Linguistic problems in the theory of man-machine communication in natural language. A study of consultative question answering dialogues. Empirical approach. Brockmeyer, Bochum (1989)
11. Vetulani, Z.: Corpus of consultative dialogues. Experimentally collected source data for AI applications. Adam Mickiewicz University Press, Poznań (1990)
12. Vetulani, Z.: A system for Computer Understanding of Texts. In R. Murawski, J. Pogonowski (ed.): Euphony and Logos (Poznań Studies in the Philosophy of the Sciences and the Humanities, vol. 57) Rodopi, Amsterdam-Atlanta (1997) 387--416.
13. Walker, D. (ed.): Understanding Spoken Language, Elsevier North-Holland, New York (1978)

Dialogues for Embodied Agents in Virtual Environments

Rieks op den Akker and Anton Nijholt[1]

Centre of Telematics and Information Technology (CTIT)
University of Twente, PO Box 217
7500 AE Enschede, the Netherlands
{infrieks,anijholt}@cs.utwente.nl

Abstract. This paper is a progress report on our research, design, and implementation of a virtual reality environment where users (visitors, customers) can interact with agents that help them to obtain information, to perform certain transactions and to collaborate with them in order to get some tasks done. We consider this environment as a laboratory for doing research and experiments with users interacting with agents in multimodal ways, referring to visualized information and making use of knowledge possessed by domain agents, but also, in the future, by agents that represent other visitors of this environment. As such, we think that our environment can be seen as a laboratory for research on users and user interaction in (electronic) commerce, educational and entertainment environments.

1   Introduction

We report about the progress of our research on dialogue agents in a virtual reality environment. The environment is a virtual theatre, implemented in VRML and Java-based extensions that allow inter-agent communication, speech recognition, speech synthesis, database access and animation. In this environment visitors can get information about theatre performances by asking questions in natural language (using the keyboard) to an information agent (Karin is her name) and they can make reservations. A second agent (the navigation agent) knows about the environment, can answer questions about the environment (using speech recognition and synthesis) and can guide the visitor to locations or information presentations. Obviously, any visitor has the freedom to walk around in this 3D environment and in this way, and not necessarily goal-directed, explore the theatre.

As will become clear from section 2, our approach in designing this environment has been bottom-up. At this moment we are in the process of designing, using an agent-oriented approach, a new version of this environment. In the new environment we want to exploit current technical possibilities that allow a multi-user environment, where both users and artificial agents (with the possibility to have both of them

---

[1] The research reported in this paper has been financed by the Dutch Telematics Institute (U-Wish project) and the VR Valley Twente Foundation in Enschede.

D.N. Christodoulakis (Ed.): NLP 2000, LNCS 1835, pp. 358-369, 2000.
© Springer-Verlag Berlin Heidelberg 2000

visualized as humanoids, i.e., 3D objects that resemble humans, both in their appearance as in their behavior) are part of a multi-agent system. This allows interaction between people who are virtually present in a scene, interaction between people and artificial domain agents and interactions with (shared) objects in the environment.

It will be clear that the aim to model and build such environments is a rather ambitious one. Research on many interesting issues can be pursued in such an environment. From a computationally linguistic point of view it is of course the presence of multiple dialogue partners that constitutes a challenge. Moreover, they may know about each other, they sometimes may see each other and they see their environment, inviting references to this visualized environment, shared behavior and shared tasks. Multimodality in interactions between agents (whether they are human or artificial) is another issue. Any utterance of a user may invoke an action of one or more agents, including speech output and synchronous lip movements, performing a certain task (made visible by animation of a humanoid), a change in an agent's facial expression, change of gaze direction, etc. Agent technology is another issue at hand. How can we 'control' the interaction between agents, the users and the (objects in the) environment, how can we allow users to introduce their own agents (see e.g. [10] in such a way that they can participate in the already existing environment? Moreover, our agents are designed to have some kind of 'interaction intelligence'. How can we integrate this intelligence in models of believes, desires and intentions? From an agent-oriented design to software engineering issues is a small step. In [11] some preliminary research is reported on the specification of our and similar complex virtual environments that allow interactions between multiple agents. Last but not least, standards have to be developed in order to be able to assemble independently developed components of inhabited virtual worlds.

2   Background

In [2] we reported about the original aims of our project and the approaches we took at that time. We discussed a natural language dialogue system that offered information about performances in some (existing) theatres and that allowed visitors to make reservations for these performances. Based on Wizard of Oz experiments we designed a system that incorporated rather traditional theory and approaches in computational linguistics and natural language processing. Unfortunately, theory and approaches did not allow to build a system that could be accessed by the general audience. That is, an audience interested in visiting cultural events and making reservations for these events, but not at all familiar with (shortcomings of) information and language technology and not at all ready to adapt its behavior to rather primitive interaction behavior of the interface to the theatre information system.

In the next phase of our research we decided to introduce a model of natural language interaction between system and user that was much more primitive from a linguistic point of view, but much more intelligent from a practical and pragmatic point of view. In [6] this system was discussed.[2] In short, we introduced a natural language understanding system between the user and a database containing information about performances, artists and prices. The intelligence of this system showed in the pragmatic handling of user utterances in a dialogue. The 'linguistic intelligence' was rather poor, however the outcome of a linguistic analysis could be given to pragmatic modules which in the majority of cases (assuming 'reasonable' user behavior) could produce system responses that generated acceptable utterances for the user. With this we don't mean that for any user utterance the next system utterance could be considered as a satisfactory answer or comment. Rather it should be considered as an utterance containing cues how to continue the dialogue in order to come closer to a satisfactory answer. The general idea behind this system was that users learn how to phrase their questions in such a way that the system produces informative answers. Certainly, we can design systems such that they 'teach' (preferably in a non-intrusive way) the users to do so. For instance, the system prompts can be designed in such a way that users adapt their behavior to the system, the prosody of system utterances (in a spoken dialogue) can invite users to provide once more information that they already assumed to be known by the system and, more generally, the system's quality may improve by assuming that the user addresses context information that has been made available by the system, for example because information concerning the dialogue or its content has been visualized on the screen.

3 Embedding: A Dialogue System in a Virtual Reality Environment

We embedded our theatre information and booking system in a virtual reality (3-D) environment that allowed visitors to walk around in the theatre, to approach an information desk with an agent (Karin) with a talking face that is able to address the user in a natural language dialogue about available performances [7]. The theatre has been built, using the Virtual Reality Modeling Language VRML, according to construction drawings provided by the architects of the building. Visitors can explore this building and its environment, walk from one location to another, ask questions to available agents and objects, click on objects, etc. Karin, the receptionist of the theatre, has a 3-D face that allows simple facial expressions and lip movements that synchronize with a (Dutch) text-to-speech system that mouths the system's utterances to the user. Presently, in our implementation of the system, there is no sophisticated synchronization between the (contents of the) utterances produced by the dialogue manager and corresponding lip movements and facial expressions of the Karin agent.

In Figure 1 we see Karin behind her desk. Near her we see some posters and a floor map of the theatre. Someone just entered the theatre. Therefore the door is open and it allows a view outside the theatre. Not shown is a monitor on the desk which allows previews of performances that may be suggested by Karin. Visitors do not necessarily

---

[2] The 'parser' of this system has become part of some commercial systems available from Carp Technologies (http://www.carp-technologies.nl). Among these systems are an automatic summarizer of arbitrary text and an assistant for navigating on a company's website.

have to talk to Karin (using the keyboard for input). They can explore the building,

Fig. 1. Karin Behind the Information Desk

enter the performance halls, watch the stage from a particular position, play with the stage lights, etc. The view on the virtual world is part of a screen where there is a control panel for controlling and navigating this world. In addition there are some menu windows in which the user can type questions for Karin, where Karin's answers are displayed (besides being synthesized) and where a table (to which the user can make references) displays alternatives when there are too many performances that satisfy a user's request. These additions make the interaction between system and visitor multimodal.

The dialogue system, represented by Karin, has been embedded in the virtual world. However, no changes were made to the dialogue model. Clearly, this is necessary. The virtual theatre invites visitors to make references to the visual context (e.g., to the posters or the floor map), and to, for example, the visual appearance of the Karin agent. The dialogue system should allow this. We will return to this problem in the following sections.

It is not difficult to think of other agents that can play a useful role for visitors of our environment. Most obvious is an agent that helps the visitor to find his or her way in the virtual world. For that reason we introduced a navigation agent and an agent platform. The current navigation agent knows about the building and can be addressed using speech and keyboard input of natural language. No real dialogues are involved. The visitor can ask about existing locations in the theatre and when recognized a route to this location is computed and the visitor's viewpoint is guided along this route to the destination. The navigation agents has not been visualized as an avatar. Its viewpoint in the theatre is the current viewpoint from the position (coordinates) of the visitor in the world. The Java based agent framework provides the protocol for communication between agents. It allows the introduction of other agents. For example, why not allow the visitor to talk to the theatre seat map or to a poster displaying an interesting performance? Unlike its predecessor, the version of the virtual theatre with a speech recognizing navigation agent has not been made accessible to the general audience by putting it on the Web. Although speech recognition is done at the server (avoiding problems of download time, ownership, etc.) there are nevertheless too many problems with recognition quality and synchronization with the events in the system. However, further work on the navigation agent is in progress. Part of this work is on user preferences on navigation in virtual worlds, part is on modeling navigation knowledge and navigation dialogues, part is on adding instruction models to agents (Evers [4]) and part is on visualization (Kiss [5]).

4   Dialogues with Agents in a Virtual Environment

In this section we discuss the consequences for the design of virtual environments if we allow human users to communicate with human-like agents (like Karin and a Navigation agent in our virtual theatre) using natural language. First notice that in any communication by means of natural language, there is an imaginative ('virtual') world: the worlds of objects and relations between them about which the participants communicate. The main problem we are confronted with when we allow users to communicate in their natural language with a software 'agent' do not come from embedding the agents in a virtual environment. Natural language is unlike a formal language a vague notion, and any formal language model will necessarily be incomplete. Even natural dialogue systems for such restricted domains as theatre information show how difficult it is to define a satisfying user, dialogue, and language model. This means that in designing natural language models for dialogue systems it is very important that the system can be extended and adapted easily on the basis of experiments with earlier versions.

Communication situated in a visible or otherwise observable (virtual) shared environment allows the communicating partners to support there communicative acts by other means of directing (like gazing or pointing) than linguistic reference. Introducing this multi-modal support for language communication in some cases helps the agents to understand each other but it introduces some new and challenging problems as well. One of them is the problem of coreferencing to shared visible objects. The phrase "that door" should be attached to some visible object in the environment and assumes that the agents share the visibility of this object. The 'geometrical' virtual environment (described in VRML code or in whatever virtual modeling language) must be described on an abstract conceptual and linguistic level as well. The agent should somehow be able to know what object the user points at even in case it is not in direct view of the agent and it should therefore be able to match this way of referring with the linguistic reference ("that door").

Natural language understanding is more than keyword recognition; we need syntax, i.e. a grammatical model of the language and pragmatics, i.e. a model of communicating agents. The grammatical model describes the relation between the order in which words and phrases in a linguistic utterance appear and their function in the whole utterance. It assumes that the words that occur in a user utterance are somehow related in a sensible way. This grammatical model underlies the first step in natural language understanding. In our case the parser for unification grammars (PATR like format) outputs a set of features structures: a syntactic/semantic analysis of (parts of) the input 'sentence'. The grammar and lexicon need to be easily adaptable for other domains, so different agents that can dialogue about different domains can share the general parts of the (Dutch) grammar and the lexicon.

The pragmatical model underlies the second step in understanding. This model assumes that an utterance is in a rational way related to the dialogue: it is a linguistic utterance of some communicative act that "fits" in the dialogue. This 'fits in the dialogue' does not exclude communicative acts that have the intention to control (in particular start or stop) the dialogue. A dialogue is a sequence of conversational acts. In a conversational act the actor addresses himself to an agent by means of an utterance. This level of conversational acts and pragmatics is in great part independent of the particular natural language that is used for communication. The agent is confronted with two problems: a) where do the words and phrases refer to and b) what is the intention of the actor with his act, i.e. what is (are) the conversational act(s) that underlies this utterance? The pragmatical model specifies the relation between the output of the parser - a message representing the syntactic/semantical structure of the user utterance - and the possible conversational acts as the possible source of this message.

An example: in our theatre information system the utterance "Are there any other opera performances tonight?" is interpreted as being an utterance that points to a conversational act in which the actor wants to know about opera performances tonight in a particular theatre (default, i.e. if not otherwise stated) because he is interested to go there in case there are such performances (default). The word "other" is only rational in case this utterance fits in a dialogue in which there was already spoken about opera performances. Moreover, the act assumes that the actor believes that the addressee can provide him the requested information. It will be clear that the pragmatical model should contain this knowledge about conversational acts in order to be able to deny this implicit assumption so the addressee can answer with: "I'm sorry I don't know anything about opera performances" or to react by querying the database for other opera performances, than the one mentioned earlier in the current dialogue, or to react by: "What do you mean by 'other'?" in case the agent does not know about other operas being discussed in the current dialogue.

The agent knows the structure (features and possible values) of the output delivered by the parser (by means of a type description) and can search for denotations of the values: in dialogue context, in the database of theatre information or in the set of actions it can perform. In most cases the parser will not give an unambiguous analysis of the input presented by the agent. For robust interpretation of elliptic utterances and non-grammatical input the agent has a conceptual model representing the relations between concepts in the domain. These concepts are referred to by words that occur in the lexicon of the parser.

The dialogue context consists of a focus stack containing linguistic items that can be referred to later on. Also references to objects in the virtual environment that are pointed at by the user (by mouse) are put on this focus stack, allowing simultaneous multi-modal interaction.

Unlike in the current implementation in which the dialogue acts of the agent are directly called by the user utterance, in the new design the agent decides what action to perform on the basis of his context-dependent interpretation of the user utterance. This allows a more flexible and intelligent system for action selection by the agent, based on his belief (dialogue and user knowledge) and his own intentions, supported by the knowledge in the pragmatical model.

Experiments with current dialogue systems show that it is important to distinguish between knowledge about the user that is confirmed, denied or only guessed by the agent on the basis of general (default) rules. The agent must decide whether to ask for confirmation in a implicit or explicit way, so the user can correct the agent if he has misunderstood him. This implies that the pragmatical model should model the intention of utterances like "No, I didn't mean that" or "You are wrong" or the like. The recognition of conversational acts that are not about the primary domain (theatre performances, or objects in the virtual world) but about the acts, beliefs, or intentions of the participating agents in dialogue, is one of the most challenging problems in building useful natural language dialogue systems.

Any natural dialogue system - however restricted its primary domain - should allow the user to refer to these aspects of dialogue itself: language (naming; "I don't know what you mean"), the participating agents ("What is your name?") and the dialogue process itself ("As I said before ..."). This implies that these aspects of communication itself need to be modeled explicitly in a dialogue system.

5   Distributed Multi-user and Multi-agent Environment

In our environment we have different human-like agents. Some of them are represented as communicative humanoids, more or less naturally visualized avatars standing or moving around in the virtual world and allowing interaction with visitors of the environment. In a browser which allows the visualization of multiple users, other visitors become visible as avatars. We want any visitor to be able to communicate with agents and other visitors, whether visualized or not, in his or her view. That means we can have conversations between theatre agents, between visitors, and between visitors and agents. This is a rather ambitious goal which can not be realized yet, not only due to lack of theory as exemplified in the previous section, but also because current web technology does not allow free speech communication between multiple users and agents in virtual environments.

One of the main shortcomings from our point of view is the poor state of multi-user technology and the slow progress in establishing standards. VRML itself has become an ISO standard. It allows the modeling and implementation of 3D environments and of simple animations of objects. The environments can be visited with a standard web browser equipped with a VRML plug-in. More complex functionality can be obtained by connecting Java Applets to the plug-in using VRML's External Authoring Interface (EAI). For example, in our virtual theatre the EAI has been used to build a version including speech recognition and in the current publicly web-accessible version it allows speech synthesis and synchronous lip movements for sentences that are generated by Karin's dialogue system. Related to VRML other standards have been proposed or are under development. For our purposes, we are interested in:

- Humanoid Animation (H-Anim) standard [14]. This standard defines a structure and interface for humanoid like agents in VRML. It does so by defining a number of VRML node prototypes: Humanoid Node, Joint Node, Segment Node and Site Node. These nodes describe the visualization of the agent, the stiffness and rotation of the joints (e.g., shoulder, elbow, knee), the segments (e.g., upper arm, jaw) and a viewpoint of the agent. An agent that conforms to the H-Anim standard can be plugged into a VRML world and controlled through its interface. Animations (not yet part of the standard) can be specified for the H-Anim agents.

- Living Worlds Standard [13]. At this moment Living Worlds is a working group rather than a standard. The aim of the working group is to define a conceptual framework and specify a set of interfaces to support the creation of multi-user and multi-developer applications in VRML. In [13] two concepts are mentioned: Interpersonal and Interoperable. The first concept refers to applications which support the virtual presence of many people in a single scene at the same time: people who can interact both with objects in the scene and with each other. Just to mention an example, when someone's avatar moves from one location to another, this movement should cause updates in the world that have to be made visible to all the clients that are connected to the world. The second concept refers to the possibility that such applications can be assembled from libraries of components developed independently by multiple suppliers. As a simple example, a user should be able to introduce his or her own VRML avatar in a world built by someone else. This requires control and adjustments of size, animations and possible interactions with the environment.

After some preliminary experiments with VRML multi-user environments (Sony Community Player, Blaxxun Contact, VNet) we now use the DeepMatrix system [9]. DeepMatrix is a multi-user virtual environment system based on Java and VRML. It has a client-server architecture which uses standards as TCP and UDP and which is compliant with the Living Worlds specifications. DeepMatrix offers users a choice of avatars. A user can supply his or her own avatar by providing a URL pointing to the VRML code of the avatar. Users (their avatars) are related to zones or rooms in the virtual world. Users that are related to the same room are updated on changes in this room. For example, a new user can enter the room, avatars move around, they initiate events (a door that opens because one of the avatars comes close to it), etc. The interface offered by DeepMatrix contains a chat area. Here users can type and read messages, see what other users are in the current room and they can explicitly activate some previously defined avatar behavior.

In Figure 2 we show a view of the stage of our virtual theatre using DeepMatrix. It shows an animated baroque dancer performing on the stage. This dancer has been imported and manually scaled down into our world (with permission) from the Baroque Dance Project of the Università degli Studi, Milano [1]. Close to the dancer we see a visitor's avatar which has been so impertinent to climb the stage in order to look at her more closely. This latter avatar has been built according to the H-Anim standard mentioned above. Its animations allow it to walk around following the coordinates of its owner's viewpoint position.

In the previous sections we talked about agents acting in our own virtual theatre. Karin was introduced as a 'visualization' of our existing dialogue system. She has extensive knowledge of performances that play in the theatre. She can move her lips and have some simple head movements in function of the dialogue. Once we had Karin it became clear that we needed an agent framework and we introduced a navigation agent with some geographical knowledge and speech recognition capabilities. In fact, we have a multitude of potential agents. There is a piano player on stage with some simple predefined animations, there is a baroque dancer with animations synchronized with audio and there are visitors, able to move around, displaying walking movements with hands and legs. It will be clear that in order to maintain a virtual environment where we have a multitude of domain and user-defined agents we need some uniformity from which we can diverge in several directions and combinations of directions: agent intelligence, agent interaction capabilities, agent visualization and agent animation.

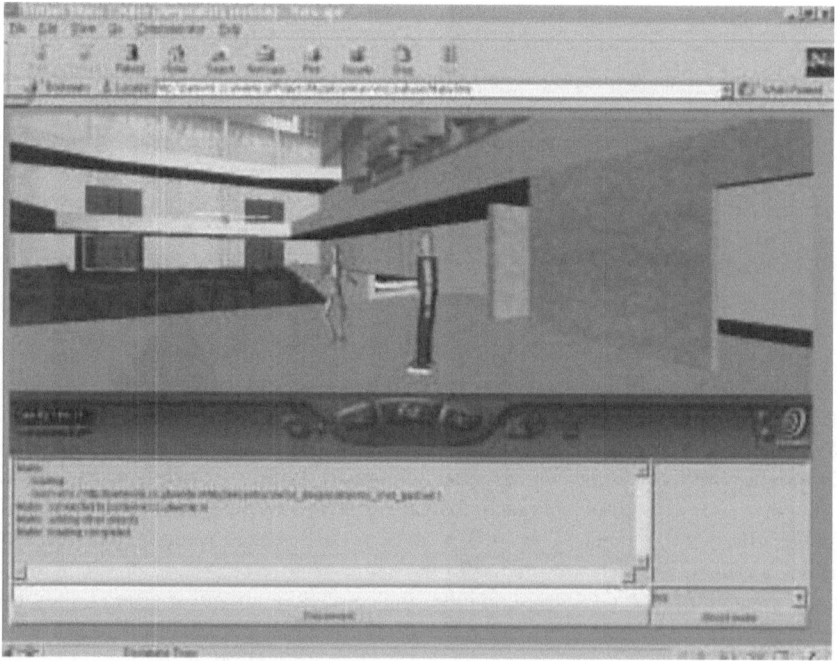

Fig. 2. The Virtual Theatre Stage in DeepMatrix: Visitor meets Baroque Dancer

Apart from dealing with problems in all kinds of subareas (e.g., those mentioned in section 4 of this paper) for our environment the following two lines of research have to be taken simultaneously in order to allow further useful research and extensions of our environment:

- Redesigning and extending our agent framework such that individual agents can represent (human) visitors (e.g., movements, posture, nonverbal behavior) and can stand for artificial, embodied domain agents that help visitors in the virtual environment (using multimodal interaction, including speech and language).

- Designing 3D VRML agents that are controlled according to the protocol of the agent framework, that can walk around in the virtual environment (either acting as a domain agent, hence displaying intelligent and autonomous behavior, or representing a visitor and its moving around in the environment). The geometry of the agents should be based on the H-Anim specification for a standard humanoid.

- Relating our agent framework to the theory of multi-agent systems and issues of autonomy, reactivity, pro-activity, social ability and learning. Some general frameworks for intelligent agents have been developed, among them the theory of belief-desire-intention agents which seems to be a good candidate (with different levels of abstraction) for our environment.

No existing multi-user environment system allows this advanced approach. When using DeepMatrix, to mention an example, we need separate channels for communicating with system agents and for communicating with other visitors using the chat extension. One reason to mention it again is that it is at least a serious attempt to comply with the Living Worlds specifications. The main elements of this specification deal with data distribution and scene synchronization. Below these elements are standards dealing with network and application protocols. Beyond these elements are standards dealing with the issues in the three lines of research mentioned above.

6   Gaze Behavior among Multiple Conversational Agents

Among the in- and output modalities we want to deal with in our future distributed virtual environments is gaze direction. This modality can help to resolve the problem to which of the visible agents a user directs a question. The role of gaze in dialogue and conversation has been studied by Cassell et al [3]. In Nijholt and Hulstijn [8] it is discussed how we can incorporate such results in annotated templates that are used for generation of system utterances in a dialogue system. Presently, we are doing experiments with a desk-mounted LC Technologies eyetracking system, where knowing where the visitor is looking at is detected by an infrared camera. On top of this camera is an infrared source projecting invisible light into the eye. This light is reflected by the retina and the cornea of the eye. These reflections make it possible to determine where a person is looking at. In particular, it is possible to determine to which agent a user is looking. This allows management of multi-user conversations in a virtual environment, where each user knows when and which other users are looking at him or her. This leaves to a certain degree open how the user is represented in the environment, but at least user gaze directional information can be conveyed. This approach allows visitors of our environment to address different task-oriented agents in such a way that speech recognition and language understanding are tuned to the particular task of the agent; therefore quality of recognition and understanding can increase considerably, since the agent may assume that words come from a particular domain and that language use is more or less restricted to this domain. That is, we can restrict lexicon and language model to the utterances that are reasonable given the agent. Obviously, we should try to visualize agents in such a way that it is clear from their appearance what they're responsible for and what a visitor can ask them. An attempt should be made to ensure that any agent is able to determine that he or she isn't the right agent to answer a visitor's questions and therefore should direct the visitor to an other task-oriented agent or to an agent having global knowledge of the task-oriented knowledge of the other agents in the virtual environment.

In the prototype we are using 3D texture-mapped models of humanoid faces. Muscle models are used for generating accurate 3D facial expressions. Each agent is capable of detecting whether the user is looking at it, and combines this information with speech data to determine when to speak or listen to the user. To help the user regulate conversations, agents generate gaze behavior as well. This is exemplified by Fig. 3. Here, the agent speaking on the left is the focal point of the user's eye fixations. The right agent observes that the user is looking at the speaker, and signals it does not wish to interrupt by looking at the left agent, rather than the user. In this set-up we want to model a user and two agents, where the agents have related tasks. For reasons of experiment we want to make an explicit distinction between the information task and the reservation task of our information and transaction agent Karin.

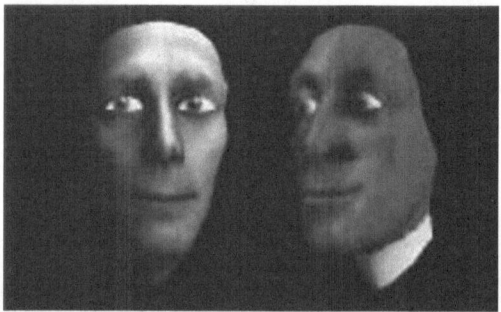

Fig. 3. Gaze modelling in Conversations with More than One Agent

Hence, we have a Karin_1 and a Karin_2 who have to communicate with each other and with the visitor. Clearly, when during the reservation phase with Karin_2 it turns out that the desired number of tickets is not available or that they are too expensive, it may be necessary to go back to Karin_1 in order to determine an other performance. Although the separation of tasks may look a little artificial, it gives us the opportunity to experiment in the prototype environment and with a (modified) existing dialogue system, rather than being obliged to develop two new dialogue systems. Nevertheless, we can not expect a straightforward transfer of the research results in this prototype to the web-based environment of our virtual theatre. Depending on research on the agent framework and the design of human-like agents in this framework some of the results can be expected to be incorporated in the foreseeable future.

7   Conclusions

We surveyed our framework of research on issues related to dialogues with agents in virtual environments. Integration and scaling down of advanced research results to web-based environments are among the issues that play. Unlike many other virtual environments the public version of the environment has been made available to the general audience. This WWW environment (http://parlevink.cs.utwente.nl/) uses a database containing the performances that play in the local theatres of our home town. People can recognize the building, its performance halls and its environment. They can get information, by asking Karin, about performances, including reviews that are read by Karin. No real reservations can be made. The navigation part of the current system is also under scrutiny by the TNO Human Factors Research Institute in the

Netherlands. User evaluation studies will give directions for further research on navigation assistance in this particular environment. The original approach in our project was bottom-up. Now that we have gained sufficient experience we have decided to start a more comprehensive and top-down approach to agent-based virtual environments where we take our existing theatre environment again as a case study.

References

1. M. Bertolo, P. Maninetti and D. Marini. Baroque dance animation with virtual dancers. *Eurographics '99* Conference, Short Papers and Demos, Milan, 1999, 117-120.
2. S.P. van de Burgt, A. Nijholt, T. Andernach, H. Kloosterman and R. Bos. Building dialogue systems that sell. Proceedings *NLP and Industrial Applications*, Moncton, New Brunswick, June 1996, 41-46.
3. J. Cassell and K.R. Thórisson. The power of a nod and a glance: envelope vs. Emotional feedback in animated conversational agents. *Applied Artificial Intelligence*, to appear.
4. M. Evers. The Jacob Project. URL: http://wwwhome.cs.utwente.nl/~evers/jacob/index.html
5. Sz. Kiss. Development of human-like agents in virtual environments. Manuscript, March 2000, University of Twente, Enschede, the Netherlands.
6. D. Lie, J. Hulstijn, R. op den Akker and A. Nijholt. A Transformational Approach to NL Understanding in Dialogue Systems. Proceedings *NLP and Industrial Applications*, Moncton, New Brunswick, August 1998, 163-168.
7. A. Nijholt, A. van Hessen and J. Hulstijn. Speech and language interaction in a (virtual) cultural theatre. Proceedings *NLP and Industrial Applications*, Moncton, New Brunswick, August 1998, 176-182.
8. A. Nijholt and J. Hulstijn. Multimodal Interactions with Agents in Virtual Worlds. Chapter in *Future Directions for Intelligent Information Systems and Information Science*, N. Kasabov (ed.), Physica-Verlag: Studies in Fuzziness and Soft Computing, 2000, to appear.
9. G. Reitmayr, S. Carroll, A. Reitemeyer and M.G. Wagner. Deep Matrix: An open technology based virtual environment system. *The Visual Computer Journal*, to appear.
10. N. Richard, P. Codognet and A. Grumbach. The InViWo virtual agents. *Eurographics '99* Conference, Short Papers and Demos, Milan, 1999, 50-52
11. B.W. van Schooten. Process- and agent-based modeling techniques for dialogue systems and virtual environments. CTIT Report, March 2000, University of Twente, the Netherlands.
12. R. Vertegaal, R. Slagter, G. van der Veer and A. Nijholt. Why conversational agents should catch the eye. In: Proceedings. ACM SIGCHI Conference *CHI 2000 - The Future is Here*, The Hague, April 2000.
13. VRML Living Worlds Working Group proposal draft 2: Making VRML 97 Applications Interpersonal and Interoperable. URL: http://www.vrml.org/living-worlds, 1998.
14. VRML Humanoid Animation Working Group proposal draft 1.1, URL: http://ece.uwaterloo.ca/~h-anim/, 1998.

Concordancing Revised *or* How to Aid the Recognition of New Senses in Very Large Corpora

Dimitrios Kokkinakis

Språkdata/Department of Swedish Language
Göteborg University
Box 200, SE-405 30, Sweden
svedk@svenska.gu.se

Abstract. This paper describes the application of a framework for text analysis to the problem of distinguishing *unusual* or *non-standard* usage of words in large corpora. The need to identify such novel uses, and augment machine-readable dictionaries is a constant battle for professional lexicographers that need to update their resources in order to keep up with the development of the dynamic and evolving aspects of human language. Of equal importance is the need to devise automatic means upon which we can evaluate to what extent a (defining) dictionary accounts for what we find in corpus data. A combination of both semi-, and automatic means have been explored, and it seems that Machine Learning might be a plausible solution towards the stated goals.

1   Introduction

This paper deals with ongoing research efforts to create a methodology that will aid professional lexicographers to distinguish *novel, non-standard* usage of (lexicalized) words. The process is automatized to a large extent, using state-of-the-art implemented Natural Language Processing (NLP) software for written Swedish, such as different kinds of annotators and analyses tools, coupled with large repositories of static and dynamic lexical knowledge. The NLP tools are geared towards the goal of distinguishing non-standard senses applied on very large bodies of texts. The obtained results, that do not conform to the *norm* according the lexical resources and the method used, need manual inspection in order to make a decision regarding the actual, or not, identification of a new or extended usage. However, the inspection process can be automatized, and accelerated, as soon as large portions of texts have been appropriately marked and analyzed, since Machine Learning techniques can be applied to count the distance between previously analyzed and newly processed material. A distance to the nearest marked instance for each test item over a certain threshold, might indicate that an unusual or novel usage is identified, while under a threshold might indicate a prototypical usage.

D.N. Christodoulakis (Ed.): NLP 2000, LNCS 1835, pp. 370–381, 2000.

The presentation that follows is not about word sense disambiguation (WSD), sense or semantic tagging *per se*, it is rather about how to use WSD, and other lingware, in a practical situation. Along these lines, a typical scenario for many scholars, such as professional lexicographers, is the need to have sophisticated software in their every-day work in order to cope and organize the rapidly growing bulk of large corpora in electronic form, to automatically aid the evaluation of (defining) dictionaries against textual data, and to automate the process of discovering non-standard usage of words.

This paper is organized as follows. First, background efforts towards the goal stated in the title of this paper are given, chapter (2); then a brief presentation of various static and dynamic lexical resources as well as annotation and analyses tools for written Swedish will be presented, chapter (3); chapter (4) describes the method explored for the discovery of non-standard senses; while chapter (5) presents a worked example and discusses some preliminary results obtained; finally chapter (6) end the presentation by giving some general conclusions and directions for future research.

2   Background

2.1   What is Novel Use?

There is a justified need to distinguish new senses and novel usage of words, and accordingly augment defining dictionaries with such material. This is regarded as a constant battle for professional lexicographers that need to update their artifacts in order to keep up with the development of the dynamic and evolving aspects of human language, and its constant and rapid change. Here the term *sense* is used to refer to *dictionary sense*, more specifically "...any numbered section of a defining dictionary entry which supports its own definition or requires separate treatment from the surrounding material ...", [2].

The definition we adopt for the experiments presented in this paper regarding what might constitute a new, novel or non-standard use of a particular word, is based on the lexical resources in disposal, more specifically the Gothenburg Lexical Database (GLDB). Thus, if a word in a specific context does not fit the sense descriptions, provided by the lexicographers, in this specific dictionary, then it will be worth examining it manually, in order to establish if a non-standard use has been detected. For a similar experiment, but with manually inspecting large text instances for the purpose of evaluating the Generative Lexicon see [7].

Comparisons between established machine-readable dictionaries (MRDs) and text collections have shown that there is a gap between the two in different dimensions. Since accurate, robust analysis tools were rare, until recently, even for over-explored languages, such as English, only a very coarse estimate of the coverage of the dictionaries has been studied. This is usually taking the form of identifying 'new' words, words not in a 'master wordlist' of 'existing' words, or counting how many of the words found in various text collections were in various machine-readable resources, such as the Longman Dictionary of Contemporary English (LDOCE) and the COLLINS dictionary, [13], [19].

The lack of greater sophistication in the software tools that were available for working with large corpora has been prohibitive for researchers to go a step further and actually try not only to discover new words but new senses of existing, lexicalized words. [3] comments that if one had software that could reliably categorise citations (i.e. concordance lines[1]) into semantic subsets, one could find answers quickly and easily to questions such as which citations out of the set do not appear to match any of a pre-defined set of word sense categories. Accordingly, potentially *new* uses of this word could be identified. After all, in the very relevant research area of WSD the interest has been persistently focused, until very recently[2], on quality WSD of a handful of target words, rather than quantity ([14], [22]).

2.2   Previous Research

The idea of employing automatic techniques dealing with the topic of discovering new or novel usage is not new, on the contrary. In early work by [20], within the developed "Preference Semantic" system, methods for dealing with extensions of word-senses are discussed. These are based on the incorporation of richer semantic structures, called *pseudo-texts*, and the observation of unexpected contexts. The shortcoming of the approach presented there however, was the inadequacy to deal with many forms of lexical ambiguity, since the elaborated mechanism of templates for all part-of-speech had to be both too general, for the creation of semantic representation, and too specific, to aid disambiguation. In his experiments, however, [20] observes that extended or new usage is actually the *norm* in ordinary language use (for English).

Syntactic cues are used by [5] for the derivation of semantic information and augmenting on-line dictionaries for novel verbal senses. The syntactic cues are divided into distinct groupings that correlate with different word senses. For a very large number of verbs, the syntactic signature (syntactic patterns) is used, compared with Levin's, [15], verb classes and information from LDOCE. According the algorithm presented in [5]: if a verb is in Levin's lists it is classified accordingly; if not, Word-Net synsets are used (lists of synonym semantic concepts, [17]), and if the synonym is in Levin's classes they select the class that has the closest match with canonical LDOCE codes; if there are no synonyms, or LDOCE codes, a new verb class i created. Syntactic signatures are of the form: 'X broke the vase to pieces' which, according to [5], becomes '[np, v, np, pp(to)]'.

Similarly, [21] describe a method, quoting an unpublished manuscript by Jim Cowie at CRL-NMSU, on an effort to piggyback a dictionary from a corpus and a *seed* MRD. By applying the described method, all the occurrences of a word in a corpus are classified as belonging to sets of senses defined by a lexcographer who has examined a subset of the occurrences of the word using concordances. The authors

---

[1] A concordance line is a formatted version or display of all the occurrences or tokens of a particular type in a corpus, the type is usually called the keyword or target or search item.

[2] Some large scale WSD efforts on all content words are described in [8].

argue that after a sufficient number of example senses have been marked it should be possible to classify the remaing instances of a word using different techniques. More interestingly, it may be possible to highlight unusual usages (or different *unclassified* senses) by identifying instances where the overlap occurrence is low, and subsequently it is necessary to examine these instances manually. Cases where the overlap is high may indicate archetypical example usages.

Finally, [6] argues that the semantics of verbs are determined by their complementation patterns, discussing an empirical, semi-automatic approach, where it is necessary to identify typical subjects, objects and adverbials, and then group individual lexical items into sets. In creating the behavioural profiles of verb lemmas, such as 'urge' in large corpora, [6] showed that 10% of the uses of 'urge' are metaphors and figuratives, while the most common patterns account for 61% of the occurrences "a person urging another person to do something". Moreover, [6] proposed, that for unusual uses of words it is advisable to statistically sort their collocates into relevenat sets, to give a name and note possible correlations among different sets in particular roles (subject, object), and explain the relation by appealing to criteria of ellipsis, rhetoric, etc.

3   Lexical and Algorithmic Resources

3.1   Lexical Resources

The lexical resources that are used in this work consist of the GLDB, which is the largest, most comprehensive lexical resource for modern Swedish, upon which a number of defining dictionaries have been produced, [16], and the extended content of the Swedish SIMPLE semantic lexicon, about 25,000 entries, [12]. For the classification of proper names into semantic classes, a named-entity recognizer (NE) is used, [9]. The semantic classes in the NE recognizer fall into the categories LOCATION, HUMAN, TIME and ORGANIZATION. Proper names are both frequent and have a serious impact for the disambiguation of the surrounding context. The NE module is also classifying personal pronouns referring to humans as well as appositive nouns (e.g. he, she, professor) to the class HUMAN.

3.2   Algorithmic Resources and Machine Learning

The most important NLP tools that comprise the algorithmic resources are a rule-based part-of-speech tagger; a semantic tagger, [12]; a sense tagger (for content words), [10]; and a cascaded finite-state parser, [11]. Moreover, various finite-state based software that identify and mark idioms, multiword expressions, phrasal verbs, and perform heuristic compound segmentation and lemmatization are used.

The idioms consist of approx. 4,500 different ones, according to the GLDB. Compound segmentation is based on the distributional properties of graphemes, trying to identify grapheme combinations that are non-allowable when considering non-compound forms in the Swedish language, and which carry information of potential token boundaries. The heuristic behind the segmentation is based on producing 3-gram and 4-gram character sequences from several hundreds of non-compound lemmas, and then generating 3-gram and 4-grams that are not part of the lists produced. Some manual adjustments have also been imposed. Ambiguities are unavoidable, although the heuristic segmentation has been evaluated for high precision. Finally, lemmatization is based on the output from the part-of-speech tagger and the rich feature representation that can be found in the part-of-speech tags.

Machine learning techniques, [18] are used in order to automate the calculation of the overlap of the contexts between word that are candidates of defining a novel sense. More specifically, we adopt a supervised, inductive, classification-based variant of Machine Learning called Memory-Based Learning (MBL), and a specific implementation by [4] called TiMBL. Using such techniques, the contexts (or instances or analyzed, modified concordance lines) can be *sorted* by calculating the distance of a new processed context with the distance to the nearest instance (or neighbour) of each test instance already processed. Here, the distance of two contexts is defined as the difference between the features within the instances.

Training and test instances consist of fixed-length vectors of symbolic n feature-value pairs (in the study presented in this paper n=37), and a field containing the classification of that particular feature-value vector. During classification an unseen example X, a test instance, is presented to the system and a distance metric   between the instances of the memory Y and X is calculated,   (X,Y). The algorithm tries to find the *nearest neighbour* and outputs its class, as prediction for the class of the test instance, as well as the distance from the nearest neighbour in the training instances.

4   Design and Methodology

The methodology and design proposed in this report consists of an integrated approach to unify the results of the software outlined previously, that manipulate the content of lexical and textual resources, in order to aid the recognition of potential non-standard use of lexicalized words. The method is inspired by the previously description of the work by Jim Cowie discussed in [21] (pp. 240) and the work in [7]. In particular, I am interested of producing different modified views of typical concordance lines (see figure 1) and then use a combination of manual and automatic techniques for inspecting the obtained results. Moreover, when enough modified concordance lines have been produced, inspected and marked, given a particular sense from the available lexical resources, the overlap between old and new material can be measured, and aid towards the identification of novel senses, according to the lexical resources used, here the GLDB.

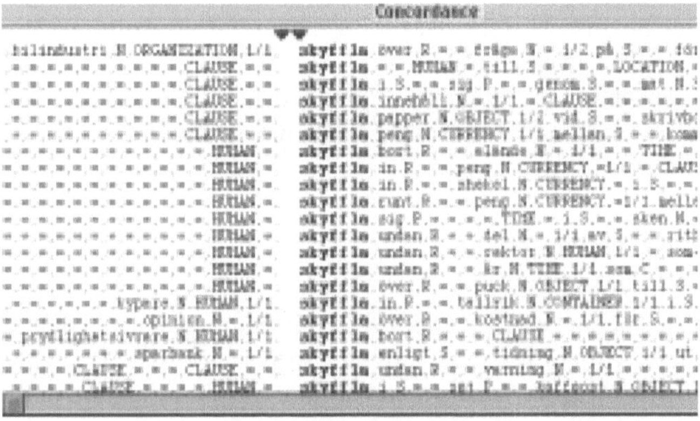

Fig. 1. A More Abstract Representation of Concordance Lines

Thus, the following processing steps are considered:
- Gather a large number of sentences (or concordance lines or contexts) for every word to be examined from a (newspaper) corpus
- Annotate these sentences with any possible type of information available (such as part-of-speech, sense and semantic information)
- Parse with a syntactic analyzer
- Normalize the information obtained by the different tools (lemmatization, uppercase to lowercase conversion, keeping the head of long chunks recognized during parsing, etc.)
- Decide the format for the MBL vectors
- Create the fixed-format vectors, by gathering the information provided by the steps (2), (3), and (4) above, and use them as training data
- Perform the same steps again, this time on sentences taken from another text genre and use the result as test data
- Use MBL with the training and test data, and calculate the distance between the test and training instances
- Inspect the results: zero distance? (identical instances), small distance? (prototypical sense), large distance? (non-standard sense)

By applying these steps, concordance lines can be transformed from raw text to a more abstract, annotated representation, upon which MBL can calculate the overlap between the material, see a worked example in chapter (5).

4.1   Thresholds

Using MBL different threshold values are tested depending the provided algorithms. For instance, one is using the normalized Information Gain, (i.e. Gain ratio), which is measured by computing the difference in uncertainty (i.e. entropy) between the situations without and with knowledge of the value of a feature. Another threshold is used when the algorithm tested is the nearest neighbor search (k-NN or IB1), using weighted overlap and information gain weighting. Accordingly, the instances with the highest threshold values produced by the TiMBL software are manually examined, (identical instances, complete overlap, produce '0' zero distance). Of course, the returned values are dependent on the amount of training data, therefore, for each test performed the thresholds are adjusted in accordance with the results.

5   A Case Study and Results

In order to test the applicability of the proposed architecture, and methodology, I chose to use two different types of texts, namely 'newspaper' and 'data technology'. The reason to it, is that merely testing such an architecture in a multi-million newspaper corpus, requires rather long time efforts to analyze the results, since the system has been recently completed, and the material, that has been used for developing some of the tools, has been also used by the lexicographers for the production of the static resources, particularly the GLDB. Thus, it is more difficullt, at this stage of the development, to test the functionality of the system in a single-genre corpus, and I intend to show that the system works in principle, using two text collections from different genres, and in the future concentrate on a single text collection such as newswire texts. Although the tested hypothesis may sound trivial, namely that since the two text collections belong to different genres, it is more likely that the method *will* highlight difference in usage between senses clearer than a single-genre corpus, this is the simplest way to illustrate the functionality of the architecture and test my hypothesis. However, there is nothing that excludes that there might be cases in the training material alone where one can find non-standard sense or use of words, nor that the 'data technology' does not contain prototypical use of the words. After all, defining dictionaries are limited physically, and thus it is impractical to give descriptions of all possible sense nuances even in a single genre corpus, regardless of the model incorporated in the dictionary. Nevertheless, it is a useful exercise to devise automatic methods for evaluating to what extent a dictionary account for whatever we can find in corpora.

5.1   A Worked Example

In order to make the methodology described in chapter (4) clearer I will provide some examples showing how different tools process few sample instances. The key word under investigation in the small sample given, is the verb skyffla, which according to the GLDB has two senses, the first is similar to 'to shovel' while the second is most similar to 'to shove (away)'. All instances are taken from the Swedish language bank (http://www.spraakdata.gu.se/lb), while the annotations provided are, in some cases, simplified. Four such lines, with a very approximate interpretation, are:

Socialdemokraterna försöker skyffla diskussionen om EMU under mattan.
'The social democrats are trying to shovel the discussion about EMU under the rug.'
Han försökte också skyffla ansvaret för utvecklingen rörande Cypern på EU.
'He also tried to shove the responsibility regarding the development in Cyprus on EU.'

Sakic skyfflade över pucken till Ozolinsh.
'Sakic shovelled the puck to Ozolinsh.'
Morfar skyfflade kol i fabriken i femtio år.
'Grand father has shovelled coal in the factory for fifty years.'

5.1.1 Tokenization, Part-of-Speech Annotation and Lemmatization.

Tokenization not only identifies graphic words (tokens) but also recognizes idioms, phrasal verbs and multi-word expressions. The part-of-speech tags shown below are simplified for the sake of simplicity and readability. The original tagset is using a slightly modified version of the Swedish version of the PAROLE morphosyntactic description, (http://spraakdata.gu.se/parole /lexikon/swedish.parole.lexikon.html).

```
Socialdemokraterna/NOUN försöker/AUX-VERB skyffla/VERB diskus-
sionen/NOUN om/PREP EMU/ABBREVIATION under_mattan/IDIOM ./PUNC
Han/PRONOUN försökte/AUX-VERB också/ADVERB skyffla/VERB ans-
varet/NOUN för/PREP utvecklingen/NOUN rörande/PREP Cy-
pern/PROPER-NOUN på/PREP EU/ABBREVIATION ./PUNC
Sakic/PROPER-NOUN skyfflade/VERB över/PARTICLE pucken/NOUN
till/PREP Ozolinsh/PROPER-NOUN ./PUNC
Morfar/NOUN skyfflade/VERB kol/NOUN i/PREP fabriken/NOUN i/PREP
femtio/NUMERAL år/NOUN ./PUNC
```

Lemmatization is based on the output from the previous tool, and it is implemented as a finite state mechanism with three distinct states, one for verbs, one for nouns and one for adjectives. The suffix of the content words, along with the rich morphosyntactic features returned by the tagger suffices to establish the base-form of each content word with over 98,5% accuracy.

```
Socialdemokraterna[socialdemokrat] försöker[försöka] skyffla
[skyffla] diskussionen[diskussion] om EMU under_mattan .
Han försökte[försöka] också skyffla[skyffla] ansvaret[ansvar]
för utvecklingen[utveckling] rörande Cypern på EU.
Sakic skyfflade[skyffla] över pucken[puck] till Ozolinsh .
Morfar[morfar] skyfflade[skyffla] kol[kol] i fabriken[fabrik] i
femtio år[år] .
```

5.1.2 NE-Recognition and Semantic Annotation.

The named-entity labels are obtained by the NE-recognition, these are underlined in the sample below. The semantic annotation is following the SIMPLE model, colon ':' designates the hyper-hyponym relation in the semantic hierarchy, e.g. IDEO:HUMAN:CONCRETE means that the class IDEO "humans identified according to an ideological criterion" is hyponym of the semantic class HUMAN, which in turn is hyponym of the class CONCRETE. Note, that not all nouns get a semantic class annotation since the entries in the SIMPLE lexicon (at the time this work was completed) did not acount for more than 25,000 noun senses.

```
Socialdemokraterna/IDEO:HUMAN:CONCRETE försöker skyffla diskus-
sionen/ABSTRACT om EMU under_mattan .
```

378   Dimitrios Kokkinakis

Han/<u>HUMAN</u> försökte också skyffla ansvaret/COGNITIVE-FACT:ENTITY:
ABSTRACT för utvecklingen rörande Cypern/<u>LOCATION</u> på EU/AGENCY:
ENTITY:ABSTRACT .
Sakic/<u>HUMAN</u>   skyfflade   över   pucken/ARTIFACT:OBJECT:NON-
LIVING:CONCRETE till Ozolinsh/<u>HUMAN</u> .
Morfar/BIO:HUMAN:CONCRETE   skyfflade   kol/MATTER:NON-LIVING:
CONCRETE   i   fabriken/FUNCTIONAL-SPACE:LOCATION:NON-
LIVING:CONCRETE i femtio år/<u>TIME</u> .

5.1.3 Chunking.

Chunking, or shallow parsing is based on the output from the part-of-speech tagging. During analysis, only the lemmatized head of each chunk (noun, adverbial, and adjective phrases and verbal groups) is preserved, as well as particles and the preposition heading a prepositional phrase. Here 'NP' is a noun phrase, 'VG' a verbal group, 'PP' a prepositional phrase 'RP' temporal adverbial phrase. Chunking is used for a couple of reasons; to obtain the head of the chunks, since phrases can be arbitrarily long and complex, and to give a shorthand name to constituents lying at a certain distance on the left and right of the word under investigation, e.g. different types of clauses.

```
NP[Socialdemokraterna/NOUN]  VG[skyffla/VERB]   NP[diskussionen/
NOUN] PP[om/PREP NP[EMU/ABBREVIATION]] IDIOM[under_mattan/IDIOM]
./PUNC
NP[Han/PRONOUN]  VG[skyffla/VERB]  NP[ansvaret/NOUN]  PP[för/PREP
NP[utvecklingen/NOUN]]  PP[rörande/PREP  NP[Cypern/PROPER-NOUN]]
PP[på/PREP NP[EU/ABBREVIATION]]  ./PUNC
NP[Sakic/PROPER-NOUN] VG[skyfflade/VERB över/PARTICLE] NP[pucken
/NOUN] PP[till/PREP NP[Ozolinsh/PROPER-NOUN]]  ./PUNC
NP[Morfar/NOUN]    VG[skyfflade/VERB]    NP[kol/NOUN]    PP[i/PREP
NP[fabriken/NOUN]] RP[i/PREP NP[år/NOUN]]  ./PUNC
```

5.1.4 Sense Annotation.

Sense annotation is given for content words, nouns, main verbs and adjectives. The notation provided, according to the GLDB, gives the lemma number followed by the lexeme or sense number. The underlying model adopted in GLDB is the so called *lemma-lexeme* model described in [1]. The *lemmas* are grammatical paradigms, comprising formal data, e.g. technical stem, spelling variations, part of speech, inflection(s), pronunciation(s), stress, morpheme division, compound boundary, abbreviated form(s) and much more. The *lexemes*, are the numbered senses of a lemma, and are divided into two main categories, a compulsory kernel sense and a non-compulsory set of one or more sub-senses, called the *cycles*.

```
Socialdemokraterna:1/1 försöker skyffla:1/2 diskussionen:1/1 om
EMU under_mattan.
Han försökte också skyffla:1/2 ansvaret:1/1 för utvecklingen:1/1
rörande Cypern på EU.
Sakic skyfflade:1/2 över pucken:1/1 till Ozolinsh.
Morfar:1/1 skyfflade:1/1 kol:1/2 i fabriken:1/1 i femtio år:1/1.
```

5.1.5 Creating Vectors.

The vectors are of a fixed-format, consisting of four 'contexts' to the left and four 'contexts' to the right of a word under investigation.

```
KEY-WORD Part-of-Speech BYTE-OFFS
        {LEFT-CONTEXT} KEY-WORD {RIGHT-CONTEXT} CLASS
```

The left and right 'contexts' are defined as clusters of four features of the form:

```
TOKEN:MORPHOSYNTAX:SEMANTIC-TAG+NE:SENSE-TAG
```

With 'MORPHOSYNTAX' is meant a part of speech (if the context concerns a single token, which is the head of a chunk, within the clause where the keyword appears) or a larger syntactic label (if the context concern a syntactic unit outside the keyword's own clause, e.g. 'CLAUSE'). With 'SEMANTIC-TAG+NE' is meant the result obtained by the semantic annotation and the NE-recognition, while with 'SENSE-TAG' is meant the result from the sense annotation (a GLDB lemma and lexeme number). Any of the features, or even all, can be absent, in this case a missing feature is marked with a 'dummy' character, an equal sign '='. The reason to it is that MBL requires that the vectors are of equal size, one of the few disadvantages of the method in general.

Given the sample of the worked examples, the results are gathered in the format below, and then converted to a fixed format of equal size for all vectors. 'BYTE-OFFS' is simply the position of the key-word in the discourse, a mechanism that is inhereted by the tokenizer and helps linking the results with the original text from where it was taken.

```
SKYFFLA  VERB  BYTE-OFFS  =  =  =  socialdemokrat:NOUN:HUMAN:1/1
skyffla:VERB:=:1/2 diskussion:NOUN:ABSTRACT:1/1 om:PREP:=:= EMU:
ABBR:=:= under_mattan:IDIOM:=:=

SKYFFLA VERB BYTE-OFFS = = = Han:PRONOUN:HUMAN:= skyffla:VERB:
=:1/2  ansvar:NOUN:ABSTRACT:1/1  för:PREP:=:=  utveckling:NOUN:=
:1/1 rörande:PREP:=:=  Cypern:PROPER-NOUN:LOCATION:= på:PREP:=:=
EU:PROPER-NOUN:AGENCY:=

SKYFFLA VERB BYTE-OFFS = = = Sakic:PROPER-NOUN:HUMAN:= skyffla:
VERB:=:1/2  över:PREP:=:=  puck:NOUN:ARTIFACT:1/1  till:PREP:=:=
Ozolinsh:PROPER-NOUN:HUMAN:=

SKYFFLA VERB BYTE-OFFS = = = morfar:NOUN:HUMAN:1/1 skyffla:VERB:
=:1/1  kol:NOUN:MATTER:1/2  i:PREP:=:=  fabrik:NOUN:FUNCTIONAL-
SPACE:1/1 i:PREP:=:= år:NOUN:TIME:1/1
```

5.2   Small Scale Evaluation

I carried out a small evaluation of the presented approach by producing vectors such as the ones given in section 5.1.5, for a large sample of both training (newspaper articles) and testing material ('data technology' domain), for three verbs. More specifically, I looked at the verbs skyffla 'to shovel, to shove away' (2 senses, 100 training contexts and 15 test contexts), publicera 'to publish' (1 sense, 300 training contexts and 20 test contexts) and the phrasal verb hoppa in 'to step in, to interfere' (2 senses, 200 training contexts and 10 test contexts). The results produced by MBL were sorted according the distance to the nearest instance in the training sample, a distance calculated on the metrics gain ratio and information gain, using the IB1 algorithm. The instances with the highest distance from the training material in every case were:

ColorFusion-kortet skyfflar hela 9 MB videodata per sekund.
'The ColorFusion-card shovels 9 megabyte video-data per second.'
Framtidens taxibolag publicerar sina bilars positioner på Internet.
'The future's taxi companies publish their car's positions on the Internet.'
Vid trafikavbrott kan den ena ringen hoppa in och ersätta den andra.
'During interruption of traffic the one ring can interfere and replace the other.'

The characteristic for the test instances with the longest distance, in all three cases, has been the fact that a concrete object (e.g. 'card', 'ring') is initiating an action usually performed by a human or organization in the training material. While the longest distance for the instance of the verb 'to publish' has to do with publishing a 'location' or 'position' while the majority of the cases in the training sample has been to publish a concrete object (e.g. 'article', 'report'). Over half of the test instances for the verb 'to publish' had short distance to the training material, explicitly refering to prototypical usage, while the opposite could be observed with the other two verbs.

6   Conclusions and Further Research

This paper has outlined an approach to create a framework for aiding the identification of *novel* senses of words in large corpora. Empirical, preliminary results applied on two distinct types of texts have shown that although a lot of *noise* is produced by the different modules of the system, in the form of errors in part-of-speech, sense or semantic annotation, sense differences between the annotated concordance instances can be observed under the threshold conditions briefly outlined.

The design is dictionary-dependent but the methods is not specific to Swedish, as long as there are tools that can contribute with various types of morphological, syntactic, lexical and semantic information. The future direction for the work presented will operate on a specific type of corpus and on a larger sample of the language.

References

1. Allén, S.: The Lemma-Lexeme Model of the Swedish Lexical Database. In Rieger B. (ed): Empirical Semantics. Bochum (1981) 376–387
2. Atkins, B.T.: Semantic ID Tags: Corpus Evidence for Dictionary Senses. Proceedings of the 3rd OED. Waterloo, Canada (1987)
3. Clear, J.: I Can't See the Sense in a Large Corpus. In Kiefer, F., Kiss, G., Pajzs J. (eds.): Papers in Computational Lexicography, COMPLEX '94. Budapest (1994) 33–45

4. Daelemans, W., Zavrel, J., van der Sloot, K.: TiMBL: Tilburg Memory Based Learner, version 2. ILK Technical Report 99-01. Paper available from http://ilk.kub.nl/~ilk/papers/ilk9901.ps.gz (1999)
5. Dorr, B., Jones, D.: Role of Word Sense Disambiguation in Lexical Acquisition: Predicting Semantics from Syntactic Cues. Proceedings of the 16th COLING. Vol. 1. Copenhagen, Denmark (1996) 322-327
6. Hanks, P.: Contextual Dependency and Lexical Sets. Journal of Corpus Linguistics. Benjamins 1(1) (1996) 75–98
7. Kilgarrif, A.: Generative Lexicon Meets Corpus Data: the Case of Non-Standard Word Uses. In Bouillon P., Busa F. (eds): Word Meaning and Creativity. Cambridge UP (2000)
8. Kilgarriff, A., Palmer, M.: Introduction to the Special Issue on SENSEVAL. International Journal of Computer and the Humanities. Special Issue on SENSEVAL. Kluwer Academic Publishers (2000)
9. Kokkinakis, D.: AVENTINUS, GATE and Swedish Lingware. In Proceedings of the 11th NODALIDA Conference (Nordisk Datalingvistik). Copenhagen, Denmark (1998) 22–33
10. Kokkinakis, D. and Johansson-Kokkinakis, S.: Sense Tagging at the Cycle-Level Using GLDB. In Proceedings of the NFL Symposium (Nordic Association of Lexicography). Gothenburg, Sweden (1999a). Paper available from: http://svenska.gu.se/~svedk/publics/nfl.pdf
11. Kokkinakis, D. and Johansson-Kokkinakis, S.: A Cascaded Finite-State Parser for Syntactic Analysis of Swedish. In Proceedings of the 9th EACL. Bergen, Norway (1999b). Paper available from: http://svenska.gu.se/~svedk/publics/eaclKokk.ps
12. Kokkinakis, D., Toporowska-Gronostaj, M. and Warmenius, K.: Annotating, Disambiguating & Automatically Extending the Coverage of the Swedish SIMPLE Lexicon. In proceedings of the 2nd LREC. Athens, Hellas (2000)
13. Krovetz, R.: Learning to Augment a Machine-Readable Dictionary. In Proceedings of the EURALEX '94. Amsterdam, Holland (1994) 107–116
14. Leacock, C., Towell, G., Voorhees, E.M.: Towards Buidling Contextual Representations of Word Senses Using Statistical Models. Boguraev, B., Pustejovsky, J. (eds.): Corpus Processing for Lexical Acquisition. Bradford (1996) 98–113
15. Levin, B.: English Verb Classes and Alternations: a Preliminary Investigation. UCP (1993)
16. Malmgren, S.G.: From Svenska ordbok ('A dictionary of Swedish') to Nationalencyklopediensordbok ('The Dictionary of the National Encyclopedia'). In Tommola H., Varantola K., Salmi-Tolonen T., Schopp, J. (eds). Proceedings of the EURALEX '92, Vol. 2. Tampere, Finland (1992) 485–491
17. Miller, G.A. (ed.): WordNet: An on-line Lexical Database. International Journal of Lexicography Special Issue 3(4) (1990)
18. Mitchell, T. M.: Machine Learning. McGraw-Hill Series on Computer Science (1997)
19. Renouf, A.: A Word in Time: First Findings from the Investigation of Dynamic Text. Aarts, J., de Haan, P., Oostdijk, N. (eds.): English Language Corpora: Design, Analysis and Exploitation. Rodopi (1993)
20. Wilks, Y.: Frames, Semantics and Novelty. In Metzing, D. (ed): Frame Conceptions and Text Understanding. de Gruyter (1980) 134–163
21. Wilks, Y., Slator B. and Guthrie L.: Electric Words, Dictionaries, Computers, and Meanings. MIT (1996)
22. Yarowsky, D.: Unsupervised Word Sense Disambiguation Rivaling Supervised Methods. In Proceedings of the 33rd ACL. Cambridge, MA (1995) 189–196

Learning Rules for Large-Vocabulary Word Sense Disambiguation: A Comparison of Various Classifiers

Georgios Paliouras, Vangelis Karkaletsis,
Ion Androutsopoulos, and Constantine D. Spyropoulos

Institute of Informatics & Telecommunications, NCSR "Demokritos",
Aghia Paraskevi Attikis, Athens, 15310, Greece
{paliourg,vangelis,ionandr,costass}@iit.demokritos.gr

Abstract. In this article we compare the performance of various machine learning algorithms on the task of constructing word-sense disambiguation rules from data. The distinguishing characteristic of our work from most of the related work in the field is that we aim at the disambiguation of all content words in the text, rather than focussing on a small number of words. In an earlier study we have shown that a decision tree induction algorithm performs well on this task. This study compares decision tree induction with other popular learning methods and discusses their advantages and disadvantages. Our results confirm the good performance of decision tree induction, which outperforms the other algorithms, due to its ability to order the features used for disambiguation, according to their contribution in assigning the correct sense.

1   Introduction

The meaning of a word may vary significantly according to the context in which it is used. For instance the word "bank" will have a completely different meaning in financial text than in geological text. This is a case of a clearly identifiable sense distinction, but there are cases where different senses of a word may be harder to distinguish, e.g. "bank" as a financial institution and as a building. Both senses are likely to appear in the same context and one needs to take into account the details of their use, in order to distinguish between them. The process of distinguishing between different senses of a word is called word-sense disambiguation (WSD). Word-sense disambiguation is necessary for a number of tasks in natural language processing (NLP), such as machine translation, query-based information retrieval and information extraction.

In general, the rules for distinguishing between the senses of different words differ. For instance, a valid disambiguation rule for the senses of the word "bank" would examine the occurrence of the words "river", "financial", etc. in the context of the ambiguous word. This evidence would be completely irrelevant for most other words. Thus the disambiguation rules are in general word-specific. Furthermore, it is difficult to construct such rules manually, especially when the difference between the senses is not great, e.g. "bank" the institution and the building. For this reason, the automatic construction of disambiguation rules is highly desirable. One way to

D.N. Christodoulakis (Ed.): NLP 2000, LNCS 1835, pp. 383-394, 2000.
© Springer-Verlag Berlin Heidelberg 2000

achieve this aim is by applying machine learning techniques to training data containing the various senses of the ambiguous words.

An important aspect of the work presented here, as compared to related work, is that all content words (rather than a handful of them) in the training texts are subject to disambiguation. This step towards large-vocabulary disambiguation is necessary if WSD systems are to be used in practice. However, the automatic construction of large-vocabulary disambiguators is hard, due to the sparseness of the training data for each individual word. An important issue that arises in this context is the ability of the learning method to construct simple general rules that apply to all words, capturing regularities in less frequent words in the data.

In an earlier study [15], we have shown that good results on the task of large-vocabulary disambiguation can be achieved with the use of decision tree induction. In the study presented here we compare decision tree induction with a variety of other learning methods. All of these methods are general-purpose, i.e., they were not designed for this particular task and they are implemented in the platform WEKA, which is publicly available for research purposes.[1]

Section 2 presents related work in WSD. The WSD task, as this is realised in our approach, is presented in Section 3. The learning methods that are used in the study are briefly presented in section 4. Section 5 presents our experiments (i.e., experimental set-up and results). Finally, in section 6, we summarise the work and present our future plans.

2   Related Work

Early efforts in automating the sense disambiguation task made use of Machine-Readable Dictionaries (MRDs) and thesauri, which associate different senses of a word with short definitions, examples, synonyms, hypernyms, hyponyms, etc. A simple approach of this type is to compare the dictionary definitions of words appearing in the surrounding text of an ambiguous word with the text in the definition of each sense of the ambiguous word in the dictionary. Clearly, the higher the overlap between the dictionary definitions of the surrounding words and the definition of a particular sense of the ambiguous word, the more likely it is that this is the correct sense for the word. Some of the methods that are based on MRDs and thesauri are presented in [11], [19], [4]. The resources that are commonly used in these studies are: the WordNet, Longman's Dictionary of Contemporary English (LDOCE), Roget's thesaurus and Collins English Dictionary (CDE). A more thorough account of this work can be found in [7].

Despite the useful information that they contain, MRDs and thesauri are often inadequate for WSD, e.g. MRD sense definitions are often non-representative of the context in which the sense is met. As a result, the focus of WSD research has recently turned to *corpus-based* methods. According to this approach, a corpus of text is used as training data for the construction of disambiguation rules for different words. The construction of these disambiguation rules is achieved by a variety of machine learning methods.

---

[1] URL: http://www.cs.waikato.ac.nz/ml/weka/index.html

An important distinguishing feature for machine learning methods is the extent of supervision provided for training. Supervision is provided in the form of hand-labelling the examples that are used for learning. In the case of WSD, a fully supervised method requires that all occurrences of an ambiguous word in the training text be labelled with the correct sense. The sense labels are typically taken from a dictionary. Given this information, a supervised learning algorithm constructs rules that achieve high discrimination between occurrences of different word-senses. Examples of supervised learning methods for WSD appear in [1], [6], [9], [22], [18]. The learning methods used in those studies are general-purpose, including: decision-tree induction, decision-list induction, feed-forward neural networks with backpropagation and naïve Bayesian learning. Their results are very encouraging, exceeding 90% correct sense labelling in some cases.

However, this high disambiguation rate is achieved at the expense of disambiguating only a small number of words. In all of the above-mentioned studies only a handful of words are included in the evaluation experiments and for each of these words a sufficient number of examples are provided, covering all senses of the word. This is an unrealistic scenario, when aiming to construct a system to be used in practice. The results presented here are on a much larger scale, considering all content words of a corpus.

In addition to the supervised approaches to learning WSD systems, unsupervised learning has been used for the same purpose, which does not require hand-tagging of the training data, e.g. [21], [10], [17]. As expected, the performance of the unsupervised learning approaches is lower than that of their supervised counterparts. However, performance evaluation of unsupervised learning methods is not straightforward, as there are no correct tags against which to compare the results of the disambiguation.

A compromise solution between supervised and unsupervised learning is the use of a small number of tagged examples, together with a large set of untagged data. Such partially supervised learning methods are presented in [23], [18], using rule-learning and neural networks respectively.

An important issue for any WSD learning algorithm is what features will be used to construct the disambiguation rules, i.e., what evidence is relevant for WSD. Since syntactic information is not considered useful for hard WSD tasks, the evidence commonly used consists of words that can be found in the neighbourhood of the ambiguous word. The question that arises then is how large this neighbourhood ought to be, i.e., how broad a context is needed for disambiguation. According to this criterion, the WSD methods in the literature can be divided into two large groups: *local* and *topical* WSD. In local WSD only the close neighbourhood of the word (<10 words on each side) is used. Topical methods on the other hand use a larger context window (> 50 words on each side). None of the fairly recent approaches presented above uses purely local information. Yarowsky [21] and Schütze [17] present purely topical methods, but in both papers the value of local information is noted. Most of the recent approaches, e.g. [22], [18], combine local and topical information, in order to improve their performance.

A critical component of any application of machine learning is the representation of the training examples and the generated model, i.e., the disambiguator here. The most popular representation for training examples in machine learning is the feature vector, i.e., a fixed set of features, taking values from a finite set. Examples of such features in WSD may be collocated words, within a window surrounding the ambiguous word. These types of feature dominate the literature on learning methods for WSD. Despite the encouraging results obtained in most studies, features of this type cause a combinatorial explosion in the space of possible solutions. This is due to the unbounded value set of the features, e.g. almost any word can be a collocate of any other word. Little work has been done so far on alternative forms of representation. Yarowsky [21] looks at classes of words and Schütze [17], groups words that occur in similar contexts.

3   The Word Sense Dismabiguation Task

The data used in this study are extracted from the SEMCOR corpus, which is a selection of various texts from the Brown corpus. The important feature of this corpus is that the content words, i.e., nouns, verbs, adjectives and adverbs, have been hand-tagged with syntactic and semantic information, as part of the WordNet project. A subset of SEMCOR is used here containing only financial news articles. We have chosen this subset of SEMCOR, because a previous study [14] has shown that better disambiguation performance can be achieved by focusing on a specific thematic domain.

The SEMCOR corpus is tagged with WordNet sense-numbers. However, the information extraction system for which we want to use the WSD methods,[2] makes use of the Longman Dictionary of Contemporary English (LDOCE). For this reason we translated the WordNet tags into their equivalent in LDOCE. This translation was supported by a resource that was constructed in the WordNet project: a mapping between the senses in the two dictionaries [2]. The mapping between WordNet and LDOCE senses suffers in several respects. Two important problems are:

- there is a large number of senses in both dictionaries that have not been mapped onto senses in the other dictionary;
- the mapping between senses is hardly ever one-to-one, e.g. seven different Wordnet senses for the verb 'absorb' are mapped onto the same LDOCE sense, while the word has four LDOCE senses.

Due to these problems, there is a loss of information in the translation of the data from WordNet to LDOCE tags. In average, only a quarter of the words in the corpus can be assigned LDOCE senses.

The SEMCOR text is translated into training data using the feature-vector representation. For each word, each of its LDOCE senses with the correct part of speech is represented as a separate example case for learning. The correct sense is labeled as a positive example and all other senses as negative. Each example case contains the following characteristic information about the word and the context in which it appears: the lemma of the word, the rank of the sense in LDOCE corresponding to how frequently the sense appears in general text, the part-of-speech tag for the word and ten collocates (first noun/verb/preposition to the left/right and

---

[2] The work presented here was part of the project ECRAN (Extraction of Content: Research at Near-market), LE-2110, Telematics Application Programme.

first/second word to the left). For instance, the word "bank" in the following example:

If you destroy confidence in banks you do something to the economy.

is being used with LDOCE sense rank 1. The feature vector representation of the positive example extracted from this sentence is:

{"bank", 1, noun, "confidence", "destroy", "in", "economy", "do", "to", "in", "confidence", "you", "do"}

where "bank" is the lemma, 1 is the sense rank, noun the part of speech, "confidence", "destroy", "in", the noun, verb, preposition on the left, "economy", "do", "to", similarly on the right and "in", "confidence", "you", "do", the four words surrounding the word "bank". In addition to this positive example a number of negative vectors are generated, one for each alternative sense for the noun "bank".

The evidence used in the disambiguation of different words differs significantly. This is because the disambiguation evidence consists of specific words that commonly occur in the context of the ambiguous word. Due to this fact, almost all work in WSD has considered words individually, i.e., a different disambiguator is built for each word. In the work presented here we test this hypothesis by attempting to construct a common disambiguation system for all content words in SEMCOR, using the lemma of the ambiguous word as a feature in the training examples. Depending on the use of the lemma by the disambiguation system, we can judge whether the system performs word-specific disambiguation, or whether the learning procedure has identified word-independent patterns in the data. The identification of such general patterns is particularly useful when disambiguating rare words, for which there is insufficient training information in the data. This is unavoidable when performing large-vocabulary WSD.

4   Learning Methods

The main aim of this article was to investigate the applicability of different machine learning methods on the task of large-vocabulary disambiguation. In order to achieve that, we wanted to examine as many different algorithms as possible, under the same conditions. For this purpose we chose the experimental system WEKA, which provides a large number of algorithms on a common platform. Furthermore, it incorporates useful experimental tools, such as k-fold cross-validation. WEKA is publicly available for research purposes and all the algorithms in the system are presented in detail in [20].

The algorithms that were chosen for this study can be grouped into three broader categories: *symbolic induction algorithms, probabilistic classifiers* and *memory-based classifiers*. Symbolic induction algorithms, use heuristic search methods to construct symbolic classification models, which generalise the information in the training data. In a similar vein, probabilistic classifiers build probabilistic classification models, based on a statistical analysis of the training data. Finally, memory-based classifiers do not perform considerable generalisation of the data. They keep the training data in a well-organised memory and classify unseen instances, by finding the most-similar training instances in memory.

Each of the three categories is represented by its most popular members. Thus, we have used: two symbolic induction algorithms (decision tree and decision rule induction), one probabilistic classifier (naïve Bayesian) and two memory-based classifiers (decision table and instance-based). All five of these algorithms have been applied successfully in a variety of other tasks and it has been observed that none of them is universally better or worse than others. The performance of the algorithms varies significantly, according to the nature and the representation of the problem. Thus, our aim is not to evaluate the quality of the algorithms as such, but to examine which of them are suitable to the WSD task, represented as explained in section 3.

Decision Tree Induction (J48). The decision tree induction algorithm used here is called J48 and it is an improved version of the C4.5 algorithm [16] that we used in [15]. Given example cases in the format described in section 3, J48 constructs a decision tree, which can then be used to assign sense tags to unseen data. J48 generates decision trees, the nodes of which evaluate the descriptive features of words, i.e., the lemma, sense-rank, part-of-speech tag and the values of collocates. Following a path from the root to the leaves of the tree a sequence of such tests is performed, resulting in a decision about the appropriate sense for the word. The decision trees are constructed in a top-down fashion, by choosing the most appropriate feature each time. The features are evaluated according to an information-theoretic measure, which provides an indication of the "classification power" of each feature. Once a feature is chosen, the training data are divided into subsets, corresponding to different values of the selected feature, and the process is repeated for each subset, until a large proportion of the instances in each subset belong to a single class. This process is also known as "iterative dichotomization", although it usually produces multi-branch (i.e., not binary) splits at each node. J48 provides an option for binary splits, which we evaluate separately here. The binary-split version of J48 will be henceforth called J48b.

Decision Rule Induction (PART). Large decision trees can become incomprehensible. For this reason, a number of algorithms have been devised that construct a list of decision rules for classification, rather than a tree. Some of these algorithms, such as AQ15 [3] and CN2 [12], construct decision rules directly from the training data. However, it is also quite straightforward to construct rule lists from decision trees. Each path from root to leaves is a conjunctive rule, the conditions of which are the individual nodes. Alternative paths are combined disjunctively. This naïve approach can be improved by optimizing the structure of the resulting rules. This process was first introduced in the program C4.5rules [16], which translates decision trees that have been constructed by C4.5 into rule lists. The rule lists that were constructed by C4.5 were even shown to achieve better classification performance than the original trees in some cases. The algorithm that we use here is a variant of this approach and is called PART. It translates trees that are generated by J48 into rule lists.

Naïve Bayesian Classification (NB). The Naïve Bayesian [5] is arguably one of the simplest probabilistic classifiers. The model constructed by this algorithm is a set of probabilities. Each member of this set corresponds to the probability that a specific feature value f_i appears in the instances of class c, i.e., $P(f_i|c)$. These probabilities are estimated by counting the frequency of each feature value in the instances of a class in the training set. Given a new instance, which assigns specific values to the descriptive features, e.g. lemma, sense-rank, part-of-speech tag and collocates, the classifier estimates the probability that the instance belongs to a specific class, based on the product of the individual conditional probabilities for the feature values in the instance. The exact calculation uses Bayes theorem and this is the reason why the algorithm is called a Bayesian classifier. The algorithm is also characterized as Naïve, because it makes the assumption that the features are independent given the class, which is rarely the case in real-world problems. Despite this strong assumption, the algorithm performs surprisingly well on a range of tasks.

Instance-Based Classification (IBk). Instance-based (or memory-based) classifiers [13] do not build general models from the training data. Instead of that, they store *all* training instances in a memory structure, and use them directly for classification. The simplest form of memory structure is the multi-dimensional space defined by the features in the instance vectors. Each training instance is represented as a point in that space. The classification procedure is usually a variant of the simple k-nearest-neighbor (k-nn) algorithm. k-nn assigns to each new unseen instance the majority class among the k training instances that are closest to the unseen instance (its k-*neighborhood*). Euclidean distances are typically used to measure the similarity between two instances. The implementation of the k-nn algorithm in WEKA is called IBk and provides several parameters, which can be used to improve the performance of the algorithm, e.g. weighting the instances in the neighbourhood according to their distance from the test instance, when deciding on the class of the test instance.

Decision Table Classification (Dtable). Decision tables [8] are reduced versions of the original training set. The data set can be viewed as a table, the rows of which correspond to different instances and the columns to the different features. Reduction is done in both directions, by removing instances and features. The end-result of this process is a smaller table, which can be used for classification in a similar manner as the original training set in the k-nn algorithm. The only difference is that some of the features in the test instances are ignored, as they have been removed from the table. The selection of instances and features to be kept in the decision table is usually based on information theoretic measures, as in the inductive learning algorithms. In this manner, a decision table can also be viewed as a list of decision rules, all of which have the same length.

5   Experimental Results

5.1   Experimental Set-Up

The measures that were chosen for the evaluation of the algorithms are those typically used in the language engineering literature: *recall* and *precision*. The recall measure is based on the number of positive examples that were identified as such by the WSD system. These are called True Positives (TP). The actual recall measure is the ratio of True Positives to the total number of positives (P) in the test data:

$recall = $ TP/P.

On the other hand, precision is the ratio of True Positives to all examples classified as positive, i.e., True Positives (TP) plus False Positives (FP) by the system:

$precision = $ TP/(TP+FP).

In all of the figures presented in the following sections, the performance of the system is measured on unseen data. Furthermore, in order to arrive at a robust estimate of performance, we use ten-fold cross-validation at each individual experiment. According to this experimental method, the data set is divided into ten equally sized pieces and the learning algorithm is run ten times. Each time, nine of the ten pieces are used for training and the tenth is kept as unseen data for the evaluation of the algorithm. Each of the ten pieces acts as the evaluation set in one of the ten runs. Thus, each recall and precision figure presented in the following sections is an average over ten runs, rather than a single train-and-test result, which can often be accidentally high or low. Finally, it should be noted that, unlike MRD-based approaches, the constructed disambiguators make no use of external resources.

5.2   Results

The financial news articles of SEMCOR consist of 3,613 word occurrences, of which 1,987 have been tagged with WordNet senses, resulting in 753 word occurrences with LDOCE senses and 355 distinct words. The LDOCE polysemy of the dataset is 3,516/753=4.67, and the ratio of word occurrences to distinct words, i.e., the average word repetition is 753/355=2.12. Word repetition is one indication of the richness of the vocabulary in the text. The closer the ratio is to 1, the richer the vocabulary.

Table 1 presents the results for the algorithms examined in this study. In order to set the results in context, we examine the following simple base case: we consider as appropriate the first sense of each word in LDOCE, i.e., the most frequently used sense. The shaded row in Table 1 shows the performance of this simple rule. Clearly, any results close or below the performance of this simple rule are not acceptable as a solution to the problem.

Table 1. Performance of different classifiers on large-vocabulary word-sense disambiguation.

Classifier	Recall	Precision
J48	77.4%	82.6%
J48b	77.7%	76.7%
PART	71.1%	77.5%
Dtable	60.8%	78.0%
NB	55.4%	63.8%
IBk	49.0%	66.3%
baseline	48.0%	65.0%

The performance of symbolic induction methods is clearly better than that of other methods. In particular the decision tree induction algorithm (J48), with the use of multi-way splits has achieved the highest recall and precision results. Recall is slightly lower than precision, which is an indication that the trees are conservative in labelling instances as positive. This bias towards negative instances is due to the disproportionately large number of negative instances in the data set: 2,489 out of 3,516 instances.

One of the questions set initially was whether word-independent rules can be constructed, i.e., whether general patterns can be identified that are independent of specific words and still can be used for disambiguation. This question can be answered by examining the decision trees constructed by J48. In general, the constructed decision trees represent collections of word-specific disambiguators, i.e., they are composed of subtrees that focus on specific words. The only exception to this phenomenon is the use of the sense rank to group words that appear less frequently in the training set. For most of those words, the learning algorithms decide to select the most frequent sense (highest rank), rather than building complex disambiguation rules, using the collocates. This combination of general and word-specific disambiguation is desirable for large-vocabulary WSD.

When imposing the use of binary splits in the decision trees, the precision of the classifiers falls by 6 percentage points. The explanation for this fall in precision can be given by comparing the structure of the decision trees generated by J48b, with the structure of the trees generated by J48. As mentioned above, the trees generated by J48 perform primarily word-specific disambiguation, which means that the feature 'lemma' appears near the top of the tree, producing a broad tree. On the other hand, J48b is forced to produce binary trees, which have limited breadth. Each value of the feature 'lemma', i.e., each ambiguous word, is treated as a separate feature. In this manner, it becomes difficult to build a word-specific disambiguator.

The rule induction algorithm PART suffers from a similar problem. Although it starts with a broad decision tree it breaks it into path-size segments and tries to optimise it by removing whole rules or parts of them. Each rule can only treat a single value of the feature 'lemma', which is equivalent to binarising the feature. However, it should be noted that the fall in performance observed for J48b and PART is accompanied by a much larger fall in the size of the disambiguation models. J48 generates trees in the order of a few thousand nodes (around 4,000 nodes), while J48b generates trees containing a few hundred nodes (around 850 nodes) and PART generates a few hundred rules (around 500). As a result, the models generated by J48b and particularly those generated by PART are much easier to understand than the trees generated by J48.

Outside the symbolic induction family, the algorithm that performs best is the one constructing decision tables. Its performance is not much lower than that of PART, which illustrates the fact that simple decision rules in the form of a table can be effective classifiers, approaching the performance of more expressive rule representations, such as that used by PART. At the same time, the large difference between this algorithm and IBk shows that the generalisation achieved by reducing the training set into a decision table can make a very important difference.

Finally, the Naïve Bayesian classifier and IBk perform very poorly. In particular, the performance of IBk is hardly above the baseline. The best result that we achieved for IBk was for $k=1$, i.e., adopting the class of the closest neighbour. The low performance of NB and IBk shows that generalisation is essential in order to arrive at an adequate solution to the WSD problem. This result may be affected significantly by our choice of representation for the data. In particular, one known problem with the instance-based classifiers is that they do not perform well when the instance space is sparse. This happens when there is a large number of features or feature values. In our representation we have used a small number of features. However, each feature can take many values. As a result, the instance space is very sparsely populated. In order to test the importance of this problem, we translated all of the multi-valued discrete features into a large number of binary features and selected a part of them, using an information theoretic measure (Information Gain). By doing that, in effect, we aimed to approach the representation used in J48b. Feature selection reduced considerably the sparseness of the instance space and improved the performance of NB and IBk. The results shown in Table 1 use the reduced binary feature set. Despite the improvement, the performance of the two algorithms has remained low, due to their inability to produce generalisations of the data.

6   Concluding Remarks and Further Work

Machine learning algorithms are a promising approach to the automatic construction of word sense disambiguators. In the study presented here we performed a comparative evaluation of various supervised learning methods, which require that the training texts are hand-tagged with the correct senses for ambiguous words. Five learning algorithms were evaluated on financial news articles from the SEMCOR corpus. The textual data were translated into feature-vector training instances, as needed by the learning algorithms. 10-fold cross-validation was used to gain an unbiased estimate of the performance of the algorithms.

An important difference of the work presented here from previous work on this subject is the size of the vocabulary being disambiguated. Rather than restricting the attention of the system to a handful of words, all content words in the data were considered for disambiguation. This is a more realistic scenario, introducing the problem of sparseness of the training data. The reaction of the best-performing learning algorithm to this was to combine a simple general disambiguation filter for the words that appear less frequently in text, with word-specific disambiguation rules for the remaining words. This combination of word-specific and general disambiguation rules is an interesting outcome of our experiments that deserves further study.

The comparative evaluation has shown that inductive learning methods, which construct disambiguation models, by generalising the training data, perform best on the WSD task that we examined. In contrast, memory-based algorithms and a simple probabilistic one did not perform as well. This is attributed to the large number of values that each feature is allowed to take in the representation that we have used. This characteristic of the representation favours the algorithms that are able to perform flexible feature selection and ordering in the frame of an expressive model, such as a decision tree or a list of decision rules.

The above-mentioned observation presents an interesting direction for further work. Namely, the choice of an appropriate representation of the training data. In addition to the coding of the large number of feature values, we are concerned about the coding of the different senses for each word. The representation that was used here separates word instances into different senses, which are then treated as individual instances. Alternative representations that would allow the grouping of all senses related to a single word should also be examined.

Another important issue in WSD is the extent of the context used for disambiguation. Only local context was taken into account here. Topical evidence has also been shown to help in WSD and should be examined. Finally, we would like to test the learning methods in other sense disambiguation problems, in order to confirm the relative performance results that we presented here.

References

1. Black E.: An experiment in computational discrimination of English word senses. IBM Journal of Research and Development, v.32, n.2, (1988) 185-194
2. Bruce, R. and Guthrie, L.: Genus Disambiguation: A study in weighted preference. In Proceedings of the International Conference on Computational Linguistics, (1992) 1187-1191
3. Clark, P. and Niblett, T.: The CN2 algorithm. Machine Learning, 3(4), (1989) 261-283.
4. Cowie, J., Guthrie, J. A. and Guthrie, L.: Lexical disambiguation using simulated annealing. In Proceedings of the International Conference on Computational Linguistics, (1992) 359-365
5. Duda, R. O. and Hart, P. E.: Pattern Classification and Scene Analysis, John Wiley, (1973)
6. Gale, W. A., Church, K. W. and Yarowsky, D.: A method for disambiguating word senses in a large corpus. Computers and the Humanities, v.26, (1993) 415-439
7. Ide, N. and Veronís, J.: Introduction to the special issue on Word Sense Disambiguation: The state of the art. Computational Linguistics, v.24, n.1, (1998) 1-40
8. Kohavi R: The Power of Decision Tables. In Proceedings of the European Conference on Machine Learning, (1995) 174-189
9. Leacock, C., Towell, G. and Voorhees, E. M.: Corpus-based statistical sense resolution. In Proceedings of the ARPA Human Languages Technology Workshop (1993)
10. Leacock, C., Chodrow, M. and Miller, G. A.: Using corpus statistics and WordNet relations for sense identification. Computational Linguistics, v.24, n.1, (1998) 147-165
11. Lesk, M.: Automated sense disambiguation using machine-readable dictionaries: How to tell an pine cone from an ice cream cone. In Proceedings of the SIGDOC Conference, (1986) 24-26
12. Michalski, R. S., Mozetic, I., Hong, J. and Lavrac, N.: The multi-purpose incremental learning system AQ15 and its testing application to three medical domains. In Proceedings of the National Conference on Artificial Intelligence, (1986) 1041-1045.
13. Mitchell, T. M., Machine Learning, McGraw-Hill (1997)
14. Paliouras, G., Karkaletsis, V. and Spyropoulos, C. D.,:Machine Learning for Domain-Adaptive Word Sense Disambiguation. In Proceedings of the Workshop on Adapting Lexical and Corpus Resources to Sublanguages and Applications, International Conference on Language Resources and Evaluation, Granada, Spain, May 26 (1998)
15. Paliouras, G., Karkaletsis V. and Spyropoulos, C. D.: Learning Rules for Large Vocabulary Word Sense Disambiguation. In Proceedings of the International Joint Conference on Artificial Intelligence (IJCAI '99), v. 2, 674-679 (1999)
16. Quinlan, J. R.: C4.5: Programs for machine learning, Morgan-Kaufmann (1993)
17. Schütze, H.: Automatic word sense discrimination. Computational Linguistics, v.24, n.1, (1998) 97-124

18. Towell, G. and Voorhees, E. M.: Disambiguating highly ambiguous words. Computational Linguistics, v.24, n.1, (1998) 125-146

19. Wilks, Y. A., Fass, D. C., Guo, C. M., MacDonald, J. E., Plate, T. and Slator, B. M.: Providing machine tractable dictionary tools. Machine Translation, v.5, (1990) 99-154

20. Witten, I.H. and Frank, E.: Data Mining: Practical Machine Learning Tools and Techniques with Java Implementations, Morgan-Kaufmann (1999)

21. Yarowsky, D.: Word-sense disambiguation using statistical models of Roget's categories trained on large corpora. In Proceedings of the International Conference in Computational Linguistics, (1992) 454-460

22. Yarowsky, D.: Decision lists for lexical ambiguity resolution: Application to accent restoration in Spanish and French. In Proceedings of the Annual Meeting of the Association for Computational Linguistics, (1994) 88-95

23. Yarowsky, D.: Unsupervised word sense disambiguation rivaling supervised methods. In Proceedings of the Annual Meeting of the Association for Computational Linguistics, (1995) 189-196

Greek Verb Semantic Processing for Stock Market Text Mining

John Kontos[1], Ioanna Malagardi[1], Christina Alexandris[2], and Maria Bouligaraki[1]

[1] Athens University of Economics and Business, Department of Informatics,
76 Patission St., 104 34 Athens, Hellas
jpk@aueb.gr, imal@gsrt.gr, bouligaraki@ath.forthnet.gr
[2] National and Capodistrian University of Athens, School of Philosophy, Hellas
calex@ilsp.gr

Abstract. In the present paper we present the implementation and application of a system for computer semantic processing of Greek verbs occurring in Greek Stock Market Texts. The system has been implemented with the programming language Prolog and it accomplishes functions like the automatic detection of circular definitions and the automatic transformation of definitions into special forms in which verbs that express basic concepts are used. The application of the system concerns the interface of a user with an Intelligent Information Extraction and Text Mining System, which is under construction. The Computational Lexicon constructed supports the Deductive Mining of Knowledge from Texts about the behaviour of companies. The knowledge acquired is used for the answering of questions about the behaviour of companies from the texts using the ARISTA method.

1 Introduction

In the present paper we present the implementation and application of a system for computer semantic processing of Greek verbs occurring in Greek Stock Market Texts for the purpose of text mining using the ARISTA method. The system has been implemented with the programming language Prolog and it accomplishes functions like the automatic detection of circular definitions and the automatic transformation of definitions into special forms in which verbs that express basic concepts are used.

The application of the system concerns the interface of a user with an Intelligent Information Extraction and Text Mining System, which is under development. The system uses our novel approach based on the ARISTA method described in [7] and [10]. The approach was introduced for the implementation of question-answering systems for the extraction of information and mining knowledge from texts and which differs from the dominant formal representation approaches such as described in [6], [12] and [13]. The Computational Lexicon constructed supports the Deductive Mining of Knowledge from Texts about the behaviour of companies. The knowledge acquired will be used for the answering of questions about the behaviour of the companies for which information is presented in the texts.

D.N. Christodoulakis (Ed.): NLP 2000, LNCS 1835, pp. 395-405, 2000.
© Springer-Verlag Berlin Heidelberg 2000

The methods used for our system are described and the operation of the system is illustrated using instructive examples of questions. Our question-answering based approach serves the aim of creating flexible information extraction tools accepting natural language questions and generating answers that contain information extracted from text either directly or after applying deductive inference [10]. This approach corresponds roughly to what are called "Adaptive IE Systems"[14].

2   The Verb Definition Processing Subsystem

The implementation of the system of computer processing of Greek verbs from Stock Market Texts uses the tools that we have developed for the semantic processing by computer of the definitions of verbs. The tools developed for verb processing exhibit some novel features with some basic features being the creation of the lexicon automatically using a machine readable dictionary, the learning of the correct interpretation of verbs with more than one meaning using machine learning by supervision techniques based on user feedback.

The system has been implemented with the programming language Prolog so that satisfactory portability can be achieved. The system accomplishes the function of the automatic detection of circular definitions and the automatic transformation of definitions into special forms in which verbs that express basic concepts are used by following chains of definitions connected through verbs common to the entries being chained. A machine-readable dictionary with possibly ambiguous entries is used, which provides the analysis of complex verbs into basic ones. In particular, in one case of Greek verb processing about 600 motion verb definitions were analysed automatically and they were re-expressed in terms of about 50 basic verbs. Every time a verb is processed which is amenable to more than one interpretation the system allows the user to interact with the system and state its approval or disapproval of the interpretation chosen by the system, which helps the system to learn by supervision. Another computational lexicon that was created with our techniques was a Medical one of about 2000 words.

Our system exhibits some novel features i.e. the creation of the lexicon is accomplished automatically using a machine readable dictionary, learning of the correct interpretation of verbs with more than one meaning is accomplished using machine learning by supervision techniques based on user feedback.

3   The Verb Subsystem Illustration with an Agent-Guiding System

The Agent-Guiding system was implemented with Turbo Prolog, which has some simple facilities for computer graphics. Using these facilities the system displays a room with a door, some furniture and some objects that may be manipulated by the agent. These are objects such as a table, a door, a desk, a bottle, a box and a book. The bottle, the box and the book are examples of objects that may be manipulated by the agent. It is supposed that there is an invisible agent in the room, who can move around and execute the user's motion commands. These commands may refer directly or indirectly to the movement of specific objects or the change of their state. The agent knows the names of these objects and their position in the room displayed on the screen. The agent also knows how to execute some basic commands.

When the user submits a command, the agent, in order to satisfy the constraints of the verb's meaning, may ask for new information and knowledge about objects and verbs, which may be used in the future. A machine-readable dictionary with possibly ambiguous entries is used, which provides the analysis of complex verbs into basic ones. In particular, in the case of Greek about 600 motion verbs were analysed automatically in terms of about 50 basic verbs. Finally every time a command is executed which is amenable to more than one interpretation the system allows the user to observe the graphical output and state its approval or disapproval that helps the system to learn by supervision.

4   Architecture and Operation of the Definition Subsystem

The system is composed of a number of modules each one performing a different task. These modules are:

- Machine readable dictionary processor
- Lexical processor
- Syntactic processor
- Semantic processor
- Basic verb processor
- Graphics processor
- Learning module

The operation of these modules is supported by a number of databases. These are:

- Machine readable dictionary
- Basic Lexicon
- Stems Base
- Objects Attributes Base
- Knowledge Base

The texts processed consist of sentences with one or more verbs that declare the action of an agent and some other words like nouns, prepositions or adverbs. Prior to the syntactic and semantic analysis of the sentence the system checks if each word of the sentence belongs to its lexicon. Stemming is used at this stage because of the multiple forms of the Greek words. When the command contains a word unknown to the system then the system produces a message for the user and terminates the processing of the present sentence and continues with the processing of the rest of the present text.

After having recognized all the words in a sentence the system performs the syntactic analysis of it. If the input sentence is syntactically correct, the system recognizes the main verb, the object or objects of it and the adverbs or prepositions connected with it. After this the module for "processing basic verbs" tries to satisfy all the constraints and the conditions put by the selectional restrictions of the verb. This processing requires searching in the knowledge base from where the system retrieves information about the object's properties. At this point, when some information is unavailable or ambiguous, the system interacts with the user in order to acquire the missing knowledge.

There are two different types of questions that the system may ask. The first type includes questions for which there is no information in the knowledge base and the user must supply it. The second type refers to questions that demand a Yes or No answer. This happens when more than one interpretation of an input verb is possible and the system cannot decide which is the correct one. In these cases, the system, using the machine learning mechanism, suggests each time one of the different solutions and requests an answer from the user. The Yes or No answers generate appropriate entries in the knowledge base and can be used next time a similar sentence is processed without requesting for information any more. This process is based on the "learning by taking advice" technique of machine learning.

5   Examples of Operation of the Lexical Subsystem

Suppose that the system processes the imperative sentence "open the door". The system isolates the words of the command and recognizes the verb "open" and the noun phrase "the door". The verb "open" appears in the lexicon with a number of different definitions. E.g. in the LDOCE we find among others the following two senses of "open": a) to cause to become open, b) to make a passage by removing the things that are blocking it. The Greek dictionary we used contains similar sets of senses for this verb and the sense selection mechanism is practically the same for the two languages. The main difference is the wording of the sense selection rules for the two languages where the objects and their properties have different names. The system selects the sense "b" because it knows that a door blocks a passage. The next decision the system has to take concerns the way the opening action is executed.

The system finds in the knowledge base that there are two alternative ways of interpreting the verb "open", using either a "push" or a "pull" basic motion. Then, it selects the first one and asks the user if this is the right one. If the answer is "No", the system selects the next available interpretation and prompts again the user for an answer. When the answer is "Yes", a fact is recorded in the knowledge base which denotes that for the verb "open" and the object "door" the appropriate motion is e.g. "pull" in case that the "Yes" answer was given for the "pull" interpretation.

The second example refers to the movement of a book that exists in a virtual microcosm of the system. When the system is given the imperative sentence "put the book on the desk" it searches the knowledge base to find a side of the book that can be used as a base for it. The book has 6 sides and when the system selects one of them it presents graphically the book on the desk having this side as base. Then, it asks the user if the result of the motion is the correct one. When the user enters a "Yes" answer, this is recorded in the knowledge base and the process terminates. When the user enters a "No" answer, the process continues trying sequentially all the available sides of the book until the user gives a "Yes" answer.

The graphical user interface that was implemented was very helpful during the development. It was easier to see the result on the screen, graphically rather than reading lists of the knowledge base to find the changes that were recorded during the program execution and the machine learning process.

6   Verb Selectional Restrictions

In the present paper an attempt is also made to exploit theoretical insights on the selectional restrictions for the purposes of the system. The verb subcategorization frames involve selectional restrictions on verbs and their arguments and modifiers, which may be noun phrases, prepositional phrases, infinitives and participles. Specific classes and subclasses of verbs are related to a specific set of arguments and modifiers. These elements form subsets within the set of elements determined by the sublanguage processed by the system. Our analysis concerns different types of selectional restrictions such as selectional restrictions on verb complements and selectional restrictions on noun phrase and participle complements.

Although they have been regarded as a 'static' representation of encoded semantic information (i.e. in computational lexicons) [1], selectional restrictions (or "domain-specific constraints") of various types have been used in a wide range of domains in the field of NLP processing.

The selectional restrictions in respect to verbs contribute to the hierarchical conceptualization of the temporal relations of elements in a text fragment. Apart from adverbs and prepositions indicating time, temporal relations are expressed by the finite verb (or infinitive) and its modifier (participle), its arguments (i.e., an infinitive) and the modifiers of its arguments (a secondary clause or another participle).

In the corpora processed by the present system, direct temporal relations to the finite verb or infinitive of the sentence are actually expressed by the relation between the finite verb/infinitive and the participle modifying it. Participles may refer to an event that happened before (i), after (ii) or during (iii) the event expressed by the finite verb or infinitive/infinitive. The determination of the temporal relation between the finite verb and another verb's participle is based on the type of participle involved, in particular, the type of verb the participle is derived from. In the restricted domain of the corpus, specific participles paired with verbs or infinitives express a specific type of temporal relation between these two elements. The types of temporal relations are, therefore, determined by the type of participle only and are independent from the finite verbs or infinitives. The available templates correspond to the subcategorization of these verbs.

The criteria that are used to express temporal relations are either semantic or sublanguage specific and are valid and applicable only in the particular domain of the corpus, namely financial texts. A list of illustrative examples follows:

(i) Event expressed by the participle precedes the event expressed by the finite verb:

Παρουσιάστηκε αύξηση της τάξης του 308,3%, φθάνοντας τα 294,6 εκ. δρχ.
(A raise of 308,3% was indicated, reaching 294,6 million DRS.).

(ii) Event expressed by the participle follows the event expressed by the finite verb:

Ενώ οι εξαγωγές αυξήθηκαν στα 1.394 εκ. καλύπτοντας το 34% του συνολικού τζίρου *(While the rate of exports rose to 1.394 million DRS, covering 34% of the turnover).*

(iii) Event expressed by the participle occurs at the same time as the event expressed by the finite verb:

Κατά τη χθεσινή γενική συνέλευση της Πειραιώς, ο πρόεδρος της τράπεζας δήλωσε "παρών" όσον αφορά τη διεκδίκηση της Ιονικής, τονίζοντας ότι δεν πτοείται από σενάρια. *(During the last general assembly of the Bank of Piraeus, the president of the bank stated his "presence" in respect to the contest of the Ionian Bank, pointing out that he is not daunted by scenarios).*

In the domain of the present corpus it has been observed that sub-groups of verbs, classified according to their semantics, constitute three groups of participles formed from these verbs. The first group involves participles indicating precedence over the act expressed by the finite verb or infinitive they refer to. Participles of verbs expressing semantic relations of (I) "arriving at a point" (reaching (φθάνοντας), surpassing (υπερβαίνοντας), exceeding (ξεπερνώντας), terminating (τερματίζοντας), closing (κλείνοντας)), (II) "foreseeing" (aiming at (στοχεύοντας), foreseeing (προβλέποντας), assuming/considering (υπολογίζοντας)), aiming at (αποβλέποντας)) are classified in the first group.

The first group also includes a group of verbs that cannot be classified according to a particular semantic criterion. In case, the classification criterion is purely sublanguage specific, restricted within the domain of the microcosm of financial texts. This group is constituted by the following verbs: purchasing (εξαγοράζοντας), participating (συμμετέχοντας), having designed, having implemented (έχοντας σχεδιάσει, έχοντας υλοποιήσει), distributing (διανέμοντας), issuing (εκδίδοντας).

The second group is constituted by participles that indicate an act following the act expressed by the finite verb or infinitive they modify. It involves participles of verbs expressing the following semantic relations: (I) "showing" (indicating (σημειώνοντας), demonstrating (παρουσιάζοντας), showing (εμφανίζοντας)), "accomplishing" (completing (ολοκληρώνοντας), achieving (επιτυγχάνοντας), accomplishing (πραγματοποιώντας)) and (II) "raising" (raising (ανεβάζοντας), increasing (αυξάνοντας)).

Similarly to the first group, the second group includes another set of verbs that are not classified according to semantic criteria, but according to criteria of the sublanguage domain. This group is constituted by the following verbs: covering (καλύπτοντας), obtaining (αποκομίζοντας), registering (καταγράφοντας), re-adapting (αναπροσαρμόζοντας), reacting (αντιδρώντας), offering (προσφέροντας), choosing (επιλέγοντας), intervening (παρεμβαίνοντας), having (now) (έχοντας (πλέον)).

The third group involves the cases of participles where it is not clear whether there is precedence or antecedence over the act expressed by the finite verb or infinitive. These participles are participles of verbs involving speech and speech acts. Since these verbs involve speech acts, the temporal order is dependent on the speaker. For instance, in the following example (iv) the participle "expressing" may refer to time before or after the verb "predicted"

(iv) Η Morgan Stanley προέβλεψε περαιτέρω μείωση των επιτοκίων στα ομόλογα, διατυπώνοντας θετικές εκτιμήσεις για την Ελληνική αγορά. *(Morgan Stanley predicted a further decrease of rates of interest in bonds, expressing positive estimations for the Greek market).*

The group of verbs related to speech acts includes the following verbs: pointing out (υπογραμμίζοντας), emphasizing (τονίζοντας), suggesting (προτείνοντας), clarifying (διευκρινίζοντας), contradicting (διαψεύδοντας), declaring (δηλώνοντας), formulating, expressing (διατυπώνοντας), condemning (καταγγέλοντας).

7   Event Ordering Determination

The role of an element in the sentence and its semantic type determines its precedence or antecedence in relation to another element of the sentence. In the present corpus, precedence relations between actions conveyed by the sentence are in many cases expressed by the relation between the main verb of the sentence and the participles connected to the main verb. Participles may have a complement or argument that is available before or after the event expressed by the main verb of the sentence.

For instance, in the sentence "Η υπεραξία του χαρτοφυλακίου στις 31/3/99 ξεπέρασε το σύνολο των   κερδών και ανήλθε σε 1.759,2 εκ.δρχ. σημειώνοντας αύξηση κατά 124,6%", the main part of which is translated in English as *"The value rose to 1759.2 million, demonstrating a raise of 124.6%"*, the word "demonstrating" which is the translation of "σημειώνοντας" (an "ontas" participle in Modern Greek) refers to an event which refers to a quantity (124.6%) that is the result of a calculation based on the event expressed by the verb "rose". Different precedence relations are expressed with "reaching" in the sentence "Αύξηση της τάξης του 308,3% παρουσίασαν τα καθαρά κέρδη φθάνοντας τα 294,6 εκ.δρχ." the main part of which is translated in English as *"A raise of 308.3% was indicated, reaching 294.6 million"*. In the latter example "reaching" has an argument with computational precedence over the argument of "indicated". In the corpora analyzed these two verbs were always temporally related to the main verb on the sentence in the same way. The participle "demonstrating" (σημειώνοντας) always follows in "computational time" the main verb of the sentence, while the participle "reaching" (φθάνοντας) always precedes the main verb of the sentence. We call "computational time" an axis analogous to the real time axis on which events are placed according to the order that the quantities involved are computed or obtained.

8   Text Mining with the ARISTA Method

A final important point of our approach is the processing of text directly avoiding any kind of formal representation when inference is required for the mining of facts not mentioned explicitly in the text. This idea of using text as knowledge base was first presented in [2], [3] and further elaborated in [5], [7], [8] and in [9], [10], [11] as "the ARISTA method". This is a new method for knowledge acquisition from texts that is based on using natural language itself for knowledge representation. The Computational Lexicon constructed supports the Deductive Mining of knowledge about the behaviour of systems like companies.

A form of sentences found in the corpora used for text mining contained two verbs one of which was in the "ontas" form that has replaced participles of Ancient Greek in Modern Greek. In some of these sentences the complements of the two verbs are related through some arithmetical or sorting operation that supports the deductive generation of answers to the users questions. In the section "Event Ordering Determination" above the determination of the order of events was discussed. In this section the answering of questions from such sentences based on the ARISTA method will be discussed.

Our question-answering based approach aims at the creation of flexible information extraction tools, which accept natural language questions and generate answers that contain information extracted from text either directly or after applying deductive inference. Our approach also addresses the problem of implicit semantic relations occurring either in the questions or in the texts from which information is extracted. These relations are made explicit with the use of domain knowledge. The foundation of our method can be found in [4]. Examples of application of our method are presented in [7], [10] concerning three domains of quite different nature. These domains are: Oceanography, Medical Physiology, Aspirin Pharmacology and Ancient Greek Law. Questions are expressed both in Greek and English.

9   The Question Grammar

The information extraction task can thus be performed interactively enabling the user to submit natural language questions to the system and therefore allowing for greater flexibility than template based systems. Our method uses a question grammar combined with a text grammar for the extraction of information. These two grammars use syntax rules and domain dependent lexicons while the semantics of the question grammar provides the means of their combination. The semantics of a question grammar may provide the means of the combination of question processing with information extraction. An illustrative question grammar production is presented below for English questions:

```
q(Q,SComp):-  f(Q,who,VP),f(VP,V,ANP),f(ANP,the,NP),

              f(NP,VN,OB),f(OB,of,C),f(C,Company,""),

              syn(V,SV),is_a(Company,ObComp),

              t(VN,SV,SComp,ObComp).
```

The predicate t(_,_,_,_) which was given this name in order to remind one the role played by templates in other methods of information extraction, connects the question grammar with the text grammar .

The predicate f(_,_,_) is a shorthand version of the inbuild Turbo Prolog predicate fronttoken(X,Y,Z) which gets the first word Y of a string of words X and returns the remainder of the strimg of words Z.

Using this predicate we effectively recognize with the above production questions written following the pattern:

<who><VERB><the><DEVERBAL><of><NAMED_ENTITY_CLASS>

Examples of such questions are:

q1="who plans the purchase of companies ?"

q2="who plans the purchase of industries ?"

q3="who completed the purchase of commercial ?"

The predicates syn(_,_) and is_a(_,_) exploit verb and named_entity taxonomies respectively.

e.g. a verb taxonomy fragment would be:

plan
  interested
  decide
  announce

and a named_entity taxonomy fragment would be:

companies
  commercial
        company name 1
        company name 2
        company name 3
  industries
        company name 4
        company name 5
        company name 6

10   The Text Grammar

The text analysis performed by the system that was implemented on the computer is based on logic grammars appropriate for each text domain. An original parsing method appropriate for languages with relatively free word order was used for the Greek text. This method consists of the automatic translation of every sentence into a number of logical facts written in Prolog and the recognition of syntactic constituents as logical combinations of these facts. These facts take the form of a logical predicate with three arguments. The first argument specifies the number of the sentence that contains a given word, the second argument specifies the position of the word in the sentence and the third specifies the word itself.

In traditional methods of syntactic analysis by computer, which is mainly used, for the analysis of English texts one syntactic rule must be written for every particular sequence of words. This means that if we apply such a method for the syntactic analysis of Greek a plethora of syntactic rules will be needed for the same constituent due to the word order freedom of this language. On the contrary the method followed in the present system allows the statement of a single syntactic rule for the parsing of two or more equivalent syntactic structures that differ only in the relative position of the words involved. The form of sentences that can be analyzed by the rules developed for the present system consists of one verb and its complements.

The complements of the verbs are recognized by syntactic rules that analyze the following basic forms of noun phrases:

- Noun
- Article + Noun
- Article+ Participle
- Adjective+ Noun
- Noun in Nominative+ Noun in Genitive
- Noun+ Pronoun+ Article+ Noun

11   Conclusion

In the present paper we presented the implementation and application of a system for computer semantic processing of Greek verbs occurring in Greek Stock Market Texts for the purpose of text mining with question answering using the ARISTA method. The system has been implemented with the programming language Prolog and it accomplishes functions like the automatic detection of circular definitions and the automatic transformation of definitions into special forms in which verbs that express basic concepts are used. The methods used for our system are described and the operation of the system is illustrated using instructive examples of questions. Our question-answering based approach serves the aim of creating flexible information extraction tools accepting natural language questions and generating answers that contain information extracted from text either directly or after applying deductive inference.

References

1. Boguraev B., Pustejovsky J.: Lexical Knowledge Representation and Natural Language Processing, in: Artificial Intelligence 63, Elsevier (1993) 193-223
2. Kontos, J.: Syntax-Directed Processing of Texts with Action Semantics. Cybernetica, 23, 2 (1980) 157-175
3. Kontos, J.: Syntax-Directed Plan Recognition with a Microcomputer. Microprocessing and Microprogramming. 9, (1982) 227-279
4. Kontos, J.: Syntax-Directed Fact Retrieval from Texts with a Micro-Computer. Proc. MELECON '83, Athens (1983)
5. Kontos, J.: Natural Language Processing of Scientific/Technical Data, Knowledge and Text Bases. Proceedings of ARTINT Workshop. Luxembourg (1985)
6. Kontos, J., Cavouras, J. C.: Knowledge Acquisition from Technical Texts Using Attribute Grammars. The Computer Journal.,Vol 31, No 6, (1988) 525-530
7. Kontos, J.: ARISTA: Knowledge Engineering with Scientific Texts. Information and Software Technology, Vol. 34, No 9, (1992) 611-616
8. Kontos, J.:. Artificial Intelligence and Natural Language Processing (In Greek) E. Benou, Athens, Greece (1996)
9. Kontos, J., Malagardi, I.: Information and Knowledge Extraction from Medical Texts. Health Telematics Education Conference, Athens (1998)
10. Kontos, J., Malagardi, I.: Information Extraction and Knowledge Acquisition from Texts using Bilingual Question-Answering. Journal of Intelligent and Robotic Systems. Kluwer Academic Publishers, 26(2), (1999) 103-122
11. Malagardi, I.: Computer Determination of Relations between the Elements in Noun Phrases of Sublanguages. 17th annual meeting of the Department of Linguistics. Aristotle Univ. of Thessaloniki (1996)
12. MUC-6: Proceedings of the Sixth Message Understanding Conference. J. Aberdeen et al. (1995)
13. Wilks, Y.: Information Extraction as a Core Language Technology. In Pazienza, M. T. Information Extraction. LNAI Tutorial. Springer, (1997) 1-9
14. Wilks, Y., Catizone, R.: Can we Make Information Extration More Adaptive? Proccedings of ES99, The Nineteenth SGES International Conference on Knowledge Based Systems and Applied Artificial Intelligence, Springer (1999)

Extracting Semistructured Data - Lessons Learnt

Udo Kruschwitz, Anne De Roeck, Paul Scott, Sam Steel,
Ray Turner, and Nick Webb*

Department of Computer Science, University of Essex
Wivenhoe Park, Colchester, CO4 3SQ, United Kingdom
{udo,deroe,scotp,sam,turnr,webbnw}@essex.ac.uk

Abstract. The Yellow Pages Assistant (YPA) is a natural language dialogue system which guides a user through a dialogue in order to retrieve
addresses from the *Yellow Pages*[1]. Part of the work in this project is concerned with the construction of a *Backend*, i.e. the database extracted
from the raw input text that is needed for the online access of the addresses. Here we discuss some aspects involved in this task as well as
report on experiences which might be interesting for other projects as
well.

1 Introduction

The YPA is a directory enquiry system which allows a user to access addresses
and other information of advertisers in a classified directory [4]. A substantial
part of the work on this project has been the extraction of data from the source
files to create a *Backend* database. This source data is *semistructured*, in other
words "data that is neither raw data, nor very strictly typed as in conventional
database systems" [1]. A second notable fact is that we do not have access to
vast amounts of data, our sources are in the range of a few megabytes. The solution is to construct a *Backend* such that the *online* query processing is midway
between theorem-proving and *Information Retrieval (IR)*. The theorem-proving
is about metafacts (e.g. relations between different indices) rather than entities
like addresses or single index entries. In this paper we will describe aspects of
the *Backend* construction and what has been learnt in this process.

The structure of this paper will be as follows. First we will give a general
overview of the architecture of the YPA system (section 2). In section 3 we will
point to related work. Section 4 focusses on the *Backend* component of the YPA.
Finally we describe recent experiences and evaluation results (section 5) and
conclude with an outline on future work (section 6).

---

* Now at University of Sheffield (n.webb@dcs.shef.ac.uk)
[1] Yellow Pages and Talking Pages are registered trade marks of British Telecommunications plc in the United Kingdom

D.N. Christodoulakis (Ed.): NLP 2000, LNCS 1835, pp. 406–417, 2000.

2   System Overview

The YPA is an interactive system for querying a database of addresses in a classified directory. A query can consist of simple keywords, phrases or can look like this:

I need the addresses of hotels with en suite bathrooms in Wivenhoe please!

Figure 1 is an overview of the system architecture (depicting the data flow).

A conversation cycle with the YPA can be roughly described as follows. A user utterance (recognised by the *Speech Recognition* or typed in via the *Graphical User Interface*) is sent to the *Dialogue Manager*. The *Dialogue Manager* keeps track of the current stage in the dialogue and controls the use of several submodules. Before handing back control (together with the relevant data) to the *Toplevel*, the input is first sent to the *Natural Language Frontend* which returns a so-called *slot-and-filler query*. The *Dialogue Manager* then consults the *Query Construction Component*, passing it the result of the parsing process (possibly modified depending on the *Dialogue History* etc). The purpose of the *Query Construction Component* is to transform the input into a *database query* (making use of the *Backend* and possibly the *World Model*), to query the *Backend* and to return the retrieved addresses (and some database information) to the *Dialogue Manager*. Finally the *Dialogue Manager* hands back control to the *Toplevel* which for example displays the retrieved addresses. It could also put questions to the user which were passed to it by the *Dialogue Manager*, if the database access was not successful (i.e. did not result in a set of addresses). At this stage the cycle starts again.

3   Related Work

If we look at the YPA as a system, then it is comparable with natural language dialogue systems. A lot of online dialogue systems have been described mainly for dealing with times or train schedules , for example [3,18,14,10,7]. This is of little interest for the YPA. However, dialogue systems have also been built for retrieving addresses from *Yellow Pages*, for example *Voyager* [24,22,6] and *Galaxy*, but the implementations are restricted to sample domains or small-scale address databases (e.g. 150 objects in *Voyager* [6] or 2400 tourist related listings in *Galaxy* [23]). This is of course not unrelated to the fact that these are *spoken* language dialogue systems.

However, the task of extracting and representing *semistructured* data within such a system can be tackled in different ways. Different communities approach the problem of dealing with this sort of data in different ways. From the perspective of database management systems (*DBMS*) there has been a research interest in how to represent this data as well as how to extract parts of it. The *Lore* database management system [11] is designed specifically for the management of semistructured data. The *Information Manifold* system [8] allows the

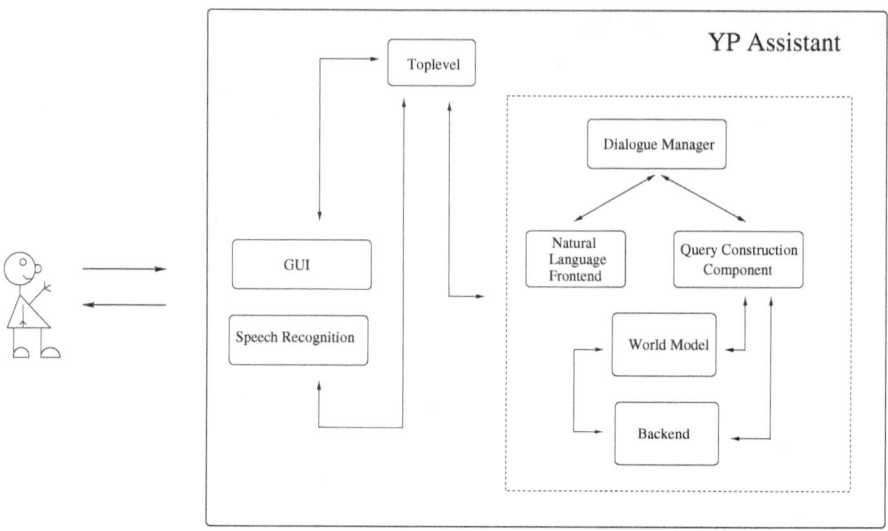

Fig. 1. Architecture of the YPA

access to data in heterogeneous sources. By declaratively describing the contents and the query capabilities it allows a uniform access to various resources.

On the other hand, a typical *IR* approach tackles the problem in quite a different way. The traditional task is to select a set of documents from a large collection so that the selected documents satisfy a user's query. It is not necessary to think about actually accessing semistructured data in an *online* system, but to preprocess this data *offline*. It is therefore reasonable to extract data from the corpus of documents that can then be represented by a traditional relational database system. The remaining problem is then *how* to represent the content of the source documents. The *NLIR* system [16] which is a *Natural Language Information Retrieval* system uses parallel indices which represent the same document using different indexing methods. Natural language processing (*NLP*) has been incorporated into *IR* systems (lexical processing, stemming, POS tagging etc.) [9,15] but "NLP techniques used must be very efficient and robust, since the amount of text in the databases accessed is typically measured in gigabytes" [21]. *IR* systems usually rely very much on statistics. As we pointed out earlier, the amount of data in the YPA system is in the region of just megabytes. But we could abstract the YPA to an *IR* task involving *short queries* for the access of *short documents* which is quite different to classical *IR* tasks like those considered at TREC [17].

From this point of view there are at least two approaches that should be mentioned here. *Publishers Depot* [5] is a commercial product that allows the retrieval of pictures based on the corresponding caption.[2] That means the doc-

---

[2] http://www.picturequest.com

uments are very short compared to standard *IR* tasks. Some points are worth mentioning here as we are concerned with similar problems. First of all, *WordNet* [12] is the base for semantic expansion, i.e. synonyms, hypernyms etc. are used to broaden the search. For this purpose *WordNet* was tailored. Among other things, that included the deletion of "bad" words, the removal of odd links and addition of new terms which do not exist in the *WordNet* lexicon. Overall *WordNet* is seen as well suited for *IR* tasks like this.

On the other hand there has been work on *conceptual indexing* [20]. A knowledge base is built that is based on the observation that there are few true synonyms in the language and usually there is a generality relationship like: *car –> automobile –> motor vehicle* which can be expressed as a *subsumption* relationship. [20] employs an example from the *Yellow Pages*:

- The *Yellow Pages* do not contain a heading "automobile steam cleaning".
- There are basic facts (axioms): (1) a *car* is a *automobile* and (2) *washing* is some kind of *cleaning*.
- The algorithm has to infer that *car washing* is some sort of *automobile cleaning*.

Such a knowledge base has been applied to precision content retrieval knowing that standard *IR* approaches are not very effective for *short* queries [2].

Our approach can finally be placed somewhere between the one used in [5] and [20].

4   The Backend

4.1   Input Data

The *Backend* construction process takes the raw data (the so called *YP printing tape*) and creates a database that retains as much information and relations as possible for the online enquiry system. This was described in detail in [4]. The input data is *semistructured* in a sense that a record structure for the addresses and headings does exist but the internal structure of these entries is not formally defined. Usually this consists of partial English sentences, address information, telephone patterns etc. Several types of adverts exist: *free, line* and *semidisplay* entries with *semidisplay* adverts carrying more information than just the name and the address of the advertiser. Here is a typical *semidisplay* entry as it appears in the printed directory (in this case listed under *Hotels & Inns*):

```
┌─ UDO, THE ──────────────────────┐
│                                  │
│   TOWN CENTRE BED & BREAKFAST    │
│   EN SUITE ROOMS-AMPLE PARKING   │
│     High St,Wivenhoe,01206 827735│
└──────────────────────────────────┘
```

The actual source code in the *printing tape* does not give us much more structured information than what can be seen in the printed advert:

```
195SS15SBZS9810289N955030800 0 0150UD0,THE^
195SS15SBZS9810289B935020800C0     TOWN CENTRE BED & BREAKFAST^
195SS15SBZS9810289B935020800C0     EN SUITE ROOMS-AMPLE PARKING^
195SS15SBZS9810289B935020800C0     CHigh St,Wivenhoe,01206\$_827735^
```

When comparing this data with a typical user request it is often hard to find adverts which do actually satisfy the complete user query. In our initial example the user asked for *hotels with en suite bathrooms,* something which cannot be found in the list of adverts. But the above example is still a very good match.

We see the task of the dialogue system as narrowing the gap between a user request and what the index database of the system can supply. Figure 2 presents a different example for this task.

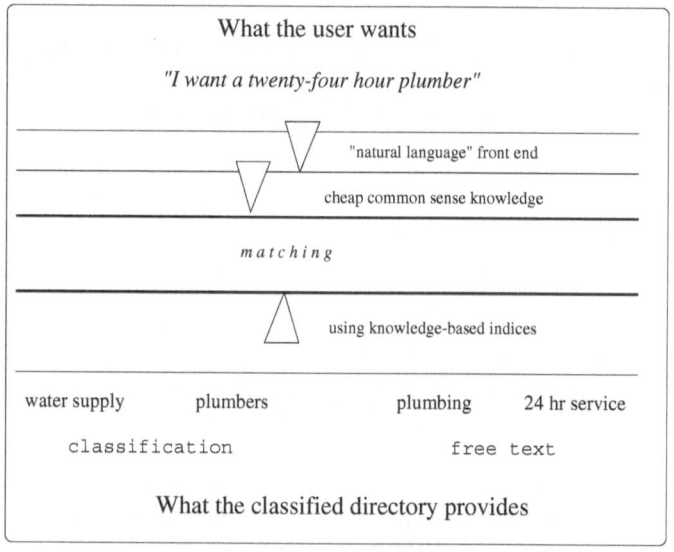

Fig. 2. Narrowing the Gap

Thus, the input data must be transformed into an appropriate representation which does allow to match user queries to adverts as good as possible combining various sorts of information like the name of the heading, the keywords in the free text of an entry (*TOWN CENTRE BED & BREAKFAST* ...) etc.

In order to obtain such a *Backend* database of indices we can distinguish two extreme positions for the construction process: *Knowledge Representation,* i.e. express the data in logic and do theorem proving in the online YPA system or *Information Retrieval,* i.e. use morphology and string matching. The intermediate position that we have chosen extracts relatively flat relations from the incoming data and uses text-retrieval-like methods for this *offline* process, while we can still apply theorem-proving-like methods in the *online* system.

4.2   Data Representation

The *Backend* database which is compiled *offline* consists of a set of different tables. The indices in these tables are represented as normalised representations of (stemmed) base forms of simple keyword or phrases, but the relations between index tables can be used in the online system which goes beyond string matching. Threrefore we speak about *knowledge rich* indices. The performance of the retrieval depends on how well the *Query Construction Component* (YPA-QCC) and the *Dialogue Manager* (YPA-DM) exploit this knowledge.

For the above example the simplified information stored in the various tables for this advert includes the following: *location indices* ("wivenhoe"), *heading indices* ("hotels", "inns"), *business name indices* ("udo"), *free text indices* ("bed_breakfast", "en_suite_rooms" ...), *heading reference indices* (for "guest houses" see also the heading "hotels & inns"), *street indices* ("high_street").

An extract of this information as encoded in our Prolog database is shown here:

```
keyword_heading('hotel_inn', 33264).
keyword_heading('hotel', 33264).
keyword_heading('inn', 33264).

entry(33264, 33302, 'udo,the').

keyword_entry('bed_breakfast', 33302).
keyword_entry('bed_breakfast_suit', 33302).
keyword_entry('room_suit', 33302).
   ...

see_also(31136, 33264).
```

Some of the information is easy to find, for example the heading name and the references, but on the other hand information like the street name must be spotted within the free text, this is not marked.

With a database created like this it is now the responsibility of the YPA-QCC to decide how to combine the different index tables in the retrieval process. Several cases are possible given the following user request:

Are there any guest houses in Ipswich?

First of all, the list of adverts listed under *Guest Houses* could be displayed. But with the given reference to *Hotels & Inns* the list of addresses might be extended. However, if this list becomes too big, should the user be given a choice of different headings to select from or should only be the *best* matching adverts displayed? What if all adverts have the same ranking?

Some strategies for the YPA-QCC can be triggered by different setup options available to the user. For example it might be that the user is interested in high *recall* rather than *precision*, in which case the strategy employed by YPA-QCC and YPA-DM will look different to the default strategy (in the example that could mean that adverts under the heading *Hotels & Inns* will always be retrieved when asked for *guest houses*).

4.3   Interaction with Other Components

We referred to the *Backend* as a database of *knowledge rich* indices. It remains the task of the other components in the system to actually apply this in a sophisticated way. In parallel to the work on the database creation we revised the *Query Construction Component* and the complete *Frontend* to be able to exploit the *Backend* knowledge. But how much does the *Backend* influence these components?

First of all, it turned out that we can still use a very flat and robust parser which then calls the slot filling process to group the information in a domain dependent second processing step (some slots are: *location*, *transaction* and *products & services*). That means only very general syntactic structure and almost no semantic information is preserved in the process of transforming the input query into some internal representation except the implicit semantics of the slots. This was explained in more detail in a separate paper about the *Frontend* [19]. For the *Query Construction Component* this flat structure seems sufficient, because to solve the task of retrieving information from the *Backend* the *Query Construction Component* mostly relaxes or constrains a database query and this is triggered by simple assumptions:

- Simple syntactic information (like the detection of prepositional phrases or modifiers) is exploited to relax queries. This works very efficiently.
- The semantics of the slots can be used to relax or constrain queries. This knowledge can be encoded declaratively, for example:
  - A slot *streetname* has some relation to a slot *location* in a way that relaxing a query can be achieved by emptying the *streetname* slot and leaving *location* untouched.
  - A slot *products & services* is more important than the *methods of payment* slot, this is of course part of the domain dependent customisation.
- Finally, other metafacts (knowledge about the *Backend* database) which are not encoded as semantics of slots can be used.

After all, the *Query Construction Component* is responsible to combine these flat but heterogenous knowledge sources in the retrieval process.

4.4   Applying the Backend Database

We want to report some experiences gained while working on the YPA which involve the usage of the *Backend*.

Initially we went for a high *recall* because a lot of queries could not be answered just because the query terms could not be mapped to the indices in the *Backend*. When testing the system with real users we soon noticed that a high *precision* is much more desirable than a high *recall*, something that has also been reported by [5]. Nothing seems more irritating for a user than addresses whose retrieval cannot be explained. As an example a user asked for *car magazines*. The results that the system offered as the best it could find came from under the headings of *Scrap Metal Merchants*. That resulted from expanding both the query terms *car* and *magazine* using synonyms, hypernyms and cross references in the directory because nothing matched the initial query:

- The word *product* is a hypernym of *magazine*.
- The heading *Reclaimers - Waste Products* cross-references to *Scrap Metal Merchants*.
- The heading *Car & Commercial Vehicle Dismantlers* cross-references to *Scrap Metal Merchants*.

As a result, we had to restrict the query expansion procedure. Addresses that are now retrieved are filed under *Newsagents*, though these do not match the complete query.

A different example is the request for *kitchen cupboard specialists in Ipswich*. In an old version of the YPA the result was not very user friendly. What happened was that there was no match for the complete query but trying partial matches resulted in *too many* adverts, because the only partial match that was considered was looking for *specialists* which of course gives *too many* addresses. And that was exactly the information given to the user with the request to relax the query. In the latest version of the system the user now still does not get any addresses with this query but rather than just asking the user to relax the request there is now a dialogue step that offers relaxations in several ways. In this example you would get:

1. *Do you want to see matches in a wider area?*
2. *Should I search for kitchen specialists?*
3. *Should I search for cupboard specialists?*

For each of these options a corresponding checkbox is displayed. However, the default input field allows the user to continue the dialogue in a different way in case none of the displayed options make the user very happy (in this case the user might input *Restart please!*).

Finally, a last example: In a version with a brutal but simple stemmer we were able to match a query for *press photography* to a heading *Photographers – Press* (which would not work with the Porter stemmer, another simple stemming algorithm [13]), however at the same time a user querying for *hospitality* retrieved addresses that contained a list of *hospitals*, not the best match. We are still experimenting with two different stemmers, but are convinced that too little stemming is better than too much stemming.

5   Recent Experiences and Evaluation

5.1   Other Input Data

In a recent development we created a similar system using much richer data which however still fits into the same *Backend* structure only that new relations are added. Look at this extract which represents only a part of the information stored for one advert:

```
PRODUCTS AND SERVICES
* MPA Regional Wedding Photographer of the year, 1997
* Commercial, PR and legal photography at competitive prices
* Wedding and portraits a speciality
  ...


HOURS OF BUSINESS
8.00-21.00 7 days a week including Bank Holidays by arrangement
24 hour answerphone

FACILITIES
Small studio with studio lighting, photographic framing
  ...
```

It proved to be very simple to convert the new data files once the set of scripts had been developed. Minimal customisation of the scripts were needed. Essentially we extended the extraction process by additional steps.

The main advantage of accessing the new data is that the *free text* in the advert is much longer. In this version there is more information than printed in the directory. Addresses are still very short if we see them as documents in an *Information Retrieval* task. But for the *free text* we discovered:

- The information they contain is still very dense, i.e. every phrase is meaningful.
- The information is often grouped under different labels which are just words or phrases but highlighted in certain ways (e.g. capital writing followed by a line break or underlined). The text can then be split into subunits containing information of type *Products, Opening Hours, Brands* etc. Now different sorts of *free text* indices exist. This task is based on pattern matching and performs well for the data we have so far.
- The different types of information extracted in the former step can be treated differently, for example a word like *Monday* cannot be ignored when creating indices for the type *Opening Hours*, but it can in all other cases.

- The distribution of keywords for *all* adverts under a given heading shows that the most frequent keywords describe that heading generally very well, i.e. these keywords can be associated with that group of adverts even if they do not occur explicitly in the name of the heading (e.g. the keyword *ticket* is very frequent under the heading *Travel Agents*).

We quickly built a system based on this new data and the first results are very promising though they must be validated by more data.

5.2   Evaluation

For the evaluation we used the YPA version 0.7 for the Colchester area with about 26.000 addresses.

We performed two sorts of evaluation, one technology focussed one precision-based. While the technology based evaluation is of particular interest to find problems in the different components of the YPA, the precision based evaluation is appropriate to see how the system performs overall comparing the results with the user query. Note however, that this is not a trivial task. We cannot just adapt a standard *IR* method of measuring *precision* at certain *recall* points because the YPA is a dialogue system and will not display addresses as long as it cannot find an appropriate set of addresses. We therefore applied simple metrics for the evaluation described here.

We used a query corpus of real user queries, in this case our *Bristol corpus* of 75 user queries. We measured how many of the resulting addresses are appropriate. This was done as a *black box* evaluation where the whole system was hidden. For the results presented here we only queried the database once and did not continue the dialogue if there was one initiated by the system. We then evaluated the system under different assumptions simplifying the evaluation:

1. If the initial user query is successful then calculate the average precision of the addresses by counting appropriate results as *100%* and everything else as *0%*. The average precision should be *0%* if no addresses are retrieved after the initial query. This gives us a baseline.
2. The same, but define the average precision as *100%* for those cases where the query does not give a result. This might seem unrealistic, but in most of these cases the request cannot be satisfied at all because there are no matching addresses as for example in the query *Skydiving in Colchester*.
3. Ignore those queries in the corpus which cannot be matched to any addresses in the database and then calculate the average precision as explained before.

The average precision that we calculated for each of the three assumptions is 61% for assumption 1, 79% for assumption 2 and finally 74% for assumption 3. These are the results of a very simplistic evaluation. One aspect for example is not reflected at all, that is the order and ranking values of the adverts in a successful user query.

We continue with evaluating the YPA. At the moment we are most concerned about a more detailed evaluation and measuring the *recall* as well.

6   Outline

We continue work on the YPA system. One of the interesting parts is to extract more structural information from the new (richer) data files. At the same time this will influence the other components in particular the *Query Construction Component* and the *Dialogue Manager*, because a more varied *Backend* database allows a refined query construction and a more user friendly dialogue.

We also noticed that the function of the *Dialogue Manager* changed quite a lot in the process of the overall development of the YPA. More and more tasks which were initially located in the *Dialogue Manager* have been implemented as customisations of the *Query Construction Component*. It could well be that in future we will merge those two components to just one.

We also plan to make the developed data extraction tools more generic so that they can be applied to completely different domains.

As a major task for the future remains a deep evaluation of the system which involves another user trial once we have developed a framework for this.

Acknowledgement

We want to thank all test users at BT Laboratories, Martlesham Heath, for bravely querying the system at various stages without giving up.

References

1. ABITEBOUL, S. Querying Semi-Structured Data (invited talk). In *Proceedings of the 6th International Conference on Database Theory (ICDT)* (Delphi, Greece, 1997), pp. 1–18.
2. AMBROZIAK, J., AND WOODS, W. A. Natural Language Technology in Precision Content Retrieval. In *Proceedings of the 2nd Conference on Natural Language Processing and Industrial Applications (NLP-IA)* (Moncton, Canada, 1998), pp. 117–124.
3. AUST, H., OERDER, M., SEIDE, F., AND STEINBISS, V. The Philips automatic train timetable information system. *Speech Communication 17* (1995), 249–262.
4. DE ROECK, A., KRUSCHWITZ, U., NEAL, P., SCOTT, P., STEEL, S., TURNER, R., AND WEBB, N. YPA - an intelligent directory enquiry assistant. *BT Technology Journal 16*, 3 (1998), 145–155.
5. FLANK, S. A layered approach to NLP-based Information Retrieval. In *Proceedings of the 36th ACL and the 17th COLING Conferences* (Montreal, 1998), pp. 397–403.
6. GLASS, J., FLAMMIA, G., GOODINE, D., PHILLIPS, M., POLIFRONI, J., SAKAI, S., SENEFF, S., AND ZUE, V. Multilingual Spoken-Language Understanding in the MIT VOYAGER System. *Speech Communication 17* (1995), 1–18.
7. HEISTERKAMP, P., MCGLASHAN, S., AND YOUD, N. Dialogue Semantics for an Oral Dialogue System. In *Proceedings of the International Conference of Spoken Language Processing* (Banff, Canada, 1992).

8. LEVY, A. Y., RAJARAMAN, A., AND ORDILLE, J. J. Querying Heterogeneous Information Sources Using Source Descriptions. In *Proceedings of the 22nd VLDB Conference* (Mumbai (Bombay), India, 1996).

9. LEWIS, D. D., AND SPARCK JONES, K. Natural language processing for information retrieval. *Communications of the ACM 39*, 1 (1996), 92–101.

10. MCGLASHAN, S., FRASER, N., GILBERT, N., BILANGE, E., HEISTERKAMP, P., AND YOUD, N. Dialogue Management for Telephone Information Systems. In *Proceedings of the International Conference on Applied Language Processing* (Trento, Italy, 1992).

11. MCHUGH, J., ABITEBOUL, S., GOLDMAN, R., QUASS, D., AND WIDOM, J. Lore: A Database Management System for Semistructured Data. *SIGMOD Record 26(3)* (1997), 50–66.

12. MILLER, G. Wordnet: An on-line lexical database. *International Journal of Lexicography 3*, 4 (1990). (Special Issue).

13. PORTER, M. F. An Algorithm for Suffix Stripping. *Program 14*, 3 (1980), 130–137.

14. SIKORSKI, T., AND ALLEN, J. F. A task-based evaluation of the TRAINS-95 dialogue system. In *Proceedings of the Workshop on Dialog Processing in Spoken Language Systems, ECAI-96* (Budapest, 1996).

15. SMEATON, A. F. Using NLP or NLP Resources for Information Retrieval Tasks. In *Natural Language Information Retrieval*, T. Strzalkowski, Ed. Kluwer Academic Publishers, 1997.

16. STRZALKOWSKI, T., GUTHRIE, L., KARLGREN, J., LEISTENSNIDER, J., LIN, F., PEREZ-CARBALLO, J., STRASZHEIM, T., WANG, J., AND WILDING, J. Natural Language Information Retrieval: TREC-5 Report. In *Proceedings of the Fifth Text Retrieval Conference (TREC-5)* (NIST Special Publication 500-238, 1997).

17. VOORHEES, E. M., AND HARMAN, D., Eds. *Proceedings of the Sixth Text Retrieval Conference (TREC-6)* (1998), NIST special publication 500-240. TREC web site: http://trec.nist.gov.

18. WAHLSTER, W. Verbmobil: Translation of Face-to-Face Dialogues. In *Proceedings of the 3rd European Conference on Speech Communication and Technology* (Berlin, Germany, 1993), pp. 29–38.

19. WEBB, N., DE ROECK, A., KRUSCHWITZ, U., SCOTT, P., STEEL, S., AND TURNER, R. Natural Language Engineering: Slot-Filling in the YPA. In *Proceedings of the Workshop on Natural Language Interfaces, Dialogue and Partner Modelling (at the Fachtagung für Künstliche Intelligenz KI'99)* (Bonn, Germany, 1999). http://www.ikp.uni-bonn.de/NDS99/Finals/3_1.ps.

20. WOODS, W. A. Conceptual Indexing: A Better Way to Organize Knowledge. Technical Report SMLI TR-97-61, Sun Microsystems Laboratories, Mountain View, CA, 1997.

21. ZHAI, C. Fast Statistical Parsing of Noun Phrases for Document Indexing. In *Proceedings of the 5th Conference on Applied Natural Language Processing* (Washington DC, 1997).

22. ZUE, V. Toward Systems that Understand Spoken Language. *IEEE Expert Magazine February* (1994), 51–59.

23. ZUE, V. Navigating the Information Superhighway Using Spoken Language Interfaces. *IEEE Expert Magazine October* (1995), 39–43.

24. ZUE, V., GLASS, J., GOODINE, D., LEUNG, H., PHILLIPS, M., POLIFRONI, J., AND SENEFF, S. The VOYAGER Speech Understanding System: Preliminary Development and Evaluation. In *Proceedings of IEEE International Conference on Acoustics, Speech and Signal Processing* (1990).

A Term-Based Methodology for Template Creation in Information Extraction

Kalliopi Zervanou and John McNaught

Department of Language Engineering,
University of Manchester Institute of Science and Technology
UMIST, PO Box 88, Manchester M60 1QD, UK
{kalliopi,jock}@ccl.umist.ac.uk

Abstract. In this paper, we are concerned with the problem of automatic template creation for Information Extraction (IE) and we present a methodology for the creation of IE templates. Our approach proposes the semi-automatic construction of a semantic representation of textual information based on recognition of multi-word and nested terms and Named Entities (NEs) and subsequent exploitation of term and NE context for the induction of Information Extraction template rules.

1 Introduction

The increasing amount of information stored in texts in electronic form has made imperative the need to distinguish information salient to our purposes. Research in Information Extraction (IE) focuses on this problem. IE aims at the detection and extraction of pre-specified categories of information in a natural language document. A key element for the selection of salient pieces of information is a set of shallow text analysis rules which are typically based on pre-defined linguistic patterns. These involve syntactic relations between words or semantic classes of words and express in this way *concepts* and *events* of interest that are to be extracted from the text.

As global understanding of any natural language text is still beyond the reach of current technology, each IE system is tailored to particular users' needs for specific domain information. Nevertheless, the acquisition of this domain-specific knowledge and the development of domain-specific rule sets constitute not only tedious and time consuming tasks, but also tasks innately restricted to specific applications. In response to this knowledge-engineering bottleneck, various systems attempt to learn information extraction rules automatically (Auto-Slog [13] and Auto-Slog-TS [14], [16], CRYSTAL [19], WHISK [18], RAPIER [5]).

Within this research framework, we shall consider the potential for learning generic extraction patterns. Our research on information templates, which is being carried out within the context of the CONCERTO project [10], focuses on the systematic identification of *all* possible IE events, based on textual patterns and without use of extensive semantic information. It is based on the hypothesis that, on the one hand, terms are one of the most particular characteristics of

D.N.Christodoulakis (Ed.): NLP 2000, LNCS 1835, pp.418-423, 1998.
Springer-Verlag Berlin Heidelberg 1998

the sublanguage elements used in a particular domain and they are therefore likely to convey the principal concepts of the document. On the other hand, the evaluation of existing IE systems in the Message Understanding Conferences has shown that considerable progress has been made in the task of recognition of Named Entities, namely the identification of names of persons, companies and dates of importance in the text. Therefore, the combination of term extraction and Named Entities recognition with other textual structure and syntactic cues can provide a reliable basis for the conceptual representation of domain specific texts and the definition of what constitutes an IE template in linguistic terms.

In the second section of this paper we shall consider the problem of automatic template creation and present previous research approaches. The third section presents the stages of our methodology and our research tools for implementation.

2   The Automatic Template Creation Problem in IE

The need for development of practical and portable IE systems for real-world applications has prompted a growing research interest in automatic or semi-automatic rule acquisition. In general, the problem is considered through a twofold perspective, namely:

i. construction of a dictionary of template rules
ii. construction of a dictionary of semantic information

For template rule acquisition, most systems rely on annotated training data of some sort, which are subsequently exploited by different learning techniques. One of the first dictionary construction systems was Auto-Slog [13]. Auto-Slog initially relies on CIRCUS, a conceptual sentence analyser that is based on a domain-specific dictionary of *concept nodes*. A concept node is a case frame triggered by a lexical item in a specific syntactic context. Based on a training corpus of manually tagged noun phrases that form part of the targeted information, Auto-Slog constructs an enhanced concept node dictionary. The rules that determine trigger words and context in order to activate a concept node are based on domain particular heuristics [15]. Its extension, Auto-Slog-TS [14], [16] uses a pre-classified corpus of relevant texts and the domain particular heuristics derived by Auto-Slog. In this case, Auto-Slog-TS ranks the linguistic patterns based on the frequency of occurrence of the pattern in relevant texts when compared to its presence in the full training corpus [14]. CRYSTAL [19] also generates extraction patterns using a training corpus where domain specific targeted information is annotated by the end user, whereas the recently developed WHISK system [18] does not require prior syntactic or semantic annotation when applied to structured or semi-structured text.

Semantic lexicons are mostly manually constructed. There have been attempts to make use of existing general purpose relational lexicon resources such as WordNet [12]. The RAPIER system [5], for example, incorporates in its induced regular expression patterns (such as POS tagger output) semantic class information provided by WordNet. WordNet is also used by another IE system architecture presented by Bagga et al. [1]. They attempted to use WordNet noun ontologies for building both the semantic database and the extraction rules. They base their generalisation rules on the enumerated *sense lists* of WordNet and a graphical user interface to semi-automate the procedure. However, as also claimed by Riloff & Jones [16] *"general-purpose resources, such as WordNet, do not contain the necessary domain-specific vocabulary"*.

Other attempts for automatic construction of semantic dictionaries are mostly based on training sets of keywords or key concepts verified manually or semi-automatically. In CRYSTAL [19], an existing domain specific semantic lexicon defines the semantic classes of words. In Auto-Slog [13], [15] concept node trigger words are domain-specific and in essence keywords are verified manually. Interestingly, domain specific terminology extraction was implemented by keyword recognition to test Auto-Slog in the domain of microelectronics and the results have shown that terminology recognition through this keyword method can be also used to identify relevant information independently from the concept nodes [15].

To sum up, we observe that these approaches rely on initial semantic annotation of the targeted information to build case frame-like rule templates. In Auto-Slog, noun phrases referring to targeted information are annotated; in Auto-Slog-TS, all noun phrases are annotated and then concept nodes are selected based on their relevance weights; and, in CRYSTAL and WHISK, a domain-specific semantic lexicon is required. Subsequently, rule induction is based on the initial concept nodes for Auto-Slog and Auto-Slog-TS, based on heuristics and observation of the source text domain, whereas in WHISK an algorithm for rule generalisation is further applied based on the semantic hierarchies of the domain specific lexicon.

Our hypothesis is that semantic information can be obtained automatically through Named Entities recognition and term extraction in order to built the initial case frame-like conceptual nodes instead of mere keywords or other key concepts and without having any target information annotated. Moreover, linguistic rules need not be based on mere observation of the source text domain and heuristics. Systematic corpus analysis of the domain texts could provide more reliable and coherent rule patterns for the extraction of important information.

3   A Term-Based Methodology for Template Creation

In our approach, we attempt to investigate whether semantic dictionaries can be based on extracted terms instead of keywords and make use of POS and partially syntactically annotated text to create term-based extraction patterns. Our methodology for template creation consists of four main stages:

1. Automatic term recognition and Named Entities recognition for content representation, extraction of collocated VPs, NPs etc.
2. Feature analysis (object/relationship)
3. Identification of position in text structure and syntactic information
4. Template leraning algorithm

Terms form an important feature, although not the only one, of any sublanguage domain and IE applications typically target domain specific information. Terms are theoretically the embodiment of specialised concepts [17]. Therefore, terms are more likely to convey the domain specific information in a document. The identification and the extraction of terms is, according to Boguraev & Kennedy, *"one of the better understood and most robust natural language processing technologies within the current state of the art of language engineering"* [2]. Their research has shown that linguistic processing targeted at term identification, such as the TERMS algorithm [9], can be applied for content characterisation in domain specific texts and can be extended as *discourse notion* to cover domain independent representations for automatic summarisation purposes [2], [3]. We can therefore take advantage of the research done in the area of term extraction for information extraction purposes and make use of existing tools.

There are various techniques for automatic term recognition, based on linguistic and statistical methods. We have chosen to use the *C-value/NC-value method* tool [8]. This method combines linguistic and statistical information to extract multi-word and nested terms from English corpora. The *C-value* component identifies multi-word, nested terms and collocations, whereas the *NC-value* part incorporates a method for the extraction of term context words. The statistical part defining the termhood of the candidate strings outperforms the common statistical measure of frequency of occurrence used for term or mere keyword extraction, making it sensitive to nested terms.

In our approach, the extraction of complex terms is important for it does not only give a more accurate representation of concepts in the source text, but also, according to the principle of syntagmatic derivation in terminology, the term constituents can be divided into two constituents, where the head constituent often represents a super ordinate concept [4]. For instance, *a cellular fibrous tissue* is a type of tissue, and this semantic hierarchy information can be further used for eventual generalisation of our template patterns. Moreover, the extraction of term context words and collocations is expected to give us additional information for the case frame of the term.

Named Entities is another important element of the information that has to be recognised and extracted. According to the MUC-7 task definition, the Named Entity task consists of three subtasks: the annotation of *unique identifiers* of entities (organisations, persons, locations), times (dates, times), and quantities (monetary values, percentages)[6]. The existing research in Information Extraction has shown that the Named Entities recognition task has achieved the highest accuracy of all IE tasks, as defined and evaluated in the Message Understanding Conferences. In particular, Named Entities can be extracted with reliability of $F < 97\%$, in MUC-6, and $F < 94\%$, in MUC-7 (where F-Measure is Recall and Precision weighted equally) [7]. Moreover, according to a recent study by Mikheev et al. [11], Named Entities recognition does not constitute a knowledge bottleneck, since relatively small gazetteers and a judicious use of internal and external evidence for Named Entities recognition rules are sufficient for satisfactory results.

Therefore, term and Named Entities extraction can provide a reliable linguistic basis for the identification of extraction templates when this information is combined with other syntactic and grammatical category information.

For Named Entities recognition we make use of the Basic Semantic Element Extraction (BSEE) module of the CONCERTO project [10]. The BSEE module carries out the tokenisation and morphological analysis of input text. Named Entities are identified and recognised by a combination of database look up and context-sensitive linguistic rules. These rules build up syntactic and semantic structural representations and also find instances of co-reference between names [10]. At this stage of our research, the BSEE entities database will be enhanced with recognised terms and subsequently feature analysis of the resulting structural representations will be carried out. Then, based on these results, we shall attempt to investigate eventual regularities in the position of the extraction pattern in the text structure and we shall use all resulting features to induce pattern extraction rules.

4   Conclusion

In this paper, we were concerned with the problem of automatic template creation in Information Extraction. We have presented current approaches and we have proposed a methodology for template creation based on term recognition and systematic investigation of the source text structure and linguistic patterns. Our approach proposes an initially exhaustive identification of *all* possible linguistic patterns that express domain specific information. Although the result of such a process is not readily applicable for user-specific IE purposes, we believe that the subsequent exploitation of such patterns will not only facilitate knowledge acquisition in the development of IE systems, but it will also provide a reliable training basis for the automation of template rule acquisition. Moreover, term-based investigation of the sublanguage domain linguistic features, syntactically and morphologically, can be beneficial for other areas of natural language processing. Our work is currently in process and further work must be done in order to test and evaluate our methodology in Information Extraction applications.

References

1. Bagga, A., J. Y. Chai and A. Biermann: The Role of WordNet in the Creation of a Trainable Message Understanding System. In *Proceedings of the Fourteenth Conference on Artificial Intelligence (AAAI/IAAI-97)*, (1997) 941–948
2. Boguraev, B. and C. Kennedy: Technical Terminology for Domain Specification and Content Characterisation. In *Information Extraction: A multi-disciplinary approach to an emerging information technology. International Summer School, SCIE-97, Frascati, Italy, July 14–18.1997, M.T. Pazienza (ed.)* Springer, (1997) 27–96

3. Boguraev, B. and C. Kennedy: Salience-Based Content Characterisation of Text Documents. In *Proceedings of ACL/EACL'97 Workshop on Intelligent Scalable Text Summarisation*, Madrid, Spain, (1997) 2–9

4. Bourigault, D.: LEXTER, a Terminology Extraction Software for Knowledge Acquisition from Texts. In *Proceedings of the Ninth Knowledge Acquisition for Knowledge Based System Workshop (KAW'95)*, Banff, Canada, (1995)

5. Califf, M. E. and R. J. Mooney: Relational Learning of Pattern-Match Rules for Information Extraction. In *Working Papers of ACL-97 Workshop on Natural Language Learning*, (1997) 9–15

6. Chinchor, N. A.: MUC-7 Named Entity Task Definition. Version 3.4, 13 July 1997.

7. Chinchor, N. A.: Overview of MUC-7/MET-2. In *Science Applications International Corporation (SAIC)*, (1998)
   http://www.muc.saic.com/proceedings/muc_7_proceedings/overview.html

8. Frantzi, K. T. and S. Ananiadou: The C-Value/NC-Value Domain Independent Method for Multi-Word Term Extraction. In *Journal of Natural Language Processing*, **6**(3) (1999) 145–179

9. Justeson, J. S. and S. M. Katz: Technical Terminology: Some Linguistic Properties and an Algorithm for Identification in Text. In *Natural Language Engineering*, **1**(1) (1995) 9–27

10. McNaught, J., W. J. Black, F. Rinaldi, E. Bertino, A. Brasher, D. Deavin, B. Catania, D. Silvestri, B. Armani, P. Leo, A. Persidis, G. Semeraro, F. Esposito, G. P. Zarri and L. Gilardoni: Integrated Document and Knowledge Management for the Knowledge-based Enterprise. In *Proceedings of Practical Application of Knowledge Management 2000 (PAKeM 2000)* (forthcoming), Manchester, (April 2000) 10–14

11. Mikheev, A., M. Moens and C. Grover: Named Entity Recognition without Gazetteers. In *Proceedings of EACL'99*, (1999) 1–8

12. Miller, G. A., R. Beckwith, C. Fellbaum, D. Gross and K. Miller: Introduction to WordNet: An Online Lexical Database. In *Five Papers on WordNet*, (1993) 1–9
    ftp://ftp.cogsci.princeton.edu/pub/wordnet/5papers.ps

13. Riloff, E.: Automatically Constructing a Dictionary for Information Extraction Tasks. In *Proceedings of the Eleventh National Conference on Artificial Intelligence (AAAI-93)*, (1993) 811-816

14. Riloff, E.: Automatically Generating Extraction Patterns from Untagged Text. In *Proceedings of the Thirteenth National Conference on Artificial Intelligence (AAAI-96)*, (1996) 1044-1049

15. Riloff, E.: An Empirical Study of Automated Dictionary Construction for Information Extraction in Three Domains. *AI Journal*, **85** (August 1996)

16. Riloff, E. and R. Jones: Learning Dictionaries for Information Extraction by MultiLevel Bootstrapping. In *Proceedings of the Sixteenth National Conference on Artificial Intelligence (AAAI-99)*, (1999)

17. Sager, J. C., D. Dungworth and P. F. McDonald: English Special Languages: principles and practice in science and technology. Oscar Brandstetter Verlag KG, Wiesbaden, (1980)

18. Soderland, S.: Learning Information Extraction Rules for Semi-structured and Free Text. In *Machine Learning, C. Cardie and R. Mooney (eds.)* Kluwer Academic Publishers, Boston (1999) 1–44

19. Soderland, S., D. Fisher, J. Aseltine and W. Lehnert: CRYSTAL: Inducing a Conceptual Dictionary. In *Proceedings of the Fourteenth International Joint Conference on Artificial Intelligence (IJCAI '95)*, (1995) 1314–1319

A System for Recognition of Named Entities in Greek

Sotiris Boutsis[1,2], Iason Demiros[1], Voula Giouli[1], Maria Liakata[3],
Harris Papageorgiou[1], and Stelios Piperidis[1,2]

[1] Institute for Language and Speech Processing
Artemidos 6 & Epidavrou, 151 25, Athens, Greece
tel: +301 6875300, fax: +301 6854270
{sboutsis,iason,voula,xaris,spip}@ilsp.gr
[2] National Technical University of Athens
[3] Cambridge University
ml257@cam.ac.uk

Abstract. In this paper, we describe work in progress for the development of a Greek named entity recognizer. The system aims at information extraction applications where large scale text processing is needed. Speed of analysis, system robustness, and results accuracy have been the basic guidelines for the system's design. Pattern matching techniques have been implemented on top of an existing automated pipeline for Greek text processing and the resulting system depends on non-recursive regular expressions in order to capture different types of named entities. For development and testing purposes, we collected a corpus of financial texts from several web sources and manually annotated part of it. Overall precision and recall are 86% and 81% respectively.

1   Introduction

In this paper, we present a system that recognizes and classifies named entities (NE) in Greek text. The system has been developed in the framework of the EPET II "oikO-NOMiA" project, which aims at the construction of a pipeline integrating NE recognition, shallow parsing, and co-reference resolution technologies. The pipeline will analyze text to produce a shallow semantic representation suitable for template filling in scenario based information extraction (IE) applications.

Natural Language Processing (NLP) systems performing information extraction have gained the focus of attention of both the academic and the business intelligence community. NERC is the first task in the information extraction task series. Several factors contribute to its complexity. Name-list based recognition is not adequate, since unknown names should be dealt with in addition to names appearing in the lists. Moreover, known names may be of several types; commonly used Greek names can be of type person, organization, location, or none of the above. Moreover, the name classification schema can vary significantly across domains and applications. Thus, there are two aspects in NERC: 1) recognition and classification of known names, and 2) spotting and classification of new names. It should be noted that the creation, adaptation, and maintenance of name databases comes at a significant cost; new text

D.N. Christodoulakis (Ed.): NLP 2000, LNCS 1835, pp. 424-435, 2000.
© Springer-Verlag Berlin Heidelberg 2000

needs to be scanned for names or name aliases, which should be linked to the entities they refer to. This is common in dynamic news scanning and routing.

We followed the MUC-7 NE task definition with certain adaptations. We capture organization, person and location names (ENAMEX), date and time expressions (TIMEX), percent and money expressions (NUMEX). The system is composed of a series of basic language technology building blocks for Greek developed in ILSP. The tools are modular with streamed I/O which enables their combination in a pipeline. A common Tipster-like annotation and data representation model underlies the whole application.

An initial finite state preprocessor performs tokenization and sentence boundary identification. A part-of-speech Brill tagger trained on a manually annotated corpus and a lexicon-based lemmatizer carry out morphological analysis and lemmatization. A lookup module matches name lists and trigger words against the text, and, eventually, a finite state parser recognizes NE's on the basis of a pattern grammar. A corpus of 130.000 words was used to guide system development.

System evaluation and testing was carried out against a manually annotated corpus of 20,000 words. Performance was measured with the recall (R), precision (P), and F-measure (F = 2PR / (P+R)) scores. The system achieves P=86%, R=81% and F=83%. Systems participating in MUC-6 and MUC-7 typically report F-measures around 90%, approaching human performance. We have to note, however, that our system was tested in a more diverse corpus than the MUC data set. Present performance is encouraging, but there is certainly room for improvement.

2   Background

Several successful systems for large-scale, accurate named entity recognition have been built. The majority of the systems operate on English text and follow a rule-based and/or probabilistic approach, with hybrid processing being the most popular.

The NYU system for MUC-6 [11] uses sets of regular expressions which are efficiently applied with finite state techniques. The system records the initial appearance of each name and its type; subsequent appearances of substrings of previously seen names are recorded as aliases. The F-measure is 80%. IsoQuest's NetOwl pattern based system [15] has been commercialized and performs around 90%. The NERC system developed in DFKI [17] for German text processing is based on FST's and performance ranges between 66% and 87% for different NE types.

The LaSIE system used in MUC-6 and MUC-7 [9] processes the input text by performing list-based matching and parsing with a special proper name grammar produced by hand. The LaSIE parser is a bottom-up Prolog chart parser. LaSIE's F-measure is 92%. An approach similar to the one in LaSIE is taken by NCSR Demokritos [13] for Greek and scores 73% and 97% for Recall and Precision respectively. Rule-based NE recognition is also followed by Umist in FACILE [3]. The MITRE Alembic system [1] relies on sequences of phrase rules, both hand-crafted and automatically learned through the application of Brill's error-reduction learning algorithm [5]. The system achieved 85% success rate in MUC-6.

A probabilistic language model built from a training corpus is employed in the Kent Ridge Digital Labs system [20]. Nymble [2] is another statistical approach to NERC using a variant of the standard Hidden Markov Model. It achieves an F-measure of 91% in English and 90% in Spanish.

The NYU MENE system [4] for MUC-7 is based on maximum entropy (ME) modeling. ME modeling facilitates the combination of diverse pieces of contextual evidence for the estimation of the probability of a linguistic class, and consequently lends itself to NERC. The system has been trained on a manually annotated 270K word corpus, makes use of a broad array of dictionaries, and contains no hand-generated patterns. MENE exhibits performance of 92% for the dry-run test and 84% for the formal test. The LTG system makes use of several stages of rules and pre-trained ME models [16], achieving an F-score of 93%.

There have been several efforts to apply decision-tree techniques to the NERC task. A. Gallippi approached multilingual NERC [10] using an initial core set of linguistic features and a decision tree classification scheme. A system optimized for English (F=94%) has been ported to Spanish (F=89%) and Japanese (F=83%). Sekine et al. ([18], [19]) describe a system using a decision tree to classify names in Japanese. The CLR/NMSU team propose [7] two NE recognition systems for MUC-6. The first is a data intensive method that uses human generated patterns. The second uses training data to develop decision trees.

3   Specifications

Specifying the annotation schema for the Greek NERC task, we followed the MUC-7 guidelines [6]. In particular, we cater for the identification of NE's of types ENAMEX (PERSON, ORGANIZATION, LOCATION), TIMEX (TIME and DATE) and NUMEX (MONEY, PERCENT). A brief summary of our guidelines is given here under:

We mark entities appearing in the text with their full-name, an abbreviated/reduced form of this name (e.g. "Εθνική Τράπεζα της Ελλάδος/National Bank of Greece – Εθνική / National"), or a word/phrase - usually a metonymy - consistently used to describe it (e.g. "Ηρακλής (soccer team) - ο Γηραιός", "Χρηματιστήριο Αξιών Αθηνών / Athens Stock Exchange – Χρηματιστήριο / Stock Exchange – Σοφοκλέους / (the street where ASE is located)"). Of course, simple pronominal or nominal references to NE's are not marked. NE's connected through part-whole and possessor-possessed relations are marked independently, e.g. "To [org Τμήμα Ανάλυσης και Μελετών /org] της [org Εγνατίας ΑΧΕ /org] / The [org Research Department /org] of [org Egnatia Securities /org]". Quotes are included in the NE when they are embedded in it, or when they cover it exactly.

Person: It is quite common for a company owner's name to appear in the company title. Thus, caution should be taken to correctly identify whether a person name refers to a person or a company, e.g. "o κ. [person Μυτιληναίος /person] παρουσίασε τους αναπτυξιακούς στόχους της [org Μυτιληναίος /org] μέχρι το τέλος του έτους / Mr. [person Mytilinaios /person] presented the growth target of [org Mytilinaios /org] for this year". As it is specified in the MUC-7 guidelines, titles such as "κ., κος, κον / Mr.", "κα./Miss,Ms", "πρόεδρος/president", "διευθύνων σύμβουλος/CEO", etc. are not marked as part of the NE. Also we do not mark person names included in the names of prizes, products, methods etc. E.g. "τεστ Παπανικολάου/pap test", "βραβεία Ωνάση/Onasis awards".

Organization: Councils and committees are marked as NE's only when they are written with their first letters in capital, e.g. "[org Υπουργικό Συμβούλιο /org] / [org Council of Ministers /org]", "[org Διοικητικό Συμβούλιο /org] / [org Board of Directors /org]". NE's of type location are included in an organization name only when they function as NP modifiers in genitive, e.g. "η [org Τράπεζα της/det Ελλάδος /org] / the [org Bank of Greece /org]". On the contrary, location names in complement position of prepositional phrases modifying organizations are not included in the organization NE's, e.g., "η [org Ελληνική Πρεσβεία /org] στα/prep [loc Τίρανα loc] / the [org Greek Embassy /org] at [loc Tirana /loc]". Organization designators, e.g. "εταιρεία / [company, society], οργανισμός / organization", are included in the organization name only when they are written with a capital first letter. E.g. "εκδόσεις [org Σάκουλα /org] / [org Sakoula /org] publications" vs. " [org Εκδόσεις Ερμής /org] / [org Ermis Publications /org]". Only "υπουργείο / ministry" and "χρηματιστήριο / stock exchange" are excluded from this rule, e.g. "[org υπουργείο Εξωτερικών /org] / [org ministry of Foreign Affairs /org]", "[org χρηματιστήριο της Φρανκφούρτης /org] / [org Frankfurt stock exchange /org]". Company prefixes and suffixes, e.g. "Αφοί", "Α.Ε.", "Α.Χ.Ε.", etc. are included in the organization name when present.

Location: According to the MUC-7 guidelines, location names used to refer to organizations are marked as locations: "Η [loc Ιταλία /loc] νίκησε τη [loc Βραζιλία /loc] / [loc Italy /loc] won [loc Brazil /loc]". In contrast to the MUC-7 guidelines, locative specifiers accompanying location names are always included in the named entity, e.g. "[loc αεροδρόμιο Αθηνών /loc] / [loc Athens airport /loc]", "[loc λιμάνι του Πειραιά loc] / [loc Piraeus port /loc]". Adjectives modifying a location name are included in the named entity only when they are written with a capital first letter. E.g. "[loc Βόρειος Αμερική /loc] / [loc North America /loc]", "βόρειο [loc Αιγαίο /loc] / north [loc Aegean /loc]". Adverbs are not included in the named entity unless they are part of the formal name, e.g. "πρώην/adv [loc Σοβιετική Ενωση /loc] / former [loc Soviet Union /loc]", but "[loc πρώην/adv Γιουγκοσλαβική Δημοκρατία της Μακεδονίας /loc] / [loc former Yugoslavic Republic of Macedonia /loc]".

Date and Time: Following the MUC-7 guidelines, we mark absolute date and time expressions, e.g. "[date Παρασκευή 23 Ιουλίου 1999 /date] / [date Friday 23 July 1999 /date]", "[time 10 μ.μ. /time] / [time 10 pm /time]". We also mark relative expressions indicating a specific date or time, e.g. "[date σήμερα /date] / [date today /date]", "[date χθές /date] / [date yesterday /date]", but not vague expressions that do not point to a specific date or time, e.g. "πριν μερικές ημέρες / a few days ago". Decades and centuries are marked, too. Names of seasons, months, days, holidays, and heads with date/time modifying expressions are included in the date/time. E.g. "[date δεκαετία του '80 /date] / [date the 80's /date]", "πριν την [date Πρωτοχρονιά του 2000 /date] / before the [date new year's day of 2000 /date]", "το [date οικονομικό έτος 2000 /date] / the [date fiscal 2000 /date]", "το [date σχολικό έτος 2000 /date] / the [date school year 2000 /date]". Also "[time 10πμ ώρα Ελλάδας /time] / [time 10 am Greek time /time]". Expressions such as "αρχή/beginning", "τέλη/end", "μέσα/mid" are marked with the date following them. We do not mark nouns expressing duration, e.g. "περίοδος [date 1990-1995 /date] / period [date 1990-1995 /date]". Unlike MUC-7, temporal units such as "πρωί/morning", "απόγευμα/evening" are marked even if they are not followed by an absolute temporal expression. E.g. "[time 10 το πρωί /time] / [time 10 in the morning /time]", "το [time πρωί /time] / in the [time morning /time]".

Money and Percent: We mark only numeric expressions followed by a currency expression or a percent. Currency names which are not followed by a specific numeric expression are not marked. Country names post-modifying the currency name are marked too: "[money 10 εκατ. δολάρια ΗΠΑ /money] / [money 10 million USA dollars /money]". Unlike MUC-7, we do not mark monetary expressions modified by multipliers such as "αρκετά εκατομμύρια δολάρια / several million dollars". Percent ranges are marked as one entity. Approximators, e.g. "περίπου / about", are not marked. E.g. "περίπου [percent 10%-15% /percent] / about [percent 10-15% /percent]".

4   The Corpus

A corpus of Greek texts of ca. 12,000,000 words in total comprising articles from financial newspapers and magazines (Express, Naftemporiki, Isotimia, Oikonomikos Tahidromos, and Vima) was downloaded from the web. As we wanted to use text with a high density of named entities, only the articles with the highest percentage of words with an uppercase first letter were chosen. The selected articles formed the training and testing corpus, which amounts to ca. 150,000 words. This corpus was then manually annotated according to the annotation schema described in the "Specifications" section. A TclTk graphical user interface facilitated the manual annotation of NE's in the text. Following MUC, document sections were delimited by SLUG, DATE, NWORDS, PREAMBLE, TEXT and TRAILER tags. The annotated corpus was used for both development and evaluation: 130,000 words were used to guide system development, e.g. evaluate rule performance, while the remaining 20,000 words of text were put aside for testing purposes.

5   System Architecture

System architecture is illustrated in Figure 1. The main system components are: Tokenizer, POS Tagger & Lemmatizer, Name Lookup, and NE Parser. All processing modules share a common Tipster-like [12] data model that facilitates efficient interoperation and addition of new annotation. The system runs under the PC/Windows operating system.

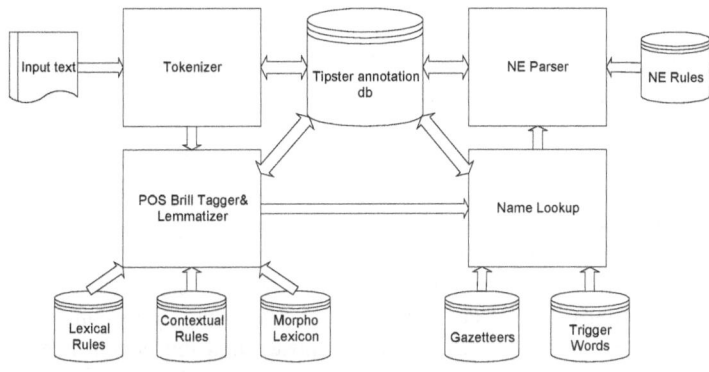

Figure 1: System Architecture

5.1   Tokenizer

Recognizing and labeling surface phenomena in the text is a necessary prerequisite for most Natural Language Processing (NLP) systems. At this stage, texts are rendered into an internal representation that facilitates further processing. Basic text handling is performed by a MULTEXT-like tokenizer [8] that identifies word boundaries, sentence boundaries, abbreviations, digits, and simple dates. Following common practice, the tokenizer makes use of a regular-expression based definition of words, coupled with downstream precompiled lists for the Greek language and simple heuristics. This proves to be quite successful in effectively recognizing sentences and words, with accuracy up to 95%.

5.2   Part-of-Speech Tagger and Lemmatizer

We use the Brill tagger [5] trained on Greek text. Rules were automatically learned from a manually annotated Greek corpus of 250K words. We use the PAROLE tagset, which, conforming to the guidelines set up by TEI and NERC, captures the morphosyntactic particularities of the Greek language. There are 584 different part-of-speech tags, so the usually reported Brill tagger accuracy is degraded down to 90%. First, the tagger assigns initial tags, looking up in a lexicon created from the manually annotated corpus during training. A suffix-lexicon is used for initially tagging unknown words. 799 contextual rules are then applied to improve the initial phase output. After part-of-speech tagging has taken place, the lemmas are retrieved from a Greek morphological lexicon containing 70K lemmas.

5.3   Name Lookup

At this stage, a set of static pre-stored names and regular expressions are matched against the tokenized, tagged, and lemmatized text in order to identify known named entities and trigger words.

We compiled lists of person, organization, and location names, combining material from several different sources such as yellow pages, company lists and place name lists available from the Athens Stock Exchange, the Technical Chamber of Greece, the Hellenic Telecommunications Organization, the National Statistical Service of Greece, etc. The name lists were also enhanced with names extracted from 130,000 words of manually annotated text. After all additions, the company name list had 1,059 entries, the location name list 793 entries, and the person name list 1,496 entries.

Furthermore, we formed lists of words, multi-words and regular expressions which are indicative of the existence of named entities in their surrounding, such as company designators, person titles, currency units, occupations, etc. This was done by automatically extracting indicative words through the application of word count and mutual information statistics to windows of 3-5 words to the left and to the right of each named entity in the training corpus and then manually clustering extracted words according to their use and semantics. These clusters were manually edited and further augmented during NE grammar development. At the name lookup stage, words appearing in a cluster get a specific tag which fires corresponding rules during the parsing phase. There are also regular expressions matching more than one words. In total, we use 57 clusters containing 920 words, multiwords, and regular expressions.

Name lookup is implemented on the basis of finite state recognizers, scanning the text at high speed for the existence of strings and regular expressions appearing in the name lists and clusters.

5.4   NE Parser

This is the last component of the NERC pipeline and finalizes the annotation added at previous stages.

Although a name in the text may appear in one of the lists, this does not necessitate that the name is of the corresponding to the list type. Context should also be taken into account to reach a safe conclusion. For instance, a company designator following a location name, could be used to correctly recognize the preceding name as of type company. To this end, rules are applied to the output of the name lookup stage to finalize named entity typing, as well as to recognize names not in the lists. Rules operate on the basis of: names recognized at the lookup stage, capitalization information, POS tags, and tags corresponding to the clusters mentioned in the previous section. Rules are written in the form of regular expressions [14] which are compiled into finite state transducers that transform input text by inserting or removing special markers. Rules are sequentially applied to the text using longest match. We make use of the FSA6 package [21] for compiling rules into finite state transducers and a C parser for efficiently applying them on the text.

The grammar consists of 110 rules in total: 17 for person, 19 for location, 37 for organization, 23 for date, 5 for time, 7 for money and 2 for percent. There are two types of rules: simple and composite, the latter being the ordered composition of two or more rules applied at the same pass. Rules may or may not take context into account. An example of a composite rule is given below:

```
markup (
[geosign+, atdf_ge^, {cap_aj, locadj_cap}^, abbr^, {const({'[person', '[loc'}, {'/person]',
'/loc]'}), cap_word, cap_rg}+, dig^],
'[loc', '/loc]')

o

conditional_markup_upward(
[{cap_rg, cap_word}+ ], '[loc', '/loc]',
[{geosign, indiclocverb}, as_se],
[] )

<EOR>
```

This rule recognizes structures such as "[loc Οδός Σίνα 4 /loc] / [loc 4 Sina Street /loc]" , "[loc νομός Θεσσαλονίκης /loc] / [loc prefecture of Thessalonica /loc]", "ορυχείο στο [loc Πότι Ρουμανίας /loc] / mine at [loc Poti, Romania /loc]", "πυρηνικός σταθμός στο [loc Τσέρνομπιλ loc] / nuclear plant in [loc Chernobyl /loc]", "Φθάνουμε στα [loc Σπάτα /loc] / We arrive at [loc Spata /loc]", ΄γεννήθηκε στην [loc Αθήνα /loc] / he was born in [loc Athens /loc]", etc. The first rule marks with "[loc", "/loc]" brackets the following: one or more geographical designators (geosign) such as "βουνό / mountain, αεροδρόμιο / airport, οδός / street" etc., optionally followed by a definite article, optionally followed by a capitalized adjective or a capitalized adjective indicative of location (locadj_cap) such as "βόρειος/north, νότιος/south" etc., optionally followed by an abbreviation, followed by one or more person NE's and/or location NE's and/or capitalized words, optionally followed by a digit. In this first rule the context of the NE is not taken into account. In the second rule, one or more capitalized words and/or capitalized foreign words are recognized as of type "location" only if they are preceded by a verb indicative of location such as "φθάνω/arrive" or a geosign followed by the Greek compound preposition "στον/[at, in]". [const(X,Y) is a macro for strings starting with X and ending with Y].

System development follows an iterative process. After each run, a Java graphical interface is used by the developer to view named entities spotted in the text. The interface identifies differences between automatically and manually recognized NE's and calculates precision and recall figures for each NE category. This facilitates fast NE grammar development.

6   Evaluation

30,000 words of the manually annotated corpus were used solely for evaluation. The performance of the system for each NE type is shown in Figure 2. There are no benchmarks for NE's of type time since only two time expressions appear in the test corpus. Figure 3 displays the error distribution over common error sources.

A significant number of errors (18.4%) are due to preprocessing (tokenization, tagging, lemmatization). As can be seen, the system did not perform particularly well in recognizing persons. 46% of errors in recognizing persons are due to preprocessing. For example, a sentence delimiter is sometimes inserted after initials which are naturally followed by periods. The same can happen in organization and location names containing abbreviations. Ambiguity between certain NE types (usually person – organization and location – organization) in the absence of clarifying context is a usual source of errors credited to the NERC stage itself.

We have taken action to deal with problems in preprocessing, as well as expand the NERC module so as to increase recognition performance per se. This includes fine-tuning the preprocessing chain, tailoring some aspects of preprocessing to NERC, expanding the NERC module to take into account gender information, and incorporating an NE cache. For example, let's consider the following:

Η [person Γερμανός / person] εξέδωσε 1.000.000 νέες μετοχές. / [person Germanos / person] issued 1,000,000 new shares.

"Γερμανός" is both a person name and a company name. Here, it was mistakenly recognized as person. Ambiguity could have correctly been resolved, if gender information were taken into account. Article "Η" is feminine whereas "Γερμανός" is masculine. This seeming violation of agreement (ellipsis in fact) could have been exploited to correctly raise the ambiguity. Furthermore, the NERC module is expanded with the incorporation of an NE cache storing instances of already recognized/classified names. This will facilitate the recognition of NE's which have been encountered and classified in other parts of the text.

Spelling mistakes account for another 11.5% of the errors. There are also words with letters from both sets, since some letters are shared by the Greek and Latin alphabets, but a script is used to map characters to the appropriate character set.

When no lists of known NE's (persons, organizations, locations) were used at the lookup stage, performance dropped dramatically. Precision and Recall figures are given in Figure 4.

NE Type	Precision	Recall	F-Measure
Person	0.71	0.71	0,71
Loc	0.85	0.82	0,83
Org	0.80	0.72	0,76
Money	0.99	0.95	0,97
Percent	1.00	0.98	0,99
Date	0.89	0.84	0,86
Time	?	?	0
Total	0.86	0.81	0,83

Figure 2: NERC Performance

NE Type	Error Distribution			
	% of errors due to preprocessing	% of errors due to spelling	% of errors due to ambiguity	Other
Person	46.0%	00.0%	12.6%	41.4%
Loc	12.5%	00.0%	09.7%	77.8%
Org	09.2%	15.7%	06.1%	69.0%
Date	15.1%	23.3%	00.0%	61.6%
Money	81.9%	00.0%	00.0%	18.1%
Total	18.4%	11.5%	06.6%	63.5%

Figure 3: Distribution of Error

NE Type	Precision	Recall	F-Measure
Person	0.80	0.34	0.47
Org	0.77	0.36	0.49
Loc	0.82	0.14	0.23
Date	0.89	0.84	0.86
Money	0.99	0.95	0.96
Percent	1.00	0.98	0.98
Total	0.75	0.45	0.56

Figure 4: NERC performance when the name lookup is omitted

7 Conclusion

In this paper, we presented a Greek named entity recognizer oriented towards large scale information extraction applications. We implemented finite state techniques favoring efficient text processing and adopted a modular design allowing fast customization to the needs and particularities of specific applications. We also carried out an elaborate evaluation of the system's output and identified the design and implementation aspects we should enhance. Since work is still in progress, we expect that benchmarks will further improve; the system, however, has already reached a level of performance (F=83%) which is satisfying for many real-world applications.

References

1. Aberdeen J., Burger J., Day D., Hirschman L., Robinson P., Vilain M. 1995. Mitre: description of the Alembic system used for MUC-6. Proceedings of Sixth Message Understanding Conference (1995)
2. Bikel D., Miller S., Schwartz R., Weischedel R.. Nymble: a high-performance learning name-finder, Conference on Applied Natural Language Processing (1997)
3. Black W., Rinaldi F., Mowatt D. Facile: description of the NE system used for MUC-7. Proceedings of Seventh Message Understanding Conference (1998)
4. Borthwick A., Sterling J., Agichtein E., Grishman R. 1997. Description of the MENE Named Entity System as used in MUC-7. Proceedings of Seventh Message Understanding Conference (1998)
5. Brill E. A corpus-based approach to language learning. Doctoral Dissertation, Univ. of Pennsylvania (1993)
6. Chinchor N., MUC-7 Named Entity Task Definition, Version 3.5 (1997)
7. Cowie J. 1995. Description of the CLR/NMSU systems used for MUC-6. Proceedings of Sixth Message Understanding Conference (1995)
8. Di Christo, P., S. Harie, C. De Loupy, N. Ide, and J. Veronis. Set of programs for segmentation and lexical look up, MULTEXT LRE 62-050 project Deliverable 2.2.1 (1995)
9. Gaizauskas R., Wakao T., Humphreys K., Cunningham H., Wilks Y. 1995. University of Sheffield: Description of the LaSIE system as used for MUC-6. Proceedings of Sixth Message Understanding Conference (1995)
10. Gallippi A., Learning to recognize names across languages. Proceedings of the 16th International Conference on Computational Linguistics (1996)
11. Grishman R. 1995. The NYU system for MUC-6 or where's the syntax. Proceedings of Sixth Message Understanding Conference (1995)
12. Grishman R., Tipster architecture design document version 2.3. Technical report, DARPA (1997)
13. Karkaletsis V., Spyropoulos C., Petasis G. Named entity recognition from Greek texts: the GIE project (1999)
14. Karttunnen L., The Replace Operator. In Finite State Language Processing, ed. Roche Em. and Schabes Yv., MIT Press (1997)
15. Krupka G., Hausman K. IsoQuest: description of the NetOwl extractor system as used for MUC-7. Proceedings of Seventh Message Understanding Conference (1998)
16. Mikheev A., Grover C., Moens M. 1997. Description of the LTG System used for MUC-7. Proceedings of Seventh Message Understanding Conference (1998)

17. Neumann G., Backofen R., Baur J., Becker M., Braun C. 1997. An information extraction core system for real world German text processing. ACL (1997)
18. Sekine S., Grishman R., Shinnou H.. A decision tree method for finding and classifying names in Japanese texts, Sixth Workshop on Very Large Corpora (1998)
19. Sekine S. NYU: description of the Japanese NE system used for MET-2. Proceedings of Seventh Message Understanding Conference (1998)
20. Yu S., Bai S., Wu P. Description of the Kent Ridge Digital Labs system used for MUC-7. Proceedings of Seventh Message Understanding Conference (1998)
21. Van Noord Gertjan and Dale Gerdemann. An Extendible Regular Expression Compiler for Finite-state Approaches in Natural Language Processing. WIA, Potsdam, Germany (1999)

Author Index

Lecture Notes in Artificial Intelligence (LNAI)

Vol. 1674: D. Floreano, J.-D. Nicoud, F. Mondada (Eds.), Advances in Artificial Life. Proceedings, 1999. XVI, 737 pages. 1999.

Vol. 1688: P. Bouquet, L. Serafini, P. Brézillon, M. Benerecetti, F. Castellani (Eds.), Modeling and Using Context. Proceedings, 1999. XII, 528 pages. 1999.

Vol. 1692: V. Matoušek, P. Mautner, J. Ocelíková, P. Sojka (Eds.), Text, Speech, and Dialogue. Proceedings, 1999. XI, 396 pages. 1999.

Vol. 1695: P. Barahona, J.J. Alferes (Eds.), Progress in Artificial Intelligence. Proceedings, 1999. XI, 385 pages. 1999.

Vol. 1699: S. Albayrak (Ed.), Intelligent Agents for Telecommunication Applications. Proceedings, 1999. IX, 191 pages. 1999.

Vol. 1701: W. Burgard, T. Christaller, A.B. Cremers (Eds.), KI-99: Advances in Artificial Intelligence. Proceedings, 1999. XI, 311 pages. 1999.

Vol. 1704: Jan M. Żytkow, J. Rauch (Eds.), Principles of Data Mining and Knowledge Discovery. Proceedings, 1999. XIV, 593 pages. 1999.

Vol. 1705: H. Ganzinger, D. McAllester, A. Voronkov (Eds.), Logic for Programming and Automated Reasoning. Proceedings, 1999. XII, 397 pages. 1999.

Vol. 1711: N. Zhong, A. Skowron, S. Ohsuga (Eds.), New Directions in Rough Sets, Data Mining, and Granular-Soft Computing. Proceedings, 1999. XIV, 558 pages. 1999.

Vol. 1712: H. Boley, A Tight, Practical Integration of Relations and Functions. XI, 169 pages. 1999.

Vol. 1714: M.T. Pazienza (Eds.), Information Extraction. IX, 165 pages. 1999.

Vol. 1715: P. Perner, M. Petrou (Eds.), Machine Learning and Data Mining in Pattern Recognition. Proceedings, 1999. VIII, 217 pages. 1999.

Vol. 1720: O. Watanabe, T. Yokomori (Eds.), Algorithmic Learning Theory. Proceedings, 1999. XI, 365 pages. 1999.

Vol. 1721: S. Arikawa, K. Furukawa (Eds.), Discovery Science. Proceedings, 1999. XI, 374 pages. 1999.

Vol. 1724: H.I. Christensen, H. Bunke, H. Noltemeier (Eds.), Sensor Based Intelligent Robots. Proceedings, 1998. VIII, 327 pages. 1999.

Vol. 1730: M. Gelfond, N. Leone, G. Pfeifer (Eds.), Logic Programming and Nonmonotonic Reasoning. Proceedings, 1999. XI, 391 pages. 1999.

Vol. 1733: H. Nakashima, C. Zhang (Eds.), Approaches to Intelligent Agents. Proceedings, 1999. XII, 241 pages. 1999.

Vol. 1735: J.W. Amtrup, Incremental Speech Translation. XV, 200 pages. 1999.

Vol. 1739: A. Braffort, R. Gherbi, S. Gibet, J. Richardson, D. Teil (Eds.), Gesture-Based Communication in Human-Computer Interaction. Proceedings, 1999. XI, 333 pages. 1999.

Vol. 1744: S. Staab, Grading Knowledge: Extracting Degree Information from Texts. X, 187 pages. 1999.

Vol. 1747: N. Foo (Ed.), Adavanced Topics in Artificial Intelligence. Proceedings, 1999. XV, 500 pages. 1999.

Vol. 1757: N.R. Jennings, Y. Lespérance (Eds.), Intelligent Agents VI. Proceedings, 1999. XII, 380 pages. 2000.

Vol. 1759: M.J. Zaki, C.-T. Ho (Eds.), Large-Scale Parallel Data Mining. VIII, 261 pages. 2000.

Vol. 1760: J.-J. Ch. Meyer, P.-Y. Schobbens (Eds.), Formal Models of Agents. Poceedings. VIII, 253 pages. 1999.

Vol. 1761: R. Caferra, G. Salzer (Eds.), Automated Deduction in Classical and Non-Classical Logics. Proceedings. VIII, 299 pages. 2000.

Vol. 1771: P. Lambrix, Part-Whole Reasoning in an Object-Centered Framework. XII, 195 pages. 2000.

Vol. 1772: M. Beetz, Concurrent Reactive Plans. XVI, 213 pages. 2000.

Vol. 1775: M. Thielscher, Challenges for Action Theories. XIII, 138 pages. 2000.

Vol. 1778: S. Wermter, R. Sun (Eds.), Hybrid Neural Systems. IX, 403 pages. 2000.

Vol. 1792: E. Lamma, P. Mello (Eds.), AI*IA 99: Advances in Artificial Intelligence. Proceedings, 1999. XI, 392 pages. 2000.

Vol. 1793: O. Cairo, L.E. Sucar, F.J. Cantu (Eds.), MICAI 2000: Advances in Artificial Intelligence. Proceedings, 2000. XIV, 750 pages. 2000.

Vol. 1794: H. Kirchner, C. Ringeissen (Eds.), Frontiers of Combining Systems. Proceedings, 2000. X, 291 pages. 2000.

Vol. 1805: T. Terano, H. Liu, A.L.P. Chen (Eds.), Knowledge Discovery and Data Mining. Proceedings, 2000. XIV, 460 pages. 2000.

Vol. 1810: R. López de Mántaras, E. Plaza (Eds.), Machine Learning: ECML 2000. Proceedings, 2000. XII, 460 pages. 2000.

Vol. 1822: H.H. Hamilton, Advances in Artificial Intelligence. Proceedings, 2000. XII, 450 pages. 2000.

Vol. 1831: D. McAllester (Ed.), Automated Deduction – CADE-17. Proceedings, 2000. XIII, 520 pages. 2000.

Vol. 1835: D. N. Christodoulakis (Ed.), Natural Language Processing – NLP 2000. Proceedings, 2000. XII, 438 pages. 2000.

Vol. 1849: C. Freksa, W. Brauer, C. Habel, K.F. Wender (Eds.), Spatial Cognition II. XI, 420 pages. 2000.

Lecture Notes in Computer Science